POLITICAL ASSASSINATIONS BY JEWS

SUNY Series in Deviance and Social Control
Ronald A. Farrell, Editor

SUNY Series in Israeli Studies
Russell Stone, Editor

POLITICAL ASSASSINATIONS BY JEWS

A Rhetorical Device for Justice

NACHMAN BEN-YEHUDA

State University
of New York
Press

Published by
State University of New York Press, Albany

© 1993   State University of New York

For information, address State University of New York
Press, State University Plaza, Albany, NY 12246

Production by Susan Geraghty
Marketing by Fran Keneston

Library of Congress Cataloging-in-Publication Data

Ben-Yehuda, Nachman.
    Political assassinations by Jews : a rhetorical device for justice
/ Nachman Ben-Yehuda.
        p.   cm. — (SUNY series in deviance and social control) (SUNY
series in Israeli studies)
    Includes bibliographical references and index.
    ISBN 0–7914–1165–6 (hc : acid-free) : $59.50. —   ISBN
0–7914–1166–4 (pb : acid-free) : $19.95
    1. Jews—Politics and government. 2. Assassination.
3. Assassination—Palestine. 4. Jews—Palestine—Politics and
government. 5. Palestine—Politics and government.
6. Assassination—Israel. 7. Israel—Politics and government.
I. Title. II. Series. III. Series: SUNY series in Israeli studies.
DS140.B42   1993
364. 1'524'08992405694—dc20
                                                                    91–36690
                                                                    CIP

10 9 8 7 6 5 4 3 2 1

To
Einat Usant and
Vered Vinitzky-Seroussi
Whose help enthusiasm and support
made this book possible

CONTENTS

PART 3: ANALYSIS, DISCUSSION, AND SUMMARY

ACKNOWLEDGMENTS

Researching and writing this manuscript was a very long and demanding process. I could not have managed to cope with this task if it were not for the unconditional love, help, patience, and support of Etti, Tzach, and Guy. My gratitude is to Dina, Hanna, and Yehuda, our parents, whose help and support were indispensable.

I am grateful to Menachem Amir, Ada Amichal-Yevin, Gideon Aran, Said Arjomand, Yoram Bilu, Moshe and Illana Brendell, Naomi Chazan, Erik Cohen, Gerald Cromer, Shlomo Gal, Don Handelman, Eliahu Hassin, Ami and Beatrice Heilbruun, Sarit Hellman, Dan Horowitz, Baruch Kimmerling, Paul Kooistra, Simcha Landau, Gary Marx, David Niv, David Rapoport, Mordechai Rotenberg, Ya'acov Scholl, Leslie Sebbah, Adam Seligman, Michael Shalev, Boas Shamir, Ehud Sprintzak, Israel Tamari, Austin Turk, Jean and Carolyn Wittenberg, Idan Yaron, and Yael Zerubavel. All provided essential help, support, constructive criticisms, and good advice which were most crucial for developing the ideas presented in this work.

It is a real pleasure, indeed honor, to extend my deepest gratitude and admiration to the best, most dedicated research assistants I ever had—Vered Vinitzky-Seroussi and Einat Usant. Their good spirits, curiosity, reliability, dedication, persistence, help, constructive criticism, support, and uncompromising devotion to the project were of the most significant and valuable quality.

The following archives provided indispensable information: Archion HaHagana, Beit Jabotinski, Beit Ariella, Mercaz Letiud Hahevra Haisraelit, Archion Hakibbutz Hameuchad, Archion "Ha'aretz," Archion "Monitin," Archion "Kol Ha'ir," the center for oral documentation in the institute on contemporary Judaism at Hebrew University, Ginzach Hamedina, and Beit Yair. I am grateful to all of them for their most substantial help. I am par-

ix

ticularly grateful to Anshell Shpillman and Hanna Armony from Beit Yair whose help was most essential.

I would like to use this opportunity to thank all of our interviewees, without whose good will and help this research could not have been carried out. For most of them, talking about the subject was not easy, and many asked to remain anonymous. I trust that this book will not give them a reason not to be satisfied. To those who did not express their wish to remain anonymous I would like to express my gratitude in the most explicit way: Shmariahu Guttman, Moshe Savorai, Itzhak Zelnik, Levi Avrahami, David Almog, Mordechai Ya'akubovitz, Alexander Hess, Uri Dromi, Aharon Amir, Uri Avneri, Meir Vilner, Yoram Aridor, Shoshana Geffner, and Isser Harel.

Many have pointed out that the subject matter of this book is something that we—perhaps—should not discuss, because it is GOAL NEFESH (meaning, in Hebrew, "disgusting"). I obviously disagree. As a Jew and an Israeli, I feel that it is my obligation to find out and understand the conditions under which political assassination events take place. This is a lesson that we—as well as others—should know. I truly believe that those who are ignorant of history are doomed to live it all over again.

Victor Azarya, Robert Cooper, Moshe Lissak, Mota Kremnitzer, Stanley Cohen, and Calvin Goldscheider read the entire first draft of the manuscript thoroughly. Their comments were of the best quality. The book would not have been what it is were it not for their constructive and most essential comments and criticism. My discussions with Erich Goode, his warmth friendship, detailed comments, valuable and generous help and support are gratefully and deeply appreciated and acknowledged.

I am grateful to Advanced Communications in Jerusalem for typing the manuscript.

The funds to begin this research were provided by the research fund of the Hebrew University. I am particularly grateful to Nava Enosh whose advice was most fruitful. The study was also funded by the Israeli Foundations Trustees, research contract no. 86-01-007. I am very grateful to both for their support. My gratitude is to the Department of Sociology at the State University of New York, Stony Brook. This department provided the necessary means which helped me to start thinking about this research during one fruitful Sabbatical. The firm, enthusiastic, and continuous support, sometimes during difficult times, of my colleagues at the department of Sociology and Anthropology at Hebrew University most certainly gave me the strength to continue and finish the project. Finally, I am very grateful to the department of Sociology at the University of Toronto, and particularly to John Simpson. The department extended to me a wonderful and warm welcome that enabled me to work on, and finish, the manuscript during my Sabbatical stay. I am particularly indebted to the members of what has become known during the fall of 1991 as the "war council": John Simpson, Isajiw Sev, and Witold Morawski; and to John Hagan, Ron Gillis, Raymond Breton, Charles Jones and Bob Brym who were all most kind in providing help, advice, and an intellectually and socially warm, supportive, and challenging environment.

Cyrill Levitt's, William Shaffir's, and John Simpson's endless patience, support, constructive challenges and criticisms, and friendship are very deeply appreciated.

I am indebted to the most constructive and helpful comments made by the three anonymous reviewers for SUNY Press. This is also the place to express my deepest gratitude and appreciation to Rosalie M. Robertson, my SUNY Press editor, for her patience, support, kindness, good advice, and a wonderful sense of humour in some very difficult moments.

The practical, emotional, and moral support given enthusiastically by Goggie and Al Blitstein, our most cherished and deeply loved second family, helped transform this project from the realm of the imagination into the realm of reality.

LIST OF CASES

INTRODUCTION

The nature and patterns of political assassinations constitute one of the most interesting, challenging, and frustrating enigmatic riddles for social research. This book aims to solve this riddle by an in-depth inquiry into the nature, scope, meaning, and results of political assassinations within one complex cultural matrix. The book focuses on political assassinations by Jews in Palestine-Israel. The nature of the inquiry is social-historical, from a sociology of deviance perspective, and it employs a methodology which relies on both primary and secondary sources.

The inquiry found that there were quite a few cases of this particular form of killing in the cultural matrix of Judaism and in Palestine-Israel. However, the prevalence of political assassinations is not very high as compared to some other cultures.

In the overwhelming majority of known cases we are *not* dealing with a lone fanatic killer, but with a premeditated, planned act, committed by a group or by a representative of a group. In most cases the assassin is linked very intimately to a *group* which plans the assassination, gives the assassins a much needed moral support, the vocabularies of motives needed to perform the task, as well as shelter and the means required to execute the plan of assassination. In many cases the victim was warned, sometimes more than once.

In each of the assassinations, the act signified the boundaries between different symbolic-moral universes. Political assassinations by Jews in Palestine and Israel are connected with a similar pattern that had existed in Europe: an assassin who operates as part of, or representing, a larger more or less crystallized symbolic-moral universe.

Two clear "reasons" for the assassinations are salient: (a) revenge and a warning signal; (b) prevention of, or interference in, a process of social or political change represented or proposed by the victim. The fact that many cases occurred *after* the potential victim did something, was warned, and that therefore most cases were considered as *revenge* as well as a warning sign implies that there is an alternative system of "justice" in operation here.

Before 1949, most cases were committed by the three main pre-state underground Jewish groups. However, the overwhelming number of persons assassinated were other Jews. After the State of Israel was formally established, the incidence of political assassination events declined very sharply and significantly. The reason for this is that before 1949 political assassinations were used to explain and justify acts that seemed like justice to the assassins in situations where they felt that they could not get a fair justice because the opportunities for such justice were blocked. After 1949, a new system of political and judicial justice came into being as the State of Israel was established, hence the need to resort to political assassinations declined sharply. Since 1948 instead of political assassinations we have cases of state sponsored assassinations: political executions.

PART 1

Theoretical Background and Methodology

CHAPTER 1

Theoretical Orientation, Plan of the Book, and Main Findings

THE PUZZLE

The nature and patterns of political assassinations constitute one of the most interesting, challenging, and frustrating enigmatic riddles for social research. The riddle of political assassinations is linked intimately with a few fascinating research questions. For example: What "determines" history, personal actors, or so-called "objective" processes? What is the impact of a political assassination (if any)? If political assassinations do have a significant impact, in what sense, then, can we understand it? What, exactly, *is* the nature of a political assassination? Under what conditions do political assassinations take place? Can political assassinations be considered characteristic of particular cultures, or are they a product of more universalistic sociological processes or conditions regardless of particular cultures?

The empirical, analytical, and intellectual puzzle this book addresses is indeed that of political assassinations. This book is based on a research that, deliberately and intentionally, attempted to answer the above questions.

The riddle of political assassinations, however, is not the only, or exclusive, focus of this book. The overwhelming majority of previous works on political assassinations were done by either political scientists, historians or psychiatrists/psychologists.[1] With some very few exceptions (e.g., see Wilkinson 1976; Turk 1983; Wagner-Pacifici 1986), hardly any sociological work was done on political assassinations. Hence, the "sociology," or "criminology," of political assassinations" as well as the methodological "know how," simply do not exist. Moreover, because prior work focuses on diverse issues associated with political assassinations, the lack of a unified, substantial, and method-ological paradigm is even more pronounced. Furthermore, in a recent paper, Gurr (1988) points out the problematic state of academic research into terrorism more generally. While we'll see later that a clear distinction needs to be made between political assassination events and terrorism, Gurr's criticism is valid for both. One goal of this work is to rectify this deficiency and pro-vide a possible new analytical look at a sociological construction of political assassinations.

An important question is *what* sociological perspective can be utilized to provide a meaningful interpretation of political assassinations? While Wilkinson (1976) was inclined to adopt Smelser's theory of collective behavior for this purpose, Smelser's elaborate theory (1962) was not constructed to explain this type of violent behavior. The fact is that this theory did not become a major (or minor) tool in explaining political assassinations. First and foremost, political assassinations constitute a form of violent and aggressive human behavior. This behavior is focused on tak-ing somebody else's life against the wish of that somebody, like what happens in similar forms of behavior: murder, killing, blood-revenge, executions, and the like. As such, the most natu-ral field in sociology to address in order to find a theoretical base for interpreting political assassinations is that of deviance and the close discipline of criminology. Thus, a unique feature of this book is its interpretative analytical framework. Political assassi-nations will be interpreted by using approaches which were developed in the sociological study of deviance and criminology and never before applied to political assassinations. This applica-tion will yield a new definitional approach to political assassina-tions, as well as a new interpretation of this phenomenon.

Furthermore, recent formulations in the sociology of deviance have repeatedly pointed out that for this type of sociol-ogy to develop, it has to interpret its empirical cases within a dynamic analytical context of morality, power, and history (Ben-Yehuda 1989, 1990). Another major goal of this work is to achieve exactly that.

The book aims to solve the puzzle of political assassinations by an in depth inquiry into the nature, scope, meaning, and results of political assassinations within what may be considered a more or less integrated, albeit infinitesimally complex (e.g., see Goldscheider and Zuckerman 1984; Cohen and Mendes-Flohr 1987), cultural matrix. Hence the book focuses on political assassinations by Jews in Palestine-Israel. The nature of the inquiry is social-historical, from a sociology of deviance perspective, and it employs a methodology which relies on both primary and secondary sources.

To have a full, gestalt type of, comprehension of the puzzle of political assassinations requires a broad knowledge in two areas. First, an analytic understanding of what political assassinations *are*, and what is their place *within* the sociology of deviance. Second, an understanding of the cases themselves, as they occurred within the relevant time period is required. In this respect, this is a study in "natural" deviance, that is deviance as it happened within its natural setting.

Choosing this approach requires the researcher to understand, and present in an intelligible manner, the natural setting within which deviance takes place. I shall later provide a fairly thorough documentation of *all* the known cases of political assassinations between the 1890s and the 1980s. These cases are not merely an attempt at historical reconstruction and are of more than "historical" interest. As case studies, these pieces of evidence can, and will, be examined as part of the clarification of the sociology of deviance that enhances our understanding of general social processes. Consequently, I shall present a theoretically rich set of case studies and illustrations that, in addition to serving as the basic documentation of a rare and interesting phenomenon, represents a major basis for understanding more general issues of the sociology of deviance, as well as of political assassinations.

The above two delimiters require a full exposure of both levels—the analytical and complex setting. The structure and content of the book reflect these two concerns: an in-depth inquiry into the nature of political assassinations *and* an emphasis on the sociology of deviance as the appropriate explanatory base of this particular form of human lethal aggression.

Since I take it that the sociology of deviance is a crucial perspective for interpreting political assassinations, I shall present a general analytical discussion of the sociology of deviance in order to establish the general analytic framework and focus our cognitive map on a set of rhetorical devices that will be employed to cope with the empirical and intellectual puzzle of this research.

The type of political assassination that we shall uncover in this research is not the "typical" assassination many of us may have in mind: an irrational assassin who kills an important political figure. This research has uncovered a sociological pattern of political assassinations, which must be conceptualized within a popular system of justice, operated (and justified) typically by a relevant collective group (and not the individual). Vengeance and revenge which are typical reasons for initiating a political assassination in this system (for example, as reactions to suspicions of treason) thus become identified with systemic moral and rational characteristics (and not individual irrational idiosyncrasies).

DEVIANCE

The General Orientation within the Sociology of Deviance

Since its inception, the sociology of deviance[2] (Schur 1979; Goode 1984; Rock 1985; Thio 1988) seems to have suffered from at least two major problems. The *first* is a theoretical chaos (Mills 1943; Piven 1981; Scull 1984; Terry and Steffensmeier 1988:60). The *second* is the fact that the sociology of deviance failed to consider total social structures and fell into a deep (yet interesting) trap of small scale studies about various esoteric, sensational types of deviance (Mills 1943; Scull 1984). Rock (1973a) even claimed that the emphasis in the sociology of deviance on studying these phenomenon has given rise to a radical type of *phenomenalism* which views society as a collection of small units lacking an overall structure. Later, Rock (1974) also claimed that the sociology of deviance had created an artificial contradiction between phenomenalism (emphasizing the need for an accurate and reliable reconstruction of the social world as seen by those living in it) and *essentialism* (searching for the underlying properties of the social order).

In order to try and solve the above problems, the sociological study of deviance must consider total social structures and/or processes by examining deviance as a relative phenomenon and as part of larger social processes of social change and stability.

This examination can be conceptualized within the theoretical context of looking at the myriad of symbolic-moral universes (Berger and Luckmann 1966) which constitute the wider societal cultural mosaic and their boundaries (Ben-Yehuda 1985, 1990). This approach is indeed consistent with the suggestions made by Piven (1981) and Scull (1984) in maintaining that the study of deviance should be reframed (Goffman 1974) within general societal processes, in a dynamic historical and political perspective.

Consequently, the analysis of political assassinations, as a particular form of deviance, will be made within a parallel analysis of power, morality, change, and stability. This is done explicitly in order to push the analysis in the direction of much-needed essentialism.

Hence, we shall next clarify a few theoretical issues which are focused on the problems of deviance, social change and stability, morality and power, and relativity. All these concepts are key terms in the sociological interpretation of political assassinations.

Deviance, Change, and Stability:
A Model of Culture and Symbolic-Moral Universes

Culture consists of all the shared material and nonmaterial objects and artifacts. Culture is eternally "changing more or less, acting as a point of reference for people engaged in interaction" (Becker 1986, p. 19). While culture implies consensus, solidarity and cooperation, dissension and conflict also are implied.

To interpret the concept of political assassinations in a societal and cultural context requires the assumption of a model of culture. Such a model should allow justifiable symbolic and interpretative analysis, while not being too complicated, a pattern originally suggested by Berger and Luckmann's concept of symbolic universes (1966).

An inherent quality of all cultures is that what is regarded as valued behavior changes, hence it becomes relativized—between and within cultures. One way of conceptualizing, and sociologically interpreting, this kaleidoscopic and eternally changing complex was indeed suggested by Berger and Luckmann (1966) and Scott (1972). Their emphasis is on the concept of symbolic universes.

Berger and Luckmann (1966, p. 113) characterize symbolic universes as:

> bodies of theoretical tradition that integrate different provinces of meaning and encompass the institutional order in a symbolic totality...symbolic processes are processes of signification that refer to realities other than those of everyday experience...the symbolic sphere relates to the most comprehensive level of legitimation.

These analysts further suggest the concept of "universe maintenance," claiming that when two, or more, contradicting symbolic universes (i.e., moral sets) meet, a conflict is unavoidable:

> heretical groups posit not only a theoretical threat to the symbolic universe, but a practical one to the institutional order legitimated by the symbolic universe in question (p. 124).

In other words, a specific symbolic universe helps its inhabitants to better understand their reality; to make sense out of what might otherwise seem senseless. A symbolic universe therefore provides its inhabitants with the necessary vocabularies of motives which are utilized by the inhabitants to explain and justify their past and future behavior. The different rhetorical devices used by inhabitants of different symbolic-moral universes would necessarily expose the cultural variance between these groups.[3]

Suggesting nihilation as a viable means to interpret, Berger and Luckmann (1966, p. 132) refer to attempts by inhabitants of one symbolic universe to use their power and legitimacy in order "to liquidate conceptually everything *outside* the same universe." A process of nihilation denies the legitimacy of reality constructions and interpretations, rhetorical devices and vocabularies of motives, which originate in other symbolic universes.

Complex cultures are characterized by the existence of multiple elective centers (Ben-Yehuda 1985, 1990; Cohen, Ben-Yehuda, and Aviad 1986), each enveloped by a specific symbolic-moral universe which demarcates its moral boundaries. These symbolic-moral universes promote alternative value and belief systems and advocate alternative lifestyles. Societal reactions to different behaviors, whether assumed or observed, will either redefine the moral boundaries of these symbolic-moral universes in a rigid way, or help to introduce elements of flexibility and hence change. The social meaning of deviance in such societies becomes essentially and situationally problematic, both to members of society and to the sociologist (Rock 1973). Criminal law in a complex society, then, becomes increasingly relied upon as a formal mechanism of social control, integrating all those who live within its political jurisdiction (Hills 1980, p. 35). This conceptualization fits very well with the more general theoretical orientation of viewing deviance as a relative phenomenon within the context of societal change and stability. The perceived threat of real, imaginary, or assumed deviance is an important issue for basic boundary-maintaining or boundary-changing functions of deviance.

Viewed in this way, deviance and deviantization become central phenomena when two, or more, symbolic-moral universes meet, compete, negotiate, and clash. Members in each universe are interested not only in its survival but also in showing its moral superiority. Thus, members in different symbolic-moral universes are engaged in generating power and in attempts to widen their basis of legitimacy—that is, members in these symbolic-moral universes are involved in moral, power, and stigma contests (Schur 1980). The ability of members from different symbolic-moral universes to generate and use power, as well as their ability to legitimize their claims, will eventually determine who will be deviantized and criminalized and where and when this will occur. Thus, general consensus and acceptance of moral statements become difficult as the meaning and interpretation of various behaviors becomes problematic. The primary trait of such multi-centered cultures is change, with much effort invested to create feelings of likeness, common cause and cultural heritage.

The notion of deviance which emerges from this conceptualization is focused on an *interpretative analysis*[4] (Geertz 1973; Orcutt 1983, pp. 59–62; Walzer 1987) which implies that *deviance will be treated as a relative label, (or a rhetorical device), which is socially constructed.* A successful, enforceable social construction of deviance depends on the ability of one or more groups to use power to enforce their definition of morality on others. This process involves delineating and emphasizing boundaries between different symbolic-moral universes. In turn this theoretical approach implies that the process of negotiating a moral meaning of rhetorical devices is continuous and ongoing between those who are defined as deviants and the social environment in which they live and function. Deviance, in this analytical perspective, always results from negotiations about morality *and* the configuration of power relationships.

In recent years a theoretical distinction developed within the sociology of deviance: between the so-called "objective" and "constructionist" views (for more on this see Best 1989, 1990; Goode 1989; Rafter 1990). The objective view is a variant of the positivist approach, quite close to functionalism. It assumes that "deviance" (or, more generally, "social problems") constitute an objective, measurable reality and particularly, that deviance consists of objective conditions and harm. On the other hand, we have the "constructionist" approach (also referred to as "subjective" or "relativist"). This approach maintains that deviance does not present the characteristics of a so-called objective reality and that deviance is the result of social collective definitions of what some organized members of a culture see as a harmful or dangerous condition(s). That is, the nature of what is, and what is not, defined as deviance is not a result of some objective conditions, but rather, is a social construction of different cultures. As Goode puts it: "to the subjectivist, a given condition need not even exist in the objective sense to be defined as a social problem" (1989:328). Both Goode (1989) and Best (1989) agree that there are two variants of the constructionist perspective. There is *strict* constructionism, and there is *contextual* constructionism. As Goode (1989:328–329) points out, the first variant argues that the expert, or scientific evaluation, of deviance as such simply represents one "claim making" activity out of many such activities. This view argues that scientific claims are also socially constructed, as other claims, and can be studied as such. The second variant argues that while deviance and social problems are the results of claim making activities, the so-called objective dimension can be assessed and evaluated by an expert, on the basis of some scientific evidence. Sociologists working from this theoretical perspective typically contrast the objective and the "constructed" versions of reality.

The theoretical view taken in this book is very close to contextual constructionism. While chapter two focuses on claim making—part 2, chapters 11 and 12 also present the facts that form the basis for constructionism.

Deviance as a Relative Rhetoric

The implication of this theoretical stand is relativistic, and negates the opposite absolutist, or normative and narrower approach which basically takes the existence of deviance as an objective, nonproblematic (and typically measurable) reality.[5] In Thio's terms (1988:21), the perspective presented here is modern, emphasizing relativism, subjectivism, and voluntarism. In simpler terms, this work emphasizes that deviance is a relative phenomenon, that the subjective perspectives of the social actors who are intimate partners to the deviance process is of crucial importance and, finally, that so-called "deviants" are not primarily products of processes over which they had little, or no, control but instead that—to a large extent—the process of becoming deviant is voluntary.

While the constructionist and relative conception of deviance seems almost self evident, especially for modern sociologists of deviance, it has been attacked. Theoretical approaches which typically take the existence of deviance as nonproblematic (e.g., positivism) do not usually adopt the relative position. In 1975, Wellford attributed to the labeling approach (which has been *the* carrier of the relativistic flag in the sociology of deviance) the following stand: "no act is intrinsically criminal...[because]...crime is a form of behavior defined by the powerful to control the powerless" (p. 334; see also Pearce 1976). The concept of deviance which is presented in this book implies that the designation of a particular form of behavior as deviant is the result of a long process of negotiation. This process means that the powerless can resist deviantization. Political assassinations provide a splendid example for how, in fact, the powerless can use a pointed deadly force to try and change the course of history.

There is, perhaps, nothing better than political assassinations to realize how deviance can, indeed, be conceptualized as a socially constructed and relative rhetorical device. What one particular individual, or group, may zealously view as a fully justified political assassination, other individuals, or groups, may view (in no

less zeal) as a simple, cold-blooded, and totally unjustified, murder. In chapter three we shall survey quite a few existing rhetorical
devices which are employed, in different cultures, to interpret acts
of taking other people's life against their will. "Political assassination" is just one more device, among many.

Deviance and Moral Boundaries

The analytical approach taken in this analysis entails an implicit
assumption that deviance, and reactions to it, do not necessarily
have to be viewed as "bad" but can be viewed as "good" as well.
The definition and evaluation of the results of deviance become rel-
ativised and depend, to a large extent, on the point of view, and
interests, of the evaluator. In other words, the symbolic-moral universe of the evaluator becomes a crucial variable when it comes to
an assessment of the act. The problem of deviance and moral
boundaries is one of conceptualization. Is the social construction of
deviance, and reactions to it, aimed primarily to stabilize moral
boundaries and help induce moral and normative rigidity, or is it
aimed primarily to help induce change in moral boundaries and
help to create moral and normative flexibility? In a short micro-
level question we can re-phrase this dilemma: Is the assassin
(deviant) a negative and dangerous *criminal*, or is he/she a *revolutionary* hero? As I have already indicated before (1990), the answer
to this question is quite complex and depends on the specific combination of a few variables. This, perhaps, is one of the *most* problematic questions regarding political assassinations, and some bitter arguments focused around it. For example, do we interpret the
behavior of the assassins of such figures as Archduke Ferdinand,
Trotsky, Sadat, Bernadotte, Kennedy, Aldo Moro, Olaf Palme as
political? criminal? insane? religiously fanatic? revolutionary? No
less important is *who* is making the interpretation and *why*.
  Traditional theories of deviance have either emphasized the
"negative" aspect of deviance (that is, its capacity to produce
processes which enhance social rigidity), or took it for granted.
The view that deviance can be "positive," even in the sense of
helping a process of societal change into being and change societal symbolic-moral boundaries as well, not to mention power, is
less widespread.[6] This positive side of deviance was illuminated

originally by Durkheim's statements on deviance—that is, that deviance can be "functional" in helping a societal reaction into being in a way which either reaffirms moral boundaries and hence promotes social rigidity, or changes them thereby inducing cultural flexibility. These different viewpoints were further amplified by Erikson's work (1966), as well as by others. Political assassinations can be viewed as a form of negative deviance, however, it may also be viewed as a positive deviance. For example, the murder of a brutal, cruel, corrupt, and stupid tyrant, or as speeding up a necessary and positive revolution.[7]

While many scholars followed the idea of reactions to deviance as attempts to enhance social stability and rigidity (e.g., Erikson 1966; Bergesen 1984), fewer followed the idea of deviance as producing normative change and flexibility. Coser (1962) and Douglas' works are clear exceptions. Coser pointed out that deviance may contribute to what he called "normative flexibility." Douglas, much more explicitly, suggests the term "creative deviance": "Deviance is the mutation that is generally destructive of society, but it is also the only major source of creative adaptations of rules to new life situations" (p. 60). Political assassins, in fact, frequently have in mind the idea of inducing or preventing a process of social and political change by their act.

I have indeed examined previously (1985, 1990) how social constructions of deviance, and societal reactions to it, could be *interpreted* as important and essential ingredients in social processes of change and stability. As we shall see later, the topic of political assassinations includes both aspects of Durkheim's idea in it; that is deviance as a major ingredient in processes of social change and of social stability. This particular topic provides a critical focus for power struggles and for bitter arguments about the moral boundaries of the Jewish community in Palestine (Yishuv) and in Israel. Political assassinations mark the boundaries of the acceptable and unacceptable, of good and bad, of deviance as leading to change or to stability.

Politics and Deviance; Power and Morality

Analyzing political assassinations from a sociological point of view places this study not only within the general area of the sociology of deviance, but within the particular subarea of politics and deviance. This is so because in that area power and morality play an open and explicit role in determining what would, and what would not, be considered as deviance. Viewing political assassinations as such (and not as "murder" for example), typically involves bitter, and explicit, arguments about morality and power.

The concept of power is essential to the area of politics and deviance because it basically helps us to understand who can deviantize who. The concept of power alone, however, is insufficient. Power must be legitimized, and symbolic-moral universes (or morality) provide that legitimacy. In this perspective, we may view many different centers enveloped by corresponding symbolic-moral universes, which confront, conflict, and negotiate with one another. During the negotiations among symbolic-moral universes power may be generated and moral boundaries compromised. This conceptualization means that it is not always the case that the powerful would necessarily deviantize the powerless. The powerless may persuade inhabitants of other symbolic-moral universes of the "truth" of their cause, and/or be engaged themselves in the generation of power, and negotiate a settlement. Discussing politics and deviance necessitates using the concepts of power and morality in the most explicit way (see Ben-Yehuda 1990).

As I have pointed out elsewhere (1990:62–63): "the area of politics and deviance [can be characterized] as follows: Problematic behavioral acts, which take place at the realm of the seams, where different moral boundaries touch, or from the periphery of a moral universe towards its center and vice versa, and which involve challenges (or abuse) of power and morality would fall into the area of politics and deviance." This area was divided into two separate divisions: political elements in so-called regular deviance (1990:65–71) and political deviance proper (1990:71–94). Generally speaking, the degree to which a particular form of deviance will be regarded as political depends, first of all, on how explicitly and clearly this act challenges the power structure and symbolic order, of a particular symbolic moral universe. Political deviance proper consists of three classes of deviant acts. One class consists of acts done by one person, or a group, in the periphery and which challenge the authority and legitimacy of those in the center. Such assassinations as those of Robert Kennedy by Sirhan Sirhan on June 5, 1968, Julius Caesar in March of 44 B.C., Martin Luther King by James Earl Ray on April 4, 1968, and Mohandas K. Gandhi on January 30, 1948, exemplify this class. Political assassinations as a tool to change policy was used by the Sicarii (to be discussed in chapter 5), some Bulgarian (particularly during the 1920s, see Ford 1985: 259–261) and prerevolution Russian underground movements (e.g., the *Narodnaya Volya* from 1878 onwards, see Ford 1985:227–230). These acts usually aim at transforming symbolic-moral universes and changing moral boundaries. The second class consists of deviant acts by those in the center who were invested with power and legitimacy and are, supposedly, the guardians of the symbolic-moral universe and its boundaries. Sometimes these guardians may abuse their power and twist and mock their moral obligations, committing despised and harmful acts of deviance. State sponsored terrorism, executions, and assassinations fall into this class. The reign of terror induced by Stalin is an illustration. The third class involves a clash between social actors from two or more different and opposing symbolic-moral universes (or cultures) (1990:256). Genocide will be in this category. As we shall see later in this book, political assassinations and executions can be found in these classes.

The designation of particular behavioral patterns as deviant contains some important, although often implicit, political elements—that is, elements of power and morality. Exposing these elements is not always an easy task. Thus, the very attempt of defining a particular behavioral pattern as deviant is inherently a political act. This attempt is based on using power to impress the view of a specific symbolic-moral universe upon other universes. Applying a process of deviantization does not, however, necessarily mean that the application would be successful and culminate in the actual identification of one person (or group) as deviant because this process can be reversed (e.g., see Ben-Yehuda 1987).

The Natural History of Crime Approach

Faithfulness to one of my original delimiters, that of adhering to an approach which describes and interprets deviance within its natural setting, necessitated choosing a particular approach: that of the natural history of crime approach.

I deliberately and intentionally will not only give the descriptive information required to understand each of the cases of the political assassinations, but will also adhere—whenever possible—to the natural history of crime approach in each case. In each of the cases I will try to describe the "reasons" given for the assassinations, how the decision to assassinate was made, and what happened later. I also tried to assess the impact of the assassinations. I thus followed the above approach, trying to observe how the pattern of deviant behavior emerged, how and when it flourished, and how the pattern of political assassinations weakened or died.[8] Adhering to this approach would yield a rigorous historical reconstruction of the period under question, focusing on political assassinations, as well as on the relevant political and social events and processes which are required for a better understanding and interpretation of the assassinations.

Cullen argues that it is not sufficient to describe a particular form of deviance. He maintains that it is equally important to try and find out why a *specific* form of deviance was chosen rather than another form (1983). Following Cullen's work, I shall try indeed to answer the question of why were political assassinations "chosen" as a particular form of deviance, and not something else. Partially, this approach would also help us to avoid the problem of falling into the interesting trap of fascinating phenomenalism proper (mentioned earlier), and to consider total social structures. This is so because the problems of functional equivalents and alternative courses of action, are linked to issues which are inherent to social structures (e.g., opportunities and pressures to deviate, as well as questions of social justice).

PLAN OF THE BOOK,
LOGIC AND ORDER OF PRESENTATION

Previous works on political assassination events either focused in detail on one particular case (e.g., the assassination of J. F. Kennedy, Abraham Lincoln, Aldo Moro, etc.), or gave very brief and telegraphic information about many cases from different cultures (e.g., Ford 1985; Heaps 1969; Kirkham, Levy, and Crotty 1970:301–325). Some gave relatively much information about a few cases (e.g., Havens, Leiden, and Schmitt 1970; Hyams 1969). These approaches are often quite confusing and unsatisfactory because they provide a problematic basis for generalizations.

Clearly, one must have enough information to allow justifiable and persuasive generalizations to be made. Since I am committed to the approach that deviance must be presented and interpreted within the broader cultural matrix where it occurred, political assassination events must also be understood and interpreted within the culture in which they have taken place. Lack of a true understanding of the relevant culture, and a reification of the background for the assassination, would limit any meaningful interpretation. For example, even in one of the very few cases in this study where we could attribute an assassination plot to a certified "crazy" person, as in the case of Galili's attempts on Uri Avneri's life in 1974 and 1975 (see case no. 89), the historical and political background became crucial for verifying and understanding the case. It is important, even in this case, to understand who Avneri was, what was the background of Galili as this understanding gives us a much better insight into the motivations of the different actors who participated in this dramatic assassination, and the vocabularies of motives which they used.

In addition, the chronic lack of a good working definition of political assassination events helped to confuse the issue even further. Hence, we started this research project with a very strong theoretical emphasis that gave us the necessary, and indispensable, clear cut and replicable criteria required for the decision about which cases to include in the study.

The above considerations dictated a strategy which emphasized the need to provide short—however accurate, reliable, and dependable—descriptions of the different cases, as well as the *relevant* social context in which they happened. The value of this approach rests with several considerations.

This book is divided into three major parts. The first part consists of three chapters which introduce the reader into the theoretical framework, the definition of political assassinations (in a comparative perspective) and the methodology. The second part presents all the cases we have located of political assassinations and executions. The third part integrates the first and second parts into one analysis. It presents the statistical description of the aggregate cases, and provides a detailed sociological interpretation for the data. In this structure, the major premises of a contextual constructionist perspective are met. While somewhat unusual in structure, the structure of this book is meant to answer all the deficiencies of previous texts that were, and will be, mentioned. I would strongly urge the reader to read the sociological and historical tales in the second part. There is nothing better in terms of acquainting oneself with the historical reality in question than reading this part. Moreover, because of the theoretical approach adopted here, that is a natural history of crime and a grounded theory, reading this part will reconstruct the historical reality in a vivid and detailed manner. It will make reading the third part much more meaningful. However, those wishing to skip reading part 2, are more than welcome to read parts 1 and 3 only.

The book is structured in a way that is meant to highlight the important aspects of an historical-sociological study of political assassinations in one culture.

First, it is meant to expose the reader to the major facts (including references for possible future work), hence providing an important resource for a detailed analysis of cases of political assassination events within one cultural matrix, something which has never been done before in this scope and magnitude. Second, the detailed descriptions would provide a deeper understanding of, and insight into, the nature of the different competing symbolic-moral universes, their clashings, negotiations, and co-existence. As we shall see, victims of assassination plots always marked the boundaries between different symbolic-moral universes. Third, it would provide the reader a strong, fascinating and interesting, entrance into the history of the State of Israel from a very peculiar and unique point of view and vivify the background atmosphere for the different periods, so necessary to understand the cases. Fourth, this background becomes crucial when it comes to reaching conclusions. The information gathered from the different cases enables one to draw much broader sociological conclusions regarding the nature of political assassinations within a particular culture. Finally, the story of political assassination events has a few dozen of good and fascinating sociological plots which simply need to be told.

Obviously, descriptions of the different cases is limited. The wealth of information about some assassinations (e.g., those of De Hahn, Arlosoroff, Giladi) is such that one could easily write a whole book on each one of them. Other cases are very poorly documented because the relevant information was not available. Thus, the presentation of the different cases is not always balanced in terms of length of presentation and information about the cases themselves. The danger of creating only an encyclopedia for the subject is counter balanced by the theoretical emphasis.

The order of presentation is historical—from the first cases to the most recent ones. I found this type of presentation the easiest to digest, as well as the most comprehensible, fluent, and coherent. An important analytical commitment of this work is to present the natural history of crime, and to view deviance within the natural historical and political context in which it occurred. This commitment requires a chronological order of presentation. Furthermore, and as far as was possible, each case can be read and understood independently of other cases. The "price" of choosing this strategy was that a minimal level of some repetition in a few cases could not be avoided. However, the gain in the creation of independent presentations justifies this strategy.

We shall cover in this survey a period of about one hundred years of renewed Jewish life in Palestine-Israel. The chronologically ordered sequence of presentation is grouped in part 2 of the book and is divided into seven chapters. Chapter 4 gives a brief general historical background. Chapter 5 will give the necessary background of political assassinations in the Tanach (the Hebrew Bible), the Sicarii and in Europe up to 1948. Chapter 6 covers a period which ranges from 1892 until 1918. It includes the period of renewed Jewish settlement in Palestine under Turkish occupation and ends with the British conquest and occupation of the land. Chapter 7 covers a period which ranges from 1919 till 1948, which includes the most important period of the British occupation of Palestine. Chapter 8 covers a period which ranges from 1949 till 1988, which is the period of the establishment, crystallization and consolidation of the State of Israel. Chapters 6, 7, and 8 report on a total of ninety-one cases altogether. To make the ninety-one cases appear in a more condensed way, the reader will find in the Appendix three diagrams which detail in brief *all* the ninety-one cases. The diagrams are useful for a quick search for particular cases. Chapter 9 details the cases we have of state sponsored political executions. Finally, in chapter 10 I shall compare terrorism to political assassinations, I shall review two problematic categories: those that look like political assassinations but are not, and unconfirmed cases. This part of the book will present the empirical base for this study. The actual analysis, descriptive statistics and interpretations, will be provided in part 3. Faithfulness to the *contextual constructionism* approach necessitates a presentation of the objective data, the way they were socially constructed, and an integration of the historical data with the sociological interpretation. Part 3 of the book is aimed to achieve this integration.

Researching and writing the different cases demonstrates the validity of the analytical stand which states that it is very difficult to have a good understanding of deviance without understanding the relevant context in which it took place. Hence in each case we tried, within a limited space, to provide such a construction so that the total effect of the cases would be that of a "reliving the past" experience (Zunz 1985). Whenever I could, I went to the actual places where the assassinations took place, especially in Jerusalem, to the point where my colleagues began to refer to my trips in the city as the "assassination tours." Whenever possible, I gave the contemporary name of the street, placed together with the older one.

Many of the assassinations were committed by actors from particular groups, characterized by specified symbolic-moral universes. When the involvement of a group was confined to one case only, I usually described the group within the account of the case itself. However, there were groups which were involved in many cases. Chapter 4 provides a short and general description of these groups. Following the presentation of the different cases in part 2, it becomes possible to extract the position and apparatus these groups had regarding political assassination. This presentation, which is an extension of the discussion in chapter 4, will appear in part 3 (chapter 12). There, its digestion will become easier.

Choosing the cases was completely guided and dictated by the definition developed for the characterization of political assassination events (chapter 2). All the cases were classified into the four categories presented in chapter 2: (1) "preplanning"; (2) "planning"; (3) "unsuccessful"; (4) "successful."

MAIN RESULTS OF THE STUDY

To make reading of the following chapters more productive, this section details the main findings of this study, so that the reader would be more sensitized to the construction of the cases themselves. The *full* set of findings, and the sociological interpretations will be presented in part 3.

The first cluster of conclusions refers to the pattern of political assassination events as a particular form of killing. These events exhibit a unique pattern: the "typical" political assassination event tends to take place in the morning or the evening of a Monday or a Friday, in the month of March (or May). The frequency of the assassination events was magnified in the years 1939, 1947, and less so in 1944 and 1946. The overwhelmingly preferred weapon was a hand gun (or a bomb). Typically, the event took place in one of the large urban centers. Tel Aviv came first, to be followed by Jerusalem and Haifa. While most British targets were hit in the Jerusalem area, the Jewish targets were hit, typically, in the Tel Aviv area (and much less so in the Haifa area). Chances were that only the specific target was hit. However, the use of a mine/bomb, or explosive envelops, increased the probability that innocent bystanders would be hit. Most victims were not very prominent males, over forty years old with families. Only a very small and insignificant minority of the victims were females, reflecting the fact that females remained overwhelmingly outside the major Jewish-Arab-British conflict before 1948. There were no female victims after 1948.

The second cluster of findings relates to the events and their interpretation. The rhetorical device "political assassination" can in fact be used to describe quite a few cases of this particular form of killing in the cultural matrix of Judaism, in Palestine-Israel. However, the prevalence of political assassinations is not very high *compared* to some other cultures (e.g., in some South American societies, where one could even find so-called "assassination squads"; or in some Muslim Mediterranean societies).

The majority of known cases do *not* involve a lone fanatic killer, but constitute a premeditated, planned act, committed by a group or by a representative of a group. Thus, the specific pattern of assassinations which emerges from this research is a very interesting one. I chose to call it *collective political assassinations* since most cases involve more than one assassin. While the actual assassin may be only one, in most cases this person is linked very intimately to a *group* which plans the assassination, gives the assassins a much needed moral support, the vocabularies of motives needed to perform the task, as well as shelter and the means needed to execute the plan of assassination. In many cases the victim was warned, sometimes more than once. The fact that most cases involve a group, usually quite secretive, makes it very difficult to fully and thoroughly document the cases.

The assassins typically felt as part of a specific symbolic-moral universe, and the act signified the boundaries not only of that universe but of a larger cultural matrix as well (e.g., see Ben-Yehuda 1985). The rhetorical device called political assassination, as it has existed among Jews in the land of secular miracles, is associated to a similar pattern that had existed in Europe: an assassin who operates as part of, or representing, a larger more or less crystallized symbolic-moral universe.

Two "reasons" for assassinations are salient: (a) revenge and a warning signal; (b) prevention of, or interference in, a process of social or political change represented or proposed by the victim. Moreover, the fact that many cases occurred *after* the potential victim did something, was warned, and that therefore most cases were considered as *revenge* as well as a warning sign implies that there is a "strange" system of "justice" in operation here.

Political assassination, as a particular rhetorical device, is invoked to explain and justify acts that seem like justice to the assassins in situations where they felt that they could not get a fair justice because the opportunities for such justice were felt to be blocked. It is as if an alternative system of justice was put into operation. Being secret and collective, however, makes it very difficult to fully expose in detail the ways through which this system works.

The dramatic fact which emerges from the study is that after the State of Israel was formally established, the incidence of political assassination events declined very sharply and significantly.

Before 1949, most cases were committed by the three main pre-State underground Jewish groups, with Lehi the most prominent one. However, the overwhelming number of persons assassinated, especially by Lehi, were Jews. This conclusion is quite surprising to say the least. A major challenge to the sociological interpretation will be directed at resolving this puzzle.

CHAPTER 2

Political Assassinations: Theoretical Background

INTRODUCTION

Having laid out the general theoretical foundations for developing a systematic sociology of deviance approach to political assassinations—this chapter will integrate the previous conceptualizations in order to spell out this approach.[1] Eventually, three questions will be answered as this chapter unfolds: (1) What is the relationship between political deviance and political assassinations? (2) How does our understanding of political deviance clarify political assassinations and vice versa? (3) How does the study of political assassinations illustrate some of the broader issues associated with the study of deviance in general, and political deviance in particular?

Havens Leiden and Schmitt (1970:xi), as well as Ivianski, (1977:59) note that the area of political assassinations lacks clear definitions and systematic research; the sociology of political assassinations does not constitute an exception. It really does not exist. Hence, a major goal of this work is to document, analyze and *interpret* (e.g., Geertz 1973; Walzer 1987) acts of political assassinations by Jews in Palestine-Israel and use this case in order to develop a new and systematic social approach to the sociology of political assassinations.

The way in which the name "political assassinations" was used implied that a variety of killings have been included in it, which have, at times, lacked a valid common denominator.

Furthermore, *before* starting to collect cases of political assassinations for this study, we had to have a clear criteria to help select the cases, and decide which cases to include in the study. Thus, the goal of this chapter is to provide a clear and working definition of political assassinations that is methodologically sound and theoretically justified.

The major reasons for limiting the scope of this study to one particular culture were (a) accessibility to data, and (b) an opportunity to examine in depth a particular form of deviance within what may be considered as a more or less similar, albeit infinitesimally complex (e.g., see Goldscheider and Zuckerman 1984; Cohen and Mendes-Flohr 1987) culture.

However, one can not simply present a sociological approach to political assassinations without first reviewing, even briefly, the comparative wisdom on this issue. Hence, the next four subsections are devoted to a critical review of the relevant scholarly literature.

HISTORICAL AND THEORETICAL BACKGROUND

Assassinations and Assassins

The rhetorical device "assassination" refers to a very particular form of taking somebody else's life against his/her will. It has, by now, become almost a tradition for works on political assassinations to try and locate the source of the term. Let me, therefore, continue this tradition and delve—very briefly—into the term itself. The exact source and original meaning of the term "assassin" does not have a *crucial* importance for us. Admittedly, there is *some* importance (as well as curiosity) for charting how the rhetorical device assassination came into being, and what it may have meant originally. However, finding out what the original meaning was, and comparing it with the meaning being given to it in contemporary cultures is most certainly not the focus of this study. Indeed, while there is much resemblance between the original terms and its contemporary usage, the contemporary definition which is to be developed in this chapter, is *based* on relativism and thus the possibly true and original meaning of "assassinations" gains only secondary importance.

As Rapoport points out, the word assassin has an Arabic origin, and refers to a particular pattern of killing which was practiced by an Islamic religious cult which called itself the Ismaili. The goal of the early Ismaili was to help purify Islam by terror, and by killing major officials who the Ismaili saw as corrupt and wrongdoers (1971:3–4). The Ismailis, however, had no exclusive rights on this form of killing. There were past movements which used assassination as part of their struggle. Well-known groups are the Thugs (who killed for Kali—e.g., see Rapoport 1984; Hurwood 1970:13–16), or the Sicariis (to be discussed next chapter). The order of Assassins, however, is probably the most famous of them all.

Describing and analyzing the history of the order of Assassins was done by other scholars, and a *full* account of their history and activity is clearly beyond the scope of this work (e.g., see Hodgson 1955; Lewis 1967). A brief account, however, is in order.

The death of the Islamic prophet, Mohammed, came at 632 and created a crisis. One result of solving the crisis was the creation of the Caliphate, which institutionalized the Prophet's charisma. Abu Bakr became the Khalifa. There were those, though, who disagreed, and felt that Ali—the cousin and son-in-law of the Prophet, had a better and stronger claim than Abu Bakr. This particular dissenting group became known as the *Shiatu Ali* (Ali's party), and later as *Shia*. That early conflict gave birth to a most important cleavage in Islam (Lewis 1968:20).

Around the year 760 a particular group broke away from Shiism. They called themselves Ismailis, after Ismail, son of Jafar al-Sadiq, great grandson of Ali and Fatima. At the end of the eleventh century, a secret society of the Ismailite sect was founded in Persia by Hassan-i Sabbah. Hassan-i Sabbah was born, at an unknown date, in the Persian city of Qumm, and died in 1124. Hassan apparently traveled extensively in the Middle East, North Africa, and Egypt, winning converts. His goal was to disseminate heterodox doctrine and battle the Seljuq Empire.

Hassan needed a base and by 1090 he had enough followers to help him conquer (1090–1091) the fortress of Alamut in the Elburz mountains (in northern Persia, south of the Caspian sea). Alamut became the headquarters of Hassan's sect and Hassan himself became known as the Old Man of the Mountain, or the Grand Master. Hassan, however, wanted to gain more converts and have more bases. He apparently felt that Islam could, and should, be purified by assassinating in a systematic way, all of its major officials, whom he chose to define as corrupt. Hassan clearly aimed to unify Islam into one coherent and integrated community. Hassan and his sect have thus developed the "art of assassination."

They were quite successful in spreading fear and trembling (Rapoport 1984). Hassan's ruthlessness was justified on religious grounds. He chose young, intelligent, and able people, full of enthusiasm and faith. They were then trained and taught the principles of Hassan's interpretation of the faith and then sent on their deadly missions.

The groups of these young men were called *Fidais*. There are uncorroborated reports (traced to Marco Polo) that Hassan's young assassins, at Alamut, were led into a so-called "garden of paradise" where they consumed Hashish. The purpose of this supposed ritual was to persuade the converts that paradise awaits them, even if they get caught and executed after carrying out their assassination plots. Better yet, the ritual led them to believe that it was in their interest to be caught and die and thus hasten their entry to paradise. Hence the name Hashishin became synonymous with Hassan's sect.

There are a few good reasons to suspect the validity and truthfulness of the story about the Hashish consumption (e.g., see Lewis 1968:12; Rapoport 1984; Ford 1985:100–104), but the fact that it was socially constructed, told, and possibly believed, created a dynamic of a self-fulfilling prophecy.

The Assassins, as they became known to the West by the Crusaders, were quite successful, and gained almost full control of Syria. Furthermore, in the Muslim context the basis of power was personal. Hence, when a Sultan, or an Amir, were assassinated (or died), this base of power disintegrated (Rapoport 1984). Assassinations within this cultural context were thus a powerful weapon.

At the twelfth century the Assassins were led by the last Grand Master—Rukh-al-Din Khurshah. The end of Rukh, and of the Assassins came under the double assault of the Mongols and of the Mamluk Sultan of Egypt, Baybars.

In 1256 the fortress of Alamut fell. Later, and throughout the 1270s, many other fortresses of the Assassins throughout the Middle East fell. Thousands of Assassins where killed. That was the end of the ruthless organization which threw an ugly shadow over the region for almost two centuries. While the thirteenth century marked the virtual end of the Assassins as a sect, the stories and reports about them, their ideology and methods, were carried into Europe by the Crusaders.[2]

Hence, Hassan helped into being one of the strangest, most bizarre and interesting, groups of Assassins, as well as the name.

The assassins developed an organized attempt, and policy, which exhibited one of the most important features of political assassination: a carefully and nonrandom selection of a target, coupled with a carefully planned assassination plot.

The pattern of assassination, however, was very interesting and unique. The assassins killed unprovoked, in a particularly vile manner, and after they had befriended their victim (Rapoport 1971).

While the Ismaili enriched the English language with an important rhetorical device, they were neither the first, nor the last, to use the tool of killing a specific person in the context of a political struggle. This route of action was practiced in Biblical times, during the Graeco-Roman times, in medieval Europe and in other times, cultures, and places (e.g., see Rapoport 1971; Ford 1985). Hence, in some instances assassins were hired, in other cases assassinations were used in the context of a revolution (the French, Russian and others). Furthermore, rulers and governments found themselves involved in assassination plots.

The word assassination in English, following the Ismaili practice, was focused not on the person attacked so much as in the *manner* of attack. It was conceptualized to be a premeditated form of killing, committed by stealth or by lying in wait—the opposite of a duel. The victim was *not* always a prominent person, and the assassin was often hired. There generally was not a personal relationship between assassin and victim. The Ismaili assassins' main "crime," in this context, was conceptualized as one of betraying a trust and ignoring natural sentiments created by an intimate relationship (Rapoport 1971:4). One has to notice that it must be the combination of planning the assassination *and* the intimate relationship which must have been so bizarre.

It is clearly the case that one can see, without much difficulty, that a dazzling variety of phenomenon may exist under the names political assassination, assassination, political murder, individual terror, and the like. In fact, one may even claim that the interpretations of the phenomenon we refer to as political assassination is *so* diverse and culturally dependent that we may be in a better analytical position if we do not attempt to define it altogether. Indeed, Kirkham, Levy, and Crotty (1970:1) chose exactly this approach. I rejected this route. I had to decide *what* did and did not constitute a case of bona fide political assassination. Without such a definition no real or precise empirical progress could be accomplished. I was convinced that the basic underlying characterization of what may seem like a variety of phenomenon is there, giving a platform for a possible and uniform, clear definition. Hence, I decided to try and develop a definition and characterization of political assassinations which would *assume* diversity and would transcend it, from a sociology of deviance perspective. The rest of this chapter reflects this effort. I shall touch the subjects of the impact and results of political assassinations, the theoretical background and various definitions of political assassinations. Then I shall develop, in gradual stages, my own definition and characterization for political assassinations.

I will focus on a definitional approach which will converge not so much on the *manner* of killing, but on the *specificity* of the target. Most of the other meanings of assassination (as mentioned previously) will be kept.

THE IMPACT AND RESULTS OF POLITICAL ASSASSINATIONS

The question of the impact, or usefulness, of political assassinations occupied the attention of most scholars who worked in this area. Some even blended the question of the *impact* with the question of the *morality* of political assassination (e.g., see Hyams 1974:14–17; Ford 1985).

Havens, Leiden, and Schmitt (1970:36) point out that assessing the impact of political assassinations is very difficult. They distinguish between (a) the immediate impact of the act and the significance that history ultimately assigns to it, and (b) the personal impact versus the systemic impact. They (pp. 37–39) suggest six possible types of systemic impacts of political assassinations:

1. No discernible changes are produced.
2. Personal changes occur that would not have taken place otherwise (e.g., the succession of Lyndon Johnson after Kennedy's assassination).
3. Some change induced in a particular policy.
4. Inducing profound alteration in the political system (e.g., the assassination of Rafael Trujillo Molina in the Dominican Republic, (May 30, 1961), Patrice Lumumba in the Congo, (January 1961), Julius Caesar.
5. Inducing an actual social revolution (e.g., the assassination of Alvaro Obregon in Mexico in 1928)
6. Helping a whole political system to collapse and disappear (e.g., the assassination of Engelbert Dollfus, Austria's Chancellor in 1934; that of Archduke Francis Ferdinand and his wife on June 28, 1914 by Gavrilo Princip in Sarajevo).

Taking all this into consideration it may be easier, and more fruitful, to discuss the *results* of political assassinations and not so much the impact. Rapoport rightly points out that: "The lone assassin can set furious political forces in motion, but only conspirators have a reasonable chance of controlling them, and the best way to exploit the opportunity provided by an assassination is to usurp the powers of government" (1971:22). That is, Rapoport implies that the chances of an assassination to achieve a meaningful change (if that has been the original goal at all), depend on the ability of the assassin(s)/conspirators to follow it up by a meaningful political action. One simply must be reminded, though, that assassinating for revenge, for propaganda and assassinating a tyrant (e.g., see Laqueur 1978:7–43) may all achieve their explicit goals, and significant results, even without following it up with an immediate and integral (to the assassination) political process.

Summarizing his work, Ford (1985:387) asks "Is assassination ever justified?"; "Does assassination work?" and "Has assassination proved that it can solve problems, not only in the short but also in the long run?" Ford unequivocally answers that "the history of countless assassinations, examined with an eye to comparing apparent motives with actual outcomes, contains almost none that produced results consonant with the aim of the doer, assuming those aims to have extended at all beyond the miserable taking of a life." Put, perhaps, in different terms one could rephrase and dramatize Ford's rhetorical device into stating that "political assassination is morally wrong and pragmatically useless." Judging by his most impressive and scholarly work, one must cope with this strong generalization.

The contents of morality is something which is specific to particular symbolic-moral universes—hence, its relative interpretative nature. However, being opposed, in principle, to murder, how could anyone oppose the moral statement, based on universalistic principles, that political assassination is morally wrong? One simply can not do this. However, the other question is whether political assassinations can be *justified*, and if so, on what grounds. A specific (particularistic) symbolic-moral universe can, no doubt, justify assassinations on moralistic grounds. However, there are other grounds as well. When it comes to social constructions in the form of justifications, that is the *pragmatic* aspect, Ford's position is more difficult to accept and defend. Obviously, numerous political assassinations had results—both on the personal and on the system level. Even Hassan's Assassins achieved, for a while, some very impressive results. We certainly may not always like those results, but we cannot simply deny their existence.

Hence, political assassinations which were aimed as revenge, as propaganda by deed or for elite substitution, were certainly pragmatic in the sense that more than once, they achieved some clear results. Had it not been the case, how are we to explain the persistence of the acts? Furthermore, the fact that political assassinations achieved results more than once is amply documented. We shall have, however, to reexamine this issue very closely later, in light of the results of this study.

Leiden (in Kirkham, Levy, and Crotty 1970:9–10) argued that: "An assassination can have a high impact when (a) the system is highly centralized, (b) the political support of the victim is highly personal, (c) the 'replaceability' of the victim is low, (d) the system is in crisis and/or in a period of rapid political and social change, and (e) if the death of the victim involves the system in confrontation with other powers." It is not entirely clear whether *all* these conditions must co-exist simultaneously for an impact effect to exist, or whether only part of the conditions must be present, and if so what part. For example, it is not obvious whether condition (b) was valid for the fateful June 28, 1914 assassination of Archduke Francis Ferdinand in Sarajevo. Likewise, it is not obvious that condition (d) was valid for the July 20, 1944 attempt to assassinate Hitler. Both events did have severe impacts. Hence, the above characterization may be overinclusive. Furthermore, the word impact is problematic. As argued before, the word result serves us much better. However, once we switch from thinking in terms of impacts into thinking in terms of results, the question of "under what conditions are results achieved?" takes on very different meaning. Such conditions would be difficult, if not impossible, to chart. But nevertheless, one *can* still ask some questions about results for the short and long run, as well as for the different social actors who were involved in the assassination. While such impact as "revenge" is meaningless, as a result it is very meaningful.

Theoretical Background for Political Assassinations

As noted earlier, with very few exceptions, the overwhelming majority of works on political assassinations were written by either political scientists and historians, or by psychologists and psychiatrists. These perspectives, especially that of political theory and science, tend to emphasize the power dimension. In this section I shall review, very briefly, the main findings of these efforts.

A major discussion in the literature is the typical association between terrorism and assassinations. Most authors tend to analyze assassinations as part of terrorism (e.g., see Snitch 1982; Rapoport 1971).

Snitch (1982) identified five *basic* goals for terrorism and, in his approach, for political assassinations as well. These goals are:

1. to receive popular recognition for a cause/group.
2. to receive official recognition for a cause/group.

3. to gain recruits.

4. to undermine the morale and prestige of the government.

5. to provoke the government to use such harsh and desperate measures as martial law, curfews, massive arrests, so that popular discontent would take place and help throw the government.

Rapoport (1971) distinguishes between assassinations which are simply assassinations and those that are part of a terrorist campaign. The former are a legitimate, useful means in power struggles.

In the West, over time, three justifications developed for assassination (p. 7). The *first* was a purely instrumental one, developed by the Greeks and Romans, stipulating that the moral value of an assassination depends entirely on the end(s) achieved. The *second*, developed by Christian philosophers, stipulates that political assassination is evil in itself, but nonetheless can be justified on the grounds that it can prevent a greater evil. The *third* was developed solely to justify an assassination which was part of a terrorist campaign. Participation in the struggle, or assassination, was a good thing in itself regardless of the particular results achieved.

A few scholars associated political assassinations with terrorism and political instability in particular (e.g., Kirkham, Levy, and Crotty 1970; Crotty 1971). The value of this approach is that it does not attribute assassinations primarily to "crazy" and "irrational" individuals. It negates, for the most part, what Clarke (1982:5) labeled the "pathological theory of assassination," namely theorizing that "assassins are acutely disturbed persons who suffer from such a diminished sense of self that their lives become increasingly isolated, bitter and unbearable." (See also Conklin 1986:157–158). This approach received much support from a few studies which suggested that most of those "who have assassinated, or attempted to assassinate Presidents of the United States...have been mentally disturbed persons who did not kill to advance any rational political plan" (Kirkham, Levy, and Crotty 1970:78). However, this position can be challenged easily and repeatedly, both on the grounds of the diagnosis and as not characterizing accurately assassins who were sent by groups.

Kirkham, Levy, and Crotty (1970:148–211), Crotty (1971), Clarke (1982), Feierabend et al. 1971; Feierabend and Feierabend (1976) all try to understand political assassinations as a possible *systemic* property of specific cultures, or social orders, at particular times. The conditions under which political assassinations flourish hence becomes an important issue for these scholars.

It may well be that destabilization and chaos result from many political assassinations. But the reverse is conceivable too; and deciding which variable is dependent, and which is independent, can theoretically be solved by resorting to history. Furthermore, this approach does not tell us much about the criminological and sociological *nature* and particular *pattern* of assassination.

Havens, Leiden, and Schmitt (1970:4–46) conclude that the level of societal institutionalization of the political system is a crucial variable. Stable societies experience fewer political assassinations, and the systemic impact of such events—if they happen—is minimal. Rapoport (1971) offers a dissenting position noting that the extraordinarily high number of assassinations of U.S. presidents compared to that of Latin America suggests that the centralization of administrative and symbolic authority in the hands of one person may be a more important condition.

Many of the cross-cultural studies on political assassinations suggesting the above conclusions are based only on U.S. newspaper coverage of such events (e.g., the *New York Times*). However, this source is very problematic (more on this in the next chapter), thus the conclusions are problematic.

Definitions of Political Assassinations in the Literature

One major primary problem in this area appears in the form of a deceptively simple question: what exactly *is* the nature of a political assassination? The relevant literature[3] does not provide a crystallized consensus regarding this issue. A major reason for this confusion may be due to the fact that it is not at all clear whether different scholars were defining the *same phenomenon*. Hence, it may be that "individual terror," as defined by Ivianski, is an altogether different phenomenon than political assassinations as defined by Lerner, or others.

A major and typical problem in this area has been the analytic tendency to blur between the concept of political assassination with that of *terrorism* (e.g., see the deliberations of Wardlaw 1982; Hyams 1974:15–17, 166–167; Clutterbuck 1977:31, 96), mass murder, political executions, and the like. To exemplify the complexity of this problem, let us use a few illustrations of some prevalent definitions. The following definitions were chosen deliberately because they *all* focus on events which appear, prima facie, as political assassinations in nature. The various definitions interpret these events in different ways. Our use of "rhetorical devices" later in this chapter, is meant to bypass the painful, confusing, and to some extent even hopeless, problem of a definition.

Defining and characterizing political assassination was attempted by a few scholars. One frequently quoted, and early, definition was suggested by Lerner (1930:27): "Assassination refers to those killings or murders, usually directed against individuals in public life, motivated by political rather than by personal relationships.... Assassination is the deliberate, extralegal killing of an individual for political purposes." Lerner's definition includes some very important elements, and was adopted by Wilkinson (1976:4). Kirkham, Levy, and Crotty (1970), writing some forty years after Lerner, stated that "we do not undertake to define precisely what is meant by an 'assassination,' nor do we limit consideration in this Report to a particular consistent definition of 'assassination.' There are at least three separate elements woven into the concept of 'assassination' which identify it as a particular kind of murder: (1) a target that is a prominent political figure; (2) a political motive for the killing; (3) the potential political impact of the death or escape from death, as the case may be" (p. 1).

Padover (1943:680) defined assassination as "the trucidation...of a political figure without due process of law." Havens, Leiden, and Schmitt (1970:2–6) suggest that assassination refers to "the deliberate, extralegal killing of an individual for political purposes" (p. 4). Hurwood (1970) chose a broader approach, stating that "what generally distinguished assassination from ordinary homicide...was an assumption that the assassin acted on behalf of others, or out of fanatical devotion to some cause or faith" (p. 1). Crotty (1971:8) broadened this approach even further and defined political assassination as "the murder of an individual, whether of public prominence or not, in an effort to achieve political gains."

Lester avoided the problem of the definition by stating that: "Assassins fall into three categories: murders by a hired killer who has no personal involvement with the victim, conspiracies for political change, and killings based on personal animosities" (1986:216). The emphasis on a "hired assassin" and on categorizaion evades the core question—what *is* a political assassination?

The broadest definition is located in Ford's 1985 book. There he states: "Assassination is the intentional killing of a specified victim, or group of victims, perpetrated for reasons related to his (her, their) public prominence and undertaken with a political purpose in view" (p. 2).

Ivianski uses a most interesting rhetorical device: individual terror. Although he never defines the opposite (e.g., "collective terror"?), the definition he provides for individual terror is: "a system of modern revolutionary violence aimed at leading personalities in the government or the Establishment (or any other human targets). The motivation is not necessarily personal but rather ideological or strategic" (1977:50). In 1981 he repeated this claim and stated explicitly that individual terror was different from political assassination in that the former aimed to hit the state or the regime which was represented by the target, and not the target per se (p. 409). However, already on the first page of his 1977 paper he falls into what may be an unavoidable trap when he states that: "One act of 'individual terror'—the assassination of Archduke Francis Ferdinand at Sarajevo." Thus, although Ivianski may give the impression that he discusses a theory which is aimed to explain late nineteenth-century terror (especially Russian and the infamous *Narodnaya Volya*), he is in fact discussing political assassinations proper as well (also in his 1981 paper). If we confine his definition only to nineteenth-century terrorism (which is doubtful), than obviously fewer generalizations can be made. If we do not, than his definition is too broad and lacks specificity as far as political assassinations are concerned. Political assassination is not just "violence," it is the use of deadly force. Also, it does not have to be defined as "revolutionary" (e.g., Sirhan Sirhan's 1968 assassination of Robert F. Kennedy). Some of the assassins may, perhaps, *want* to use this particular account, or rhetorical device, but we do not have to accept this for more than what it really is. Furthermore, Ivianski fails to take notice of the fact that governments may in fact commit acts of political assassinations (e.g., the assassination of Trotsky in August of 1940), not to mention individual terror and terrorism in general (e.g., see Stohl and Loppez 1984; Cline and Alexander 1986), and genocide and mass murder (e.g., see Chalk and Jonassohn 1990; Harff and Gurr 1984; Kuper 1982, 1986).

Although Turk is quick to point out that motivation is extremely difficult to establish, he nevertheless defines assassination as: "a politically motivated killing in which victims are selected because of the expected political impact of their dying" (1983:83). Turk's definition is close to my definition, particularly with its emphasis on the *selection* of the victim. I will add to this the element of the *specificity* of the victim as well. Furthermore, there are a few more elements which need to be introduced into the definition of political assassination than what is implied by Turk's economical definition.

Finally, Rapoport suggested one of the most elaborate and thoughtful definitions. For him, an assassin: "means murderer but more than that, it means an unprovoked murderer who kills in a particularly vile manner. In the common law assassination is murder committed without warning by stealth, surprise, or lying in wait. The assailant has been hired for the occasion, or he undertakes it for political purposes. In any case the victim, usually though not necessarily a prominent person, has not provoked the assault by offering the assassin a personal offense" (1971:4).

It is thus evident that defining/characterizing the concept of political assassination has become an Herculean and Sisyphian task. Different definitions focus on a range which goes from a specific target to a collective target, and from a 'prominent' political target to any target. Such an analytical mix is not very useful.

TOWARD A NEW DEFINITION
OF POLITICAL ASSASSINATIONS

The Sociology of Taking Somebody Else's Life

One common element which clearly marks political assassination is the fact that it revolves around the attempt, sometimes successful, to take the life of somebody else. This element has constituted one of the classical subjects for the sociology of deviance.

The biblical injunction "Thou Shall Not Murder" could be interpreted to mean that taking another human being's life is a universal crime. It is not. Such a command is defined differently in different times and/or cultures (Nettler 1982; Lester 1986). It is also defined differently in the same culture. Hence different types of accounts and rhetorical devices (e.g., see Potter and Wetherell 1987) are used to make such an act "explainable" or "justifiable." These, in turn, depend on the interpretation of the circumstances. Thus, while the act of taking somebody's life against his/her wish may appear to the lay person as universally forbidden, the interpretation of such acts is culturally dependent and hence, very relative. Consequently, taking somebody's life is not universally forbidden. Killing other people, in short, is not always interpreted as a negative and stigmatized act—it can certainly be interpreted as positive deviance.

The type of rhetorical device which will be used to describe the death of an actor will, first of all, depend on whether we view that death as natural. A natural death would usually mean that the actor has finished what we may consider his/her natural life span and dies, without any intentional (e.g., suicidal, criminal), or unintentional (e.g., accidental), help from him/herself or another person. The rhetorical devices "deceased," "passed away," or simply "died," would typically be employed in this case.

When death is not defined as natural, other rhetorical devices are invoked. One very basic distinction in this case is whether the potential victim agreed, or even willed and wished, to die. If the answer to this question is positive, then a small pool of rhetorical devices becomes available. For example, the rhetorical device called "suicide" and its variations (e.g., Hara-kiri), euthanasia (with consent), and the like. This category, however, is not very relevant to political assassinations.

The other possibility is that the potential victim does not agree, or wish, to die. The act of taking the victim's life against his/her wish thus becomes a typically forceful and violent act. In such a case, another cultural pool of rhetorical devices becomes available to make a culturally meaningful interpretation of the act of taking another person's life against his/her will.

When a situation is defined using the rhetoric device of war, then taking other humans' life is not only excusable, it is mandatory for so-called "combat soldiers." It is even rewarded by powerful symbols and can be defined as "positive deviance." Hence, under normal combat circumstances, we do not say that a soldier murdered his enemy, or vice versa. Wars, however, do have some rules, and some acts of taking other peoples' life—even in a war situation—may in fact be regarded as murder (e.g., killing prisoners of war).

Such rhetorical devices as "infanticide" (e.g., Piers 1978), "child homicide" (Fiala and LaFree 1988), "self-defense," or "blood revenge" in some Middle Eastern (and other) societies (e.g., Ginat 1984; Daly and Wilson 1988:221–251; Bohem 1984), as well as "genocide" (e.g., Kuper 1982, 1986; Walliman and Dobkowski 1987; Chalk and Jonassohn 1990) and "lynching" (e.g., Olzak 1988) may also be used to justify and/or explain acts of taking other peoples' life, as well as such other ritualistic situations defined as vendettas, human sacrifices, and duels.

The famous rhetorical device called *Homicide* may itself be classified into criminal and noncriminal. Each of these devices is further divided into finer distinctions. *Criminal homicide* is defined differently in different countries and states. Goode (1984), for example, draws our attention to the legal accounts used in New York state for this particular rhetorical device: murder, voluntary manslaughter, involuntary manslaughter, and criminally negligent homicide. He also draws our attention to two forms of *noncriminal homicide*: *excusable* (e.g., in specified car accidents) and *justifiable* (e.g., a policeman shooting what may be defined as a fleeing felon—see, for example, Scharf and Binder 1983; Lester 1986:61–71). Furthermore, some people view abortion as homicide. We can realize, therefore, that acts of taking other people's life get different labels as different rhetorical devices are utilized to describe them. Thus, Goode's (1984:221) conclusion that *"the taking of human life is tolerated under certain circumstances"* is clearly valid (emphasis in original). (See also Reid 1982:214–219; Bonn 1984:187–191; Barlow 1984:135–147; Conklin 1986.) Circumstances, however, are not just "given" and typically require definitions and interpretations. Hence, cultures provide a variety of rhetorical devices, vocabularies of motives and accounts (some of which are institutionalized in the law) aimed at defining differentially acts of taking other peoples' life (for a review, see Nettler 1982). Furthermore, murderers tend to develop their own vocabularies for justifying murder (e.g., see Dietz 1983; Hepworth and Turner 1974; Levi 1981).

There are two sets of variables which may help us get out of the problematics of the definition. First, the term assassination is focused on the specificity of the act. Unlike the impersonal and indiscriminate acts of terrorism, political assassination is selective, discriminate, and has a very specific target.

Second, the term assassination implies something very different from criminal homicide (e.g., see Wolfgang 1958; Goode 1984:219–228). While the rhetorical device called criminal homicide is used within what is defined as the criminal context, and other types of homicide within other contexts, the rhetorical device called assassination seems to be used mostly in noncriminal contexts and is closely affiliated to power politics and morality in an explicit way. Hence, while the rhetorical device called a "typical murder" (as a specific subcategory of criminal homicide) refers to something which "takes place between intimates, not strangers, and is usually unplanned" (Goode 1984:222), the rhetorical device called a political assassination refers to something which is diametrically opposed: it is planned and typically takes place between strangers. Thus one important element in the characterization of assassination is what assassination is not—it is not a "typical" murder (see also Hyams 1969; Heaps 1969).

Political assassination is a *name* given to a particular form of taking somebody else's life against his/her wish. Therefore, we have first to delineate the *theoretical* parameters which are needed to understand those characteristics that constitute this distinct form of killing.

Political Assassination Events and Their Interpretation

Political assassinations, no doubt, form a particular pattern of deviance. As such, we can distinguish between the *act* of political assassination itself, and its *interpretation*. While the act constitutes part of what some will define as "objective reality," its interpretation is culturally dependent. Dostoyevsky's imaginary hero-victim Raskolnikov (in *Crime and Punishment* [1866]), illustrates this point when he tries to construct a variety of some very different accounts in order to "justify" the murder he committed.

Kirkham, Levy, and Crotty suggest the use of an important and useful term: *Assassination Events*. The term *event* is useful for two reasons. First, it helps to demarcate the act from its *cultural interpretation*. Second, it helps reveal the important distinction between executions and assassinations. The concept refers to:

> an act that consists of a plotted, attempted or actual, murder of a prominent political figure (elite) by an individual (assassin) who performs this act in other than a governmental role. This definition draws a distinction between political execution and assassination. An execution may be regarded as a political killing, but it is initiated by the organs of the state, while an assassination can always be characterized as an illegal act" (1970: Appendix A).

A political assassination event thus refers to the act of taking someone's life against the wish of that person. This definition, however, emphasizes a "prominent" figure. We shall get rid of this emphasis. The next question obviously is what *makes* this form of killing unique? How is such an event interpreted culturally in a way which makes sense to members of that culture and to the members of the relevant symbolic-moral universes? The *working definition* regarding the nature of political assassinations and executions which emerges from the analytical discussion so far, *and which we shall use,* is as follows:

> The characterization of a homicidal event as a political assassination or execution is a social construction. It is a rhetorical device which is used to socially construct and interpret (that is, to make a culturally meaningful account of) the discriminate, deliberate, intentionally planned, and serious attempt(s), whether successful or not, to kill a specific social actor for political reasons having something to do with the political position (or role) of the victim, his/her symbolic-moral universe, and with the symbolic-moral universe out of which the assassin/s act(s). This universe generates the legitimacy and justifications required for the act, which are usually presented in quasi-legal terms. However, decisions to assassinate are typically *not* the result of a fair legal procedure, based on a "due process"

Let us dissect this important definition to its component parts, and explain them. First, political assassination is a rhetorical device. It is a *name* which we use to interpret (and, for some, to justify) a particular act of killing. This name helps us to make sense of what otherwise is a terrible situation, and to construct a culturally meaningful account. The words rhetorical device obviously do neither mean an abuse of language, a linguistic trick, nor an attempt to disguise the "real" meaning of an event (Rapoport 1982).[4] The point is that there is no real or "objective" meaning because meaning is negotiable and culturally dependent. The term rhetorical device is utilized here precisely because the real meaning of an event is socially constructed and interpreted. The term means that the interpretation of a political assassination event is not objectively given. It is culturally constructed. What for one person (or group) is a political assassination bona fide, may be interpreted as a simple murder for another person (or group). For example, the assassination of Baron Walter Edward Guinnes Moyne, British Minister Resident in the Middle East, on November 6, 1944, in Cairo by two members of Lehi was defined by the British as an act of simple murder. However, the very same act was defined by Lehi as a legitimized and justified act of individual terror. Here we find deviance as a relative concept and interpretation. Using the term rhetorical device enables us to keep some distance from the event itself and yet, give room for a real and indigenous cultural interpretation. This term also helps us transcend the so many different and divergent definitions of political assassinations and suggest a more unified approach.

Second, political assassinations are not "crimes of passion." They constitute attempts to kill which are very carefully planned. This is why the definition emphasizes the deliberate and the intentional. Third, political assassinations are target specific. It is the *specificity* of the target which distinguishes political assassination from other acts of indiscriminate terrorism. Fourth, the definition emphasizes that the attempt to assassinate must be serious. It is not important whether the attempt was successful or not (that is, whether the specific target died or not). The "seriousness" of the attempt will be translated, in this study, into four distinct types, (see the last section in this chapter): preplanned,

planned, unsuccessful, and successful. Fifth, the reasons for which the potential victim is targeted are political, and are associated with the political role, or position, of the victim. This definition does not assume that the victim must be a *prominent* target. The elements of power and morality enter this definition in the front door because this part of the definition emphasizes that political assassinations events *are* the expression of power in the form of lethal force, whose use is justified on the basis of political-moral reasoning. Political assassination events can be directed from the periphery or from the center—both between and within different symbolic-moral universes.

Sixth, the symbolic-moral universes out of which the assassin(s) act(s), and of which the victim is part, are crucial elements in the interpretation. The elements of power and morality, which are so salient and explicit in political assassination events, consequently place these events squarely within the area of politics and deviance. Seventh, while the justifications for political assassinations tend to be presented by the assassins in quasi-legal rhetorical devices, decisions to assassinate are typically not the result of a procedure which is based on a "due process." The victim typically does not stand a fair chance to defend him/herself properly. This definition does not make a distinction whether the assassin(s) was/were hired or not, and it does not stipulate the existence of specified technical methods (or procedures) of killing (e.g., whether the assassin befriend his future victim). Finally, the definition neither makes assumptions about the relationships between assassin-victim (i.e., if they should, or should not, know each other); nor that the assassination be (or not) the result of a situational provocation (e.g., that one stranger provoked another in a specified situation, a struggle developed, and one of the strangers was killed).

It is often (but not always) in the interest of the assassin(s) to publicize the act (but usually not to expose the specific assassin, in cases where *groups* are responsible for the assassination), and the reason(s) for it, so that the function of demarcation of the boundaries of symbolic-moral universes will be accomplished. Thus, in all the cases that we located, 90 percent of the assassins were never caught. Only 5 percent were caught, brought to trial, and found guilty.

The concepts of power and morality, as explained in chapter 2, are crucial for understanding the nature of assassinations. The rhetorical device political assassination clearly has something to do with the use of power, on the one hand, and with the definition of symbolic-moral universes and with the maintenance of the boundaries of those universes, on the other hand.

Furthermore, the concept of "nihilation" has been suggested to refer to attempts by inhabitants of one symbolic-moral universe to use their power and legitimacy in order "to liquidate conceptually everything outside the same universe" (Berger and Luckmann 1966:132). A process of nihilation denies the legitimacy of reality constructions and interpretations, rhetorical devices and accounts, which originate in other symbolic-moral universes. Using the rhetorical device political assassination means that nihilation does not stop at the symbolic level.

The most important variable, which distinguishes political assassination from terrorism, is the specificity of the target.

Assassination always involve a serious attempt (whether successful or not) to use what is considered by the assassin, or by those who send him, as a legitimized deadly force against a *particular* target. This attempt is usually carried out without the nonsecret legitimacy and approval of the official, or appropriate, organ(s) of a state (or what is considered as its equivalent) which can bestow such a legitimacy (e.g., a court; a government). It is the death of actor X the assassin desires, and not the explosion of, say, an airplane per se.

"Assassination, no matter how narrowly or broadly defined, belong among a larger class of politically aggressive and violent behavior" (Kirkham, Levy, and Crotty 1970:164). The legitimacy for assassination is anchored in a different symbolic-moral universe than that of a state or a country, usually opposing or disagreeing with it in a most fundamental way. An execution is anchored in a secret process activated by specific organizations (or individuals) of a state (e.g., a secret intelligence service) or its equivalent (in terms of legitimizing the act). Thus, Hurwood (1970:34) states that only the *king* had the authority to give the legitimacy (and the order) for a political execution. Hence, as we shall show (in chapter 9), when the Israeli secret service set out to execute members of "Black September," the authorization for those acts came from the Prime Minister. It also appears that in the United States decisions to commit political executions involve the highest echelons of the military and political elites (e.g., see *Los Angeles Times*, April 12, 1989). Lehi, Etzel, and the Hagana, the three pre-state Jewish underground groups, committed many acts of political assassinations, and insisted that the authorization for these acts came from the political centers of those groups.

A country, a state, sometimes even a society, has—or generates—the legitimacy to use power. Thus, a country may legitimize the use of deadly force in war, death penalty, or define other situations where taking an actor's life is considered legitimate, even mandatory. Such legitimacy, however, can be generated also by much smaller and integrated ideological groups.

The existence, or nonexistence, of legitimacy (and who grants it) refers to a few related questions:

a. Whether a state or a country, through its official organs, approves a particular act of killing.

b. How is the decision arrived at; secretly or through an open public and fair due process (e.g., where a proper defense is presented and the potential victim has a chance of presenting his/her case in a persuasive way).

c. Whether the potential assassin(s) accept(s) the right of that state, or country, to give such a legitimacy.

Relating the variables of the specificity of the target to the legitimation to use deadly force enables us to draw a classificatory scheme:

The diagram cross-tabulates two distinct analytical levels: a state and an individual. No need for an intervening level variable is called for because the two levels in the diagram are sufficient to explain the different possible outcomes.

On the left side of the diagram two questions are answered; (a) whether the country/state approves, or does not approve, the assassination/killing; (b) whether the potential assassin/killer accepts, or does not accept, the legitimacy of the country/state to grant such authorization.

The differences between terrorism and political assassinations are evident. Terrorism usually aims at a general and collec-

DIAGRAM 2–1
SPECIFICITY OF TARGET
AND LEGITIMATION TO USE DEADLY FORCE

Legitimation to use Deadly Force	*Target*	
	Specific	*General*
State approves secretly, potential killer accepts	political execution	state sponsored terror; genocide
State approves openly, potential killer accepts	death penalty	war
State approves, potential killer does not accept	(no case)	(no case)
State does not approve, potential killer accepts	regular homicide (criminal and noncriminal)	multiple murders mass murders serial murders
State does not approve, potential killer does not accept	political assassination	terror

tive target. Political assassination is highly discriminative. It seeks the death of a very particular actor, and does not aim at the collective, or at an indiscriminate target. The above chart indicates that political assassinations and political executions are similar. The major difference between them is the issue of who legitimizes and authorizes assassination and why.

Some explanations about the diagram are needed at this point. A very sharp distinction is made in the diagram between a *specific* and a *general* target. This is the basis for distinguishing between terrorism and political assassinations. Another distinction is between terror and *State* sponsored terror. Both are directed against a nonspecific target. However, while terror is typically directed from the periphery toward the center, or the mainstream of society, State sponsored terrorism is directed from the State's center to the mainstream (e.g., the Stalinist terror; Pol Pot's terror/genocide) or the periphery (e.g., the campaign against the Ixil in Guatemala). There is an important analytical distinction between the late nineteenth-century Russian revolutionaries— *Narodnaya Volya* (and its tactics of terror), and Stalin's mass terror, or the mass terror aimed by the Guatemalan government against the Ixil. There, more than twenty thousand Guatemalans died between 1966–1978 at the hands of "death squads" (see van der Bergh 1988; Amnesty International Reports for 1978:123, 1980:140, 1981:149, 1982:140). Likewise, in the 1970s, at least fifteen thousand "disappeared" in Argentina (Amnesty International Report 1978:95), and death/assassination squads operated in El Salvador. Much worse and horrendous State sponsored terror and genocide campaigns were carried out by Nazi Germany against Jews, by Pol Pot's regime in Cambodia (Kampuchia) against millions of Cambodians (e.g., see Ngor and Warner 1987; *Time*, August 1, 1988:12). In one case the lethal force is aimed from the center; in the other case from the periphery (see also *Political Killings by Governments*, 1983; Harff and Gurr 1989).

Somewhere between political executions and State sponsored terrorism we can find the following examples concerning Iran and Iraq. Amnesty International Newsletter of October 1983 reports that: "The total number of executions in Iran since the 1979 revolution must be considerably higher than the 15,000-plus officially announced so far" (vol. 13, no. 10:10). Another Amnesty International Report state that between January 1977 and the end of 1977 "over 200 Iraqis were executed" (1978:250).

In a similar fashion, the column under specific target makes a distinction between a political execution, which is a political assassination sponsored by a State (e.g., Stalin's ordered assassination of Trotzky in 1940, or his "assassination squad" which was active during the late 1930s in Europe [Ford 1985:269–270; Schwartz 1988]), and a political assassination, which is not. Both are not dissimilar, but there are some important analytical and methodological differences between the two. To begin with, a *major* difference is the fact that States (totalitarian or democracies) have a very different basis of legitimacy than individuals, or groups. The amount, and type, of power which they can generate and use is very different too. Second, while political assassinations are typically directed from the periphery, political executions are directed from the center. While the above two points make political executions different from political assassinations, there are some substantial methodological differences too. The process of decision making in each case is very different; the methods of killing vary; and it is relatively easier to identify and validate cases of political assassinations than cases of political executions. States are typically very secret about cases of political executions.

While the previous definition of political assassination does not make a distinction between political assassinations and political executions, for the reasons mentioned here, I shall discuss the two separately (chapters 6–8 and 9).

Another relevant question is whether explanations invoked for the micro, individual level, of murder (e.g., why murderers kill) may be applicable to political assassinations and executions. In principle, such comparisons are not—prima facie—useful. There are, however, some cases which may be used. A *revengeful* political assassination may, in some general philosophical aspect, remind us of a *blood revenge*. In both cases there is a planned act of killing. However, while political assassination events are very target specific, blood revenge is specific only on the family level, that is the choice of a specific target is less important than hitting the specific collective.

One other comparison may be with "hired killers" (for non-political reasons), or with organized crime sponsored murders (e.g., see Sanders 1983:245–247; Levi 1981). The cold blood planning of the killing of a specific target must remind us of political assassination. Indeed, some may even identify similar "political" aspects in both cases. However, the similarities end here. Political assassination events are initiated by—and from—an *ideological* point of view. The conflict there is between opposing symbolic-moral universes struggling to change something meaningful and of significance in society. Hired killers (as defined above) *have* no political ideology. The act is done for a fee, and typically there is no group which may give legitimacy to the act. Even if such a group exists, (e.g., organized crime) its goal is not to achieve any kind of social change. On the contrary, hired killers are typically employed to "solve" local problems (e.g., of area) which are usually focused on such down-to-earth problems as monetary interests, intimidation of opponents, or gaining control over a territory.

One must add that the history of political assassinations and executions (for political reasons) provide us with enough cases of hired assassins, either by a government or by other groups. Our definition of political assassinations and executions does not exclude this possibility.

Another possible comparison may be with "compulsive" killers. It may be argued that groups which committed a few assassinations are compulsive killers. Leyton (1986) basically argues that "compulsive killers" suffer from an acute sense of status frustration, as if these killers are on the fringes of respectability and they commit their atrocities against those who they view as representatives of the social class which excluded them and denied them status. Our classificatory chart shows why both multiple and mass killers (e.g., see Levin and Fox 1985) cannot be compared to political assassination events on purely theoretical grounds. The evidence that political assassins resemble, even remotely, compulsive or mass killers does not exist. Furthermore, the application of the word compulsive, taken from *individual* behavior, to describe a group's *social* behavior is very problematic. While again, the "status frustration" hypothesis—applicable to the individual level—may in some philosophical sense resemble "frustration" of a social group which aspires to change society, the comparison ends here. The dynamics of making a decision to assassinate, the "reason" given, the specific choice of targets—all render the comparison as not valid.

While the above working definition/characterization of political assassination events seems exclusive and capable of providing generalizable and distinct guidelines, there are two additional categories of taking other people's life which may appear, prima facie, close. These are mass murders (e.g., see Levin and Fox 1985) and serial murderers (Holmes and DeBurger 1988). While these types of killing may, sometimes, share some common characteristics with political assassinations (e.g., the fact that a few groups committed *some* political assassinations), there are some very significant differences between them. Mass and serial murderers (as well as compulsive killers) do not typically select their victims on a basis characterized by a strong political "reasoning." The murders are usually hidden, and the personal pathology of the murderers is also typically present and emphasized.

Political assassinations thus exhibit almost all the traits of what we have come to know as general deviance, and of deviance and politics particularly.

Political assassinations, and executions, are culturally relative. Some may view them as a very negative form of deviance, while others would view them as a positive form of deviance. Some individuals, and organizations, most certainly view political assassinations and executions as an important political tool. These assassinations form the moral and political boundaries between the legitimate and illegitimate, the powerful and the powerless. In a society which is characterized by the existence of a multiplicity of centers, enveloped by their symbolic-moral universes, who conflict, clash and negotiate, political assassinations and executions may become not only important boundary markers, but a conflict resolution technique.

It is not uncommon for individual assassins, and their sponsoring groups, to view themselves as participants in a moral crusade. Typically, the last words of Princip (assassin of the Austrian Archduke Francis Ferdinand) before he was executed proclaimed his innocence and belief that his death was required by Serbia. He obviously felt himself a very righteous moral crusader. Individual assassin(s), and sponsoring groups, typically reject the prevailing hierarchy of morality and credibility, and project an alternative hierarchy. Political assassinations and executions thus explicitly refer to issues of power and morality. It should not surprise us to discover that bitter arguments are waged over the social construction and interpretation of the meaning of political assassinations. The debate is focused on turning a particular form of killing into a political statement. Consequently, political assassinations, and political executions, involve—in the deepest sense—arguments about power, and social and political justice. In some instances, political assassinations may involve political trials and political prisoners—if the assassin(s) is/are caught and brought to trial, which is not very common.

Terror and Assassination

Assassination as "propaganda by deed" was a strategy which was used in the nineteenth century (although it was also used by the Sicarii in the 60s A.D.) and it is typically associated today with terrorist movement's activities (Rapoport 1984).

A major source for confusion about the nature of political assassinations has come from the concept of terror. The word assassination can *legitimately* be used to describe an act of a terrorist. Rapoport and Ivianski argue that the theory of modern terror developed from the concept of tyrannicide which was, after all, a theory of assassination (1971; see also Ivianski 1977). Likewise, it is not difficult to conceptualize the Islamic Ismaili-Nizari ("Assassins") as terrorists. Ivianski's individual terror perhaps illustrates this possible confusion in the sharpest sense.

An illustration for the confusion between terror and assassination can be found in Clark's account about acts of terrorism/assassinations: "From June 1968, through December 1980, ETA ...[killed] 287...In Argentina...more than 2,300 persons were killed between July 1974 and August 1976. In Northern Ireland, more than 1,600 persons were killed...between 1969 and 1976" (1986:126). No distinctions are made here between victims of acts of assassination and acts of terror.

The modern tendency has been to view political assassinations exclusively within terrorism. Indeed, many terror movements and groups have advocated the use of political assassinations. One reason for why the concepts of "terror" and political assassination have been confused is not only because the concept of political assassination can be used to describe an activity of a terrorist group, but also because many terror movements used tactics of political assassinations (e.g., the *Narodnaya Volya*, *Lehi*). The distinction here is between political assassination and terror, as discrete activities. Terrorist groups however, can—and have—used political assassinations. While this work does not deny the validity, legitimacy and usefulness of viewing political assassinations within the context of terror, it is also worth our while to try and examine political assassinations as a separate analytical and empirical entity, as one more specific form of lethal violence. In this way, a magnified (and more sensitive) perspective of this particular phenomenon will emerge.

The distinction made here between an act of terrorism and political assassination and execution, as it emerges from the previous section, is very clear: the target of a political assassination plot *is a very specific individual*. The target of terrorism is not. It is the death of a particular social actor which the assassin(s) desire(s) and it is that particular person toward whom the gun/bomb/knife is aimed. The assassin would not search for a substitute to that target. In contradistinction, an act of terror is not aimed to hit a particular individual. This, obviously, does not mean that terrorists are not involved in acts of political assassinations. This distinction, based on the nature of the target (individual versus collective) is very sharp, and to the best of my knowledge has not been developed or utilized in this way before. Retrospectively, this distinction proved to be a very powerful and useful tool for this research.

David C. Rapoport has tried to develop one of the most interesting, thoughtful and intriguing distinctions between terrorism and assassination. Since his attempt is unique in the literature, and somewhat different than the one suggested here—it is necessary to consider it in more detail (1971:37, and continued in 1988). Rapoport contends that: "there is close relationship between the assassin and the terrorist," however, "there are profound differences between the assassin and the terrorist, differences which can be appreciated best by focusing on the meaning of their actions rather than on the acts themselves.... In his mind, the assassin destroys men who are corrupting a system while the terrorist destroys a system which has *already* corrupted everyone it touches.... Assassination is an incident, a passing deed, an event; terrorism is a process, a way of life, a dedication. At most assassination involves a conspiracy, but terrorism requires a movement" (1971:37–38).

The above definition, however, presents several obstacles. First, Rapoport seems to hover between two separate analytical levels without making an explicit distinction between them. On the one hand, he talks on the assassin and the terrorist, and what may happen in their *mind*, that is, his focus is on subjective meanings. This is a difficult intellectual exercise, bordering on psychological reductionism, and apparently unsatisfactory. On the other hand, Rapoport resorts to *the acts* (incident versus process) themselves: those of terrorism and assassinations. Hence, we have here two distinct categories: the mind and the act itself. The discussion does not clear the connection between these categories. Second, this general approach will most certainly cause him to be inclined to include assassinations within terrorism, and consequently views such groups as the Sicarii, Ismaili and others primarily as *terrorist* movements (indeed, a tendency shared by many modern researchers of terrorism). The major drawback of such an approach is that it may lead to less than sensitive findings and to cruder generalizations. This tendency may blur the difference(s) between terrorism and assassinations. Third, making a distinction only on the basis of the meaning of the action on the micro level may become problematic. If we interpret "meaning" as the one imputed to the act by the assassin(s), than we may end up with a classification which will have non mutually exclusive types (e.g., see next section).

Furthermore, it would be very difficult, if not impossible, to distinguish terrorism from assassination only on the basis of subjective meanings. Even Rapoport must have been aware of this problem and he suggests another nonsubjective distinction—one between an "incident" (assassination) and a "process" (terrorism). One of the pre-state underground Jewish groups—Lehi—had an explicit ideology in favor of political assassinations. One *can* argue that the nineteenth-century Russian *Narodnaya Volya* had some of this as well. It is no mere coincidence that Ivianski, who feels so uncomfortable with political assassinations but very comfortable with individual terror, was a former member in Lehi. The interpretative rhetorical device political assassination is more threatening and derogatory than individual terror. The latter terms "allows" Ivianski, and Lehi, to connect Lehi's assassinations to the nineteenth-century Russian revolutionaries. In fact, and as we shall see in a later chapter, most assassination events by Jews in Palestine and Israel were committed by ideological groups and movements. Hence, and at least for Lehi, assassination was not an incident but a process. It can be also argued that for the Hagana (see chapter 4), at some periods, assassination *was* a process and not an incident.

The above discussion does not deny the fact that many terror movements and groups resorted to assassinations. However, rather than view assassinations within the context of terror exclusively, this study will focus on assassinations exclusively. Putting assassinations under the magnifying glass gives us the benefit of developing a greater sensitivity to the phenomenon itself.

While using the specificity of the target as the distinguishing criterion may too be problematic and perhaps difficult to apply in some rare instances, its major advantage is that it is replicable, clear, obvious, easy to use, powerful and sharp.

Classification and Categories of Political Assassination Events

Choosing the cases was completely guided and dictated by the above definition and characterization of political assassination events. We shall present here two typologies.

The first typology is close to a much older typology developed originally by Machiavelli (see Rapoport 1971:12–22), and focuses on the *modus operandi*. He suggested that assassinations have two stages: preparation and execution. Each of these stages is characterized by a specific set of problems. For example, the danger of informers in the preparation stage is magnified when a group of conspirators conspires to assassinate someone. The advantage of this classificatory scheme is heuristic. We generally classified the cases into *four* different categories. The first two are closer to the preparations stage; the last two are closer to the execution stage. It gives us a much more powerful, sensitive and magnifying tool with which we can interpret the different stages of assassination.

The *first* is "*preplanning.*" In this category we have cases of serious deliberations and discussions whether or not to assassinate a specific social actor. In some cases, the potential act of assassination was halted at this stage (e.g., see cases no. 10 and no. 11). In some other cases a decision to assassinate was made. Having made a decision usually means that planning for the act must begin. The emphasis in this stage, however, is on how serious were these deliberations, and the nature of the decision which was made. One could claim that we may see in death threats a stage preceding preplanning. For example, Hashomer threatened to assassinate Ben-Gurion (Nakdimon and Mayzlish 1985:220–231), or Lehi's threat to assassinate Abba Hushi—a famous and influential political figure from Haifa (*Davar*, January 1, 1949:1), as well as other threats.[5] If, however, the threat was not accompanied by a serious and credible plan, or a pre-planning discussion (and not just contemplating or making a threat per se), it was not taken into account.

The *second* category was "*planning*," that is, when the assassination plot passed the preplanning stage and a decision and commitment to assassinate was made. However, planning means that for some reason, sometimes technical and sometimes substantial, the plan was not executed. For example, in the case of John Shaw (case no. 46), there was an assassination plan but just before the assassination itself the main assassin (and planner) was arrested by the British for a reason totally unrelated to the assassination and so the plan was not executed. In the case of Lyttelton (case no. 29), although a decision to assassinate was made, it was not executed because the potential assassins felt that the damage may outweigh the benefits.

The *third* category is "*unsuccessful.*" In this category we have cases which passed the first two stages but that no assassination, or even physical injury to the victim, was made. The usual reason is technical—a mine that did not explode, a gun that malfunctioned at the critical moment (e.g., see the cases involving Ford [no. 41] and Gordon [no. 17]), a mailed envelope with a bomb that did not reach its destination (or, reached the wrong target). In many cases the victim was not even aware of the attempt(s) (e.g., see some of the assassination plans against Lt. Col. Barker [case no. 60] or Sir Harold MacMichael [case no. 47]). In some other cases the victim was very well aware of the fact that what stood between him and death was a small mechanical problem with a gun (e.g., see case no. 17 with Gordon), and thus he had time to escape, or that somebody else died instead of him because a booby trapped envelope reached the wrong hands (e.g., see case no. 81 with Roy Farran).

The *fourth* category is "*successful.*" In this category are those cases which passed the first two stages and culminated in an execution of the plan which was either fully successful (victim died) or partially successful (victim wounded in a serious way). Cases where the victim was barely even scratched—for example, the case with Ford (no. 41) or with MacMichael (no. 48)—were classified as "unsuccessful." There is no way for the victim not to be aware of the assassination attempt in this category. The fact that the intended victim sometimes did not die is usually attributable to technical, or chance, factors and not to the lack of intent.

It is well worth noting that the above categorization is very different from legal categorizations about forms of killing and wounding. For example, the above categorization does not use the concept of a conspiracy, or the fact that successful includes both killing and serious wounding. The major rational for the above categorization is the question of *how far?*, or *to what extent?* did the assassination event proceed. Viewed in this way, the classification is helpful.

The above classification is based on a description of the event itself, regardless of the motivation of the assassin(s). However, Gross (1970); Kirkham, Levy and Crotty (1970:3–11); Crotty (1971:10–13), and Bensman (1971) all seem to share a particular form of a classification of political assassination events, which is based on the *motivation for the act*. This classification has five types:

1. *Elite substitution*—the assassination of a political leader in order to replace him. Usually, without aiming to create any substantial systemic or ideological change. This type of assassinations typically refers to a power struggle when a particular leader is assassinated in order to replace him/her or those he/she represent in power with an opposing group at the same level.

2. *Tyrannicide*—the assassination of a despot in order to replace him with a better, usually less repressive and oppressive, more rational ruler. This is one of the oldest forms of assassination as well as the one which has many moral and philosophical justifications.

3. *Terroristic assassination*—assassination on a mass and indiscriminate basis in order to demonstrate the government's inability to rule, or to let a minority govern a majority.

4. *Anomic assassination*—assassination of a political figure for private reasons. This type usually refers to the "crazy" lonely assassin who may use a political rhetoric to justify the act, but appears to demonstrate a psychiatric disorder.

5. *Propaganda by deed*—assassination which is carefully planned for a particular political figure and which aims to draw and direct attention to a specific problem.

The above classification, however, demonstrates at least two problems. First, the different types are *not* mutually exclusive. Second, the third type obviously attempts to combine—on one analytical level—assassination and terror. In itself, this type can not be useful for our purposes.

Furthermore, the research which is reported in this book clearly points to at least one additional category based on *motivation*, that needs to be added in order to interpret the cases collected for this study:

Revengeful assassination—a political assassination, as defined earlier, which is aimed at some form of revenge. Included in this act is the fact that this type of assassination may serve as a warning sign to others. There is something of a "propaganda by deed" here, but not in the sense defined earlier.

The detailed discussion of these five types is because they seem to be so prevalent in the literature. They can be used in each of the previous categories of political assassination events. Thus, we can take preplanning and examine within this category how many cases can be explained by any of the five types. This classification, however, is so problematic that it can not be used as a major analytical tool. However, I shall examine later in the book the usefulness of the above five types. We shall see, in fact, that the original five types are not very useful to explain or interpret the majority of our cases.

CHAPTER 3

Methodology and Research Experience

Scope and Timing

The methodology of this research consists of a combination of deductive and inductive methods.[1] I began working without any clear definition of the nature of political assassination thinking that, like most other people, I "knew" what it was. Very quickly it became apparent that without a very clear working definition, I would be setting myself for an impossible, and hard to justify, "salad" of cases. The literature was not very helpful. So, based on about twenty cases of what I thought were political assassinations bona fide I embarked on a long and painful intellectual journey, looking to develop a working definition. That journey culminated in the definition of what I considered was a political assassination (chapter 2), and hence we could begin a thorough and systematic search.

This study is focused on assassination events by Jews in Palestine and in Israel. The major reasons for limiting the scope of this study were: (a) accessibility to data; (b) an opportunity to examine *in-depth* a particular form of deviance within what may be considered as a more or less similar, albeit complex, culture; and (c) during this time period, in Palestine and Israel, we have a case of an attempt to rebuild a new Jewish culture and society. This attempt involved some profound social and political changes for Jewish collective life, as well as profound changes in the personal identity and consciousness of Jewish individuals. Deviance in general was conceptualized to be a product of the conflicting, clashing and negotiating symbolic-moral universes. Political assassination events were put squarely within this context. No meaningful and valid sociological interpretation for political assassinations in this cultural matrix could be developed without a full understanding of the culture itself, and its history. The different symbolic-moral universes, and total social structure, of that culture must be made explicit and comprehensible, within a dynamic political and historical context of social change and stability. Political assassinations, in this culture, always marked the boundaries between different symbolic-moral universes. Thus, in a very special and important sense, by examining such an unusual and infrequent form of deviance as political assassinations we gain a better insight into the nature of Jewish culture and society in Palestine and Israel.

Another problem was when and where to begin the search. The "when" was easier. It made sense to begin our search for political assassinations by Jews in Palestine-Israel with a time period which coincided with what is considered as the renewal of modern Jewish life in the land. That period began in the last three decades of the nineteenth century, and lasted until what is usually called by historians the first Jewish immigration wave to Palestine (1882–1903). However, as we began our research, it became very clear that we lacked an essential historical and comparative background. Again, we stopped collecting information and started to look for cases of political assassinations in the history of the Jewish people in general, from Biblical times onwards. As we shall see (chapter 5), most relevant information was found in preIsrael Europe. That, perhaps, should not have been a surprise because at the end of the last century about three quarters of all the Jews in the world lived in Europe (Goldscheider and Zuckerman 1984:3). This research yielded some most fascinating cases, and patterns which were to be emulated later. There, again, once the inductive stage was finished—we turned back to our original research goal; to the period marking the beginning of a pronounced, aggressive and salient presence of renewed Jewish life in Palestine-Israel, from 1882 until today.

Problems of Sources of Information

Once the definition, timing, and location of political assassination was clarified, the next problem was how to locate and find the actual cases. Like any other study, the issue of the sources for information—the basis for generalizations and substantive conclusions—is very important. Unfortunately, reliable methodology does not exist in this area. While the information about some assassination events (e.g., as in Tyrranicide, or in killing "foreigners" in a struggle for independence) is available, the name for most of the data required for this research was coined by Gary T. Marx's provocative essay as "hidden and dirty data," that is: "The data...runs contrary to widely (if not necessarily universally) shared standards and images of what a person or a group should be" (Marx 1984:79) Indeed, one thing which became very obvious was that getting information about cases of political assassination was extremely difficult—sometimes even impossible, totally corroborating Marx's categorization of hidden and dirty data.

How does one find about political assassination events? This is an area where individuals and organizations frequently have a vested and obvious interest *not* to disclose information. Furthermore, no central registries for political assassination events exist. One simple method was employed by Kirkham, Levy, and Crotty's team (1970:301–325, based on data collected by Leiden's and Feierabend's groups). Their goal was to collect the *maximum* number of cases of political assassination events—in a global perspective—for macro comparative purposes, within a relative short period of time. Hence, surveying the *New York Times* for items which looked like political assassination events became a major method. The list given by Kirkham, Levy, and Crotty includes 1,409 political assassination events, world wide, between 1918–1968.

Let me use this list to illustrate some of its shortcomings. The list has twenty cases which took place in Palestine (1.4%) and an additional three cases which took place in Israel (0.2%). In this study, which focused *only* on political assassination events committed by Jews, we identified ninety-one cases (that is, we had nearly four times more cases[!], not including all the more problematic cases) and that, for a very limited search. Had we taken into consideration political assassination events by Arabs, the numbers would have been significantly higher. We went further and rechecked all the twenty-three cases. Four (17.4 percent) cases could not be confirmed; 11 (47.8%) cases were committed by Arabs; five (21.7%) cases were committed by Jews. One case (MacMichael) was listed twice. The assassinations of Count Bernadotte and of Colonel Serot appear in Kirkham, Levy, and

Crotty's list as two separate cases. However, while Bernadotte's assassination was planned and executed by "Hazit Hamoledet" (a "front" organization for Lehi, one of the pre-state Jewish underground groups), Colonel Serot's death was not planned by the assassins. He was shot accidentally by the automatic weapon used to assassinate Count Bernadotte. Hence, *the overwhelming majority* of cases in our study never even came to the attention of Leiden's and Feierabend's groups. This conclusion illustrates vividly the severe limitations of using a superficial methodology. On the other hand, precisely this severe limitation highlights the specific advantages of making an in-depth probe and inquiry into the scope, nature and interpretation of political assassination events within *one* cultural matrix.

Methods Used

The closest methodologies that could be used in this study are those employed in social-historical research and in regular police work, that is, a combination of qualitative and quantitative methods. One of the very first decisions made was to try and focus on open, accessible, available, and corroborated sources. Obtaining secret and classified information (and consequently unpublishable and uncommunicable) was very problematic, and was ruled out.

We also decided to rely only on Israeli, or other Western and reliable open sources. In this way, we could be assured that whatever cases we had were in fact bona fide cases. Obviously, this strategy meant that we could not locate all cases (or examine all cases from every possible angle), but only all the cases in open sources. Basically, this decision ruled out Arab sources and classified information. In the few times we looked for Arab sources, we never got very far. Barriers of language; unreachable locations, archives, and sources all combined to make Arab sources virtually nonexistent for us. The problem of classified information was already mentioned above. One must remember that this methodological strategy may provide a somewhat biased basis for generalizations.

The first methodological strategy we used was simply to talk with fellow scholars working on the political history of the State of Israel. A few such conversations yielded an initial list of cases. We often received only a name (usually the person assassinated) and a wrong time or "reason"; sometimes what initially appeared as a political assassination turned out to be a simple act of undistinguished terror.

Second, we tried to locate every book of either memoirs of active important political or military actors in Palestine and Israel who lived during the century beginning in 1882, and secondary works analyzing the period (including M.A. and Ph.D. dissertations). Going through them was much more time consuming, but was also more fruitful and helpful. Secondary works proved better sources than biographies and autobiographies. The latter typically lacked accurate dating and demonstrated confusion about events and dates. The problematic, sometimes confusing, accounts given in some of the biographies and autobiographies, are probably due—in some major way—to the fact that some of these autobiographies were written thirty to forty years after the event(s) took place. In some sources, code names of actors were still used. Deciphering code names was not always an easy task. Another problem is more objective. Until 1948, most authors worked in secret and in conspirational conditions. In many cases, when writing the book the author really did not know what was going on and what may appear as an important event in the late 1980s, was not viewed in this way in the 1930s or 1940s. Furthermore, the heated ideological arguments between different groups often helped to bias the report. Among the best available research documents on Hagana and Etzel (two important pre-state underground Jewish groups) are two monumental sources. One is the eight volumes authoritative history of the Hagana ("Sefer Toldot Hahagana," referred to in this book as S.T.H.) and the six volumes of what can be considered as the official history of Etzel, written by the Jerusalemite historian David Niv (referred to in this book as Niv). I used both sources quite extensively. A similar history for Lehi (the third underground group), unfortunately, does not exist.

Third, we went to major archives—Beit Jabotinski, Beit Yair, Beit Ariella, the Hagana's archives, *Ha'aretz* (an influential daily newspaper) archives, the State of Israel Archives ("Ginzach Hamedina"), *Kol Ha'ir* (a Jerusalem weekly newspaper) archive,

Monitin (a weekly magazine) archive, and the Center for Oral Documentation at Hebrew University. The best and most open archives were those of *Ha'aretz* and "Beit Jabotinski."

Although much effort was spent with the Hagana's archives, not much useful information was derived from it. Officially, data about political assassinations simply "do not exist" there. The Hagana archive, and the archive of the Hakkibutz Hameuchad (at Yad Tabenkin. Also associated with the Hagana) were the most evasive in their answers. Inquiries to the two archives were typically answered by such answers as "we do not have any information on this topic," or by sending us to a list of persons who send us to other persons who send us to other persons, and so on, but who never gave us any useful information (that is, except inquiring why we are doing this study, who funded it, and how much did we "really know"). That, despite the fact that we *had* on record (from other sources) at least fifteen cases of possible political assassination events in which the Hagana was involved. In one case we inquired about operation ZARZIR, which was a 1948 plan of a Hagana unit, Hashachar, to assassinate many of the contemporary Arab leaders. We were lucky in this case because we were told that information about this operation was still classified (forty years after the plan was made).

Hence, the Hagana's potentially important archives were virtually useless for this research. Judging by these archives, one may erroneously (and obviously wrongly) come to the conclusion that the Hagana may have not been involved in political assassination events at all, or minimally involved and did a better job of covering up. The Shai's (the Hagana's department of intelligence) archives simply *must* have a real wealth of data. Unfortunately, these archives either do not exist, or are hidden. Rumor has it that these important archives are now part of the archives of the Israeli Secret Service. Lehi does not have a real archive yet (at the time of writing this book, Lehi's archives are in the process of collecting and processing data). However, some ex-members of Lehi wrote detailed biographies, and Anshell Shpillman (head of the Lehi's museum) was helpful. "Beit Jabotinski," where Etzel's archives are, has more information on political assassination events than the two other archives. The information there, however, is typically telegraphic.

Fourth, we checked contemporary newspapers, both local and foreign. We used extensively *Ha'aretz*, and to a much lesser degree the *Palestine Post* and *Davar*. On most occasions these sources were used to corroborate dates and enrich the information we had about suspected cases. We tried to locate unknown cases of political assassination events in contemporary newspapers but very quickly encountered an unsolvable problem of how to decide whether a report of a murder, or an attempted murder, reflected a regular criminal act or the more unusual category of political assassination. Sometimes the case was very clear; other times it was not possible to decide. That observation led to a decision to cross check all sources, whenever that was possible.

Fifth, whenever we could locate relevant actors, we tried to interview them. Such interviews were frequently very helpful, but also problematic. The most difficult part was the interviewees' typical inability to remember accurately names, dates, places, and processes of decision making. However, frequently these interviews yielded golden information.

Another related method was to look for interviews which were given by key actors to other researchers and/or journalists. Frequently I found that I could utilize these interviews in a variety of useful and productive ways.

The "dirty" nature of some of these sources, however, also came in to focus. Let me use two examples only. In 1979, Eldad Sheib, who was one of Lehi's main figures and obviously involved in the decision process which led to the decision to assassinate Bernadotte granted an interview to Harel, a journalist from *Monitin*. In that interview, Eldad disclosed some very important details about the Bernadotte 1948 assassination (case no. 83). Unfortunately, when we tried to locate the relevant issue of *Monitin* in the library, we found out that, typically, the specific volume was mutilated in such a way that the specific pages containing the interview were cut out. Eventually, we had no choice but to go to *Monitin*'s editorial offices in order to zerox the relevant pages. The second illustration concerns testimony of 154 pages given in 1968 by Avraham Tehomey, an extremely important actor in the history of the Hagana and Etzel. The testimony (tape and transcript) was deposited with the Center for Oral Documentation, Institute for the study of Contemporary

Judaism, Hebrew University. The testimony simply "disappeared." That testimony may have been crucial for a better understanding of the assassination cases involving De Hahn (case no. 6), Rotstein (case no. 12), and perhaps a few others.

Whenever a trial took place, we tried to locate the verdict and the justifications, as well as the appeals, if there were any (e.g., as in the cases involving Pinkas; Vilner; Avneri and Kasztner—as victims).

Eventually a file was opened for each case. In each file we put together all the information we could gather on that case. As mentioned, in some cases, when actors were still alive, and the case was not clear enough, we resorted to interviewing. Cross checking data, dates, events from all the different sources and bringing them to bear on one case yielded a crisper, more focused and sharper understanding of the case itself. Working in this way meant that much of this research focused on solving puzzles and riddles, closer to police work. Thus, sometimes we knew we had a case, but we had to look for the date, method of assassination, given reason, and the like. Sometimes finding the date (or the method) of the assassination attempt proved to be a very tedious job. Some resources "missed" dates by a whole year.

Finally, let me report on an interesting process of "dripping" information which developed as the research was progressing. On a few occasions, we were offered information which we were not supposed to use. I tried this route a few times and discovered that it lead nowhere. In all of the cases we were offered oral information, without any supporting documentation. In a few cases, after checking, it turned out as inaccurate, sometimes even misleading, information. After more than two years of hearing such "stories," one simply gets tired of chasing wild geese. This problem can be referred to as dripping:[2] individuals "dripped" to me, or to my research assistants (or to others) partial information. Let me give four salient, and documented, illustrations of this dripping.

The *first* case concerns *Altalena*. *Altalena* was a ship (actually a landing craft) which was purchased by Etzel (one of the three pre-state Jewish underground groups). It was loaded with weapons in Europe and sent to Israel. Ben-Gurion and other commanders of the emerging IDF (Israel Defense Force) felt that the ship brought weapons to Etzel only and they apparently suspected (and feared) that Etzel was planning a coup. On June 21, 1948—after the *Altalena* arrived in front of the beach near Tel Aviv—Ben-Gurion ordered the IDF to open fire on the ship and blow it to pieces. The order was executed and in the afternoon the ship was fired upon. A few members of Etzel were wounded, others were killed and the *Altalena* was burning and smoldering. Nakdimon, who wrote one of the books on the affair, states (1978:280) that Dov Orbuch, who was involved in the shelling of *Altalena*, left his son Joseph a *written note* which was supposedly written by Ben-Gurion and in it a *direct order* from Ben-Gurion to Dov to open fire on the "Altalena." The son, according to Nakdimon, refuses to give this most important note to historians.

A *second* illustration also involves Nakdimon. Nakdimon (1986) maintains that Joseph Hecht, one of the most important commanders of the Hagana got a *written order* from Itzhak Ben-Zvi (originally from Hashomer, and later the President of Israel) to assassinate De Hahn (see case no. 6). According to Nakdimon, Hecht's son has this most important note and refuses to give it to historians.

The *third* illustration involves the account given by Etai Be'ery that his father left him with some *very* important documents which he refuses to reveal (see footnote no. 120 of chapter 7). This is an important issue because Etai's father was accused in court (and found guilty) in the unjustified assassination of Captain Tubianski (see case no. 82).

The *last* illustration is more personal. One evening after I gave a long talk on this research in Jerusalem, an older male approached me after the talk. He presented himself as a former Hagana/Shai (one of the pre-state Jewish underground groups) agent and told me that he, and other agents, could swear that Tubianski (who was shot to death in 1948 after he was suspected in espionage, and cleared of the suspicion later, case no. 82) was, in fact, a spy. This is simply contrary to *all* available facts. I asked him for some solid evidence, more details, or to meet with the people he mentioned. It was not forthcoming.

In all the above illustrations potentially *crucial* important documents (or information) supposedly "exist" but are conveniently "unavailable." Personally, I very much doubt even the existence of the documents in the first two illustrations.

In all the above cases, as well as in a few others, dripping the information was clearly intended to create a particular impression through information control. In all the cases, the implication of the "hidden" information, if ever proved valid (which, I must reiterate, I doubt), is a dramatic and different interpretation of the case. This possible alternative interpretation typically serves the interests of one of the parties involved in the case (or, even the interpreter). After two years of being exposed to such "drippings" I must confess a *most* definite irritation and wariness at this manipulative technique.

Some Methodological Consequences

Unfortunately, and despite the effort, there are still a few cases where all the information is very telegraphic—just the name of the person who was assassinated, method (sometimes not even that), date, the rhetorical device(s) given as justifying the assassination (usually in one or two sentences) and the organization which legitimized the act. In some cases, even such basic information is lacking. This lack of information characterizes more the cases involving the Hagana, than any other organization. We typically could not get more information about the nature of the process culminating in the decision to assassinate, or by who. In some cases, finding the accurate date of the assassination was difficult. While the Hagana's archivists "could not find" relevant materials, and dodged our questions, it had no monopoly on doing that. We encountered similar reactions (although to a much lesser degree) in other archives.

Whenever we had information about a possible case, but no information available about at least the name of the person who was supposed to be assassinated, the reason, the date, and so forth, but just a general reference to a case—I decided not to utilize the case because it was useless for any further processing. There were about eighteen such cases. For example, Niv (vol. 5:78) reports on a death sentence Etzel declared against a British policeman, no. 1617, because he abused prisoners. While policeman no. 1617 was under surveillance for a while, no real attempt on his life was ever made. Since information about the rank, name, date, nature of plan was lacking, I decided not to include the case.

Hence, while I view the major orientation of this work as sociological, there was no escape from doing social-historical research as well. The list of cases included in the survey which appears in the next part reflects all (and only) the cases that I felt had enough information (including corroboration) to justify inclusion in the analysis.

Sampling

Choosing the cases was completely guided and dictated by the definition developed for the characterization of political assassination events which was given in chapter 2.

An interesting and important question is how many of the total number of cases was the methodology used successful in capturing? In other words, do the cases included in this study consist of the entire universe of cases, or do they constitute a sample of that universe; and if so, what is the nature of the sample, and are there clear biases?

It is virtually impossible to give accurate and authoritative answers for the above questions. Generally speaking, it is difficult to assert that the cases included in this study consist of the *entire* universe of cases, and this conclusion is probably valid for all four categories.

The number of evasive answers we got, the nature of the hidden and dirty data we deal with in this research is such that the above conclusion is simply unavoidable.

The majority of political assassination events which occurred between 1920–1948 were committed in large part by by the main three pre-state underground groups—the Hagana, Etzel and Lehi. I feel fairly confident that the cases reported here, and which were committed by Etzel and Lehi, either cover all the cases, or are very close to cover it all. I have no doubt, however, that there were probably *many* more cases committed by the Hagana, about which we know nothing. There are a few reasons for this conclusion. While Lehi and Etzel typically publicized their activity in this area, the Hagana typically kept very quiet. The Hagana maintained that it was *against* political assassinations, Etzel and most certainly Lehi were not against it. Furthermore, at different times the Hagana had specialized units for assassination (e.g., Pum, Hashachar, the Pelugot Meiuchadot in Tel Aviv, or the three "death squads" they had—see chapter 7). An organization the size of the Hagana would not have created and maintained such organizational specialized units just to have them. The variety and persistence of such units certainly indicates on a consistent thought in the direction of assassination. Operation ZARZIR (see case nos. 58 and 77) is another indication toward this direction. Thus, one cannot avoid the conclusion that the amount of dirty and hidden data protected by the Hagana in this area is larger than what is known. The above disparity between ideology and reality certainly gave rise to *discreditable information* and *dark secrets* (e.g., see Hepworth 1971), a la Marx's charaterization of "hidden and dirty information." Obviously, what we encounter here are attempts at *information control* (Goffman 1963:57–128).

However, the degree to which each of the categories above is closer to a "sample," or to the "entire universe" varies. The methodology used, and the available information in the "preplanning" category, makes this category closer to a sample. Not every preplanning is reported, and one may safely assume that what we encountered here was probably under-reported. The category of "planning" is probably better in terms of reporting, and the one of "unsuccessful" even better than planning, even in the sense that reports of public unsuccessful attempts typically appear in a few independent sources. The category of "successful" is probably closest to represent the entire universe of political assassinations in that category. However, whether this category "covers" 80 percent, 70 percent, or 95 percent of all the cases is a question to which a definite answer can not be given, with any degree of confidence or certainty. The cases with Kurfirst (no. 52), or Ben-Betzalel (no. 59) indicate that there may have been cases which were not reported anywhere (unless the researcher knew exactly where to search), or severely under-reported. Estimation of how many cases we, in fact, missed can not be given.

The one thing which can be said with a very high degree of certainty is that I do not believe that there are many more cases hidden in public, open resources. Furthermore, even if a few cases were missed, the ones we have constitute such a large group, and the emerging patterns are so clear, that it is doubtful whether a few more hidden cases would make a real difference. Thus, even if we do not have the entire universe of cases, our sample probably represents the reality of the whole without an obvious bias.

An indirect corroboration for the above statement is that whenever we went to interviews, especially at the later stages of the research, when we had most of the information, we were never "surprised" to discover new cases. Sometimes, I was even able to surprise the interviewee. In one case (Wolf Fiedler, no. 48), I totally surprised Niv with the case itself, and partially surprised him with the details about the case of Kadia Mizrachi (no. 61), where some of the information is simply puzzling (e.g., that she betrayed her son to the British).

As can be expected, the available information on political executions is indeed meagre. All of it is based on open and previously published sources.

Reasons for Low Availability of Information— *"Dirty and Hidden Information" and the "Tubianski Syndrom"*

That data on political assassinations and executions is in Gary Marx's (1984) terminology both hidden and dirty is obvious. However, why is such an information "dirty and hidden" in the specific context of political assassinations and executions in Palestine and Israel? There are a few reasons for that. I suspect that one major reason for this—despite the dozens of years which elapsed—is the fact that those involved are not always comfortable with, or proud of, what they did.

While the information about assassinations of non-Jews is, relatively speaking, easily available, similar detailed information about the majority of the cases involving Jews as victims is virtually nonexistent. In many cases, all we have is a date and a laconic reason, typically involving the use of such rhetorical devices as "traitor" or "squealer," to account for why the victims were killed. One is certainly puzzled by this phenomenon.

A few answers come to mind. One obvious reason given by some interviewees was that some of the people involved in the cases were still alive and why bother them? This answer, however, is very problematic. If the assassination was originally justified, beyond a shadow of a doubt (as some of the contemporary accounts indicate) then there should be no problem disclosing the relevant information. I suspect, however, that those involved in the cases do not feel very comfortable about the cases because the "proven guilt" of the accused was not proven "beyond a shadow of a doubt." Indeed, how could it be? Most cases occurred before 1948, and were committed by the three pre-state underground Jewish groups. They did not have real "prisons," they could not "arrest" and have a long legal procedure to prosecute anybody. They all operated under conspirational conditions, in secret and under a grave danger of being detected and caught by the British (which usually meant torture, a long period of imprisonment arrests, and even death sentences). They had to deal very fast and in a swift and decisive manner with what they considered dangerous. Fast decisions had to be made. However, even under the difficult circumstances, the Kurfirst case (no. 52) took a few good weeks. The case involving Vera Duksova (no. 80) took two days and the case involving Tubianski (no. 82) took one day.

Although in justifying assassinations all three major pre-state underground Jewish organizations use the account that the accused were brought "before a court," there really is no hard evidence or documentation which corroborates the actual existence of such courts, the procedures they used, or the way they reached a verdict. In only four cases (Kurfirst [no. 52], Hilewitz [no. 42], Levi [no. 75, although this case is very problematic], and Tubianski [no. 82]) there is mention in some details of such a "court." The accused were typically not represented by a lawyer and "appeal" was not a real alternative. The decision to assassinate appears to be a command decision, sometimes following a discussion, but not a result of a real court decision. It seems that the use of the word/account court in these cases is usually unjustified. Some good support for this hypothesis may be found in such cases as those of Zvi Frenkel (no. 9), Walter Strauss (no. 24), Michael Waksman (no. 25), Yaacov Soffiof (no. 26), Major Shlomo Schiff (no. 27), Binyamin Zerony (no. 28), Avraham Wilenchik (no. 37), Eliahu Giladi (no. 38), Wolf Fiedler (no. 48), Moshe Ben-Betzalel (no. 59), Michael Schnell (no. 62), Vitold Holianitzky (no. 78) and it came to the clearest focus in the case of Tubianski (see part 2). If one may generalize from Tubianski's case, then there may be a good reason to suspect that there were other cases like this, giving rise to a possible "Tubianski Syndrom" which may explain a large part of the reluctance to disclose details even today. There is less reluctance to disclose information about non-Jewish victims, but a very high degree of reluctance to disclose information about in-group victims—that is, other Jews.

Tubianski was suspected of espionage. In the twilight time zone of June 1948, during the passage of Israeli society from a pre-state stage to a formal state, captain Tubianski was brought to a "field court," was "found guilty" and shot at the same day. Later, at the request of Tubianski's wife, Ben-Gurion—Israel's first prime minister—launched a full scale investigation which cleared Tubianski of all suspicions, accusations, and charges. In fact, the person held responsible for the investigation and execution of Tubianski was brought to trial, and found guilty (see case no. 82).

This particular case is, perhaps, more instructive than what may appear. It probably represents the type of "justice" prevailing among the three pre-state underground Jewish organizations than the type of justice which emerged, crystallized and prevailed after 1948, which was based on open and formal procedures grounded on facts, evidence and due process. Other "in-group" victims before 1948 probably did not even have the same "procedure" as Tubianski had. One is simply left pondering about how many of the other victims could have been spared had they faced an open and public trial with a proper defense, and not a secret procedure which, in most cases, can not even be traced today (see also case no. 19).

Further support for this hypothesis was added in the case of the assassination of Wagner (see case no. 54). There, we found and interviewed one of the assassins. Before answering our questions, he wanted to know what we knew about the case. Having heard what we knew, and especially Wagner's number in the Nazi party, our interviewee seemed more relieved. During the interview it became apparent that he and his assassin colleagues knew, at the time, that their action was based on partial information. The assassination seemed justified at the time, *based* on that partial information. As more information was gathered, and from a perspective of about forty years, their act of assassination seemed even more justified to him. The support from this case to the above hypothesis is that the rhetorical device called "political assassination" was sometime used *as an answer to a question*— should actor x be assassinated? This answer was probably, and typically, based on *partial* information. Hence, the reluctance to give information in detail. What would happen if, as in the Tubianski case, it would be discovered that in a large number of cases, or in any particular case, the assassination was not justified?

In other words, a real "danger" of making the data about political assassination events fully open may lie with the fact that—in quite a few instances and cases—these data may prove to be "guilty knowledge" (Hughes 1971), damaging and discrediting (e.g., see the cases involving De Hahn [no. 6], Giladi [no. 38] and Pritzker [no. 39]).

Some Research Experience

Despite the above, and since some of the actors involved are still alive, some interviewing was expected. Despite the fact that in some cases more than thirty years have passed, we had great difficulty arranging for interviews. When interviews were granted, interviewees were typically very careful and evasive. In one case, for example, after we had an okay for an interview from the former chief of the so-called "Zrifin Underground" (which, among other things, planted a bomb in the Soviet embassy in Israel in the 1950s), he threw us out of his Tel Aviv office (very politely, I must add) on our arrival. In another case, it took us three months to get an interview with a former Chief of the Jerusalem Police. He had held that position in the early 1950s, a period during which a few Orthodox Jews, supposedly belonging to a group who wanted to create a theocracy in Israel, were caught "with a bomb" in the Knesset building. It took us about two hours of interviewing to get out of him that, in fact, there was no bomb! It was difficult to get more information, as the interviewee pointed out again and again that some of the actors suspected of belonging to this group have since become very "important." One of them is now a chief Rabbi, who refused our requests for an interview.

In case no. 38 we managed to interview the daughter of Giladi's sister. Giladi was a Lehi member and was apparently shot in 1943 by his friends in Lehi, supposedly because they felt he constituted a threat (ideologically and pragmatically) to the group. Our data suggest that another "real" reason was probably a struggle for leadership in the group. The person who emerged as the leader was Yazernitsky, or in his more known name Y. Shamir, currently (1988–1991) prime minister of Israel. Giladi's nephew told us that the family, and herself, tried to find where Giladi's body was buried and to force some form of recognition in Giladi's memory. Their attempt was only partially successful. Giladi's picture appears now in the Lehi museum (with the neutral rhetorical device "killed" attached to it), but they still do not know where he is buried. Furthermore, she told us that when she was more active, in the early 1980s, she and her family were threatened to leave the issue, to the point that she expressed her amazed (dis[?]) belief that the "underground still exists" (taped interview May 5, 1987)—that is forty-four years after the assassination!

In case no. 85, Keinan and Ben-Yair were acquitted in court. However, there are enough clues, and information, indicating that it is very plausible that they were, in fact, those who planted the bomb in the home of then Minister of transportation D. Pinkas. Unfortunately, we could neither obtain the original transcripts of the trial nor the trial exhibits. A contemporary ballistics expert's examination of the remnants of the bomb could shed a new light on the case. Keinan himself refused an interview, in a very rude way.

Final Note

Despite all the many difficulties, an unexpected large pool of cases was discovered, which serves as the basis for the analysis. While it is difficult, indeed impossible, to estimate what accurate percentage of the real universe of assassination attempts this methodology enabled us to discover, it is large enough, and sufficiently representative, to warrant the conclusions as valid. Compared to other research projects on political assassination events, there are clear advantages of the approach taken in this study. Finally, no systematic biases due to omitted cases have been observed.

PART 2

Actual Cases

CHAPTER 4

Historical Background

The period which is covered in this study goes from Biblical times to 1988, with a special emphasis on the 1880s–1988 period. Some background must be provided about this period so that what follows will make sense to the readers who may be less familiar with the major historical events. Obviously, I have no intention of rewriting Jewish history, only to give a broad sketch, painted with a very crude brush, and focused on the relevant issues for this study.

Commitment to the natural history of crime approach compels one not only to describe that history in a natural sequential order, but also telling the historical "tale" as those participating in it saw it, much like other research in deviance where the point of view of the deviant(s) is taken into consideration and presented "as is" (prostitution, drug use, etc.). As we shall see later, much Israeli nationalism is obviously behind the historical tale of the context and of the assassinations and executions. The reader, however, is asked to bear in mind that this book should not be taken as a praise or critique of that Israeli nationalism.

This chapter is divided into two parts. These parts are intended to serve as a necessary background that will help further reading of the book more understandable. The first part charts the general historical background needed to understand the context in which the different cases of assassinations and executions are being interpreted. The second part provides a brief historical description of the main pre-state Jewish underground groups who committed most of the assassinations.

THE GENERAL HISTORICAL CONTEXT

Following the Biblical period, the area referred to, in broad terms, as Palestine and Israel was occupied by the Greek and the

Roman empires. During 167–160 B.C. the Hasmoneans revolted against the foreign rule. The Hasmoneans (the name given to the Maccabees by Josephus Flavius, in the Mishna and the Talmud, but not in the book of Maccabees) were a priestly family who lived in Modi'in. The Hasmoneans' revolt against the Seleucid forces, their alliance with Rome (established in 161 B.C.), all resulted in a prolonged period of independence for Judea, under the Hasmonean rule. The Hasmoneans crystallized and consolidated their rule over the land and their State came to its peak of power and territory under the rule of Alexander Yanai (103–76 B.C.). In the early 60s B.C. Pompeus ended the rule of the Hasmoneans. Following some inner wars, and changes in the political figures in Rome (e.g., the assassination of Julius Caesar in March of 44 B.C.), Herod I was appointed as the emperor of Judea in 37 B.C. and lasted in this position till 4 B.C. The years following Herod's death witnessed a growing unrest, riots, destabilization and a series of cruel and corrupt Roman rulers. The so-called Jewish "big revolt" began around 66 A.D. and lasted till around 73 A.D. The Jews were totally defeated by the Roman legions. This is an important period because it gave rise to the first known group of Jewish assassins—the Sicariis (more about them in the next chapter). During this revolt, the second Jewish temple was burnt, as well as Jerusalem. However, despite the horrendous destruction, another Jewish revolt began around 132 A.D. lead by Bar Kochba. Again, the revolt ended with a Roman victory in the summer of 135 A.D. when the last Jewish resistance was crushed. While the casualties among the Jews were very high (probably on the magnitude of 580,000), the Roman army suffered very heavy casualties too. These revolts were basically focused around attempts of different Jewish groups to maintain Jewish independent sovereignty over their land, as well as bitter, sometimes lethal, arguments between different Jewish groups and factions about how to attain this political, religious, and cultural independence.

While a few Jews remained in the land, the majority of Jews were forced to leave Zion. For the next eighteen hundred years, the Jewish people survived mostly in the diaspora, harboring prayers and dreams of returning to Zion. At the turn of this century, the majority of Jews lived in Europe, suffering at different times and localities, from various degrees of anti-semitic persecutions.

The long Jewish exile (Galut) was explained by Jews as: (a) a divine trial for the survivability of the Jews, (b) a divine punishment for the sins of the Jews, (c) a way to be purified towards redemption, (d) the Galut is a temporary state, at the end of which the Jews will return to Zion. Longing for Zion were expressed in different ways: contributions to the small Jewish community which survived in Zion, individual immigration to Zion, maintaining rituals associated with the future return to Zion and the like. However, *no* systematic, planned and aggressive attempts, or ideologies, that Jews, as a people, should return to Zion prevailed (except for some small Hasidic sects in the eighteenth and nineteenth centuries).

Zionism, as a pragmatic ideological movement, was conceived of, and created, in the late nineteenth century by *secular* Jews. Zionism's main goal was to advocate an active and militant policy that Jews should return to Zion, their homeland and natural place.

The anti-semitic image of the Jew, as it crystallized in Europe, implied that Jews were afraid to fight, exploited their neighbors, were eternally involved in questionable financial and monetary transactions (and in loaning at high rates of interest). Jews were described as a despised, degraded, lazy, mean and miserable people. Zionism, which emerged on the background of anti-semitic pogroms, and of various and other nationalistic struggles in Europe, aimed to change this stereotype in the most radical way. It aimed to create a new type of Jew: fighter, proud, and working his/her own land.

The Zionist movement advocated Jewish immigration to Zion and had to cope with different problems regarding the future blue-print of Israel. The major issues were whether this new Jewish State would be socialistic or more capitalistic; the possible balance between secular—democratic values and religious values and dealing with the Arab population which resided in Zion for hundreds of years.

Since the sixteenth century, Palestine was part of the Ottoman empire. In the nineteenth century, there were only about 10,000 Jews in Palestine, and about 365,000 others (about 35,000 Christians, and the rest Muslims). The first Zionist immigration wave to Palestine was between 1882–1903. This new wave emphasized Jewish settlement in small communities called Moshavot, to be based on agriculture, and work the land. Some of the new Moshavot received financial support from Rothschild (see case no. 1). Without that support they could not have possibly survived. More immigration waves followed, as well as the crystallization of the Jewish Zionist movement in Europe and the establishment of a Jewish political lobby which eventually geared itself toward help- ing to reach the goal of creating a new Jewish state—Israel.

When the first World War began, the Jewish population in Palestine (the so-called Yishuv), was on the magnitude of 85,000 (out of a total population of around 700,000). From those, only 12,000 lived in villages and the rest lived in towns. During the war, the Turkish authorities were not too sympathetic to the Yishuv, an attitude which culminated in the expulsion of Jews from Jaffo in March of 1917 (see cases no. 2 and no. 3). The peri- od of the Turkish occupation constitutes one chapter in the book.

The British army which was commanded by General Allenby, advanced from the south, defeated the Turkish army and con- quered Palestine. Jerusalem itself surrendered in December of 1917. Until 1948, the British ruled Palestine.

While under the Turkish occupation, the Zionist effort was beginning to crystallize; under the British occupation a fight for Jewish independence took place; culminating in the establish- ment of the State of Israel in 1948.

The main conflicts involving the Yishuv during the British occupation focused along a few issues. A major conflict devel- oped with the British themselves. The British foreign policy towards Palestine was inconsistent. On the one hand, it reflected the British, sometimes limited, commitment to help the Zionist movement establish a new Jewish homeland. On the other hand, and especially during and after World War II, the British did not want to antagonize the Arabs who objected to the creation of a new Jewish homeland in Palestine. As time passed, the British policy became much more hostile to the Zionist movement. Jew- ish immigration to Palestine was the heart of Zionism. It became especially crucial for Jews who wanted to escape from the Nazi hell. The British did not cooperate and they did not allow Jewish refugees from Nazi occupied Europe to enter Palestine in any significant numbers. Hence, one major conflict with the British focused on the Yishuv continuing attempts to help Jews immigrate to Palestine, despite British objection. The name "illegal immigration" was used to describe that immigration. Second, the British maintained an extensive bureaucracy in Palestine, including police forces, so that they could maintain their occupation. Many Jews worked in these bureaucracies, and were loyal to their British employers. As the second World War continued and the anti-Zionist British policy became more apparent, the three underground Jewish groups—Hagana, Etzel, and Lehi—intensified their struggle against the British, putting the many Jews who worked for the British in a very problematic position. To whom were they loyal? As we shall see, quite a few cases of assassinations were directed against Jews who worked for the British and were defined as "traitors" by the Hagana, Etzel, or Lehi.

Another struggle crystallized with the Palestinian Arab national movement. Arab national Palestinians objected and expressed a growing resistance to Zionism and to the returning Jews.

The third major struggle developed between different factions within the Jewish community in Palestine. There were struggles between the old Yishuv and the new immigrants; between left and right (socialists versus capitalists); between more and less militant groups.

During this period, the intensity of the struggle between the Hagana, Etzel, and Lehi reached, at some years, dangerous proportions. However, at other times they cooperated. These three groups aimed their struggle for the creation of a new Jewish State, but they were divided very bitterly on how exactly to achieve it. These three groups used military and guerrilla tactics against the Arabs, British, and against one another. In some respects, all three groups relied on the legacy of earlier defense groups, which crystallized during the Turkish period: Bar Giora, Hashomer and Hakibbutz. Since the majority of political assassination events were committed by all of these groups, and especially by Lehi, Etzel, and the Hagana, we shall have to examine, in more detail, but very briefly, the main Jewish underground groups which existed, and operated, in Palestine prior to the formal establishment of the State of Israel. All these groups/organizations chose to describe themselves by the rhetorical device "Jewish Defense Groups." The groups will be described in the next section in the chronological order of their development. Hence, the period of the British occupation forms another important and long chapter in the book.

The State of Israel was created officially after the British forces left (May 14, 1948; e.g., see Louis and Stookey 1986) when, on the same date, in Tel Aviv, Ben Gurion declared the establishment of the State of Israel. Israel's Arab neighbors did not accept the establishment of the State, and a major war broke out between invading Arab armies, irregular forces and the newly established Israeli Army, the IDF (Israel Defense Force). Many Jews who escaped the Nazi holocaust, and survived the Nazi death and concentration camps found themselves in Israel's bloodiest, longest, and most fierce war: what became known as the war for independence.

After 1948, and the war, Israel began to lick its wounds and try to consolidate itself as a democratic State. It is still doing that. As a new State, Israel had to face many internal, and external, threats and problems. Of those, three major conflicts are relevant to this study. The first has been the continuing conflict with the Arabs. Second, the need to cope with what happened in Nazi occupied Europe, with the holocaust, and the relations with Germany created conflicts between different ideological groups. Third, a potentially explosive conflict developed between secular and religious Jews in Israel. All these conflicts yielded political assassination events. Other conflicts, such as a potentially explosive ethnic conflict between "Ashkenasic" Jews (whose origins are from Western and Northern Europe, America, Canada and Australia) and "Sephardic" Jews (whose origins are from the Arab peninsula, and from Northern Africa; see, for example, Ben-Yehuda 1987), between rich and poor, right and left, did not yield assassination events (although they did yield other violent reactions). The period following the establishment of the state of Israel forms another chapter.

All the political assassination events which will be detailed in the next six chapters are within the general historical context described here, and form together the historical foundation upon which this study is based.

JEWISH DEFENSE GROUPS 1907–1948
BAR GIORA, HASHOMER, HAKIBBUTZ, HAGANA, ETZEL, AND LEHI

Introduction

This part will describe briefly the main Jewish groups which existed in Palestine prior to the formal establishment of the State of Israel in 1948. All these organizations chose to describe themselves by the rhetorical device: Jewish Defense Groups. An accurate and short analytical description of these groups is not an easy task. The following description touches only the main characteristics of these groups. One very important question is the position of these groups toward political assassinations. Unfortunately, none of these groups ever published such a clear "policy statement." To present such a "policy" to the reader requires a summary of fragmental information, but much more important, it requires a fairly intimate knowledge with the actual cases of assassinations. The way we could deduct what the policy of the different groups toward assassination was focused on collecting the different cases of assassinations in which these groups were involved and crossing it with different statements issued by leaders of those groups. In this sense, the "policy" of these groups toward assassinations was inferred by resorting to a "grounded theory" approach (Glaser and Strauss 1967; Strauss 1987: chapter 10; Corbin and Strauss 1990). Hence, in this part a general description of the different underground groups will be given and the way these different groups handled assassinations will be given in chapter 12 where the findings of the research are analyzed, *after* the presentation of the different cases of assassinations. Such a split presentation has obvious advantages in presenting and interpreting the findings within the context of a grounded theory approach.

Bar Giora—Hashomer—Hakibbutz: 1907–1920

The organizers of Bar Giora were a group of Jews who lived in Palestine and were clearly influenced by left wing revolutionary movements in Russia. On September 29, 1907 some of the founders met in Yitzhak Ben-Zvi's home in Jaffa, sharing their moral and political conviction that a new revival in national independent Jewish life in Palestine is imminent. These people[1] shared a common ideological core, and also the view that Jews had lived a long enough time under other people's rule. The name "Bar Giora" was chosen as a replica of the name of Shimon Bar Giora, one of the main leaders of the Jewish revolt against the Romans during the last days of the second Jewish Temple (circa 69-70 A.D.). Unlike the Sicariis, they did not want to use terror but they did want to create a reliable and active self-defense group, coupled with a strong feeling of "shelihut" (or "mission").

Specifically, they criticized the reliance of the new Jewish settlements in Palestine on Arab guards. The Bar Giora group intended to monopolize ("conquer" in their contemporary terminology) work; to provide Jewish guards and to develop the Jewish settlements. They used the slogan: "In blood and fire Judea fell— in blood and fire Judea will rise" which is a direct reminiscent of the days of the second Jewish temple. In short, these people created a secret and small ideological social group, with a very strong moral and political consciousness, emphasizing the collective sharing of ideas and goods. Members were concentrated in the agricultural farm in Segera in the lower Galilee in the north.

The few successes the group had in defending Jewish settlers against Arab attacks crystallized and integrated the group even further. A major event was the successful defense of Mescha.

On April 12, 1909 another organization was created out of Bar Giora—the famous Hashomer ("the guard"). The head of Hashomer was Israel Shohat. This organization was still small, conspiratorial and acceptance of members was highly selective. Its members basically accepted the defense goals of Bar Giora but added more political goals. While it *is* somewhat difficult to see the fine differences between the two organizations, members did feel that these organizations were different, mostly also because of the different personalities involved in the different groups. In 1914 Hashomer had about forty members and another fifty candidates and hired hands. The social composition of the organization was, to a very large extent, determined by a meticulous selection process, which was done by Israel and Mania Shohat. Due to this selection process, there can be no doubt that Hashomer was a rather small, secret, and elitist group. In its peak, it did not have more than three hundred members. Hashomer certainly viewed itself as an integral part of the Zionist movement.

When World War I began (August 1914), Palestine was under Turkish occupation. The Turkish army planned to use the land as a base for a military movement south towards Egypt and the Suez Canal. Palestine and Syria had to supply the fourth Turkish army. The Turks obviously wanted all the available weapons, and Hashomer went underground. Mania and Israel Shohat were expelled to Turkey and Hashomer began to disintegrate. The Nily affair (see case no. 3) did not make life easy for Hashomer's members because the Turkish authorities persecuted and jailed members. This situation changed after the British conquest and occupation of Palestine in 1917, especially since some of Hashomer's members joined the British security forces.

The annual meeting of the Hashomer in 1920 witnessed some bitter arguments. Israel Shohat and his group wanted to keep Hashomer as an elite and exclusive organization and Tabenkin and Golomb wanted a popular, widespread organization. The decision was to dissolve the Hashomer and become part of a larger and newer organization, the Hagana.[2]

While Hashomer dissolved in 1920, its core members kept in touch with each other, particularly the group around Mania and Israel Shohat, previous director of the Hashomer. Gradually, they formed an opposition group within the Hagana called "Hakibbutz."[3] This small group consisted of about sixty to seventy members. Hakibbutz was evidently an active group, influenced ideologically by Russian leftist revolutionaries. One of its most important explicit goals was to provide self defense and to socialize members as revolutionary elements. Hakibbutz maintained special connections with "Gdud Ha'avoda" (the Work Battalion).

Gdud Ha'avoda existed between 1920–1929 in the northern part of Palestine. Its main goal was to prepare the conditions for Jewish mass immigration to Palestine and to create a strong self defense group. During its existence, about twenty-five hundred people moved through its ranks; in its peak in 1925 it had around 665 members. After economic crises and heated political debates between its left and right parts, Gdud Ha'avoda disintegrated in 1927 and ended its existence in 1929 (see Margalit 1980).

The security problems of Gdud Ha'avoda were handled by old members of the Hashomer who were organized in their new group—the Hakibbutz. Hakibbutz obviously tried to continue the tradition which had been crystallized and established by the Hashomer, and tried to maintain its strong political and ideological platform. As case no. 5 points out, it was the Hakibbutz which assassinated Tufik Bay.

Because of ongoing disputes between members of the Hakib-butz and the leaders of the emerging Hagana, investigating committees were established to resolve these disputes. In 1926 a particularly harsh debate was in process, as a new committee started its work (August 8, 1926). In January of 1927 the committee published its conclusions and the disintegration of the Hakibbutz began. It was complete and full in 1929 with the mainstream of the Hagana ascending to prominence (see S.T.H., vol. 1:219–241; Rechav 1963: 747–748).

The Hagana

Clearly, the largest and most influential pre-state Jewish underground group was the Hagana (meaning "Defense"). Contrary to the other pre-state underground groups, the Hagana was the operational arm of a political organization, the Jewish Agency, and was used and controlled by that political organization. Hence, decision making processes in the Hagana, especially regarding important issues (e.g., political assassinations) were probably very different than in the other pre-state organizations. The Hagana was a very big and complex organization with many diversified units. While the two most distinct units were the political branch and the military branch, there were other branches and units. Many books were written on the history of the Hagana. The reader is referred to S.T.H.; Cohen 1981; Pail 1979. For a *very* short review, see Rabinov 1969. I shall provide here a very brief sketch of the Hagana, based on Rabinov 1969; and the more curious reader is urged to read the eight volumes of S.T.H.—the history of the Hagana.

Generally speaking, the history of the Hagana parallels the history of the renewed Jewish settlement in Palestine. From the early days of the settlement (as well as from lessons learnt in

Europe) the need for a Jewish defense organization became evident. Bar Giora, Hashomer, and the Hakibbutz were such primary organizations. The beginning of the Hagana can be traced to 1919–1921. After the Arab attacks on Jews in Palestine in May of 1921, the social kernel for the Hagana crystallized. The Hagana drew its membership from large groups of politically left oriented Jews in Palestine, and was intimately associated with the labor union—the Histadrut. The first commanding committee of the Hagana was created in 1921.

The early 1920s witnessed a relative peace in Palestine. However, the Hagana and the Hashomer got into a serious debate about the nature of the defense and in 1922 Hashomer members severed their relationships with the Hagana. Hashomer's security perception was active and aggressive, the Hagana was more passive. The Arab attacks on Jews in 1929 caught the Hagana (as well as the British Army) by surprise. Ex-members of Hashomer (the organization did not exist in 1929) helped the Hagana in attempts to cope with the Arab attacks. The defense concept which evolved was one which emphasized the *national* (not local) basis. The Jewish Agency[4] decided to take responsibility for the Hagana.

In the 1930s the Hagana experienced a severe crisis: some of its old and most experienced commanders refused to accept the moral and military authority of the Jewish Agency. Consequently, a few of these commanders were asked to leave their command posts. More severe was the problem in Jerusalem where a group headed by Avraham Tehomey (and others) split from the Hagana and created another organization (Hagana, or Irgun Beit), which later became the Etzel.

In the early 1930s, the Hagana created the National Command ("Mifkada Artzit"). In those years the Hagana emerged and crystallized as a national organization. It began to provide military training and courses for its recruits, purchase weapons, establish a modest basis for a military industry, as well as laying the foundations for departments for medical help, law, intelligence, and it was getting into attempts to help bring Jewish immigrants to Palestine ("Aliya").

When Arab attacks on the Yishuv were renewed again in 1936 the Hagana was more prepared. It gradually moved from a local and static defense to a dynamic and more aggressive defense, based on strike forces. In 1937 strike forces were created ("Posh-Pelugot Sadeh") and in 1939 they were replaced by other units. In 1938, a British officer—Charles Orde Wingate—helped to create, train, and lead specially and carefully selected strike force units who specialized in assaults during the nights. During those years, the Hagana helped a massive effort to create new Jewish settlements.

The events of the late 1930s helped the Hagana to reorganize and create a vital organization, as well as establish new patterns of defense and assault.

1939 saw the nomination of the first head of the Hagana's National Command—Yohanan Rattner, and in 1939 the establishment of the Matcal, the general military command of the Hagana. Ya'acov Dori was nominated as the first chief of staff.

The Hagana began to use its newly established, and organized, military power from 1938–1939. It created a special strike force—the Pum in 1939 (see case nos. 19 to 24 and Pail 1979:175–180) to act against Arab attacks and against the British occupation forces.

The basic policy of the Jewish leadership during World War II was not to interfere with the British war effort which was aimed to crush the Nazis. The Jewish Agency pressed the British authorities to create a Jewish Brigade. The idea was to help create a partnership with the British, so that after the war, the British would help to establish a Jewish state. The British, however, tried to dismantle the Hagana. They were not very successful. Clearly, the British suspected that the military experience gained by Jews in combat in a special Brigade may be translated later into the Jewish struggle for statehood. These suspicions, one must add, were not baseless.

Changes in British personnel, as well as the bad situation of the British army in North Africa in 1941 helped to create better relationships between the Hagana and the British authorities. On May 19, 1941 the Hagana created the Palmach ("Pelugot Machatz," meaning shock or storm troops). It consisted of a brigade of striking and assault units. The Palmach was the Hagana's military structure that was mobilized all the time. The British felt that the Palmach was a very reliable force and used it in some combats during 1941–1942. The British victory at Al-Alamain in November of 1942 ended this period of cooperation and the Palmach went underground. The British eventually established a Jewish Brigade group within the British army in 1944 (see chapter 5 on the Nokmim).

When World War II was coming to an end, there were increasing signs of an anti-Zionist British policy (e.g., fierce objection to the mass immigration of Jews to Palestine). Consequently, the Hagana and the Palmach turned more and more attention into actions against the British. Consequently, the British army tried, in June 29, 1948 ("The Black Saturday"), to disarm, by force, the Hagana and Palmach. That attempt was not very successful, although thousands of members were arrested.

The Palmach, no doubt, grew as a very strong military organization. When the State of Israel was established in 1948, the Palmach's brigades carried most of the weight of the bloody defense against the attack of the Arab neighbors of Israel in what became known as the Israeli war for independence. The Hagana contributed to the Israeli army between forty thousand to sixty thousand soldiers.

Etzel: Irgun Tzvai Leumi (National Military Organization)

One basic principle of the Zionist movement was the wish to recreate the Jewish state. Herzl, *the* founding father of Zionism, projected this goal very forcefully in Basel, Switzerland in 1897 when the first Zionist Congress met.

Beginning in 1925, Ze'ev Jabotinsky headed the opposition to the established, left-winged Zionist movement. This opposition demanded a revision in the Zionist movement's goals and means, while at the same time sharing the idea that Jews should re-create their own state. The main demands for a "revision" focused a much more aggressive, determined, and dynamic policy, as well as emphasizing an aggressive military orientation. The contradiction and friction between the oppositionary movement and the main body of the Zionist movement grew till a real faction began to gain momentum in 1931, and culminated in the 1935 elections. Then, a new right-wing Zionist organization was created (Niv, first volume; S.T.H., vol. 2, part 1:488–499).

In 1931 a group with fascist inclinations which called itself "Brit Habiryonim," headed by Abba Ahimair, was created (see case no. 7), and was dissolved in 1933 after some of its key members were arrested by the British, and the rest were stigmatized by the Hagana. The charge was that this group was involved in the assassination of Arlosoroff.

In the spring of 1931, Avraham Tehomey and a few others, who felt totally dissatisfied with, and alienated from, the Hagana, left it and created an independent defense organization in Jerusalem, (Irgun Beit). This was the actual beginning of the Etzel, which contrary to the Hagana (that was politically left wing) was politically a right-wing, active defense group, affiliated to the revisionist faction. The initial group consisted of around three hundred members, and had branches in Jerusalem and in other locations. Such people as David Raziel, Abraham Stern, and Avraham Tehomey were very active in this group.[5]

Following the Arab riots of 1936, and in April of 1937, Etzel was divided again. Against the background of a deep ideological controversy, about half the members (around fifteen hundred) returned with Tehomey to reunite with the Hagana (April 1937), and the other half, headed mostly by Abraham Stern, David Raziel and Moshe Rosenberg emerged as the new Etzel. Robert Bitker became the first Commander of this group, but was asked to leave his command in October of 1937 (see case no. 9), and was replaced by Moshe Rosenberg. Etzel, in 1937, was not larger than two thousand members.[6] Rosenberg quit his position on May 28, 1938[7] and David Raziel became the commander of the Etzel.

In May of 1939, David Raziel was arrested by the British (Niv, vol. 2:235, see also case no. 44), and Hanoch Kalai became the temporary commander of Etzel (ibid., p. 736). On September 1, 1939, the five high commanders of Etzel were arrested by the British. As the second world war began, Raziel and Jabotinsky decided that Etzel would not fight the British any more but would join instead their efforts to fight Nazi Germany. Their policy was rejected by Abraham Stern and others. On June 19, 1940, after most of Etzel's commanders, including Stern, were released from British jail (on June 18, 1940), they had a meeting in Tel Aviv (Yevin 1986:187) where severe and harsh accusations were directed at Raziel. Subsequently, he resigned.

Jabotinsky did not accept Raziel's resignation and renominated him as commander (July 17, 1940). Abraham Stern did not accept this decision and continued to crystallize a group of members around him. Stern was elected, on June 19, 1949, as commander (Niv, vol. 3:43) of Etzel. As can be seen, Jabotinsky's instructions did not make much difference, as the Etzel was in a real crisis. The crisis was ideological and not only a clash between different personalities and temperaments (see also Naor 1990:203–253).

Stern's group basically rejected Jabotinsky's and Raziel's position that cooperation with the British was required, and that lowering the level of the guerrilla warfare was something they had to do as long as British were fighting the Nazis. Stern's group was characterized by members who wanted to fight the British, be active and not lower the profile of the guerrilla warfare. It appears that this particular group may have been somewhat inclined to a possible and limited cooperation with the Italians (Yevin 201–213).

On June 26, 1940, Stern initiated the publication of a document (no. 112) which stated that Etzel would not cooperate with the British and encouraged Jews to evade the draft to the British army.[8] Document no. 112 endorsed an active and aggressive approach, contrary to what it portrayed as the passivity of the Hagana. Stern's group wanted to stop the connections with British intelligence, disconnect from the leaders of the revisionist movement and renew the struggle against the British (Lankin 1980:52–54; Yellin-Mor 1974:57–70; Yevin 1986).

Jabotinsky died on August 3, 1940 but his death did not calm the controversy. In August (August 14, Bauer 1966:112), Stern and his group left the Etzel (a process which actually began already in March of 1940) to establish Lehi. At that time Stern's group called itself "the Etzel in Israel."

This crisis was painful for both Etzel and Lehi and continued to serve as a seedbed for animosities as well as feeding hatred. Yevin (1986:106) states that Etzel had around two thousand members after the split in the summer of 1940.

Etzel reorganized and regrouped under the renewed leadership of Raziel. In 1941 a pro-Nazi revolutionary process began in Iraq. Haj Amin Al-Huseini (the Arab Mufti; see case nos. 11

and 55) was actively involved in it. The British asked Etzel to help them cope with it and Raziel and a few others volunteered to go east and help. There Raziel died during an air raid on May 20, 1941.[9] After his death Etzel was under the command of a group of Etzel's commanders, headed by Ya'acov Meridor.

During 1941–1943 Etzel was in a very problematic state—socially, politically, and operationally, attempting to redefine itself. As part of that re-organization, on December 1, 1943, Meridor quit his position, admitting that "nothing of significance was achieved in the last two years" and on January 1, 1944 Menachem Begin was appointed as the last commander-in-chief of Etzel (S.T.H., vol. 3, part 1:493).

The period of low activity for Etzel ended and under Begin's leadership Etzel entered a renewed period of activity. Etzel was active against British and Arab targets (ibid., pp. 520–543; Livni 1987; Niv). During 1945–1946 Etzel enjoyed a membership of about two thousand members. During 1945–1947 more activities followed (e.g., see also Begin 1950; Meridor 1950). When the Israeli Army (IDF) was created in 1948 and the Lehi, Hagana, and Etzel basically ended their separate and independent existence, Etzel had between three thousand to five thousand members to contribute to the Israeli army. From these numbers, about three thousand were actual fully trained soldiers.[10]

Lehi: Lohamei Herut Israel (Fighters for the Freedom of Israel)

In August of 1940, the split of Stern's group from the Etzel was final. Stern's group saw itself as continuing the Etzel and even called itself Etzel in Israel. This group's explicit goal was to be the factor that would control Palestine politically by force of weapons, in the name of the "fighting Jews." In September of 1940, Abraham Stern changed the name of the group into Lehi (Yevin 1986:216). Since this group became known as Lehi, and for reasons of convenience and consistency, this is the name I have used throughout the text.

In September of 1940, Stern published Lehi's first announcement (Yevin 1986:315) and in November of 1940 the movement's "principles" (Yevin 1986:316). Both documents clearly delineate the symbolic-moral universe and boundaries of Stern's

Lehi. The documents are saturated with mystic statements regarding the divine nature of the people of Israel, their divine right to their land, based totally on Biblical sources, even to the point of building the third Jewish Temple. Stern changed his name to AVI—Abraham Ben Yair. He explained his choice of this particular name as a symbol which continued the tradition of the Sicariis (see chapter 5). Stern's new name reflected the name of the Sicariis' last commander on top of the doomed fortress of Masada—Elazar Ben-Yair. Stern's name became very quickly identified with "Yair."

In the summer of 1940, and after the split from Etzel, Yair found himself commanding a very devoted, talented and dedicated group of zealots, including some of the best, most qualified and experienced commanders of Etzel. On September 16, 1940, Lehi committed a most successful bank robbery in Bank APAK (Anglo Palestine Bank) on Ben-Yehuda Street in Tel Aviv. As a result of the robbery Lehi acquired a very large amount of money which enabled the young organization a decent start as an underground and revolutionary movement.[11]

Compared to the Hagana and Etzel, Lehi always was a much smaller organization. It was estimated that, in 1946, the Hagana had about 80,000 members, the Etzel 1,000 active members (plus around 4,000 in the reserves), and Lehi had around 200 members (Avidor 1970:232).

In the early 1940s the attrition rate from Lehi was apparently very high. Many felt that breaking Etzel into two organizations was useless; many members were unemployed and had to find a job. Hence they could not devote their time to Lehi. moreover, the atmosphere of mutual suspicion became unbearable (Yevin 1986:215). Yair was apparently not very effective in closing his ranks and keeping his initial advantage. Lehi began to transform into a small, unique type of organization, almost a sect.

One of Yair's main efforts was ideological. He tried to make the symbolic-moral boundaries of Lehi distinct. He met (probably in 1941) with Abba Ahimair who headed in 1933 the semi fascist and defunct Brit Habiryonim (Yevin 1986:253, see also case no. 7). He also met with Israel Sheib (Eldad) who later became Lehi's ideologist, and with Uriel Shelach who was then a bubbling, original and stormy Israeli poet. He met with Shelach first at Hebrew

University where they had studied. Shelach was on his way to develop a unique moral perception and symbolic moral universe that was supposed to help into being a new type of Jew. Shelach's ideology, and followers, became later known as the "Canaanites" (e.g., see case no. 84). Shelach helped to draft some of Etzel's and Yair's publications (Yevin 1986:98–99, 106). He was also involved in some of the ideological debates between contemporary leaders of Etzel (ibid., 209–210). After Yair was killed, Shelach wrote a powerful poem in his memory (e.g., see Yevin 1986:7–8).

From 1940 till 1942 Lehi, under the leadership of Stern, committed quite a few anti-British and other (urban) guerrilla activities, including robberies of money and acts of personal terrorism. Lehi did not accept the idea that the raging second world war called for a temporary cooperation with the British occupation army. Its core ideology was focused on a relentless struggle with the British, and with a spice of mysticism and elements of messianism. Lehi explicitly wanted to chase the British out and reestablish a Jewish state—the sooner, the better.

Lehi, at that time, was a small group, not popular with the British, Hagana and Etzel. Consequently, its members were persecuted. When the British intelligence discovered Stern's hiding place, the British officer Morton (see case no. 33) shot him to death—on February 12, 1942. When Yair was killed, most of Lehi's members were already in prison. The movement was in an advanced state of disintegration.

In September of 1942, Yitzhak Yazernitzki-Shamir and Eliahu Giladi escaped from the British detention camp in Mazra, and together with Yehoshua Cohen, Anshell Shpillman and others recreated Lehi. After the assassination of Giladi (see case no. 38) in the summer of 1943, a collective leadership for Lehi began to emerge. The group was headed by Shamir, Eldad Sheib, and Nathan Yellin-Mor (after his escape from the British detention camp in Latrun on November 1, 1943). Sheib was arrested by the British in April, 1944, and in July, 1946 Shamir was also arrested (see case no. 56). Hence, the time period when the three actually lead Lehi together was short, and command responsibility fell mostly on the shoulders of Shamir and Yellin-Mor.

Shamir and Yellin-Mor understood quite well that it would be impossible for Lehi to behave as it did while under Stern's leadership. They realized the need for popular and widespread support—and they acted toward that direction. Hence, from the autumn of 1942 till 1944 Lehi committed many acts, focusing—again—on personal terrorism. A turning point was the November 6, 1944 assassination of Moyne (see case no. 49). As a result, the persecutions against Lehi began again, and Lehi toned down some of its activities.

Between the autumn of 1945 till September of 1946 all three underground Jewish groups in Palestine—Lehi, Etzel, and the Hagana, cooperated in the struggle against the British. This cooperation collapsed in September of 1946 and Lehi continued its own activities.

When the state of Israel was established in 1948, Lehi accepted the authority of the new state and was formally dismantled on May 29, 1948. Lehi contributed to the Israeli army about eight hundred members.

While formally Lehi ceased to exist, some of its members continued their subversive activities. The assassination of Bernadotte on September 17, 1948 in Jerusalem (see case no. 83) was an illustration. That assassination, among other things, roused such a severe reaction from the new Israeli government that basically the actions taken by the government put an end to the existence of even the more militant remnants of Lehi.

In the 1950s, some militant groups and cases of political assassination events, had assassins who were formerly members of Lehi. For example, the cases involving Pinkas (see case no. 84) and Kasztner (see case no. 85). Some of these groups certainly gained much support and legitimation from Sheib, who continued to harbor and maintain his right-wing ideology.

While Lehi tried to establish a political party after 1948, the attempt failed. Shamir himself began a late and very successful political career. In 1970 he joined Herut party and became a parliament member for Gahal (Begin's party) in 1973. In 1977 he was elected as the chairman of the Israeli parliament—the Knesset. In 1980 Shamir was appointed as the minister of foreign affairs. Shamir became Israel's prime minister from October 1983 till September 1984. He became prime minister again from October 1986 till September 1988. Following the summer of 1988, Shamir became prime minister again.[12]

CHAPTER 5

Political Assassinations by Jews in the Bible, the Sicariis, and in Europe

GENERAL BACKGROUND

Clarifying the exact nature of political assassination events is not enough. There are at least two additional problems which are connected to the problem of characterizing political assassination events, and which require clarification as well. The *first* problem is an historical one—at what time period does one start looking for cases of political assassination events in Palestine-Israel? As mentioned earlier, I decided to begin the research with the new Jewish settlement in the land. That is, the last decades of the nineteenth century. This timing seems justified because it fits the revival of national Jewish life in what Jews feel is their homeland. This brings forth the second question.

As data collection began, it became evident that the *second* problem we had to deal with was the general attitude toward, position of, and actual cases of political assassination events within the cultural matrix of Judaism. Because the State of Israel is viewed, by Jews and others, politically, religiously, and socially, as the homeland of the Jews, it becomes essential to find out how Judaism regards political assassination events.

While it may be difficult to define the symbolic-moral universe of Judaism, two clear boundary markers are the Tanach (the Hebrew Bible) and the actual history of the Jewish people.

There are a few cases of political assassinations in the Tanach. For example, Ehud of the tribe of Benjamin who assassinated Eglon, the king of Moab and then won Israel eighty years of freedom (Judges 3:9–11; Heaps 1969:37–39). Another case involved Yael, Heber Hakeini's wife who assassinated Sisera (who oppressed the people of Israel cruelly for twenty years), after his defeat in the battle against Barak (Judges, chapters 4–5; Heaps 1969:39–42); Another case is the assassination of Joab, King David's chief of army, by Benaiah, son of Jehoiada, by orders from David himself. This is a well-known famous case because Joab "fled to the tent of the Lord and caught hold of the horns of the altar." This did not help because at King David's insistence, Benaiah killed Joab (I Kings, chapters 1–2, and 2:28). There are few other cases in the Tanach which focus on assassinations as a pragmatic way of getting rid of political opponents, and as a tool in struggles for the royal throne (for a lucid short review see Ford 1985:7–24; The Books of Kings report on quite a few cases).

One of the most famous cases of political assassinations involved Gedaliah. In the year 586 B.C. Nebuchadnezzar (ruler of Babylon between 605-562 B.C.) conquered Jerusalem and destroyed the first Jewish Temple. Having deported most of the officials, Gedaliah, son of Ahikam son of Shaphan, was appointed by Nebuzaradan as governor of Judea. Gedaliah's family was pro-Babylonian and may have objected to the revolt in the first place. Gedaliah encouraged the rest of the surviving Jews to return to Zion, repopulate the empty cities, work the land and to reconciliate and resign themselves to live under the yoke of Babylon. Many Jews listened to the call and returned to Zion. Unfortunately, Ishmael, son of Nethaniah, son of Elishama, who was a member of the royal family, was apparently not too thrilled with Gedaliah who became head of state without being a member of the royal family. Hence, Ishmael (with the support of Baalis, king of Ammon) assassinated Gedaliah (either in 586 B.C. or five years later). The Babylonian's reaction did come and more violence and new deportations took place. The assassination of Gedaliah was regarded by the people of Israel as a national disaster and the third day in the first month of the Jewish year (Tishre) was set as the "Fast of Gedaliah" (Jeremiah 41, 2) which is still being observed today.[1]

May one draw any definite conclusions from the Tanach? The reasons for the different assassinations seem to indicate that these assassinations were used as a means for social and political control—in different situations, with some very pragmatic ends. David and Yael got rid in this way of those they did not like.

Ehud, very pragmatically, killed Eglon and freed Israel from a rule of a tyrant. Baasha assassinated Nadav, and Zimri assassinated Elah because both assassins aspired to become kings and killed those who were destined to become kings so that they could take their place. Likewise, Ismael assassinated Gedaliah because apparently *he* wanted to become the king. It appears, therefore, that political assassination was viewed as a tool to be used for achieving some specific results, which many a time they did regardless of how the late twentieth-century reader may interpret their moral justification.

This "pragmatic" nature of political assassinations events (depending, of course, on the point of view of the observer) repeated itself many years later. For example, the rule of King Herod I, king of Judea from 37 B.C. until his death in 4 B.C., was characterized by quite a few political assassination events, especially against those that Herod I suspected of plotting against him. Thus, Herod I assassinated all Hasmoneans whose existence he suspected may have endangered his hegemony. One of the most dramatic of these assassinations took place at 36 B.C. when, on direct orders from King Herod I, soldiers drowned Aristobulus in a swimming pool in Jericho (e.g., see Encyclopedia Judaica, vol. 8:378–387).

It is difficult to examine the nature, or the impact, many of these assassinations had later. The reason is probably not that they did not have any impact, but that information regarding the decision-making process leading to contemporary assassinations is—many a time—not accessible (for more on this see part three). Lehi, which was involved in most of the assassination events prior to 1948, used Biblical examples in an explicit way in its socialization processes—for example, Ehud and Yael were presented as giving legitimacy and morality to terrorism and political assassinations (see Tzameret 1974:90–91). Interesting to note though that the utilization of Biblical cases of political assassination events within *an ideological* context, which is directed to justify an ideological commitment to terror and political assassinations, constitutes an attempt to use a the Biblical stories in a *very* different context than the meaning of these stories in the original context. There are plenty of reasons to suspect that other groups used the Biblical example in a similar fashion.

The other boundary marker is located within the history of the Jews. The question is whether there is anything in that history which may help us understand better political assassinations by Jews in Palestine and Israel in the last one hundred years. Having delved into that history, it appears that there are two chapters in this history which are relevant to political assassinations and which consequently should require our attention. The first concerns the Sicariis; the second concerns what happened in Europe before the State of Israel was established in 1948.

One of the main conclusions from this section, which will focus on Jewish history, is that there was, in fact, an ideological group of Jews who advocated the use of both terror and political assassination not only against "outsiders" but against Jews as well.

THE SICARIIS

Were there Jewish ideologies, or movements, which sanctified political murder, as did, for example, the Assassins among the Muslims, who saw their goal as fulfilling and purifying Islam, and the Thugs who killed for Kali, the Hindu goddess? Surprisingly perhaps, the answer is yes: the Zealots—Sicarii—who flourished around the time of the destruction of the Jewish Second Temple (69–70 A.D.)

Between the years 66–74 A.D., the major and most dramatic part of the so-called "Big Revolt" of Jews against the Romans, who occupied Judea then, took place.[2] The Romans responded with full force—they burnt Jerusalem to the ground, destroyed the second temple and in short reconquered the land with brutal force. The Big Revolt became one of the most traumatic events in the collective memories of the Jewish people. On the one hand, this was a period of revolt, of brave and proud men and women who stood up for their rights and tried to be free from foreign rule. On the other hand, the end result of that revolt was failure, and the heroic effort ended in a mass scale blood shed of the Jews by the Roman army. The Masada myth (e.g., see Shargel 1979) is a result of that period. No understanding of modern Israel can be achieved without understanding this sad, heroic period, of which the Sicariis were part.

A major source for this period are the writings of Josephus Flavius. Flavius' writings, however, are not free from bias and are considered by many as problematic—less so today than a few years ago (e.g., see Flusser 1985; Rapoport 1982, 1988). However, without Flavius there simply is not very much we know about the period. In what follows I shall try to describe the Sicariis, based on different sources. I trust that my description is faithful to the different sources. The events and processes I describe took place almost nineteen hundred years ago. Flavius' writings are obviously an indispensable source.[3]

One may perhaps start dating the Big Revolt in the year 6 A.D. when the Romans wanted to carry out a census in the province. One of the main objectors to the census was Yehuda from Gamla (also identified as Yehuda from the Galilee) who, with Zadok Haprushi, kindled the fire of resistance. They developed and spread what Flavius called the fourth philosophy. The first three philosophies were the Essenes, Sadducees, and Pharisees. The fourth philosophy emphasized the value of freedom, and adherents felt allegiance only to God. It seems reasonable to assume that Yehuda was killed by the Romans, but the "fourth philosophy" did not die and spread in the country. It became the ideology of the Sicariis, and was identified with the aspiration to be free of, and totally resistant to, the rule of the Roman Emperor.

We first find the name Sicariis mentioned by Flavius in connection to events which took place between 52–62 A.D.. The name of the Sicariis derives from the word "sica," meaning a small dagger, which the Sicariis supposedly carried beneath their robe and which they used to knife and assassinate those that they saw as their opponents in Jerusalem, especially during the holidays. One of their very first victims was Yonatan Ben-Hanan, the former high priest. The Sicariis also kidnaped hostages which they exchanged for their own people who were sought after by the Romans.

In 66 A.D. the Sicariis took Masada by force and helped conquer the upper city in Jerusalem. They set fire to Hanania's house (the high priest) as well as burning the central archives where the legal, business and I.O.U. documents and notes were kept. Hanania and his brother Hizkiahu were killed, as well as a host of Roman soldiers who surrendered. These acts not only signified the beginning of the Big Revolt, but also helped to split the Jews into "zealots" and "moderates." It seems that the fourth philosophy adopted by the Sicariis was also accompanied by what we might call today "socialistic ideas."

Menachem, who was the leader of the Sicariis in Jerusalem, was killed by members of Elazar Ben-Hanania's group, who killed other Sicariis as well. The rest of the Sicariis, headed by Elazar Ben-Yair, fled to Masada, where they remained after the fall of Jerusalem (in 70 A.D.) until 73 A.D., when Silva's Roman Legion conquered Masada and those who were there committed collective suicide prior to the Roman final victory. The Sicariis in Masada, according to Flavius, attacked the settlement of Ein Gedi (at the foot of the mountains nearby Masada), chased the men out and killed the women and children—about seven hundred people and possibly more. Furthermore, Flavius mentioned that the Sicariis robbed and destroyed other nearby villages.[4]

While the Sicariis were involved in quite a few indiscriminate terror activities, they did not shy away from committing acts of discriminate political assassinations. For example, assassinating the ex-high priest of Jerusalem. This pattern, of using both means of terrorism and political assassinations, was repeated 1,870 or so years later—in the same land, sometimes in the same city. "Brit Habirionim" was a small Jewish group (which was established by Abba Ahimair) in Palestine of the 1930s. This group was characterized by fascist tendencies, and adopted very explicitly the Sicariis as their inspiration (see also cases no. 7 and no. 8). A book for Brit Habirionim is called "We the Sicariis" and is begun by a poem by Uri Zvi Greenberg, glorifying the Sicariis. In no place does the book explain who exactly were the Sicariis, or what they did. Lehi drew much of its inspiration from Brit Habirionim, and "Yair," Lehi's legendary leader, chose his name to reflect the name of the commander of the Sicariis on Masada (Elazar Ben-Yair). The Sicariis thus won popularity in the pre-state (1948) days, among some groups. What was usually emphasized was their craving for freedom from foreign rule, at any cost (including the mass suicide of the Sicariis on top of the Masada) and their claims for social justice and socialism. Forgotten was the murderous nature of the Sicariis, their use of terrorism and political assassinations against others Jews, their murderous raid on Ein Gedi, and the fact that the revolt they helped to start ended in an horrendous catastrophe for the Jews.[5]

One, however, must also remember that the activities of the Sicariis were much smaller and limited in scope and magnitude as compared to the activities of possibly similar groups like the Thugs and the Assassins (e.g., see Rapoport 1984 for a comparison).

While for years the memory of the Sicariis and of Masada was repressed, the renewal of national Jewish life in Israel also sparked renewed interest in both the Sicariis and Masada. Living for hundreds of years under foreign rule outside their own land, and being often subjected to virulent anti-Semitic discrimination and persecutions, the memory of the Sicariis probably gave some new Jewish groups a sense of belonging; a sense that hundreds of years ago, and against tremendous odds, Jewish freedom fighters fought and died heroically in Israel. The powerful analogy with the Sicariis gave some twentieth-century Jewish groups a vigorous and vital sense of historical continuity, belonging and a shared and mystical feeling of transcendental integration. The Masada heroic calamity only added to this.

It is difficult and improper to downplay the role of the Big Revolt in the collective Jewish consciousness, particularly in the new era beginning from around the 1930s. Masada, the Sicariis and the Big Revolt all played a crucial role in socialization processes of Jewish youth in Palestine and Israel. Masada was a place that almost every youngster in Israel heard about. Many also climbed to the top of that ancient fortress. It became a very central and powerful symbol of Jewish heroism and martyrdom, particularly so for all the pre-state Jewish underground groups. A symbol to live by. Yair, commander of Lehi, chose his name after the name of the Sicarii commander of Masada, Brit Habiryonim called itself in the 1930s, We, the Sicariis. And yet, the most unpleasant aspects of the Sicariis deeds and policies were totally repressed in the modern era. In a strange resemblance, most of the political assassinations committed by the three pre-state Jewish underground groups were aimed against other Jews, very much like the Sicariis. Hence, most political assassinations were carried out by groups for whom Masada and the Sicariis were very central socialization symbols.

Interesting to note too that, supposedly, the Israeli's Mossad assassination unit was called Metzada (or Masada, see chapter 9 and Hoy and Ostrovsky 1990:34, 117–119).

PRE-ISRAEL (1948) EUROPE

Were there cases of political assassinations by Jews as such before the renewal of Jewish national life in Palestine? The place to look into is where there was a very large Jewish population: Europe. Europe deserves this particular attention because, as demographers have pointed out, "at the end of the last century, three quarters of [the Jews] lived in Europe" (Goldscheider and Zuckerman 1984:4). However, since this study is not aimed to focus exclusively on Europe, only a modest and brief inquiry regarding the nature of political assassination events by Jews in Europe took place. We surveyed the existing literature pinpointing the well-known cases, plus a few which were not that well known, as a necessary background. Thus, and for example, while the *Narodnaya Volya* became an important example for the pre-state Jewish underground groups in Palestine, the involvement of Jews in that Russian group (and in others)—as Jews—is quite problematic. In what follows, these cases are documented individually (for a condensed summary of these cases, see diagram 2 in the Appendix).

CASE A

Hirsch Lekert (May 18, 1902)

Hirsch Lekert was born in 1880, in a small Jewish town in Lithuania—Hanoshishok (near Kovna), and was trained as a bootmaker. Lekert was active, since his youth, in the Bund organization (a Jewish socialist party which was established in 1897 and remained active in Europe).

In June 1900, Hirsch Lekert was already involved, as a leader, in a raid on the prison in Novogorod, when his group freed political prisoners. He was caught, sentenced to prison and sent for exile to Yekaterinoslaw. A few days before May 1, 1902, he escaped and came to Vilna where his young wife and widowed mother lived.

On May 1, 1902, a group of Jewish workers went in a procession from the Jewish ghetto into Vilna, the town, carrying the red flag. Army and militia forces attacked the demonstration and by orders of von Val, the county executive, fifty demonstrators were arrested. On May 2, von Val ordered the flogging of twenty-eight of the prisoners, twenty of whom were Jewish.

The Bund published a pamphlet stating that: "the Jewish proletariat will give rise to the hand that will revenge the terrible insult inflicted on them (the flogging)" (Basok 1944:5).

A group of four to six Bund members, with Hirsch Lekert, decided to revenge. While the local Bund's committee never officially approved of the activities, Lekert's group most certainly felt as if it was acting on behalf of the Bund. They bought weapons, trained themselves in the forests outside Vilna and put von Val under surveillance.

On May 18, 1902, in the evening, when von Val came out of a circus show, Hirsch Lekert shot him in the arm and leg. However, von Val did not die. Lekert did not try to escape. He was caught, arrested, put on trial before a military court and sentenced to death. At 2:00 A.M. in the morning of June 10, 1902, he was hanged, refusing to ask for clemency.

Lekert was hailed by different Jewish groups as a martyr and as a proud Jew who fought to the end.[6]

The lesson from Lekert's deed was carried into the 1940s Palestine. In an editorial which was published by Lehi, Lekert was hailed as a prototype of a Jewish hero (Lehi's writings, vol. 1:525–526). Menachem Begin, who was the commander in chief of Etzel, and years later Israel's prime minister, writes in his memoirs about a few of Etzel's members who were brought before a British military court in 1946 and sentenced to flogging (Begin 1950: 318–323).[7] Begin used the case of Hirsch Lekert to warn the British mandate forces not to degrade Etzel's members by flogging them. The British ignored the warning. On December 29, 1946, Etzel kidnaped one British major and three sergeants and flogged each one of them. Etzel warned that the next flogging of Jewish underground fighters would be retaliated by opening fire on British soldiers. The British forces never used flogging again.

CASE B

Pinhas Dashewski (June 4, 1903)

April 1903 witnessed one of the worst pogroms directed at European Jews till that time—the Kishinov pogrom. During this pogrom, about fifty Jews were murdered, hundreds were wounded, and much property was destroyed. This pogrom shook Russian Jews, as well as some of the Russian intelligentsia (e.g., Tolstoy; Gorky). As a result, Jewish self-defense societies were established (Encyclopaedia Hebraica; vol. 29:695–696).

Pinhas Dashewski was born in 1879 to an assimilated Jewish family in Korostyshev, Ukraine. As a student, he joined an activist Zionist group in 1897 and became one of the founding figures of an activist socialist student group in Keyov. The Kishinov pogrom was taken by Dashewski as an insult to his human and national pride. There are contradictory versions as to what happened next.

According to the Encyclopaedia Hebraica (1952, vol. 13:222–223), the "Jewish self-defense in Keyov decided to take revenge from the initiator of the pogrom"—Pavolaki Krushevan, and Dashewski volunteered. S.T.H. (vol. 1, part 1:160) states that while Jewish youth accepted—with pride—Dashewski's deed, he did it "on his own." The Encyclopaedia Judaica (1971, vol. 5:1310) does not attribute responsibility to anyone except Dashewski. However, Dashewski was clearly a member of an activist Jewish Zionist group and it is very difficult to accept that he had some sort of self-inspiration and decided to act on his own.

Dashewski came to St. Petersburg and started to follow Krushevan, who was the editor of two anti-semitic newspapers. Dashewski was equipped with a handgun and a knife. He did not trust that his hand would not shake when shooting (and thus, possibly hitting an innocent bystander), so, he decided to use the knife.

On June 4, 1903, he jumped on Krushevan and stabbed him in his neck. Krushevan was wounded lightly. Dashewski turned himself in to a policeman who was on duty nearby. In his trial, Dashewski admitted the fact of a premeditated attempt to assassinate Krushevan. He explained that he "felt a duty to act like this as a Jew whose national sentiment was offended" (S.T.H., vol. 2, part 1:161).

Dashewski was found guilty and sentenced to five years hard labor in prison. He was released, however, in 1906. He visited Palestine in 1910 where he was welcomed enthusiastically by the Yishuv. After the Bolshevik revolution he remained faithful to Zionism. He was arrested by the Soviet authorities and died in a Siberian prison in 1934.[8]

CASE C

Mania Shochat (Vilbuschevitz)—
Three Cases Between 1903–1905

Mania Shochat (Vilbuschevitz) was born in a small village near Grodno in 1879 to a wealthy Jewish family. Members of the family took active part in the renewal of Jewish interest and settlement in Palestine. Mania chose to get closer to the workers and get acquainted with the socialist revolution (S.R.) as well as to the "Bund" (a Jewish socialist organization). Being politically active, she was arrested in March of 1900. She was later released and joined the political activities of a questionable organization called "the independent worker's party," apparently a competing organization to the Bund. This party began to get closer to Zionism. In 1903 the Kishinov pogrom happened and the Russian authorities forbade Zionist activities in Russia. The party itself was dissolved in 1903 (S.T.H., vol. 1, part 1:199–201. For more on Mania see Goldstein 1991).

Ben Zvi (1976:39) reports that Mania was upset with the disintegration of the party, and the arrests of some of its members. She took a gun, went to the prison where the main party's supporter—Zubatov—was arrested and threatened to kill him because she thought he betrayed the party. Having talked to Zubatov she finally did not kill him.

After the collapse of the above mentioned political organization, as well as the personal political aspirations of Mania, she joined a small group of social revolutionaries who planned to assassinate Fleve, the minister of the interior. She, together with other members of "Poalei Zion," analyzed what they thought were the real reasons for the Kishinov pogrom. Their conclusion was that Krushevan, who was the major agitator for the pogrom, was only a tool, and that the real culprit was Fleve. They decided, therefore, to assassinate him, as revenge.

Fleve, however, was well protected and one member of the group—Sergei—suggested to dig a tunnel under Fleve's house, penetrate the house and assassinate him. Money was certainly needed to execute this plan. It was decided that Mania would go abroad to locate donors and towards the end of 1903 she traveled to Berlin. She met there a Jewish banker who was so shook by the Kishinov pogrom that he was willing to contribute the money. Mania remained in Berlin, under the camouflage of being a student in economics and began sending money to Russia.

Unfortunately, the group that Mania was a member of had one member called Azaf (or Azev). That Azaf was a planted agent for the Russian intelligence (Ford 1985:243–244; Gaucher 1968:57–70). He betrayed the whole group to the Russian authorities and they were all arrested. Mania, who was in Berlin, escaped that fate (Ben Zvi 1976:42–43; Shva 1969:46–47). Consequently, no attempt was made on Fleve's life.

Mania later left Berlin to Palestine and at the age of twenty-five years, in January 1904, she arrived in Jaffo port. She became very active in the crystallizing of the political and defense organizations of the new Jewish national life in Israel.

Ben Zvi (1976:59), Shva (1969:64), and Mania Shochat herself (1957:385–395) mention that after Mania arrived to Palestine in 1904, she went to Paris (probably in 1905). When she was in Paris she was approached by Meir Cohen from Minsk asking her to help him purchase weapons for Jewish self-defense groups in Russia. Mania agreed to help. They approached a weapons factory in Liege, Belgium and purchased weapons.

One day, at an unspecified date, Mania was traveling to Odessa with boxes of weapons and ammunition and stayed in a house of friends. She tells that on that day, in the afternoon, she heard the doorbell ring. When she opened the door, she saw a young, pale, and tired man who asked for Akimov. Mania told him that no such person was there and then the stranger collapsed and lost consciousness. Mania treated him, and he later awoke and for two hours told Mania his life story.

Suddenly, he asked Mania "did you not hear that they brought today to this house boxes with weapons for the revolutionaries?" Mania was frozen, scared, and shocked. She realized that the stranger was probably an intelligence agent and that if he would leave the house all would be lost. Mania writes that (1957:387) "I had a small hand gun in my pocket, a gift from the factory, with a silencer. I shot. The guy fell. He looked at me with his eyes full of sadness and was quiet. After a few minutes he died." Mania, with the help of her girl friend—Bat Zion—got rid of the body later that day.

Mania was thus involved in one case of a political assassination event in the planning stage (Fleve), and in another problematic assassination proper. Assassinating the suspected agent does not quite fit all aspects of our definition of a political assassination event (especially the seriousness and planning aspects), but it does fit other aspects of the definition (the motivation).

CASE D

Shalom Schwartzbard (May 25, 1926)

After the Bolshevik revolution in Russia, a short-lived (between 1919–1920) Ukranian Republic was established and its capital was Keyov. Simon Peteliura was the chief Ataman[9] of the Ukrainian Republican Army until it was defeated by the Red Army in 1920. During Peteliura's reign, Ukrainian Jews were subjected to pogroms and slaughters "on a scale unknown since the massacres of 1648–1649 under Bogdan Chmeilnicki" (Nedava 1979:70). Nedava (1979:78) estimates that the number of pogroms in the Ukraine during 1918–1921 was about 2,000 in seven hundred towns, costing the life of anywhere between 50,000 to 170,000 Jewish victims.

Shalom Schwartzbard was born in 1886 in Ismail, Beserabia. He was active in an underground socialist Jewish movement in Balta (Ukraine). In 1906 he escaped to Paris, where he worked as a watchman. He joined the French foreign legion, was wounded and received a few commendations. In 1917 Schwartzbard returned to Russia to join the Red Army which fought the "whites." During his service in the army, he witnessed the

Ukrainian pogroms on Jews. In Ukraine, he joined Zionist groups and took an active role in various attempts to organize self-defense groups. Being disappointed and disillusioned by the new Russian social order and regime, Schwartzbard returned to Paris in 1920.

On May 25, 1926, Simon Peteliura lived a life of a respectable political refugee in Paris. At approximately 1415 Peteliura was coming out from a restaurant located in the Latin quarter of Paris. Schwartzbard approached Peteliura, identified him and with a hand gun shot him five times. These shots killed Peteliura. Schwartzbard yelled at Peteliura that it was a revenge for the pogroms in the Ukraine. Policemen who came to the scene arrested Schwartzbard.

Schwartzbard was put on trial beginning in October 1, 1927. The defense turned the trial into a political event and used it to demonstrate Peteliura's responsibility for the pogroms. After a dramatic political trial, on October 27, 1927, Schwartzbard was found not guilty and acquitted. This verdict was acclaimed by many contemporary journalists and intellectuals.[10]

CASE E

Yankoviak, Feldman, and Blai (May 27, 1926)

The Ataman Askilko was Peteliura's right hand in 1919 in the Ukraine, and was held personally responsible for the pogrom perpetrated on the Jews in Berditchev. He was certainly considered a poisonous anti-Semite and had a reputation for abuse and maltreatment of Jews. Gildenman (1956:50) mentions that when a delegation of Jews once came to Askilko's office to ask for protection against Ukrainian ravaging gangs, he replied that "I would not want to confront my brave soldiers on behalf of a few hurting Jews."

Despite his past, in 1926, Askilko chose to live in the village of Uvarov, near Rovno, enjoying all civil rights and publishing an Ukrainian weekly magazine called *Dilo*. All this, with no interference from the Polish authorities.

Dilo published anti-semitic articles and the day after Peteliura was assassinated by Schwartzbard, it published a warm salute to

Peteliura in which Peteliura was portrayed as a great national and political hero. The salute attributed responsibility for Peteliura's death to Jews and called Ukrainians to revenge his death. Implicitly, the salute clearly called for new pogroms. Jews in Rovno were obviously anxious.

On May 26, 1926, a day after Peteliura's assassination, three young Jews were sitting in cafe "Zabrowski" in Rovno, reading *Dilo*'s salute. The three—Yankoviak, Feldman, and Blai—felt that all which was needed for new anti-semitic pogroms were two or three more such articles or salutes. They decided that to prevent such a danger, it was necessary to assassinate Askilko.

The three went to Uvarov, acquainted themselves with where Askilko lived, and found out his comings and goings. After two days, on May 27, 1926, they approached the house where Askilko lived, in the night. Askilko was sitting in front of his desk writing something. One of the three climbed on the shoulders of the other two, and with a hand gun shot Askilko dead. The three fled the scene.

Although the Polish authorities started an intensive investigation—they never found the assassins. The police file was eventually closed for lack of evidence (Gildenman, 1956).

CASE F

David Frankfurter (February 4, 1936)

David Frankfurter, the son of a rabbi, was born in 1909 in Daruvar in Croatia (Yugoslavia). He was very much immersed in Jewish culture and involved with Jewish groups, including the Zionist group of Jewish students in Germany, and very conscious of himself being a Jew.

He started to study medicine in Germany, in Leiptzig University, in the autumn of 1929. In 1931, he moved to Frankfurt and in 1933 he witnessed how Germany voted Hitler and the Nazis into power. Frankfurter gives numerous accounts in his autobiography (1984) of how the rising tidal wave of anti-Semitism in Germany scared and shook him. Frankfurter saw, personally, the crowds of Germans being heated by anti-Semitic propaganda; he experienced the hatred and danger of the Nazi menace and became keenly aware of the grave danger for Jews. Frankfurter left Germany and continued to pursue his studies in Switzerland.

In November of 1935, in Switzerland and while pursuing his career as a student for medicine, Frankfurter first heard the name Wilhelm Gustloff. Gustloff lived in Davos, Switzerland, and was the leader of the Swiss branch of the Nazi party. Frankfurter viewed Gustloff as a dangerous person (1984:72–74). He decided to assassinate Gustloff to save the violated honor of Jews; to give the world a warning signal, and to protect what he saw as "free Switzerland" from the oppressive Nazi totalitarianism (p. 73).

On the evening of February 4, 1936, David Frankfurter came to Gustloff's home in Davos. Gustloff's wife opened the door and let Frankfurter in. Frankfurter waited for Gustloff, and when he entered the room, Frankfurter used his hand gun, shot and fatally wounded Gustloff. Frankfurter ran out of the house, considered suicide, and eventually gave himself up to the police.

Frankfurter was put on trial in a local court, was found guilty and sentenced to eighteen years imprisonment. He served nearly nine years and was pardoned after the Nazi defeat.[11]

CASE G

Herschel Feibel Grynszpan (November 7, 1938)

Grynszpan was born in Hanover on March 28, 1921, the third child of Zondel and Rivka Grynszpan who immigrated from Poland to Germany. In 1938 Herschel Grynszpan left Germany and lived for a while in Brussel, and later moved to live in Paris. In August of 1938, the French authorities refused to renew his permit to stay in France and since then he remained in Paris (with his relatives) illegally. Meanwhile, and in October 1938, the Polish government declared that all the passports of Polish citizens who were living outside Poland would become invalid. This "order" was obviously meant against about seventeen thousand Polish Jews who lived in Germany. The Germans acted quickly and decisively. They told all the relevant non-German Jews to leave Germany immediately. Thus, Herschel Grynszpan's parents, together with about seventeen thousand other Jews, were expelled from Germany in the most humiliating way in sealed train cars. They were thrown into the no man's land between Germany and Poland, where they remained with no shelter, food, or supplies, being kicked back and forth by German and Polish border police. Eventually, the Polish authorities let them stay near a Polish village adjoining the border.

While Herschel could hear about this horrendous event in the media, he also received letters from his parents describing their, and other Jews, ordeal.

On November 7, 1938, Herschel Grynszpan, who was then seventeen years old, bought a gun and at around 10:00 went to the German embassy in Paris. He asked to meet the German ambassador under the pretext that he had a few important documents to offer the Germans. He was referred to the first secretary of the embassy, twenty-nine years old, Ernst von Rath. When the two were alone in the room, Grynszpan took out his recently purchased hand gun and fired five times. He missed three times, but one of the other bullets hit von Rath and wounded him fatally. Von Rath died two days later, on November 9.

While Grynszpan was a member of a Jewish youth movement in Germany (Maccabi), he claimed that he carried out the assassination purely on his own initiative (*Davar*, November 28, 1938:2). Grynszpan, according to all sources, did his act because of Jewish nationalistic feelings, and as a protest and revenge against the Nazi treatment of Jews, and the expulsion of Polish Jews from Germany (*Palestine Post*, November 8, 1938:1). In a letter to his parents, Grynszpan wrote that his main motive was indeed revenge (Nevo 1988c:26).

Grynszpan was arrested by the French authorities who decided to begin his trial in September of 1939. But this never materialized. World War II began and Grynszpan was transferred from one French prison to another. In July of 1940, the French pro-Nazi authorities extradited him to the Nazis.

The Nazis apparently wanted to use Grynszpan in a dramatic and grandiose political trial which was supposed to "prove" the existence of a global Jewish conspiracy. The trial was scheduled to begin in May 11, 1942.[12] However, the Nazis finally decided against the trial. The reasons for not sentencing Grynszpan are not known, but Fuerstein (1986:107) and *Ha'aretz* (October 5, 1961 and December 11, 1960, p. 10) imply that the reason was that the Nazis perhaps suspected that von Rath and Grynszpan had a homosexual affair and that the assassination occurred against that background. While this suspicion may be valid, on the face of it this claim does not seem too credible for the following reasons: (a) immediately after the assassination Grynszpan did not use this claim; (b) Grynszpan wanted to assassinate the German ambassador, and it seems that he met von Rath only by chance. It may also be that Grynszpan's French lawyers told him to use this account knowing that the Nazis would not want to face an account which attributed the assassination to a homosexual affair between a Jew and a Nazi (see Fuerstein 1986:107). Furthermore, von Rath was not a Nazi, and may have even been under the Gestapo surveillance, because of suspicions of anti-Nazi activities on his part. In fact, von Rath's father claimed that his son's death was a Nazi provocation (Harpaz 1988).

The whereabouts of Grynszpan after the end of World War II, or whether he survived the Nazi prison, are not known. It is quite reasonable to assume that he was killed, or died, in a Nazi prison or a concentration camp.[13]

The assassination of von Rath, however, did not go unnoticed in Nazi Germany. On November 13, 1938 Joseph Goebbels accused all German Jews of being responsible for the assassination of von Rath (*Davar*, November 14, 1938:1). The Nazis used the assassination as an excuse for what they presented as a retaliation and launched the brutal "Crystal Night" (Kristallnacht—began on November 9, 1938 and lasted till November 11; e.g., see Read and Fisher 1989) which was a wave of pogroms, an officially sponsored terror campaign against Jews. That night, Jews were beaten, wounded, raped, killed, and arrested. About two hundred synagogues (at least) were burnt down or destroyed; hundreds of stores, public buildings, and private houses were destroyed. About thirty thousand Jews were arrested and sent to concentration camps. About one hundred Jews died during the events themselves, another five hundred were murdered when they arrived to the concentration camps, and a few hundred other Jews who could not take it committed suicide. The shattered windows caused the name of that night.[14] Ford (1985:272) notes that "Herman Goering, Hitler's special commissioner to assess more formal penalties, first imposed on (Germany's) Jewish community a fine of one billion Marks, then confiscated for governmental use all insurance payments due owners of property destroyed or damaged on Kristallnacht, and finally issued the climactic decree providing, as its title proudly announced, for 'The Elimination of Jews from German Economic Life'."

Although this case has usually been portrayed as a case of political assassination bona fide, one must note that there are a few open questions which make this case somewhat problematic. The issue of homosexuality is one. A second question concerns the *personal* involvement of Grynszpan as a victim of the Nazi persecutions, as well as the sufferings and humiliations of his parents. Third, the question about the selection and specificity of the victim is not fully solved.

The literature reveals a few other cases, less known, and clustered around two axes.

JEWISH DEFENSE DURING WORLD WAR II

The first axis focuses around a few cases which typically took place in Jewish Ghettoes in Europe during the Nazi occupation. Living in those Ghettos posed a particularly painful and impossible dilemma. On the one hand, there were a few active and militant Jewish defense organizations (e.g., in the Jewish Ghetto in Warsaw). On the other hand, there were those Jews who cooperated with the Nazi regime. Some cooperators did not know or did not believe that the Nazis really intended to murder all Jews; they may have even believed that cooperation could mean survival; some cooperated perhaps because they suspected the truth but wanted to save their own (and their families') life, and thought that such cooperation could actually achieve that.

Some documentation exists which points out that a few Jewish defense organizations, especially in the Warsaw Ghetto, assassinated actors who they felt cooperated with the Nazis, to the point of treason. Thus, on the twentieth of August 1942, Israel Kanal from Warsaw Ghetto shot, and seriously wounded, the commander of the local Jewish police—Joseph Sherinski (Zuckerman 1990:174). That occurred after the Nazis began to evacuate 300,000 Jews to the death camps—an evacuation which lasted from July 12 to September 12, 1942. Kanal was a member of an organization of young Jews that was founded in the Warsaw Ghetto on July 28, 1942 to protect Jews and fight the Nazis. That organization also assassinated other cooperators with the Nazis[15] Political assassinations were also used by Jewish defense in the Cracow Ghetto in 1943 (e.g., an assassination attempt against Shimon Shpitz and other Gestapo agents—see Maimon et al. 1984, pp. 15 and 17).

Niv (vol. 3:214–215) adds that one of the underground groups in the Warsaw Ghetto—Etzi—followed Gestapo agents, Jews and Poles, put them on trial and executed them if they were found guilty in treason. According to Niv, many Gestapo agents were executed—among them a group of eight males and three females, in June of 1942. Later, Jewish collaborators were executed as well. After the evacuation of the Ghetto, on October 20, 1942, Ya'acov Leikin, the deputy police chief was executed and on November 29, 1942, Israel Furst was executed on charges of corruption and cooperation with the Nazis. A planned execution against Shmerling, a Jewish police officer, was never carried out. Etzi located other traitors and executed them as well. (See also Zuckerman 1990:179–180, 207–209, 574.)

In a recent book (1990), Itzchak Zuckerman who was one of the major figures in the leadership of the Jewish revolt in the Warsaw Ghetto,[16] states very clearly that there were violent struggles among different groups of Jews in the Ghetto and that the leadership of the revolt decided to "eliminate" (meaning, to kill) those Jews that the Jewish leadership thought were collaborating with the Nazis.[17] These were mostly Jewish members of both the Nazi controlled Jewish police and from the Judenraete.[18]

It is likely that similar actions took place in other locations. For example, *Rovno—A Memorial Book* (which was published in 1956 in Tel Aviv by "Yalkut Wohlin"—the organization of people who came from Rovno, [in Hebrew]) which is a collection of anecdotes about Jewish life in Wohlin, describes a few such cases (p. 5). However, accessibility to data is difficult and so, we shall restrict our survey and use the above cases as illustrations for what were probably more widespread contemporary trends.

THE JEWISH BRIGADE—'HANOKMIM'

The second axis is focused around a few cases involving a group which was called Hanokmim (the avengers in Hebrew), that was active after World War II. Its members came from the Jewish Brigade.

Beginning in 1939, the British recruited Jews from Palestine into the British army. These soldiers were placed in different units in a variety of roles and duties. In the summer of 1942, the Jewish Agency began to apply pressure on the British to create a Jewish Brigade, where all the Jewish soldiers would serve. At first, the British were very hesitant. However, after the British victory in the battle of Al-Alamain (November, 1942), the progress of the British-American front in North Africa (1943) and the growing distance of the fighting fronts from the Middle East—the British government announced, in September of 1944, that it would create a Jewish Brigade Group. It had about five thousand Jewish soldiers. Following training, the Brigade was transferred to North Italy, where it was placed in the front where the British 8th army fought, near the Senyo river.

The Brigade took an active role in the last attack on the Germans, before their final surrender to the allied forces in Italy. At the end of the war, the Brigade was stationed near the borders of Italy, Yugoslavia, and Austria. It was transferred to Belgium in July of 1945. Overall, the Brigade existed for twenty months and was dismantled in June of 1946.[19]

When the war was over in 1945, a group of Jewish soldiers from the Brigade organized a few groups of *Nokmim* (avengers). These groups were organized by Israel Carmi, Chaim Laskov, Robert Grossman, Marcel Tubias, Shalom Giladi, Meir Zorea ("Zero"), Shaike Weinberg, as well as a few others. While the most active members of Hanokmim came from the Brigade's second battalion, soldiers from other battalions helped too.

Carmi, who was one of the main figures, worked with the British military intelligence. Under this camouflage, the Avengers reached, located, identified and assassinated ex-Gestapo and S.S. officers, but not Jews. They assassinated them because of their participation in the Nazi effort to exterminate Jews, and as a revenge. These activities were carried out secretly; even the commander of the Brigade did not know about, and was not aware of, them. It seems evident that Israel Carmi and Chaim Laskov made many of the decisions.

Members of Hanokmim tried to locate Adolf Eichman. At an unknown date and place one unknown member of Hanokmim (possibly Shimon Avidan, Segev 1991:133) thought that he had found Eichman and killed that person. As it turned out later, he killed the wrong person. Eichman was caught only in 1960 by the Israeli secret service and brought for trial to Israel. One of his captors, supposedly, was a member in Hanokmim (Naor 1988:147–148). Naor also reports that Hanokmim wanted to assassinate the Arab mufti Haj Amin Al Husseini (1988:149-150; for more on this see case no. 55).

It is estimated that Hanokmim assassinated a few hundred Germans and other Nazis.[20] The Avengers obviously used the Nazi extermination policy of Jews as the pretext and justification for their acts, as well as other bloody events in Jewish European history—for example, the Kishinov pogrom (Ben Horin, 1987). While Hanokmim were Jews who came from Palestine and as such their acts could be counted as bona fide cases of political assassination, in reality this is a very difficult classification. The most important difficulty is that we have no detailed accounts of the numbers of the assassinations, dates, times, and accurate mechanism of decision making and modus operandi. In principle, however, the pattern and "reasons" used by Hanokmim fit the earlier European pattern, as well as the pattern which was to be developed in Palestine-Israel.

Furthermore, it is evident that there were similar attempts, by other Jewish groups, to avenge Nazis after the end of World War II, including an attempt to poison the food in a war prisoner camp of thirty-six thousand S. S. prisoners.[21]

While the Hagana's command probably knew in fairly good details what it was that Hanokmim did (and may have even approved, or prevented, some of the assassinations—e.g., see case no. 55 later in the book), its attitude toward these assassinations was ambivalent. Laskov himself may have expressed this ambivalence when he stated that: "Having revenge is the business of weak people. Nothing to be proud about. We, in fact, lost the war. We lost six million Jews. Those who did not see these places, the concentration camps and crematories, will not understand what was done to us. Since we were weak, and we neither had a state nor power—we took revenge. It was not the nice/proper thing to do, but in the situation given then, each one used the working tools he had" (Naor 1988:150).

CONCLUDING DISCUSSION

Although the Bible does have a few references to political assassination events—it is difficult to generalize from the anecdotal cases to a broader perspective. Most political assassinations in the Bible seem to be characterized by their pragmatic nature. The Sicariis and cases of political assassination events by Jews in Europe before the formal establishment of Israel in 1948 are more generalizable and significant. Ideological militant Jewish groups in pre1948 Israel, who fought for the establishment of a new Jewish state, used the cases to socialize members and as a pretext for some of their actions. Hence, the historical and essential links between the Sicariis, acts of political assassinations in Europe before 1948, and the ideology and actions of important Jewish groups which took part in shaping—and bringing into existence—the new State of Israel, can be observed.

The above cases suggest that in the majority of cases and incidences (Lekert, Shochat, Dashewski, Askilko, Schwartzbard, Grynszpan, Warsaw Ghetto, the Avengers) the major motive was revenge. In the cases of Frankfurter and Askilko, there were also attempts to prevent and stop what was felt as a dangerous social and political process-threatening Jewish existence.

The element of revenge in the majority of the above cases comes across as very salient, and the assassinations occurred, therefore, following events which were perceived by the potential assassins as worthy and deserving revenge. When viewing this particular pattern of political assassinations one must be reminded of the special situation of Jews in Europe. Of particular interest is anti-Semitism which was so virulent in some places and times that it culminated in pogroms and in the Nazi attempt to exterminate all European Jews. While not too many cases occurred, it is more than plausible to assume that feeling persecuted, with no real protection in many places, could indeed lead a few actors to political assassinations as a route, possibly the only one from the assassins' point of view, to what they felt was a revengeful justice.

Most of the assassins in the first seven cases were part of distinguishable symbolic-moral universes, in the form of active collective political groups (Lekert, Dashewski, Shochat-Vilbuschevitz, Schwartzbard, Yankoviak-Feldman-Blai, Grynszpan; Frankfurter was probably not part of any such groups). While these groups did not explicitly send them to assassinate, and when such a "mission" can be inferred (e.g., Dashewski), the organization felt uncomfortable about admitting to it, they nevertheless provided the ideological background, moral support, and psychological state of mind which enabled the potential assassin to plan and execute the act. The label "crazy" was not invoked by anyone in describing any of the assassins. The last two clusters of cases—Jewish resistance under Nazi occupation and Hanokmim—exemplify and reinforce the conclusion that most assassins were deeply immersed in definable collective political groups encompassing a distinguished symbolic-moral universe.

The assassination events in Europe from around the turn of the century and which were mentioned in this chapter can be conceptualized too as acts of a persecuted minority against a prosecuting majority. In this sense, the idea of looking at these assassination events as a mechanism of justice is reinforced even further.

What were the results of the above assassination attempts? Measuring the results of "revenge" is difficult, if not impossible. However, Ehud's assassination won Israel eighty years of freedom. The Sicariis were quite effective in causing insecurity, havoc, and paranoia in Jerusalem.

The strongest motive in recent times for assassination events was revenge. However, revenge has to do primarily with a psychological state of mind, and secondarily with propaganda as a possible warning sign to others. Thus, if the assassin wanted to revenge and his/her act succeeded, one may say that the act was "successful." Were these incidences also successful in achieving a warning effect? This question is virtually impossible to answer.

Some other results, however, can be detected. Thus, the assassination incidence in Wohlin (Rovno) was obviously inspired by the assassination attempt of Schwartzbard. That act may have prevented pogroms. The Nazis clearly used Grynszpan's act in Paris as a pretext to justify, organize, and launch the horrendous Crystal Night, which was portrayed as a retaliation for Grynszpan's act (although Ford [1985:272] rightly points out that even without Grynszpan's act the Nazis would "almost certainly have found another pretext for adopting the same course of action." This shows again that to justify an act does not necessarily mean it initially "caused" the act or had consequences).

Furthermore, in the cases involving Lekert, Dashewski, Schwartzbard, Frankfurter, and Grynszpan, the assassins made no real plan(s), or attempt(s), to escape and hide. The chance to present their case in public was something they all did not want to miss. The publicity could enable them to cope openly with conflicting symbolic-moral universes, with their grievances, and to justify their particular choice of a revengeful "justice." The best illustration is embedded in the case involving Schwartzbard. There, in a very dramatic political trial, Schwartzbard was found not guilty by the French court, although he admitted the act itself.

A different strategy was chosen by Shochat, Yankoviak, Feldman, and Blai, Jewish defense organizations in Nazi occupied Europe during World War II and by the Nokmim. Publicity and exposure, in all these cases, could have won the assassins the same chance and satisfaction won and shared in the above mentioned cases, however it would have also prevented them from continuing their actions. The feeling of being involved in a continuous, grave and dangerous struggle was also characteristic of the assassins in these cases. Publicity would not have served their purpose.

The major conclusion from the cases in Europe hence indicates that a few cases of political assassinations by Jews did in fact occur there. Most of these acts were committed by actors who were part of an ideological group. In most cases, the act was meant as a revenge since the assassins felt that their opportunity to have access to a just and fair justice was effectively blocked. The acts of revenge probably achieved the micro goal of avenging. Frankfurter's assassination of Gustloff, and particularly the assassination of Askilko probably also achieved an effect in either halting, or at least slowing, a dangerous social political process for the symbolic-moral (as well as physical) universe of Jews.

Furthermore, some of the pre-state underground movements—notably Lehi and Etzel—used some of the cases during their socialization processes (e.g., Lehi used Lekert and Schwartzbard, see Tzameret 1974:89); and in a pretext to justify some of their own acts (e.g., Etzel used Lekert's case to justify the flogging of British soldiers).

Thus, important sociological and historical links between the Sicariis, acts of political assassinations in Europe before 1948, and the ideology and actions of important Jewish groups which took part in shaping—and bringing into existence—the new State of Israel, can be observed.

CHAPTER 6

Political Assassinations by Jews in Palestine between 1882–1918

CASE NUMBER 1

Gedalia Vilbuschevitz' Attempt on Eliyahu Scheid's Life
Somewhere between 1892–1899—Unsuccessful

Baron Edmond James De Rothschild (1845–1934) was of French origin, a philanthropist and patron of Jewish settlement in Palestine. In the early 1880s the new Jewish settlements in Palestine were in a serious crisis which threatened their very existence. Farmers from Rishon Lezion (a small settlement in the middle of Palestine) appealed to Baron Rothschild for help and from 1883 he began to pour financial aid to help the settlements. Between 1883–1889 Baron Rothschild invested more than five million Sterlings (British pounds) into the settlements. His support was mediated by a bureaucracy of clerks which he sent from France, and by agricultural experts. As time passed, Baron Rothschild found himself in a conflict with the emerging Zionist movement, and especially in the midst of heated debates which focused on criticisms of the settlements he supported, and the integrity and efficiency of the bureaucratic system of support which he established. In 1901 Baron Rothschild decided to eliminate the bureaucracy and to shift the managing and supervising functions of the settlements to a different organization—JCA (Jewish Colonization Association). In this way, much of Rothschild direct involvement—as well as its accompanying patronage system—ceased to exist in its original form and new patterns emerged.[1]

Eliahu Scheid was born in 1841. He was married in 1865 to Leontin Ah. Scheid was selected by Baron Rothschild in 1883 to help organize and supervise the Jewish settlements. Scheid was involved in this role between 1880–1899. He visited Palestine about twenty-two times and stayed in the country for different periods of time in different settlements. Scheid wrote for the Franco-Jewish press, and conducted several historical studies.[2] Scheid took care of all the administrative needs of the settlements, as well as conducting political negotiations with the Turkish authorities on behalf of Rothschild.

Scheid was a controversial figure. He did not find a common language with many of the settlers and was in a conflict with Theodore (Binyamin Ze'ev) Herzl (the founding father of the Zionist movement) over a few central issues concerning the new Jewish re-settlement in Palestine.[3]

From the many accusations raised against Scheid, two deserve special attention. The first was that he supported, and took part in, the corruption of Rothschild's clerks. Second, that he chose young Jewish women from the settlements and sent them to Paris to study and that under this guise he exploited them—sexually and otherwise.[4] All accusations were denied by Scheid and his family.

Gedalia Vilbuschevitz was Mania's brother (see chapter 5 on European cases of political assassinations). He was a hard working Russian engineer in Minsk who immigrated to Palestine in 1892, a few weeks after his marriage. Gedalia used his skills to help dig water wells and design irrigation systems. He observed the settlements which were supported by Baron Rothschild's funds and was impressed, bewildered, and frustrated by what he saw as the corruption and the abuse of authority and morality of the clerks. Heading this corrupt machinery, in Gedalia's view, was Scheid. In one of his letters Gedalia wrote: "Scheid chooses a few young girls to be trained as teachers in Paris. However, when they arrive to Paris he uses them as his lovers" (Shva 1969:19).

Gedalia, who absorbed the atmosphere of Russian revolutionaries (and was certainly exposed to the influence of his stormy sister), decided to do something dramatic about the corruption he saw; something that would call everyone's attention to the corrupt system. He decided to assassinate Scheid. This is a case which illustrates how a social actor from the periphery felt that he discovered that a member of the center had abused the trust and authority invested in him, and decided to act.

In one of Scheid's regular visits to Palestine (no date is available), Gedalia went to the ship with a hand gun, explicitly intending to assassinate Scheid. However, many other people were on that boat too in the reception for Scheid's arrival. Gedalia, who was anxious not to hit innocent people, decided not to execute his assassination plan (Shva 1969:19). As far as we know, he did not repeat his attempt.

While Gedalia certainly saw himself as a Zionist, and as taking part in the actualization of the Zionist ideology, it is not clear whether his attempt was an entirely individualistic attempt, or whether he discussed his plan with others who may have supported him and given him legitimation. Due to lack of more precise information, a safe solution would be to classify this case as an individualistic case of revenge and propaganda by deed.

CASE NUMBER 2

Assassination of Aref El-Arsan by David Tidhar and Yehoshua Levi Sometime between 1916–1917

David Tidhar is reputed to be the first Jewish detective in Palestine, and one of the most colorful figures in the Jewish Yishuv in Palestine until 1948 (and particularly during the 1920s and the 1930s). He was active in the service of the Turkish authorities and later served in the British police force in Palestine. His career was certainly intriguing and interesting.

In his 1938 book, Tidhar mentions (p. 31) a Bedouin by the name of Aref Effendy who served as an aid to a Turkish commander by the name of Hassan Back. Tidhar specifically states that Effendy was a short guy with twisted legs and a crooked heart. He used to throw chairs on the heads of people in coffee shops and "He was terribly stupid and evil...terrible with his cruelty to his victims whom he used to beat with his hands, legs, with his whip, and his gun until they fell on the ground and then he used to dance on their bellys and backs." Tidhar tells his readers that after one year in the service of the Turkish government, Effendy was killed by Arabs who escaped from the army service.

A somewhat different account appears in Tidhar's 1960 book (pp. 28–31). There, Tidhar uses the name Aref El-Arsan. However, the physical description, as well as the other details about the cruelty of the man, and his boss (Hassan Back) make it clear that this is probably the same person. Tidhar states that (p. 30) "one day, Meir Dizengoff[5] told me in a conversation 'how do we get rid of this man'" meaning Aref El-Arsan. Tidhar did not need more than this hint. He and his friend, Yehoshua Levi, ambushed Aref El-Arsan on his way home, about three hundred meters before Ramla (where El-Arsan lived). They shot El-Arsan and his escort, as well as their horses. Hassan Bay did not suspect Tidhar and decided that El-Arsan's murderers were probably Arab AWOLS who were previously tortured by El-Arsan.

Corroborating this account in details is not possible. However, the general description of Hassan Bay and Aref El-Arsan—and their activities—was corroborated (S.T.H., vol. 1, part 1:323–325). Attempts to survey contemporary newspapers or find people who may have known Tidhar (or Yehoshua Levi) proved unsuccessful. Tidhar's version, therefore, must be taken as it is.

There are other accounts given by Tidhar. He mentions that he poisoned the secretary of Hassan Bay; he may have planned, or wanted, to assassinate Hassan Bay himself. He mentioned (1960:50–55) that sometime between 1918–1920 a few Arabs disguised as Yemenites penetrated a few Jewish settlements (for the purpose of espionage and preparation for future attacks) and that he killed some of those impostors. It is virtually impossible today to assess correctly the validity, or accuracy, of these accounts independently.

The account about El-Arsan's assassination seems more detailed and persuasive. The 1960 version is probably more acceptable than the 1938 as Tidhar probably felt more free to tell the truth. It is possible, though, that he boasts of something he did not actually do.

Dating this story is difficult too. It must have happened between 1916, which is the closest date in Tidhar's book and 1917, when the Turks were driven out of Palestine by the British. Dizengoff's term as mayor of Tel Aviv does not contradict this dating.

Granted that the story is valid, then Tidhar clearly acted on behalf of what he felt was an implicit hint by a major contemporary political leader. He certainly saw himself as an active, devoted, and dedicated actor for the cause of Jewish defense, and he states that Levi was from the Maccabi, which was also an active Zionist organization.

CASE NUMBER 3

Assassination Attempt on the Life of Joseph Lishansky from Nily by Hashomer—October 9, 1917

Nily stands for "Netzach Israel Lo Yeshaker" which could be interpreted to mean "the Glory (Eternal) of Israel will not fail" (I Samual 15, 29). This name was chosen by a group of Jews in Palestine who formed a small intelligence unit between 1915–1917, that spied for the British against the Turks. Most members of the group were locally born. Their main concern was that the Turks may eliminate the Jews in a way similar to the one taken previously to eliminate the Armenians. They also felt that there would be no future for Jewish resettlement under Turkish rule and that a British rule would be more favorable towards such resettlement. While members of Nily originally wanted to organize a full scale revolt, this plan was abandoned and replaced later by a more ardent intelligence activity.

The group's activities lasted from 1915 to 1917, despite different difficulties, and it was connected to British intelligence headquarters in Egypt. Nily had about thirty to forty members. Its headquarters was near Atlit, at the agricultural experimental station of Dr. Aharon Aharonson, who was Nily's undisputed leader. The summer of 1917 saw the end of the group. The Turks found out about the existence of Nily and tried to find Nily's members. Major arrests were made in October of 1917.

When World War I began, members of the "Yishuv" had to choose their loyalties, either to Turkey, or to its enemies. Many Jews left Palestine and there was a campaign by the remaining Palestinian Jews to persuade other Jews to remain in Palestine and become Turkish citizens. On this background, Nily at the time was not liked. The groups' actions challenged the authority of the leaders of the Yishuv, and the existence of Nily was interpreted by many contemporary Jewish leaders as posing a great danger to the Yishuv.[6]

While Nily, therefore, was not regarded very highly by the Jewish community in Palestine during World War I and for some time afterwards, this attitude changed later. Certainly the right wing national revisionist movement saw in Nily's members national heroes.[7]

One of the most tragic figures in Nily was Joseph Lishansky. He was born in 1890 in the Ukraine. As a child he came to Palestine with his parents who died after a short time. He later married Rivka. When he grew up he worked in Hashomer (see chapter 4) but was not accepted as a full member. Consequently, he established a rival organization which he called Hamagen ("the shield." See Nadav 1954:122–129). In 1915–1916 he met some of Nily's leaders and joined the group in 1916. Lishansky escaped a major Turkish blockade and search on October 1, 1917 and made contact with some old friends from Hashomer asking for their help in hiding him from the Turks. They took him to the northern part of Palestine, near Metula.

On October 4, 1917, Hashomer's committee in Yavneal met to discuss Lishansky's fate (Livneh 1961:288–289). They faced three choices: give him to the Turks; kill him; hide him. Hashomer's members obviously had to cope with a real difficult dilemma. The Turkish occupation was very corrupt and ruthless, very far from being benign or democratic and when the Turks searched for Nily's members generally, and Lishansky in particular, they meant business. The memory of the Turkish "treatment" of the Armenians was fresh and there was a strong sense and feeling of an imminent danger. Furthermore, neither Nily nor Lishansky were exactly popular with Hashomer (Nedava 1977: 21–30; Nadav 1977:30–32). Hashomer's meeting finally decided to move Lishansky near Metula and hide him there temporarily. This decision did not exclude the possibility that Lishansky could be assassinated later. It seems as if members of Hashomer were trying to buy precious time before being actually forced to make a fatal decision.

The Turkish pressure on the Jewish community, however, was growing stronger. On October 6 or 7, some local members of Hashomer, who probably felt that they were running out of time and had to make up their minds, decided to assassinate Lishansky so that he would not give the Turks information about

Hashomer. The decision, made by Nachmani, was given to Israel Giladi who accepted the verdict. The actual order to assassinate Lishansky was given to his two guards.

On Monday, October 9, the two guards—Shabtai ("Shepsil") Ehrlich and Meir Kozlovsky—took Lishansky for a trip and Shepsil shot him twice.[8] Although the two guards thought at the time that Lishansky died—he did not. Despite his bad wounds, he managed to bandage himself, ran to the mountains and went later to a house of friends in Petach-Tikvah (e.g., see Levinson 1987). Lishansky left Petach-Tikva later and tried to work his way south to the British lines. Unfortunately, he was caught on October 20 by a few Arabs, given to the Turkish authorities and was transferred by them to Damascus, where other members of Nily were in Turkish prison too. Lishansky gave the Turks all the information about Nily they wanted, as well as giving them information about Hashomer (which caused severe problems for Hashomer).

On December 16, 1917, Lishansky and another Nily member, Belkind were hanged in Damascus. Twelve other members were given sentences which ranged between one to three years in prison and thirty members were sent to serve in the army. Sarah Aharonson committed suicide and died on October 9, 1917. Aharon Aharonson himself died when his plane crashed into the English Channel on May 15, 1919. That was the end of Nily.

The attempt on Lishansky's life by members of the Hashomer was made by actors who got the legitimation for their act from an organization on whose behalf they acted. Furthermore, it is evident from the different sources that Hashomer was not too happy with either Nily's activities or its ideology. Their attempt on Lishansky's life may be thought of as epitomizing the clash between these two very different symbolic-moral universes. One leftist, radical revolutionary, the other radical and revolutionary—but much much closer to the right.

CHAPTER 7

Political Assassinations by Jews in Palestine between 1919–1948

CASE NUMBER 4

Attempts to Assassinate Sir Ronald Storrs in the Spring of 1920 by Hashomer—Planned

On April 4, 1920, a Sunday, a crowd of a few hundred Arabs gathered near the Jaffo gate in Jerusalem, preparing for the Arab holiday of Nebi Mussa's celebrations. After hearing some agitating speeches, they started to hit Jews. The crowd entered the Old City of Jerusalem and a riot against the Jewish inhabitants began. The riot continued until Tuesday. The British authorities reacted very slowly and only toward the weekend, and the following week, were they effective in calming the riot down. Six Jews were killed, more than two hundred were wounded, women were raped, much Jewish property was destroyed, synagogues and Yeshivot were set ablaze and tombstones were desecrated. The Jews tried to protect themselves, and consequently four to six Arabs were killed and a few dozen others were wounded. No reports of damages are available in the same sources (S.T.H., vol. 1, part 2:609–615).

While the Arabs tried to present the April 1920 events as an Arab reaction to a Jewish-Zionist provocation (S.T.H., vol. 1, part 2:615), the Jewish community in Palestine attributed the responsibility for the events to the heads of the British military in Palestine. Of special significance is the fact that following the events, the British authorities started a chain of trials against key Jewish political figures, and against local Jewish defense organizations. Thus, on April 7, Ze'ev Jabotinsky—a major Jewish leader—was arrested. Despite apparent information (and British

133

assessments) that the Jews in fact reacted to Arab provocations, Jabotinsky (and Mordechai Malka) were sentenced to fifteen years in prison. Other Jews were sentenced to periods of three years in prison. These sentences were reduced later to twelve and six months respectively and even that was reduced after a general clemency in July of 1920.

One very clear demand of the Jewish community was for the resignation of those British officers they saw as responsible for the events: Sir Ronald Storrs and major general Sir Louis J. Bols.

Sir Ronald Storrs (1881–1955) came from a distinguished British family and had a very strong sense of an historical mission (e.g., see his memoirs which were published in 1937). He was appointed on December 28, 1917 as the British military governor of Jerusalem (after Colonel Borton Pasha, who was the first appointment for this job, got bored and tired with it [Makover R. 1988:46, 69]), and between 1920–1926 he served as the district commissioner of Jerusalem. Major general L. J. Bols (1867–1930) replaced, on January 1, 1920, General H. Watson as the chief of the British military administration in Palestine. Both were accused by Jewish leaders of deliberate leniency towards the Arab rioters. In some written columns in contemporary press (e.g., by Nachman Sirkin) Storrs was even called Pontius Pilatus. However, the appeals for their resignation, especially for that of Storrs, were rejected by the first British high commissioner to Palestine and transJordan, Sir Herbert Samuel[1] (McTague 1983; S.T.H., vol. 1, part 2:609–615; Makover R. 1988).

Niv (vol. 1:133) and S.T.H. (vol. 1, part 2:620, 786) report that a few members from Hashomer planned to assassinate Sir Storrs as a revenge. They followed him for a few months and planned the details. Then, they discussed the whole idea again and decided against the assassination.[2]

The details of this assassination plot are as follows. Nadav (1954:272–277), who was an important member of the Hashomer, describes how much he wanted a revenge in the form of assassinating Storrs "like you kill a poisonous snake" (p. 273). After some deliberations he decided to assassinate Storrs both as revenge and for propaganda. He guessed, however, that the Jewish Zionist leadership would object to such a deed and decided therefore to talk to a few members of the Hashomer into joining him. Before he did that, he was joined by another member, Harit, who was sent by Israel Shochat—head of the Hashomer—to "organize" (p. 276) the assassination. Both began to follow Sir Ronald Storrs, and even worked out an assassination plan. However, Israel Shochat told Harit to delay the assassination—an order which Nadav and Harit obeyed. The reasons for the delay, and eventual cancellation of the plan, are not entirely clear but they may be related to two processes. The first may have had something to do with the Hashomer's perception that the British government was going to appoint a Jew for the position of a high commissioner in Palestine. The second reason can be related to the contemporary political struggles between the Hakibbutz and the Hagana, which ended with the Hagana's victory (see chapter 4).

This case illustrates a serious assassination plot by a group, as an act of revenge, and of propaganda by deed.

CASE NUMBER 5

Assassination of Tufik-Bay by Yerachmiel Lukatcher from Hashomer on January 1, 1923—Successful

In May of 1921 Arab groups (gangs of rioters) attacked Jewish neighborhoods in, and around, Tel-Aviv, Jaffo. Of particular interest are the events of May 1, 1921, which were focused around "Beit Haoleh" (translated as "Immigrants' House") in Ajamy, Jaffo. "Beit Haoleh" hosted, on that day, about one hundred new Jewish immigrants. It was attacked by an Arab mob around noon. A few Arab policemen who arrived at the scene joined the mob, and they all broke into the house. Consequently, eleven Jews were murdered, twenty-six were wounded (two died later). Despite the arrival of British troops later that day, the riots did not subside and continued throughout the next day. Consequently, the British governor declared an emergency situation and the British army took over (S.T.H., vol. 2, part 1:77–109).

Hashomer's members were very active during the May 1921 events, especially Mania Vilbuschevitz-Shochat (see chapter 5).

However, while Hashomer was formally dissolved in 1920, some members created a small secret suborganization (based on personal ties) within the Hagana: "Hakibbutz" (see chapter 4).

The first act of Hakibbutz was to assassinate Tufik Bay. Tufik Bay was an important police officer during the Turkish occupation of Palestine. After the British drove the Turks out of Palestine during World War I, and occupied the land, Tufik Bay continued his role as a police officer in Jaffo, and was on active duty on that fateful day: May 1, 1921.

Shva (1969:302) states that Mania Vilbuschevitz-Shochat, who was an active member in Hakibbutz, investigated who headed the mob that entered Beit Haoleh and discovered that he was Tufik Bay. Tidhar (1960:99) states that Tufik Bay was the one who forced the immigrants in "Beit Haoleh" to open the gates thus making the pogrom there possible. Israel Shochat (1957:64), Mania Shochat (1957:391), and Shneurson (1957:292) all state that once they discovered that Tufik Bay headed the mob they decided to assassinate him as an act of revenge and as a warning signal. While Shneurson states that the British high commissioner to Palestine—Sir Herbert Samuel—dismissed Tufik Bay from the police force after he had found about Bay's role in the pogrom of Beit Haoleh, that was not satisfactory for members of Hakibbutz. It took Hakibbutz two years to carry out their decision.

Responsibility for the execution was given to Yerachmiel Lukatcher—a member of "The Kibbutz." He asked for the help of his friend, Binyamin Bickman, and got it.

On Friday, January 17, 1923 at 1715 Bickman escorted Lukatcher to Manschia, where Tufik Bay lived; Lukatcher waited for Tufik Bay outside his home, during a sand storm. When Tufik Bay went out of his home, Lukatcher began to follow him. As the two were walking, Lukatcher got closer and called Bay's name. When Tufik Bay turned around, Lukatcher used his revolver to shoot Bay in the head and kill him.[3]

This assassination was carried out by two active members of an underground secret organization—The Kibbutz. They acted on behalf of the organization which decided on the act and gave the assassins the legitimation for the act. This assassination was viewed both as a revenge and as a warning.

CASE NUMBER 6

*The Assassination of Dr. Ya'acov Israel De Hahn by the Hagana
on June 30, 1924*

Israel De Hahn was born in the small Dutch town of Smilda to
an orthodox Jewish family on the thirty-first of December, 1881.
His father was active in the life of the local Jewish community,
but was not doing very well economically and turned into a very
bitter person. Israel's sister, Carey, was born before him, on January 21, 1881. Carey and Israel were apparently gifted and very
talented children. As both grew up they turned their backs to the
Jewish orthodox atmosphere in which they grew.

Having finished school, and at the age of nineteen, Israel De
Hahn decided to move to Amsterdam and to become completely
secular. There he studied law and at the age of twenty-one
received his Ph.D. in law. In Amsterdam he also joined the socialist party. De Hahn's political and academic career in Amsterdam
was very strong and stable. There were also indications for his
developing (or actualizing) a homosexual identity. Despite the
above, De Hahn was involved with, and got into, a problematic
and stormy marital relationship with a Christian physician
named Johanna Van Marsphain. De Hahn traveled to Russia a
few times. The experience and knowledge which he gained from
these travels about Russia and Jewish life there, apparently persuaded him to return to orthodox Judaism and later he even
decided to immigrate to Palestine.

In February of 1919, De Hahn left his family in Amsterdam
and began his long journey to Palestine. He arrived to Palestine
later, and moved to live in Jerusalem. While De Hahn obviously
moved to Palestine out of a Zionist ideology, he very quickly
became disillusioned with the local Zionist political and social
leadership. He drifted very slowly into the circles of the most
extreme anti-Zionist Jewish orthodox groups in Jerusalem. Later
he began to write to newspapers in Holland very critical essays
on the Zionist work in Palestine, as well as getting involved in
local anti-Zionist activities. This line of De Hahn's activities crystallized in 1920 and during 1921 he attacked not only the Zionist elite, but the new immigrants as well. For example, after the

1920s riots in Jerusalem (see case no. 4) De Hahn supported Sir Ronald Storrs when most of the Jewish community demanded his resignation. There were other anti-Zionist activities in which De Hahn was involved and which were regarded by contemporary and important Zionist figures as either treason, or close to it. These activities did not make De Hahn a very popular figure within the Yishuv (mostly to the non ultra Orthodox community, but to some members of the ultra Orthodox community too).

This process came to a peak when in 1922 some of these debates received public attention outside Palestine. Local newspapers (secular and religious) even published pieces calling to revenge De Hahn for his activity. De Hahn began to receive threats and in May of 1923 he got a direct death threat demanding that he should leave the country. All this did not stop De Hahn and he continued his activities, as well as continuing to publish extremely critical essays abroad. As Nakdimon and Mayzlish (1985:139) states: "De Hahn was hated. In fact, they loved hating him." De Hahn continued to receive written threats and warnings urging him to stop his activities.

On Monday, June 30, 1924, De Hahn went to pray in the evening in the synagogue which was located within the old structure of the "Sha'arei Zedek" hospital in Jaffo Street in Jerusalem. De Hahn left the synagogue at 1945 approximately. As he left the synagogue, and was walking down the street, he was shot three times and died a few minutes later in the operating room of the hospital at the age of forty-three.

While there were rumors that the background for De Hahn's assassination was his alleged homosexuality, it became quite evident that the real background was political. He simply stepped on too many people's toes, so to speak, and was particularly perceived as a real threat and danger for the crystallizing Zionist movement.

Who assassinated De Hahn? Three versions exist as possible answers for this question. One version attributes the assassination to Mania Shochat (who was even arrested after the assassination—e.g., see Halevi 1987:178). This version is discredited by most researchers. The more or less consensual interpretation is that the Hagana gave the order to assassinate De Hahn and that Avraham Tehomy, from that organization, with some aids did it (e.g., see Halevi 1983; Z. Meshi-Zahav and Y. Meshi-Zahav

1985; Nakdimon and Mayzlish 1985). This version received a very dramatic expose' when on Monday, February 19, 1985 the Israeli television devoted a whole program to the assassination of De Hahn. There, Tehomy (who lived then in Hong Kong) was interviewed. He almost admitted the assassination, and attributed responsibility to the leaders in the highest echelon of the Hagana (probably Rachel Yanait Ben-Zvi, or her husband Itzhak Ben-Zvi, who became many years later the president of Israel). Another version, no less credible, is that of Arzi (1982), who attributes the assassination to a small underground revolutionary cell within the Hagana (called "Hamiphal").[4]

The argument about who exactly gave the order to assassinate De Hahn, and who in fact carried it out, continues to interest contemporary Israeli society, regardless of the fact that more than sixty-three years elapsed since the assassination. The main reason is that a few modern and influential journalists (especially S. Nakdimon) keep raising the De Hahn affair in the written and electronic media. While these questions are interesting, indeed intriguing and important, they are not *as* important for this study. It is quite obvious that De Hahn was assassinated because he was perceived, and defined, as presenting a real danger, and as posing an immediate threat to (a) group(s) of dedicated, active, and revolutionary Zionists who occupied important positions in the leadership of the contemporary and organized Jewish community in Palestine. S.T.H. (vol. 1, part 3:251–253) explicitly accepts the responsibility, and admits openly, that the assassination of De Hahn was carried out by orders from the high command of the Hagana, because De Hahn was "a traitor." Most of the modern literature about the assassination of De Hahn tries to figure out how this decision was made, and who exactly it was that actually assassinated De Hahn. However, despite the relative wealth of information about this case, it is still not known with certainty how exactly was the decision to assassinate made and exactly by whom (see also Rubinstein 1985).

Thus, the assassin(s) came from a particular ideological group, definable by a particular symbolic-moral universe, on whose behalf he/she/they acted and which provided the legitimation for the act. It was this group which gave the assassin(s) shelter and support.

The assassination obviously stopped De Hahn's activities. It also gave some groups among the ultra orthodox Jews ("Haredim") a reason and a cause to rally together and close ranks on behalf of the victim. Hence between 1985–1987 (sixty-one years after the assassination) the Israeli public witnessed, again, the bitter arguments about De Hahn's assassination and again, each side to the argument used the case to project the moral boundaries of its own symbolic-moral universe (for theoretically similar contemporary cases see Cromer 1985 and 1986).

CASE NUMBER 7

The Assassination of Dr. Haim Arlosoroff on June 16, 1933

This particular case is probably the most complex, emotionally loaded one in the modern history of the state of Israel. It is virtually impossible to determine in any definite and indisputable way, that it even was, or was not, a political assassination. It was, however, an important event. While I chose to enter the case into the study because of its being so problematic, it will not be used in later statistical, or analytical discussions.

The Zionist movement in the 1930s was sharply divided between two polar groups. One large, socialist in orientation, group with such leaders as Ben-Gurion, Ben Zvi, Arlosoroff. The other group, much smaller was the "revisionist," emphasizing a right-winged, national orientation and headed by Ze'ev Jabotinsky. In the 1930s the debate between the two groups about social, political and economic issues was very strong and bitter. The tones were high, and many accusations were frequently made. Dr. Arlosoroff, considered as a brilliant young leader and intellectual, was a formidable opponent to Jabotinsky's group.

Within the "revisionist movement" Abba Ahimair, together with the poet Uri Zvi Greenberg and Yehoshua Yavin, established in October of 1931 a militant group with fascist tendencies (probably closer to the early Italian fascism) which called itself "Brit Habirionim."[5] Their historical model was the Sicarii movement mentioned earlier and, to a much lesser extent, the contemporary fascist European movements—especially in Italy. Brit Habirionim started its operation already in 1930 (with a public demonstration on October 9) and was formally established probably sometime in October of 1931. While small, this particular group presented a more or less coherent ideological symbolic-moral universe, and some of its publications could be interpreted as giving legitimacy to political assassination—much like the Sicariis. Some most poisonous propaganda which was manufactured by this group was aimed at Arlosoroff personally.[6] The murder of Arlosoroff in 1933 also marked the disintegration of Brit Habirionim. Many of the members joined years later the Etzel and Lehi.

Dr. Haim Arlosoroff was born on February 23, 1899 in Romny, Ukraine. He was considered a brilliant student and received his Ph.D. from the University of Berlin. He joined the Zionist movement while he was still a student and in 1924 moved to Palestine. Due to his natural talents, he very quickly moved to become one of the main political figures in the left oriented labor movement.

In June of 1933, Arlosoroff returned to Palestine from a long trip to Europe, which focused on political and social issues (particularly on a possible transfer of the property of German Jews to Palestine). On Friday, the sixteenth of June, Arlosoroff and his second wife, Sima, returned separately to Tel Aviv. They went together to eat dinner at the Ketty Dan restaurant and at 2130 approximately left the place for a long stroll along the Mediterranean beach. As they were walking, they were followed, part of the way at least, by two unidentified men. Later, on their return trip, they were approached by the two men. One of them lifted a flashlight and asked for the time. The other one took out a hand gun and shot Arlosoroff. That happened at around 2215–2230. Arlosoroff was rushed to a nearby hospital but died later due to loss of blood.

The Labor movement, and Ben-Gurion, used this murder/ assassination against Jabotinsky's group in general and particularly against Brit Habirionim, and vice versa. While the police accused three members of Brit Habirionim (Abraham Stavsky, Abba Ahimair, and Tzvi Rosenblatt) of the act, Ahimair and Rosenblatt were found not guilty, and Stavsky was cleared in a higher court (he died later on the ship *Altalena*). Later there were suspicions that Arlosoroff was assassinated by two Arabs (e.g., see Ornstein 1973:111–115).

It is still not known who exactly killed Arlosoroff, but it seems that some groups may have had a good motive to do it. The Arlosoroff case tortured the Yishuv in Palestine in the 1930s, and its echoes continue to haunt this society in the 1980s and 1990s.

On March 14, 1982 the government of Israel, headed at that time by Prime Minister Menachem Begin, decided to create a national and official inquiry committee to investigate the murder/assassination of Arlosoroff, almost forty-nine years [!] after the incident. The committee worked hard, finished and signed its final and detailed report, consisting of 202 typed pages, on June 4, 1985. Those who expected some new revelations were totally disappointed. The committee could not determine who were the killers, or whether Arlosoroff's murder/assassination was political or not.[7]

The last punch in this riddle was delivered in May 30, 1991. During an evening talk show in the main channel of the Israeli Television Shmuel Dothan told the listeners that in a book he published he identified the killers. According to this version, the Soviet communist party planned the assassination and send the killers too. The reason, according to Dothan, was that the communists were concerned about a joint plan among the French, British Japanese and the Zionist movement to "eliminate" the Soviet Union. Arlosoroff was thought by the communists to be the organizer of the military part of the plot in Palestine, and he was consequently assassinated (e.g., see *Yediot Aharonot*, May 31, 1991, front page. See Dothan 1991:184–195). It is virtually impossible to verify or negate this new theory. The intelligent reader must draw his/her own conclusions whether this theory makes sense or not.

While the question regarding the nature of the murder/assassination has never been satisfactorily resolved, it certainly had some very manifest political ramifications. First, it did get Arlosoroff out of the political arena, in one of the most critical periods of the crystallization of the new Jewish State in Palestine. Second, it no doubt helped the political campaign of the Labor movement to win seats in the Jewish Congress, especially against the right-wing movement which focused its efforts around Jabotinsky, as well as putting the latter in a very awkward and apologetic stand. Third, it helped to divide Jews along a bitter and explosive debate, which heightened animosities and hostilities, regarding the question of who killed Arlosoroff and why.

Since the riddle of Arlosoroff's death has not yet been solved, We shall stop here.

CASE NUMBER 8

An Assassination Plan on Jordan's King Abdallah—
Probably in 1933—Planned

In October of 1918 the British conquered Syria and Lebanon. However, the Sykes-Picot secret treaty[8] stipulated that these areas would be under French rule and influence. This treaty did not prevent the British from encouraging Faisal to create an Arab government in Syria and from becoming the King of Syria on March 11, 1920. The French, however, insisted on having Lebanon and Syria, and the San Remo meeting upheld the French claims (April 25, 1920). Faisal did not accept the French demands and the French attacked his forces, defeated them and on July 25, 1920, conquered Damascus causing Faisal to escape.

In November of 1920, Abdallah Ibn Hussein (1882-1951), second son of the Sheriff Hussein appeared in the middle East, with a force of more than a one thousand Bedouins, having in mind a revenge for the deportation of his brother Faisal from Syria. Abdallah Ibn Hussein wanted to attack the French in Syria and in March of 1921 he arrived in Amman, Jordan. The British saw in Abdallah's leadership a promising aspiring and moderate political force and begun to negotiate with him. At a meeting in Jerusalem in March of 1921, Winston Churchill, then British Colonial Secretary, offered Abdallah the administration of Transjordan. In 1921 he became the Amir of Transjordan. Eventually Abdallah was crowned in 1946 King of Jordan, a post he held until 1951. In 1933 Abdallah was a central figure in the British political plans for Palestine-Jordan. In January of 1933 he even signed an agreement about land-leasing with the Jewish Agency (the agreement was canceled later under pressure from Arab Nationalists, and Haj Amin Al Husseini in particular—see cases no. 11 and no. 56). Abdallah was a target for a political assassination plan in 1933.

Raia Berman (Regev) was born in 1909 in Lita. She moved to

Palestine, and under the influence of Abba Ahimair joined Brit Habirionim (see previous case). After the assassination of Arloso- roff in 1933, Brit Habirionim basically disintegrated. Berman states in her memoirs (Ahimair and Shatzki 1978:99-100) that "after the disintegration of the 'Brit,' we—a group of members— got together in Tel Aviv to discuss different ideas for action. One of the plans was to assassinate Abdallah. The British wanted, at the time, to make him king for all of Eretz Israel, and we thought that we ought to kill him before he becomes such a king, other- wise he would have a heir. According to the plan, I had to assassi- nate Abdallah in Nes Ziona, when he visited a local Sheikh. I traveled to Nes Ziona to visit two guys who worked there as guards. I checked the possibilities. I was supposed to dress like an Arab woman, to enter the house of the Sheikh and hit Abdallah. The plan was not executed after we fought amongst ourselves, particularly because we were young." This is one of the very rare and few instances where we have a potential female assassin.

Dating this plan is difficult, but 1933 seems reasonable because Brit Habirionim was dissolved that year (see case no. 7).

We have here a group of people, united by an ideology, plan- ning an assassination which they felt was necessary because of their commitment to their ideology—which stated that a right- wing, national and exclusive Jewish state should be created in Palestine. What they saw as the British plan to make Abdallah king clearly contradicted their ideology—hence, an assassination plan followed.

The historical irony is that on July 20, 1951 King Abdallah was actually assassinated by an Arab in Al Aksa mosque in Jerusalem. The assassination was probably planned and executed by Arabs close to Haj Amin Al-Husseini (see case nos. 11 and 55).

CASE NUMBER 9

The Assassination of Zvi (Ben-Amram) Frenkel in Tel Aviv by Etzel on September 6, 1937

In the year 1937, Etzel was still a young organization headed by its first commander, Robert Bitker (Naor 1990:96) who appar- ently was not a very successful leader.[9]

Zvi Frenkel (Ben-Amram) was an active member in Etzel. He owned a hand gun which he kept in his home. Sometime probably in August or September of 1937, Zvi Frenkel used his gun to kill an Arab, as an act of retaliation, near the Arab village of Sumeil, in the northern part of Tel Aviv (in the area where the University of Tel Aviv is located today). The British police, who investigated the case, reached Frenkel's home. While he managed to escape, his gun was found and his mother was arrested. Zvi Frenkel asked Etzel to help him hide. Initially Etzel agreed. However, hiding Frenkel became problematic. The British police spread rumors that Frenkel's mother was tortured so as to force her son to give himself in. Consequently, Frenkel wanted to see his mother, and later decided to give himself to the British police.

On September 8, 1937, a few people who took a boat ride on the Yarkon river in Tel Aviv discovered Frenkel's body. Frenkel's legs were tied with a metal wire and the body was apparently in the water for three days (which means that he was probably drowned on Monday, the 6th),

Frenkel's "friends" in the Etzel felt obviously threatened, and were afraid, that he might reveal their identity to the British police and disclose details about the organization. They decided, therefore, to assassinate him—apparently by drowning—in the Yarkon river.[10] The public account given at the time by Etzel was that Ben-Amram "went abroad."

B. Eliav, an important member in the revisionist movement, stated in his written memories (1990) that Bitker was a "ridiculous" and dangerous person (1990:107). However, Eliav also states that the decision to drawn Frenkel was not only Bitker's, and a few unidentified others were involved in making this decision (1990:108). Clearly, Eliav regarded this affair as a "crime" and he characterized Bitker's mentality as that of a criminal (1990:109).

This assassination was decided and executed by an ideological group for what one may call inner organizational reasons and needs. The organization was involved in this case in a preemptive strike against Ben-Amram, fearing he might turn into a squealer and betray his friends. This case is similar to Hashomer's attempt on Lishansky's life (see case no. 3), or to Lehi's assassination of Levi (see case no. 75).

The assassination of Frenkel was perceived by contemporary

Etzel's political leadership as a second, most tragic, mistake committed under Bitker's command (the first was a Bank robbery which had failed). Bitker was asked to leave his command and was replaced in October of 1937 by Moshe Rosenberg (see Naor 1990:101). Rosenberg (1968:3) himself stated that: "The Frenkel affair, to this day, has remained veiled, and I prefer not to comment about it..."

CASE NUMBER 10 AND CASE NUMBER 11

Preplanning the Assassination of Jardine and the Arab Mufti—1939

The Arab attacks on Jewish settlements, particularly in the Haifa area, became intolerable in 1939. The high command of the Hagana decided to create special units—called Pum ("Peulot Miuchadot"—special action)—to cope with this particular problem, using specialized aggressive activities in terms of assaults and retaliations for Arab terrorism. These units were created secretly probably sometime in March of 1939. The units consisted of specially selected volunteers, special arms and equipment (S.T.H., vol. 2, part 2:830–832). The Hagana's high command had to authorize each and every action of Pum before it took place. Although no real good detailed account of the activities of the Pum exists, it is evident that these units operated quite efficiently and that the Hagana's high command was concerned about the nature of these activities and their meaning, especially regarding terrorism and personal individual terror. Thus, Mardor (1970:26–30) describes acts that were aimed at specific targets (e.g., house of the chief of a specified Arab village—Sasa—which hosted an Arab gang) and acts of revenge and retaliation (see also Mardor 1988).

Furthermore, Mardor (1970:75) states that some Pum members in fact wanted to use the strategy of political assassination against a few British officers whom they saw as particularly cruel. However, their suggestions were not authorized and their pressure did not persuade the Hagana's high command. Apparently there was also some pressure to use the Pum to deal with Jewish "traitors," "squealers," and the like. In September or

November of 1939, only seven to nine months after its establishment, the Pum was dissolved.[11]

In 1939, the British police created a special Brigade (commanded by Mosgrave) to cope with what the British saw as the illegal Jewish immigration into Palestine. They recruited a few "Jewish squealers and traitors" (S.T.H., vol. 2, part 2:1045). "Some of the Jewish traitors were shot or beaten by the Etzel and by the Hagana's Pum" (S.T.H., vol. 2, part 3:1253). Unfortunately no report exists about who exactly "was shot" where or when, or how the shooting was authorized.

Pum was apparently involved in preparing assassination plots against squealers, and against the governor of Lod and of the southern parts of Palestine (Bauer 1966:53).

The fact that the Pum was so tightly controlled by the Hagana's high command meant, among other things, that: "The Hagana's courts were very careful with verdicts, and with the exception of squealers the Hagana did not execute people" (Bauer 1966:54).

Bauer (1966:54) mentions that (probably in 1939) Berl Katzenelson, one of the main figures in the Labor movement and the Hagana, demanded that both Robert Frier Jardine (born in 1894)—the British director of settlements and registration of Titles to Land in Palestine between 1936–1948 (Jones 1979:67)—who acquired a reputation for his hostility to Jews, and the Arab Mufti—a poisonous and formidable anti-Zionist and anti-Jewish opponent (see also case nos. 11 and 55)—be assassinated. David Ben-Gurion (who became the first Israeli prime minister in 1948) opposed and vetoed the decision. Because of his intervention both preplanned assassination plots did not pass this stage. Pum may have planned more assassinations but no more information is available on Pum.

CASE NUMBER 12

The Assassination Attempt on Moshe Rotstein in 1939 by Etzel—Unsuccessful

After the April 1937 split in Etzel, a special intelligence department was created in Etzel, the Meshi (department of information service). A first priority goal for the Meshi was to infiltrate British intelligence. Heading the Meshi was Arie Posek, and in charge of Haifa was Israel Pritzker (see case no. 39) (Niv, vol. 2:260–265).

Even before the 1937 split, Etzel established contacts with Moshe Rotstein and Joseph Davidesku who worked as Jewish agents in the Service of the British intelligence, and continuously provided Etzel with information. Etzel, likewise, fed through these two agents information to the British intelligence (Niv, vol. 2:263). Before the 1937 split Nachum Lewin was the contact person for these two, and after the split—Israel Pritzker, in Haifa. Davidesku, (see case no. 50), an ex-Nily member (see case no. 3), who worked for the British intelligence (in the department on Arab and communists affairs) was the operator of Moshe Rotstein (who was an Etzel member) (Yevin 1986:201, 212 nl).

While Avraham Tehomy (a very important contemporary figure for both Hagana and Etzel) wrote to Yevin (1986:205) that: "I expelled M. Rotstein from the organization after it was disclosed that he had embezzled the organization's money..."(probably in 1936), I (ED.) doubt that such events actually happened. One has to be very careful with statements coming from Tehomy (mostly because of his political and ideological jumps, as well as his indecisiveness and his evasive and elusive personality) and in any event, Rotstein obviously continued to work as a double agent.

The Meshi expanded its activities during 1940, and particularly active was Pritzker. He, with Davidesku and Rotstein, adhered closely to Jabotinski's and Raziel's conception and policy of close cooperation with the British. Some of this cooperation was, as we shall see, problematic. Thus, Michael Waksman, who was in contact with the British on instructions from Pritzker, was assassinated (Niv, vol. 3:41; see case no. 25). It may be possible that the cooperation with the British in 1940 was perceived by many as too far-fetched (Niv, vol. 3:40).

It was clearly the case that Pritzker used Rotstein, on at least two occasions, to create provocations. One within the Hagana. There, he tried to make the Hagana's headquarters suspect a member of collaboration, supposedly to reignite the inner feuds. The Hagana arrested Rotstein on October 7, 1941 and he was interrogated "long and hard" (as a result, A. Tehomy and M. Kaplan were charged and put on trial. Tehomy later left the Hagana. See S.T.H., vol. 3, part 1:244–245). The second provocation followed the division between "Etzel" and "Etzel in Israel" (later Lehi) in the summer of 1940. Rotstein tried "to sell" to Abraham Stern, "an agreement" of cooperation between Stern's group and fascist Italy (what became known as "the Jerusalem Agreement"—Yevin 1981:201–205, 311–314 and Eliav 1983:188–189). The essence of this "agreement" was that Mussolini would help and support the creation of a Jewish state in Palestine. In return, this future state would support Italy, and even provide a naval base in Haifa for Italy's navy. There is good reason to suspect that this agreement was fabricated by Pritzker or Rotstein so as to present Stern's group in a bad light—as if conspiring with the Italians against the British.[12]

While it is possible to guess that Rotstein acted alone, it is more than reasonable to assume that he acted on Pritzker's and Davidesku's instructions. The Etzel in 1940 was no friend to either the Hagana or the newly created Lehi.

Furthermore, when most commanders of Etzel were arrested and detained by the British in Mazra Camp in northern Palestine,[13] Rotstein "leaked" to them, while in Mazra, information that Etzel's headquarters were penetrated by a provocateur, or a traitor. He may have leaked this information on British instructions (so as to confuse and instigate Etzel's leadership), or in an attempt to divert attention from his own activities, or because he suspected (or knew) that there *was* a provocateur in Etzel's headquarters. The suspicion fell on Binyamin Zerony (see cases no. 18 and no. 28) (Yevin 1986:246, 251; Eliav 1983:190; Illin 1985:91).

Eliav (1983:187–191), a member of Lehi, states that when the magnitude and nature of Rotstein's activities came to the attention of Abraham Stern, Eliav himself and a few others (probably sometime in 1939, see Eliav 1983:189) conducted a "serious discussion" and their verdict was "a death sentence." The responsibility for the execution was given to Eliav. He went to Haifa and carefully planned the execution. "Although Rotstein was married and a father to children, he was very careful.... He used to change his place of sleep, hardly, if ever, came home and was frequently out of Haifa. Once, we almost had him when he was at home, but his family members were in the house and fearing that one may hit [innocent] others and not Rotstein caused us to cancel the action. Then, he disappeared and I delayed the execution to some other time. The execution was never carried out" (Eliav 1983:189–190).

It may be the case that Rotstein's role was more complex. In the winter of 1941 he asked for a meeting with Abraham Stern. Although Stern was warned not to come to the meeting, he apparently wanted to know the truth behind the Jerusalem agreement. Escorted by friends, Stern met with Rotstein. Although we do not know the content of their discussion, we do know that Rotstein warned Stern ("Yair") that the British were going to make his (and his friends) pictures public and offer sizable monetary rewards to anyone giving information leading to their arrest. The pictures were actually made public in January of 1942 (Yair was killed by Morton on February 12, 1942). Why would Rotstein give such valuable information and warning to Yair? Either his role and loyalties were more complex than what they may appear, or, he wanted to clear himself from any future guilt or accusations when it would be found out that the Jerusalem Agreement was nothing but a provocation (Yevin 1986:243).

It is well worth noting that Davidesku and Pritzker were assassinated by Lehi in August 21, 1945 and September 3, 1943 respectively (cases no. 50 and no. 39).

CASE NUMBER 13

An Assassination Plot by Itzhak Shimkin on Adolf Hitler's life on March 15, 1939—Unsuccessful

Itzhak Shimkin, a member of the Hagana in Haifa, was extremely concerned about the fate of Jews in Europe after the Nazis entered Austria in March of 1938. In an article Shimkin published he expressed those concerns. Very gradually he came to the realization that Hitler (1889–1945) had to be assassinated. Shimkin approached the Hagana's commander in Haifa— Ya'acov Dori—and asked for help and support. Shimkin was then sent to a higher commander—Shaul Avigur. He later even talked to Moshe Shartok (then head of the political department of the Jewish Agency). Shartok was skeptical. He was concerned that something worse than Hitler could emerge and that the assassination could endanger German Jews. Shimkin felt that he could not get any further support. He took two hand grenades from the Hagana's armory and traveled to Prague where he stayed for two weeks.

On Wednesday, March 15, 1939 the Nazis entered Czechoslovakia. At 1400 the Fuhrer's convoy passed in the streets. Shimkin prepared himself to throw the grenades. Unfortunately for Shimkin, the convoy which passed by consisted of five closed Mercedeses and Shimkin could not tell in which car Hitler was. Shimkin realized that he failed and quickly got rid of the grenades enroute back to Palestine (Eshel 1978:176–178).

While Shimkin did not act as a representative of an organization, he was obviously a member of the Hagana, and took the hand grenades from the Hagana's armory. His moral conviction that Hitler had to be assassinated as early as 1938 indicates a very alert and acute political mind, keen on collective problems facing Jews and coupled with a strong determination and commitment to follow his idea with action—despite lack of organizational approval, authorization or help.

According to Eshel (1978:178), the Israeli ministry of defense awarded Shimkin a citation for his attempt. The ministry of defense refused to confirm or deny this.

This is, perhaps, the only case where something close to "Tyrannicide" was the motivation for a political assassination event. However, in 1939 Hitler was not, yet, a full "tyrant." Furthermore, Shimkin was planning the assassination not so much because of what Hitler *had* done up to 1939, but out of his fear of what Hitler *might* do in the future. The motivation in this case was propelled by a desire to prevent what Shimkin saw as a dangerous trend, and as a revenge. One must be reminded that in 1939 Hitler had a large popular support by many non-Jews who certainly did not see the Nazi beast for what it really was.

CASE NUMBER 14

The Assassination of Joseph Brawerman on May 3, 1939 by Etzel in Tel Aviv

When the British police forces occupied Palestine, their local police force employed Jewish, as well as Arab, policemen and detectives. Both Etzel and Lehi assassinated some of those Jewish policemen, for different "reasons." The first victim may, in fact, have been Joseph Brawerman.

In the spring of 1931, Abraham Tehomy and some of his men left the Hagana to create "Irgun Beit" (the actual precedent to Etzel) in Jerusalem. Tehomy also contacted a group of around eighty Hagana members in Tel Aviv, headed by Abraham Halperin. Consequently, a national center consisting of Tehomy, Uri Nadav from Jerusalem, Y. Warshawski and Joseph Brawerman from Tel Aviv was established (S.T.H., vol. 2:575).

Joseph Brawerman, a former Jewish Beitar's (Jabotinsky's group) member, joined the British Haifa Police as a corporal. In 1936 he was stationed in the Jaffo police in the department for investigation of severe crimes. Among other duties, he had to find out how the illegal immigration of Jews to Palestine took place and to collect and give information on Etzel in Tel Aviv and its neighborhoods. Etzel decided to assassinate him because of his alleged cooperation with the British police against Jews. On Wednesday, May 3, 1939, after midnight in Tel Aviv, Joseph Brawerman was shot. He was fatally wounded and died later in a hospital (Niv, vol. 2:251).

CASE NUMBER 15

The Assassination of Arieh Polonski on May 29, 1939 by Etzel in Jerusalem

Arieh Polonski came to Palestine in 1929 from Kovrin, Poland. In 1939 he was married, twenty-nine years old, and served as a Jewish policeman (at the rank of a police corporal) in the British mandate police since 1931. He joined the British police on the instructions of the Jewish Agency and served as a "go between man" between the Jewish Agency and the British intelligence.[14]

Etzel sentenced Polonski to death because they claimed that he had "squealed" on their members to the British police (Niv, vol. 2:251; Jabotinsky's archives file number 1/21 4כ). Polonski was shot and hit by four bullets near "Beit Hama'alot" in Jerusalem (which is located at the intersection of Hama'alot and King George streets), on the evening of Monday, May 29, 1939

(S.T.H., vol. 3, part 1:60). Polonski was fatally wounded and died in hospital the next day, May 30. In that incident, an innocent Jewish bystander—Asher Nemdar (a twenty-two-year-old Jewish immigrant from Iran)—was also accidentally hit and later died.[15]

After the assassination, and on June 17, 1939, Arieh's father—Ephraim—published a long open letter to Etzel demanding an explanation for his son's death (Jabotinsky's archives, file number 7/19 4ב). Etzel replied (ibid) that Arieh was a squealer on their members and advised the father to direct his complaint to the Jewish Agency who sent his son to do "their dirty work." Etzel advised "other fathers to prevent their sons from doing errands for the Jewish Agency in the area of squealing on members of Etzel" (ibid.).

On the background of this assassination, and on July 7, 1939, the political department of the Jewish Agency published a pamphlet called "Do not Murder," signed by some of the most important contemporary Jewish political figures, calling Jews not to kill other Jews (Niv, vol. 2:250; S.T.H., vol. 3, part 1:60). Furthermore, Golomb—from the Hagana—met with Jabotinski in London on July 9, 1939 and warned him that such acts would lead to an inner war between the different underground pre-state Jewish groups.[16]

CASE NUMBER 16

The Assassination of Valentin Back on June 22, 1939 in Haifa by Etzel

In the context of the last days of the Arab revolt of 1936, Niv (vol. 3:258) reports of one Valentin Back, a Jew from Russia who spoke a few languages fluently. According to Niv, Back was recruited by the British intelligence to give them information for a large fee. Niv states that Back became friendly with members of Beitar but was not successful in discovering much about their underground activities. Niv accuses him though, of being very effective in squealing to the British about Ya'acov Kutik.

On August 20, 1938, at about 1900, Kutik, an old member of Beitar, came to the office of Etzel in Tel Aviv to take a suitcase with weapons and ammunition. As he took the suitcase, a small group of British detectives in plain clothes, with Valentin Back, appeared and arrested Kutik. On September 29, Kutik was charged in the British military court in Jerusalem with illegal possession and transportation of weapons and ammunition. He was sentenced to death by hanging. Due to pressures of Jewish leaders in Palestine and abroad, his sentence was replaced by life in prison. He was in prison for five years and was released on February 20, 1943 (Niv, vol. 3:258).

After the Kutik case Back moved, for obvious reasons, to Haifa. This did not help. Members of Etzel in Haifa found where he lived. On Thursday, the 22 of June 1939 he was shot to death in Haifa by Etzel's members.[17]

CASE NUMBER 17

An Assassination Attempt on the Life of Gordon in Jerusalem on August 18, 1939 by Etzel—Unsuccessful

The British police force in Jerusalem had a dedicated and devoted Jewish officer—Gordon, who for a while, was in charge of the police station in the Generally Building in Jaffo Road, downtown Jerusalem (Katz 1966:73).

"Yashka"—Eliav—then an important member of Etzel—(1983:132–133) states that prior to the assassination of Ralph Cairns (see next case) he decided to assassinate Gordon: (a) to "warm the barrel" in his language, (b) because Gordon had a lot of information on Etzel's people, was associated with squealers, took part in arrests and torture (e.g., was involved in Zerony's brutal investigation; see Eliav 1983:125 and case nos. 18 and 28). Eliav suspected that following a possible failure in the execution of the plan to assassinate Cairns, Gordon would cause trouble. Because Gordon was married to an English woman, Eliav felt that he fully identified with the British cause.

After checking his home in Kerem Avraham in Jerusalem, Eliav decided to carry out the assassination plot on a Friday night, close to Gordon's home. A group of four Etzel's members waited for Gordon on the evening of August 18, 1939. David Ilan was to be the actual assassin. When Gordon was about five meters from him, Ilan stepped in front of him, aimed his automatic revolver at Gordon and pulled the trigger twice. Nothing happened because the revolver malfunctioned. Gordon, who "was frozen, lifted his hands, his body shook and his eyes were popping" (ibid. p. 133) realized that the gun was malfunctioning and started to run away. Eliav and his group retreated. According to Eliav, two weeks later, Gordon and his family left Palestine and thus "in fact, we achieved what we wanted and he (Gordon— ED.) was removed from the arena of activity" (ibid. p. 133).

CASE NUMBER 18

The Assassination of Inspector Ralph Cairns on August 26, 1939 with a Mine in Jerusalem by Etzel

Binyamin Zerony, a member of Etzel, (see also case no. 28) was caught by the British in Jerusalem on August 5, 1939 after he broke into a shop which stored explosives. Zerony was brought to the British prison in Jerusalem and was tortured there in the most cruel and violent way for five nights and days. The officer who was personally in charge of torturing Zerony was Inspector Ralph Cairns. Inspector Cairns was appointed the director of the Jewish department in the British intelligence in 1939. Prior to that appointment, Cairns had been working for British intelligence for a period of about ten years.[18]

Cairns was apparently carrying out his role with a particularly zealous fervor. Zerony was not the first, or only, person to be severely tortured by him (Niv, vol. 2:272). Zerony, however, was able to use the services of a double agent and smuggled the news of his being tortured outside. He also managed to escape from prison on August 8, 1939. The report about his tortures became shocking news to the leaders of Etzel.

The British intelligence had been warned against the continued use of such methods (Niv, vol. 2:275). Since the warning did not work, Etzel's leadership decided to assassinate Cairns.[19]

Inspector Morton who served in the Palestine British intelligence, and knew Cairns, indeed states in his memoirs (1957:60–61) that Cairns was an important officer and that the warnings got to him, "They warned him that he was in danger."

Eliav, who was very active in demanding the assassination of

Cairns, was given the job (Eliav 1983:132). A few members of Etzel followed Cairns and discovered that he lived in "Gan Rehavia" in Jerusalem. They also discovered that he used to walk on a certain path to Gan Rehavia; that he was always armed and wore armored plates. Consequently, Eliav decided to use a powerful land mine. Eliav and his men constructed a mine consisting of fifteen kilograms blasting gelatin, six detonators with accelerators plus five kilograms of metal pieces. All of this deadly explosive contraption was wired with a twenty meter electric wire to an operator, and buried in the ground underneath the path which Cairns used to take in Gan Rehavia. The device was installed on Friday night (2300), the 25th of August, 1939. Next day, Saturday the 26th, Etzel's members were waiting for Inspector Cairns. At around 1430 Ralph Cairns, with a friend— Inspector Ronald Barker (head of the Arab department in the British intelligence)—walked the deadly path. The mine was exploded by Etzel member Chaim, and Cairns and Barker were blown to pieces (Niv part 2:275–276; Eliav 1983:133–138).

A few days later Etzel published a pamphlet (e.g., see Weinshall 1978:133–134) stating that Cairns was executed because he tortured prisoners and that "any British detective who would dare to torture a Jewish prisoner would be executed."

Torturing members of the pre-state Jewish underground groups seemed to constitute a very clear moral boundary marker (as well as a clear danger to the group that the tortured member would reveal vital information). Thus, S.T.H. (vol. 3, part 1:274–275) states that in 1945 a member of the Hagana—Eliezer Goldberg—was caught by the British army and tortured severely and cruelly for four days. After he was released, "and the details of how Goldberg's interrogation was carried out, the national headquarters (of the Hagana—ED.) authorized 'retaliatory acts' against his 'investigators' but, as it turned out, the (British—ED.) army transferred them immediately after their 'work' to India" (see also Levi 1959). British officer William R. Bruce was in fact executed in 1946 (by Hagana-Palmach) for having tortured members of the Hagana (see case no. 58).

Interesting to note that following the assassination of Cairns, the British felt quite threatened and decided to act against Etzel. Naor (1990:220) indeed reports that a few days after the assassination the British located and were able to arrest the members of Etzel's high command (31 August 1939), in the middle of an important meeting they held (Naor 1990:224–224).

CASE NUMBER 19

Assassination of Baruch Weinshall in October of 1939 in Haifa by Hagana-Pum

Case nos. 10 and 11 imply that the Hagana created the special units, Pum, among other things to combat those they defined as squealers and traitors (see case nos. 10 and 11 for a description of Pum). Not all squealers and traitors, however, were treated in the same manner. Some were beaten, some were threatened, and some were assassinated.

A small unit from Pum went on October 12, 1939, in Haifa, to either beat (S.T.H., vol. 3, part 1:76) or assassinate (Eshel 1978:267) a Jewish British undercover agent named Baruch Weinshall. According to Eshel (1978:267) the reason for the act was that Weinshall helped the British intelligence in its efforts against what the British defined as the illegal Jewish immigration to Palestine. The Pum's planned act, however, was not successful. Baruch Weinshall had a gun and used it to kill one of the Pum members who came to attack him: Uri (or Joseph) Urkivitz (see *Ha'aretz*, October 30, 1940:4). The Pum was now more determined and anxious to assassinate Weinshall. One attempt did not work out when Weinshall managed to hide and escape from two Pum agents (Avinoam Slutzky and Alexander Kun). A few days later, however, Weinshall was shot and killed.[20]

In a 1990 report,[21] Geva hints that a similar episode took place with a person he calls Carmi. According to Geva, there was a person by the name of Baruch Carmi in Haifa who worked for the British intelligence. Carmi was a bachelor, twenty-six years old, a policeman in the transportation unit of the British Haifa police. In the late 1930s Baruch took a trip to Poland to visit his family. After his return he was transferred to the British intelligence. There were "stories" that he was seen in Warsaw in or around the office for Aliya (Jewish immigration to Palestine). The Hagana suspected that Carmi was squealing and giving the

British information on the illegal Jewish immigration to Palestine. There is a good question whether there was any proof for that.

However, the Hagana decided to warn Carmi and sent a few members to beat him. One of those beaters was Uri Urkievitch. The Hagana's unit managed to get Carmi into an isolated place and Uri began hitting him. Carmi got his gun out, shot and killed Uri. Arieh Glickman, who witnessed the incident, told Geva that Uri hit Carmi in the head with a steel pipe causing a severe hemorrhaging. Carmi was scared and shot Uri.

Azriel Rudman, who worked in the British intelligence but was actually a double agent for the Hagana, remembers that Carmi asked for the Hagana's mercy because he was going to get married to a woman named Yonah. Rudman forwarded the information to Levi Avrahami who was the commander of the Pum in Haifa.

However, it was evident that killing Urkievitch marked the end for Carmi.

The regular members of the special "elimination unit" were (according to Geva), Haim Laskov, Uri Urkievitch, Hillel Oldag, Dov Goldman, Arieh Katz, Alik Friedman, Ephraim Buchman, Avinoam Slutzky, and Alex Kun. According to Geva, Kun said that Avrahami sent Slutzky, and Kun to kill Carmi. Geva mentions that Slutzky also says that Avrahami told him to kill Carmi. According to Kun there were three attempts on Carmi's life. Two failed but finally Hillel Oldag and Dov Goldman killed him.

According to Geva, Carmi was shot and killed on the 25th of June 1940, in Hashalom Street in Haifa, very shortly after he was married to twenty-one-year-old Yonah.

Geva located the son of Yonah's sister. Yonah herself died a few years ago after she was remarried. The son told Geva that after the failed attempts against his life, Carmi talked to Yonah's father and denied vehemently that he had anything to do with squealing to the British or giving them information on the illegal Jewish immigration to Palestine. Carmi also planned to bring his parents to Palestine which may explain why he was seen in the immigration offices in Warsaw.

Clearly, Geva hints that it may have been the case that Carmi was killed in vain and that there was no evidence against him.

The story and details are such that it is almost evident that Baruch Carmi and Baruch Weinshall are the same person. Unfortunately, our attempts to corroborate this version failed. No mention of the killing of one Carmi (or Weinshall) are mentioned in the contemporary press. In an interview, Levi Avrahami refused to answer questions on this topic.

Weinshall or Carmi, what we have here is an act of assassinating a specific target, on an order from an organization in the obvious context of revenge and warning.

CASE NUMBER 20

The Assassination of Oscar Opler in January of 1940 by the Hagana

In his memoirs, inspector G. J. Morton (1957:119–121), one of the most important British intelligence officers in Palestine, tells about a careless young Jewish informer which he used, and paid to, who lived in "Mishmar Shalosh" in the Galilee. He called this informer "Jacque."

On Saturday, January 6, 1940, a group of British policemen arrived at Mishmar Hashlosha in the Galilee for a search. Under the public house, which also served as a station for the guards, the British policemen found some fifteen rifles, hand grenades and other weapons and ammunition (S.T.H., vol. 3, part 1:126; Morton 1957:119). Corporal Haim Leitner (Jewish) who was in charge of the station was arrested, accused, found guilty in court and sentenced to eight years in prison. S.T.H. (ibid) states that all the signs pointed to a squealing. After a long investigation, the Hagana discovered that the squealer was a Jew named Oscar Opler. Following a "trial" [?], he was sentenced to death (S.T.H., vol. 3, part 1:141 and part 3:1630). Morton (1957:120–121) states that Opler (Jacque) was shot in Tel Aviv "with six bullet holes in him, and the usual notice pinned to his chest—"Tried by a Jewish Military Court, found guilty of treason, sentenced to death and duly executed." Morton has no doubts as to who did this—the Hagana.

The Hagana's archivists denied having any information about the case. S.T.H. provides no date for the execution. However, Morton (1957:120) and S.T.H. (vol. 3, part 1:127) reports on another informed and successful British search in Ben-Shemen on January 22, 1940. That search yielded again many illegal weapons and ammunition. According to Morton, his source in this case was again Jacque, so one must assume that Opler was not caught, or executed before the end of January, maybe February 1940. Judging by S.T.H., the Hagana may have not been aware of the fact that Opler was also the one who gave Morton the information about the secret illegal armory in Ben-Shemen.

CASES NUMBERS 21, 22, 23, 24, AND 35

The Assassination of Moshe Savtani, Itzhak Sharanski, Baruch Manfeld, Walter Strauss, and Moshe Ya'acov Marcus on Different Dates by the Hagana

S.T.H. (vol. 3, part 1:141) details, in seventeen lines, the story of "Uprooting the squealers." This short paragraph can not possibly be considered satisfactory. However, all of our efforts to find more information were totally unsuccessful, hence, all I can do is give the information available.

In the above mentioned paragraph, S.T.H. states that in 1940 it became evident that the British authorities were using what S.T.H. refers to as careless and innocent talkative Jews, but that they were also recruiting, for a fee, Jewish squealers. The Jewish radio station, "The Voice of Israel," warned Jewish detectives and agents that they should stop their activities, or pay with their life. The counter espionage service of the Hagana (the SHAI) tried to find them. According to S.T.H., once the Shai had enough incriminating information and/or evidence, the suspects were brought before a special legal committee. S.T.H. (ibid.) states that death sentences were given, and executed in five cases. The executions were carried out by small groups of Hagana's commanders, or by specially selected members, and the personal composition of the groups changed.

The Hagana provides an interesting account as to what it felt was the nature of the symbolic-moral boundaries whose violation it considered punishable by death. Death sentences, according to the above source, were limited either to detectives who worked in the service of the British and whose guilt was proven, or to squealers who gave the place of the Hagana's secret armories to the British. S.T.H. (ibid.) is careful to state that the suspects who were interrogated, and executed, penetrated the Hagana in the regular and mass recruitment process, which enabled them to escape careful scrutiny. According to S.T.H. these suspects were typically marginal "elements," lacking proper political consciousness.

The appendix given by S.T.H. (vol. 3, part 3:1630) gives the following names and dates for those who were sentenced to death and executed:

20. Oscar Opler (see previous case).

21. Moshe Savtani, executed on Friday, May 3, 1940, in Haifa.

22. Yitzhak Sharanski, executed on Sunday, May 12, 1940, in Tel Aviv.

23. Baruch Manfeld, executed on Tuesday, June 25, 1940, in Haifa.

Searching contemporary newspapers, neither confirmed the cases above nor yielded additional information.

24. Walter Strauss, twenty-five-year-old immigrant from Italy, was shot to death in Mea Shearim Street in Tel Aviv, on Wednesday, July 3, 1940. He was suspected to be the one who gave the British the information which led to their search for the Hagana's secret armories in Gan Yavne on March 3, 1940 (see also S.T.H., vol. 3, part 1:127 and *Ha'aretz*, July 5, 1940:8 and July 7, 1940:4)

35. Moshe Ya'acov Marcus, a twenty-two-year-old soldier in the British army, was found dead from three gun shots in a sack near the village of Ata on Tuesday, August 25, 1942. The medical examiner dated the death to the previous Friday, August 21, 1942 (*Ha'aretz*, August 30, 1942:4). Eshel (1978:268–271) describes a case where the Pum in Haifa executed a Jewish soldier. Eshel identifies the soldiers as Y.K. The nature of the description is such, that it seems safe to assume that Y.K. was, in fact, Ya'acov Marcus.

Although not specifically mentioned, judging from the Opler's case (see case no. 20) and that of Kurfirst (case no. 52), it seems safe to assume that all victims were shot with guns.

Also, one cannot escape noting the somewhat strange fact that out of the six victims, five were located, identified, interrogated and executed within a relatively short period of six to seven months (January–July 1940). Hardly any cases before, or after that. One is left pondering whether this reflected a real increase in the numbers of squealers in the first part of 1940, or reflected an activity of a particular agent/group during that period.

We tried to look for more possible cases in other sources, usually with very little success. One may safely assume that the Hagana's intelligence department—the Shai—was either involved, or at least knew, about cases of assassination (e.g., see case nos. 53 and 82). Unfortunately, the Shai's archives either disappeared physically or exist somewhere with absolutely no accessibility to them.

Dekel (1953) provides one of the few, rare and highly selective, exposes of the Shai. There, one can find mention of two cases. Both cases appear with no names, no dates and lacking other identifying information. They could be included in the cases we know, and they could be additional cases. In one case Dekel (1953:272–273) mentions a traitor who was charged in a Hagana's "court" with treason, found guilty and the verdict was that the man had to leave Palestine. According to Dekel, that man was so ashamed of his treason that instead of leaving he committed suicide by shooting himself to death with a hand gun. A second case (ibid., 274–275) involved another male traitor who gave information to the British as well as giving them the secret location of an Hagana's armory. According to Dekel, the man was put in front of what he called a "military court," found guilty and sentenced to death. This unknown and anonymous traitor was executed later at an unknown date, probably by shooting. No publicity was given to any of these cases.

Apparently, S.T.H., which details the official "history" of the Hagana, and the Hagana's archives, are extremely cautious and reluctant to provide information. There is an explicit attempt to minimize publicity about these cases. Although more than forty-seven [!] years have elapsed since these assissinations took place, one is still faced with high barriers when trying to find out what exactly happened, why and how. This state of affairs obviously requires at least a good speculation as to why the secrecy. One reason which is usually given is that "some of the people involved are still alive." That however, cannot be taken too seriously. Both Lehi and Etzel give plenty of details about their executions without giving any names. The real reason, I suspect, has to do with guilt and insecurity about the validity and reliability of the decision to execute. I shall expand on this later, after detailing the cases of Wagner (no. 54) and Tubianski (no. 81).

CASE NUMBER 25

The Assassination of Michael Waksman on May 16, 1941 in Tel Aviv by Etzel

Israel Pritzker headed, from Haifa, Etzel's intelligence department (Meshi). One of the men working for him was another Etzel's member—Michael Waksman. Waksman was nineteen years old, and under Pritzker's orders he took part in surveillance of communists and others (Niv, vol. 3:41). Under the same orders he was also in direct contact with the British intelligence, probably as part of his loyalty and commitment to the original strategy delineated by Jabotinsky (who died in August of 1940) and Raziel (then Etzel's commander) and which was expressed in a general policy of cooperation with the British.

It seems that, perhaps, along the way, Waksman got mixed up about his loyalties and obligations. He began to follow Etzel's members and give information to the British intelligence. S.T.H. states that in April of 1941, the British police found an Etzel secret armory in Bat Yam (near Tel Aviv) and the Etzel attributed this British "knowledge" of the armory to information Waksman provided them (vol. 3, part 1:483). There were other allegations that Waksman was a homosexual and corrupt (e.g., see Koren 1986:11). Waksman was warned a few times—to no avail (ibid.).

Finally, on Friday May 16 1941, Waksman—who was then nineteen years old was shot three times in his back at 0830 on the corner of King George and Betzalel streets in Tel Aviv.[22]

One thing which makes this case particularly interesting is the fact that a suspect in the assassination was caught and brought to trial on June 16, 1941—David Rosenzweig. Etzel threatened the witnesses and Rosenzweig was acquitted (S.T.H., vol. 3, part 1:483). He was, however, sent to the detention camp in Mazra and later deported to Africa. Rosenzweig himself denied that he assassinated Waksman. He repeated his strange denial to a reporter who interviewed him in 1986 (Koren 1986).

It is obvious that Waksman was assassinated by orders given by Etzel, and that the assassin was probably Rosenzweig (Koren 1986:11).

As an interesting episode, it is well worth noting that the two British Jewish officers who investigated the case—Schiff and Goldman, were assassinated by Lehi on January 20, 1942, and on September 3, 1943. Israel Pritzker was assassinated too by Lehi (see case nos. 27, 30, and 39).

CASE NUMBER 26

The Assassination of Ya'acov Soffioff on November 16, 1941 in Rehovot by Lehi

Soffioff was a Jewish officer detective working for the British police. He was accused by Lehi of giving its members to the British and was "sentenced" to death.

On the evening of Sunday, November 16, 1941, as Soffioff was coming out of a theater in Rehovot (south of Tel Aviv), having seen a movie, he was shot to death. In a public announcement Lehi stated that his death "was to be a warning to all detectives—professional and amateurs alike " (S.T.H., vol. 3, part 1:503; *Ha'aretz*, November 18, 1941:1, and November 21, 1941:6).

In his autobiography Morton (1957:142–143) states that he knew that Zelik Zak, from Lehi "was the man who had murdered Constable Soffioff" (p. 142). Morton himself shot Zelik Zak (and Abraham Amper) to death on January 27, 1942, when he and Inspector Day broke into a Lehi hiding place in Tel Aviv.

It is quite possible that Morton wanted to justify killing Zak by attributing Soffioff's assassination to him. However, if Morton is telling the truth, then one may arrive at an interesting conclusion. Abraham Amper and Zelik Zak were in charge of guarding Abraham Stern Yair, Lehi's first legendary leader (who was also killed by Morton on February 12, 1942) and "their devotion to him was limitless" (Yevin 1986:271). Zak would probably have not assassinated Soffioff without getting authorization which, judging by the closeness of the two, in this case, may have come directly from Yair, or his group of commanders.

CASE NUMBER 27

The Assassination Attempt on the Life of Major Shlomo Schiff in 1941 by Etzel—Unsuccessful

Shlomo Schiff, a Jewish officer with the British police, was born in 1895 in Kishinev Beserabia and at the age of thirteen immigrated, with his family, to Palestine. He joined Trumpeldor's Battalion during World War I and later joined the British army and took part in conquering Palestine from the Turks. He rose in the army's ranks and reached the rank of a sergeant major. After the war he was employed in public works and later joined the Palestine punitive police. In 1922 he joined the British police. There, he was cited for his good service and was promoted. He served as an Inspector in the Tel Aviv police and became an officer (major). During the 1936 Arab revolt/riots in Palestine, he took part in some of the most dangerous activities in riot control (*Ha'aretz*, January 21, 1942:1)

Livni, who was a very important member of Etzel, and in charge of operations, tells in his memoirs about an attempt to assassinate Schiff. According to Livni (1987:27–28), sometime during 1941, Etzel's headquarters decided to assassinate Schiff because "he was the senior Jewish officer in the (British) mandate police and helped the hard (and cruel) persecutions against Lehi's members" (p. 27). Livni added (interview, March 11, 1988) that Schiff was also personally interested in, and enthusiastic about, persecuting members of Lehi. He added that an effect of deterrence was sought by the assassination. According to Livni, Schiff was for a while under surveillance and he and Moshe Zomberg planned to throw four kilograms of explosives from a roof of a building on Schiff's car. Livni states that they waited for three nights (interview, ibid.), but every time Schiff showed up he was accompanied by his wife—and they did not want to assassinate her. They finally decided to give up the plan.

Schiff was, in fact, assassinated by Lehi on January 20, 1942 (see case no. 30).

CASE NUMBER 28

An Assassination Plot against Binyamin Zerony on January 18, 1942 by Lehi—Planning

Binyamin Zerony was a member of Etzel, who during the upheaval of 1940 (when Etzel and Lehi separated), joined Lehi. While still a member of Etzel he was arrested by the British in Jerusalem on August 5, 1939 (see case no. 18). Zerony managed to escape from prison on August 11, 1940, and was hidden with the help of Abraham Stern, Ephraim Illin, and his sister, Batia Goren (see case no. 44).

There were some suspicions that Zerony did not "just" escape and that the British let him go in return for his cooperation. The source of these suspicions was probably Rotstein (e.g., see Illin 1985:91; see also case no. 12). However, the suspicions were not crystallized at that time. Niv (vol. 2:261) clearly negates this interpretation. According to Niv, the British were very suspicious of Zerony's 1939 escape too, and suspected that Jo Refaeli—an Etzel double agent—who worked in the British intelligence helped Zerony to escape. Refaeli was in fact arrested by the British, released after three months and left Palestine.

During the upheaval in Etzel in 1940 Zerony took a consistent aggressive position against David Raziel, campaigned against him, and even quarreled with him. Zerony obviously leaned towards Stern's group. Pritzker (see case no. 40), from the Etzel's intelligence, even started to collect information against Zerony (Yevin 1986:179–180). In 1940 many Etzel's members were in the British detention camp in Mazra. They received there information from Moshe Rotstein (see case no. 12) that a provocateur has penetrated their headquarters (Yevin 1986:246; Eliav 1983:189) and that the provocateur was Binyamin Zerony, whose escape in August of 1939 from the British prison was planned by the British. According to Eliav (1983:189) Yair rejected this information, and they "sentenced Rotstein to death." This account, however, appears to be too simplistic.

In the autumn of 1941 Lehi's commanders got together for a meeting which lasted for a few days. That meeting proved particularly stormy. Stern was blatantly accused by Zerony of incompetence and he even suggested that Itzhak Zelnik (the "engineer" see also case no. 34) should replace Yair. The end of that super long meeting was that Binyamin Zerony and H. Kalay stated that they were both leaving Lehi,[23] not without threats against Zerony (and Kalay—"Noach"—who left with him) (Weinshall 1978:202).

Although Zerony was no longer a member of Lehi after that fateful meeting, the suspicions against him did not subside, and even intensified (e.g., Yevin 1986:251, 256, 266). Even Stern himself began to suspect Zerony, and a Lehi member ("Falach") was sent to his home to square out the differences—to no avail (Weinshall 1978:208). The suspicions against Zerony are mounting, growing, and solidifying, if only in member's minds.

Eventually, a meeting of Lehi's commanding group was called on January 18, 1942, and, having discussed Zerony, they decided that Zerony should be assassinated (Weinshall 1978:209; Yevin 1986:266) for his "treason." While it appears that Zelnik volunteered to shoot Zerony (Weinshall 1978:209; Yevin 1986:267), Zelnik himself denied (a) that there was a death sentence against Zerony, and (b) that he volunteered to do it (Yevin 1986:266–267). Weinshall states that despite the death sentence, the execution itself was delayed indefinitely and was conditioned upon Zerony's future behavior (1978:209). Zerony himself stated that he had heard about the verdict from Zelnik (Zelnik denies this) who told him that there was no one available to do the execution and that since then he (Zerony) always carried a gun "so everyone knew it was not going to be easy to hit me" (Yevin 1986:266). Zerony was later arrested by the British. The execution was never carried out.

CASE NUMBER 29

The Assassination Plot against Oliver Lyttelton on January 18, 1942 by Lehi—Planning

On January 18, 1942, Lehi's high command, which at that time consisted of Itzhak Zelnik, Ya'acov Eliav and Moshe Savorai— led by Abraham Stern, had their last meeting managed by Stern (who was killed on February 12, 1942). A few decisions were made then (e.g., to assassinate Zerony—see case no. 28). One decision was "to assassinate the Secretary of State Oliver Lyttelton who was in Cairo. Yair said then that he had a contact with a few of our soldiers who were recruited then to the British army in Egypt, and that we shall be able to get their help in assassinating Lyttelton" (Yevin 1986:266).

In an interview in his home in Haifa (October 22, 1987) Yitzhak Zelnik remembered their 1942 decision to assassinate Oliver Lyttelton. Zelnik stated that Lyttelton was the British minister in charge of the Middle East affairs and "if not against (assassination—ED.) the British Prime Minister or the Minister of Settlements than against who?" Lyttelton eventually was not assassinated. According to Zelnik the reason was that Lyttelton was Australian and not British. Australians were viewed favorably by the Jewish Yishuv which was very sympathetic to the Australian soldier. The Australian soldier behaved "very nice and we did not want all of the Yishuv against us." Thus, the decision to assassinate the (British) representative in charge of the Middle East was executed much later when Baron Moyne was in Cairo" (see case no. 49). Zelnik stated that Lehi used tactics of "personal terrorism" and that Lyttelton was "the most salient target."

Yellin-Mor (1974:211–212), one of Lehi's three contemporary leaders, states that already in the spring of 1941, after the British government created the new position of resident Minister of State in the Middle East (in Cairo), Stern thought about assassinating the minister resident. According to Yellin-Mor, Churchill's first appointment for the job was Richard Casey. Since Casey was Australian, Stern decided that assassinating an Australian "would not serve the cause and would not create the necessary impression upon the World" (1974:212).

We tried to confirm the above information and so we looked for an Australian resident minister in Cairo in 1941–1942 by the name of Lyttelton. We simply could not locate such a person within this time frame in Cairo. However, conversations with Yevin (18 November 1987), Moshe Savorai (18 November 1987), and Zelnik (22 November 1987) all yielded that Lehi in 1942 aimed at Lyttelton.

Untangling this problem was not easy. However, the facts are the following. In 1941 Churchill decided to create the special position of a resident Minister of State for the Middle East, to be stationed in Cairo. Churchill's first nomination for the job was Oliver Lyttelton. Lyttelton was British. He was elected to the British Parliament in 1940 and was the Minister of Commerce until 1941. He was appointed Resident Minister of State for the Middle East on June 28, 1941 (Gilbert 1983:1125, 1295) and was replaced in May of 1942 by Baron Richard Gardiner Casey (1890–1976) who was, in fact, an Australian diplomat and Cabinet Minister, appointed by Churchill for this job already in March. Casey filled this position from March 1942 till January 1944. His deputy was Baron Walter Moyne, who in January of 1944, became the minister resident himself. Baron Moyne was assassinated by two Lehi's members on November 6, 1944.[24]

Reconstructing the events now may give us the following picture. It is possible that when Churchill created in 1941 the new position of the resident minister in Cairo, Stern may have thought to assassinate the minister as an act of propaganda by deed. The actual decision to assassinate the incumbent came in January of 1942, during Lehi's (then, Etzel in Israel) commanders' last meeting with Stern. The incumbent was Lyttelton. Stern himself was persecuted then by the British and was killed by Morton in February. As his men were trying to regroup, Lyttelton was replaced by Casey, the Australian, in March. Zelnik, who was Lehi's commander after Stern's death, probably realized that assassinating Casey was not going to get them anywhere, for the reason he gave in his October 22, 1987 interview, and the assassination was postponed until Moyne was in office.

CASE 30

The Assassination Attempt on Major Shlomo Schiff (Died) and Nachum Goldman (Died), Ze'ev Dichter (Wounded), and Turton (Died) on January 20, 1942 in Tel Aviv by Lehi

In a meeting of Lehi's commanders, probably in 1940, they decided to assassinate Morton (see case no. 33) and Wilkin (see case no. 45), who were perceived as Lehi's worst enemies. Planning of these assassinations was given to Eliav.[25]

Eliav's idea was to create a trap at 8 Yael street in Tel Aviv. He planned to begin with a small explosion so as to call the attention of the British police. It was hoped that its chief inspectors, hopefully Morton and Wilkin, would show up. There was a room on the roof of the building, and a powerful bomb was put inside that room. That bomb was supposed to be detonated and blow everyone around to pieces. Detonation was to be made by a remote control wiring, by a Lehi agent (Baruch) who was supposed to activate it upon sight of the British officers. A third bomb was hidden in the entrance to the house and was meant for more British officers that were expected to come after the death of Wilkin and Morton. That bomb was also meant to be exploded by a remote control device, by a different Lehi member (probably Yehoshua Cohen).

It so happened that the first officers to come after the first small explosion (around 0900) were Schiff, Goldman, Dichter (all Jewish), and Turton. Lehi's operator did not identify the officers correctly and detonated the bomb. Schiff died immediately; Goldman died the next day at 5:30 A.M.; Dichter was miraculously only slightly wounded. Turton, for whom January 20, 1942 was the first day on his new job in Tel Aviv, was badly wounded. His legs were amputated and he died a week later.

When Morton and Wilkin arrived to the scene, Yehoshua, the one who was supposed to detonate the second mine decided—against Eliav's explicit instructions (1983:200, 203)—not to detonate the bomb fearing that many innocent bystanders would die together with Morton and Wilkin.

Schiff was a very well liked officer, and Goldman also won respect as a serious and dedicated policeman. The Yishuv was shocked and angered by this act and Lehi was severely criticized. The anger, however, at this act of Lehi was so bad that it helped the Jewish community in Palestine, and the British Police, legitimize and cooperate in a coordinated effort to eliminate Lehi.[26]

So far, this case may seem to verge on the boundary between political assassination (target specific) and terror. It leans, however, toward assassination for two reasons. First is Livni's (1987:27–28) account of the unsuccessful attempts to assassinate Schiff already in 1941 (see case no. 27). Second is Stern's reaction once he found out what happened at 8 Yael Street.

It is evident that Stern (Yair) was quite shaken when the news about what happened on Yael Street reached him (e.g., see Yevin

1986:267–268). After all, his group meant to assassinate Morton and Wilkin and not Schiff, Goldman, Dichter, and Turton. Furthermore, the reaction of the Yishuv to the action caused him, and rightly so, to be alarmed. Yair knew that already in December of 1941 Schiff told all the Jewish guards in the Hasharon area to find and bring Stern to him "alive or dead" (Yevin 1986:268).

Yair decided to publish, and distribute, a pamphlet explaining why Lehi hit Schiff and Goldman. The pamphlet was signed as Etzel in Israel which was then the name of Lehi (e.g., see Yevin 1986:268–269; Eliav 1983:203). There, Yair wrote that "officers Schiff and Goldman were sentenced to death by the supreme court of the organization. This verdict was confirmed by the leader and commander of the Etzel in Israel and carried out on...20/1/42 at 0920...in Tel Aviv. This...verdict should serve as a warning to the police, its officers, policemen and agents that they should not touch the messengers of the organization when these messengers carry out their national duty. Etzel in Israel's supreme court decided upon this harsh sentence paying attention to the fact that our friends Yehoshua Becker and Nissim Reuven, who were arrested while performing their duty, were tortured by the police and officers Schiff and Goldman are directly responsible for their torture. The Etzel in Israel warns again the police from the revenging hand of the organization" (Yevin 1986:268–269). One must note, however, that no record exists which confirms that Etzel in Israel's so-called "supreme court" actually decided on the assassination, or that such a court existed at all.

Eliav (1983:203) quotes another pamphlet where the organization explained the action on Yael Street. There, it is declared that the British mandate government is the enemy of Zionism and should be fought. It states that Jews who work with the British police are traitors. Thus, Schiff, Goldman, and Turton were declared as traitors and as helping in the worst form of the British suppression. This pamphlet ends with a similar warning as the first one.

This assassination plot obviously raised against Lehi many members of the Yishuv. Aharonson (1988) implies that it helped the persecution of Lehi members into being, and gave birth to the fuller persecutions after the assassination of Moyne (no. 49)—the so-called Season (see also case no. 49).

CASE NUMBER 31

The Assassination Attempt against Michael Joseph McConnell on Wednesday, April 22, 1942 by Lehi—Unsuccessful

Abraham Stern Yair, Lehi's commander, was killed by Inspector Morton (see case no. 33) on February 12, 1942. Lehi members who survived certainly looked for revenge. One target they chose was Michael Joseph McConnel, chief of police, who lived in Jerusalem.[27]

In the night of April 21, 1942, a powerful mine was attached to McConnel's car. Moshe Bar Giora, who planted the mine underneath the car rigged it to the car's back wheel. The plan was that when the car would start to roll, the mine would roll too, an electric circuit would be closed and detonation would follow (Eliav 1983:227–228). Unfortunately, the next morning at 0815, McConnell's Arab driver got into the car, which was in the house's parking garage, and started to roll it out. The mine exploded as planned, killing the Arab driver for whom the mine was not meant (Eliav 1983:227–228; *Ha'aretz* April 24, 1942:1; Yellin-Mor 1974:86).[28] McConnell was not hurt physically, but was apparently quite shocked psychologically.

According to Niv (vol. 3:192) and Eliav (1983:227–228), the attempt on McConnell's life was in retaliation and revenge for Stern's killing. Eliav, however, adds that McConnell was "chosen" as a target because he was an Irishman who escaped from Ireland after the Irish Republican Army sentenced him to death. "In this way we would have achieved two goals; paying the British intelligence for its murders and paying the debt to the Irish Republican Army" (Eliav 1983:227).

CASE NUMBER 32

An Assassination Attempt on the Life of Alan Saunders, April 22, 1942 by Lehi

Colonel Alan Saunders (1886–1964) was the District commander of the Jerusalem Palestine Police between 1920–1926 and Deputy Inspector General between 1926–1935. Between 1937–1943 he served as the Inspector General of Police and Prisons in Palestine (Jones 1979).

Already in 1939, David Raziel—then chief commander of Etzel—crystallized an agreement of cooperation with Saunders between Etzel and the British police (Yevin 1986:171). That agreement resulted from Jabotinski's and Raziel's understanding that because of World War II, and the British war effort against the Nazis, the Etzel should join and help the British (see also Naor 1990:230–233).

During the war years, attempts were made by different Jewish groups to bring Jews from Europe to Palestine because their presence in Europe—simply put—meant death for them. The British authorities objected to this effort and called this "illegal immigration." In November of 1940, the Gestapo allowed a convoy of three ships with Jews to come to Palestine. One of these ships, the "Atlantic" came in on November 24, 1940, after a very hard and dangerous trip with about seventeen hundred Jewish refugees aboard. The British arrested all immigrants and on December 9, 1940, deported them in the most cruel manner to Mauritius (S.T.H.,vol. 3, part 1:151–152 and Mardor 1957:53–57). Supervising the cruel and violent deportation was Alan Saunders. Mardor (1957:75), who was active in the Hagana/Pum states that as a Hagana member, he and his friends demanded already in 1940 "to punish" the British officers responsible for the horrendous deportation but their suggestion was not accepted.

On Wednesday, April 22, 1942, in the morning, Lehi attempted to assassinate Saunders by planting a big bomb on the road near his home. The bomb was discovered before it exploded and was dismantled (Niv, part 3:192). This assassination attempt was already done in order to revenge Abraham Stern's assassination in February 12, 1942, much like the attempt to assassinate McConnell (see case no. 31), and as a revenge for Saunder's behavior.

CASE NUMBER 33

Assassination Attempts on Jeffrey Morton's Life on Different Dates in January through May of 1942 by Lehi—Unsuccessful

All available sources indicate that Jeffrey Morton was one of the

most important British policeman in Palestine. He was particularly active, and successful, in hunting down Stern's group and in
killing Zelik Zak, Abraham Amper (see case no. 26) and Abraham Stern himself on February 12, 1942, as well as torturing
Jewish prisoners (see e.g., Shomron 1980:21). His importance,
zeal, and activities made him an obvious target for political
assassination, especially by Lehi, Stern's group.

Morton lived in a British camp in Sharona. He used to carry
a gun and wear armored plates. Assassinating him meant using a
bomb or a mine. One plan of assassination preceded Stern's murder and took place at 8 Yael Street on January 20, 1942 (see case
no. 30). After Stern's death, Lehi decided to retaliate and assassinate Morton, Stern's killer (Yellin-Mor 1974:85).

The second assassination attempt took place on February 24,
1942 (Bowyer-Bell 1987:93), when Morton and a few soldiers
were patrolling a road near Arab Jenin. A land mine exploded
under the armored car, destroying the car (Morton 1957:90–91)
but no one was seriously injured. Alas, as this attempt is not
recorded in the literature published by Etzel or Lehi, and judging
by the place where the incident happened, I tend not to attribute
this attempt to Lehi.

The third attempt occurred on Friday, May 1, 1942. In the
morning Morton got into his car, with his wife, to drive to his
office. On the way, Lehi's members detonated a powerful mine
underneath the car. The car was wrecked, but no one was hurt.[30]
Ziv Shimon, a former member of Lehi, states that they wanted to
revenge Stern's assassination and that (1973:13–14) "I took part
in this.... The mine was put in the ground...(together with
Hisia)...and detonated, again with no luck. When Morton's car
got close, it had to by-pass a bicycle...consequently, Morton's car
remained in the middle of the road. When the mine was detonated, the car was hit...but nothing happened to the passengers..."

Weinshall (1978:271) implies that prior to this third attempt,
there was a similar attempt near Petach Tikva. There, the bomb
did not explode. No other mention of this attempt can be found.

All in all Lehi tried three to four times, unsuccessfully, to
assassinate Morton. In August, the British high command—fearing for Morton's life—informed him "that it had been decided
that I had been working too hard and that for the sake of my

health my wife and I were to be sent home on leave by air immediately" (Morton 1957:157).

CASE NUMBER 34

The Assassination Plot against Itzhak Zelnik in February through May 1942 by Lehi—Preplanned

After Abraham Stern Yair, was killed by Inspector Jeffrey Morton in Tel Aviv on February 12, 1942, Itzhak Zelnik ("engineer") one of Stern's closest friends assumed command. At that time Stern's group was persecuted and its members were in constant danger. In May 1942, Zelnik could not take the pressure any more, and with the aid of a lawyer, gave himself in to the British authorities.[31]

Nathan Yellin-Mor (1974:86–87) states that a long line of failures in Lehi's activities (e.g., failure to assassinate Saunders, Morton, McConnell, see case nos. 31, 32, and 33) made some contemporary Lehi's members think that Lehi was penetrated by a provocateur. Some thought that the fact that Zelnik was always "lucky" and was never hurt indicated that he was the provocateur.

Tuvia Chen-Zion told Tzameret (1974:114) that he and his friends, members of Lehi, actually planned to assassinate Zelnik. This is also the place to note that Tuvia Chen-Zion, and his group (probably around one hundred members), were on the verge of splitting from Lehi due to profound ideological differences. This group was posed against a much smaller group of thirty to forty members, headed by Zelnik, Zvi Frunin and Yehoshua Cohen. According to Tzameret (1974:12–13), it was Chen-Zion's group which first called itself Lehi. In a testimony to Tzameret (dated February 2, 1973) Chen-Zion told the latter that he was threatened with a death sentence if he and his group were to split from Lehi. None of the threats was ever actualized (ibid., p. 13).

In an interview (October 22, 1987, Haifa) Zelnik told us that when he gave himself in to the British in May of 1942, he was not aware of the plan to assassinate him. However, the plan to assassinate him was discussed in a group meeting (e.g., Yellin-Mor 1974:87) and Yellin-Mor (1974:86) even states that Yehuda-Leib Shneursohn told Zelnik about it.

Even if one takes Zelnik's account as valid, the suspicion in February through May of 1942 must have changed members' attitudes and behavior toward Zelnik and he must have felt it. Furthermore, he knew—from first hand experience—that Lehi's members *were* perfectly capable of passing a death sentence even on those to who they felt very close (e.g., see the case with Zerony, no. 27) and Zelnik himself told us that it would have been stupid on his part (during February through May of 1942) not to suspect members because the general atmosphere in contemporary Lehi was such that those defined as traitors had to be assassinated. In addition, Zelnik himself admits that he was warned by Shneursohn and others to be careful, especially with Tuvia Chen-Zion and his group.

In the 1987 interview Zelnik described his gradual realization that his authority over members was disintegrating. He finally could not take it any more and decided to give himself in to the British. While never saying it, he may have felt safer with the British than with some of his friends who were obviously planning to assassinate him.

CASE NUMBER 36

The Assassination of Kasem Taubash in the Autumn of 1943 by Hagana/Palmach

Alexander Zeid was born in 1886 in Russia. In 1904, at the age of eighteen, he immigrated to Palestine out of his deep belief in Zionism. In 1907 he became one of the founders the Jewish defense organization Bar Giora (see chapter 4), which served as the seed bed organization for the establishment of the Hashomer in 1909. Zeid became one of the legendary and mythical figures of the period and his name became associated with numerous stories focusing on Jewish self-defense and heroism. While being on a guard duty in the Israel valley (in the northeast part of Israel) on July 10, 1938 Zeid was attacked and murdered by anonymous attacker(s).[32]

The Hagana/Palmach discovered that a Bedouin tribal chief by the name of Kasem Taubash was the one who murdered Zeid, as well as a few other Jews in the Israel valley. Taubash lived in a

Bedouin camp near the German colony Waldheim (near Alonim, in the northern part of Israel).

According to Zerubavel (1955, vol. 1:602) and a television interview with Itzhak Hankin—one of the actual assassins[33]—in the autumn of 1943, a platoon from company A of the Palmach penetrated the Bedouin camp and assassinated Taubash. Argaman, however, places that assassination in March of 1942 (1991:99).

According to Argaman (1991:88–102) and to the Palmach book (Gilad 1955, vol. 1:602), there can be no question about the fact that the main motivation for the assassination was revenge. Moreover, the authorization for the assassination came from the higher command echelons of the Hagana (Argaman, ibid.). Although the Bedouins were seeking revenge for Taubash's assassination (Argaman 1991:100–192), Zerubavel (ibid.) states that the assassination of Taubash achieved another goal as well: "as a result, a few known heads of Arab gangs escaped from…[Palestine]…they were afraid that the long punishing arm would reach them too."

CASE NUMBER 37

The Assassination of Abraham Wilenchik on February 25, 1943 by Lehi in Herzelia

Wilenchik was one of Lehi's first members, and one of the first to be arrested by the British (after Lehi robbed Bank APAK [Anglo Palestine Bank] in 1940). He spent twenty-six months in the British detention camp in Latrun and was released in February of 1943 (Niv, vol. 3:196). Wilenchick apparently took a neutral position and may have agreed to leave Lehi and possibly give the British information about Lehi for his release (Resnik 1986:179). Niv (vol. 3:196) and Resnik (1986:179) indicate that Wilenchik was accused of being a traitor and a squealer. Okev (1949:9–10) presents a somewhat different interpretation. According to Okev, while still in Latrun Wilenchik told people he wanted to leave Lehi and return to Etzel and said that other Lehi's members wanted to follow the same route.

On Thursday, February 25, 1943, a few days after Wilenchik was released from Latrun, at 4:15 P.M., a Lehi member came to

Wilenchik's home in Herzelia (north of Tel Aviv) and asked for Abraham. When Abraham got out he was shot three times and died immediately. He was twenty-six years old when he was assassinated and left a wife and a daughter. Although an inner Etzel's bulletin dated March 12, 1943, denied that Wilenchik squealed (Okev 1949:9)—this became a side issue. Okev (1949:10), Resnik (1986:179), and S.T.H. (vol. 3, part 1:506) all agree that Wilenchik's assassination's main function was to give a new, final, and frightening meaning to Lehi's slogan that "only death would release from the organization" and that members who thought about defection should think twice. A somewhat similar case would happen again in 1947 (see case no. 75).[34]

Shmuelevitz provides a somewhat different account. He states that in 1969 he met with Inspector Day, formerly of the British intelligence in Palestine. According to Shmuelevitz, Inspector Day told him that Wilenchik in fact gave the British intelligence valuable information and that in return he was released from the British prison (1973:17).

CASE NUMBER 38

The Assassination of Eliahu Giladi (Green) in the Summer of 1943 by Lehi

Lehi after Yair's violent death (February 12, 1942) and Zelnik's arrest (May 1942, see case no. 34) was basically disintegrating. Most other members were arrested by the British. The only significant member—Yehoshua Cohen—was hiding in an orange grove near the Kefar Saba—Ra'anana area (northeast of Tel Aviv) trying to keep "something" going. On this background, two prominent leaders escaped from the British detention camp of Mazra, and on September 2, 1942, they met with Cohen and tried to revive Lehi. The two were Eliahu Giladi ("Shaul") and Itzhak Yazernitzky-Shamir ("Michael"), who many years later became Israel's minister of foreign affairs and prime minister.

Giladi is one of Lehi's most enigmatic figures and not much is known about him. Eliahu Giladi was born under the name Albert Green in 1915 in Transylvania. Eliahu was his Hebrew name. At the age of twenty-one he was drafted to the Rumanian army. After some time he ran away to Palestine in 1937 (or 1938). Letters that he wrote his family indicated that he joined the Jewish underground and was committed to fight the British. Giladi joined "Beitar"'s company in Zichron Ya'acov.[35] Giladi proved himself a dedicated member of Etzel, courageous and charismatic (ibid., and Geffner Shoshana, interview May 5, 1987). When Lehi separated from Etzel in the summer of 1940, Giladi chose Lehi (Ziv 1973:17).

Giladi took an active part in one of Lehi's first actions—robbing/confiscating a large sum of money from Bank APAK in northern Tel Aviv (September 16, 1940, see Eliav 1983:174–177). Giladi also played a very central role as the director and instructor in what was probably Lehi's first political indoctrination course which took place in an orange grove in Magdiel sometime in the winter of 1940 (possibly in November). Giladi emphasized there the importance of "inner discipline" and the main points of "Hatchia," a document drafted by Abraham Stern in November of 1940, which outlined the main ideological themes of Lehi, as Stern saw them.[36] Yellin-Mor states that Giladi served as a personal example in his modest living, "he lived on bread and margarine, onion and salt" (1974:91; Gilboa 1986:107 challenges this account).

No documentation is available regarding the question of when or where exactly was Giladi arrested by the British. We only know that he was arrested under the false name of Ezra Levi (Yellin-Mor 1974:106), probably in 1941 in Netanya, and his name surfaced again in the context of being in the British detention camp of Mazra.

In Mazra, Giladi gained reputation and followers and emerged as a courageous and charismatic leader. He certainly was the motivating focus of a group of youth.[37] Kotzer (1977) describes Giladi as handsome, determined, and sensitive, totally dedicated to Lehi's cause—as he saw it. Gilboa (1986) mentions some differences of opinion between Yazernitzky-Shamir, Yellin-Mor, and Giladi. Giladi planned to escape from Mazra and was clearly the driving force behind it.[38]

On August 31, 1942, Yitzhak Yazernitzky-Shamir (Michael) and Eliahu Giladi (Shaul) escaped from Mazra. Once out of the camp, they made contact with Anshell Shpillman[39] who gave them food, shelter, and clothes and then they moved to meet Yehoshua Cohen, who survived in the orange grove near Kefar Saba. They started to reorganize Lehi. That was the beginning of how Lehi reemerged, like a phoenix, to become a renewed and vital revolutionary movement under the triumvirate leadership of Yazernitzky-Shamir, Yellin-Mor, and Eldad. Ziv (1973:17) states that after the escape from Mazra, Giladi played a very central role in reorganizing Lehi.

From September of 1942 there was an obvious competition of leadership in Lehi. Yellin-Mor was in Mazra. There remained Yazernitzky-Shamir, a grayish, serious, and thorough person. Shamir liked to double check and be very sure before acting; he consulted a lot, was thoughtful, and noncharismatic. Almost the exact opposite of Giladi who was stormy, self-assured, charismatic, and fast. What exactly happened is difficult to know. Giladi did not leave anything in writing, and no account from his point of view was written. The sources available portray Giladi in a very problematic light.

Pesach Levi ("Shchori") was appointed as Giladi's connection. Yellin-Mor states that Giladi humiliated and insulted him in front of other Lehi's members. Levi wrote to his girl friend Shulamit (Sarah Shamir) that there was no value to his life without Lehi, and that there was no place for him in Lehi the way Lehi was. He committed suicide in November of 1942 (Yellin-Mor 1974:450–451). This, obviously cast a dark and unpleasant shadow over Giladi.

Another incident is reported by Banai (1958:143–144). He describes the preparations he, Giladi, and Yerachmiel Aharonson ("Elisha") were making for an operation. Giladi asked Aharonson if Aharonson did something which he was supposed to do. Aharonson said no and Giladi "cold bloodedly, got close to Elisha (Aharonson—ED.)...cursed him...and hit him in his face.... He (Giladi—ED.) drew a 'Colt' revolver, aimed it at his (Aharonson—ED.) chest and said 'I'll hit you like a dog'..." According to Banai, Giladi acted like a "simple murderer."

A similar incidence is reported by Yellin-Mor (1974: 123–125). In this case Yitzhak Yazernitzky-Shamir (Michael) canceled an order given by Giladi for an action (attacking British soldiers with explosives during a demonstration). After Giladi found out, and confirmed, that it was Shamir who canceled his orders, he "threatened Michael in front of others that 'this would be the last time. If you dare change an order of mine, I'll hit you like a dog!'" and, according to Yellin-Mor, Giladi pointed his American "Colt" to Shamir.

There are other accounts in Yellin-Mor (1974:125, 441–442) and Banai (1958:144) which portray Giladi's suggested operations as very risky, dangerous and on the verge of suicide. The accounts emphasize Giladi's brutality and problematic attitude towards females (no specific details, however, are given). Ginosar, who was Giladi's bodyguard in Haifa, states that "I hated him and demanded to separate from him. He was violent, despotic and humiliated his friends. I used to eat in restaurants with him, I don't know where he got the money for it. I hardly had money for bread and Lakerda [a fish]. If I ever had thought about committing suicide—that was during 'Shaul's period.... 'Shaul's planning was adventurous and did not take into account human problems. I witnessed his humiliating attitude toward Anshell Shpillman. 'Yair' liked 'Shaul' because of his courage..."

Shmuelevitz (1973:16), one of Giladi's friends, also echoes the usual, almost stereotypical, accusations. He states that he was told that Giladi began to drink alcohol excessively and reached the point of demonstrating a lack of what he calls "mental balance." According to Kotzer (1977:190), it is possible that one of Lehi's women, who slept with Giladi, may have heard him brag about different grandiose "plans" he may have had, and spread the word about them.

I must admit that having followed some of the accusations against Giladi, I could not help wondering to what extent Lehi may have created here an Orwellian type of the infamous "archenemy Goldstein." In any event, and judging from the different accounts, there is no question that Giladi's reputation was eroding among some central members of Lehi.

Ziv (1973:17–19) states that he was considered as Giladi's best friend. When Giladi was assassinated Ziv was still in Mazra. After he got out he was told that following Giladi's escape from Mazra "something happened to [him], that in my opinion was a mental illness which attacked him.... I did not know Giladi the way he was described to me.... Michael [Shamir] called me...he was the one who told me all these things about Giladi.... I was truly shocked.... I found it hard to believe such things on Eliahu...later I was persuaded that there was no other way..."

There was an ideological problem too. Lehi before and after Stern's death was quite different (e.g., see Resnik 1986). Yellin-Mor, Shamir, and Eldad apparently learned the bitter lesson from the time when Lehi under Stern's leadership became one of the most hated groups in the "Yishuv" in contemporary Palestine. They decided to change that.

Yellin-Mor (1974:101) states that Giladi leaned towards revolutionary ideas, nihilism and specifically towards ideas developed by Dimitry Ivanowitz Pisarev (1868–1940) who was one of the main figures in the Russian nihilist movement. Giladi is said (it sometimes sounds almost like an accusation) to have wanted to use personal political assassinations. He is particularly reputed to have wanted to assassinate the heads of the Hagana and the Jewish Agency.

One, of course, can not fail to notice the similarities between Giladi and Stern, especially both leaders' determination and stands on issues of political assassination and general ideological orientations (e.g., see Yevin 1986:205–206), as well as some of the main points of the Hatchia (e.g., see Yevin 1986:316). These similarities are even more salient because they emerge from descriptions of people who can not possibly be considered as sympathizers of Giladi. As an illustration, let me quote from Kotzer (no date:270) who quotes Stern "I know, many would come and point out dark spots in our very essence. They will show moral defects, point to plots and indecencies as we orient and direct ourselves to our goal. They will find lack of generosity, of friendship and an ingratitude.... It is true! We are not trying to hide this truth. We repeat and emphasize: if moral dirt, lies and deception, prostituting our sisters and wives and [using] degraded means would lead us to the goal-we shall use them !!!" Furthermore, Ginosar (1973:3) states that Stern knew Giladi and liked him.

It is not clear, or documented, when exactly Giladi began to voice his ideological "deviance." One may suspect that prior to his escape with Shamir in 1942 there were already some differences of opinion. According to Yellin-Mor, however, this ideological "shift" found its expression in the summer of 1942 (1974:101). Yellin-Mor (1974:102, 122–125), who remained in Mazra, states that he was very concerned and even warned Shamir about Giladi. Shmuelevitz's (1973) and Ziv's (1973) interviews do not lend support to Yellin-Mor's account. According to them, Giladi's behavior in Mazra was not abnormal.

If the ideological tendencies attributed to Giladi were in fact true—nihilism, extreme revolutionary ideas, political assassination of Jewish leaders on a large scale, suicidal operations—then one can easily see why Yellin-Mor, Shamir, and a few others viewed Giladi as dangerous. Furthermore, it seems safe to assume that the personal conflicts between Shamir and Giladi became intolerable. It is also true that Giladi, the charismatic figure, attracted many young followers around him and most certainly threatened Shamir's position as Lehi's leader, if in fact Shamir was the indisputable leader then (which is not quite clear).

Eventually, Shamir had to make a decision. Considering Shamir's natural hesitance, reluctance and slowness, one almost must assume that he probably consulted a few close friends and even wrote to Yellin-Mor to Mazra asking for his advice. The letter to Yellin-Mor indicates that Shamir felt neither pressed with time to act, nor was he sure about his position as *the* leader. However, before Yellin-Mor could respond, the decision to assassinate Giladi—before Lehi was to be torn apart—fell (perhaps because some unknown event happened which made such a decision a necessity). Shamir himself (1973:3) states that "The execution of Giladi was necessary. Many members came to me and complained that there was no other way. The operational decision was mine personally. I consulted with friends." Yehoshua Cohen (1973:9) also implies that the decision to assassinate Giladi was hurried "that was a matter of minutes in my opinion, and if the decision to assassinate him would not have been made and executed, he [Giladi] would have fired. I have no doubt about it..." and "...if a decision would not have been made, Lehi would have been destroyed..." (p. 8); "...Shaul could have reached the stage where he would have assassinated Shamir, and then Lehi would have disintegrated" (1972:12).

There are *three* versions about how Giladi was executed. According to S.T.H. (vol. 3, part 1:507), Giladi was invited to a class on weapons in the sands of Bat-Yam (south of Tel Aviv) and there he was assassinated, probably in the summer of 1943 (Segev 1981) which means he was twenty-eight when he died. It is not known how the editors of S.T.H. knew how or where Giladi was executed. We do not know by what weapon, the exact date or how exactly was the decision made. Second, Baruch Nadel, in his allegorical and confused book (1976), hints[40] that Giladi was shot at Lehi's headquarters (1976:45–46). Third, Kotzer (1977) states that Giladi was shot in his back. In a rare interview, all Shamir—who was most certainly a prominent figure in the assassination plot—was willing to say was "it was a tragic, very tragic, affair, that is very difficult to talk about. Under the conditions prevailing then, we did not see any other way" (Segev 1981:8). According to this report, Shamir later called his daughter Gilada.

After the assassination, Shamir received Yellin-Mor's approval. He also called thirteen leaders from Lehi to the sand dunes in Bat Yam and told them about Giladi's assassination. The fact that Shamir did not do it before the assassination, but only after it, indicates that the conspirational nature of Giladi's assassination (even Eldad did not know—Yellin-Mor 1974:140) was probably due to Giladi's popularity and Shamir's lack of confidence in the support of other members of Lehi. Yehoshua Cohen (1973:10) implies that there may have even been contemporary suspicions that he, together with Giladi, would go against Lehi's center—that is, Shamir. All thirteen leaders confirmed the decision and the assassination (Banai 1958:145; Yellin-Mor 1974:125). These acts certainly crystallized Shamir's position as leader of Lehi and, implicitly, gave a very strong signal to potential opposers. Giladi's death was not disclosed to everyone and the "cover" story was that Giladi left for a mission abroad. Obviously, Kotzer (1977: see also Segev 1981) and Eliav (1983:175, 258–259) were not too happy with the assassination. Eventually, even such important members of Lehi as Yehoshua Cohen, Matitiahu Shmuelevitz, and Shimon Ziv, who were closest to Giladi at one time, were persuaded and made to believe and accept the accounts given about the assassination by the assassins, post factum (e.g., see Geter 1967:114; Cohen Y. 1973:7–10; Shmuelevitz 1973; and Ziv 1973).

The question of who exactly assassinated Giladi haunted some of those who wanted to decipher the case. Kotzer told Segev (1981:9) that two members of Lehi did it—Yerachmiel Aharonson (who was killed by the British on March 19, 1944, see case no. 42) and another anonymous person. According to Kotzer, they shot Giladi from his back because "Had they come in front—he would have drawn first" (ibid).

As Shamir rose to prominence in the Israeli political system—first as a "Likud" parliament member (from 1973), then as the minister of foreign affairs (in March of 1980), and finally as Begin's inheritor as Israel's prime minister (September 1983-September 1984, and again from October 1986)—the Giladi affair continued to haunt him. In 1981 there was a theater show in Israel ("The death of a revolver-man") depicting the Shamir-Giladi conflict. Due to the family's pressure, Lehi museum agreed to recognize Giladi as a casualty (1981) and in 1984 the Ministry of Defense told Giladi's sister's daughter that the state of Israel would recognize Giladi's death as the death of a regular soldier who fell during the struggle for Israel's independence. That happened about thirty-eight years after his assassination. Unfortunately, his place of burial is still unknown.

Although some may try to put the Shamir-Giladi dispute within a personal context (and thus turn Giladi's death into a murder) I think that there can be no question that Giladi was assassinated on the background of a very deep, real, and painful power struggle within the leadership of Lehi during 1942–1943, and the crystallization of the nature of its future activities.[41]

CASE NUMBER 39

The Assassination of Israel Pritzker on September 3, 1943 by Lehi

After the April 1937 division in Etzel, a special intelligence department was created: the Meshi (Department of Information Service, later known as the "Delek"). Meshi was headed by Arie Posek, and in charge of Haifa was Israel Pritzker (Niv, vol. 2:260–265). When World War II began, Raziel who was then commander of Etzel, and Jabotinski, felt that Etzel should cooperate with the British and help them combat and defeat Nazi Germany. Pritzker apparently felt very strongly about helping the British and instructed his agents to help the British find information about both the Hagana and Lehi (Eliav 1983:158–159; Yevin 1986:178–180). Hence, and as an example, Pritzker was "collecting information against Zerony" (Yevin 1986:180; see case no. 28). Pritzker, no doubt, became not only instrumental but also very important in this cooperation (e.g., see Bauer 1966:265). Bauer (1966:113) states that already in 1940 "according to one source, Stern declared a 'death sentence' on Pritzker, and if to trust a report from the Hagana's sources, a few Etzel members threatened to kill Stern if anything would happen to Pritzker..." Thus considering, and perhaps preplanning, the assassination of Pritzker may have already taken place three years before the actual assassination.

According to Niv (vol. 3:59–60), in November of 1940, when Raziel was reappointed as Etzel's commander, a reorganization took place, and Pritzker was reassigned (in the winter of 1941). He continued to maintain contacts with British intelligence agents in Haifa. Among the agents Pritzker used were M. Rotstein (see case no. 12), Joseph Davidesku (see case no. 51), and Michael Waksman (see case no. 25).[42]

It appears that Israel Pritzker may have been involved in an attempt to "trap" Stern and Lehi into signing a fabricated document which was supposedly an agreement with Mussolini's Italy (Yevin 1986:201–208; Bauer 1966:141). Another and similar attempt was to help create some disorganization in the Hagana's high command by hinting to them that their headquarters were penetrated by a traitor (Bauer 1966:141–142; S.T.H., vol. 3, part 1:244–245). Moshe Rotstein was the active agent in both cases (see case no. 12).

Thus, it seems safe to assume that Pritzker was involved in giving information about Lehi's members to the British intelligence, information that led to their eventual arrest (Bowyer-Bell 1987:85; Niv, part 3:180). Pritzker, however, may have done this as a result of his tragic assumption that this secret cooperation "was in line with the general line of the party" (Shavit 1976:58).

Obviously, members of Lehi did not like Pritzker's activities[43] and they decided to assassinate him after they had accused him of betraying their members to the British. Lehi declared a death sentence against him.

However, before the actual assassination Lehi's agents approached Ya'acov Meridor, commander of Etzel de facto between 1941–1943, and informed him about their intention. Meridor told them that "We have nothing against him, but if Lehi has an interest to prosecute him—that is their business." One can easily infer from this that Etzel's high command at that time did not approve of Pritzker's activities. Furthermore, Meridor told Amrami (1954) that when he took over the command of Etzel, he was identified with a group of commanders that opposed Pritzker (and others) who, so they felt, were too pro-British. Eventually, Pritzker and his associates were neutralized and Meridor told Pritzker to stay away from Etzel. Lehi's command[44] did not come to a different conclusion. Moreover, the assassination of Michael Waksman—who was one of Pritzker's agents—on May 16, 1941 by Etzel (see case no. 25) could only lend more credibility to Lehi's assessment that Pritzker's activities were no longer backed by Etzel. Assassinating Pritzker implied for Lehi that the organization was not forgetting or forgiving and that their betrayed members were not forgotten or abandoned but revenged. Shmuelevitz (1973:6) states that after Pritzker's assassination the relationships between Lehi and Etzel improved considerably. The time lag, however, is important. Pritzker was not as active or influential in 1943. Nevertheless, he fell victim to his past loyalties.

Moreover, it seems safe to assume that Lehi's "invoice" with Pritzker was not limited only to betraying their members to the British intelligence. It was also due to his part in the provocation which was presented by Rotstein (Pritzker's agent) and which aimed to smear and stigmatize Stern and Lehi as collaborators with fascist Italy.

Resnik (1986:186–187) points out that Pritzker was a "neutral" victim. His assassination could help Lehi "ventilate" past hostilities against Etzel and indicate that Etzel was not backing up any more cooperation with the British. Resnik states that although Meridor may have not known that Pritzker would be assassinated, Meridor also stated that even if he had known, he would have probably not prevented it. Thus, Resnik concluded that Meridor and/or Etzel probably had an actual interest in Pritzker's assassination. The fact also remains that three other assassination attempts were directed against three of Pritzker's agents—Moshe Rotstein, Michael Waksman, and Joseph Davidesku (the last two, successful).

Israel Pritzker was born in Russia and came to Palestine in 1923. He was thirty years old at the time of the assassination. On Saturday evening, September 3, 1943, at around 2030, he was shot about five times and killed by Lehi's members as he was leaving his home in Peretz Haiut street in Tel Aviv (*Ha'aretz*, September 5, 1943:4 and September 6, 1943:2). He was survived by his pregnant wife and young daughter. Following his death, some contemporary leaders of the revisionist movement (e.g., Dr. Unitchman and R. Rosov) expressed full confidence in his innocence. Meridor, however, never retracted his fateful sentence, despite pressures from Pritzker's surviving wife to clear her husband's name for the sake of their children (Koren 1986:11). Obviously, this assassination created much embarrassment for Etzel (see also Okev 1949:11–13).[45]

CASES NUMBERS 40 AND 43

The Assassination of Zeev Falsh on March 13, 1944, and of Chaim Gotowitz on May 10, 1944 by Lehi

Lehi made quite a few efforts to find out who exactly were the Jewish agents/detectives who were used by British intelligence against them (Niv, vol. 4:42). Lehi usually defined such Jewish detectives as traitors and squealers—common rhetorical devices used to justify an assassination (e.g., see Katz 1987:32).

Gotowitz and Falsh were viewed by Lehi as particularly dangerous (Banai 1958:259). On Monday, March 13, 1944, in the evening, Zeev Falsh who worked for the British intelligence for about five years, was shot to death near his home on Herzl street in Ramat Gan and died immediately.

Gotowitz, who worked for the British intelligence for about twelve years, was shot to death around 0800 on Wednesday, May 10, 1944, near his home on Hayarkon street, Tel Aviv. Both were assassinated by Lehi's agents who were never identified or caught.[46]

Lehi's announcement from 1944 told the public that Falsh and Gotowitz were assassinated because they were "hired detectives, squealers, agents of the enemy's intelligence." On that same announcement, Lehi gave the names of nine other traitors and squealers who were warned to stop their activities—or else. Among the names on the list were Max Schindler (see case no. 70) and Ya'acov Hilewitz (see case no. 43). No record exists about assassination plots against the rest (Lehi, *Ketavim*, [A]:531). An editorial in *Davar* (May 18, 1944:1) strongly denounced the assassinations and the threats made in Lehi's announcement. These were important events. The phenomenon against which Lehi's rhetoric was addressed to must have been prevalent and probably occurred again and again. The idea of revenge was prominent in conjunction with the use of the above rhetorical devices. It is thus evident that the motivation to utilize such rhetorical devices as traitor, squealer, and cooperator was gaining prominence and importance as boundary maintenance markers. Clearly, the function of this activity was not only to signify the moral boundaries of the collective, but to keep the integrity of the group intact against external threats and challenges. Furthermore, Lehi's use of the above rhetoric implies that a very specific and peculiar system was in operation here, a system of intra organizational justice. It was as if a mini-version of the criminal process was working here. As we shall see later in the analysis, the amount of political assassinations in this specific context was the highest.

CASE NUMBER 41

The Assassination Attempt on the Life of Major Y. P. W. Ford in Tel Aviv on April 10, 1944 by Lehi—Unsuccessful

In 1944 Yerachmiel Aharonson was a student in the Technion in Haifa. He was the son of a wealthy family from Warsaw who came to Palestine and joined Lehi, where he was called Elisha. Yazernitzky-Shamir transferred Elisha from Haifa to Tel Aviv and asked him to organize the civilian background support for Lehi, a job Elisha was apparently delighted to do. On March 19, 1944, Elisha was walking along Maza Street in Tel Aviv when he was stopped by a British patrol. Since Elisha carried a gun, he took it out and started to shoot. Consequently, the British policemen began a pursuit after him, shooting with their submachine guns. Elisha was later cornered, shot, and killed.[47]

Lehi responded violently as its command group gave the order to "clean the city streets from every person who wears a uniform which means he is British" (Yellin-Mor 1974:155). What followed were numerous attacks against British forces (ibid.; *Ha'aretz*, March 24, 1944:1)). One act of revenge was discriminately and specifically aimed at Major Y. P. W. Ford, the commander of the Tel Aviv police, who was selected as a target because of his official role.

On Monday, April 10, 1944 in the morning, three Lehi's members (Immanuel Hanegby, Ya'acov Bentov, and Nechama Cohen) waited for Ford very close to the building of the Tel Aviv police. As Ford's car got close to the ambushers, Hanegby sent a long burst of bullets from his automatic "Tommy gun" at Ford. The bullets broke through Ford's car windows and pierced Ford's shirt sleeves. Ford himself was miraculously unharmed. The plan stipulated that in case of a failure on Hanegby's part, Ya'acov Bentov was supposed to use his handgun and shoot Ford. Bentov executed his part but his hand gun got stuck and did not fire. Ford's life was saved. A few weeks later Ford left Palestine.[48]

CASE NUMBER 42

The Assassination Plot against Ya'acov Hilewitz in March–May 1944 by Etzel—Planned

Ya'acov Hilewitz was born in Rasien in Lithuania. As an adolescent, he joined the revisionist movement (Beitar) and gained there a reputation of an embezzler. In the late 1930s he immigrated to Palestine and joined the Etzel. In Palestine he worked in the daily newspaper *Hamashkif* and later became active as a fundraiser. He gained an additional reputation as a gambler and as a person who liked to live luxuriously, loved good food and nice clothes.

In 1938, Hilewitz was arrested by the British and as a result of his prison experience in the Acco prison he probably decided not to be arrested again. In October 1942 he was involved in a plan whose goal was to expose Arabs who supported the Nazi cause. The plan failed and Hilewitz could either go underground, or become an informer for the British intelligence. It seems that he chose the latter route.[49]

Beginning in March of 1944, Hilewitz's behavior began to arouse suspicions in Etzel's intelligence department. There were a few incidents involving the British intelligence which indicated that they knew too much (Niv, vol. 4:43; Livni 1987:116; Yellin-Mor 1974:182–184). Yellin Mor (1974:182–184) indicates that he was the one who was instrumental in exposing Hilewitz's double role.[50] Niv (vol. 4:43) states that a sympathetic Jewish officer told Arie Posek, previous head of Etzel's intelligence, about a letter sent from the British intelligence to the British chief secretary (probably John Shaw) detailing Hilewitz's connection with the British intelligence. That officer even gave Posek a copy of the letter. Posek gave the letter to Ya'acov Tavin, head of the Delek (contemporary Etzel's intelligence service).

On March 23, 1944, Etzel attacked the headquarters of the British intelligence in the Russian Compound ("Migrash Harusim") in Jerusalem. British officer John Scott (head of the Arab Department) was killed in the attack. Asher Benziman from Etzel was wounded and later died.[51] This attack, and others, marked a sharp turn in Etzel previous policy of limited cooperation with the British.

According to S.T.H. (vol. 3, part 1:524), Bethell (1979:129) and Nedava (1983:29), following the attack Hilewitz called Sir Richard Charles Catling, then senior officer in the Palestine Police force (between 1935–1948; Jones 1979:22–23) and asked for a meeting in Jerusalem. He told Catling that Etzel's attack on March 23 was a mistake which "hurt the Jewish cause" (Bethell 1979:129). He also told Catling that he would tell the British all he knew about Etzel if the British police would guarantee his safe passage out of Palestine and would give him enough money to enable him to begin a new life in the United States (ibid.). The British approved, and the Americans helped.

Hilewitz was given a large sum of money, probably between two thousand to five thousand English pounds. He gave the British intelligence a list of seventy-nine names of Etzel's high commanders and sympathizers. He even visited Begin's (then commander of the Etzel) secret hiding place in Jerusalem.[52] On March 31 (and April 1), 1944 the British arrested about sixty members of Etzel from that list. Begin himself, and Ya'acov Meridor, managed to escape being arrested by chance. On that very day, March 31, in the morning, Catling took Hilewitz in his own car south via Cantara to Cairo. There he waited in the Continental Hotel for a vacant seat in a flight to the United States (Nedava 1983:29; Shavit 1976:75).

Ya'acov Meridor, who was in Cairo, wanted to follow Hilewitz, assassinate him and throw his body into the Nile. However, he did want to consult Begin first and get his approval (Nedava 1983:29). Begin fiercely objected to assassinate Hilewitz without being absolutely sure of Hilewitz's guilt. He asked that Hilewitz be asked to return to Palestine so he could have a chance to defend himself. Two Etzel members, Itzhak Zuckerman and Shmuel Krauskopf were sent to deliver the invitation. Hilewitz told them to come the next day. When they came, they were told he could not come. When they left the hotel, they were approached by agents of the British military intelligence and were barely able to escape and cover their tracks (Niv, vol. 4:44–45).

Ya'acov Tavin, contemporary head of Etzel's intelligence department, began a full scale investigation. His findings were presented on May 25, 1944, before a special court of Etzel. Chairman of the court was Ya'acov Meridor, with two other judges—Shlomo Lev-Ami and Betzalel Amizur. Prosecutor was Eliahu Lankin and the defense was represented by Haim Landau. The court heard the case, and after deliberations found Hilewitz guilty of a provocation, and sentenced him to death (Niv, vol. 4:45; Nedava 1983:29). This, I cannot avoid commenting, is one of the very few detailed accounts, in all the cases, of anything which comes close to a legal procedure in court.[53]

Unfortunately for Etzel, at that time Hilewitz was not in Cairo any longer—he was flown to the United States. There, Hilewitz tried to present himself first as a member of Etzel. Very quickly, however, he realized that his life was in danger and he kept a very low profile. He later changed his name to Hill and began to work for a stationery store in New York (Katz 1966:366). He was married in 1946, had a son and continued to stay in the United States.

Hilewitz was contacted in 1944 by Shmuel Merlin, Etzel's representative in the United States and was advised to return to Palestine to clean his name—he refused.

Etzel's members in the United States informed Etzel's headquarters in Jerusalem about Hilewitz's arrival to the United States and asked for instructions. They did, however, recommend not to touch him because they were concerned that an action against Hilewitz might trigger the United States authorities to put an end to Etzel's activities in the United States. Tavin told Nedava that the recommendation was accepted and Hilewitz was not assassinated.

Another opportunity Etzel had to assassinate Hilewitz was in April of 1948 but was again not actualized. Shmuel Katz, who was then Etzel's representative in the United States refused again to authorize Hilewitz's assassination, for much the same reasons which were valid in 1944 (see Katz 1966:365–367, particularly pp. 366–367). Begin's "hesitation," however, frequently won him harsh criticisms from his own fellow members (e.g., see Begin 1980:154; Lankin 1974:70–71).

Hilewitz was contacted again in 1958 by Dr. Herzel Rosenblum, then chief editor of the Israeli influential daily newspaper *Yediot Aharonot*. Dr. Rosenblum was so impressed by Hilewitz's account, and his fierce denial of the charges against him, that he was actually willing to help him clean his name.[54]

Hence, we have here an example of a person who was accused and found guilty in treason without a fair trial. It is possible that Hilewitz, who probably knew the nature of his friends in Etzel and the type of "justice" which awaited him, refused to go back and face the charges because he suspected that he would not stand a chance to have a fair and unbiased trial. The fact that he was so effective in persuading Dr. Rosenblum (as well as his behaviour after coming to the United States, that is in contacting Etzel members there), may indicate that Etzel's interpretation that he was simply a traitor, felt guilty and escaped, may be too simplistic. The reality may have been *much* more complicated.

It is difficult to decide whether Hilewitz did, or did not do much, or whether what he was accused of being involved in, was from purely ideological or personal-economic motivation. Probably both. One thing which is very obvious is Begin's carefulness and mature judgment. He obviously wanted to be absolutely sure before permitting an assassination event to happen, despite a strong opposition from his own men, and was willing later to weigh the benefits of not assassinating Hilewitz in the United States against revenge. He did insist on collecting evidence and having a trial. Considering the dangerous conditions and the damage Hilewitz may have caused, one can only commend Begin's mature judgment and action.[55]

CASE NUMBER 44

The Assassination Attempt on Ephraim Illin in the Winter of 1944 by Lehi—Unsuccessful

The newly established (April 1937) intelligence service of the Etzel was in contact with a few Jewish agents who served in the British intelligence. One of the agents who kept contacts with the British intelligence was a businessman Ephraim Illin who "gave Yair direct reports and Yair used to give him different assignments" (Niv, vol. 2:263).

Illin rendered some important services to the underground. On August 11, 1939, Binyamin Zerony from Etzel escaped from the Jerusalem British Prison he was in (see case nos. 18 and 28). After his escape he was transferred in Illin's car, driven by a cab driver, and followed by Illin in another car, to Tel Aviv to hide for a while in the house of Illin's sister—Batia Goren.[56] Illin also helped to get visas for immigrants and in purchasing weapons (Yevin 1986:150). Years later, Illin tried to help Etzel to buy weapons in Europe (Lankin 1974:270).

On February 22, 1939, David Raziel, then chief commander of Etzel, returned to Palestine from a trip to Poland, with a phony passport. In Lod Airport[57] he aroused the suspicion of a custom officer who wanted to arrest him. Raziel managed to escape and after some adventures, managed to arrive to Tel Aviv on the 23rd, and assumed his command position (Niv, vol. 2:233–234; Naor 1990:183–184).

Raziel scheduled a meeting for Friday, May 19, 1939, in Haifa with Pinhas Rotenberg. Since the roads were tightly inspected by the British, Raziel and his escort, Ephraim Illin, decided to by-pass the road blocks by flying to Haifa. The two took an inner flight from Tel Aviv to Haifa. The flight made a stop over in Lod Airport—supposedly in order to take additional passengers. There, Raziel was rediscovered by the same British custom officer whose suspicions had been aroused three months earlier when Raziel came back from Poland. Raziel was arrested immediately by the British intelligence and sent to prison in Jerusalem (Niv, part 2:235; Naor 1990:207–215). Illin was not arrested. More suspicions were aroused against Illin in August. On the night of August 31, 1939 the command of Etzel grouped in 31 Aharonowitz St. in Tel Aviv for a special session. The apartment was rented for them by Illin. The British police apparently found out about this meeting and British detectives surrounded the apartment and arrested everyone. That arrest raised suspicions that Illin had something to do with it. As it turned out to be, Illin was probably innocent (Naor 1990:223–224).

Anshell Shpillman told the author in an interview (July 5, 1987, Beit Yair) that "we tried to assassinate Illin because he was the only one who knew about Raziel's flight to Haifa...we suspected that he was cooperating with the CID....we also asked his help to meet Wilkin but Wilkin did not show up..." According to Shpillman, Lehi's center decided to assassinate Illin. The assassin who went to kill Illin at his home in Shderot Chen, aimed his rifle at Illin. However, Illin's mother was walking in the room and was getting in and out of the firing line. The assassin was concerned that Illin's innocent mother might be hit and "thanks to his mother Illin remained alive." Shpillman admitted that Illin later left the country to Europe and helped Etzel and Lehi to buy weapons. The witness even recalled a conversation with Menachem Begin who questioned Shpillman about the trial Lehi made to Illin. In any event, no more assassination attempts were made on Illin's life. Kotzer (no date:201) implies that Illin was also suspected of causing the main arrest of the Etzel leadership (in 1939) and that "if it were not for David Raziel who defended him, he would have been executed. Raziel demanded proof..."

In 1985 Illin published his memoirs. There, he discusses at length the suspicions against him (pp. 94–101 and 262–272) and provides a very persuasive account for his innocence, denying that he had anything to do with Raziel's arrest.

Some interesting observations can be made from this case. First, different actors were well aware of the suspicions against Illin regarding his suspected role in Raziel's arrest on May 19, 1939. Thus his help to hide Zerony (Yevin 1986:160) and to buy weapons in Europe (Lankin 1974:270) were attributed to Illin's attempts to clear his name. Abraham Stern, who knew about those suspicions, rejected them (Yevin 1986:160). Second, Illin had no real chance to present *his* position and explanation regarding Raziel's arrest. According to Illin (1985:264–268) he demanded from Begin to investigate the suspicions against him. In 1960, Begin appointed an investigation committee who, according to Illin, found him innocent (for more on this complicated issue see Naor 1990:208–210). Illin maintains that the death sentence that Lehi passed against him was not based on facts, but on vicious rumors, gossip, unfounded conjectures, and hearsay. Third, Shpillman's testimony attributed the assassination attempt to Lehi in the winter of 1944, and associated it to Lehi's attempts to meet Wilkin, a British intelligence (CID—Criminal Investigation Department) officer. Lehi in fact did try to assassinate Wilkin in September of 1944 (see case no. 45). It is then quite possible that Lehi's center (which did not exist until at least August–September of 1940) did not like Illin to begin with and "remembered" past suspicions against him. It may also be that in the winter of 1944 they tried to get Wilkin through Illin, and when Illin "did not deliver the goods," that is Wilkin did not show up for the meeting, they felt that their worst suspicions were confirmed and they decided therefore to assassinate Illin. It is not known why the assassination attempts did not continue. It is possible that the efforts involved in the successful assassination of Wilkin on September 29, 1944, and the success itself (see next case), may have calmed down Lehi's zeal to assassinate Illin.

CASE NUMBER 45

The Assassination Attempts on T. I. Wilkin in Tel Aviv and Jerusalem by Lehi: June 1941, Tel Aviv—Unsuccessful; and September 29, 1944, Jerusalem—Successful

T. I. Wilkin arrived to Palestine in 1930 as a policeman and for a long time served in the Tel Aviv Police force. He had many social contacts with Jews and spoke Hebrew fluently. Kotzer (1977: 234) and Eliav (1983:196) even state that he had a Jewish lover—Borochov's daughter.[58] Since 1938 he served in the British intelligence, where he was promoted and was transferred from Lod to the intelligence headquarters in Jerusalem. There he was appointed as head of the Jewish department (Eliav 1983:24; Katz 1987:39).

Like Morton (see case no. 33), Wilkin's activities against the pre-state underground Jewish groups, especially Lehi, made Lehi view him as a most dangerous and deadly enemy. It did not take long for Lehi to decide that Wilkin should be assassinated.[59] An unsuccessful attempt was already made at 8 Yael Street in Tel Aviv on January 20, 1942 (see case nos. 30 and 33).

Wilkin was involved in the arrest and torture of Zerony (Yevin 1986:159, see also case nos. 30 and 18); in the interrogation of Kotzer (1977:233–235); arrested Yair and the Etzel's headquarters on August 31, 1938 (Weinshall 1978:140–143; Yevin 1986:161, 163); and was present in the incident on January 27, 1942 when Morton shot Zelik Zak and Abraham Amper (Yevin 1986:270–271; see also case no. 26) when he kicked Savorai who was wounded (Eliav 1983:24); finally he was involved in the last action against Yair, when on February 12, 1942, Morton killed Yair.[60]

Already in June of 1941, Lehi's commanders met with Yair and decided to assassinate Wilkin, who was then stationed in Tel Aviv. Wilkin was put under surveillance, but he kept such a chaotic schedule (possibly as a deliberate step to avoid assassination) that no assassination plot could be planned or executed (Weinshall 1978:214–215; Yevin 1986:244–245).

In the summer of 1944, "Machlaka Vav"—Lehi's intelligence department—received information that Wilkin was in Jerusalem. Members of Machlaka Vav in Jerusalem began to look for him until they confirmed that he was seen in the King David Hotel. Matitiahu Peli was assigned with the task of putting Wilkin under surveillance.

Lehi discovered that Wilkin lived in the dormitory for police officers in the Rumanian Church. Wilkin's path and pattern of walking to his office were learned and documented. At that stage Peli took a bus to Tel Aviv to meet Itzhak Yazernitzky-Shamir

(Michael) to get final approval for the assassination. He got the approval on the same day and returned to Jerusalem.

Lehi's center sent Ya'acov Banai ("Mazal") to join David Shomron ("Ali") for the assassination, and it also sent an escape car. Itzhak Yazernitzky-Shamir gave Banai the direct order to shoot Wilkin (Banai 1958:256). The two assassins were equipped with Polish made "Nagan" hand guns for the assassination (each with seven bullets) and other automatic hand guns, for self-defense—if necessary.

At around 0800 on Friday, September 29, 1944 (two days after "Yom Kippur"), the death trap for Wilkin was set. Matitiahu Peli, seated and dressed like an Arab, waited to see Wilkin come out from the police officers' dormitory in the Rumanian Church and walk in Saint George Street (Shivtei Israel Street today). When he saw Wilkin, he signaled Banai and Shomron (by throwing his hat) that their victim was following his usual path of walking. The escape car passed the assassins, signaling that everything was progressing according to the plan. The car made a left hand turn into a parking spot in front of the Armenian Church in Melisanda Street (today Heleni Hamalka Street), close to its intersection with Saint George Street. Banai and Shomron waited for Wilkin to arrive at the intersection of Saint George Street and Melisanda Street. The two assassins walked toward Wilkin. The three passed each other and the local Lehi's men from Machlaka Vav gave a final confirmation of Wilkin' identity. The two assassins turned back, took out their Polish Nagan's and started to shoot at Wilkin. Wilkin was surprised. He turned, tried to draw his own gun, but collapsed. Out of the fourteen bullets fired at him, eleven hit. Wilkin died immediately. Although the escape plan did not work as previously arranged, all involved in the assassination managed to escape and none was ever caught.[61]

After the assassination Lehi published an announcement taking full responsibility for Wilkin's assassination and stating that "T. I. Wilkin (called 'Wilkin'), officer of the enemy's intelligence, super-hunter of the Palestinian Gestapo...was attacked and killed.... Due to the means he used: abominable cheating, atrocious lies cruel torturing and unjustified murder, he became one of the pillars of the oppressive regime in our homeland" (Lehi, *Ketavim* [A]:717–718).

CASE NUMBER 46

The Assassination Attempts on Sir John Valentine Winston Shaw's Life from October–December 1944 by Lehi—Unsuccessful

In 1944, sometime between October and December, Lehi planned to assassinate Sir John Shaw (then fifty years old), who was the chief secretary of the British mandate forces in Palestine between 1945–1946 (Jones 1979:115), and a promoter of a "strong hand" against the pre-state underground Jewish groups (Bethell 1979:128, 142–143).

After the assassination of Wilkin in September, Lehi planned to assassinate Shaw. It is not entirely clear why and a safe guess may be that the main reason was to try and achieve a "propaganda by deed" effect. Lehi's agent in charge of the operation was Yehoshua Cohen and he was helped by David Shomron (Ali). John Shaw was put under surveillance. Shomron and Cohen planned to ambush him near the lepers' hospital in Jerusalem (near where the Jerusalem theater house is now) on his way from home to work in the morning. Since final confirmation for the assassination from Lehi's center in Tel Aviv did not arrive—the assassination was not carried out. Meanwhile, Shomron was asked by Cohen to come to Jerusalem to pay his apartment rent. When Shomron arrived to Jerusalem he met Cohen and they both went to have breakfast in a small Arab restaurant near the Y.M.C.A. building. As they were eating, a British detective entered the restaurant, identified Cohen, and arrested him. Shomron managed to escape. Since Cohen did not carry a gun at that time, he could not resist arrest. The arrest of Cohen, which was totally unrelated to the assassination plot, effectively stopped the plan.[62]

Although one may suspect that one of Etzel's goals in blowing up the King David Hotel in Jerusalem on July 22, 1946,[63] was to kill Sir John Shaw too, there is no direct proof for that (this act indeed should be classified as terrorism because of its indiscriminate nature).

Thurston Clarke (1981:231) states that about two months after the King David Hotel was blown up by Etzel, Sir John

Shaw was appointed as high commissioner in Trinidad and Tobago, "a short while after that Etzel sent a booby-trapped letter to his new address. It was discovered in the post office and dismantled." No additional confirmation for this "attempt"[?] could be found.

In an interview Sir John Shaw gave in 1954 to Philip Ben in London, he did not mention any assassination attempts on his life. He stated that he was trying to implement a contradictory, inconsistent, and an impossible British policy. He emphasized that he was only a government clerk, an administrator, and not a politician. He added that he had no personal responsibility for what happened during his term in Palestine and that he only obeyed orders he received from the British high commissioner for Palestine and from London.

CASE NUMBER 47

Seven Assassination Attempts against Sir Harold MacMichael, mostly by Lehi

Sir Harold Alfred MacMichael (1882–1969) was the fifth British High Commissioner for Palestine, and served between 1938–1944 (Jones 1979:83)). He began his appointment on March 3, 1938, after serving for many years in Sudan. MacMichael most certainly shared the British perspective and policy which held that the future of Britain was tied very intimately with the Arab world, and hence viewed revived Jewish attempts to resettle Palestine as interfering in that policy.

According to Ben-Gurion, Israel's first prime-minister, and S.T.H. (see vol. 2 part 2:783 and vol. 2 part 3:1217) MacMichael was "a cruel and narrow minded clerk...showing cold blooded cruelty and lack of a human spark..."

Two Jewish tragedies connected with MacMichael were associated to two refugee ships. In November 1940, with the Gestapo's approval, about thirty-six hundred Jewish refugees arrived in Palestine from Europe on three boats called *Milos, Pacific,* and *Atlantic.* The British authorities took about 1770 Jewish refugees and put them aboard the ship *Patria,* intending either to deport them to Mauritius, or to turn the *Patria* into a floating prison. MacMichael refused to let the refugees stay and when the *Atlantic* arrived (November 24, 1940), the British began to transfer its passengers to the *Patria* too.

The Hagana decided to blow a hole in *Patria* to prevent deportation. Unfortunately, because of some miscalculations, the "hole" turned into a two by three meter hole and *Patria* sunk within ten to fifteen minutes and more than two hundred refugees died (Elam 1990:93–125; Naor 1990:258–259). MacMichael still refused to let the rest of the refugees stay (S.T.H., vol. 3, part 1: 152–158; see also case no. 32). Consequently, Lehi viewed Mac-Michael as a real and dangerous enemy (e.g., Lehi, *Ketavim* [A]:645–646 and 647–648).

The other incident involved the ship *Struma*. *Struma* was an ancient 180 ton wreck which, for some unknown reason was still called "a ship." It sailed from Rumania on December 12, 1941 on the initiative of the revisionists, carrying aboard a precious load of seven hundred sixty-nine Jewish refugees—women, men and children—away from the Nazi deadly hell. The *Struma* aimed to bring all of its refugees to Palestine.

The ship never reached a Palestinian port. It was stranded in a Turkish port. MacMichael refused again to allow the Jewish immigrants to enter Palestine. While the negotiations about the fate of the *Struma* were going on, the Turkish authorities became impatient and on February 23, 1942, towed the ship into the Black Sea and left it there, without food, water, fuel and with a broken engine. There she was probably torpedoed by a Russian submarine and sunk (Ofer 1988:244). Only one passenger survived. MacMichael was perceived as directly responsible for sinking the *Struma*. Anonymous ads with MacMichael's picture on them were publicized in Palestine with the explanation "Wanted for Murder of 800 Refugees drowned in the Black Sea on the boat 'Struma'" (e.g., see S.T.H., vol. 3, part 1:159–161; Ofer 1988:235–285).

Another tragic event occurred in 1944. In March of 1944 the Nazis invaded Hungary. Adolf Eichman was assigned with the gruesome task of murdering the 800,000 Hungarian Jews (S.T.H., vol. 3, part 1:562–563). On April 25, Eichman called Yoel Brand, an Hungarian Jew, and told him that the Nazis were willing to leave about one million Jews alive if the allies would provide the Wehrmacht with ten thousand trucks (see Bauer 1982:148–191). On May 15, Brand left Hungary with this diabolical "blood for trucks" offer to go to Turkey and from there to Syria. The plan was to present this "deal" to the British. Contrary to given British promises, when Brand arrived in Syria he was arrested by the British authorities. From there he was sent to Cairo where he was imprisoned for three and a half months. Bowyer-Bell states that it was an order from MacMichael which authorized Brand's arrest and shipment to Cairo. By doing this, MacMichael violated a previous promise he gave to Moshe Shartok, from the Jewish Agency, that Brand would not be arrested. The only explanation supposedly given by MacMichael for violating his commitment was that "it is war now" (Bowyer-Bell 1987:95; Katz 1966:185; Bauer 1982:148–191; Hadar 1971).[64]

However, one must notice that the role Brand played was very complicated and the debate whether he, and Kasztner (see case no. 86) were pawns used by Eichman to expedite the extermination of Hungary's Jews, or whether there really was there a blood for trucks deal, has not been entirely resolved.

In any event, Brand's mission failed and from May 1944 the Nazis deported about 450,000 Jews from Hungary to the death camp Auschwitz, where they were systematically gassed and cremated. That happened despite appeals from Jewish leaders to bomb (by air) the railroads leading to Auschwitz, and the camp itself. The appeals were rejected.[65]

It appears that an original reaction to MacMichael was planned by Eliahu Beit-Zuri, Amichai Faglin, and David Danon who developed two different plans to assassinate MacMichael— one with a gun, the other with a knife or an ax. However, this particular group disintegrated before any action was taken.[66]

Another reaction, in November of 1943, was by "Am Lochem" (a short-lived underground Jewish group, which tried to combine members from the three different pre-state Jewish underground groups into a coordinated and focused action. It existed between the autumn of 1943 till January of 1944. See Niv, vol. 3:263–273; S.T.H., vol. 3, part 1:488–492). That group, together with Etzel, planned to kidnap MacMichael and put him on trial as personally responsible for the fate of *Struma,* and then bargain with the British for political concessions. The plan was canceled in the last minute because of the unexpected arrival of a number of British army officers to Jerusalem. Etzel, at that time, did not want to hit British army officers and personnel who fought the Nazis.[67]

The next reactions to MacMichael was more focused, by Lehi, on political assassination. The first unsuccessful attempt occurred on February 3, 1944. Then, Lehi planted a mine in the sewer pipe at the entrance to Saint George Cathedral in Jerusalem. Lehi meant to detonate it by a hundred meter remote control wire when MacMichael was visiting the Church. Eliahu Beit-Zuri was supposed to activate the mine. He received the signal that MacMichael was in the right spot, he activated the trigger, but the mine did not explode. Later, the Church's gardener noticed the unusual marks on the ground and the mine was discovered and dismantled.[68] From this first unsuccessful assassination attempt until August of 1944, a period of seven months, five more unsuccessful attempts against MacMichael were carried out by Lehi's members.

The second unsuccessful attempt occurred near the Protestant Church where the government printing press house in Jerusalem was (near the old, Turkish train station). There, a group of Lehi members waited equipped with submachine guns and camouflaged as painters and geographical surveyors. This group waited in two different days and nothing happened. During their wait in the second day they drew the attention of a nun from a nearby Church and had to quit this plan.[69]

A third unsuccessful attempt focused on a few Lehi's members who waited for MacMichael near the government printing press building in Jerusalem aiming to shoot him with a submachine gun. On the third day of waiting, they had some problems with the escape car and the plan was canceled.[70]

A fourth attempt was made in February of 1944 (Nedava 1974:70). MacMichael planned to visit Cinema Rex in Jerusalem to watch the British propaganda movie *Spitfire*. Lehi's plan was to wait for MacMichael's car and throw a hand grenade into it. The plan was canceled after the apparently irrelevant arrest of a Lehi member, and Lehi's suspicion that the arrest may have been connected to the plan (Shomron 1985:73–74; Yellin-Mor 1974:192).

A fifth unsuccessful attempt was based on the path of MacMichael's morning trip to his office. The idea was based on the fact that at a particular place, MacMichael's car was slowing. The plan was to use submachine guns and hand grenades. However, as the potential assassins were waiting for MacMichael, they were approached by an unsuspecting British patrol and asked to leave the area (without even searching them. They were "loaded" with weapons...). Lehi's members decided not to press their luck and left.[71]

A sixth unsuccessful attempt took place when Lehi learned that MacMichael was planning to attend a concert at the Evelyn De Rothschild school. Banai got a ticket and planned to shoot MacMichael in the theater. MacMichael did not show up (Yellin-Mor 1974:193; Banai 1958:247–248; Shomron 1985:75–76).

On August 8, 1944, the public in Palestine learned that MacMichael was to be replaced. Lehi intensified its efforts. Lehi found out that on Tuesday, August 8, 1944, MacMichael planned to attend an Arab farewell party in Arab Jaffo municipality. Having checked the route to Jaffo, Lehi's members, headed by Yehoshua Cohen, prepared an ambush on the fourth kilometer of the road from Jerusalem to Jaffo, near the Arab village of Lifta. The ambush consisted of three positions each manned by three men, and two signaling posts. At 1620, MacMichael's convoy passed through the ambush. They were attacked by hand grenades and submachine gun fire. While the impression Lehi's members had was that MacMichael could not have possibly survived—he did. His driver drove the car into a rock and outside most of the heavy fire. MacMichael was slightly and insignificantly wounded, his adjutant was very severely wounded, the driver was wounded slightly, and MacMichael's wife was not hurt.[72] None of the participants in the assassination attempt were ever caught.

According to Bowyer-Bell (1987:97), at an unspecified time in 1944, Etzel planted a remote controlled bomb in the road to Jaffo, near Mikve Israel (an agricultural school) aimed to be detonated when MacMichael's car would pass near it. Bowyer-Bell states that Lehi's August 8, 1944, attempt preceded Etzel's attempt and so Etzel had to dismantle the bomb.

From all the attempts on his life, MacMichael could only know about the first and the last. According to Yellin-Mor (1974:195–196) the August 8 attempt made MacMichael very paranoid (and reasonably so) and his departure from Palestine on August 30, 1944 (Niv, vol. 4:54) was under heavy guard, shameful, and without honor.

Yellin-Mor (1974:189–197) Banai (1958:252–253) and Bowyer-Bell (1987:95) all justified the assassination attempts by attributing direct and personal responsibility for the *Patria* and *Struma* tragedies to MacMichael, as well as attributing to him a consistent anti-Jewish position, and blocking the passage of tormented Jewish refugees to Palestine. He was held responsible for Stern's death as well as for the deaths of other Lehi's members. However, the assassination attempts were not only meant as a revenge. They were clearly aimed at the symbol of the British occupation forces, and at a person that Lehi at the time felt was one of the worst enemies of the Jewish struggle to reestablish a Jewish state.

As Cohen G. (1975) showed, almost thirty years later, and as an historical irony, MacMichael was not very sympathetic to the idea of a Jewish homeland until the summer of 1943. However, from the autumn of 1943 he changed his mind and supported a partition plan (as well as Baron Moyne—see case no. 49), which eventually meant supporting a Jewish homeland.

In 1954, Philip Ben interviewed MacMichael in his home in England. MacMichael did not indicate any awareness of the numerous assassination attempts on his life. He denied any responsibility for the *Struma* tragedy and generally tried to minimize his role in Palestine. He told Ben that he was trying to implement an impossible, inconsistent, and contradictory policy and that he was not responsible for the British Mideast policy. One simply *has* to be reminded, at reading MacMichael's lack of memory, evading and "innocent" answers to Ben, that for eight[!] fateful years he was the British high commissioner for Palestine. In essence, the highest British official in Palestine and its actual ruler. Certainly his reports and evaluations, which were sent to London, had a significant impact on crystallizing the British Mideast policy.

CASE NUMBER 48

The Assassination of Wolf Fiedler on October 4, 1944 in Tel Aviv by Etzel

Document 1/21 4ב, page one, in the Jabotinski archives entitled "Executions of Cooperators with the British Intelligence" states that on Wednesday, October 5, 1944, in Tel Aviv, Etzel executed Wolf Fiedler (probably Jewish) after he was found guilty and sentenced to death on charges of giving information to the British.

Ha'aretz (October 5, 1944:4) informed its readers that on October 4, two anonymous males came to Fiedler's house and called him out. Fiedler was single, twenty-three years old and was employed as a cleaning man at Hayarkon hospital. Fiedler came out and walked with the two strangers. On Nachmani Street they shot him five times. He was wounded critically and died shortly after he was brought to a hospital.

Fiedler, who was conscious until he died, told policemen that he did not know who shot him or why. *Ha'aretz* states that Fiedler was a member of Beitar (Jabotinski's group), served for a year and a half in the British airforce and then worked as a guard. About six months before his assassination, he was accepted to work in Hayarkon hospital (October 6, 1944).

Unfortunately, no further information is available about this case. It appears, prima facie, that Etzel may have assassinated, in this particular case, an actor who, ideologically at least, may have been very close to them and even part of their group.

CASE NUMBER 49

The Assassination of Baron Walter Moyne on November 6, 1944 in Cairo by Lehi

Baron Walter Edward Guinness Moyne, British, was born in 1880. He performed several important political roles. Among them, the Minister of state for the Colonies and Leader of the House of Lords from 1941 to February of 1942. He was the Deputy Minister of State, Middle East, between August 1942–January 1944. In January of 1944 he was appointed as Minister Resident in the Middle East, in Cairo.

Yellin-Mor (1974:211–212) states that when in 1941, the British government created the position of the Minister Resident in the Middle East, Abraham Stern (Yair) considered the possibility of assassinating the minister. However, for a variety of reasons, Lehi did not assassinate the first minister Lyttelton, or the second—Richard Casey of Australian origin (for details, see case no. 29). When in 1944 Moyne, the Britisher, replaced Casey, it seemed that Lehi had the "right" target.

At an unspecified date, sometime after Yazernitzky-Shamir escaped from the British detention camp in Mazra on August 31, 1942, he and Israel Sheib (Eldad), as two contemporary and prominent leaders of Lehi, decided to actualize Lehi's policy of personal terror by assassinating Moyne. Three reasons were given for the assassination. One was that Moyne was personally responsible for what the two considered as an anti-Jewish and anti-Zionist British policy. Two, the next person in this job would be careful before repeating Moyne's policy. Three, Lehi would have a public opportunity to explain its cause to the world (Frank 1963:21–23; Shavit 1976:79). In a public announcement, publicized after Moyne's assassination (Lehi *Ketavim* [A]:737-738), Lehi repeated the claims, stating that Moyne was an avowed enemy of the freedom of the Jewish people but added more details: that he was also personally responsible for the disaster of the refugee ships *Patria, Struma,* and others (see the details in the case of MacMichael, no. 47)); that he helped the Arab cause and did not help the Jewish refugees from Europe. In fact, while we know now that Macmichael objected to let the *Patria* get to Palestine. Moyne's objection was *fierce.* It seems that the British could guess what would happen to the *Struma* once it gets to the open sea. They did not want to let its Jewish passengers get to Palestine, but were concerned that the responsibility for the tragic end of that ship would fall squarely on their shoulders (see Ofer 1988:252).

Lehi had a few "good" reasons (from its point of view) to try and hit Moyne. Yazernitzky-Shamir and Sheib, however, did not make any definite, or practical, plans for the assassination.

On the night between October 31 and November 1, 1943, Yellin-Mor, another Lehi leader, escaped from the British detention camp in Latrun. This escape accelerated the preparations for

Moyne's assassination. There was one more development which may have accelerated the preparations even further and that was the blood for trucks deal offered by Eichman (see case no. 47).

As can be recalled, when Brand came from Nazi occupied Hungary with Eichman's "offer," he was arrested and sent to Cairo where he was imprisoned for three and a half months. In Cairo he (may have) met with Moyne to discuss Eichman's offer. Brand states that when Moyne heard about the Nazi offer to release about one million Jews he responded by saying "How do you imagine it, Mr. Brand. What shall I do with those million Jews? Where shall I send them?" (Brand 1957:155; Brand 1960:49–79; Niv, vol. 4:80–81; Ayalon 1980; Rosenfeld 1955; Bauer 1982:148–191; see also Hadar 1971). In 1949 Yellin-Mor in fact testified in court that Moyne was assassinated because of his involvement in the *Struma* affair and the Brand affair (see *Ha'aretz*, January 23, 1949:1).

Wasserstein (1982) argues that the "account" supposedly given by Moyne to Brand was a propaganda fabrication by Lehi, and that Moyne and Brand probably never met. Even if this interpretation is true, the fact remains that Lehi used the account. Hence, true or not, the use of Moyne's supposedly account to Brand was embedded in, and supported by, a particular social construction of reality, which must have been very plausible to Lehi's command, and members.

One can safely assume that Lehi's high command was not aware of Moyne's supposed account to Brand when it decided to assassinate Moyne (e.g., see Eldad 1962:31). However, and from Lehi's retrospective point of view, this certainly could mark the culmination of what they already saw as Moyne's committed anti-Jewish and anti-Zionist stands. He was also active in consistent and systematic actions, and speeches (e.g., see S.T.H., vol. 3, part 1:655–657; Lehi *Ketavim* [A]:458–460), against the creation of a Jewish homeland (Niv, vol. 4:81; Kanaan 1975). For Lehi, 1944 seemed ripe for his assassination.

Lehi had a branch in Egypt, which was organized by Binyamin Geffner. He was given instructions to put Moyne under surveillance and to start making the necessary preparations for the assassination. When Geffner left Cairo he was replaced by Joseph Sittner (see case no. 50) who continued the preparations.

Two other Lehi's members were sent to Cairo for the actual act—Eliahu Beit-Zouri, twenty-two years old, and Eliahu Hakim, seventeen years old. They were given full authority to devise and execute the assassination.

On Monday, November 6, 1944, at around noon, Beit-Zouri and Hakim waited for Baron Moyne near the entrance to his home. Moyne returned in his car with his military aid, and secretary, at around 1310. As Moyne's driver got out of the car to open the door for Moyne, Hakim and Beit-Zouri, armed with hand guns, jumped from their nearby hiding place. Hakim shot Moyne three times, and Beit Zouri shot and killed the driver who tried to protect Moyne.

Hakim and Beit-Zouri tried to use their escape plan. They took their bicycles and began their escape ride. A motorcycled Egyptian policeman who happened to be nearby started to chase them. Hakim tried to shoot the policeman, he shot back. Hakim was hurt and fell. Beit-Zouri returned to help him. Both assassins were surrounded now by an angry mob. The policeman arrived very quickly to the scene and both assassins were arrested.

Baron Moyne was badly injured. He was taken to the military hospital in Cairo where he received blood transfusions and was operated on. However, his wounds were too severe. He died later that day at around 2030.

After their arrest, Hakim and Beit-Zouri were charged with murder before an Egyptian court. Hakim and Beit-Zouri certainly saw themselves as political prisoners (Ben-Yehuda 1990:90–93) and turned the trial into a political event. Both assassins presented a a defense that was based on using what apparently were proud and uncompromising national accounts. They admitted that they assassinated Moyne because of his, and his government's, involvement in the massacre of hundreds of thousands of Jews and in robbing the Jewish homeland. Both admitted that they were "soldiers in Lehi."

There cannot be any question regarding the fact that their proud stand in court amplified Lehi's ideology and cause worldwide. Both were found guilty and on January 11, 1945, were sentenced to death. Hakim and Beit-Zouri were hanged in Cairo on March 23, 1945, in the morning. They were buried in Egypt. In 1975 their remnants were brought for burial in Israel, and in

1982 the government of Israel decided to issue special stamps dedicated to their memory.[73]

Were there any results to this assassination? The answer is yes. First, there can be no doubt that the publicity which Lehi gained as a result of the assassination and of Hakim and Beit-Zouri's defense, was of global proportions.

Second, the Yishuv, the Etzel and the Hagana, reacted very negatively to the assassination. Ben-Gurion, Weitzman, and Shartok—all major contemporary Jewish leaders—were apparently shaken and appalled. Weitzman even told Churchill's secretary (John Martin) that Moyne's assassination shook him more than the loss of his RAF (the British Royal Air Force) pilot son in 1942. Ben-Gurion stated explicitly that no British interest was endangered by the act but that "it was like sticking a knife into the Jewish people's back." The assassination marked the beginning of the "Season," the "hunting season," when members of the Hagana publicly and openly began to harass and kidnap, torture, and give to the British especially members of the Etzel, (the Hagana may have simply used the opportunity "to close its account" with Etzel). Following the assassination, Lehi buried itself even deeper underground and was inactive for almost a year. The strange fact is that the hunting season, much provoked by the assassination, was directed by the Hagana primarily against Etzel and not against Lehi.[74]

Third, Wasserstein (1982), Bauer (1970:90-91; 1974), Ayalon (1982) and Cohen M. J. (1979) all state that before Moyne's assassination, the British Cabinet received a report from its Palestine Committee. "The report, which would have recommended giving to the Jews a state of their own in Palestine, had been minuted for the Cabinet's agenda on 3 November 1944.... After the assassination on 6 November, Churchill gave orders to hold the item, it was impossible to discuss the future of Palestine while such outrages continue" (Cohen M. J. 1979:370). It is not clear whether the Cabinet would have had—in fact—cleared the way for establishing the state of Israel already in 1945, however the assassination—very clearly—gave a few very good excuses to the opposition (ibid.).

It may thus be that in 1944 both MacMichael and Moyne supported the establishment of a Jewish state, not because they were such great supporters of the Zionist-Jewish cause, but because they supported what they thought were the British interests and realized that a Jewish state could, perhaps, promote those interests. Furthermore, Churchill who traditionally supported the Zionist-Jewish cause, was so appalled by the assassination of his close friend Moyne, that he started to drift away from his traditional support. For the above mentioned particular group of scholars, Moyne's assassination symbolizes a loss of opportunity for the Zionist movement—that of the possibility that Israel could have been a reality already in 1945. More support for this speculation may be found in the Yalta summit which took place in February of 1945. There, Stalin and Roosevelt seemed supportive of the idea of a Jewish state, but Churchill—in the brief occasion when the subject was discussed—was "roaringly" quiet (Wasserstein 1982:16–17). Moreover, Churchill's position that Moyne was not such an enemy of the Zionist cause did receive some substantiation (e.g., see Cohen M. 1978:169; see also Cohen M. 1978 for the complementary details, including Harold MacMichael's stand. See also case no. 47).

For a rebuttal, pro-Lehi interpretation of Moyne's assassination see Hakim (1982). Hakim maintains that even without Moyne's assassination, the British government would not have created a Jewish homeland in 1945.

CASE NUMBER 50

The Assassination of Joseph Davidesku on August 20, 1945 by Lehi

As can be recalled from the assassination of Israel Pritzker (on September 3, 1943, see case no. 39), of Valentin Back (on June 22, 1939, see case no. 16) and the attempts on Moshe Rotstein's life (in 1939, see case no. 12), Davidesku was another agent of Pritzker.

Davidesku had an interesting personal history. He was born in 1891 and at the age of twenty-two he joined a local (near Haifa) Jewish defense group: the "Gideonim."[75] A picture from 1913 of the Gideonim shows Davidesku as part of the group. When First World war began, Davidesku joined the Turkish Army. He got out of the service after a short time and began to work for Nily (see case no. 3), and supplied the British with vital information. In 1919, he won a British citation and a letter of gratitude from the Hanhala Zionit in Jerusalem for his help to the British empire. From the beginning of the British occupation of Palestine, Davidesku was active in various intelligence activities, especially good was his reputed ability to disguise himself as an Arab and secure information about the Arabs. Hence, Davidesku worked in the British intelligence within the Arab department.[76] From 1921, Davidesku's intelligence activities included also help to the Hagana, and later to Etzel and Lehi too. It seems that his ideological committment was to help the Yishuv generally, and not any particular group within it (Karpel 1990).

As was mentioned in case no. 49 (assassination of Moyne), Lehi's representative in Cairo, who was partly responsible for the planning and execution of Baron Moyne there on November 6, 1944, was Joseph Sittner (later Galili). After the assassination the British began to search for the actors involved in the assassination, including Sittner. According to Banai (1958:342) and Eliav (1983:274–275)—two members of Lehi—British intelligence agents discovered that Sittner was in Palestine and they instructed Davidesku to locate him. Davidesku agreed but told the British that he would do it under one condition—that after Sittner would be in British hands he, Davidesku, would leave the country.

Tidhar's account is very different (1960–61:309–312). Tidhar states that during all of Davidesku's years of work for the British intelligence he gave the Hagana, Etzel, and Lehi information (for a fee). In 1945, the son of a woman named Koblancz was arrested by the British intelligence on suspicion that he was a member of Etzel. His mother, a woman from Zichron Ya'acov (near Haifa) pulled all the strings she could in order to get her son out. Davidesku, himself from Zichron Ya'acov, was put under a lot of pressure to help Koblancz. Koblancz was arrested in Yaffo, so Davidesku went to Yaffo to plead for him. There, officer O'Sullivan who was in charge, promised him that Koblancz would be released. O'sullivan did not keep his promise, but did put Davidesku under surveillance. While Davidesku probably told O'sullivan that he met with Sittner he did not tell him where. That was not necessary because Davidesku was under British surveillance. Thus, after one of Davidesku's meetings with Sittner, British detectives sprang into the coffee house where they met and arrested Sittner. Tidhar's account does not mention whether Davidesku asked the British intelligence to get him out of Palestine.

Karpel (1990) offers a somewhat different interpretation, more suitable perhaps to the dark world of intelligence and counter intelligence scheming. She suggests the following interpretation. Rafael Sadovsky, an Egyptian Jew who was also part of the Lehi organization in Egypt, was arrested in March 1945. Under investigation, he gave his British interrogators the names of all the members of Lehi's group in Egypt, including Sittner. Consequently, Sittner was arrested too. Somehow, Sittner managed to escape from the prison, defected from the British airforce (which he had previously joined) and returned to Palestine. There, he met with Ya'acov Banai (Mazal) and Itzhak Yazernitzky-Shamir (Michael), from Lehi and gave them his version of the events in Cairo. In Palestine, Sittner assumed a new identity and met with Davidesku once a week to get information. According to Sittner, Davidesku was giving the British information about their conversations. After one of their meetings, the British ambushed and arrested Sittner. From his prison cell, Sittner managed to smuggle a letter to Lehi's headquarters in which he accused Davidesku in the squealing that led to his arrest. Lehi's headquarters felt that Davidesku was a traitor and had to be executed.

Karpel raises a few disturbing questions regarding Sittner's role. First, it may be possible that he worked for the Hagana's Shai before he joined the British Air Force and gave the Hagana information on Lehi. Second, his unclear "escape" from British detention in Egypt is strange too. Finally, following Sittner's second arrest by the British (in Palestine), he was not tortured, and was not bitter (about Davidesku), and got "only" a two years sentence for his role in the assassination of Moyne.

Be it Banai's and Eliav's versions, Tidhar's or Karpel's, Lehi was not the type of organization to take lightly Sittner's arrest. From the minute Davidesku was held responsible for Sittner's arrest his fate was sealed. On Monday, August 20, 1945 at around 2045 a team of four Lehi's members: Moshe Bar-Giora and Abraham Yehudai, escorted by two females for cover, approached Davidesku's house in Zichron Ya'acov (Eliav states that he was not far behind watching the action. 1983:275–276). There Davidesku was sitting in his room talking to an acquaintance, Arie Niederman. Eliav states that Moshe Bar-Giora got to the window of the room and fired two shots which hit Davidesku in the head and killed him. Banai (ibid.) states that both—Bar-Giora and Yehudai—fired at Davidesku. According to Ha'aretz (August 21, 1945:4) and the Palestine Post (August 21, 1945:1) twelve shots were fired at Davidesku. Davidesku, fifty-four years old at the time of the incident, died immediately. After the assassination, the assassins fled the place. None was ever caught (see also Okev 1949:15–17).[77]

After the assassination, Lehi's public announcement stated that Davidesku was a squealer and betrayed Jewish fighters to the British intelligence, which were the reasons for his execution (Lehi, Ketavim [A]:1021–1022).

CASE NUMBER 51

The Assassination Attempts on Ernest Bevin's Life in 1945–1948 by Lehi—Preplanned, Planned, and Unsuccessful

Ernest Bevin (1881–1951), British, developed a political career in the British Labor party. He was appointed as the British Minister of Foreign Affairs in the winter of 1945, a position he held until 1950. While before being appointed as the minister he showed some sympathy for the Jewish-Zionist ideology and enterprise, after his nomination he demonstrated consistent and extreme anti-Zionist and pro-Arabic positions, at a period which was very crucial to the reestablishment of Israel.[78]

We found about six different recorded attempts to assassinate Bevin. Since all attempts lack dating, I must assume that they probably took place between 1945–1948 (when Bevin's activity was perceived to be at the most relevant anti Israeli peak).

The first plan was to stop Bevin's car with another car and kill him. This plan failed because the potential assassin ("Avner") lacked a car, or the resources to buy one (Ha'aretz, May 15, 1959:2; Avner 1959:115–121). The second plan involved using a "booby trapped" book. The explosive book was put underneath the first bench in the House of Lords. Unfortunately for Lehi, the woman who put the bomb there got "cold feet" and after a few weeks threw it into the river Thames (*Ha'aretz*, May 15, 1959:2; Avner 1959:130–150). The third attempt took place when Bevin went out from his car for a meeting and was supposed to be shot by a potential assassin, but a last minute unknown event prevented the assassination (Katz 1966:243). Two more attempts focused on trying to attack Bevin as he was driving in London. These attempts were not carried out because of technical problems in timing. Katz (1966:243), who reports on the last two attempts, attributes the source of the information to an anonymous female Lehi member. The last, sixth, attempt is reported by Bowyer-Bell (1987:305) who describes a plan by Herouti, a member of Lehi, to assassinate Bevin on his way to his office. However, Yellin-Mor, Lehi's commander at the time, called Herouti at the last minute and for an unknown reason(s) ordered him to cancel the plan. All six attempts were made by members of Lehi.

CASE NUMBER 52

The Assassination of Benjamin Kurfirst Sometime between January and March 1946 by the Hagana

Benjamin Kurfirst was born Jewish in Danzig, Poland, in 1919, as the youngest son in his family. He immigrated to Palestine when he was twenty years old with his mother and a few brothers in 1939.

In the winter of 1946, Mordechai Ya'akubovitz and Rafi Frumer served in the Palmach's company stationed in Kibbutz Ayelet Hashachar in the northern part of Palestine. One day, in the afternoon Kurfirst, unknown to anybody in Ayelet Hashachar, arrived to the Kibbutz and demanded to see the kibbutz's secretary. He offered to sell Italian machine guns in commercial quantities for low prices. Eliahu Lipetz, the secretary—as well as Ya'akubovitz and Frumer—became very suspicious. However, before they decided to arrest him—Kurfirst escaped. To no avail. Ya'akubovitz and Frumer chased caught and arrested him. They placed him under their guard in Kibbutz Ayelet Hashachar, and later moved him to Dardara (near the Kinneret shore).

An interrogator (probably Yehoshua Blum, one of the Hagana's most enigmatic figures, [see Edelist 1987]) from the Shai (the Hagana's intelligence service) arrived and interrogated Kurfirst, sometimes using torture. As the interrogation unfolded, it became clear that Kurfirst was hired by the British intelligence. Kurfirst told his interrogator that he was caught by the British having committed a few criminal acts. In return for suspending the charges against him, he agreed to serve the British intelligence. One of his first tasks was to persuade Kibbutz Ayelet Hashachar to purchase—illegally—weapons. His contact point was Sergeant Joseph Killy from the Haifa British intelligence (see also case no. 70). The purpose of this provocation was obvious—once the Kibbutz agreed to buy the weapons, the British would have had the excuse, and probable cause, to search the Kibbutz where, they suspected, the Hagana hid illicit weapons and ammunition.

The Hagana appointed a court, probably headed by the late Aviezer Friedman. They weighed the evidence against Kurfirst, charged him with treason, and sentenced him to death. The execution took place at night, a day after the trial. He was shot in the head and buried in an anonymous place. Kurfirst's brother claimed that Benjamin served in Lehi. I checked on July 7, 1987, with Anshell Shpillman—head of Lehi's archives—and it is quite obvious that Benjamin was not a member of Lehi. Kurfirst's interrogation took about six weeks, his trial one day. While both Ya'akubovitz and Blum claimed that a protocol of the proceedings in the trial was written—it is not available. The case itself was not publicized, and Kurfirst's family did not know, until July of 1987[!] what happened to their son/brother (see Nakdimon 1987; Ya'akubovitz 1953, 1967; and a taped interview with Ya'akubovitz from June 19, 1987). The case itself probably took place during the months of January, February, and March of 1946. Better dating is not available.

Kurfirst was assassinated by actors from a specific symbolic-moral universe—the Hagana. That organization provided the legitimation and procedure for Kurfirst's assassination. It created the processes and definition of reality which eventually led to Kurfirst's death. The strange fact is that contrary to Etzel and Lehi who made sure that when they assassinated similar actors on equivalent background charges, (e.g., see the cases involving Kadia Mizrahi, Chaya Zeidenberg, Israel Pritzker, as well as others) they tried to give wide publicity to the cases, the Hagana did not. And not only in this case (more on this particular issue in the analysis).

CASE NUMBER 53

The Assassination Attempt on Inspector Raymond Cafferata on February 15, 1946 in Haifa by Etzel and Lehi—Unsuccessful

The week of the 20th to the 24th of August 1929 witnessed some of the worst anti-Jewish attacks by Arabs in Hebron. All in all, sixty-seven Jews were murdered there. The chief of police in Hebron at that time was Raymond Cafferata (1897–1966). While S.T.H. (vol. 2, part 1:320–323) indicates that Cafferata tried to stop the Arab mob, and that he himself (with the aid of a Jewish policeman) even killed eight of the Arab rioters, Lehi (Ketavim [B]1982:553) apparently felt that—to a very large extent—he did not do enough to protect the Jews in Hebron. In total contradiction, Jones (1979:21) states that Cafferata, who was a police officer from 1922, and deputy district superintendent of police from 1936, "was instrumental in saving many ultra-orthodox Jews of Hebron from massacre during the 1929 riots..."

Inspector Cafferata was again involved in a bloody action against Jews on November 16, 1943, in Ramat Hasharon. Under some pretenses, Inspector Cafferata lead a police and army force that was supposed to search Ramat Hasharon. During the search, which was extremely violent, Inspector Cafferata and his men opened fire and fourteen Jewish citizens were wounded, one died (S.T.H., vol. 3, part 1:182–186).

Another bloody search, directed by Inspector Cafferata, took place on November 25, 1945. Then he lead British forces which attempted to search Kibbutz Givat Chaim. The search ended in a blood bath when the British police tried to enter into the kibbutz by force, killing eight kibbutzniks and wounding numerous others (S.T.H., vol. 3, part 2:862–865).

Since at least 1944, Inspector Cafferata was transferred to the Haifa police. At that time, he was already identified as "one of the most dangerous underground persecutors" (Niv, vol.

4:230). On October 16, 1944, Asher Trattner, from Etzel, was caught in Haifa pasting Etzel's wall pamphlets. He was interrogated and cruelly treated and tortured by Cafferata (Livni 1987:178). Trattner died on November 11, 1944.

In 1946, Etzel felt it had it with Cafferata. When Lehi's members (who in 1946 joined Etzel and the Hagana to form a short-lived joint command) suggested to assassinate Cafferata, Etzel agreed. The Hagana did not object as they too had a long and a bloody account with Cafferata (Livni 1987:178).

Members of Etzel and Lehi waited for Cafferata's car along Ben-Yehuda and Masada streets in Haifa. They planned to shoot Cafferata and to throw one and a half kilograms of TNT into his car. On Friday, February 15, 1946, everything was ready. However, in the last minute Cafferata's driver—who had good instincts—managed to by-pass the truck that was supposed to stop his car. The TNT exploded without causing any damage, and the shots fired at Cafferata's car did not hit anybody (Livni 1987:179; Ha'aretz, February 17, 1946:2). While Etzel tried to follow Cafferata again and execute a new assassination plan, Cafferata became very careful and left Palestine after a short while. According to Niv (vol. 5:221) Etzel in England, in 1947, considered again to assassinate Cafferata. Since Etzel members in England could not locate Cafferata, no plan to assassinate him ever crystallized (Tavin 1973:171). In any event, no more assassination attempts against Cafferata were carried out.

CASE NUMBER 54

The Assassination Attempts on Guthelf Wagner's Life in Tel Aviv on March 22, 1946 by a Palmach Unit

The Templars were a German-Christian pietist sect which established settlements in Palestine in the nineteenth and twentieth centuries. The Templars separated in 1858 from the Lutheran Church and reorganized themselves as a separate group. One of their major goals was to settle in Palestine so as to accelerate the apocalyptic vision of the prophets. The number of the Templars in 1810 reached five thousand. They began to actually establish settlements in the late 1860s and early 1870s. Despite a disheartening beginning, and severe hardships, they were able to root themselves in a few places: in Jerusalem, Haifa, and Jaffo. In 1875, they had seven hundred people in Palestine, and twelve hundred in 1914. They subsisted on their work in hotels, commerce, and small industry. In 1917–1918, and with the British conquest, the Templars were exiled as enemy citizens. After the war ended, they were allowed to return and in 1937 there were about two thousand fifty Templars in the country (Kanaan 1968:24).

The Templar movement in Germany, dissipated, more or less. In Palestine, however, they managed to keep their special identity, as well as hidden feelings of nationalism. When National-Socialism, and Hitler, appeared it seemed that most Templars joined the Nazi movement. Their position was consistently anti-Jewish[79] and very sympathetic to Nazi Germany and Hitler's National-Socialism. In 1937, about 34 percent of the Templars were formal members in the Nazi party. In 1935, Burgermeister Guthelf Wagner declared, at the Templars' general assembly in Jaffo, that the goals of Nazism were identical with those of the Templars and that therefore the Templars accepted Nazism (Kanaan 1968:57).

In 1939, when second world war began, most Templars were put by the British in detention camps (Kanaan 1968:96–110). In May of 1940, there were one thousand six Templars in four different settlements (Kanaan 1968:100). On July 31, 1941, six hundred and sixty-one Templars were sent via Egypt to Australia aboard the *Queen Mary*. They arrived to Australia in August 24, 1941, where they were put in a detention camp. There were about three hundred and forty-five Templars left in Palestine.

There is enough evidence to indicate that the Templars were involved not only in Nazi propaganda against Jews in Palestine, but were active in helping Arab groups attack Jews, as well as supplying arms, weapons, and explosives to the Arabs, and spying too (Kanaan 1968:96–110).

As the Nazi atrocities against the Jews during second world war became more and more evident, the Jewish underground groups in Palestine became more and more unhappy with the Templars presence. True, when the war broke out the British concentrated the Templars in camps, and deported many to Australia and Germany—but that was not satisfactory for the Jewish underground groups.

Of particular interest was the Templar Burgermeister Guthelf Wagner (born in Stutgart), who declared publicly his total identification with Nazism, and whose membership number in the Nazi party was 7024779 (Kanaan 1968:143). Wagner owned a mechanical plant/factory in Jaffo and intelligence reports indicated that this factory supplied Arab gangs/groups with mines, bombs, bullets, as well as repairing their weapons (Kanaan 1968:93; Dekel 1953:182–186).

Livni (1987:28–29; see also Niv, vol. 3:260–261) who was a commander in Etzel, in charge of operations, describes what was probably the first attempt on Guthelf Wagner's life on Sunday, May 16, 1943. Livni, and a few other members from Etzel, planted a powerful bomb, with a timing device, in the main assembly hall of the Templars in Sharona. While they wanted to hit the Templars generally, they clearly intended to hit Wagner because he "was known as a Nazi zealot" (p. 29; see also Kanaan 1964:372). The operation was successful, as Etzel's members managed to plant the bomb. It exploded the next morning, May 16, 1943. Part of the hall was destroyed, six members of the Templars were wounded, as well as Wagner himself. Livni states that two months after the act, all the Germans were exiled from Palestine to Australia aboard the *Queen Mary* (Livni's dates are probably incorrect. The "Queen Mary," with the Templars, left in July of 1941). While Etzel did want to hit Wagner, Livni stated very clearly (interview March 11, 1988), that the act was *not* aimed against Wagner particularly, but against the Templars generally. Hence, the May 16 act should be classified more as an act of terror.

As is evident, not all Templars left Palestine. After the war ended, the Hagana felt that the British were inclined to let the Templars stay, and even bring the exiled Templars back from Australia (Gilad 1955, vol. 1:587). The Jewish Agency sent a memo to a British-American investigation committee, demanding that the German Templars should not be allowed to stay in, or return to, Palestine. The British, however, were not as sensitive (S.T.H., vol. 3, part 2:1317–1318).

The Hagana, and its operational striking force—Palmach—

decided "to warn the authorities and the Germans themselves that we would not allow the Germans to exist in our country" (ibid.). Accordingly, a unit of Palmach reserve people from Tel Aviv was sent to assassinate Guthelf Wagner. What made this assassination easy was the fact that Wagner used to go every day to manage his factory on the border between Tel Aviv and Yaffo, escorted by British or Arab bodyguards.

Itzhak Sade, commander of the Palmach, gave the direct order to assassinate Wagner. A unit of five Palmach members (four males and one female) waited for Wagner on the morning of Friday, March 22, 1946, on Levinsky Street in Tel Aviv. They chose the place after a long surveillance which revealed Wagner's pattern of behavior. They chose the spot along the way that Wagner used to drive to his factory in Jaffo. On that day Wagner himself drove the car, escorted by an Arab armed guard and another German in the back seat. The Palmach unit stopped Wagner's car and disarmed the Arab body guard who surrendered to them. One male assassin pointed his revolver—a Parabelum—at Wagner but he had a sterile bullet. The other male assassin got into action and used his own gun to kill Wagner.[80] The Voice of Israel announced the next day that the "known Nazi Wagner was executed and that the authorities were warned that a Nazi foot would not step in Eretz Israel."

Since the Hagana thought that the warning was not taken too seriously, a unit of Palmach attacked on November 17, 1946, a group of Germans, guarded by Arabs, that returned around 1700 from Haifa to their detention camp in Waldheim. "The two German males were shot and killed. The female and Arab guards were not touched" (S.T.H., ibid.; see also *Davar*, November 19, 1946).

What was the impact of the assassination of Wagner? S.T.H. (ibid.), Gilad (ibid.) and Kanaan (1968:115) have no doubt "the assassination of Guthelf Wagner caused a severe shock to all the Templars. They understood that the probability of their return to their houses and farms in Eretz Israel was very low and thin. They began to worry for the life of the Templars in Palestine" (Kanaan 1968:115). The British apparently arrived to similar conclusions. In 1946, there were two hundred and eighty Templars and forty-eight Germans in Palestine (Kanaan 1968:117).

While the final deportation was not quick, in April of 1948, the British finally ordered the Templars to leave. On April 20, 1948, three hundred Templar and Germans left the country. The history of a long German settlement in Palestine came to an end. The very clear signals given to the pro-Nazi Templars and Germans were unmistakable.

What we have in this case are two plots. One (Etzel's) was aimed against the Templars and Wagner, the other (Hagana's) was aimed against Wagner exclusively. The reasons for the two plots were identical-to rid the country of pro-Nazi Germans. Hence, two rather different underground Jewish groups, distinguishable by dissimilar symbolic-moral universes (Etzel right wing, Hagana left wing) sponsored a similar action.

CASE NUMBER 55

The Assassination Plot(s) against the Jerusalem Arab Mufti—Haj Amin Al-Husseini in May 1946—Planned

From the Jewish point of view, the Arab Mufti—Haj Amin AL Husseini—was a particularly effective and poisonous anti-Semite and anti-Zionist.

Haj Amin AL-Husseini was born in Jerusalem in 1893. He emerged as an extreme Arab nationalist and was active politically since 1919. He was sentenced in absentia to ten years in prison for his role in the Arab, April 1920, anti-Jewish riots in Jerusalem (see case no. 4) but was reprieved in 1921. In an attempt to appease the Arabs, the British high commissioner, Sir Herbert Samuel, appointed AL-Husseini in 1921 as the Mufti of Jerusalem, the supreme religious authority of the Moslems in Palestine. In 1922, he was also appointed as chairman of the Supreme Muslim council. He used both positions to advocate and advance his extreme anti-British and anti-Jewish views and was effectively and instrumentally involved in the Arab riots and rebellion in 1929 and 1936. When these disorders subsided and deteriorated into terrorism, the British forces began a "search and hunt" operation after Al-Husseini. Dressed as a woman, he escaped in October of 1937 first to Lebanon, then to Damascus, and by using ties with German and Italian agents, he fled to Iraq.

When a pro-German coup in Iraq failed, he escaped to Germany. There he became an ardent supporter of Nazi Germany. He met with Hitler, helped to recruit and organize Arab volunteers, and aided and supported the Nazi program of extermination of the Jews. He planned to construct extermination camps in Palestine for the Jews and was probably involved in a failed Nazi attempt to poison the water wells in Palestine.[81]

There are a few recorded cases of assassination plots against the Mufti. One was preplanned (see case no. 11) by key actors in the Hagana. On another preplanned attempt reports Katz (1966:85). Although a date is not given, this particular preplanning must have been around 1936–1937. Katz reports about an Arab reporter who joined the Mufti's headquarters. That reporter made it known to an Etzel friend of his that for two hundred pounds he was willing to help assassinate the Mufti. Katz, who clearly states that for him the decision about political assassination was guided by pragmatic (not moral) issues, decided nevertheless to consult with Jabotinski. Jabotinski totally opposed political assassinations and he instructed Katz in a cable not to proceed. Katz expresses regret for having obeyed Jabotinski on this issue at the time.

In May of 1940 David Raziel—then commander of Etzel—agreed to go to Iraq on a secret mission on behalf of the British. At that time, Iraq's political leadership was very sympathetic to Nazi Germany, and the Mufti found there a comfortable home. As Naor points out (1990:268) one of the main reasons for Raziel's agreement was his hope that once in Iraq, he could capture the Mufti. That plan never worked out as Raziel was killed in Iraq during an air raid (see Naor 1990:265–279).

Another attempt, which went beyond the preplanning stage, was made by Ya'acov Eliav. In his memoirs, Eliav (1983:343) who at that time was Lehi's representative in Europe, states that after the second world war ended, and probably sometime in 1945–1946 he learned that Al-Husseini escaped from Germany and found refuge in France, near Paris. Here is his account: "Haj Amin Al-Husseini headed the Arab rioters in Eretz Israel against the Jewish settlements, since its beginning. During second world war he was in Germany and helped Hitler to exterminate European Jews, waiting anxiously for the Nazi conquest of Eretz

Israel in order to exterminate the Jews in Eretz Israel. He came to Paris to save himself. The surveillance of my men showed that the best way was to blow up the Mufti in his car. I prepared a powerful mine that would not have left much of the Mufti. However, the surveillance before actually planting the mine (in the car) indicated that the Mufti was suddenly gone. Thus, I was prevented from finishing my service in Europe with an unprecedented achievement, and as a warning to the anti-Israeli Arab states..."

Clearly Eliav had the power, authority and legitimacy as well as the man power, skills, and resources to take the initiative in planning and executing a political assassination. He was Lehi's representative in Europe and his plan was obviously based on the idea of getting rid of somebody he saw as a dangerous political enemy, as well as a warning sign.

Dating Eliav's plan is difficult. Eliav came to Europe in May of 1946 and was there until September of 1947 when he was arrested in Belgium. The Mufti landed in Berne's airport on May 7, 1945, and was deported by the Swiss authorities to France at the French frontier at Linetau. From there, he was transferred to Paris (Schechtman 1965:167). The British demanded that he be given to them and the assumption was that his stay in Paris was only a temporary short delay before his deportation to the British (ibid.). Meanwhile, Haj Amin lived, under French surveillance at the villa "Les Roses" in a Paris suburb. On May 29, 1946, the Mufti managed to escape French surveillance and boarded a TWA flight to Cairo, where he landed at the same day (Schechtman 1965:186–191) and where he remained. This dating, considering that Eliav's men surveillance was intensive, has to place the attempt somewhere in May of 1946.

Naor (1988:149) reports that Hanokmim (see chapter 5) also planned to assassinate the Mufti. According to Naor (who quotes Zorea), Chaim Laskov planned to assassinate Haj Amin Al-Husseini in Paris. He planned to use some of the best snipers he had (probably from the the second battalion of the Jewish Brigade) for that act. While the group of snipers was in Paris planning, and preparing for, the assassination, the Hagana's headquarters called them and instructed them to quit the action.[82] No further information is available on this particular action.

CASE NUMBER 56

The Assassination of Sergeant T. G. Martin on September 9, 1946 in Haifa by Lehi

Yellin-Mor (1974:403) states that Sergeant T. G. Martin was perceived as dangerous to Lehi as was Conquest (who was assassinated on April 26, 1947—see case no. 67).

Sergeant T. G. Martin was certainly one of the British experts of the CID (Criminal Investigation Department) concerning the Jewish underground. In the month of July 1946 the CID conducted intensive searches in Tel Aviv to locate and arrest members of the underground. One of the people in the lines waiting to be identified was Itzhak Yazernitzky-Shamir (Michael), who was dressed as an orthodox rabbi and camouflaged by a thick black beard—to no avail. Martin looked at Shamir and recognized him. Furthermore, to be sure, Martin sneaked secretly behind Shamir and called his underground name (Michael)—Shamir's response left no place for hesitation—he was arrested and on July 23 he was flown by the British to exile in Africa.[83] This arrest was most certainly the most important achievement of the British in that search operation. Much credit went to Martin and the whole incident received widespread coverage in the press.

Following Shamir's arrest Lehi decided that Martin had to be assassinated (Shomron 1985:208; Banai 1958:483). Martin served in the CID in Haifa and, as usual, he was put under surveillance. Martin lived in the German colony in Haifa and every day he used to walk to his work, passing the tennis courts. This habit helped Lehi to crystallize the assassination plan. On the morning of Monday, September 9, 1946, two tennis "players" staged a game. They were actually Lehi's members. They waited for Martin to pass by. Martin did not disappoint them. At the usual time he went to his work and passed near the "tennis players." He apparently became suspicious. Martin may have tried to draw his gun but was too slow. The players drew two hand guns and shot Martin to death. Both retreated successfully and were never caught.[84]

Shamir himself denies that he had anything to do with the decision to assassinate Martin but "had they consulted me—I would have approved. Martin was one of the most active people in the British intelligence and was emotionally involved in the struggle against us. The newspapers publicized the fact that it was Martin who identified me. Well, this was a challenge. Speaking from the point of view of morale it was very important for us to act. To demonstrate to the Jewish people. It can be said that he himself signed his own death sentence" (Bethell 1979:223).

CASE NUMBER 57

The Assassination of Israel Lewin on December 24, 1946 in Tel Aviv by Lehi

Israel Lewin, a twenty-four year old Jewish male from Bnei Brak (near Tel Aviv) was found dead, shot in the head, near the entrance to "Hadassa Garden" in north Tel Aviv, on Tuesday, December 24, 1946 (*Ha'aretz*, December 25, 1946:8). Lewin was born in Poland and came to Palestine during World War II. He was married and had two children.

In an announcement to the press and to the public (ibid. and Lehi's *Ketavim* [B]:359–360) it became evident that Lewin was executed by Lehi. According to Lehi's announcement, he was accused of, and confessed, the following "crimes" before a Lehi's court: (a) cooperation with the British intelligence (with an officer named Tulson) especially helping the British by giving them information about the illegal Jewish immigration to Palestine. For this activity the British supposedly offered Lewin a salary, (b) together with others (Shalom Friedman and Herman Tamary) they presented themselves as Lehi members and extorted money from a coffee shop ("Hamozeg") in Haifa, (c) Lewin supposedly betrayed a Lehi member to the british intelligence, (d) he, and others (Curtis and Sa'adia) worked out a plan to capture an important member of the Jewish underground in return for a large sum of money. Lehi's announcement states that a death sentence was given and executed, only after a thorough investigation. Lehi assured the public that Lewin was executed only on the basis of solid and reliable evidence. Furthermore, the announcement denounced and warned "traitors, squealers, provocateurs and blackmailers that they will be punished severely." No details are available regarding the nature of the "solid" evidence, the trial, its length, and so forth.

Ha'aretz (ibid:4) provides some more details. "On Saturday night, two males and one female arrived to Lewin's apartment in Bnei Brak. They told Lewin that they *were* the court of Lehi and began immediately with the 'procedure.' They accused him of cooperation with the British police and of extorting money. They said that Lewin admitted his guilt. The whole "procedure" took two hours. After consultations, they told Lewin that he was sentenced to death, because they found him guilty of treason, squealing and extortion. Lewin and his wife started to cry, pleading mercy on behalf of their young children. Following some more consultations, the three told them that they decided to replace the 'death sentence' with 'severe physical beating'. On Monday, Lewin went to Jerusalem and when he returned he was taken by a few anonymous people to Tel Aviv where he was executed. It is guessed that they decided to change the verdict back to 'death' after they found out that Lewin, despite their warning from Saturday, went to meet British intelligence officers in Jerusalem.... Lewin's partner in the extortion...in Haifa... was...severely beaten and his right hand broken" (translated by the author).

Anshell Shpillman[85] stated that Lewin was warned three times to stop his activities. According to Shpillman, Lewin was associated with Lehi and there were some very serious discussions about his case prior to the assassination.

CASE NUMBER 58

The Assassination of William H. Bruce on October 17, 1946 in Jerusalem by Hagana/Palmach

At the end of February 1946 (probably on the 28th) British police forces searched the Jewish settlement in Biria (in the northern part of Palestine) and found documents, weapons, and ammunition. As a result, all of the twenty-four settlers[86] who resided in Biria were arrested and transferred to the British prison in Acco.

On April 4, 1946, the Palmach members who were arrested

in Biria were asked to give fingerprints. They refused by insisting that they were not criminals. As a result, policemen broke their fingers and tortured them. The Hagana warned that torturing their members was not something they were willing to tolerate. Heading the interrogation was the British officer W. H. Bruce (S.T.H., vol. 3, part 2:874): "The investigators, and he personally, treated the prisoners in a very cruel way.... A Hagana court was persuaded that the man (Bruce—ED.) tortured prisoners in excess pleasure even beyond what was required by his commanders. Evidence was collected from the prisoners. The court decided on a death sentence [against Bruce] because of his totally unjustified cruel behavior toward, and violence against, the prisoners." (Dror 1986:125; see also S.T.H., vol. 3, part 3:1743).

Apparently the British took the verdict and the warning quite seriously and Bruce disappeared for about eight months. Following many efforts made by the Shai—the intelligence service of the Hagana—he was rediscovered first in Jaffo, and later in Jerusalem. Bruce was put under surveillance in Jerusalem by members of Hagana/Palmach/Mista'arvim (more on them later) for a few weeks. His habits were learnt and a plan for his execution was made (Dror 1986:125–128).

On the evening of Thursday, October 17, 1946 (S.T.H., vol. 3, part 2:874; Niv, vol. 5:44) Bruce, wearing civilian clothes, was walking, escorted by bodyguards, in downtown Jerusalem near where "Zion" cinema used to be (crossroads of Ben-Yehuda and Yaffo streets). There, in a small alley (Melisanda street [today Heleni Hamalka St.]—Niv, ibid.), three Palmach members waited for him. At around 2230 Bruce got close, and when he was in front of Rivoli store,[87] the assassins attacked him. While each one of them fired at Bruce twice, he was actually hit by three to five bullets. Although his body guards escaped, without offering any resistance, Bruce himself may have managed to fire a few shots at his assassins. The sound of shots brought British officers to the place, and Bruce was taken to the British military hospital on Mount Scopus where he died around midnight.

The assassins retreated to the Moslem cemetery in Mamilla where they buried their weapons and safely retreated from there. Although British police discovered the weapons, it never found out who the assassins were (Dror 1986:129).[88] Hagana/Palmach publicized, in the radio (transmission from October 22, 1946), that Bruce was executed because he "tortured the prisoners of Biria."[89]

Who were the "Mista'arvim"? The high command of the Hagana, in coordination with the Jewish Agency, created a special Arab department in 1942. At first, this department was called "Hashachar" (translated as "the morning"). The conceptualization of this department was clearly with an orientation toward intelligence. Members of the department (a few dozen men) were supposed to collect information about the Arabs. This department was renamed later as the "Mista'arvim." In August of 1948 this department was integrated into the newly established intelligence service of the Israeli army under the code name S.M. 18, which was under Shmaria Guttman's command. The unit was dissolved in 1950 (Granot 1981:18; Dror 1986:11–13; Black and Morris 1991:35–44). Dror describes the roles of this department explicitly as: "implanting agents, collection of information, operation of sabotage, misleading operations, eliminations of agents and/or key members of the enemy..." (1986:12). Hence, it is quite obvious that the Mista'arvim *could* be used for the purpose of political assassinations. In fact, we have two recorded and confirmed cases of political assassination events by the Mista'arvim: this case and case no. 77 which was the attempt on Nimer al-Khatib's life.

It is of utmost interest and importance to pay attention to Dror's note that: "After the war of independence began [1948—Ed.], the Hagana's Shai, as well as the Hashachar [the 'Mista'arvim' —Ed.], were busy in following salient chiefs of Arab gangs who took an active role in organizing the 'events' against the Yishuv. There were even 'elimination' orders against some of them, but for political reasons this plan—operation ZARZIR (from January of 1948)—was not made fully operational. The newspapers were aware of the attempt to assassinate sheik Nimer al-Khatib [see case no. 77—N.B.Y] near Kiryat Motzkin (he later escaped to Lebanon). The list of 'targets' included such commanders as Abdul Kader al-Husseini (who was killed later in the battle of the Kastel), Issa Bendek, Galab al-Khaldi, Hussein Shublac and others..." (1986:136; see also Black and Morris 1991:512 n. 16). This is an extremely important item of information. It admits that an intelligence unit of the Hagana *was* involved in planning and executing political assassination events, and that in January of 1948 a whole plan to 'eliminate' Arab commanders was worked out. It is not at all clear *who* made this plan, *how* the targets were chosen, and because of *who* exactly, or *why*, Operation ZARZIR was not made fully operational. All attempts to find information about this topic were, unfortunately, not successful.

CASE NUMBER 59

The Assassination of Moshe Ben-Betzalel on November 19, 1946 by Lehi

Ben-Betzalel, a Jew, was born in Zefat in 1911 and joined the British Palestine police in 1938 when he was twenty-seven years old. He worked as a policeman in Jerusalem, the northern border, Tiberias and on March 7, 1944, he was transferred to Jaffo police, where he served to his last day. He was married, with two children. He divorced in 1942 and remarried in 1946. His second wife was pregnant when he was assassinated (*Ha'aretz*, November 20, 1946:6).

Ben-Betzalel worked in the British police intelligence in Jaffo in 1946, when he got threat letters from "one of the terrorist organizations" (ibid.). On Tuesday, November 19, 1946, at 0800 Ben-Betzalel, wearing civilian clothes, was standing in line and waiting for bus number four in Northern Tel-Aviv, reading a newspaper. He was approached by two unidentified young males who unnoticed took out handguns and shot him, declaring that he was a detective and deserved to die.

An innocent by-stander, Moshe Mukov, was also wounded from a gun shot which accidentally hit his leg.

Both Okev and Galili[90] state that Ben-Betzalel was "loyal to the Yishuv and the instructions of the organization. Served the Hagana" (Okev 1949:17). Okev points out that about a week before the assassination, Ben-Betzalel was approached by Lehi's agents. They demanded that he would cooperate with them. He refused and they threatened to kill him. Okev states that Lehi had nothing specific against Ben-Betzalel and that he was assassinated because of his refusal to (a) cooperate with Lehi and (b) to influence other detectives to cooperate with Lehi too. Although Lehi never "officially" accepted responsibility for this assassination, Okev and Galili attributed this act to Lehi. Some reinforcement to this version may be found in Lehi's official publication from 1947.

Sometime after Ben-Betzalel's assassination Lehi publicized a public note entitled "Honor to the policeman—death for the detective" (Lehi *Ketavim* [B]:295–296) There Lehi stated that "if in days of peace one can be satisfied with staying away from the detective, with contempt, this can not be satisfactory during days of war, especially during underground war. A detective to the underground is what a spy is in war. And for a spy there is one sentence only—death."

CASE NUMBER 60

Assassination Attempts against General Sir Evelyn Hugh Barker from December 1946 until February 1947 by Lehi

General Barker (born 1894) was the commander, Eighth Corps from 1944–1946, and British troops in Palestine and Transjordan from 1946–1947 (Jones 1979:9); Barker was also the GOC (General Officer Commanding) in Palestine in 1946 (M. J. Cohen 1978:192 n. 15).

General Barker's record in dealing with Lehi and Etzel, from the latters point of view, was anything but what they considered fair. Let me give a few examples.

In December of 1946, a few members of Etzel were on trial before a military court in Jerusalem on charges of attempted bank robbery. The youngest of the accused was Binyamin Kimchi, then seventeen years old. He was found guilty and received a sentence of eighteen years in prison and eighteen floggings. Flogging, as a form of punishment for youth under eighteen years old, was not an uncommon punishment. Menachem Begin, however, felt that this was a demeaning punishment, as it reminded him of the Hirsch Lekert incident (see chapter 5). The British were then warned against executing this particular form of punishment. However, and despite the warning, they carried out the flogging. In return, Etzel flogged one officer and three British sergeants. Kimchi's punishment was authorized by Barker (Niv, vol. 5:70–77; Begin 1950:321).

In another case, General Barker authorized the death penalty given to Dov Gruner, a member of Etzel, for taking part in attacking a British police station (Niv, vol. 5:79–94). Gruner, and three other members of Etzel—Yehiel Drezner, Eliezer Kashani, Mordechai Alkali—were all hanged on April 16, 1947, after Barker approved (on January 24, 1947) the verdict.

Barker left Palestine in February 12, 1947, when (Niv, vol. 5:105, 219) he was replaced by General Sir Gordon MacMillan (see case no. 67).

However, Barker received his worst reputation somewhere else. On July 22, 1946, Etzel planted explosives in the King David Hotel in Jerusalem. At 1237 the explosion occurred and the five floors of the southern part of the hotel collapsed. About eighty people died and forty were wounded.[91] On July 25, 1946, Barker sent a letter-memo (which became known as the "Non Fraternization Letter"—see Jones 1979:9) to his officers. There he told them that he firmly believed that the Jews should be punished to the extent that they would experience the British feelings of contempt and disgust for their behavior. Accordingly, Barker instructed his soldiers to avoid all Jewish places—coffee shops, food stores, restaurants, vacation centers and even private homes—and stay away from them. He told his soldiers that although these measures may cause them some inconvenience, he was sure that once the Jews would be punished in the way which the Jewish race hated the most—their pockets, and by showing the British feelings of contempt toward them, the punishment would be effective. This order was rightly interpreted as anti-Semitic and caused much public resentment. It was canceled on August 9, 1946.[92] Neither Lehi nor Etzel were willing to take this type of anti-Semitism lightly. Both decided to assassinate Barker and to cooperate in this matter (Yellin-Mor 1974:368).

Barker was put under surveillance and his habits were learned. The first plan came from Etzel and consisted of shooting Barker with two heavy machine guns from an armed and moving truck. The plan was rejected as unsafe and too risky (Yellin-Mor 1974:369). A second plan involved a woman "nursemaid" ("Yael") who was to take a booby-trapped baby stroller (as if with a baby—actually a doll) with an actual "baby" consisting of forty kilograms of explosives near Barker, activate the detonator and look for a shelter while Barker would be blown to pieces. The nursemaid waited for Barker for two days and when he did not show up, the plan was canceled. The third attempt involved planting a sixty kilogram mine, with thirty kilograms of metal scrap pieces, all constructed in the form of a white barrel. This deadly contraption was put alongside the road from Tel Aviv to Jerusalem somewhere between Motza and the Arab village of Lifta. The contraption had an electrical remote control wiring. Menachem Cohen and Dov Cohen waited for some time around the ambush place to blow Barker to pieces with this device. Since Barker did not show up, and the two were concerned that by-passers may become suspicious, they eventually detonated the mine on December 2, 1946 as a British patrol in a Jeep passed near the deadly contraption, killing the four British soldiers who were in that Jeep (Yellin-Mor 1974:369–370; S.T.H., vol. 3, part 2:912).

Dating *all* these attempts accurately is virtually impossible. However, it seems safe to assume that they were all carried out between August 1946 till February 12, 1947, when Barker left Palestine (Niv, vol. 5:25).

Bowyer-Bell (1987:184) states that a fourth undated attempt was made when a trap consisting of two armed, and ready to detonate, grenades was discovered and dismantled near Barker's house.

In 1947, Etzel and Lehi tried to assassinate Barker in England. Lehi's member Aviel (who resided in Palestine) sent Barker an explosive envelope by mail (Yellin-Mor 1974:370); Etzel members were sent to try to assassinate him, and Etzel from Palestine instructed its members in England to try and assassinate Barker.[93] Tavin (1973:167–171) describes how Etzel members in England spent two month following Barker and planning his assassination. The basic plan was to drive a car parallel to Barker's car and use heavy fire from an automatic submachine gun (Tommy Gun) to assassinate Barker. However, the potential assassins encountered many difficulties: the hiding place of their ammunition was discovered; they had difficulties getting a car and finally, a key member of the group of assassins—Jo—was arrested by the British police. Consequently, the whole plan was abandoned. According to Niv (vol. 5:226), Lehi's team in Europe, headed by Eliav, sent

Barker another explosive envelope, which was discovered by Barker's military aide and dismantled. Thus, after Barker left Palestine, there were two unsuccessful attempts on his life, and one or two preplanned, or maybe planned, attempts.

Overall, there were seven or eight attempts on Barker's life. None succeeded, and none of the potential assassins was ever caught. This is also the place to mention that in this case we have one of the few cases where solid evidence for a possible woman assassin (the nursemaid) exists.

CASE NUMBER 61

Assassination of Kadia Mizrahi by Etzel on March 8, 1947

In the Jabotinski archive there is a document (file number 7/19 4ב), attributed to a so-called Etzel court and phrased as an announcement.

"Kadia Mizrahi, from Rehovot [a small town south of Tel Aviv—ED.], a basically corrupted prostitute, traitor to her people, servant of the enemy, a professional squealer, who betrayed Hebrew citizens to the British intelligence—including her son— was sentenced, after hearing testimonies and receiving evidence which left no doubt in her guilt, to death. The court delayed the execution twice and ordered its messenger to warn the criminal and let her have the chance to stop her despised activities. The criminal, however, was not attentive to the court's warnings and continued to betray young Jews to the hands of the enemy. As a result, the order was given and the verdict executed in Rehovot on March 8, 1947."

Ha'aretz (March 10, 1947, p. 2) reported that Kadia Mizrahi, a Jewish Yemenite, divorced, forty-five years old with one son and four daughters, worked in the British police in Rehovot. She worked first as a cleaning lady and later as a policewoman. She was shot eight times by two different weapons on Saturday night, at 2200, March 8, in her home, in the neighborhood of Mar- murek in Rehovot. Etzel's announcement which followed the assassination (Jabotinski archive, file number 1/21 4ב), and Niv (vol. 5:110) state that Kadia was an ex-hooker who worked for the police either as a policewoman or as an agent.

CASE NUMBER 62

The Assassination of Ernst Michael Schnell on
Saturday, March 8, 1947 by Lehi

Ernst Michael Schnell, seventeen years old, was the only son of
the Schnell family who lived in Ramat Yishai. He was religious,
and participated in the "Bnei Akiva" youth movement. He was
trained as an electrician (*Ha'aretz*, March 11, 1947).

Schnell joined Lehi's branch in Haifa, and Pinhas Ginosar
was given the task of supervising and training him. Although
Ginosar doubted Schnell's stability and ability to keep a secret
(Ginosar 1973:4), Schnell very quickly met most of Lehi's members in Haifa, including Naftali who was busy following Conquest, whose assassination was planned[94] (Yellin-Mor 1974:402).

On Saturday, March 1, 1947, Etzel attacked fifteen British
targets in Palestine, including the British officers' club—Gold-
schmidt's House—in Jerusalem. As a result, the British forces
declared that Palestine was under "a military rule" (Niv, vol.
5:102–105). One Saturday before the March 1, 1947 fateful
event, Lehi's branch in Haifa was decimated by a large number
of arrests made by the British. All in all, eight local central members were arrested, including Naftali. Lehi began to suspect that
an informer was involved. When Naftali was interrogated, the
British made a mistake and brought Schnell to recognize him.
Naftali concluded that Schnell was the squealer and sent his suspicions to his outside Lehi friends. A hunt for Schnell began.
Schnell tried to avoid Lehi members. In one occasion he was
located, interrogated and "after a long interrogation a gun was
pointed to him to kill him. The gun did not work. 'Goel' had no
choice but to turn the incident into a quasi-joke made, supposedly, to test Schnell's loyalty" (Yellin-Mor 1974:403.)

Lehi did not give up. Schnell was found again and taken,
probably by force, to a cave in the Carmel mountain (Yellin-Mor
1974:403; *Ha'aretz* March 10, 1947, p. 2). There he was interrogated by Dov "who became very angry" at Schnell's evasive
answers. In the interrogation it was found out that Schnell had a
small notebook with the names of Lehi's members. Schnell was
beaten in order to make him talk but he did not. He did not even

admit that he was the one who identified Naftali at the British intelligence Headquarters. "The boy knew what he could expect. He told his interrogators, "I know that this is my end, for what I did. Now you do with me what you want'" (Yellin-Mor 1974:403–404). At the age of seventeen, Schnell was shot four times and died. That probably took place on Saturday, March 8, 1947 (*Ha'aretz*, March 11, 1947, p. 1 and Yellin-Mor 1954:404).

According to Yellin-Mor (ibid.) members of Lehi went on the following Sunday to Schnell's parents to search in his room and to explain to them what had happened. He states that Schnell's parents were not surprised and even apologized for their son's behavior. Lehi publicized in March of 1947 the fact that Schnell was killed ("executed" in Lehi's original statement) on charges of squealing (Lehi, *Ketavim* (b), p. 413–414).

CASE NUMBER 63

The Assassination of Leon Mashiach on Friday, March 21, 1947 in Petach Tikva by Etzel

Leon Mashiach was born on September 8, 1916 in Sofia, Bulgaria, immigrated to Palestine, and became a member of the Etzel in Petach Tikva (a small town near Tel Aviv) (Jabotinski's institute archives; Niv, vol. 5:352).

The investigation department of Etzel's intelligence became suspicious after two members of Etzel from the Petach Tikva branch were arrested by the British. These arrests suggested to Etzel that squealing was involved. After an intense investigation, the suspicions fell on Leon Mashiach.

Following a long interrogation, Mashiach admitted his guilt, and attributed his cooperation with the British intelligence to his excessive drinking and gambling with cards. He said that due to the money shortage he experienced, he began to work for the British intelligence, giving them information on Etzel's armories and on members from his own group (Niv, vol. 5:110, 352).

In March, Mashiach signed a declaration which stated that: "I, the one signed below, declares of my own free will: a. I had a contact with intelligence detective sergeant Maclachlan in Petach Tikva. b. I gave him information on two training sites. One in the synagogue near the flour mill [called] Rot and one in the kindergarten in Yehuda Camp. Together with the above sergeant, I prepared plans to capture trainees with weapons in the above places. c. Also, I knew that they were going to arrest (five words are erased) Joseph Nadler..."[95] The document is "signed" by Mashiach Leon, dated, and states the place of signature—Petach Tikva.

The details of the investigation and the "confession" were delivered to Etzel headquarters for approval. On the very same day, Friday, March 21, 1947, Leon Mashiach was killed (probably shot) in one of the orange groves near the entrance to Petach Tikva.

In a statement publicized after the execution, Etzel denounced Mashiach as a traitor to his people and as a squealer who committed his acts for lucre. Etzel took full responsibility for the "verdict" and the execution on the grounds that people like Mashiach, who were capable of betraying their own people to the "Nazo-British" (expression appears in this way in the original), deserved only one punishment—death. The same document states that after the "criminal" admitted his acts, he asked the court to allow him to commit suicide so as not to disgrace his son. The court denied his request "knowing that the father's disgrace as a traitor would not fall on the son's head, who would grow to be a loyal son to his people and country" (Jabotinski's institute archives, file number 7/19 4ב, a message from "Rak Kach," supposedly the Etzel's court).[96]

CASE NUMBER 64

Assassination Attempt on Sergeant Weighorn on March 27, 1947 in Tel Aviv by Lehi—Unsuccessful

According to Niv (vol. 5:133) and Banai (1958:672) Sergeant Weighorn was a Jewish detective policeman, in charge of the Jewish department in the British intelligence in Tel Aviv. On Thursday March 27, 1947, a unit of Lehi attempted to assassinate him but they failed.

Why was there an attempt on Sergeant Weighorn's life?

In March of 1946, the Hagana/Palmach tried to bring to Tel Aviv's beach an "illegal" ship with Jewish immigrants aboard.

The ship was named *Ord Wingate*. On the night of March 27, 1946 the Hagana/Palmach stationed many forces in Tel Aviv. The night became known as "the Wingate night." The ship, however, was intercepted while still in the sea and never came to Tel Aviv.

Some small skirmishes however between British and Hagana's forces in Tel Aviv occurred. In one of those skirmishes, at 7 Marmorek Street, at around 2330, a four-member unit from Palmach was engaged in a small battle with a British armored patrol car. During the battle, three Palmach members surrendered. A fourth member, the nineteen-year-old female platoon commander, Bracha Fold, was shot to death by the British while she tried to reload her submachine gun (see S.T.H., vol. 3, part 2:876, 1225; Dekel 1953:94–97).

Hanna Armoni from the Lehi museum, told the author (on December 29, 1987) that Sergeant Weighorn was responsible for "the murder of Bracha Fold." Furthermore, she stated that he was particularly violent towards members of the Jewish underground. These were the reasons why Lehi tried to assassinate him. Mrs. Armoni added that Sergeant Flower worked with Weighorn, using the same methods, and Lehi tried to assassinate him too in December of 1947. No further details or corroboration for the possible attempt on Flower's life could be obtained.

CASE NUMBER 65

The Assassination of Joseph Frumkin on April 3, 1947 in Jerusalem by Lehi

Ha'aretz (April 4, 1947, p. 1) reports that on Thursday April 3, 1947 at 7:30 P.M., two young Jewish males arrived at Frumkin's home in the neighborhood of Mekor Chaim in Jerusalem. They knocked on the door and asked for Frumkin. When his daughter came out and told them that her father was not at home they told her not to lie. Hearing the noises, Frumkin came out and at the request of the two males they all walked to the outside corner of the house where the two strangers shot Frumkin six or seven times, wounding him fatally in front of his wife and children. The two males escaped. Frumkin was taken to Hadassah hospital where he died later. He was fifty-two years old when he died.

Banai (1958:672) and the Jabotinski's archive (file number 1/21 4⊃, p. 2) reports that on April 3, 1947, a death sentence against Joseph Frumkin was executed by Lehi's members. The "reason" given for this execution is stated as "connections and cooperation with the British intelligence."

No further information was available on the case.

CASE NUMBER 66

The Assassination Attempts on General Sir Gordon MacMillan during April–July 1947 by Lehi: April 1947—Unsuccessful (by a mine); June 30, 1947—Unsuccessful (by a mine); and July 3 and 4, 1947—Unsuccessful (by a mine)

General Sir Gordon Holmes Alexander MacMillan (born 1897) was GOC (General Officer commanding) in Palestine between 1947–1948 (Jones 1979:83–84). He replaced General Evelyn Barker (see case no. 60) on February 12, 1947. MacMillan was a tough minded commander and intended to implement a tough policy against the pre-state underground Jewish groups. One of his very first acts was to demand that the British troops would stop referring to members of Lehi, Etzel and Hagana by using such accounts as "terrorists." He insisted that such accounts and rhetorical devices as "murderer," criminal, and "robber" be used instead (Niv, vol. 5:105). Another of his acts was to sign and confirm the death sentence on Meir Feinstein (from Etzel) and Moshe Barazani (from Lehi) (see case no. 68) on April 17, 1947.[97] Lehi decided to assassinate MacMillan. The responsibility for the assassination was given to "Uzi the red" (see also case no. 70) and Ezra Yachin (Yachin 1984:178).

The first assassination attempt was made about two weeks after MacMillan signed the death sentences in April 1947 (Yachin interview, June 21, 1987). A powerful mine was planted underground (on Saturday night) in one of the curves of the Jerusalem-Tel Aviv road (close to Givat Shaul). A few Lehi's members rotated in observation, waiting for MacMillan to show up.[98] Unfortunately for Lehi, the British discovered the mine and dismantled it (S.T.H., vol. 3, part 2:956; Niv, vol. 5:45; Yachin 1984:178–187).

A second attempt focused on planning to use a cart (used by baggage movers). The plan was to fill the cart with explosives and to detonate it in Jaffo Street in Jerusalem near the old structure of "Sha'arei Zedek." A short time before the bomb was supposed to be detonated, a small unit of Hagana members came by and told the two Lehi's operators to dismantle the mine. The Hagana's goal was not to arrest Lehi's members but to prevent the assassination (S.T.H., vol. 3, part 2:956).

A third attempt was made on the third and fourth of July 1947 when a powerful mine was discovered, by Hagana members, on the road from Jerusalem to Tel Aviv (probably near Romema). The police was notified and the mine was dismantled (Niv, vol. 5:171; Yachin 1984:195).

Yachin's (1984:187–195) account conveys the clear impression that at that time (probably April–July 1947) he was literally obsessed with the idea of assassinating Macmillan and approached his local Lehi commander in Jerusalem with various ideas about how to do it, including volunteering to put himself in some dangerous and risky situations. All his suggestions were rejected by his commander.

CASE NUMBER 67

The Assassination of A. A. Conquest on April 26, 1947 in Haifa by Lehi

Not many British intelligence officers helped the Jewish struggle in Palestine, and those who helped did so for a variety of reasons. A. A. Conquest was the head of the British intelligence CID in Haifa and helped the intelligence service of the Hagana in return for a promise and commitment that he would not be hit/hurt by the Jewish underground groups (especially Etzel and Lehi) (S.T.H., vol. 3, part 1:246–247).

Lehi, however, viewed Conquest as one of their worst and most dangerous enemies, (Niv, vol. 5:135)—"he had good sources and he knew how to acquire new ones," and was involved in the case of Schnell (see case no. 62). "Avner," who later assassinated Conquest, states that another influential Lehi member, Dov, told him that "this Conquest, he's a real bastard;

don't think it's only being here that's made him so bloody tough. In Ireland they called him 'The Butcher'. When the Irish hear of his death, they'll send us their congratulations" (Avner 1959:99). Lehi's members in Haifa followed Conquest, but he was very careful. He used to disguise himself, never took the same route twice and was always escorted by an armed body guard. When Lehi decided that Conquest should be assassinated "there was no choice but to trust chance." There were daily ambushes and the plan was to use submachine guns because of their firepower and because one of the assassins knew how to use this weapon particularly well (Yellin-Mor 1974:410; Banai 1958:586).

Finally, on Saturday, April 26, 1947, A. A. Conquest was spotted by the two Lehi's assassins as he was coming out of the CID building in Haifa. He took an army car and took the road to the Carmel mountain. There, he stopped at Spinney's (in the German colony) to buy merchandise. Lehi's two assassins[99] followed him. The plan was that as he got out of the shop, Lehi's car would drive by and he would be shot. That is exactly what happened as a whole barrel of Tommy gun submachine gun bullets found their way into Conquest's body. Here is how "Avner," Lehi's assassin, described the event: "I raised my submachine gun and stuck the barrel out of the window. Conquest was right in front of us.... He turned his head and realized what was happening.... I pulled the trigger. Three bullets hit him in the stomach.... Yigal [the driver—ED.], seeing Conquest fall, threw the car into gear to try and get up speed. I had time to fire one more burst" (Avner 1959:103). Niv (vol. 5:135) states that Conquest did not die immediately but was brought to a military hospital where he died a few hours later.

Unfortunately for the assassins, as they were retreating via Um Boulevard towards Hadar Hacarmel in Haifa, they were spotted and fired upon heavily from the government building. They were also pursued by British army cars. The driver was hit in his back, and as he made a left-hand turn, the car got stuck. The two assassins got out of the car and continued to retreat on foot. While the two assassins were separated during the flight, and one thought that the other had died, they eventually got together on the same day, and received medical treatment. Neither was caught (Banai 1958:586–587; Yellin-Mor 1974:410-411).

Following the assassination Lehi published an announcement taking responsibility for Conquest's assassination because in their view he was "responsible for a long list of war crimes against the Jewish fighting underground."

CASE NUMBER 68

Assassination Attempt against Hans Reinhold ("Yanai") on May 13, 1947 in Belgium by Etzel

Hans Reinhold ("Yanai"), thirty-one years old, joined Etzel after his release from the British army's Jewish Brigade. He began to work in Etzel as an instructor and specialist on explosives and field training in the Haifa branch. He took part in some of Etzel's guerrilla actions in the northern parts of Palestine (e.g., blowing up railway tracks, planning to sink a British destroyer in Haifa's port—see Eliav 1983:333) and thus gained the trust and confidence of his superiors in the organization.

In March of 1946, he was transferred by Etzel to Jerusalem. There he started to climb up the ladder of Etzel's organization and reached very close to the top commanding echelon.

In Jerusalem, he took an active part in the blowing up of the King David Hotel (on July 22, 1946).[100] His behavior there, however, aroused suspicion. Yanai was supposed to activate the trigger of the explosives. In the last minute he refused, and his commander did it. Following the action, Yanai disappeared for a few hours. In October of 1946, Yanai took part in planning the attack on, and blowing up of, the Central railway station in Jerusalem. On October 30, 1946, at 2:00 P.M., the attack was indeed carried out (Niv, vol. 5:47–49), but the British captured four of the attackers, possibly due to squealing by Yanai (*Ma'ariv*, July 23, 1954, p. 4). Yanai himself disappeared completely after the attack. Meir Feinstein, with the others who were arrested, was put on trial before a British military court in Jerusalem on March 25, 1947. Moshe Horowitz and Masud Buton presented an alibi and were acquitted. Meir Feinstein and Daniel Azulai were found guilty and sentenced to death. Azulai's sentence was changed later to life imprisonment. Feinstein, who was waiting to be executed with another Lehi member (Moshe

Barazani), received in their prison cell a grenade which was smuggled in by Lehi. The two used the grenade and blew themselves up on April 21, 1947.

Etzel became very suspicious about Reinhold-Yanai, as various members felt that there was something very strange about Reinhold's behavior. Etzel's intelligence department, the Delek (previously Meshi) began to investigate. They found a strong connection between Reinhold and Max Schindler (see case no. 69). Reinhold's past behavior in Jerusalem and Haifa was analyzed, especially concerning his alleged role in various failures. The analysis gave credence to the hypothesis that Yanai was, in fact, a spy/traitor/provocateur. More evidence was collected, especially Reinhold's possible role in betraying members of Etzel to the British and giving the British details about secret ammunition and weapons depots. Consequently, Etzel appointed a special investigative committee, consisting mainly of Ya'acov Amrami and Shmuel Tamir (who between October 1977 and August 1980 became Israel's minister of law). As a result of the investigation, Etzel's headquarters passed a death sentence on Reinhold.[101]

Although Reinhold disappeared around July 21, 1946, Etzel began to look for him. Etzel had no success (e.g., Niv, Volume five:50; *Ma'ariv*, July 7, 1954, p. 4). Apparently, Reinhold felt that he was in a dangerous situation and escaped. However, in the spring of 1947, Etzel's agents in Europe managed to locate Reinhold in Brussels. He was hiding there under the name of Harry Rose. Etzel decided to kidnap Reinhold-Yanai-Rose and execute him.

The local Etzel commander, Mordechai Shani, was appointed in charge of the operation, and he was joined by Eliahu Lankin—Etzel's commander in Europe then—who came from Paris (Beit Jabotinski's archives, file number 12/19 4 כ).

After surveillance, Reinhold-Yanai-Rose was captured, severely beaten, and put into a car in Brussels. On Tuesday, May 13, 1947, as the Etzel's car was speeding out of Brussels, it was spotted by a reporter who saw what happened and called a policeman. They both began to chase the kidnapers' car. The car which was driven by Etzel members got by mistake into a blocked alley and the kidnapers and "Yanai" were arrested and brought to a local police station. Yanai was later released. It is interesting to note that

according to Tavin (1973:174) when Yanai was kidnaped he identified at least one of his kidnapers and told him: "why do you do
this to me? Hoy, what do you do? You are making a mistake."
After the British intervened, "Yanai" was flown to England and
the three kidnapers were put on trial. Shani and the two other kidnapers—two brothers, George and Alex Gur Arieh—were found
guilty on charges of attempted murder and illegal possession of
weapons, and each was sentenced to three and a half years in a
Belgian prison. They were all released one year after the State of
Israel was established in 1948.[102]

In a follow-up story in 1954, in *Ma'ariv* (see July 7, 1954, p. 4
and September 3, 1954, p. 8) it was disclosed that at that time,
Reinhold-Yanai-Rose was living in New York. It was also suggested that he may have visited Israel and may even have served in the
Israeli army after 1948, without anyone knowing who he was.

CASE NUMBER 69

*Assassination Attempt against Max Schindler on May 16, 1947 in
Haifa, by Etzel—Unsuccessful*

Max Schindler was a German-born Jew who worked from 1936
till 1940 as a police officer for the British police in Zichron-
Ya'acov (southeast of Haifa) and was then transferred to the
British Haifa police. Very quickly he was integrated into the
police's Jewish department of the Haifa police intelligence office
(Niv, vol. 4:42). According to Niv (vol. 5:49), his job in the
British police was to locate, identify and arrest members of the
Jewish underground. He was suspected of being the contact
agent for Yanai—(Hans Reinhold—see case no. 68) the traitor
(Niv, vol. 5:45–50).

In the spring of 1944, Lehi published a public warning in
which Schindler was warned to stop his activities or else be punished (Lehi—*Ketavim* [A] p. 531). Schindler was considered as
one of "the most dangerous of the British intelligence people"
(Niv, vol. 5:152) by Etzel's intelligence.

Etzel appointed a special group of its members in Haifa to
assassinate Schindler. On Friday, May 16, 1947, at 0800,
Schindler rode in a police car on Aviv Street on Mount Carmel,

Haifa, escorted by a policeman. Etzel's agents managed to detonate a powerful mine near the car. The policeman who escorted Schindler was killed. Schindler himself was wounded badly and brought to a hospital where he was treated and his life was saved. On May 22, 1947, he left Palestine and never returned (Niv, vol. 5:152).

CASE NUMBER 70

Assassination Plots against Sergeant Joseph Killy in Lod and in Haifa by Lehi: July 23, 1947—Unsuccessful (by a mine); August 10, 1947—Unsuccessful (by gun shooting); and November 12, 1947—Wounded (by submachine gun)

Sergeant Joseph Killy, from the British intelligence, was considered by Lehi as a dangerous opponent (Yellin-Mor 1974:411; Banai 1958:579–585) and was even compared to Wilkin (see case no. 45) in terms of his experience and activities against the Jewish underground. Banai states that Killy was very familiar with the Jewish Yishuv.

Sergeant Killy was first spotted by the Lehi's intelligence department when he served in Lod (east of Tel Aviv) police. There, his successful activities against Lehi drew much attention (e.g., see Banai 1958:579–584). Meir Pony (Shaul), head of Lehi's intelligence department then decided, probably together with other members of the department, that Killy had to be assassinated (Banai 1958:584).

Lehi's members hid a powerful mine in a road to Wadi Rubin, west of Rishon Letzion (south of Tel Aviv), and waited for the British intelligence car taking detectives to the range to practice shooting. Unfortunately for Lehi, the plan did not work. When the British intelligence car passed by the mine there were civilians around and Lehi's members did not want to detonate the mine and accidentally hit innocent bystanders. The car thus passed unharmed. The disappointed and frustrated Lehi members waited until a convoy of trucks with British paratroopers passed on the road and blew the mine under the middle car and a few soldiers were wounded (between three to eighteen). This incident actually enabled us to date the assassination attempt to

July 23, 1947. It is very doubtful that the British knew that Killy was the original target.

Regardless of this unsuccessful attempt, the British apparently decided to use Killy's rich experience and transferred him to Haifa. Lehi branch in Haifa was instructed to carry out the assassination (Yellin-Mor 1974:411). Hence came the second attempt.

On August 10, 1947 (Niv, vol. 5:331), a unit of six Lehi's members drove to Haz restaurant in Haifa where they knew Killy used to eat. The plan called for shooting Killy with hand guns. Along the way, one so-called by Lehi "noise-grenade" (a small chemical contraption which, upon ignition, made noises that were supposed to create a diversion of attention from the real target of the attack) started to burn in the pocket of Eliahu Dahan and later exploded in the car wounding Dahan and Chaim Akheiser. They tried to escape but were spotted and arrested—Dahan was in fact arrested by Killy. Eliahu Dahan and Chaim Akheiser were brought before a British military court in Haifa on November 2, 1947, and each was sentenced to twenty years in prison. Chaim Akheiser got quite a reputation when, after the trial, he asked his judges "do you really think you'll sit in this land for another twenty years?" (Niv, vol. 5:331) (the British mandate forces actually left Palestine in May 14, 1948) (see also Yellin-Mor 1974:411–412; Banai 1958:584–585).

Three months after the above attempt, on November 12 of 1947, another member of Lehi (Uzi the Red), escorted by other Lehi's members, got into the office of "Pal Transport" (a freight company), which was located on Hamlachim Street in Haifa, above the Haz coffee shop, around 1100. Under the close watch of his friends, who guarded the office's clerks and customers, threatening them with a gun, Uzi the Red opened a violin case he was carrying and got out a "Sten" submachine gun. Killy was sitting at that time in the open yard of the restaurant near a table. Uzi the Red aimed the submachine gun at Killy and from a height of six meters fired eight rounds of two to three bullets at Killy. Killy was wounded badly, and at least one other British sergeant was killed. The assassin got quietly out of the office and into a car which waited outside, and disappeared. Despite some printed newspaper reports that Killy was "fatally wounded,"

Killy was actually taken to a hospital, treated, and survived (*Ha'aretz*, November 25, 1947, p. 3). He was sent out of Palestine after a few months.[103]

CASE NUMBER 71

The Assassination of Yehoshua Zarfati on October 30, 1947 in Tel Aviv—by Lehi

Yehoshua Zarfati was a car salesman from Jerusalem. In September of 1947, he was approached by Lehi's members and warned (and threatened) to stop his activities for the British police. Okev (1949:18–19), who provides the most detailed account available on this assassination, states that Lehi's threat was probably a way for Lehi to press Zarfati into serving Lehi and give them information about the British with whom he was in contact socially and commercially. Zarfati, according to Okev, was connected with Lehi and contributed money to the organization. Okev states that he may have become too deeply involved with the British intelligence, and when Lehi wanted that he would continue his contacts and he refused—they assassinated him. This act, according to Okev, created much fear among other merchants and importers.[104] Okev writes that Zarfati was shot in Ben-Yehuda street in Tel Aviv at the end of October 1947.

Banai, whose account is certainly given from Lehi's point of view, states very dryly, and without details, that on Thursday, October 30, 1947, Yehoshua Zarfati was shot "by members of Lehi and wounded fatally. There was a death sentence against him on charges of cooperation with the British intelligence" (1958:675). File number 1/21 4ב in the Jabotinski archives (p. 2) confirms that in the above date Zarfati was executed and shot to death by Lehi.

Ha'aretz (October 31, 1947, p. 8) confirms the details and adds that the assassination occurred at 1830, and that Zarfati was forty-one years old when he was killed. An innocent woman bystander—Margalit Taib—was wounded in her leg from the shots. Zarfati himself did not die immediately, and was in hospital in critical condition for a few days before he died on Friday November 7, 1947 (*Ha'aretz*, November 9, 1947, p. 4).

CASE NUMBER 72

The Assassination of Corporal Shalom Gurevitz on November 3, 1947, in Jerusalem, by Lehi

Shalom Gurevitz served in the British police since the late 1920s and was considered as their expert on communism.

Kotzer (1977:103), a former member of Lehi, describes in his memoirs a boat trip that he, and a few of his friends, took in the autumn of 1938 to Turkey and to Alexandria. He states that on that boat they met a squealer named Gurevitz who "stuck" to them. Kotzer expresses his wonder as to why Gurevitz followed them, and whether it had anything to do with Kutik's trial.[105] Kotzer recalls that on the first night on the ship, he and a few other of his friends, tried to throw Gurevitz into the sea. That attempt was not successful since Gurevitz hung tightly to the side of the ship ("like a leach"), and as a ship's officer came by, they had to leave Gurevitz giving him a grave warning. Kotzer states that Gurevitz caused the organization much damage (he does not, however, specify the exact nature of the damage) and that he was later executed in Jerusalem.

Okev (1949:19) provides, again, a detailed account of the case. He states that Gurevitz was assassinated because he did not want to provide Lehi with information, and that there was an unproven rumor that he caused the arrest of two members of Lehi in Jerusalem. Okev states that by assassinating Gurevitz Lehi may have wanted to demonstrate to some unknown party that they were active against the police's fight against communists (Okev does not explain this hypothesis).

On Monday, November 3, 1947, Gurevitz left the police headquarters at noon to go to his home at 8 David Yellin Street in Jerusalem; four young males knocked on his door which was opened by his wife. When Gurevitz got to the door, the visitors apologized and left. Half an hour later two unidentified males showed up again at the door and said they came from Lehi "to renew the contact"; Gurevitz invited them to his room. After a short while the sound of a burst of bullets being fired was heard and the two males escaped. Before they left, they fired eighteen bullets into Gurevitz's body. Gurevitz was forty-two years old when he was assassinated. The assassins escaped without being caught. Apparently Gurevitz tried to resist and struggled with his assassins as knife wounds were found on his arm and chest (*Ha'aretz*, November 5, 1947:6).

Banai (1958:675), without much detail, states dryly that "Shalom Gurevitz, sergeant of the intelligence, was shot and killed by Lehi members. There was a death sentence against him for charges of his activity against the underground." Okev (1949:19) states that this assassination left a strong impression among the (Jewish) policemen who were willing to render services to the Yishuv. According to *Ha'aretz* (November 4, 1947, p. 4) Corporal Gurevitz was assassinated because Lehi demanded that he would give them information and he refused.

CASE NUMBER 73

The Assassination of the Shubaki Family on November 19, 1947 by Lehi

The eleventh of November 1947 witnessed a secret course on weapons given to Lehi's youth in an isolated house near Ra'anana (north of Tel Aviv). Suddenly, the place was surrounded by British soldiers who opened fire on the young people and killed three females and two males. The rest were either wounded or arrested (Lam 1987).

Lehi was not the type of organization to let such an incident pass without a response. Among other things on November 12, 1947, Lehi's members in Haifa attacked a group of British soldiers, killing one and wounding three; on the thirteenth another attack in the Ritz coffee shop in Jerusalem left twenty-eight wounded, on the fifteenth two more policemen were killed in Jerusalem (Yellin-Mor 1974:428; Banai 1958:675).

"The British were the murderers, but they were not the only ones to be punished. How did they ever get to the place?" (Yellin-Mor 1974:428). Yellin-Mor was sure it was due to squealing. Having investigated, Lehi discovered that the information was given to the British by members of the Arab family Shubaki who lived not far away from the house where Lehi adolescents were trained. Lehi decided to punish the Shubaki family so that (a) the informers and squealers would be punished, (b) it would serve as a warning to all the Arabs in Palestine. In order to prevent rumors that punishing the Shubaki family was due to national, ethnic, racial, or religious motives, Lehi wrote and distributed an announcement (Lehi, *Ketavim* [B], pp. 1058–1086) "to our Arab brothers" dated November 21, 1947, explaining the punishment delivered to the British and to the Shubaki family. The punishment was that on Wednesday, November 19, 1947, members of the Shubaki family were shot to death. Lehi's announcement gave the names of Jews and Arabs who served the British and "advised" them to quit their dangerous practice.

The assassination itself took place in the early hours of the morning, at approximately 0430. Ten Lehi's members, equipped with automatic submachine guns, penetrated the Arab village of Arab-Shubaki (near Ra'anana) dressed similarly to the police-military men. They told the head of the village to gather all the men and selected five members of the Shubaki family. They took them to a nearby field where they shot them. Ahmed Salameh Shubaki, fifty years old, the father, his sons, Wadia (twenty-five) and Sammy (twenty-three) died instantly. His brother's sons were shot too. Sami (twenty-three) was wounded badly and Sabar Ahmed (twenty-seven) died later of his wounds. A spokesman for the Jewish Agency denounced this assassination. It may well be the case that the Shubaki family had close and good relations with the close by Jewish settlements.[106]

This particular case may be considered marginal. While the targets were specific (male members of a particular family), it is not entirely clear whether Lehi in fact was sure that all of the members in the Shubaki family were involved in squealing, so this case may be closer in concept to a blood revenge, somewhere between terror and political assassination.

CASE NUMBER 74

The Assassination of Yedidia Segal in January of 1948, intentionally by, or by default of, the Hagana

The three different pre-state Jewish underground groups did not always live in harmony. Competition, persecutions and cooperation with the British marked significant chapters of their existence (e.g., see Shavit 1976). Part of these activities were kidnaping members of the opposite group, sometimes torturing them and even giving them to the British. Such an unpleasant chapter took place in 1947 and early 1948.

The relations between the Hagana and Etzel in Haifa were strained in 1947/48. During the searches for a Hagana member in Haifa who was kidnaped by Lehi, the Hagana's agents arrested a twenty-one-year-old member of Etzel—Yedidia Segal ("Gavriel"), together with another member of Etzel. Both were suspected as involved in the earlier kidnaping of a Hagana member by Etzel.

Yedidia was born in 1926 in Palestine and joined Etzel when he grew up. There he became a Lieutenant. Both Etzel's members who were arrested by the Hagana were brought to a hiding place on Mount Carmel where they were interrogated using violent means (probably between January 10 and 12, 1948).

Early in the morning Segal managed to escape towards the Arab village Tira. The Hagana's guard fired after him but Segal disappeared. Segal's dead body was found later mutilated and shot near Tira. His body was brought to Haifa for identification.[107]

Etzel accused the Hagana of kidnaping, torturing and assassinating Segal. The "story" about Tira, they said, was an invention to "cover up" the atrocity. The Hagana stuck to the story of Segal's escape and eventual murder by the Arabs. This sad and tragic affair is still brought up in the written media every now and then (e.g., see Yerushalmi and Avituv 1986).

Which of the two contradictory versions of what happened to Segal is really true is a question to which we cannot possibly provide a valid and definite answer. I tend, however, to attribute responsibility (even indirectly) to the Hagana. It was the Hagana who kidnaped Segal and it was the Hagana therefore, who was responsible for him. Even if Segal managed to escape, they had to prevent it, and even then, why fire at him?

Another question is whether this is a case of political assassination. That the Etzel and the Hagana represent two different symbolic-moral universes is obvious. Segal was clearly a specified target and he was not just arrested randomly by the Hagana. It has not been established, however, that the Hagana intended to assassinate Segal. Thus, while I described the case here, I did not include it in the statistical analysis.

CASE NUMBER 75

The Assassination of Yehuda Arie Levi on January 15, 1948 by Lehi

Levi, thirty-three years old, single, was a Sefardi Jew who came to Palestine from Italy. He had very good technical talents and when he joined Lehi he became the manager of the technical department. He served as a guide and teacher in Lehi's courses on explosives. An industrious and inventive fellow, he developed road mines, bullets and igniting-grenades. He showed a tendency to study, was inclined to study chemistry and was about to be sent to the United States as a representative of Lehi.

In November 29, 1947, the United Nations decided that the Jewish state would be established. This created a problem for Lehi. They had to decide either to disband the organization and join the new emerging Jewish state, or continue to exist and operate as an independent organization. While originally Lehi's headquarters gave the order to disband, the order was canceled within a month (e.g., see S.T.H., vol. 3, part 2:1544). That process was not easy, and left many members of Lehi totally confused.

Yehuda Arie Levi was one of those who decided to leave Lehi and join the Hagana. He contacted the Hagana's people and told them of his intentions (S.T.H., ibid.). He did not make his decision secret and told other members of Lehi about it too. Kotzer (no date:193) states that Lehi's headquarters sent a female member of Lehi to talk to Levi to find out what exactly were his intentions and why, despite the cancellation of the disbanding order, he insisted on joining the Hagana.

That anonymous female did talk to Levi and reported to her superior. As a result Lehi's members were instructed to avoid contacts with Levi and excommunicate him. Most of his friends in fact stayed away from him. Levi did not give up—he continued to voice his opinion and demanded an explanation from Lehi's command. A clarification was needed. The process of clarification turned very quickly into a trial. However, even the judges could not find anything wrong in Levi's actions or words. The whole affair was turned over to Lehi's headquarters. Yellin-Mor (with agreement from Sheib) decided that Levi should be assassinated (Kotzer, no date:193).

At 0630 on Thursday, January 15, 1948, about fifteen armed young males broke into the Levi's apartment in Hayarkon Street in Tel Aviv and took Yehuda Arie by force with them. His body was found later, with four hand-gun bullet holes in his chest (Okev:1949:24–29).[108]

Kotzer's and Okev's descriptions provide some details. According to Okev (and S.T.H., ibid.) a few weeks passed after Levi's kidnaping and his family began to apply pressure on different political figures to help find their son. Even the Tel Aviv Rabbinate demanded to know where Levi's body was buried (after a rumor that he was killed).

An inner contemporary memo of Lehi informed members that Levi was accused of violating group discipline, telling lies, demoralizing other members of Lehi and disclosing secrets. He was brought before a special court, found guilty as charged and executed. Lehi members were told that this act could not be avoided. In an interview, Shamir (1973) said that at the time of the incident he was in Africa and added that "the court which sentenced Levi to death was the only [court] we created..."

On Friday, November 11, 1987, *Yediot Aharonot* published a long "cover story" on this case. According to the report (see Nevo 1987), on the day Levi was kidnaped by Lehi he was put before a court of Lehi and shot at the same day, after Yellin-Mor approved the sentence. The actual assassin was interviewed, under a pseudo-name "Ze'ev" and told Nevo that he shot Levi because had he not, he would have been shot himself: "what could I do? Why did those who were the judges not prevent it? I received an order, and I shot, I could not refuse." (ibid., p. 21). Ze'ev told Nevo that the order to shoot came from "Adam." The use of the nickname thirty-four[!] years after the assassination, and the reluctance to be exposed, obviously indicate that those involved certainly do not feel comfortable with their actions.

On February 15, 1977, Levi's name was added to the list of Lehi's casualties . His family wrote on his tombstone that he was murdered by bad people ("Zedim") which made some contemporary Lehi survivors (e.g., Yazernitzki ["Shamir"], Anshell

Shpillman) quite angry. Shpillman told Nevo that in 1948 Lehi had no prisons, that Levi could not be isolated and that "there was no choice...the underground could not afford such anarchy.... That was a loss, a tragedy. But he (Levi) brought the death upon himself..."

Levi was not a traitor or a squealer in the stereotypical sense of the terms. He just wanted to transfer from Lehi to the Hagana on the background of his conviction that it was about time for Lehi to become one with the new Jewish state. His execution cannot be possibly understood but as a very strong signal from Lehi's center to the other members. In a period of great confusion and contradictory messages and commands, Levi's assassination delivered an obvious signal that the coherent symbolic-moral universe which was Lehi was still intact and vibrant, and that anybody willing to violate Lehi's moral boundaries would be punished severely. Levi did not hide his opinions—on the contrary. That made his challenge to the moral boundaries more explicit and more difficult. His execution needed to be explained to Lehi's members—for exactly the same reason—to clarify and reify the moral boundaries in the most explicit manner.[109]

CASE NUMBER 76

The Assassination of Chaya Zeidenber in Tel Aviv on February 1, 1948 by Lehi

Banai (1958:628–630) describes a phone conversation between Chaya Zeidenberg, a single, twenty-two-year-old Jewish nurse who worked in the government hospital in Jaffo, and Doud Yasmini, a commander in the Arab organization Nejada (an anti-Jewish Arab organization, established in 1946—see Haber and Schiff 1976:352). That conversation was intercepted and its content given to Lehi's intelligence agents. In it, Ms. Zeidenberg promised Doud to plant a bomb in the center of Tel Aviv.

Lehi wasted no time, and located Chaya. Under interrogation she "cried" and "admitted" that she was willing to do anything for Doud who was her lover. "She admitted that she lied and that she went out a few times with him in Jaffo. Doud broke her, made her surrender. She knew that she was going to commit a crime against Jews and that she did not deserve to live.... (She)...gave Doud information about the Hagana's positions in Holon and Bat-Yam (then small suburbs south of Tel Aviv)" (Banai 1958:630). Banai states that this affair was brought to attention of Lehi's center and that a field court sentenced her to death by shooting (ibid.). She was taken to an orange grove near Tel Aviv (in Hadar-Ramataim) where she was shot (Haber and Schiff 1976:194).

In an announcement made by Lehi in February 1948 (see Lehi, *Ketavim* [B], February 1982 [2d ed.] pp. 907–908) her "confession," dated Sunday February 1, 1948, written in Hebrew supposedly in her own handwriting, and supposedly signed by her, was given: "I, Chaya Zeidenberg, living in Holon, Dov Hos Blvd., Am neighborhood, admit here that I was in touch with an Arab named David Yasmina. I promised him one day to put a bomb in Tel Aviv. This Arab has been my lover for six years.... I used to visit him frequently in Jaffo, mostly in Tel Aviv. Lately, I scheduled a meeting with him for Sunday February 1, 1948."

The Hagana was not too thrilled with the affair. Doubts were raised about the authenticity of the confession, as well as its validity. It was pointed out that the "proofs" against Chaya Zeidenberg were shaky and not corroborated. Thus, it was pointed out that Rose, a woman who helped locate Chaya, was also in love with Doud and that the whole affair may have been on the background of a simple jealousy by Rose. It was also pointed out that too much pressure may have been applied against Chaya by her interrogators and that elicited a problematic "confession." Doubt was also raised regarding the validity and nature of the court procedure(s) (Okev 1949:20–23). Lehi's announcement from February of 1948 (ibid.) stated that the Hagana's behavior was hypocritical and not serious. Lehi continued to defend this position in public (Lehi, *Ketavim*, [B], pp. 915–916).[110]

CASE NUMBER 77

An Assassination Attempt on the life of Sheik Nimer al-Khatib near Haifa on Thursday, February 19, 1948, by Hagana/Palmach —Unsuccessful

As can be recalled, the Mista'arvim was a group of Jewish Palmach warriors who pretended to be Arabs, and under this guise penetrated Arab territory and performed a variety of intelligence and operational activities (e.g., see Cohen Y. 1969; Dror 1986; Black and Morris 1991:35–34; see case no. 58). In 1948, the Mista'arvim's attention in Haifa was drawn to the activities of sheik Nimer al-Khatib.

Sheik Nimer al-Khatib, thirty-two years old, was educated in Al-Azhar in Cairo, and became later a preacher at the Istiklal mosque in Haifa. He was one of the heads of the Moslem organization in Haifa, and a member of the Arab national committee in the city (S.T.H., vol. 3, part 2:1362). He gained a reputation of an Arab national zealot (Ha'aretz, February 20, 1948, p. 4). According to Mista'arvim sources, al-Khatib was one of the chief instigators and agitators against Jews in the northern part of Israel and in Haifa particularly (S.T.H., vol. 3, part 2:1381). He chose what the Mista'arvim regarded as the main mosque in Haifa as the place from where he staged what was described as: "poisonous speeches, spiced with quotations from the Koran" (Cohen Y. 1969:57). Consequently, al-Khatib drew the attention of the Palmach.

Eventually, a decision to assassinate al-Khatib was made. It is not known how, or by who exactly, the decision was made (Cohen Y. 1969:61).

The first plan was that the Mista'arvim would assassinate al-Khatib in Haifa and retreat under fire to nearby Hagana's positions. However, because al-Khatib was very heavily guarder personally, this particular plan was canceled.

Another plan was executed on February 19, 1948. Probably in early February 1948 al-Khatib went to Damascus to recruit Arab warriors and acquire weapons and ammunition. When he returned from his trip, on February 19, on the road from Acco to Haifa around 0930, near Kiryat Motzkin (in the northern entrance to Haifa), a group of Mista'arvim was waiting for his car. Al-Khatib was traveling at the time in a taxi cab of the "Al Alamain" Arab taxi company, accompanied by two Arab escorts. The Mista'arvim identified al-Khatib and began to chase his cab with a black car of their own. After a short while, and near the old Shell Bridge (today, Paz Bridge), the Mista'arvim opened fire from automatic weapons on the taxi, hitting it with at least thirty bullets.

The Arab driver of the cab was wounded, but he managed to drive the cab to the Al Amin Arab hospital. One of al-Khatib 's escorts was wounded severely, and the other died. Al-Khatib himself, however, was wounded from three bullets which had hit his shoulder. He was operated and later recuperated (see Cohen Y. 1969:61 and *Ha'aretz* February 20, 1948:4; Black and Morris 1991:42–43).

It is not known if more attempts against al-Khatib life were ever made. With the exception of Dror's dry note implying that following this attempt al-Khatib escaped later to Lebanon, it is difficult to assess what the other results (if any) of this particular assassination event were (1986:136).

CASE NUMBER 78

The Assassination of Vitold Holianitzky in February or March of 1948 by Lehi in Jerusalem

After Robert Bitker had been asked to quit his position as commander of Etzel, Moshe Rosenberg was appointed as the new commander.[111]

Rosenberg helped to create and institutionalize good and fruitful working relationships with Vitold Holianitzky, who was then the Polish consul in Palestine. The contacts with Holianitzky included Rosenberg, Kalai and Abraham Stern (Yair), who became later Lehi's creator and commander. In the meetings, they tentatively explored the possibly common interests between the Polish government and Etzel. Stern demanded weapons and support for the illegal Jewish immigration to Palestine. Holianitzky certainly showed a positive attitude (Niv, vol. 2:163–164); Naor 1990:154–155). Holianitzky was apparently moved, and deeply impressed, by his meeting with Abraham Stern (Weinshall 1978:107–110; Yevin 1986:123–134) and they became friends. Holianitzky supported Etzel and Abraham Stern, with warm letters of recommendation directed to the Polish authorities, and helped them to get phony passports for illegal Jewish immigrants. During May and June of 1938, Stern and Holianitzky worked out a draft for an agreement between Etzel and the Polish government. When Abraham Stern was killed by British police officer Jeffrey Morton on February 12, 1942, the only flowers put on the fresh grave were those sent by Holianitzky and his wife (Kotzer, no date:p. 250).

After the Nazis invaded, conquered and occupied Poland, Abraham Stern still kept his friendship with Holianitzky. He continued to send Holianitzky small gifts on various Christian or national Polish holidays. Holianitzky, however, was left without work or income. The British helped, and he got a job, first as a censor and later as the deputy in charge of enemy property (that is property whose owner(s) were citizens of either enemy countries, or of countries occupied by the enemy) (Haber and Schiff 1976:159; Yellin-Mor 1974:473).

According to Kanaan (1958:96), in 1948 a representative (Daniel Oster) from the Jewish National Fund was in the process of negotiating with Holianitzky the fate of the German property which was left in Palestine. At that time Holianitzky lived with his wife in Rehavia, Jerusalem.

Somehow, somebody told Lehi's intelligence that Holianitzky (and Arnold—see following case) were spying for the British and for Arabs. Natan Yellin-Mor (1974:473) states that some proof was provided too. Both were taken by members of Lehi in Jerusalem to be investigated. Kanaan (1958:96) recalls that: "One day Holianitzky's wife told me that her husband was arrested.... She said that he showed them a silvered Bible he received from Abraham Stern with a warm and friendly dedication." That did not help. Kanaan guessed that members of Lehi took Holianitzky. Kanaan states that he contacted some members of the Hagana which he knew, as well as Dov Yoseph, and they all promised to help. To no avail. Holianitzky and Arnold were both sentenced later to death for their alleged activities and were executed immediately. Holianitzky's body was found in a field near Sheik Bader (Jerusalem) with his hands tied to those of Arnold (see next case) (ibid., p. 97).

None of Lehi's members who were involved in the assassination of Holianitzky was apparently aware of his warm connections with Abraham Stern, or of Holianitzky's "important contribution to the freedom war" (Yellin-Mor 1974:473).

Yellin-Mor (1974:473), Weinshall (1978:109) and Kotzer (no date:p. 250) all state that this assassination was not justified. Yellin-Mor even discusses the Holianitzky case in the same context he discusses the Tubianski case (see case no. 82), as if both are similar in some important aspect(s). Lehi's contemporary announcement, however, in 1948, clearly denounced Holianitzky as a "Polish spy and an agent of the British intelligence" (Lehi, *Ketavim* [B], pp. 963–964).

CASE NUMBER 79

The Assassination of Stephen Arnold in February or March of 1948 by Lehi

Arnold served in the Anders[112] Polish army and later arrived to Palestine. He headed the Polish news agency in Palestine. He was accused by Lehi of giving information to the British and to Arab gangs. Arnold was assassinated by members of Lehi in Jerusalem in February or March of 1948 (Haber and Schiff 1976:378; Yellin-Mor 1974:473; see also the previous case).

Yellin-Mor "explains" the two last cases on the background that in February–March of 1948, Jerusalem was under siege and many rumors were circulating in the city "explaining" how the Jordanian artillery (which shelled Jerusalem) could, sometimes, have direct hits. One explanation was that the Arabs were getting information from spies. This atmosphere, according to Yellin-Mor, gave rise both to the Tubianski tragedy, and to those of Holianitzky and Arnold.

CASE NUMBER 80

The Assassination of Vera Duksova in Jerusalem on March 27, 1948 by Lehi

According to Reicher (1968), the intelligence department of Lehi found out in 1948 that a female spy (for the British) was working in Jerusalem. After an investigation, they located Vera Duksova. Duksova, who was thirty-six years old, presented herself as Jewish and was married to a Jew. On Friday, March 26, she was kidnaped by members of Lehi from the Allenby coffee shop, which was then located on King George Street in

Jerusalem,[113] where she worked as a waitress. A boy that was taken with her, was released shortly afterwards.

She was taken to Lehi's camp at Sheik Bader, near Jerusalem (today, the area between the Jerusalem Hilton Hotel and the Knesset) and there she was interrogated. Eventually, she admitted that she worked for the British intelligence. Consequently, on Saturday night she was shot to death after she had been accused of spying for the British and of cooperating with the enemy (see S.T.H., vol. 3, part 3:1809; Ha'aretz, March 29, 1948, p. 4; Haber and Schiff 1976:130).

Lehi's announcement from March 1948 admits the assassination for the above stated reasons (see Lehi, Ketavim [B], February 1982 [2d edition] pp. 981–982) and details the confession given, supposedly, by Duksova in the Czech language, written by her, and translated into Hebrew: "Jerusalem, 27/3/48. I, who is signed below, was born in 1912 in Pribraum, Czechoslovakia. I left Czechoslovakia in 1938 and went to Turkey. In 1940 I began to work for the British intelligence. My superior was Mr. Wittold. I arrived to this land in 1941, and I was detained in Camps until 1945. In 1946, I started to work for the CID and to look for other people willing to work for the CID. The expectation from the people recruited by me was: 1. to bring information on the illegal immigration (Ha'apala) 2. to give information on the ammunition-weapons depots of the Hagana. About two months ago Inspector Stenson asked me to give him information about the road blocks in Rehavia [a neighborhood in Jerusalem—ED.] I provided the information. (Signed) Vera Duksova." The announcement ended by the declaration "Our camp should be cleaned from traitors and squealers" and "one is their fate—death." Signed, Lohamei Herut Israel—Lehi.

CASE NUMBER 81

The Assassination Plan against Major Roy Farran on May 4, 1948 in England by Lehi

Lehi had a few very young members. One of the jobs given to these young members was to glue Lehi's posters and announcements on walls in public places. One of the kids who did this was Alexander Rubowitz ("Chaim" was his underground name), sixteen years old from Jerusalem. On the night of May 6, 1947 he was, in fact, in the midst of gluing Lehi's announcements on public walls in Jerusalem.

At that time the British brought to Palestine special army units (called "Special Squads") whose soldiers and officers wore civilian clothes in an effort to use unconventional anti-terror activities against the Jewish underground groups. Major Roy Farran, an ex-commando soldier, headed one of the units.

On the fateful night of May 6, 1947, a group of plain-clothes detectives caught Alexander Rubowitz in the middle of gluing Lehi's wall announcements on Usishkin and Keren Kayemet Streets in Jerusalem. He was taken by force to a police car. As Rubowitz fought the people who arrested him, the hat of one of the detectives fell (there were actual witnesses to the incident). That hat played a crucial role in the following drama.

Alexander Rubowitz was never seen again—alive or dead. Lehi's guess was that he was tortured to death and they began to search for his murderers. The hat that was found had six English letters on it: FAR.AN. The British at first denied that the name of Farran existed, and on June 19, secretly flew Farran out of Palestine. Lehi found this out and started to attack British soldiers throughout Palestine. The British admitted then that they flew Farran to Syria. Under pressure, Farran was brought back to Palestine and had to confront a military court on October 1, 1947. In a fast procedure, the court acquitted Farran. The next day he left Palestine for good.

During this affair, Farran's behavior, as well as that of the British intelligence, was very bizarre to say the least. Farran kept appearing and disappearing, ran away from arrest, quit the police job, gave himself back again and so forth.

Lehi's intelligence sources, however, were fairly confident that Farran was in fact involved in Rubowitz's kidnaping, torture, and murder. There were rumors that Rubowitz was cruelly tortured, that Farran burnt a swastika sign on Rubowitz's chest and that his body was burnt and his ashes discarded. The incidence created much turmoil in the Palestine and British press, as well as among Jewish and British political leaders. Farran became a target for Lehi.[114]

While Farran's memoirs (1948:343–384) refer to the incident, he denies there that he had any connection to Rubowitz's disappearance.

Lehi's agents followed Farran to England, attempting to execute a death sentence passed against him by Lehi. The person in charge of the execution was Herouti. According to Yehuda Ben-Ari's account (a letter from April 15, 1977, file number 7/4 5ב in Jabotinski's archives) he helped Herouti to locate Roy Farran's address in a small village where he lived with his parents. Herouti and his men bought a book in London's Foyle's, booby trapped it with explosives and sent it to Roy Farran's address. The booby trapped book arrived at Farran's place on Tuesday May 4, 1948, almost exactly a year after Rubowitz's kidnaping. There, Roy's younger brother—Rex—opened the package. It exploded and Rex was killed (see also Yachin 1984:203; S.T.H., vol. 3, part 2:935; Niv, vol. 5:150). While Roy Farran does not mention in his book the tragic death of his brother, he left England and for many years moved from country to country.

The Rubowitz-Farran affair has refused to disappear. There are still members of Lehi who want to know what exactly happened, and Rubowitz's family in Jerusalem certainly wants also to know where their son is buried. Binyamin Geffner, an ex-Lehi member, is still actively trying to solve the case. He traced Farran to Calgary Canada and interviewed some of his friends. According to Geffner, it is possible that after Farran and his men tortured Rubowitz to death, they buried his body in a hurry in the backyard of a local church in Jerusalem (e.g., see Golan 1975).

CASE NUMBER 82

The Assassination of Captain Meir Tubianski on June 30, 1948, by an Order of a Field Court of the Israel Defense Forces

The British Mandate over Palestine ended in May of 1948, and the partition plan did not award Jerusalem to the Jews. A fierce and long battle over Jerusalem took place in 1948 and the Jewish portion of Jerusalem was under siege. The city was bombed and bombarded by the artillery of the Jordanian Legion, as well as exposed to shots by active Arab snipers. The city was hence under much pressure, militarily, economically (food was rationed), socially, and politically. The Lehi, Etzel and Hagana were very active in defending the city. During the siege, rumors about spies, collaborators, informers, and traitors abounded and the ugly ghosts of war poisoned the atmosphere. We have already seen that in 1948 Lehi alone executed four people in Jerusalem. What was perceived as the accuracy of the Jordanian artillery puzzled the Jewish defenders of the city. Their suspicions focused on the Jerusalem Electrical company. The company had the addresses of all important places in the city and some of its workers were in constant contact with the Arab side of the city, using their wireless transmitters (for legitimate reasons).

Etzel arrested five British clerks of the Jerusalem Electrical company and investigated them. The Hagana arrested Meir Tubianski.

Meir Tubianski was an engineer and a senior official in the Jerusalem Electrical company in 1948. He had the rank of a Major in the British army during the second world war. In June of 1948 he was appointed as the first commander of the Jerusalem newly established IDF (Israel Defense Forces) camp in "Schneler" near Mea Shearim (Haber and Schiff 1976:222–223). Since Tubianski did not succeed in this job, he was transferred to command the airstrips in Jerusalem (Shealtiel's testimony, *Ha'aretz*, October 19, 1949, p. 2).

During the Arab siege of Jerusalem in 1948, the three underground Jewish organizations moved their headquarters and factories in the city. The Hagana's intelligence service, the Shai, in Jerusalem headed at that time by Binyamin Gibly, became very suspicious about the accuracy of the Arab artillery in hitting targets which moved in the city (e.g., factories and headquarters). There was a strong suspicion that Tubianski gave the addresses of the places to his British colleagues in the Jerusalem Electrical company so that they could connect them to the Electrical network. This information, that was the suspicion, was transmitted to the Arab artillery which bombarded the new addresses.

Tubianski was an old member (for about twenty-two years) in the Hagana. In the early months of 1948, Isser Be'ery, the head of the Shai in Israel[115] received information that Tubianski was giving hostile British clerks information (which they supposedly passed on to the Arabs). Be'ery consulted with the head of the legal service of the IDF, then Abraham Gorally, and as a result decided to arrest Tubianski. Be'ery will later claim that he understood from Gorally that he was allowed to establish a military court against Tubianski. On the very same day Be'ery told the commander of the Palmach about his suspicions. A written request was made to the Palmach regional commander to assist Be'ery in any way possible.

The Trial

On Monday June 30, 1948, Be'ery sent one of his officers to arrest Tubianski, who was in Tel Aviv. Tubianski came willingly and without resistance. They left Tel Aviv around 1500. At approximately 1600 Tubianski faced the charge of treason in front of a military court in the deserted Arab village of Beit Giz (on the road from Tel Aviv to Jerusalem). Three judges were appointed to hear the trial.[116] Tubianski was not allowed to prepare a proper defense or to consult with a lawyer. Tubianski was shown a list of the arms and ammunition factories in Jerusalem the addresses of which he supposedly had given to his British superiors in the Jerusalem Electrical company.

At that time Jerusalem had two different networks of electricity, of which one serviced the military and both of which were serviced by the Jerusalem Electrical Company. The British manager of the Jerusalem Electrical Company—Michael Bryant—may have known about the two electrical networks, but during a conversation conducted on June 16, 1948, Tubianski gave Bryant the information. This conversation was open, and was probably overheard by other Jewish workers. Suspecting that Tubianski was giving vital and secret information to a hostile British, this information was passed on to the Hagana's intelligence. Despite the insinuations, the information provided by Tubianski could be obtained by other ways. Tubianski was also accused that the information given on the sixteenth to Bryant was passed on to the Jordanian artillery.

When Tubianski heard the charges, he supposedly admitted giving Bryant the information, thereby indirectly admitting guilt.

While there is a version that he supposedly may have even said that he deserved a death sentence, a more reliable version is that he probably admitted giving the list of places that needed electricity on both networks in Jerusalem, but maintained that the information was given only so that these places could be connected to the network and receive electrical supply and not as an act of treason. Nevertheless, the judges found Tubianski guilty of espionage and treason and decided on a death sentence. On the same day he was arrested, at around 1900, a firing squad[117] shot Tubianski to death.[118] The whole trial, conviction, and execution took about three hours.

The Clearing and Cleansing of Tubianski

Short announcements in the Jewish daily press of July 20, 1948, informed the public that on the thirtieth of June an unknown spy was executed. Tubianski's wife, Chaya (Lena), was not told what had happened but when she found out, she wrote to David Ben-Gurion (November 1948), demanding an explanation. Ben-Gurion instructed the army chief of staff to investigate. Ben-Gurion wrote Tubianski's wife in December 1948 that "I checked the procedure of his trial and I found out that it was not in order, perhaps because the underground laws were still dominant in the army" (*Ma'ariv*, July 5, 1949, p. 2).

On July 1, 1949, Ben-Gurion wrote again to Mrs. Tubianski that "it was found that Meir Tubianski was innocent (and his execution) was a tragic mistake.... Attempting to rectify the tragedy, the chief of staff decided: 1. to give Meir Tubianski a rank of a captain. 2. to give him a full military burial. 3. to pay you and your son compensations.... Your husband made a mistake and perhaps a serious one, giving his British superior a list and did not think it would fall into the wrong hands. He admitted the mistake and regretted it, but he had no bad intentions and without intent there is no treason" (Tubianski's file in the *Ha'aretz* archive). Tubianski was buried in a full military service on July 7, 1949 (*Ha'aretz*, July 5, p. 1; July 7, p. 1; July 8, 1949, p. 1).

On July 10, 1949, Isser Be'ery was arrested and charged with the illegal killing of Tubianski. The trial itself was open to the public and began in the district court of Tel Aviv on October 16, 1949, and lasted until October 30, 1949. On November 22, 1949, the verdict was given. The court stated specifically that no charges of treason against Tubianski were substantiated and that his execution was a fatal mistake. The court stated that the use of the list Tubianski supposedly had given to his British superior as evidence lacked any basis. Furthermore, some questions were raised during the trial regarding the nature of the accusations against Tubianski. For example, between June 11 and July 9, a cease fire was in effect, so the information supposedly given by Tubianski *could not* have served the Jordanian artillery. Moreover, there were some questions as to whether in fact the Jordanian artillery was so accurate (*Ha'aretz*, October 26, 1949, p. 2). In short, Tubianski was innocent of the charges of espionage and treason.

Tubianski's execution was attributed to Be'ery for three reasons: (a) Be'ery appointed three of his subordinates as judges in a "field military court" and told them that if they found Tubianski guilty they had the permission to sentence him to death; (b) After the judges had found Tubianski guilty and sentenced him to death, Be'ery approved the sentence and verdict; (c) Be'ery ordered that a firing squad be assembled to carry out the court's decision. Be'ery was found guilty as charged and was sentenced to one day in prison. (See also Bar Zohar 1970:39–45; Harel 1989:113–137; *Ha'aretz*, November 23, 1949). Clearly the court was convinced that Tubianski was killed illegally, but was equally convinced that Be'ery did not do what he did with a malicious intent.

The five British clerks kidnaped by Etzel in 1948 were given to the Hagana. Three were released for lack of evidence, two were charged with espionage. One (Hawkins) was found innocent and the other (William Silvester) was found guilty. In an appeal to the Israeli Supreme Court[119] this individual was found not guilty and was consequently released (Katz 1966, p. 427).

Ben-Gurion wrote to Tubianski's wife: "I checked the procedure of his trial and I found out that it was not in order, perhaps because the underground laws were still dominant in the army." This is an important statement because it supports our understanding of the type of social and legal justice on which Tubianski's trial was based.

The Tubianski case left a real scar in the moral fiber of Israeli society. Debates around and about it still rage. Thus, when I gave a few talks in Israel and mentioned the Tubianski case, some people in the audience came to me and told me they were in the Hagana and were willing to swear that Tubianski was in fact a traitor. They could not, however, provide any proof or unknown information.[120]

The Tubianski case is significant, interesting and instructive from another and different angle too. The trial and court, as well as the justice Tubianski received probably represent the type of justice which prevailed among the three pre-state underground Jewish organizations. The type of justice which emerged, crystallized and prevailed after 1948, and which was based on open and formal procedures grounded on facts and on due processes, and radically different than the pre-1948 justice.

The Tubianski case lights up a type of justice, which was based on insufficient and inconclusive evidence, much conjecture, a lot of pressure, fast procedures, lack of any proper attention to basic rights of defendants, no right to a real appeal, etc. What was called a trial was not a trial in the sense that we all know and understand. Tubianski really did not have much of a reasonable chance to defend himself once the trial began. Other victims of the same justice, before 1948, may not even have had the same procedure Tubianski had and were "judged" by a court they had not even confronted. One is simply left pondering about how many of the other victims which are included in this study could have been spared had they faced an open and public trial with a proper defense, and not a secret procedure which, in most cases, can not even be traced today.

What I call the "Tubianski Syndrome," that is the realization that after a thorough investigation a convicted traitor may be found innocent, is what lies, I think, at the heart of the extreme reluctance to reopen the cases, even after forty years. The discreditation yielded by the Tubianski's case was simply overpowering.

CASE NUMBER 83

The Assassination of Count Folke Bernadotte on September 17, 1948 in Jerusalem by "Hazit Hamoledet"

Count Folke Bernadotte was born in 1895 in Sweden, a son to an esteemed and respected family. He was the youngest son of Prince Oscar August Bernadotte of Sweden, a brother of King Gustav V. He served in the Swedish army until 1939 and from then on, following some bitter failures in the business world, he devoted his life to humanitarian activities. He was elected as the Swedish Scouts president in 1939 and became president of the Swedish Red Cross in 1946. He was involved in helping Danish Jews and other Scandinavians to escape from the Nazi occupation to Sweden, and negotiated the release and rescue of thousands of Scandinavians and Jews, from Nazi concentration camps. This activity, however, was not problem free. Nadel (1968), Tzameret (1988) and Leni Yahil (the *Jerusalem Post*, May 3, 1985:13) all indicate that Bernadotte was not so interested in saving Jews from Nazi concentration camps, and was much more interested in the Scandinavian prisoners. Yahil guessed that the reason for that may have been that Bernadotte was afraid that the inclusion of Jews in his efforts could render the whole operation useless. It was therefore due to the efforts of his Danish and Norwegian partners that Jews were, after all, included in the rescue operation. In April of 1945, he passed a manipulative peace offer from Himmler to the allies. The offer was rejected on April 27 (e.g., see Hewins 1950, and Bernadotte's 1945 book on that period, as well as Nadel 1968 for counter arguments).[121] However, despite his problematic record in the above negotiations and personal detachment, Bernadotte, somehow, gained a reputation of an international political celebrity.

The Arab armies and irregular forces invaded Palestine in May of 1948, in a brutal and blunt attempt to violate the U.N. partition plan. The Secretary-General of the United Nations was Trygva Lie who was very concerned about the Arab military invasion to Palestine (which he referred to as "armed aggression"—see Persson 1979:109). While it is not entirely clear from where exactly the idea of a UN mediator came, it is nevertheless obvious that Lie supported the idea and on May 14, 1948 the UN General Assembly adopted a resolution calling for the appointment of a mediator.[122] Lie chose Bernadotte, and on May 20, appointed him as the UN Middle East mediator between the Jews and the Arabs (see Persson 1979:108–111). Bernadotte actually came to the Middle East in May of 1948. Due to his intervention, a cease fire agreement was achieved and lasted between June 11 till July 9.

Bernadotte began to crystallize some ideas about how to solve the Jewish-Arab problem in Palestine-Israel. In November 29, 1947, the UN adopted a partition resolution for Palestine, basically dividing the land between the Jews and the Arabs. Bernadotte worked out a plan that deviated quite significantly from the UN resolution.

He considered giving the Negev (Israel's southern part) to the Arabs, giving the Galilee to the Jews, internationalizing Jerusalem, restricting Jewish immigration to Israel and giving permission to the Arab refugees to return to Palestine (which were considered by the Jews as major concessions to the Arabs). The government of Israel rejected (already in July of 1948) these ideas and Bernadotte was not very popular among the Jews. Lehi staged a demonstration against him, and he was warned a few times.[123]

According to Nadel (1968), Kanaan and Margalit (1968), Harel (1979) and Shaked (1988) during June or August of 1948, the leadership of Lehi (Yellin-Mor, Eldad-Sheib, Yazernitzky-Shamir), in a series of discussions, decided that Bernadotte posed a serious and real threat to the future of the emerging state of Israel. Eldad and Yehoshua Zetler suggested to assassinate Bernadotte. The suggestion was accepted. Yellin-Mor insisted that, for various reasons, Lehi should not be directly associated with the act and suggested to create a front organization called "Hazit Hamoledet" (translated as "the National Front") that would take responsibility for the act. Yehoshua Zetler, from Jerusalem, was charged with the operational responsibility. While Eldad Sheib remembers the June or July meeting fairly well, Zetler claims that he does not remember it (Shaked 1988). According to Zetler, he and Eldad Sheib went from Jerusalem to Haifa to meet Natan Yellin-Mor in the sixth or seventh of September 1948, in order to get his final approval. While Shamir was present in the first meeting, it is not entirely clear whether he was present in the second meeting. In any event, the decision to assassinate Bernadotte was made.

On Friday September 17, 1948, at around 1700, Bernadotte's car convoy was going through Jerusalem. Its movement was blocked by a jeep on Hapalmach Street, near Katamon (near

where 18 Hapalmach Street is today), and four Jewish men in
what looked like army clothes approached the convoy. No one
on Bernadotte's convoy carried arms, strictly on Bernadotte's
wish. One of the men identified Bernadotte and "he put a
Tommy gun through the open window on my side of the car and
fired point-blank at Count Bernadotte and Colonel Se'rot"
(Statement of General Aage Lundstrom, p. 268 in Bernadotte
1951). While Count Bernadotte was rushed to a nearby hospital,
he was dead on arrival. He was fifty-three years old when he
died, (as well as Colonel Se'rot who was the chief of the French
UN observers unit).[124]

The death of Bernadotte was tragic from another angle too.
Persson (1979) mentions that Bernadotte disliked, even despised,
quite a few of the Jewish and Arab leaders who he negotiated
with (something which was omitted from Bernadotte's 1951
book) and that, yet, Bernadotte was a firm believer in the importance of persons in shaping historical processes. He did not
believe in objective historical powers and processes. Ironically
the very same firm belief led to his assassination, by people he
could not possibly identify with, or like.

Bernadotte's assassins were never fully identified or brought
to trial. During the years since 1948, there were a few "leaks" to
the press about who the assassins were. It seems almost a certainty that Yehoshua Cohen was the one who actually used his
"Schmeisser" submachine gun to assassinate Bernadotte. It also
seems quite certain that the other Lehi members who were present
in the fateful September 17 assassination were Yehoshua Zetler
(as the Lehi commander in charge of the operation), Yitzhak Ben-
Moshe ("Betzaleli"), and Mechoulam Makover ("Yoav").[125]

Some former members of Lehi gave during 1988 a few interviews from which a partial reconstruction of the operational
level can be made. It seems safe to assume that Lehi member
Yehoshua Zetler ("Meir") chose the particular members of the
group of assassins. Aside from Cohen there were probably only
four other Lehi's members present in the assassination scene.
Judging by Makover's most recent and systematic testimony (see
Bender 1988 and Makover M. 1988), as well as Shaked's (1988)
detailed investigation, it seems also safe to assume that Yehoshua
Cohen, Mechoulam Makover, Yitzhak Ben-Moshe and another

(still anonymous) person took part in the actual assassination.[126] They all left Lehi's camp "Dror" (which was located in Talbia) at around 1600 with a Jeep. The Jeep of the assassins followed the "De Soto" car which was driven by Yehoshua Zetler. Zetler placed the assassins in the assassination spot and went with Stanley Goldfoot (another member of Lehi) to an observation spot on a nearby hill, from where they watched the assassination. Makover was the one who used the Jeep to block the road (Palmach Street), forcing Bernadotte's convoy to come to a full stop. Cohen was the one who identified Bernadotte in the last car of the convoy. He aimed his Schmeisser submachine gun into the car and opened fire. The first round hit, by mistake, the French Colonel Se'rot; Cohen took aim again and the second round of bullets hit Bernadotte.[127]

The information about Bernadotte's movements in Israel was obtained from Stanley Goldfoot, a reporter who was a member of Lehi, who gave it to Yehoshua Zetler. After the assassination, Gabi Badian—who was with Lehi's intelligence—called Stanley Goldfoot and asked him to draft and type a bulletin in which the responsibility for the assassination was claimed by Hazit Hamoledet, a previously unknown organization. Badian told Goldfoot that this had to be done on orders from Lehi headquarters in Tel Aviv. Goldfoot followed the instructions to the letter, and later even distributed the stenciled bulletin to all the embassies and consulates in Jerusalem.

Yehoshua Zetler, the commander of the hit team that assassinated Bernadotte, told Shaked (1988:2) that Bernadotte was assassinated because: "We believed that the man was dangerous, that he meant to create historical facts that would have determined our future. The UN had decided on internationalizing Jerusalem, and then suddenly Bernadotte appeared with a much more dangerous plan: to include the city within Jordan. There was no escape from deciding on his assassination."

Although some scholars tend to argue that the assassination of Bernadotte had either no results (e.g., Heller), or problematic results (e.g., Amitzur 1989), it is not too difficult to see that the assassination had, in fact, quite a few results. The heads of the new state of Israel (e.g., Sharet, Dov Yosef, Ben-Gurion) were shocked. An anti-Israeli propaganda wave began to roll in the world. Ben-Gurion, Israel's first prime minister, decided to act fast and firmly.

Ben-Gurion and his advisors were not misled by the decoy called Hazit Hamoledet. It is clear now that the "new" name did not fool Ben-Gurion and his staff. They sensed Lehi's fingerprints all over the case and they were fairly certain that Lehi was indeed deeply involved in the assassination. They decided to deal swiftly and decisively with Lehi and give a clear signal to other possible similar underground groups who may threaten the emerging and crystallizing fragile political structure of Israel. As a result, hundreds of Lehi's members were arrested (e.g., see *Ha'aretz*, September 24, 1949, p. 1) and finally Yellin-Mor (one of Lehi's commanders) and Matitiahu Shmuelevitz were arrested in Haifa on September 20, 1948, after a large scale manhunt (Harel 1989:110–112).

They were both accused in a military court in Acco on December 5, 1948, with violating the act of terror prevention.[128] In the trial, Yellin-Mor denied any connection to Bernadotte's assassination. According to an interview with Eldad, Yellin-Mor lied in the trial (see Harel 1979:144). On February 10, 1949, both were found guilty (although they were not found guilty as directly involved in Bernadotte's assassination). Yellin-Mor was given a sentence of eight years in prison and Shmuelevitz was given five years. On February 10, 1949, a general amnesty was declared in Israel and both were released.[129]

The reaction of the temporary Israeli government to the assassination was firm and consistent. On September 18, 1948, the government publicized a very strong denouncement of the assassination. On May 4, 1949 Abba Eban, then the Israeli ambassador to the UN told the security council that the investigation in the case continued. On April 9, 1949 Israel reported to the UN that it had paid compensations to Se'rot's family. It would also pay later a compensation of around $54,000 to the UN. On September of 1949, Israel announced that it would plant a forest commemorating Bernadotte and on May 27, 1950, Israel apologized to the UN for the fact that Bernadotte was assassinated in its territory.

A few days after the assassination, Bernadotte's final report was made public in France with a set of recommendations very similar to the ones mentioned earlier (e.g., see *Ha'aretz*, September 21, 1948, p. 1). On December 11, 1949, the UN General Assembly decided to reject those recommendations.

The two most prominent results of Bernadotte's assassination were the following: (a) the newly established state of Israel headed by Ben-Gurion, virtually eliminated the existence of Lehi as a potential dissident rival and dangerous underground group; (b) the "compromise" plan Bernadotte advocated simply died. It is possible that it would not have been accepted even had he lived. His assassination, however, eliminated the existence of an able and energetic mediator. In his absence, there were no other entrepreneurs who kept pushing his plan, and the signal of what may be the fate of advocators of similar plans was visible (see also Persson 1979; Stanger 1988).

Joseph Heller, who wrote some historical papers on Lehi, told Segev (1988; see also Heller 1979) that Bernadotte's assassination was actually a signal from Lehi to the USSR that a "capitalist," British oriented intervention, in the form of a Western imperialist mediator was unacceptable. Heller relies on what may seem to be an orientation towards the USSR in Lehi at that time. This is an interesting and refreshing look at the Bernadotte's assassination. However, this interpretation is not consistent with most works, and reports, which were published so far on Bernadotte's assassination. Judging by Lehi's ideology and activity, it is very reasonable to accept the version that Bernadotte was assassinated because Lehi's contemporary command estimated that he posed a grave danger to the emerging State of Israel. One must be reminded that Bernadotte's mission lasted almost four [!] months. During this time period, Lehi—as well as others—did not hide their dissatisfaction with the mediation. It seems that only once Lehi's command felt reasonably sure that—from their ideological perspective Bernadotte constituted a real danger, they carried out the plan of his assassination. Furthermore, Heller's interpretation is based on an interesting conjecture and not on any direct documentation, or interviews. Those involved in the assassination never gave any information which supports this hypothesis.

In the same interview, Heller also told Segev that Bernadotte's assassination did not change much because it hurt the state of

Israel very little, and that the assassination "did not at all influence on the elimination of the [Bernadotte's] plan. His plan would not have been actualized because the victories won by the Israeli army in the independence war changed the face of reality and everyone rejected the plan: the Arabs, the Soviets and the Americans too.... They could let him, that Swede, die of old age and everything would have been as it is today." This interpretation is evidently speculative. To begin with, if contemporary political powers were so unanimous in their objection to the Bernadotte's plan, especially the Soviets, than there was absolutely no reason for Lehi to want to assassinate him. Second, I very strongly doubt that the assassination "did not change anything." Bernadotte was a very powerful and prestigious person. It is not at all clear that he could not persuade the USSR the Arabs and the Americans to accept his plan (or a weakened version of it). He was asked, after all, to *mediate*, and he was very serious about his mediation. Furthermore, while his personal history of mediation was quite problematic, he nevertheless had some success in it. One must be also reminded that regarding Bernadotte, Ben-Gurion said that: "As long as Bernadotte was alive all the UN was against us, except the Russians" (see Lapidot and Leor 1988). While this may give some tenuous support to Heller's previous conjecture ("a signal to the Russians"), it most certainly does not support his second interpretation (that the assassination achieved no results). Third, Israel was not always successful (in the 1948 war, in the 1956 Sinai campaign and in the 1967 war) to translate military achievements and the conquering of territory into political gains. Heller's assertion that the victories won in 1948 by the Israel army would have "dictated the map," with or without Bernadotte, is misleading, inaccurate and constitutes an unfounded and unwarranted conjecture. Philosophically, Heller seems to take the position that historical processes transcend individual actions and apply it to the Bernadotte case.[130] This application is quite problematic.[131]

CHAPTER 8

Political Assassinations by Jews in Israel between 1949–1980

CASE NUMBER 84

The Assassination Plot against West German Chancellor Konrad Adenauer on March 27, 1952—Unsuccessful

The early fifties witnessed the total disintegration of Etzel and the hesitant emergence of "Herut" party which, supposedly, continued Etzel politically. The early 1950s also witnessed one of the deepest and most bitter controversies in the history of Israel—the "Shilumim Agreement" between the government of the Federal Republic of Germany and Israel. As a result of this agreement, Israel received vital and essential economic aid from Germany. The Herut party did not like the agreement at all, and preached relentlessly and vehemently against it. Menachem Begin, a leader of Herut, was very effective. The moral claim against the agreement was that it gave the Germans an unjustifiable rehabilitation (e.g., see Segev 1991:173–236).

On this background, a former Etzel member, Yehoshua Offir, was asked (it is not known by who) to create an underground in the city of Haifa. The goal of this "underground" was to hit ships coming to Haifa port and bringing equipment as part of the Shilumim Agreement (Lifshitz 1987). On September 6, 1953, Ben-Zion Herman (who worked for Herut's newspaper) was caught carrying a bomb into Haifa's port.[1] On October 5, 1952, Dov Shilanski from "Herut" was also caught in Jerusalem trying to put a bomb in the ministry of foreign affairs (more on this in chapter 10).

While the above two acts may be considered as acts of terror, there was a third act which did constitute a political assassination event proper.

In 1952, and following guidelines and instructions from sources in Israel, a group of five sympathizers in France (probably including Dr. Eli Tavin) sent in March an explosive envelope to Konrad Adenauer (1876–1967) who was the first chancellor of the Federal Republic of Germany (Sarna 1987). One of the reasons to use France as a base was an explicit attempt to mislead Ben-Gurion and disassociate Herut in Israel from the act.

On Thursday, March 27, 1952, the explosive parcel addressed to Adenauer arrived in Munich. A German bomb disposal expert— Karl Reichart—tried to open the envelope. It exploded and killed him, as well as severely wounding three other policemen (*Jerusalem Post*, March 28, 1952, p. 1; Sarna 1987).

Clearly, we had here an act of "propaganda by deed" committed by a group of actors aiming at a specific and prominent political actor.

CASE NUMBER 85

The Assassination Plot against David Zvi Pinkas on the Night between June 21 and June 22, 1952—Unsuccessful

The secular/religious conflict between Jews in contemporary Israeli society has been severe, problematic and explosive. It is a conflict between two very different philosophies and ways of life (e.g., see Friedman 1977; Samet 1979).

In 1952, the State of Israel was facing an acute shortage of fuel. As a result, the government of Israel decided in June that all vehicles in Israel would not travel during two full days. One day would be chosen by the owner, the other day had to be a Saturday. While the minister of transportation then—David Zvi Pinkas—stated that the choice of Saturday as one compulsory day was due to economic reasons, others interpreted it as an attempt to enforce and reinforce religious values of observing the Shabbat (Saturday). This is the place to note that observant Jews are not supposed to ride in their vehicles on Saturday.

David Zvi Pinkas (1895–1952), contemporary minister of transportation, was born in Sopron, Hungary, and in 1925 settled in Palestine. He was a Mizrachi leader and a member of religious parties ("Chazit Datit" in the first Knesset, and "Hamizrachi" in the second) who began his political career as a member in the Knesset after the elections to the second Knesset in October of 1951.

On Sunday, June 22, 1952, around 0130 in the morning, two people were caught running out of David Zvi Pinkas' home in Ramchal street in Tel Aviv. The police guards who were stationed outside Pinkas home stopped them and after a few minutes a bomb exploded at the front door of Mr. Pinkas' apartment. The damage was severe, but luckily no one was hurt (see *Ha'aretz*, June 23, 1952). The two people who were arrested coming out of Pinkas' house at that night were Amos Keinan (twenty-three years old) and Shealtiel Ben-Yair (twenty-nine years old) (see *Ha'aretz*, June 23, 1952). Both were arrested and charged in July 1952 with putting the bomb at the front door of Pinkas' apartment. Both denied the charges and after a long trial,[2] both were acquitted on September 13, 1952 (see *Ha'aretz*, September 14, 1952, p. 2). An appeal to the Israeli supreme court (no. 139/52) did not change the verdict. The judges of the supreme court stated that the prosecution had a very weak case to begin with and regardless of the question whether Keinan and Ben-Yair were telling the truth or not, the prosecution simply did not have good evidence.

Before and during the trial, Keinan's past affiliation with Lehi and the Canaanim (see below) came up.

In 1945, Keinan joined Lehi (Yellin-Mor 1974:362–363) under the underground name of "Yochanan" (after the name of a famous Jewish warrior from the days of the second Temple— Yochanan from Gush Halav. Here we have again the connection to the zealots [see Keinan 1988]). Between 1949 and 1950, he joined the group that became known as the "Canaanites" (*Ha'aretz*, July 10, 1952, p. 4). That group was established by Uriel Shelach (also called Yonatan Ratosh). Shelach was acquainted with Abraham Stern ("Yair"; see Yevin 1986:98–101, 106, 125, 174, 208–210), and even wrote a powerful poem commemorating Yair after he was killed by Morton.[3]

The Canaanites formed a small group of young idealists whose main goal was to create a new type of a Jewish identity— personal and collective—in Palestine and Israel. They called themselves the "young Hebrews," tried to reject the use of symbols which were associated with the Jewish existence in the Diaspora, and wanted to create a new, proud, nationalistic-secular and free Jew. Among other things, this group explicitly demanded a full and total separation of religion from State.[4] While the Canaanites were clearly unhappy with Pinkas' decision, Keinan was no longer a member in the group in 1952, and in their newspaper (*Aleph*) the Canaanites denounced the act. Although much less is known about Ben-Yair, it is clear that he was in Lehi too and that he and Keinan met in May of 1948 as members of Lehi (Keinan 1990:21).

On the face of it, Keinan and Ben-Yair had some "good" ideological reasons, from their point of view, for putting the bomb at the door of Pinkas' home. The "story" which they gave the court sounds even today incredible, bizarre and simply improbable and unbelievable. In an interview with one of the prominent leaders of the Canaanites[5] the interviewee expressed no doubt that Keinan was the one who in fact planted the bomb at the door of Pinkas' home. However, one must be reminded that officially in the court, Keinan and Ben-Yair were acquitted. Interesting to note that Keinan wrote—very briefly—about this affair in 1990, but failed to relate directly to the question of whether he and/or Ben-Yair were in fact involved in the bombing of Pinkas' home.

In terms of classification, there can be no doubt that Pinkas' life was threatened and in danger at the night between June 21–22 of 1952. The "reason" for that act was probably ideological. However, it is not possible—officially—to point out who the assassins were.

CASE NUMBER 86

The Assassination of Dr. Rudolf Kasztner by Dan Shemer, Ze'ev Ekstein, and Joseph Menkes in Tel Aviv on March 2, 1957

To understand this case we shall have to delve into the historical description of the Nazi extermination of Hungarian Jews.

In March of 1944, the Nazis invaded Hungary. Adolf Eichman and his group came to Budapest and began their preparations to activate the "final solution" for Hungarian Jews.[6]

The Jews in Hungary were divided among themselves into a few main groups. They were, however, aware of what the Nazis were doing to European Jews. They tried to organize help, and created a "saving committee."

One of the key members of the committee was Dr. Rudolf (Israel) Kasztner (born 1906). Kasztner was a local Zionist politician who found himself in the midst of something more dreadful than Dante's hell. Kasztner tried to negotiate with Eichman and his group of murderers and attempted to save as many Jews as he possibly could under the circumstances.

He was effective in securing the exit of the "train of the prestigious" in June of 1944. That was a train with 1684 Jews aboard which the Nazis allowed to leave Hungary to Switzerland supposedly as a sign of "good will" and indication of "intent." He was also involved in Yoel Brand's mission (see case nos. 47 and 49).

On May 25, 1953, the legal advisor to the Israeli government accused, in criminal file no. 53/124, a very questionable character named Malkiel Greenwald (e.g., see Harel 1985:113–125), with defaming Dr. Kasztner. At that time, Kasztner was the spokesman for the Israeli ministry of commerce and industry. Greenwald, in mimeographed letters accused him of cooperating with the Nazis, helping in the final extermination of Hungarian Jews, helping a Nazi war-criminal, living on funds "confiscated" from Hungarian Jews and called to kill Kasztner.

According to Greenwald's accusations, Dr. Kasztner actually helped the Nazis. The main claims were that the June 1944 train was a price the Nazis paid to buy Kasztner's silence in order to keep Hungarian Jews unaware of what was really awaiting them, and that Kasztner gained economically from the money confiscated from the Jews. Monstrous accusations indeed.

In January of 1954, the trial began in Jerusalem and Greenwald hired as his lawyer Shmuel Tamir (who was earlier a member of Etzel, and in the late 1970s became Israel's minister of Law). Tamir was very effective in turning the trial over, from a simple criminal case into a political trial and from an accused he became an accuser. This trial became one of the most dramatic and painful trials in the history of Israel. It lasted from January 1953 till June 22, 1955.[7] In the trial, the role of the Jewish leadership in 1944 Nazi occupied Hungary and in Palestine, was examined with a magnifying glass.

Tamir implied that there were many different issues in which Kasztner was involved, and on which he basically acted as a cooperator (or a collaborator) with the Nazis and hence was a traitor. I shall mention them briefly. One, the very fact that he maintained contacts and negotiated with the Gestapo and the SS. Second, that he was involved in what became later known as the prestigious June 1944 train. The implication was that rather than save many Jews, that train was the price that Eichman and his Nazi group were willing to pay for Kasztner's silence. Three, the Nazis allowed Dr. Kasztner to hide his Jewish identity in Budapest and his behavior there, according to Tamir, was disgraceful. He did not wear a yellow Magen David, he played cards with Nazis, and so forth. Fourth, that Kasztner selected and positively discriminated Jews from the Kloj Ghetto over Jews from other places and 388 Jews from that particular ghetto were on the June 1944 train, many of them were relatives of Kasztner. Fifth, that Kasztner helped to turn Yoel Brand's mission (see case nos. 47 and 49) into a failure. Sixth, that Kasztner failed to alarm and inform Hungarian Jews that they were not just being transported outside of Hungary to a new resettlement, but that they were transported to be exterminated in Auschwitz. That he failed to warn Jewish leaders outside Hungary as to the real horrendous events. Seventh, in 1944, the British army sent a few British Jewish officer paratroopers to Hungary for intelligence purposes. Three of them, Hanna Senesh, Yoel Palgi, and Goldstein clearly intended to help organize the Jews into resisting the Nazis. The claim was that Kasztner was involved in the arrest of all three by the Nazis. Eighth, that after the war ended Kasztner testified in favor of SS officer Kurt Bachar. Ninth, that Kasztner interfered with saving operations in Europe. Tenth, that Kasztner had personally used the money confiscated from Jews to live a luxurious life in Switzerland.

On June 22, 1955, Judge Halevi, in a long and detailed verdict, determined that, in fact, Kasztner cooperated with the Nazis, and thus helped indirectly in preparing the ground for the extermination of Hungarian Jews, and that he helped ex-SS officer Kurt Bachar. The judge stated that the above tenth accusation was totally groundless. Judge Halevi stated in the verdict that when Kasztner accepted "the gift" of the train "he sold his soul to the devil" (e.g., see Rosenfeld 1955:415; Segev 1991:266–267. Segev's main advantage is in his reification of the contemporary atmosphere in Israel).

The trial in Jerusalem attracted much attention. Already in the night of March 15, 1955 an anonymous pamphlet was distributed in which one of the judges—M. Peretz—was accused of being biased and of cooperating with the old "leadership" so as to help "cover up" Kasztner's supposed "atrocities" (Harel 1985:106). That there were many people in Israel in the mid-1950s who were unhappy with Kasztner's activities during the period of the holocaust is obvious.

Eldad Sheib, who was one of the triumvirate that had previously commanded Lehi, had a newspaper called *Sulam* (meaning in Hebrew "ladder") which preached a right-wing national ideology. He also formed an organization called "Hazit Hanoar Haleumit" (meaning in Hebrew "the front of the National youth") where small groups met and discussed various national topics. Eldad certainly preached doing "something" about Kasztner (e.g., see Harel 1985:47–48, 145–147).

The transition of Israel to a state in the late 1940s and early 1950s was a problematic and painful process. Different political groups who felt that the emerging state was not what they wanted, took the freedom to choose terrorism "to get their way." One of these groups was the right-wing national "Malchut Israel" ("the Kingdom of Israel"), or as it became known, the "Zrifin underground." That group was particularly active during 1952–1953. For example, on February 9, 1953, late at night, members from the group planted a bomb at the Soviet embassy which was located at that time at 46 Rothschild Street in Tel Aviv. The bomb exploded and wounded some workers, as well as causing much damage. Consequently, Moscow severed its diplomatic ties with Israel for about six months. The Israeli secret service began an investigation, exposed the group and arrested about sixteen members. They were charged in a military court. Some were found guilty and sent to prison. Two members of that group were Ya'acov Herouti and Joseph Menkes (see Harel 1985:55–73 for a short account). The lawyer for the defendants was again Shmuel Tamir. For lack of evidence, Menkes was not charged. Herouti received a ten year prison sentence. In 1955,

Herouti and others, received state clemency and were released. Herouti and Menkes were previously members of Lehi.

On Saturday night, March 2, 1957, Dr. Kasztner returned to his home in Tel Aviv (8 Shderot Shmuel Street) from his work as the night editor of a local Hungarian language newspaper. An anonymous male approached Dr. Kasztner, identified him and shot him three times with a gun. Dr. Kasztner was taken to a hospital where he fought death for about two weeks. He died on the eighteenth. The Israeli secret service, headed then by Isser Harel, started to investigate. Very soon four suspects were arrested: Ya'acov Herouti, Joseph Menkes (thirty-eight years old), Ze'ev Ekstein (twenty-four years old), and Dan Shemer (twenty-three years old) (see Ha'aretz, March 7 and 11, 1957). The police told the press on March 12, 1957 (see Ha'aretz, p. 4) that they deciphered the case.

While there were other different background actors such as Tamir, Rumak, and Sheib, only Menkes, Ekstein, and Shemer were eventually charged on May 28, 1957 of assassinating Dr. Kasztner and in being members in a terroristic organization. Herouti was charged with membership in a terrorist organization. On January 28, 1958, in a different trial, Herouti was found guilty in publicizing the pamphlet mentioned before, and was sentenced to eighteen months in prison. An appeal to the Israeli supreme court was not accepted. Menkes, Shemer, and Ekstein were found guilty in Kasztner's assassination. In responding to an appeal, the Israeli supreme court stated that it was Menkes who persuaded Ekstein to assassinate Kasztner and even gave him the gun to do it. The court stated that there was an underground which was responsible for the assassination. The three were convicted for their participation in a terroristic organization and received long prison sentences.

Meanwhile, the Israeli supreme court debated the original and old Greenwald-Kasztner trial. The five judges reconfirmed that Kasztner in fact helped SS officer Kurt Bachar by giving a falsified testimony on his behalf. However, most judges rejected all the other accusations made by Greenwald as essentially baseless.

On May 23, 1960, Israel's prime minister—David Ben-Gurion—announced in the Israeli Knesset that Adolf Eichman had been caught and would be put on trial in Israel (for a short reifying description, see Segev 1991:307–359). After a long and dramatic trial, Eichman was executed. The Kasztner affair did not become a major issue in Eichman's trial but from the few references to it (as well as from interviews Eichman gave to *Life* magazine), it appears that, from Eichman's perspective, Kasztner was obviously trying to save as many Jews as he possibly could. However, a by-product of that effort was the fact that Hungarian Jews were kept quiet. Kasztner's enigma, therefore, was not fully resolved.

Clearly, Ekstein, Shemer, and Menkes acted as a group. Their cohesion was partly integrated by their ideological convictions of Kasztner's guilt in cooperation with the Nazis. They were also united by a right-wing and nationalistic world-view which went back to Lehi and to Sheib's Sulam group. In fact, Sheib's club was located at Menkes' house (Harel 1985:138). Sheib's revolutionary right-wing propaganda no doubt helped to shape and crystallize the group into taking the lethal path leading to Kasztner's assassination.

The Greenwald-Kasztner trial, and Kasztner's assassination, served as hot platforms for different moral debates. The Greenwald-Kasztner trial examined the nature and scope of the Jewish leadership's involvement in helping to prevent (or helping) the Nazi's extermination campaigns. The assassins' trial was used by Tamir and Uri Avneri (see case no. 89) to claim that the Israeli secret service was behind Kasztner's assassination because it was too dangerous for the major political party—then Mapai—to leave Kasztner alive. Their version was helped by the fact that the Israeli secret service had penetrated the Menkes-Ekstein group and that for a short while before the assassination Ekstein worked for the service. These claims were examined and dismissed by Margalit (1982) and Harel (1985) (see also Black and Morris 1991:153–156).

Furthermore, Hadar's (1971) and Bauer's (1982:134–191) works imply that, at least in the Brand affair, Himmler probably intended to try and negotiate a peace agreement with the allies. In this context, Eichman's "offer" to spare the Jews in the "blood for trucks" deal was a by product of that initiative. Bauer's work clearly indicated that some essential parts in Brand's 1954 testimonies were not true, and points to Tamir's questionable role in helping to amplify lies.

In 1987, Dinur indicated that in a perspective of thirty to forty-three years, Kasztner's actions during World War II in Hungary which were aimed to save as many Jews as possible, were distorted by Tamir's biased and one dimensional interpretation (see also Segev 1991:239–303).

CASE NUMBER 87

Abraham Ben-Moshe's Attack on Meir Vilner on
October 15, 1967 in Tel Aviv

In the month of June 1967, Israel was involved in the six-days war which ended in a major and swift victory—militarily and politically (at least, that was how it was viewed in 1967)—for Israel. The social, moral, and political atmosphere in the country was certainly one of joy and happiness. The Russians were evidently not viewed as contemporary friends of Israel.

Parliament member Meir Vilner was fifty-one years old in 1967. He had been a longstanding major and prominent member of the Israeli communist party (Rakach). That party won a reputation for being identified with the Russian position and with the Arab-Palestinian cause. Moreover, Vilner was even personally identified with the Russian position. In the atmosphere prevailing in post-June 1967 Israel, one could hardly envy Vilner's position.

On May 15, 1967, Mr. Vilner left his home in Tel Aviv with his wife. They were walking when, at the corner of Hayarkon and Yonah Hanavi streets, at around 1800, Vilner was attacked. His assailant was Abraham Ben-Moshe, about forty-seven years old, who presented himself as an "Asir Zion," meaning he was imprisoned in Russia for being a Zionist. At the time of the attack Ben-Moshe was working at the daily newspaper *Hayom*.

He attacked Vilner by stabbing him with a nine centimeter knife. Ben-Moshe was arrested immediately. He told the policemen who arrested him that he was a prisoner of Zion, feeling the pain of Soviet Jews, and that that was why he attacked Vilner. Vilner was rushed to a hospital, where he was treated and later recuperated (see e.g., *Ha'aretz* October 16, 1967, p. 1; October 17, 1967, p. 10). Ben Moshe's attack received much coverage in the Israeli and Soviet press (e.g., see the issues of *Ha'aretz* in October of 1967). Reading the contemporary press coverage leaves one with the very distinct impression that there was an attempt on Vilner's life. In an interview (May 7, 1987), Vilner told us he had no doubt that Ben-Moshe intended to assassinate him.

On December 13, 1967, Ben-Moshe was accused in the district court in Tel Aviv with premeditated, attempted murder. During the trial, the district attorney and the lawyer for the defense got into long debates about the nature of the injury and of the accusation. Ben-Moshe admitted attacking Vilner but said that "if I had wanted to murder him, I would have done it. I had no intention to murder him.... I wanted to demonstrate against this tranquility in (Israel) that (we) let a Jew...hate his own people...be in the Knesset.... As a citizen of Israel, I followed for years Vilner's deeds.... He is not a Jew! He hates Israel.... He followed Lord Haw-Haw, the British traitor" (see *Ma'ariv*, February 6, 1968, p. 3). Vilner's wife testified that following the attack Ben-Moshe yelled "I'll finish him, this is a hater of Zion" (ibid.; *Ha'aretz*, February 6, 1968, p. 5).

On February 28, 1968, in the summarizing speech, the district attorney—Eliezer Liebson—for some unclear reasons, asked the court to change the accusation from premeditated murder (punishable by a life in prison sentence) into illegal wounding, which is considered significantly less severe (see *Ma'ariv*, February 28, 1968, p. 7).

On March 11, 1968, the district court stated that while it was not persuaded that Ben-Moshe intended to kill Vilner, it was obvious that he meant to hurt Vilner in a serious way. Hence, Ben-Moshe was convicted of causing a severe injury and sentenced to eighteen months in prison.[8]

The state attorney, Zvi Bar Niv, appealed to the Israeli supreme court. He told the court that the Tel Aviv district attorney—Liebson—was carried away in his feelings (and was reprimanded for that) and asked the supreme court to give Ben-Moshe a much harsher sentence (see *Ha'aretz*, July 15, 1968, p. 4). On September 9, 1968, the supreme court added six more months to Ben Moshe's sentence.[9]

In July of 1987, I contacted Yoram Aridor, Ben-Moshe's lawyer in the trial, to try and contact Ben-Moshe. Aridor was then a parliament member in the right-winged "Likud" party, as well as the previous powerful minister of the treasury. Aridor wrote me on July 5, 1987 (and on July 9 told me over the phone) that Ben-Moshe was no longer alive, that he could add nothing to the case and that I better not contact Ben-Moshe's family because he was acquitted from an accusation of premeditated murder and was found guilty only in incurring a severe injury. Thus, Aridor stated, there was absolutely no proof that Ben-Moshe made a real attempt to assassinate Vilner and that the whole affair was so declared by the Israeli court.

The attack on Vilner served, as in other cases, as a focal point for heated arguments about what kind of rhetoric was permitted and what was not permitted in the Israeli political scene; what was and what was not accepted in the Israeli democracy. In other words, the case served as a marker for the boundaries of symbolic-moral universes.[10]

While Vilner, and others, were convinced in 1967 and now, that Ben-Moshe actually intended to assassinate Vilner, the court did not accept this perception. Although Ben-Moshe was originally accused with premeditated murder, this accusation was replaced in the last phase of the trial with a much less severe accusation. Clearly, the public and the political atmosphere in 1967 was not conducive to such views as those expressed by Vilner. Since the intent to assassinate was not proved to the satisfaction of the court, I am forced not to include this case in my statistical analysis.

CASE NUMBER 88

The Assassination Plot by Regional Commander Brigadier Shmuel Gonen (Gorodish) on the Life of Moshe Dayan, in November 1973—Planning

The October 1973 ("Yom Kippur") war, which was initiated by Egypt and Syria on October 6, 1973 at 1400, caught Israel by complete surprise. The war ended on October 24, but its repercussions are still echoing in Israeli society. Minister of Defense before, during, and after the war was Moshe Dayan (1915–1981).

One of the main military figures in that war was the south regional commander, Brigadier Shmuel Gonen. Gonen was born in 1930 in Lithuania and immigrated to Palestine with his parents in 1933. In 1944, he joined the Hagana. He was wounded five times in the different battles he fought and was recommended for a military citation. He joined the Israeli armored forces in 1949, and won a military citation for his performance in the 1956 Israeli Sinai Campaign against Egypt. In 1966, he was appointed as commander of Brigade Seven (armored) and won everlasting fame for his leadership of that Brigade during the "Six Days War" (June 1967; see Teveth 1968). Brigadier Gonen was appointed as the regional commander of the South in July of 1973 after a long, glorious, and distinguished military career. During the war in 1973, Ariel Sharon, who was then a group commander, revolted against Gonen. Dayan suspended Gonen from his command.

Later, in November 18, 1973, the Israeli government appointed Judge Agranat then the president of the Israeli supreme court—to head an investigation committee on the Yom Kippur War. On April 1, 1974, the committee submitted its first partial report. The report emphasized, and attributed, most of the responsibility for Israel being caught by surprise to the Israeli high command. Gonen was particularly criticized. He appealed to the Israeli supreme court, but his appeal was rejected. This first part of the report recommended to suspend Gonen. The last (third) report of the committee was submitted on January 30, 1975. There, the recommendation to suspend Gonen was canceled, but it was recommended that his promotion be restricted. While much of the long report is still classified, it has raised numerous debates about the original charter of the committee, the qualifications of its members and its conclusions which located the responsibility for the surprise in 1973 to the army, leaving the political level (government) largely untouched. The role and responsibility of Dayan in the fateful events of October of 1973 are still debated. In a perspective of about fifteen years, it indeed seems that most of the immediate "political" price for that war was paid by the army.

Gonen, hurt and angry, left the Israeli army in 1977 and in 1978 arrived to Bangi (a town on Ubangi river, in the Central African Republic) as a self-imposed exile. There, in a strange, remote and removed steaming jungle he tried to make enough money to finance an attempt to reinvestigate the 1973 war, and his role in it, so as to rehabilitate his reputation in Israel. Gorodish died on September 30, 1991 from a heart attack in Italy.

In May of 1987, Israeli journalist Adam Baruch flew to Bangi to interview Gonen (see *Yediot Aharonot*, May 27, 1987, front page and long interview in the May 29, 1987 weekend supplement, pp. 22–23). There Gonen told Baruch that "After I was suspended...in 1973...I planned to assassinate Moshe Dayan.... If I had not had a political consciousness I would have done it too.... The thing which stopped me was that Dayan was a civilian, the minister of defense, and I was a soldier, I could not raise my hand on the civilian system.... I planned to arrive...(to Dayan's office).... I had no problem to enter Dayan's office and kill him.... I would have taken a hand gun and shot him.... I would have looked into his eye and shot him between his eyes.... Don't you realize that if I had done that, I would have entered a different history.... The (Israeli) people would have understood what happened. That 1973 Dayan sacrificed us (the military high command), he...simply threw us to the dogs. He betrayed the soldiers, saved his own skin from the Yom Kippur oversight.... I would have entered his office and, with a peace of mind, shot him, accurately" (*Yediot Aharonot*, May 27, 1987, front page).

Gonen obviously wanted to assassinate Moshe Dayan because he saw Dayan not only as responsible for the Yom Kippur War oversight, but because, in his view, Dayan escaped condemnation by sacrificing the army's high command, especially Gonen.

As far as we know, Gonen's planning was not related to any political or social group and he was alone in this.

One is tempted to ask whether Gonen's report is an ex post fact invention. It may, of course, be. However, judging by Gonen's personality and actions, I tend to credit him with being sincere in his report of deliberating and planning to assassinate Dayan.

CASE NUMBER 89

The Assassination Attempts on the Life of Uri Avneri on March 24, 1974 and December 18, 1975, by Eliahu Galili—Unsuccessful

Uri Avneri can certainly be considered as one of the most interesting, as well as controversial and colorful, figures in Israel (see also Black and Morris 1991:153–156).

Born in Germany in 1923, Avneri came to Israel in 1933. In

the early years of the Second World War he was a member in Etzel, but before the state of Israel was established in 1948 he left Etzel and joined the Hagana. In the War of Independence (1948) he fought with a famous striking force "the foxes of Samson" and was wounded. While he was also ideologically close to the "Canaanim" (see case no. 85) he never really joined that group and had some bitter ideological arguments with them. Avneri later joined *Ha'aretz* (a daily morning newspaper) as a reporter.

Avneri wrote much, and his book on the 1948 Israeli war for Independence (published 1949) won unprecedented popularity. In 1954 he purchased the weekly magazine *Haolam Haze* (meaning in Hebrew "This World") and became its chief editor, explicitly aiming to turn it into an Israeli version of *Time* magazine.

Haolam Haze published a combination of gossip, nude pictures and what could be interpreted as extreme political criticism (accurate more than once), and stories about corruption in the Israeli establishment. It can be safely assumed that many contemporary people in Israel, some of them very powerful, were not too happy with either Avneri or *Haolam Haze*.

When Avneri suspected that the Knesset (the Israeli parliament) was about to legislate a law against *Haolam Haze*, he established in 1965 a new party and in the elections which took place for the Israeli Sixth Knesset he won a seat (1965). In the 1969 election his party won two seats for the Seventh Israeli Knesset. He was not able to be in the Eighth Knesset because he failed to be elected. However, due to a political agreement, Avneri entered the Ninth Knesset (1977) a little late (February 5, 1979) and did not finish his term, as he was replaced in the middle of the term.

In late 1970, Avneri opened a personal campaign against Moshe Dayan (see also case no. 88), and was identified as a left-winged political fighter for many issues, including the Palestinian question.

Haolam Haze and Avneri were attacked several times. On November 26, 1952, a "scare bomb" was thrown into the offices of *Haolam Haze* in Tel Aviv, slightly wounding some workers (*Ha'aretz*, November 27, 1952, p. 4; *Haolam Haze*, December 4, 1952, p. 11 and December 11, 1952, p. 9). Warning letters were received as well. *Haolam Haze* attributed the act of throwing the bomb to a political motivation fueled by either hatred of *Haolam*

Haze's left wing stands, or to extreme religious orthodox Jews who may have objected to the secular line of *Haolam Haze*. Another possibility was attributed by *Haolam Haze* to actors influenced by Israel Eldad ("Sheib")—formerly chief ideologist of Lehi—propaganda against Avneri and *Haolam Haze* which were published in Eldad's journal *Sulam*. On the last day of November 1952, around 23:00. Uri Avneri and his deputy—Shalom Cohen —were attacked by four youngsters in Tel Aviv and severely beaten (*Ha'aretz*, December 1, 1953, p. 2; *Haolam Haze*, December 3, 1953, p. 10 and p. 2). In May–June of 1955 two explosive devices were placed near the offices of *Haolam Haze*, one was discovered and dismantled, the other exploded and wounded a worker. In November of 1971 the editorial offices of *Haolam Haze* were set on fire, causing severe damage. None of the culprits in any of the above mentioned attacks has ever been caught.

Uri Avneri was personally attacked three times, in 1974 and 1975, by Eliahu Galili. The Galili family was famous in Kiryat Shalom, a southern neighborhood in Tel Aviv. The Father, Ben-Zion, was unemployed for many years and had five sons. Two sons immigrated to the United States and one went to work as a technician at Hebrew University. The family later moved to another neighborhood—Shapira, with better living accommodations. Eliahu was born in 1948 and was an average pupil. He went to a professional school and was trained as a car mechanic. He joined the Israeli army in August of 1966 and served as a tank mechanic in armored brigade number seven (commanded by Gonen—see case no. 88). Eliahu Galili finished his army service in August of 1969. Eliahu then decided to go to the United States to try his luck there. His trip to the United States was not successful and after a stay of three years in the United States he returned to Israel.

One Friday in February of 1974, Galili waited for Avneri outside the *Haolam Haze* office. He attacked him with his bare hands and managed to scratch Avneri. Two of Avneri's friends who were there separated the two. The police were called but Galili was not formally accused. A few weeks later, on March 24, 1974, Galili arrived at Avneri's office and attacked him again with a knife. Again Galili was caught and given to the police. Galili was, consequently, hospitalized in a hospital for the mentally ill as suffering from a mental illness and as unfit to stand trial. Among other things, Galili told people that Avneri planted microphones in his head, that Avneri read his thoughts, and that these were the "reasons" he attacked Avneri.

Galili, however, did not give up. He was released from the hospital for the mentally ill after a few months. On Thursday, December 18, 1975, in the morning, Galili waited for Avneri near his home in Tel Aviv. As Avneri opened the door of his apartment, Galili attacked him with a big knife, clearly meaning to kill him. The two started to struggle and Avneri, badly cut and bleeding, managed to escape from his assailant and got help. Again, Galili was caught, certified as insane and rehospitalized.[11]

While, at that time, there were some speculations that Galili may have been sent by "an organized group" (e.g., see *Haolam Haze*, December 24, 1975, p. 28; *Yediot Aharonot*, December 23, 1975, p. 12, and December 22, 1975, p. 4)—not a surprising speculation judging by the background, it appears that, in fact, Galili *was* mentally ill and part of his paranoid symptoms were focused on Avneri. In a detailed and taped interview on May 20, 1986, Avneri in fact admitted this, despite the somewhat different accounts he used in 1975.

This case is perhaps the only recorded case where a lone and "crazy" potential assassin, with apparently no group behind him, attacked a specified target. In this particular case, a specified political target was attacked for what may be labeled as a "private reason" (crazy maybe, but private nevertheless).

The only other cases where individuals, without being sent by an ideological group, were involved in political assassination events were those involving Ben-Moshe's attack on parliament member Vilner (see case no. 87, and the problematics involved), Shimkin's attempt on Hitler's life (see case no. 13), Gonen's plan to assassinate Dayan (case no. 88) and the next case.

CASE NUMBER 90

Plans by Ze'ev-Miron Eltagar to Assassinate Anwar Sadat and Sa'ad Murtada between 1979–1980

October 6, 1973, was the first day of the 1973 war. The tank battles along the Egyptian front line were fierce. One of those fateful battles took place at around 1715. Lieutenant Miron Elt-agar, twenty-two years old, was in charge of one of the tanks. He told the crew of another tank over the wireless that he was charging. That was the last anyone has heard of him.

Miron's father—Ze'ev—set out to find out what happened to his son. According to one version, Miron and his crew were caught and surrendered to Egyptian soldiers who, cold blooded-ly, shot them to death. Officially, Miron's body was never found. The death of his beloved son hit Ze'ev very hard, and a burning desire for revenge took root.

Years later, Israel and Egypt began a process of political negotiations about signing a peace treaty between them. In the late 1970s, certainly in 1979–1980, it was obvious that Israel and Egypt were in fact going together in the peace path.

In April of 1979, Ze'ev-Miron Eltagar decided to assassinate the Egyptian president Anwar Sadat (1918–1981), or the first Egyptian ambassador to Israel—Sa'ad Murtada (born 1923). The main reasons for his motivation were two. First, he saw Sadat as personally responsible for the 1973 war and therefore for the death of his son. He certainly wanted revenge. Second, he wanted to commit an act that would shake the world. Obviously, he wanted to achieve a propaganda by deed effect. While Sadat was Eltagar's first choice, he considered Murtada as a proper substitute. Eltagar intended to use a hand gun, and planned to do the assassination in front of as many people as possible. It was clear to him that he would have been arrested immediately and planned to turn his trial into a political trial.

Eltagar was very well familiar with such examples of politi-cal assassins in Jewish history as Yael and Sisera, Schwartzbard (see case D, chapter 5) , and the attempts on MacMichael's life. He knew Frankfurter personally (see case F, chapter 5), and was a former member in Etzel. He certainly defined himself as "the last avenger."

It appears that the decision to assassinate either Sadat or Murtada crystallized in Eltagar's mind in April of 1979. He even took some practical steps toward accomplishing the planning. Eltagar, however, found the occasion to express to Moshe Dayan (see case no. 88), then the minister of foreign affairs, his protest against the peace treaty with Egypt. Dayan initiated a few talks with Eltagar and in his bright mind and sharp senses he felt, or understood, that Eltagar was probably planning (and seriously) an assassination. Dayan tried to persuade him not to do it and on June 14, 1979, even sent him a letter discouraging him from making any "practical conclusions."

In the few conversations Eltagar and Dayan had, Dayan tried to argue with Eltagar that an assassination could be very dangerous to Israel and that Eltagar should not do it. However, it may also be that Dayan was not sure whether he succeeded in persuading Eltagar and Dov Sion, his aide, probably heard about the plot and contacted the Israeli secret service. Eltagar was later contacted by an agent from the Israeli secret service. As a result of the conversation, Eltagar tried to get some important political figures to help him because he suspected that he was going to be arrested. Later, Eltagar gave his word to the head of the Israeli secret service in the Tel Aviv region that he would not assassinate the Egyptian ambassador. Hence, Eltagar's intentions did not pass the planning stage. Eltagar was apparently persuaded that an assassination was not going to get him where he wanted (see Petersburg and Kastro 1988; Eltagar 1988; interview with Eltagar from January 27, 1988, and a telephone conversation from February 2, 1988).

CASE NUMBER 91

The June 2, 1980 Attempts by the "Jewish Underground" to Hit Bassam Shaka, Karim Khalaf, and Ibrahim Tawil

The 1967 "Six Days War," with the new Israeli conquests opened many different opportunities for different groups in Israel. One hidden ideological undercurrent broke with much power and vitality to the surface—Gush Emunim. Basically, Gush Emunim is a group of right-wing religious zealots who were very effective in helping to put numerous Jewish settlements mostly in the occupied West Bank from 1967 on and living there.[12]

During 1978–1980 a large group of Jewish settlers mostly from Gush Emunim, and sympathizers, became increasingly upset about what they saw as growing Arab attacks on them, endangering their safety (Segal 1987; Litani 1980). Itzhak Geniram ("Akale"), Yehuda Etzion, Menachem Libni, Yeshua Ben-Shushan, Shaul Nir, as well as a few others, began to crystallize a "Jewish underground." All in all, the largest number of members they reached was between twenty-five to twenty-seven. Their basic "loose" ideology was right-wing, fiercely supporting Jewish settlements in areas conquered by Israel in the 1967 war, and most of them were inclined toward orthodox Judaism. The one evident unifying "ideological" element of this group was their total dissatisfaction with the protection they felt they were getting from the Israeli army. In a long, gradual and incremental, process a large group of 25–27 members committed a series of actions against Arabs. The main reason for the planned actions was revenge, supposedly to intimidate the Arabs and give them a good reason to be afraid. Some of the activities of the group were clearly acts of terrorism.

The so-called Jewish underground consisted of members from different backgrounds and walks of life. It is difficult to state in any degree of certainty the level of group integration of the members. Hence, charting the group's accurate nature and goals is a complex task. Some very very general statements about it can, perhaps, be made. To begin with, some members of the leadership core most certainly viewed Lehi as their symbol. Being nationalistic and religious, it was their conviction that the land of Israel was given by the Almighty to the people of Israel, that is the Jews. Anyone who wanted to live under, and accept, Jewish law, that was okay. However, as Gush Emunim was settling Jews in the 1967 acquired territories, Arab resistance grew. As far as members of the underground were concerned, the Israeli security forces were not providing enough protection for Jewish settlers, and the Israeli government was not making enough decisive steps toward claiming Jewish-Israeli sovereignty over what they saw as the Land of Israel (including the territories). Basically, members of the underground rejected the democratic essence which forms the basis of Israel in favor of relying on a specific interpretation of some of the Jewish scriptures. To a very large extent, the Jewish underground formed an activist vigilante group.

In July of 1983, and as an act of retaliation for the murder of Aharon Gross, a Jewish student in a yeshiva in Hebron, two members of this group opened fire and threw a hand grenade at Arab students in the Islamic College in Hebron. This indiscriminate terror attack ended with the death of three Arab students and another thirty-three wounded. Some members of the group also planned to blow up the holy Moslem mosque—Dome of the Rock, in Jerusalem. Some of the members put booby-trapped hand grenades in December 1983 near a mosque in Hebron. The Arab guard of the mosque was badly injured. On April 26, 1984, some members booby-trapped six Arab public buses. At this time, the Israeli secret service was fully aware of the activities of the group and arrested the members who even helped to defuse the bombs which they had previously put in the Arab buses. No one was hurt (see Shragai 1984; *Ha'aretz* June 19, 1984, p. 13).

The reason I put the Jewish underground here, is their possible planned attempt of political assassination of the Arab members of the "National Guidance Committee" ("Va'ada Lehachvana Leumit"). The Va'ada Lehachvana Leumit was created on October 1, 1978, during an Arab conference in Beit Hanina. The committee had twenty-four Arab members and its explicit goal was to coordinate and direct the Arab resistance activities against the Israeli occupation. Prominent and active members in the "Va'ada" were Basam Shaka (from Shchem-Nablus), Karim Khalaf and Ibrahim Tawil (from Ramalla and Al Bireh), Fahed Kawasmi (from Hebron) and Muhamed Milchem (from Halhul). It is clearly the case that the Va'ada was rather successful in its activities against Israel. It supported violent acts and preached strong and violent resistance thus giving legitimacy to various acts of violence and terror of Arabs against Jews. On March 11, 1982, the Va'ada was declared illegal by Israel. Kawasmi and Milchem were deported from Israel.[13]

Segal (1987:75–76), a former member of the Jewish underground, states that the Jewish underground decided to hit thirteen Arab members of the Va'ada Lehachvana Leumit both as a revenge and in order to stop their activities. Since time was short and there were not enough men, they decided to hit only five: Basam Shaka, Karim Khalaf, Ibrahim Tawil, Hamzi Natshe, and Ibrahim Dakak. It was decided that Menachem Libni would booby-trap their cars. The potential victims were put under surveillance.

On June 2, 1980, bombs planted in the cars of Basam Shaka and Karim Khalaf exploded. Both were inside the cars and were badly wounded. The cars of Natshe and Dakak were not booby-trapped because of last minute problems. When, on June 2, the Israeli authorities realized what was going on, an explosive expert (Suleiman Hirbawi) was sent to check Tawil's home. Although Captain Gila, then in the Israeli army, who was a member in the underground and knew about Tawil's booby-trapped car was near Hirbawi, he did not warn him. Hirbawi decided to check Tawil's car—when he did that the bomb exploded. Hirbawi was badly injured and lost his eyesight (Segal 1985, Ha'aretz, June 6, 1980, p. 3).

These events constituted, no doubt, another severe blow to the members of the Va'ada.

All fifteen members of the underground who were involved directly and indirectly in what most certainly looked like assassination attempts were arrested by the Israeli secret service in April of 1984 after a long and hard intelligence effort by the service.[14] On May 23, 1984, they were accused in court in Jerusalem of attempted murder, and other charges. After fourteen months of legal procedures, eleven members were acquitted from the accusation of attempted murder, but found guilty of causing a severe injury (e.g., see Ha'aretz, July 11, 1985, p. 2). The court stated that the leading figures in the case were Libni, Etzion, and Nir. After the trial, Gush Emunim, and others, started an aggressive campaign to bring about clemency for all of the accused. At the time of writing this manuscript (1987–1988) some were still in prison.[15]

With the exception of Segal's (1987) sympathetic book, no full account about the Jewish underground has been written yet and this book is most certainly the wrong place to do it. Some conclusions, however, are very clear. First, members of the Jewish underground acted as a group, with a division of labor, clear goals and a very loose ideology. The word commonly used to describe this group as an "underground" is perhaps too strong. In the Israeli context, an underground brings immediately an association to Hagana, Etzel and Lehi. The resemblance of the underground to these groups in terms of organization, vision, commitment and sophistication is *very* shallow indeed. However, members of the underground did act under the collective feeling of having collective goals. Second, the very existence of this underground, and its activities, helped to explode into the open a bitter argument about the nature, and definition, of Jewish-Arab relationships within Israeli society. Third, the Underground acts against Tawil, Halaf, and Shaka clearly helped to further sink and stop the activities of the Arab Va'ada Lehachvana Leumit. During their trial, members of the underground emphasized how helpless and frustrated they felt seeing their friends being killed by Arabs vis-a-vis what they saw as a lack of proper actions from the authorities (e.g., see *Ha'aretz*, April 1, 1985, p. 3). Furthermore, Libni, a central figure in the underground stated that he felt that a group of Jewish rabbis supported active and indiscriminate hostile activities against Arabs (e.g., see *Ha'aretz*, May 2, 1985). Libni even compared the underground activities to those of Lehi and Etzel (e.g., see *Ha'aretz*, May 8, 1985, p. 1). On July 14, 1985, he told the court that he helped create the underground because he felt that the state of Israel simply deserted the security of the Jewish settlers (see *Ha'aretz*, July 15, p. 3).

The very existence of the Jewish Underground, and the fact that some of its leaders and supporters identified themselves with Lehi gives credence to the observation made already in chapter two and that is that underground/terror groups frequently commit acts of both terrorism and assassination. The Jewish underground—in this sense—was not different from other similar groups, acting under similar conditions. My own guess is that had the Israeli secret service not intervened when it did, more assassinations and terror would have followed, and eventually more of this lethal aggression would have been directed against other Jews. However, to probe further into this issue—a comparative study of underground groups will have to be undertaken. This task, obviously, is way beyond the scope of this study.

Prima facie, it seems justified to include this case in the list of assassinations. However, there are two reasons against it. First, Segal (1987:76) clearly implies that the underground did not mean to assassinate their intended specific victims but "just" to incapacitate them. Second, the court did not convict any member from the underground on the charges of attempted murder (in this case). Thus, although very close to political assassination, I decided to drop this case from being included in the general statistical descriptive part. The case will become useful in the theoretical part.

CHAPTER 9

Political Executions

In the theoretical introduction to political assassination events, we made a distinction between "political assassinations" and "political executions." This chapter focuses on political executions and complements the previous chapters on political assassinations.

When we have an official organization of a state, or a country, which makes a decision to assassinate a particular actor, for political reasons (that is, a decision to assassinate *from* the center), and the decision is made not in a due, fair and open, process, then we have a case of a political execution. For example, the political execution of Leon Trotsky at his home outside Mexico City on August 20, 1940 (see also Dewar 1951; Byas 1942; Lentz 1988:78). It is also not uncommon for countries at war to try and assassinate key political and military leaders of the "other side." One such example is the assassination of the Japanese fleet admiral, Isoruku Yamamoto, also reputed for his role behind the Japanese surprise attack on Pearl Harbor. U.S. military intelligence discovered the whereabouts of Yamamoto. On April 18, 1943, Major John w. Mitchell led a squadron of sixteen P–38 Lightning fighters on a long flight to intercept Yamamoto's airplane. Mitchell's squadron identified and intercepted Admiral Yamamoto's airplane over Bougainville Island. In the air battle that developed over the Solomon Islands, and which lasted less than ten minutes, Yamamoto's airplane was hit and the admiral killed (Glines 1990; Hoyt 1990:248–249; Lentz 1988:83).

All governments seek to conceal their political execution plots (Rapoport 1971:34). Certainly, information regarding political executions constitutes hidden, dark and discrediting information. The Israeli government provides no exception when it comes to the question of whether the State of Israel was involved in political execution plots. Obviously, answering such a question in detail is very difficult. No country is overeager to expose such possibly discrediting and dark information. All we could do here was to try and collect some of the more available and credible information.

As mentioned in the second chapter, acts of political executions which are initiated by governments and performed by their representatives, *are* included in our definition of political assassinations. A major problem, however, exists with these cases. The problem is that of finding accurate information not only to validate the cases, but to find out *how* the decision was made, *by whom*, what type of units perform such acts, how are the official killers trained, how are these executions justified and many other similar questions. As we shall see, in most cases which were suspected as political executions, such information typically does not exist. Thus, one can guess that the known cases of political executions probably constitute only the tip of the iceberg of undisclosed cases.

The cases which were selected for this chapter were those that we felt, within a reasonable degree of certainty, constituted cases of political executions bona fide.

What are the official organizations in Israel which can decide on, and execute, a political assassination event? Similar to other countries, Israel as a state has a government which can decide to carry out a political execution. Like other countries, Israel has a police force, army and intelligence services who—theoretically at least—can decide on, and may be used for the purpose of, political executions.

It must be remembered that the legacy of Etzel, Lehi and the Hagana was that political assassination events were, under certain circumstance, possible and rightful. These three pre-state Jewish underground groups were definitely involved in several political assassination events. The Palmach, which was the operational military arm of the the Jewish Agency and the Hagana and, to a very large extent, the precursor of the Israeli Army, was definitely involved in a few political assassinations/executions. Thus, Gilad (1971:72–73) tells of how, at an unknown date, the Palmach hit some specific and un-named Arab actors, at unknown dates and places, for political reasons. These Arabs were considered dangerous enemies and held responsible for atrocities against Jews. Furthermore, the Hagana had *specific* units which could be used for this purpose: the Pum (see case nos. 10, 11, and 19), the "Mista'arvim" (see case nos. 58 and 77), the Pelugot Meiuchadot in Tel Aviv (see next chapter, the case with Berger), and other special units (see case no. 54 and the discussion about the Hagana in the part three). Hence the Palmach's actions can be viewed as motivated by both revenge and "eliminating" possible political and military Arab leaders (e.g., case no. 36, or the 1948 ZARZIR operation, which was meant to "eliminate" major Arab leaders). The Lehi, obviously, had an *open* and public policy of political assassinations, and the Etzel was involved in such acts too. The legacy of political assassinations, therefore, ideologically and organizationally was in existence. I remember talking to Isser Harel, Israel's former chief of the Mossad, and asking him about political executions. His response was "we stopped that." I never received a detailed answer to my question of what it was exactly that they stopped.

Since many of the main figures in the Hagana, Etzel, and Lehi found themselves, after 1948, in key decision-making positions, in various political and command posts, we can certainly expect them to continue to carry the tradition, ideology and practice of political assassinations, under a different guise, into their new roles.

Israel has three central intelligence organizations. One is the Shabac. Its main role is in internal security. Our search did not yield any known cases of planned political assassinations proper, or executions, that were carried out by this agency. Information about the Shabac in public and open sources, however, is virtually nonexistent. The second organization is military intelligence. The third agency is the Mossad. Its main role is collecting information and operations, outside of Israel.[1] There are indications that the military intelligence and the Mossad were also involved in a few cases. No involvement of the Israeli police was found in political assassinations or executions.

THE ISRAELI ARMY

The Israeli Army was involved in a few plots of political executions, mostly with intelligence operational units, and against non-Jewish targets.

Granot (1981), in fact, hints that different units of the Israeli Army's intelligence were involved in acts of sabotage and kid-naping (of enemy offices) on enemy territory.

Hassan Salame—1948

As a background case, it is easy to start with the attempts to assas-sinate Hassan Salame. Salame was a leader of Arab gangs which attacked Jews. In the late 1940s the Hagana/Palmach tried to assassinate him, probably a few times, but had no success.[2] On May 30, 1948, Etzel's members attacked the Arab village of Ras-El-Ein. During the Arab counter-attack, and purely by chance, Salame was wounded fatally and died two days later.[3]

Ali Qassem—1948

Another case is reported by Bar-Zohar (1970:37–38), Granot (1981:13–16), Nevo (1988b), Harel (1989:114–117), Raviv and Melman (1990:24), and Black and Morris (1991:59–60). They report that when Isser Be'ery (e.g., see the case involving Tubianski, no. 82) was appointed as the head of the emerging military intelli-gence in the spring of 1948 (he was previously head of the Hagana's Shai) he ordered to kill an Arab double agent called Ali Qassem because he suspected that the Arab double agent was about to give the Arabs information. That killing probably took place on November 16, 1948, by shooting, in one of the wadis (val-leys) of the Carmel mountain. When the details of the affair were found out by the IDF it created much turmoil and it was decided to charge Be'ery with the illegal killing of Qassem. The trial took place in December of 1948 before a military court, and the discus-sions were classified (that is the trial was with "closed doors"), probably between December of 1948 till February of 1949. On February 9, 1949, Be'ery was found guilty. He was sentenced to be demoted from his military role, but his military rank was not touched (Harel 1989:116). Consequently he was dismissed from his military role as the head of the IDF's military intelligence.

Attempting to Kill the Egyptian High Command—1956

On October 29, 1956, Israel invaded Sinai in the "Sinai Cam-paign" (more on this later in this chapter). One day before the operation began, Israeli intelligence sources discovered that eighteen very senior officers of the Egyptian military command were supposed to fly in one airplane from Damascus to Cairo on the night of October 28. An Israeli fighter pilot, Yoash Zidon (who became a parliament member for "Tzomet" in 1988), and his navigator, Eliashiv Brosh, were instructed to to fly their British made Meteor N. F. 13, locate the Russian made Illushin 14 that was carrying the Egyptian officers, and shoot it. The commands were given by the Israeli airforce command, and the operation was carried out.[4]

This case is very close to our definition of a political execution, however, while the target was specific, it is also true that the target was a specific group.

In the 1950s and 1960s, the Israeli Army (and particularly paratrooper units) was involved in many retaliation acts against Arab terroristic groups. Most of these acts were not against particular persons or specific targets, but some probably were (e.g., see Haber and Schiff 1976:178, 430; Har-Zion 1968;[5] Avneri no date; Milshtein 1987). Getting fairly accurate details about these activities against specific personal targets is virtually impossible. However, it is quite clear that such acts, whenever done, were either aimed as a revenge, or to prevent further actions against Jews inspired and/or organized by the particular actor.

The army—from the time of the Hagana/Palmach and later—was thus involved in hitting specific targets. The units used were either the military intelligence or commandos (no information is available on other possible units). It is more than plausible to assume, with a very high degree of certainty, that no hits by the Israeli Army after 1948 were directed against specific Jewish targets.

Some actions were publicized in more detail.

Mustafa Hafez and Salah Mustafa—1956

One famous case occurred in July 1956. Then, the head of Israeli military intelligence—Brigadier Yehoshafat Harkabi—was faced with the need to provide a good answer to the infiltration of Arab "Fedayeens" from neighboring arab countries into Israel, and their numerous acts of deadly violence and terrorism against

Israeli citizens. He suggested to hit personally those who headed the terror activities. Two of those heads were Colonel Mustafa Hafez, head of Egyptian intelligence in the Gaza strip, and Colonel Salah Mustafa who was the Egyptian military attache in Jordan. Both were considered by Israeli military intelligence as heading Arab Fedayeens terror activities against Israel. Using a sophisticated trick, Israeli intelligence agents used an Arab double agent (Mohammed Suleiman Al-Talalka) to deliver an explosive package to Colonel Mustafa Hafez. Although the package was not addressed to Colonel Hafez, the Israeli intelligence agents were quite sure he would open it. The trick was that Al-Talalka thought that the Israeli intelligence officers trusted that he worked for them. In fact, he worked for Colonel Hafez. The Israelis, however, were not misled. The package they gave Al-Talalka was addressed to the chief of police in Aza. The Israelis told Al-Talalka that the package included the secret codes for communications with the chief. Hence, the implication was that the chief of police in Aza was an Israeli agent. The Israelis suspected that instead of going to the chief, Al-Talaka would first go to his employer—Colonel Hafez—and give him the hot news. They also guessed that Colonel Hafez would do the most obvious thing for an intelligence officer and open the package. That is exactly what happened. On July 11, 1956, Colonel Hafez received the deadly package. He opened it and triggered an explosion which killed him and badly wounded Al-Talalka and Hureidi. On July 13, 1956, Colonel Mustafa received, via regular mail, a similar package. He opened it and was also killed. Both acts helped to reduce significantly the deadly Fedayeen activities almost until October 1956, when the 1956 Sinai military campaign (see next case) began.[6]

EXECUTIONS INVOLVING THE MOSSAD

An Assassination Plot against Gamal Abdul Nasser—1956

Gamal Abdul Nasser (1918–1970) was the president of what became known as the United Arab Republic (Egypt), and the spearhead of the Pan-Arabic movement. His foreign policy was characterized by its anti-Israel emphasis, and included a variety of activities which ranged from the organization of an economic boycott through armed infiltration, closing the Suez Canal to Israeli shipping and Sabotage, to open and explicit belligerency (e.g., see Encyclopedia Judaica, 12:841–843). Nasser was certainly regarded as a dangerous enemy of Israel.

We were able to locate two plots against Nasser.

The first plot took place during the Israeli withdrawal from Sinai in 1957, after the Sinai Campaign. Let us look more closely at this first plot.

In 1956, Israel, together with Britain and France attacked Egypt. Each country had its reasons for the attack. Israel was clearly fed up with the Fedayeens who were infiltrating its territory, attacking civilians sabotaging installations and mining roads. Israel's reasons and goals for initiating what became known as the Sinai Campaign were to put to an end the activities of the Fedayeens from the southern border of Israel, to open the Suez Canal for free passage of Israeli ships, and to prevent a possible military attack on Israel by Egypt and other Arab States (that is, the campaign was also defined as a preemptive strike). Israel may have also hoped that a swift and decisive military victory could destabilize the Egyptian regime and Nasser would be overthrown.

The Israeli attack in Sinai began on October 29, 1956, and was completed successfully on November 5, 1956. The military moves were successful and the victory was quick, swift, and decisive. However, no political destabilization occurred and despite the military defeat Nasser's regime seemed stable. Following strong international pressures, American and Soviet threats, Israel had to withdraw from the Sinai Peninsula which was conquered during the campaign. On January 22, 1957, Israel withdrew from most of Sinai, and in March from the other areas conquered during the campaign. Hence, Israel was forced to give up virtually all of the military achievements gained during the campaign.[7]

Oded Granot states that before the Israel withdrawal from Sinai, Israeli and French intelligence officers devised a plan to assassinate Nasser. The idea was hide powerful explosives in the office building of the Suez Canal Authority. The officers were sure that following the withdrawal Nasser would come to the building and carry a flaming speech to the Egyptians. The idea was to use a secret agent that would detonate the explosives with a remote control device (from Port Fuad) just as Nasser would come to the microphone to deliver his speech. A dramatic plan indeed. According to Granot, the plan was worked to the smallest details and then submitted for approval to the authorities (the exact nature of "the authorities" is not clear) in Israel and France. While the Israeli answer was on its way back to the planners (it is not clear what the nature of the answer was), Paris decided against the plan. The justification for not approving the plan was not political. The French claimed that the explosion would either kill or wound innocent bystanders (see *Ma'ariv*, October 24, 1986:25).

The second plot took place sometime after the end of the Sinai Campaign.

During the late 1950s and early 1960s Nasser was regarded by the Israeli political, military and intelligence elites and decision makers as *the* most dangerous enemy of Israel.

Menachem Klein implies that between 1958–1960 Israel considered the possibility of assassinating Nasser (probably by either the Mossad or by military intelligence). Apparently, Ben-Gurion decided against the assassination because he did not believe that assassinating Nasser could solve Israel's problems. Furthermore, he was concerned because of the high risk which was included in getting Israel's secret service(s) involved in an assassination attempt against Nasser (1986:45–50).

Thus, what we have here are two cases in either the "pre-planning" or "planning" stages.

While the idea to assassinate Nasser was provoked by his activities against Israel, the deliberations whether to assassinate him, and the decision not to, were also guided by pragmatic considerations which focused on the what was seen as the possible outcome and the risks involved.

A Suggestion to Assassinate Charles de Gaulle—1961

Isser Harel, former Israeli chief of the Mossad, reported that in March of 1961 Golda Meir (then minister of foreign affairs) received a suggestion from a French political figure that Israel should help him, and his group, assassinate French president de

Gaulle. The background for this suggestion was the apparent dissatisfaction of some French politicians and military officers with the de Gaulle's stand regarding Algeria. In return, the suggestion was that once in power, the conspirators would provide the Israeli Army with all its needs for free. The French politician explained that for obvious reasons, it would look bad if a Frenchman would assassinate de Gaulle and asked the Israeli secret service to provide an Arab agent for the act. Harel and Golda Meir consulted with the Israeli chief of staff and the deputy minister of defense (then Shimon Peres) and they realized that the suggestion was much too risky for Israel, not to mention the possibility of a provocation. The whole thing was brought before the prime minister (then, David Ben-Gurion) and it was decided that a warning should be delivered to de Gaulle's office about the existence of a possible plot against him. On March 29, 1961, the information Israel had was given to the director of de Gaulle's military chamber. About a month later, the famous "Rebellion of the Generals" against de Gaulle took place. The rebellion failed. Harel hints that there were a few other unsuccessful attempts against de Gaulle's life, but he does not state when or by whom (Harel 1989:291–295; See also *Ha'aretz*, September 29, 1989, p. 3; for more details see also Raviv and Melman 1990:72–73).

The Egyptian Missile Crisis—1962–1965

In July of 1962, Egypt surprised the world by announcing that it had four operational missiles with ranges of two hundred fifty to five hundred kilometers. The Israeli intelligence community, and the Mossad particularly, were caught by surprise. In the investigation which followed the Egyptian announcement it was found out that Egypt recruited, in secret, a group of German engineers who had worked for Nazi Germany's missile project, and who were developing the Egyptian missile project.

Furthermore, the information available indicated that Nasser, then Egypt's president, considered arming the missiles with unconventional warheads (e.g., biological, chemical, radiological). Israel tried to recruit, through regular diplomatic channels, the help of the Federal Republic of Germany, to stop the project, but failed. Consequently, the Israeli Mossad began a series of operations which were aimed at scaring and hitting the German engineers personally. On September 11, 1962, Heinz Krug, whose firm provided supplies for Nasser's missile project, was kidnaped from his office in Munich. In November of 1962, explosive envelopes were sent to the office of the German manager of one of the missiles's factories in Egypt, and to other German Engineers. Upon opening, the envelopes exploded killing and wounding workers. In February 1963, an attempt to assassinate Dr. Hans Kleinwachter—an engineer in the project—took place when he came from Egypt to visit his home in Germany. The "Mossad" apparently used *all* methods available to stop the Egyptian missile project, including threats, attempted assassinations, and kidnapings.

As the Israeli diplomatic pressure built up, and as the activities against the German engineers in Egypt became visible, some German engineers began to leave Egypt. In 1964–1965, the struggle continued as Israeli intelligence agents in Egypt (Wolfgang Lotz and Valtrud Neuman) sent in September of 1964—again—explosive envelopes to the German engineers. In 1965, a key German engineer—Professor Filtz—left Egypt and the project continued to deteriorate further until it came to a full stop in 1969 when the German engineers' work in Egypt was terminated.[8] The Israeli intelligence community itself was divided concerning the evaluation of the seriousness of the threat, and was therefore divided regarding the question of how to act. To summarize, this case is clustered around attempts by Israeli agents, and agencies, to hit specific personal targets in Egypt and Europe that were felt at the time to threaten Israel's national security.

The Ben-Barka Affair—1965

Steven (1980:236–252) implies that the Israeli Mossad, under the leadership of Meir Amit, was involved in another assassination event. Mehdi Ben Barka (born 1920) was a Moroccan left wing politician. In 1963, he was accused of plotting against the Moroccan King—Hassan. Consequently, he had to leave Morocco and seek political asylum in Europe. In that year, "it was claimed that Ben Barka was behind an attempt to assassinate the King, and at a special court hearing he was sentenced to death *in absentia*" (ibid., p. 241). According to Steven, King Hassan may have hinted in 1965 to General Mohammed Oufkir, his loyal tough and ruthless Minister of the Interior, that "he would not grieve the death of his former tutor (Ben Barka)" (ibid., p. 241). According to Steven, Mossad's agents helped in organizing the surveillance on Ben Barka, and in other ways. In November of 1965, Ben Barka was kidnaped in France, supposedly by French agents. Once Oufkir received the message, he came to France, "and in his presence Mehdi Ben Barka was gunned to death" (ibid., p. 244). The assassination probably took place on November 15, 1965. Hence, while the Mossad was not involved directly in the actual assassination, it was probably involved in the preparations for it. Raviv and Melman (1990:157–160) imply that as result of the involvement of the Israeli Mossad in the Ben-Barka affair, French president de Gaulle ordered that the Mossad's European "command be removed from Paris...[and he ordered]...a cessation of all intelligence cooperation between the two nations" (pp. 158–159; see also Black and Morris 1991:202–205).

The April 10, 1973 Beirut Raid

For many years, Israel has fought a deadly war with the PLO (Palestinian Liberation Organization). One of the actions Israel took in 1973, was a daring raid. On April 10, 1973 a daring specially selected unit from the Israeli Army, in full operational cooperation with the Mossad, attacked Arab-Palestinian terrorist headquarters buildings in Beirut. The military forces which carried out the land raid in Beirut on April 10, 1973, intended to assassinate, and hit, as many leaders and centers of Palestinian terrorist groups as possible. Unfortunately for the raiders, while Ali Hassan Salame (a main leader who they wanted to hit) was probably at the time of the raid in Beirut, and not very far from the places that were attacked—he was not hit. However, three other major leaders of the PLO were caught in their apartments, and were shot to death: Kamal Nasser (who was a chief spokesman for the PLO); Mohammed Yussef Najjar ("Abu Yussef") and Kamal Adwan (described as a senior commander in "Black September"). The last two were from the founders of the PLO. Another fifty or so PLO members were killed too during the raid. Although this raid was clearly meant to hit as many members of the PLO as possible, it was also meant to hit some *very* specific targets. The raiders went to specific apartments, looking for particular PLO and Black September figures.[9]

Black September and Salame—1973, 1979

The next case originated in the Olympic games which took place in Munich, West Germany in September 1972. On the morning of September 5, a group of Arab terrorists from Black September, under the leadership and guidance of Ali Hassan Salame—the son of the aforementioned Hassan Salame—murdered two Israelis and took nine others as hostages from the Israeli Olympic team in the Olympic village in Munich. Eventually, an attempt by the Germans to release the hostages ended when the terrorists massacred the nine hostages. Five of the terrorists were killed and three survived (e.g., see Groussard 1975; Bar-Zohar and Haber 1984; Black and Morris 1991:269–272). This is also the place to mention that Ali Hassan Salame was involved in another act of terror which took place on May 8, 1972, when Sabena flight 572 (Brussels-Vienna-Tel Aviv) was hijacked by members of Black September and landed at Ben-Gurion airport in Israel. The passengers were later released by an Israeli commando unit who raided the plane (see Raviv and Melman 1990:183). An interrogation disclosed that Ali Hassan Salame was the "brain" behind the hijacking.

The Israeli government was apparently fed up with both Ali Hassan Salame and Black September. According to Bar-Zohar and Haber, Golda Meir (then the Israeli prime minister) instructed the heads of Israel's secret services to hunt down and kill key members of Black September and Ali Hassan Salame (1984:149, 156–157; see also Hoy and Ostrovsky 1990:178–180; Raviv and Melman 1990:185–186; Black and Morris 1991:272).

As a result, it appears that the Israeli Mossad began to track, hunt down and execute, mostly in Europe, various prominent figures of Black September. It is obviously difficult to document and validate the cases. However, it seems that at least six to seven leaders[10] were executed, using various methods (including booby-trapping a telephone) as a result of which the activities of

Black September, as a terrorist organization, came to a standstill.[11]

At least two more attempts on Salame's life were made. One attempt took place on July 21, 1973, at around 2200 in the small Norwegian town of Lillehammer. Following intelligence reports that Salame was sighted in Lillehammer, a team of about fifteen Israeli agents arrived to the town. Instead of Salame, they misidentified Ahmad Bushiki, a Moroccan waiter who lived in Lillehammer with his seven months pregnant Norwegian wife—Toril. Thinking Bushiki was Salame, the agents shot him 14 times and killed him. This action was done in a most unprofessional manner and six members of the Israeli team were caught by the Norwegian authorities, were put on trial, and received different sentences.[12]

As mentioned in a previous section, one goal of the April 10, 1973, raid to Beirut was to hit Ali Hassan Salame. The raid failed in this particular aspect.

The next attempt was more successful. In January of 1979, a few agents of the Mossad arrived in Beirut and prepared an ambush to Ali Hassan Salame. They tracked the route along which he was traveling and parked a car full with fifty kilograms of plastic explosives along the route. The car could be exploded by a remote control device. On the afternoon of January 22, 1979, Salame and his bodyguards passed near the booby-trapped car. The agent of the Mossad (probably a woman—Erika Chambers) who detected, and identified, Salame's car passing near the booby trapped car pressed the button of the remote control device and killed Salame. Eight people died and sixteen others were wounded in the awesome blast. None of the Mossad's agents involved in the action was ever caught.[13]

Revenge for the Massacre in Ben-Gurion (Lod) Airport—1972

On May 30, 1972, remnants of the Japanese Red Army, in collaboration with a Palestinian terror group (PFLP—Popular Front for the Liberation of Palestine—Wadia Hadad's group) arrived to Lod airport in Israel (on a flight from Rome) and upon arrival opened fire on innocent passengers who were waiting for their flights. Twenty six passengers were shot to death.

According to Dani Sade and Tzvi Zinger, a short time after the massacre, different leaders of Palestinian terror organizations received explosive envelopes, especially figures who were connected to the massacre in the airport. Other attempts on the life of other Palestinian leaders were made too (e.g., booby-trapping a car). Some were killed and some wounded. The implication is that these attempts originated in Israel as an act of revenge (*Yediot Aharonot*, January 18, 1989, pp. 36–37).

Dr. Yahya El-Meshad—1980

Iraq's interest in having a nuclear capability began already in the 1970s. This interest was translated into reality when Iraq signed a few agreements with France. These agreements focused on France building an Osirak nuclear reactor at Al-Tuweitha. The Israeli secret services became quite concerned about this developing nuclear capability, and inner intelligence debates regarding assessing the danger for Israel from this reactor were developing too (Raviv and Melman 1990:251–252; Black and Morris 1991:333–334). Eventually, on June 7, 1981, Begin's ordered air raid against the Iraqi reactor was executed and a few Israeli air force jets bombed and destroyed the reactor (Nakdimon 1986a; Perlmutter, Handel, and Bar-Joseph 1982; Raviv and Melman 1990:250–252, 256–257; Black and Morris 1991:332–337).

This may have not been the only attempt made by Israel to stop the Iraqi nuclear program. On June 6, 1980, Dr. Yahya El-Meshad, a fifty-year-old senior member of Iraq's Atomic Energy Commission, arrived at Paris to discuss with the French some issues concerning sending equipment and nuclear fuel to Iraq. Dr. El-Meshad arrived to his hotel in Paris (the hotel Meridien) on the evening of June 13, escorted by a local prostitute, a thirty-two-year-old Marie-Claude Magal. Ms. Magal did not escort Dr. El-Meshad into his room, and left. On the next morning, June 14, the hotel chambermaid who came to clean the room discovered El-Meshad's dead body in his room. He was apparently murdered in a most brutal way (the murder weapon was a knife) in his hotel room. Ms. Magal was killed in a hit-and-run accident on July 12. The person(s) responsible for El-Meshad's violent death, and the one responsible for Ms. Magal's death, were never identified or caught. While it is not entirely clear who, or exactly why, Dr. El-Meshad and Ms. Magal were killed (or even if these two deaths are related), the way, and the context in which, Black and Morris (1991:334) and Perlmutter, Handel, and Bar-Joseph (1982: 71–73) report this murder gives a strong impression that one of Israel's secret services may have been involved in these cases. Hoy and Ostrovsky (1990:15–24) in fact attribute both assassinations directly and specifically to the Mossad (1990:24). They attribute the assassination of El-Meshad to the Israeli Mossad's attempts to stop the Iraqi nuclear program, and the assassination of Ms. Magal to what they term as an "operational emergency" (p. 24). It is difficult, however, to make any more definitive statements about this case for lack of more information.

Mohammed Bassem Sultan Tamimi ("Hamdi")—1988

At the age of thirty-five, Tamimi was a lietenant colonel in the PLO's military apparatus. He was involved in planning of dozens of attacks by Palestinian guerrillas inside the occupied territories, and organized a PLO group called "Islamic Holy War." Tamimi's activities drew the attention of Israeli intelligence. One of his planned action in Israel took place on October 15, 1986. At that date the Israeli Army conducted a swearing in ceremony by the Wailing Wall in Jerusalem. Present were the new recruits and their families. Tamimi's agents threw grenades into the crowd, killing one Israeli and wounding seventy (see Raviv and Melman 1990:389).

Israel Prime Minister Shamir was asked to approve the execution of Tamimi. Once the execution was approved, Mossad's agents began planning the act.

Tamimi was located in Cyprus. Mossad's agents planted a bomb in the car Tamimi was travelling with, and with a remote control device exploded the car on February 14, 1988. In the car were at the time also Marwan Kayyali, a PLO colonel and Mohammed Hassan Buheis, a PLO activist. They all perished in the explosion (Raviv and Melman 1990:389–390; Black and Morris 1991:468–469).

Khalil El Wazir—1988

On Saturday April 16, 1988, at 0130 in the morning, a group of unidentified commandos attacked the Tunis house of Khalil Ibrahim El Wazir (known as "Abu Jihad"), number two man in Al Fatah in charge of operations. El Wazir was killed in the attack which apparently was directed specifically against him. Israel had a long list of reasons to revenge El Wazir since he was behind the planning of some of the worst terrorist acts against Israel. Israel, however, neither denied nor confirmed that it was involved in this execution. It seems reasonable to assume, though, that Israel *was* involved in the act. Israel certainly had the motive for the act, and the modus operandi was similar to the one which was used by the Israeli Defense Forces in its April 10, 1973 action in Beirut mentioned earlier.[14] The U.S. State Department condemned the assassination as political, and according to the *Washington Post* (April 21, 1988) the decision to assassinate Abu Jihad was actually made by the Israeli government.[15] Raviv and Melman (1990:391–399) and Black and Morris (1991:469–472) in fact make it plainly clear that Israeli intelligence was behind this execution.

Gerald V. Bull—1990

The execution of Bull took place in 1990, that is after 1988 which is the "closing date" for this book. Yet, in light of the 1991 Gulf War, and the case itself, it is of interest to examine this execution.

During the months of March and April 1990, the world was stunned by the declaration of Saddam Hussein, president of Iraq, that his country had what he termed an advanced "binary" chemical weapons, capable of destroying half of Israel. Following news dealt with Iraq's attempts to manufacture some lethal chemical and biological weapons, as well as the means to send them to specified targets. In late March 1990, a large shipment of sophisticated electronic hardware to Iraq was seized in London airport. Supposedly, the shipment included super-sophisticated detonators for nuclear bombs. About three weeks later in that month, a shipment of huge steel pipes was seized in a port in north east Britain. These pipes were described as parts of what was termed as a "doomsday canon," a monstrosity of a canon, forty meters long, capable of sending a chemical, biological, or nuclear warheads (probably weighing around two hundred fifty

kilograms) to a target that may be about sixteen hundred kilometers away from the canon. This gun clearly constituted a
threat to Israel's national security. According to all sources, there
was only one man in the world who could design such a monstrous canon—the sixty-two-year-old Canadian ballistic expert
Gerald V. Bull. As the news about the British seizure of parts of
the gun were made (around April 12, 1990) it was also disclosed
that on March 22, 1990, Gerald Bull was shot twice in the neck
with a silencer-equipped 7.65 millimeter pistol and killed in
Brussels by some unknown people (see the *New York Times*,
April 22, 1990, front page). Some sources attributed this killing
to the Israeli Mossad (see Grant 1991; Lowther 1991; Raviv and
Melman 1990:424; and Canadian CBC "The 5th Estate" February 12, 1991 television program entitled "The Genius and the
Gun").

Bull was a renowned world expert on long-range canons. He
was involved in the 1950s and 1960s in the American-Canadian
project "Harp." Three guns were built by this project, four hundred twenty millimeters each, with a forty meters barrel. A test
with one of these guns (stationed in Barbados) managed to throw
a huge projectile into space, some one hundred eighty kilometers
away from earth (see *Yediot Aharonot*, April 13, 1990, pp. 1–2.
Similar items appeared in the British *Times*, *Daily Telegraph*, and
the *Independent*).

To remind the reader, the Israeli intelligence services tried to
hit German scientists who were developing long-range missiles
for Egypt in the early 1960s. Also, in 1981 Menachem Begin,
then Israel's prime minister, authorized an air raid against an
Iraq nuclear plant once it was suspected that the reactor was
about to be used to develop nuclear weapons. The plant was
bombed and destroyed on June 7, 1981 (see the case involving
Dr. El-Meshad, above). Hence, an Israeli involvement in the case
involving Bull seems more than likely.

To summarize the role of the Mossad in executions, it is clearly the case that the Mossad was involved in quite a few cases of
political executions outside Israel. Hoy and Ostrovsky (1990:34,
117–119) even state that the Mossad has a specialized bureaucratic unit of assassins called "Kidon."[16] This unit is, supposedly,
part of a larger operational structure called Metzada (or Masada).

Interesting to note that, if one is to attribute credibility to Hoy and Ostrovsky's book, two thousand years apart assassins are associated with Masada. According to this source the Mossad is involved in assassination plots on a regular basis. Available information indicates that decisions to assassinate involve the highest echelons of Israel's political structure. We find again and again references that imply that the Israeli prime minister had to be involved in such a decision, as well as current heads of the intelligence services. It is also possible that this decision making process may have involved, in different times, other figures such as previous heads of intelligence, and/or the minister of defense.

Hoy and Ostrovsky provide the most explicit and detailed description available of this process (1990:24–26). They state that a secret committee exists in the office of the Israeli prime minister, that "sits as a military court and tries accused terrorists in absentia, consists of intelligence personnel, military people, and officials from the justice department." Hoy and Ostrovsky state that the committee meets at various locations and holds meetings that look like a "trial," where each case for potential execution is being "tried." For each potential case, there is a "prosecutor" and a "defense" lawyer. This "court" can decide on either to bring the accused to Israel to stand trial, or if that is not possible, to execute him/her. An execution, according to this source, requires the approval of the prime minister. It is impossible to know how accurate and valid is Hoy and Ostrovsky's description[17].

ATTEMPTS TO USE ISRAELI JEWS TO ASSASSINATE POLITICAL FIGURES IN ISRAEL

The fact that major political figures in Israel (e.g., president, prime minister, ministers) were not victims for political assassinations is obvious. With some very few and rare exceptions Israeli citizens have not turned these figures into targets for assassination attempts. This is very different than what happened in other countries in Europe, South America, and the United States. Answering the question of why did this happen is not easy, but it is probably due to a few factors: the more integrated nature of Israeli society, lack of strong centrality of Israeli leaders, lack of strong cultural supports for violence of this type in Israeli society as compared to other societies (more on this in chapter 12), and the nature of the Israeli political system which, so far, has managed to be able to give expression to a variety of groups (see also Dagan 1989).

However, unofficial (and public) intelligence reports suggest that there were attempts by some of Israel's Arab neighbors to use Israeli Jews to execute Israeli political figures. Two of these attempts were publicized.

1. Husni al-Zaim, who was the Syrian president between March to August 1949, sent his deputy to approach a senior Israeli Army officer—Lieutenant Colonel Yitzhak Spector—and offered him a sum of a few million dollars if Spector would assassinate Ben-Gurion. Spector reported to his superiors in the Israeli Army about the offer and nothing happened (Tevet, *Yediot Aharonot*, April 4, 1989, p. 9).

2. In 1965, a somewhat eccentric person called Alan Stil (not his real name) crossed the border from Israel to Syria. He was caught by Syrian intelligence officers. Thesse officers planned to send Stil back to Israel in 1967 with a sniper's rifle so that he would assassinate Moshe Dayan. In 1969, Stil arrived to Israel after he was deported from Austria. The Israeli secret service apparently knew who he was and he was arrested upon arrival. Stil was charged in court with an illegal crossing of the border and intention to harm Israel's national security. He was sentenced to ten years in prison (Dagan 1989:29)

THE INTIFADA

The so-called Arab "Intifada" ("uprising") began in the occupied Israeli territories (since June of 1967) in 1987 (e.g., see Shalev 1990; Schiff and Ya'ari 1990). Basically, the Intifada consisted of a more or less controlled violent Arab behavior toward the Israeli occupation forces, Jewish settlers in the territories and Jews in general. A few sources maintained that as part of the struggle between the Israeli security forces and the Arabs, the

Israeli forces politically executed specific Arab activists. Since the information on this particular issue is too scant, recent, given in the middle of a bitter struggle, virtually impossible to corroborate or deny by independent sources, typically fragmented and biased, and lacking in good and reliable verification, we shall have—unfortunately—to leave this particular and potentially very important issue for future work.[18]

CONCLUDING DISCUSSION

Rapoport (1971:34–35) equates a government's reliance on assassinations, to a "desperate gambler's stroke" (p. 35) and states that: "assassination is the tactic of the resourceless...a government which cannot pursue foreign policy by conventional means and uses assassins instead, is also likely to be a government so vulnerable that its weapons perform like boomerangs in the hands of the inexperienced" (34). This is, obviously, a moral statement and position. At the risk of seeming to provide a "justification" for political assassination events in the form of executions, one must be reminded that selecting the route of political executions was in fact taken by governments in different cultures as a useful and pragmatic tool. Rapoport actually points that out repeatedly. The known cases which were surveyed in this research, and which involved the state of Israel, did many times achieve their stated goals. Thus, while perhaps morally questionable, the political executions were nevertheless, and often, pragmatically useful—from the point of view of those who planned and executed them. Revenge was achieved, Black September was devastated. the Arab terrorist activities in the 1950s *were* stopped, the German scientists in Egypt were intimidated.

While it is inaccurate to assert that political executions were a major tool used by Israel, it was used whenever the decision makers felt that executions could achieve specific goals like revenge, or in preventing future occurrences of aggression and violence against Israel. In fact, Raviv and Melman (1990:398) hint that one possible guideline was that only heads of rather small terrorist groups who fully controlled the group "were appropriate targets" because their execution could mean the end of the terrorist group itself.

It is also evident that decisions to politically execute must have the approval of the highest levels in the Israeli political, security and military structure.

Although in many cases mentioned in this part the available and publicly free documentation is scarce, partial and somewhat problematic, (not to mention possible cases which we were not aware of) the pattern which seems to emerge is evident. We again encounter cases of political assassinations and executions directed from the center, without a legal and "due" process, against specific actors as either an act of revenge, or aimed to stop these actors' activities which were thought to be dangerous for Israel's national security.

CHAPTER 10

Political Assassinations, Terror, and Tangential Cases

INTRODUCTION

Having detailed the more or less known and validated cases, we have to focus our attention on other categories which are tangential to bona fide cases of political assassination events. The first task is to focus and sharpen the distinction between political assassination events and terrorism. Second, there were cases in the history of the State of Israel which prima facie look like political assassination events, but are really not. Third, we have to present cases which, on the surface, look like political assassination events proper, but the information which is currently available about them is such that we could not classify them as bona fide cases.

This chapter is important because it helps us draw and emphasize the necessary boundaries between cases which, according to the definition used in this book, are political assassinations proper, those which are not and those which are undecided.

POLITICAL ASSASSINATIONS VERSUS TERRORISM

In chapter 2 we detailed our definition and characterization of political assassination events. This is the place to reemphasize the fact that acts which were not aimed at specific actors, but were rather indiscriminate and aimed at a collective target, were not included in this study. Let me give a few illustrative examples, within the context of this study, to clarify this issue.

On July 22, 1946, Etzel planted explosive devices in the King David Hotel in Jerusalem. The explosion which followed at 1237 resulted in the collapse of the southern wing of the hotel, the death of eighty and about forty wounded.[1] On April 9, 1948, Lehi and Etzel attacked Dir Yassin, an Arab village near Jerusalem. Around two hundred fifty Arab villagers were killed (out of about four hundred villagers), four members of Etzel and Lehi were killed and about forty were wounded.[2] On June 10, 1939, Etzel planted bombs in the central British post office in Jerusalem. The explosion which followed wounded a few.[3] On August 2, 1939 Etzel planted three bombs in the house of the broadcasting service in Jerusalem. The bombs exploded at 1830 wounding some, and killing an Arab engineer—Adiv Mansour—and Mai Weissenberg, a Jewish broadcaster.[4] All these activities, and many other similar acts, were part of the struggle between the three pre-state Jewish underground groups and the Arabs and the British.

Two interesting, somewhat similar acts happened after 1948. On October 5, 1952, Dov Shilanski from the "Herut" party (who became a parliament member in June 1977 for the "Likud" party) was caught by security men (probably due to a squealing) when he was trying to plant a bomb at the foreign affairs office in Jerusalem.[5] In November, Shilanski was charged in court (*Ha'aretz*, November 28, 1952, p. 8) found guilty (ibid., November 30, 1952, p. 1.) and sentenced to twenty-one months in prison. On December 6, 1953 he was released.[6]

On October 30, 1957, Moshe Duek, twenty-six years old, who was born in Syria and immigrated to Palestine in 1946, managed to enter the old Knesset building in Jerusalem (on King George Street, where the ministry of tourism is located today) and from the balcony threw a hand grenade on the desk around which the government ministers were sitting (the so-called "government desk"). No one was killed, but a few ministers (including David Ben-Gurion) were wounded. (*Ha'aretz*, October 30, 1957, p. 1). Duek was caught immediately and admitted his guilt. It turned out that prior to the incident he was under psychiatric treatment and was even hospitalized in a mental hospital (*Ha'aretz*, October 31, 1957, p. 1). In May 1958, Duek was found guilty in court (*Ha'aretz*, May 11, 1958, p. 2) and sentenced to fifteen years in prison (*Ha'aretz*, August 8, 1958, p. 8).[7]

The lethal forces used in all the above cases were never aimed at specific targets, but rather against a collective entity. Even Duek directed his hand grenade against the government and not against any particular minister. As such none of these, and similar, cases were taken into consideration in this study. Such acts and their results in terms of numbers of dead or wounded people clearly outnumbered—by a large factor—the number and results of acts of political assassination.

Acts Which May Look Like Political Assassination Events but Are Not

During the research, we encountered a few cases that prima facie looked like political assassination events—either in the literature or by various informants but after probing, they turned out not to be political assassination events. It is important to describe, analyze, and clarify those cases, and thus also clarify and amplify the analytical framework of this research. I shall next use the thirteen cases we had in order to illustrate the above argument.

1. On the night of February 14, 1944, two Lehi members in Haifa were stopped by two British Inspectors: Robert A. Green and Sergeant H. A. Yuher for a routine check. Lehi members opened fire and killed both British Inspectors (Niv, vol. 4:33; Banai 1958:176–179). The British were killed not because there was an assassination plot directed specifically against them, but because they simply happened to be the ones who checked two people whom they probably did not even seriously suspect were members of Lehi.

2. On April 1, 1944, a member of Lehi in Haifa ("Baruch" —Joseph Rosenbaum) was accidentally wounded from his own gun. The police arrived with a Jewish sergeant, Ya'acov Polanyi. In the struggle which developed, Polany was killed (Yellin-Mor 1974:156–158; Banai 1958:194–197).

3. On September 27, 1947, a member of the Hagana named Eitan Avidov in Innsbruck (Austria) was killed when a group of members of Etzel attacked and entered by force a camp of the Hagana. Etzel denied that its members were in the attacking force (S.T.H., vol. 3, part 2:1059–1062; Niv, vol. 5:256–259; *Ha'aretz,*

October 9, 1947, p. 3; *Yediot Aharonot*, September 8, 1972, p. 40, Tavin 1973:138–139).

4. On August 18, 1940, the Hagana attacked an Etzel camp and Eliahu Shlomi (Daics)—twenty-one years old—from Etzel was killed (Niv, vol. 3:55–58; Gurion 1973; S.T.H., vol. 3, part 1:472–474).

In all the above cases, no assassination plot existed as the "reason" to kill those specific actors. They were all killed because they happened to be in the midst of a violent conflict, and as parties to that bloodly conflict.

5. Okev (1949:13) and Galili's testimony (*Davar*, January 1, 1949, p. 2) imply that in the second half of September 1943, Lehi assassinated a person named Pinhas Shover in Haifa. According to *Ha'aretz* (September 19, 1943, p. 3) Shover, a thirty-two-year-old carpenter, was indeed shot on September 18 near his home in Haifa by unknown people. However, it is also evident that on October 4, 1943, Shover recovered and left the hospital (*Ha'aretz*, October 5, 1943, p. 3). Furthermore, the description available (*Ha'aretz*, September 19, 1943, p. 3) implies that it is quite possible that Shover was shot by mistake when he and his friend went outside their home to check who were the two strangers that hung out near their house in Haifa.

6. Yellin-Mor's testimony in 1948 (see *Ha'aretz*, December 21, 1948, p. 1) and Begin (1961, part 4:39) imply that the Hagana assassinated in March 1947 a thirty-eight-year-old Jewish police corporal by the name of Mordechai (Mottel) Berger in Arlozorov street in Tel Aviv. According to the *Palestine Post* (March 30, 1947, p. 3) Berger served for sixteen years in the police and was survived by his pregnant wife and a six-year-old son. According to the *Palestine Post*, Berger was beaten to death. S.T.H. has a somewhat different version. According to this source, Corporal Berger was suspected already as an informer to the British Police during the 1939–1940 demonstrations. Consequently he was beaten then by members of Pum (see case nos. 10 and 11 for a description of Pum). In 1947, the Hagana's branch in Tel Aviv was in a crisis, and its members initiated a few activities against suspects as squealers and informers. The local commander of the Hagana—Nachum Ziv-Av—instructed his Peluga Meiuchedet (meaning "special company") to get hold of Corpo-

ral Berger and beat him. Faithful to the command, on the morning of March 28, 1947, a few members of the Peluga Meiuchedet attacked Berger and beat him severely. Apparently, Berger was beaten too hard and died later. The Hagana's headquarters accused Ziv-Av of instructing to beat a man without getting previous approval and that as a result of the beatings Berger died, although there had been no intention to kill him. Ziv-Av was put before a special court of the Hagana, was found guilty and dismissed from his command. He was transferred to another command position (vol. 3, part 2:1283 and vol. 3, part 3:1786). This is an interesting case. First, it shows that the Hagana's high command tried to control fairly tightly activities against specific and individual targets. Second, the Hagana's command created a unit for special activities in Tel Aviv. The unit was commanded by Shmuel Nutov and had a few hundred members, divided into smaller groups of six to eight members. The units' activities included actions against individuals (S.T.H., vol. 3, part 2:1280–1281). Third, there was *no* intentional and/or deliberate assassination plot against Berger.

7. An interesting case occurred on November 20, 1947, again around Innsbruck (Austria). A claim was made that a member of Etzel by the name of Milu Freulich, was caught by the Hagana's members in Austria and/or by a group of immigrants, was tortured and killed. Begin (1961, vol. 3:57), as well as others, attests to this. *Ha'aretz* (November 28, 1947) gives the contemporary response of the Hagana, which investigated the case. The Hagana's version was that Freulich addressed a group of Jewish refugees on the border of Austria and promised them to guarantee their entrance to Italy for a fee. When the group tried later to enter Italy, they were all arrested by the Italian police. After their release, they accused Freulich of cheating them and taking their money for nothing. As a result they beat him severely. Freulich, as it turns out, became sick from the beating and supposedly even "died" from the beatings of the group. A later inquiry discovered that, in fact, Freulich did not die, and immigrated to Israel (see Niv, vol. 5:257 and Tavin 1973:224–225).

8. Brigadier David Marcus (Miki Stone) was born in 1902 in the United States, graduated from West Point Academy in 1924 and took part in the Allies war effort in Europe during World

War II. In 1947 he was recruited to the emerging Israeli Army and came to Israel on February 3, 1948, to help instruct and advise. On May 28, 1948, he was appointed as the commander of the Jerusalem front and won much admiration. On the night of June 11, 1948, he was shot and killed by mistake by a guard, probably Eliezer Liron Linsky, in the military camp near Abu-Gosh Monastery about thirteen kilometers west of Jerusalem. After his death there were rumors that his death was not accidental and should be attributed to the supposedly bad relations between him and the army. These rumors were not substantiated, and were later rejected.[8]

9. On February 10, 1983 in the evening, the "Peace Now" movement (e.g., see Palgi 1979, Bar On 1985) in Israel staged a demonstration near the government buildings in Jerusalem. Suddenly, at 2050, a hand grenade was thrown into the crowd and exploded. Ten demonstrators were wounded and Emile Greenzweig, thirty-three years old, was killed (*Ha'aretz*, February 11, 1983, p. 1). After a long and exhausting investigation the police arrested, in January 1984, Yonah Avrushmi. On March 27, 1984 Avrushmi was accused in the district court in Jerusalem with murder and attempted murder. He denied the charges (*Ha'aretz*, March 28, 1984, p. 6). Avrushmi tried to make a plea bargain, when he was willing to admit that he killed but did not murder (*Ha'aretz*, May 29, 1984, p. 3). On January 13, 1985 he was found guilty of murdering Greenzweig and received a sentence of life in prison (*Ha'aretz*, January 14, 1985, p. 1). The Israeli supreme court rejected Avrushmi's appeal (see *Ma'ariv*, February 20, 1987). However, Avrushmi, who was totally opposed to the ideology of the Peace Now movement, did not aim his grenade particularly at Greenzweig—but at the collective. This case is obviously an act of terrorism.[9]

10. On December 8, 1983, there was a demonstration in Arab Shechem (Nablus). A Jewish settler from Alon More, Joseph Harnoi, thirty-eight years old, who passed by around 1400, began to chase one of the children demonstrators. He entered a bakery where he thought the child was hiding and inside, in front of her father, shot ten-year-old Aisha Al-Bahash to death and wounded her girl friend with his "Uzi" submachine gun. Harnoi and a friend of his, Ephraim Segal, were arrested.

Harnoi was charged with murdering Aisha and Segal was charged with destroying evidence, threatening witnesses, and acting as an accomplice after the fact. In October 1985 both were found guilty. Harnoi got a ten year prison sentence and Segal got a seven-month prison sentence (e.g., see Ringel-Hoffman 1988). Again, in this case, Aisha was murdered not as a result of a specific assassination plot against her. A different person/child who could have been pursued during the demonstration, may have found a similar tragic end.

11. On April 12, 1984, four Palestinians boarded Israel's Egged bus no. 300 in Tel Aviv. The bus was heading to Ashkelon, a southern Israeli city on the Mediterranean coast. As the bus was on its way, the Palestinians hijacked it. Later on, Israeli soldiers stormed the bus and released the passengers. Two of the Palestinians were killed during the initial action. Two others were taken prisoners, were interrogated by the Shabac (see previous chapter) and were later killed. In what was probably the most spectacular "cover-up" operation in the history of the Israeli secret services, the Israeli Shabac initially denied that its people were ordered to, and killed, the two Palestinians. Civil servants of the Israeli Shabac lied and manipulated other civil servants. Eventually, this cover-up was exposed and some major reorganization of the Shabac took place. On the surface, this may look like a case of political execution. However, the killing of the two Palestinians was not an act of a political execution, as defined. It was much more a local, immediate, unauthorized properly (in the Israeli context) and a very problematic decision. The Shabac's "need" to stage a cover-up operation only testifies that this was not a bona fide case of a political execution. Hence, this case was not included in the previous chapter (see Raviv and Melman 1990:278–300; Black and Morris 400–409).

12. On the twenty-eighth of October 1984 a "Lau" anti-tank guided missile was fired in Jerusalem, near the cinematheque, on an Arab bus. One Arab was killed and ten others were wounded. Later, a written note was found near the place of the incident demanding the release of the Jews from the "Jewish underground" (see case no. 91) from prison and a threat to the Arab terrorists (*Ha'aretz*, October 29, 1984, p. 1). After a long investigation, a nineteen-year-old AWOL soldier, David Ben-Shi-

mol, was apprehended on November 2, 1984. He admitted firing the missile, and also throwing a hand grenade into an Arab coffee shop. He stated that he committed his acts as a revenge for Arab acts of terrorism against Jews (*Ha'aretz*, February 25, 1985, p. 9). Ben-Shimol was found guilty of premeditated murder and sentenced to life in prison (*Ha'aretz*, April 18, 1985, p. 6). In this case, Ben-Shimol clearly did not intend to assassinate anyone in particular; he aimed at a collective entity.

13. Finally, on April 22, 1985, the body of an Arab taxi cab driver, Hamis Tutanji (thirty-two years old), was found dead. In the investigation, it was found that a group of three—Danny Eisenman (twenty-seven years old), Gil Fux (twenty-one years old) and Michal Hallel (twenty-five years old) murdered Tutanji as revenge for an Arab terrorist act of murdering a Jewish taxi cab driver—David Caspi—a few days earlier. All three admitted the act and when their trial ended in Jerusalem (December 3, 1986) they were found guilty of murder and sentenced to life in prison (e.g., see for a short summary *Yediot Aharonot*, December 12, 1986, p. 9; Kafra 1986). Again, this group wanted to kill an Arab taxi cab driver, any driver. They were not particularly interested exclusively in Tutanji.

Cases Which Cannot be Validated as Bona Fide Political Assassination Events

During the research effort and process, we came across a few cases that appeared to be political assassination events. However, the information available was such that we could not establish, with a satisfactory degree of confidence or certainty, that in fact these were bona fide cases of political assassination events. The problematics involved were usually due to possibly doubtful sources, lack of sufficient details (e.g., names, dates, reason, plans, etc.). We encountered about twenty-two such cases and these are listed below:

1. On the evening of Yom Kippur, September 23, 1929 hundreds of Jews were gathered around the Wailing Wall in East Jerusalem for prayers. They partitioned the area for male and females using screens. The British deputy governor of Jerusalem, who came to visit, thought that putting the screens was illegal and

instructed officer Douglas Duff to remove it. This incidence creat-ed much turmoil in Jerusalem, and eventually also helped the 1929 anti—Jewish Arab riots into being (S.T.H., vol. 2, part 1: 304–307 and 312–340). Avraham Tehomy told Nakdimon, in an interview, that a secret group existed within the Hagana in Jerusalem in the 1920s, whose name was Hamercaz ("the cen-ter"). According to Tehomy, at an unknown time (probably in 1929) three members of the group—Zechariahu Urielli ("Zachar"), Uri Alpert, and Avraham Tehomy himself—intended to assassinate Douglas Duff for his part in the September 23, 1929 incident near the Wailing Wall, but they never carried out their intention (Nakdimon and Mayzlish 1985:178). There are a few good reasons to doubt this report. First, the reliability of Tehomy's reports is problematic at best. Second, officer Duff was obeying orders of his superior. Third, even Tehomy admits that this "plot" was not authorized by the Hagana command, and it is highly doubtful whether it would have been. Assassinating a British officer in 1929 was probably unthinkable for the Hagana. Third, no mention of this plot, or of the Hamercaz is to be found. It is possible that fifty-five years after, Tehomy is attributing to a possible and imaginary "group" something that may have crossed his own mind in 1929.

2. Bauer (1966:53 n. 49) states that the PUM (see case nos. 10 and 11), probably in 1939, planned two assassinations. One against the British district governor in Lod, the other against the British district governor of the south.

3. Eliav (1983:69) states that on July 15, 1938, Mishka Rabinowitz, who was under Eliav's supervision, assassinated an unnamed head of an Arab gang as well as his body guard.

4. Eliav (1983:75–76) tells of an unsuccessful assassination attempt against the Arab engineer Martin Huri, who was the supervisor of the orphan home in Shneller camp (Jerusalem) and who was believed to be a leader of Arab murderous gangs, and a supporter of the Arab Mufti. Huri was shot and badly wounded. No date is given for the act, but it is likely to have occurred in the 1930s. Naor (1990:102) reports probably on the same event. However, he uses the name Martin Hadad and dates it to Octo-ber 20, 1937.

5. There are reports that in July 1941, the secretary of the

communist party in Tel Aviv—thirty-two-year-old Sioma Mironi-anski—was arrested by a few Jewish officers of the British CID (Criminal Investigation Department) and beaten to death in the British intelligence building in Jaffo. In 1948 the Israeli government appointed a investigating committee to find out what had happened to Mironianski. The committee submitted its report in 1949. The committee stated that Mironianski *was* indeed arrested by a few Jewish officers of the CID. Since he refused to cooperate, he was beaten. Because he was physically weak, he died of the beating. The report stated that because Mironianski's death was unintentional and not planned, the police officers who were involved in the case were embarrassed and decided to hide the body. While it appears quite clear that Mironianski was indeed killed due to a severe beating by police officers (probably Jewish), it also seems that no real and planned assassination plot against him specifically was involved (see Nadel 1968:119, Dagan 1988 and file number 5437/10 in the Israeli "Ginzach Hamedina" [the State Archive]).

6. Eliav (1983:76) states that he and his men tried to assassinate Dr. Kanaan, a leader of Arab gangs. They wounded him. No date of the attempt is given.

7. Clarke (1981:231) states that, at an unknown date, Etzel tried to assassinate Andrew Campbell, the British military prosecutor. According to Clarke, Campbell's dog—"Punch"—discovered the assassins, barked, and woke up the people in Campbell's house thus saving their life. Punch was shot and wounded.

8. Shomron (1985:51, 57) implies that at unknown dates (possibly in February of 1944) Lehi planted a mine in the garage of the British officer Horsburg in Haifa. The mine exploded but probably did not kill him.

9. Okev (1949:13–14) implies that in the middle of the month of August 1945, Lehi may have assassinated in Haifa a forty-eight-year-old Jewish lawyer named Joseph Barnblum. Mr. Anshell Shpillman, director of Lehi archives and museum, vehemently denied (interview, December 24, 1987) that Lehi had anything to do with this. In an interview (February 12, 1988, by telephone), Barnblum's son—Ami—who tried to investigate his father's death, implied that it was more likely that his father was killed by Arabs.

10. Tavin (1973:101 n. 71) reports that in a refugee camp in

Milano, Italy, a Jewish refugee from Poland was suspected of cooperating with the British military police, and of squealing on members of Etzel. The refugee was interrogated and later sentenced to death. He was executed in February of 1947 by members of Etzel in the camp. The name of the refugee is unknown, as well as the details of the case. According to Tavin, the interrogation and execution took a whole night.

11. Margaret Truman-Daniel, claimed that in 1947, Lehi sent explosive envelopes to her father, U.S. President H. Truman. According to her claim, the FBI discovered the envelopes and dismantled them (*Ha'aretz*, December 3, 1972, p. 2) Eliav (*Ha'aretz*, December 12, 1972, p. 24) and Yellin-Mor (*Ha'aretz*, December 5, 1972, p. 15) flatly denied this. One must be reminded, though, that in 1947, Eliav and Lehi did in fact send explosive envelopes from Europe to different people (e.g., see Eliav 1983:322–326).

12. Harel (1985:38) states that on July 6, 1948, Lehi in Jerusalem executed a Jewish woman named Rosa Beizer who, according to Lehi, served as a "chief agent for the British intelligence" in Israel. Mr Anshell Shpillman, Director of Lehi archives and museum, vehemently denied (December 24, 1987) that Lehi had anything to do with this.[10]

13. In a previous chapter we noted that Herouti (case no. 86), was involved in the Zrifin underground and the Kasztner murder trial. In the trial of Herouti in December of 1952, a witness named Ariel Aliashvilli told the court that he prepared a bomb and planned to use it against Moshe Sharet. He stated that when he met Herouti and told him about his plan, Herouti told him not to carry it out (see *Ha'aretz*, December 12, 1957, p. 5).

14. Yachin (1984:162–163), a former member of Lehi, describes an unsuccessful attempt at an unspecified date, on the part of Lehi in Jerusalem to assassinate Brigadier Davis, commander of the Ninth British division. No reason is given for this attempt, and no accounting is provided as for why Lehi did not continue its attempts to assassinate Davis.

15. Okev (1949:13) implies that in early June of 1943 Lehi may have assassinated Pesach Haim Levi, twenty-two years old, in Tel Aviv. This case, however, may be a misidentification of Pesach Levi from Lehi, who had actually committed suicide (see case no. 38 about Eliahu Giladi).

16. On April 22, 1949, the body of Michael Barnt was found, shot to death, on the beach in Tel Aviv. There were rumors that Barnt was a member of Etzel, that he may have come to Palestine-Israel aboard the *Altalena* and that the "reason" for his death was political (see *Ha'aretz*, April 25, 1949, p. 1 and April 26, 1949, p. 4).

17. Isser Harel, former chief of the Israeli secret service, states (1985:50–51) that between 1950–1952 there were plans by secret groups in Israel to assassinate the U.S. water mediator, Erik Johnston,[11] and the British minister of foreign affairs, Selvin Lloyd. In a telephone interview (March 25, 1988), Harel stated that the specific group which was involved in these cases was more or less the same group which was later involved in the Kasztner assassination event (case no. 86), that is a group which was affiliated with an extreme right-wing nationalistic ideology. According to Harel, this group was infiltrated by (an) agent(s) of the Israeli secret service, and when the service learned about the plans to assassinate Johnston and Lloyd they took the necessary actions to stop it.

18. Niv (vol. 5:78) reports on a death sentence declared by Etzel against a British policeman no. 1617 because he abused prisoners. While policeman 1617 was under Etzel's surveillance for a while, no real attempt on his life was ever made.

19. In two interviews with ex-Etzel members the interviewees mentioned that Etzel had assassinated a person whose nickname was "Pinocchio" (because of a physical deformity he had) because he was suspected of squealing. Unfortunately, and despite all our efforts, we could not locate the time of the case, the real name of the victim, the weapon, the ethnicity of the victim or find contemporary corroborations for the assassination.

20. In an article by Ezra Danon in *Ma'arachot* (July 1984:294–295), it is reported that, at at unknown date and place the Hagana assassinated a commander of Arab gangs—Yoseph Hamdan. That, the article implies, was part of a policy aimed to "eliminate" the leaders/commanders of Arab anti-Jewish groups (gangs). It is stated that the "Arab Shai" (an operational intelligence unit, probably the Hashachar, or the Mista'arvim) had a few successes in this area.

21. Argaman (1991:168–180) reports that in the early 1950s, a notorious Arab gangster named Mustafa Samueli (from

the Arab village of Nebi Samuel) created much fear among Jews in the area around Jerusalem. He committed many ferocious acts of aggression against Jews (mostly robberies). According to Argaman, a military unit ambushed Mustafa Samueli and killed him. How much is this case a simple case of a criminal robber who directed his actions against Jews, and how much was a political/military challenge involved here is not at all clear.

22. In September of 1986, Yoseph Lunz, sixty-six years old from Kefar Saba, took two hitch hiking soldiers in his car. During the car ride, he suggested to the two soldiers (who were completely unknown to him), that they should assassinate parliament members Shulamit Aloni and Yossi Sarid, both members of Ratz, a left oriented party. Luntz told the soldiers that both parliament members had to be assassinated because of their political views. The soldiers who must have been amazed at the Chutzpa and the very idea, reported the incidence to the police. After some investigations, it was decided to try and press charges against Luntz. At the time of writing this report, it is unclear how this bizzare case would end. Obviously, the amount of seriousness of Luntz in "planning" an assassination event is doubtful at best. This whole episode can not be taken too seriously (*Yediot Aharonot*, June 8, 1986).

PART 3

Analysis, Discussion, and Summary

CHAPTER 11

General Criminological Parameters and Characteristics of Political Assassination Events

Introduction

I have already emphasized that one of the unique features of this research is that it views political assassination events from the perspective of the sociology of deviance and criminology. This particular perspective focuses on political assassination events as a special subcategory within a much broader type of human aggression and violence—that of taking other people's life against their will. Therefore, it becomes important, empirically, analytically, and comparatively to try and delineate what are the parameters which make this subcategory different from other, perhaps similar, forms of taking other people's life against their will. This is the goal of this chapter.

A primary issue we have to look into relates to the broadest, most general characteristics of political assassination events. Here, we shall have a macro, broad view of eighty-seven cases (see section on Sampling, Analysis, and Methodology in the next chapter) and try and see if we can generate some general characteristics. We shall later compare the emerging criminological pattern of political assassination events with those of the most famous and researched form of taking other people's life: homicide.

Time

The first questions we shall look into are about the day, date, and timing of the events.

TABLE 11–1
DAY OF THE WEEK WHEN
POLITICAL ASSASSINATION EVENTS TOOK PLACE

Day	Frequency	Rounded Percentage
Sunday	4	7
Monday	10	17
Tuesday	8	14
Wednesday	8	14
Thursday	10	17
Friday	13	22
Saturday	6	10
TOTAL	59	

CHART 11–1
DAYS AND FREQUENCIES OF
POLITICAL ASSASSINATION EVENTS

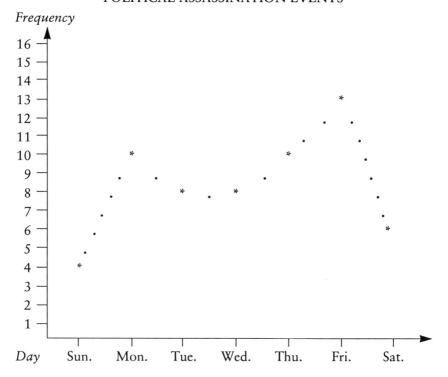

In twenty-eight cases (about 32% of the total number of cases), no information was available regarding the day. From the known cases (N = 59), there is a clear tendency for political assassination events to take place on Mondays, Thursdays, and much more so on Fridays. These two days mark the beginning and the end of the weekend and it is possible that political assassination events are planned for these two days in the hope that it may be easier to escape and not be caught as police forces are not yet fully operational because of the weekend vacation.

In forty-seven cases (about 54% of the total number of cases) no information was available regarding the accurate time in the day. The table indicates that the preferred time for a political assassination event is either the morning or the evening. There may be a few reasons for this modus operandi. First, these are also the times when people either go to, or come back from, work. Hence, prediction of routine at these particular times is easier which makes attacking more convenient. Second, identifying the victim(s) at these times may be easier and more convenient. Third, these times may be more favorable in terms of the expected ease of escape.

In twenty-one cases (about 24% of the total number of cases) no information was available regarding the month. Two months seem to be more prone than others to "host" political assassination events: March and May (actually, 41.5% of the cases occurred in the months of March–April–May). Perhaps the "Ides of March" is not, after all, a vacuous expression. On the other hand, the months which are least likely to host political assassination events are July and December.

A related question is whether the date in the month has any significance. This issue was examined and it appears that the cases are dispersed more or less evenly during the days of the month with a percentage that ranges typically between three to five per date. There are a few slight exceptions. It seems that the second and the twelfth rank low (1.7% for both) and the twenty-second and the third rank high (8.6% and 10.3% respectively). No unusual numbers for the Ides of March. However, it seems that the above deviations are not theoretically meaningful.

The next question relates to the dispersion of the cases over the years.

TABLE 11–2
TIME OF THE DAY WHEN
POLITICAL ASSASSINATION EVENTS TAKE PLACE

	Time	Rounded Frequency	Percentage
Morning	(0600–1159)	15	38
Noon	(1200–1359)	2	5
Afternoon	(1400–1759)	5	13
Evening	(1800–2159)	11	28
Night	(2200–0559)	7	18
TOTAL		40	

CHART 11–2
TIME OF DAY AND FREQUENCIES OF
POLITICAL ASSASSINATION EVENTS

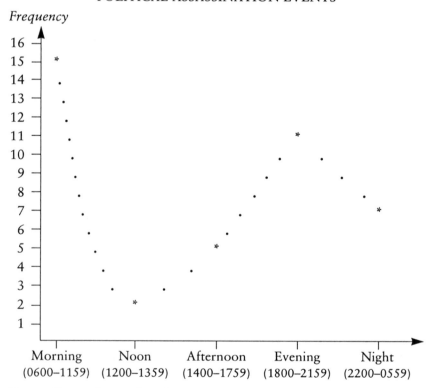

Time of Day when Political Assassinations Occur

TABLE 11–3
MONTH AND POLITICAL ASSASSINATION EVENTS

Month	Frequency	Rounded Percentage
January	4	6
February	6	9
March	11	17
April	5	8
May	11	17
June	5	8
July	1	2
August	5	8
September	5	8
October	5	8
November	6	9
December	2	4
TOTAL	66	

CHART 11–3
MONTHS AND FREQUENCIES OF
POLITICAL ASSASSINATION EVENTS

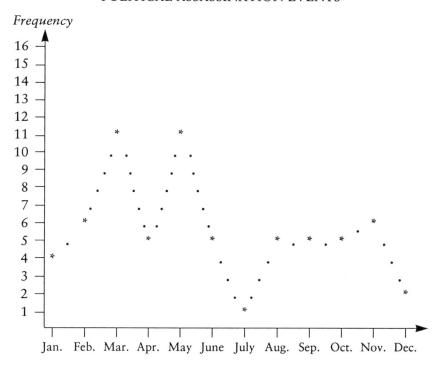

TABLE 11–4
POLITICAL ASSASSINATION EVENTS BY BLOCKS OF YEARS

Year	Frequency	Rounded Percentage
1896–1917	3	3
1918–1948	78	90
1949–1980	6	7
TOTAL	87	

Obviously, most cases are concentrated between 1918–1948, which was the period of the British occupation of Palestine. It is worth our while now to look at a more detailed dispersion:

It is easy to see from Chart 11–4 how political assassination events really picked up volume between 1939 to 1948 and than leveled off again (more on this particular phenomenon later). The years which were most characterized by political assassination events were 1939, 1944, and 1947. These three years alone count for almost 40% of all the cases. Particularly high was 1947. It is relatively easy to explain the peaks in 1939 (and 1947). 1939 marked the beginning of World War II and the turmoil, in and between, the Etzel and the Hagana as well as a fierce struggle in the *Yishuv* about the boundaries of its different symbolic-moral universes. Hence, 60% of the cases (N = 6) in 1939 were by Etzel and 30% (N = 3) by the Hagana. From all the targets at that year (N = 10), seven (70%) were Jews: five by Etzel and two by the Hagana.

In 1944, a year before the end of world war II, 80% (N = 8) of the cases were committed by Lehi and 20% (N = 2) by Etzel. Five of the targets (50%) were British, the rest were Jews (two by Etzel and three by Lehi).

In 1947, there were fourteen targets, out of which eight (57.1%) were Jews (four by Etzel and four by Lehi); five (35.7%) British (by Lehi) and one Arab (by Lehi). Nineteen forty-seven was one year before the British left Palestine and before the state of Israel was established. This year was characterized, again, by fierce struggles about definitions of symbolic-moral universes and the very nature of the emerging state. How-

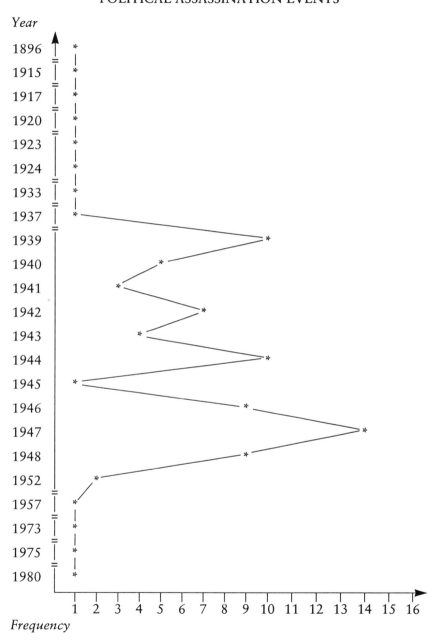

CHART 11–4
YEARS AND FREQUENCIES OF
POLITICAL ASSASSINATION EVENTS

ever, explaining the peaks in 1944 and 1946 is much more elusive and problematic and despite searches for possible external and/or interorganizational reasons, no good explanation could be developed.

The distribution of the cases over the years varies greatly. All of Lehi's cases are concentrated between 1941–1948 a period of seven years (peaking in 1944 and 1947). All of Hashomer's cases are concentrated between 1917–1923. The cases involving the Hagana are dispersed from 1924 till 1948 (peaking in 1940). Etzel's cases are dispersed between 1937–1947 (peaking in 1940 and 1947). Half of the involvement of "other groups " is between 1952–1957, and 60% of the individual cases are concentrated between 1973–1980.

Weapons

In fifteen cases (about 17% of the total number of cases) no information was available regarding the weapon(s). Obviously, the overwhelming preference was for a hand gun and for bombs. A hand gun was usually perceived as a reliable weapon. Using a hand gun, moreover, increased the probability of hitting a specific target only, which was not the case when using a bomb. An interesting question relates to the type of weapons chosen by the different groups.

Lehi's assassins, as well as individual assassins, the Hagana and Etzel, overwhelmingly preferred to use hand guns. While Lehi was the only group which used automatic weapons, the Hagana never used those fire spitters, or bombs, which Lehi felt very comfortable to use.

Another question is related to the type of weapon used and the result(s) of the events in terms of "success."

Obviously, the weapon associated most frequently with a "successful" event is a hand gun (78%). Automatic weapons and bombs are weakly associated with success (10% and 6%, respectively). The weapons least successful were explosive envelopes (although we saw in chapter 9 a very successful use of such "weapon" by the Israeli military intelligence), a combination of methods and a knife. Most of the "unsuccessful" events were characterized by the use of a bomb/mine (45%).

TABLE 11–5
TYPE OF WEAPON AND ASSASSIN(S)

Assassin	Hand Gun	Rifle	Automatic Weapon	Bomb/ Mine	Knife	Explosive Envelope	Drowning	More than One Weapon
Individual assassin	3			1	1			
Hashomer	2							
Etzel	8			3			1	
Lehi	19	1	5	7		1		2
Hagana	11	1	1					
Other groups	2	1		1		1		
TOTAL (72)	45	3	6	12	1	2	1	2
% of total	63%	4%	8%	17%	1%	3%	1%	3%

TABLE 11-6
TYPE OF ASSASSINATION EVENT AND WEAPON

Type of Assassination	Hand Gun	Rifle	Automatic Weapon	Bomb/ Mine	Knife	Explosive Envelope	Drown	Comb. of Weapons	Total
Planned	3								3
Unsuccessful	4	1	1	9	1	2		2	20
Successful	38	2	5	3			1		49
TOTAL	45	3	6	12	1	2	1	2	72

Place

TABLE 11–7
PLACE OF POLITICAL ASSASSINATION EVENT

Place	Frequency	Rounded Percent
Jerusalem	19	23
Tel Aviv-Jaffo (center)	34	42
Haifa (north)	15	19
Other (in Palestine-Israel)	5	6
Other (outside Palestine-Israel)	8	10
TOTAL	81	

In six cases (about 7% of the total number of cases) no information was available regarding the place. Clearly, most political assassination events took place in the Tel Aviv area. The second place was Jerusalem and the third was Haifa. These places basically also reflect the concentration of Jewish citizens in the crucial years 1939–1948, as well as the centers of British government.

Two interesting questions are related to the place of assassination. One question is related to place of assassination and ethnicity/nationality of victim; the other to the place of assassination and the assassin(s).

TABLE 11–8
PLACE OF POLITICAL ASSASSINATION EVENT AND
NATIONALITY/ETHNICITY OF VICTIM

Place of Assassination Event	Ethnicity of Victim				
	Jew	British	Arab	Other	Total
Jerusalem	6	10		3	19
Tel Aviv (center)	27	3	3	1	34
Haifa (north)	9	4	2		15
Other (in Palestine)	4		1		5
Other (out of Palestine)	1	4	1	2	8
TOTAL	47	21	7	6	81

Since Jerusalem was the administrative center of the British forces in Palestine between 1918–1948, it should not surprise us to find that most victims in the Jerusalem area were British (53%), and that more British were killed in Jerusalem than elsewhere. A complimentary finding is that most victims in the Tel Aviv and Haifa area (79% and 60%, respectively) were Jews, as these areas had a high concentration of Jews.

TABLE 11–9
PLACE OF POLITICAL ASSASSINATION EVENT
AND THE ASSASSIN(S)

				Area		
Assassin	Jerusalem	Tel Aviv (center)	Haifa (north)	Somewhere Else in Pal-Israel	Outside of Pal-Israel	Total
Individual		4			1	5
Hashomer	1	1		1		3
Etzel	3	6	3	1	1	14
Lehi	13	15	6	1	5	40
Hagana	2	5	6	1		14
Another group		3		1	1	5
TOTAL	19	34	15	5	8	81

Most political assassination events by Lehi and Etzel (38% and 43%, respectively) were in the Tel Aviv area. The Hagana's cases are more evenly distributed between Jerusalem and Tel Aviv. In all three major Urban areas—Jerusalem, Tel Aviv, and Haifa, Lehi's cases were the most dominant (68%, 44%, and 40%, respectively).

Accuracy of Hit

One last interesting and essential question is how accurate were the assassins in hitting their targets? After all, we have emphasized that the factor which distinguishes terrorism from political assassination is that in the latter the target is *very* specific. The results of the analysis are fascinating.

TABLE 11–10
HITTING INNOCENT BYSTANDERS

Target	Frequency	Percentage
No bystander was hit	56	79
One bystander was wounded	2	3
Two + bystanders were wounded	1	1
One bystander was killed	8	11
One bystander was killed + 1+ were wounded	2	3
The "wrong" target was killed by mistake	2	3
TOTAL	71	

In 16 cases there was no actual assassination attempt.

Checking these data against the weapons used in order to see what was the weapon which was the most "dangerous" in this context did not yield very significant differences between hand guns (four cases out of forty-five) a rifle (one case out of three) and, automatic weapons (two cases out of six). The two interesting cases were: (a) the use of a mine/bomb where in five out of ten cases of when this weapon was used, innocent bystanders were hit (three were killed) and (b) in the two cases where explosive envelopes were sent, they reached and hit the wrong targets (one must be reminded, though, that this method was used successfully by the Israeli military intelligence in the 1950s [see chapter 9]).

A related question is who "goofed" the most from the fifteen cases where innocent bystanders were hit.

Clearly, and as far as we can tell, the Hagana, individuals, and Hashomer either did not goof, or goofed very little. Lehi and Etzel were the ones who goofed the most (66% and 20%, respectively). It appears though, that when Etzel and Lehi goofed the mistakes were quite lethal. These groups account together for at least 73% (and more) of all of the "killed by mistake" cases.

To counterbalance the interpretation which emerges from tables 11–10 and 11–11, and the discussion, one must add that in a few instances (e.g., see the cases involving Scheid [no. 1]; Schiff [no. 27]; Illin [no. 44]; Killy [no. 70] as well as part of the plan about the explosions at 8 Yael Street—see case no. 30) the potential assassin(s) exercised restraint and did not activate a plan to assassinate fearing that innocent bystanders may be hit.

TABLE 11–11
HITTING INNOCENT BYSTANDERS BY ASSASSINS

			Assassins				
Type of Hit	Individual	Hashomer	Etzel	Lehi	Hagana	Other groups	Total
One person wounded			2				2
Two persons wounded			1				1
One person killed			3	4		1	8
One person killed, 1 wounded				1	1		2
Killed the wrong target				1		1	2
TOTAL			3	9	1	2	15

Apprehension

One interesting criminological question is "how many of the assassins were ever caught?"

TABLE 11–12
WAS THE ASSASSIN CAPTURED?

	Frequency	Rounded Percentage
No	78	90
Yes, but not brought to trial	2	2
Yes, brought to trial and acquitted	2	2
Yes, brought to trial, found guilty	5	6
TOTAL	87	

This table shows that the chances of the assassin to be caught were very low because very few of them were ever caught. Only 8% were charged in a court and only 6% were found guilty. The fact that the assassin(s) was/were so well protected from being captured and prosecuted can be attributed to his/their membership in ideological groups which were able to construct this most efficient protection.

It is well worth noticing that out of the nine cases were suspects in the assassination events were caught, one third (three cases) happened between 1949–1980, that is after the state of Israel was established.

Victims' (and Assassins') Characterizations

Some important questions pertain to who the victims and the assassins were. Let me point out immediately that a section on the characteristics of the assassin(s) could not be created. In about 72.4% (N = 63) of the cases, we simply do not know who the individual assassin(s) was/were. We do know, however, who was the *organization* which took responsibility for the act. In twenty-four cases (27.6%) where we know who the specific assassin(s) was/were, we typically lack essential biographical/background information. However, in the cases where we know who the specific assassin(s) was/were, we also know that in the overwhelming majority of cases she/he/they acted on behalf, and instructions, of an organization and not because the assassin(s) had anything personal against the victim(s). It is therefore unwise theoretically to make a deep probe into the characteristics/background of the specific assassins in hope of finding there possible clues for justifying the acts.

From the available information it is quite clear that there *were no cases involving hired assassins*. From the information about the background, especially the Sicariis and Europe, we can also make the same conclusion. Thus, the *hired assassin*, mentioned in the literature, does not exist in the political assassinations which were studied here. While political executions were probably planned, and carried out, by people who were on the government's payroll, it would not be valid to call them hired assassins. These government agents are probably not paid per assassination, they probably do not see themselves as hired assassins, their basis of legitimization is very different than that of a hired assassin, and their social role as assassins is only temporary.

Therefore, the rest of this section and next tables are addressed to the issue of characterizing the victims.

TABLE 11–13
AGE OF VICTIM

Age	Frequency	Rounded Percentage
17–30	11	26
31–39	7	17
40–50	13	31
51–76	11	26
TOTAL	42	

In forty-two cases (48% from the total number of cases) no information was available regarding the age of the victim. In two cases (2% of the total number of cases) there was more than one victim. The majority of victims were forty years and older. This fits well the fact that it takes time for a person to establish himself/herself as an important political actor and as "worthy" of an assassination attempt.

The overwhelming majority of the intended victims (N = 84 which is 97% of the cases) were males. The complimentary figure is that there were very few female assassins. In only one (maybe two) cases we know that there was a female assassin (case nos. 8 and 60, not including political executions), and in both cases we had unsuccessful cases. While we know that females took part in assassination teams, their role in the actual assassination was virtually nil. These low figures probably reflect the fact that females remained overwhelmingly outside the major Jewish–Arab–British conflict before 1948, and there were no female victims after 1948. While it may appear that female "deviants" were dealt with differently than males, the better explanation lies probably elsewhere. Females' power, influence and position, were so low that they apparently did not present any major threat to any of the powers involved in the struggles, hence the very low proportion of female victims. While perhaps "good" in some moralistic sense, this fact also reflects the females' low nonthreatening status. Furthermore, the fact that—as far as we can tell—there were no actual female assassins only reinforces this conclusion.

TABLE 11–14
MARITAL STATUS OF VICTIM

Marital Status	Frequency	Rounded Percentage
Single	12	32
Married, no children	5	14
Married, with children	11	30
Married, no information available on children	7	19
Divorced	1	3
Widowed	1	3
TOTAL	37	

In forty-eight cases (55% of the total number of cases) there was no information available on family status. In two cases (2% of the total number of cases) there was more than one victim with different family statuses. In only 32% of the known cases we had an unmarried victim. The majority of victims were married, with a sizable proportion having children too. This figure fits the age of the victims, most of them were old enough to raise families.

COMPARING POLITICAL ASSASSINATION EVENTS WITH CRIMINAL HOMICIDES

So far in this chapter I detailed the parameters which characterize and constitute, on the macro-criminological level, the unique pattern called "political assassination," as defined in chapter 2. However, without a comparative perspective this unique pattern may be unclear and useless. The purpose of this part is to provide this perspective.

In chapter 2 we have seen that there exists a reservoir of rhetorical devices from which we can choose particular ones to use, in specific instances, to help us interpret various acts of taking somebody else's life against his/her wish. The invocation of any of these rhetorical devices depends on the specific pattern of the act. Thus, such rhetorical devices as lynchings, human sacrifices, blood revenge, and criminal homicide attach different symbolic and moral meanings to a basically similar act.

The best documented pattern of taking somebody else's life is what has become known as criminal homicide. The differences between criminal homicide and political assassination events are striking.[1] Next I shall characterize the situation for which the rhetorical device "criminal homicide" is typically invoked. Most data are based on studies from the United States, on American populations.

Like political assassination events, homicides tend to occur in large urban centers. While Wilkinson's work (1984) implied that the average murder rate in rural areas was higher than the rate in most cities, Thio (1988:110–111) pointed out that rurality "is related to homicide only if we compare the homicide rates of rural areas with those of most cities, which are relatively small, having populations of fewer than 50,000 people...larger cities, with populations exceeding 50,000, do have significantly higher murder rates than those small cities and the rural areas..."

Most victims and offenders involved in homicide are usually *males*, and the murderers typically do not exhibit marked signs of psychopathology, like in political assassination events. However, it appears that beside these similarities we have only differences. A political assassination event is typically carefully planned and cold bloodedly executed. Criminal homicide is usually a crime of passion, and is typically unplanned. Homicides between two friends or acquaintances seems to constitute the largest category of homicides. Killing of strangers, according to one study, constituted about 25% of the urban homicides. Many criminal homicides cases involve a knife as the murder weapon (between 27% to 39% of the time), the rest use guns (typically in the United States the so-called "Saturday Night Special"), or beat the victim to death (although almost any other weapon could be used too). Alcohol is usually involved in criminal homicides. In about 60% of the cases of criminal homicides alcohol was present in either the offender or the victim or both (e.g., see Wolfgang 1958:136; Wolfgang and Zahn 1983; for an updated statement on homicides, including a call for more refined analyses see Williams and Flewelling 1988).

Von Hentig pointed out already in 1948 that in many cases of criminal homicide the homicide victim precipitated his/her own death. A victim precipitated murder involves a murderer and a victim who not only know each other, but who are engaged in a social intercourse (or in a "homicide situation") which almost "leads" to the homicide-situation. This situation is characterized by much interpersonal tension and hostility and culminates in a murder attempt. In many cases the murder, according to Wolfgang (1957 and 1958:752), is where "The role of the victim is characterized by his having been the first in the homicide drama to use physical force directed against his subsequent slayer. The victim-precipitated cases are those in which the victim was the first to show and use a deadly weapon, to strike a blow in an altercation—in short, the first to commence the interplay of resort to physical violence" (for refinements of the approach see Luckenbill:1977; Felson and Steadman 1983; Wilbanks 1984).

Technically, political assassination events are obviously *not* victim-precipitated, as defined. However, one could argue that they are "victim-precipitated" in the general, perhaps macrophilosophical, level in the sense that the acts, or positions, of the potential victim make him/her vulnerable (perhaps even precipitating) to an assassination event.

Contrary to the characteristics of the victims of political assassination events where only less than a third of them are between the ages of seventeen and thirty, a majority of victims of criminal homicide are between the ages of twenty and thirty (e.g., about 45% of the victims are below the age of twenty-five).

Criminal homicides typically take place between members of the same race (that is, they are usually intraracial), and are correlated with poverty. There is probably a relationship between a country's income *distribution* and the homicide rate. But lots of poor countries (like China, a fifth of the world's population) have fairly low homicide rates, and the United States is at least halfway up there in its murder rate. Civil turmoil is also related to a high homicide rate—Ethiopia, Northern Ireland, Colombia, and so forth, have high rates. Countries where tribal peoples come to a city, unsupervised by their elders who have no power in the new context, and where traditional culture has been destroyed, present a high homicide rate. Thio (1988:108) also associates homicides with a violent past on the part of the murderer.

Homicides tend to occur during the late evening and early morning hours (i.e., 2000-0200) of the weekend (usually Saturday night). While patterns of homicides tend not to follow con-

sistent seasonal patterns, there are small and slight increases during the late spring and summer months (vacation time), and in
December (holiday season) (see also Cheatwood 1988).

The above parameters make "the solution of a typical homicide case...relatively simple...criminal homicide shows a high
clearance rate: nationally, 76% of homicides are cleared by arrest"
(Bonn 1984:189). This observation is obviously not true for the
pre-1948 cases of political assassination events which involved a
group. The specific assassin(s) in these cases were hardly, if ever,
caught (see table 12).[2]

It is not too difficult to realize that *none* of the above patterns, so characteristic of criminal homicides, describes even
remotely political assassination events.

The unique patterns of criminal homicide enticed Marvin
Wolfgang and Franco Ferracuti (1967) to invoke the *subculture of
violence* hypothesis. This hypothesis, briefly stated, stipulates that
there are social groups which are characterized by high rates of
violence and which also have a value system that views violence
not only as tolerable and expected but also as required. The deeper one gets involved in this type of subculture, the higher is the
probability of that person being involved in violent acts. The
applicability of the concept of the subculture of violence to political assassination events is limited and complicated. On the one
hand, social disorganization, civil unrest and a struggle of various
groups who aspire to create a national entity is typically violent,
and legitimized as such. Hence the idea may be applicable. On the
other hand, Wolfgang and Ferracuti's concept was developed to
describe a subculture within a more or less integrated culture. The
use of the term *subculture* in the context of 1924–1948 Palestine
is erroneous. The cases between 1949–1980 typically did not
involve the lower class type of violent gang members described by
Woflgang and Ferracuti's concept. The *value* of violence did not
typically describe those actors who were involved in the 1949–
1980 cases. Their violence was very specific and limited.

There is one obvious limitation for this conclusion. We do
not know what *type* of person chose to join the Lehi versus what
type of person chose the Hagana or Etzel. If, for example, those
who chose Lehi were inclined to more violence to begin with,
then the above conclusion has to be altered. In such a case it may

be possible that the modus operandi of the different underground groups superimposed a self-selection process for potential recruits. Unfortunately, absolutely no reliable information is available to help us settle this problem.

SUMMARY

The pattern of taking somebody else's life called criminal homicide is very different from the one called political assassination (or, a political execution).

The "typical" political assassination event tends to take place in the morning or the evening of a Monday, a Thursday, or a Friday, in the month of March (or May). The frequency of the assassination events was magnified in the years 1939, 1947, and less so in 1944 and 1946. This fluctuation in the frequency of political assassination events in those years may be due to the intensity of the struggle of the Yishuv in those years (among different Jewish groups and with external threats, e.g., the riots of 1939). The overwhelmingly preferred weapon was a hand gun (or a bomb). Typically, the event took place in one of the large urban centers. Tel Aviv came first, to be followed by Jerusalem and Haifa. While most British targets were hit in the Jerusalem area, the Jewish targets were hit, typically, in the Tel Aviv area (and much less so in the Haifa area). This distribution parallels the concentration of the British administration in Jerusalem, and the concentration of Jews in the Tel Aviv, Haifa, and Jerusalem areas. Chances were that only the specific target was hit. However, the use of a mine/bomb, or of explosive envelops, increased the probability that innocent bystanders would be hit.

In the overwhelming majority of cases the assassin(s) was/were not caught. The available information indicates that hired assassins were not involved in the cases.

Most of the victims were males, over forty years old, with families. This fits the general idea of a political assassination event. It simply takes time to establish and succeed in a political or administrative career. Typically, those who seemed worthy of a political assassination event fit the above demographic profile. The low structural status of females (not even as informers) explains why there were so few female targets (or assassins).

CHAPTER 12

Political Assassinations
as Rhetorical Devices:
Patterns, Reasons, and Interpretations

SOME GENERAL THEORETICAL OBSERVATIONS

One of the very first observations made in this study is that the rhetorical device "political assassination" can in fact be used to describe quite a few cases of taking other people's lives against their will within the cultural matrix of Jews in Palestine and later in the State of Israel. However, the prevalence of political assassinations (and executions) there is not very high as *compared* to some other cultures (e.g., in some South American societies, where there are so-called "assassination squads"; or in some Muslim Mediterranean societies).

We have recorded ninety-one cases of political assassination events in a time span of almost ninety-five years, between the 1890s until 1988. We found different cases until 1980, and a few probable political executions until 1988. The few cases of political executions do not really change the conclusions. If we take into consideration only the "successful" cases, then the figure drops to fifty-one. As a comparison for the prevalence issue, let us use two local examples. First, it was estimated that during the so-called "Arab Revolt" in Palestine between 1936–1939 the number of Arab casualties was around six thousand. Only fifteen hundred died as a result of British or Jewish activities, and the major bulk of about forty-five hundred victims died as a result of the internal terror among different Arab groups (Arnon-Ochana 1982:139–140; Eshed 1988:55–56). Second, between 1980–1986, a period of seven years there were about twenty-three cases of Arabs assassinating other Arabs, in the same political, target specific, context, in the Israeli occupied West Bank and Gaza Strip (see *Ha'aretz*, March 3, 1986, front page). The Arab "Intifada" (uprising) began in the Israeli occupied West Bank and the Gaza strip in December 1987. Between this time and 1990, around two hundred Arabs were assassinated by other Arabs.[1] Furthermore, no contemporary Jewish leader of a significant and salient stature (e.g., a president, prime minister, etc.) was assassinated (with the possible and problematic exception of Arlosoroff [case no. 7]). The non-Jewish prominent figures who were assassinated were very few, mostly Bernadotte (case no. 83), Moyne (case no. 49), and the attempts on MacMichael's life (case no. 47).

The histories of political assassination events in the distant past of Judaism, and in the last hundred years, demonstrate some interesting connections: the use of similar names, similar ideas, and similar symbols. One need only remember such examples as "Yair" and the Sicariis, Ehud, Mania Shochat, to see this analogy. Moreover, as we shall see later on in this chapter, underlying these many and varied cases is a coherent sociological conceptualization—that of an alternative system of justice.

Studying the history and sociology of political assassinations gives one a powerful, and biased, look into the history of the Jewish people too. It is virtually impossible to understand and interpret the cases without having a fairly detailed understanding of the background. Hence, no good understanding of Vilbushevitz's attempt on Scheid's life (case no. 1) is possible without understanding the early stages of the renewed Jewish settlement in Palestine. No understanding of the assassination of Ralph Cairns (case no. 18) is possible without understanding the nature of the relationships between Etzel and the British. Likewise, the assassination events directed against MacMichael (case no. 47), Moyne (case no. 49) and Kasztner (case no. 86) cannot be fully understood without an understanding of the Jewish holocaust in Nazi occupied Europe during World War II.[2] This conclusion alone necessitates using a *sociological* perspective to interpret political assassinations.

It is thus quite evident that the "sociological story" of political assassination events by Jews in Palestine and Israel touches, in the most deep and powerful sense, some very important parts in the history of Judaism itself, and *much* more so, of the difficult—indeed heroic—struggles of the Zionist movement to reestablish the State of Israel. Hence, through the history of such a deviant pattern of behavior, one is forced to have a deep and somewhat shocking glimpse into the history of nondeviance. It would have been useless, and futile, to provide the different accounts of the cases themselves without providing the background. The complicated and long "story" of political assassination events portrayed in this book, involves other "stories"—of power and moral struggles, and of a vibrant and sometimes violent history. This is also the story of the clashings and negotiations between symbolic-moral universes.

It is not only that a valid interpretative understanding of political assassination events in Palestine and Israel is impossible without having the necessary historical and political background facts. Political assassination events, as evident from this study, were typically located on the boundaries of clashings between different symbolic-moral universes. For example, De Hahn's (case no. 6) assassination involved a clash between two radically different views about the nature of the renewed Jewish settlement in Palestine. Giladi's (case no. 38) assassination revolved, among other things, around a bitter argument about Lehi's nature and course of action. The assassination of many "traitors" and "squealers" involved marking the boundary of what was perceived as legitimate and as nonlegitimate cooperation with the British occupation forces in Palestine. The assassination of Kasztner (case no. 86) illustrates again such a clash which was focused on arguments about what was, or should have been, the "proper" behavior of Jewish leadership in Europe during the Nazi occupation. Hence, political assassination events typically took place at some very painful stitches and junctions of the Jewish Israeli social structure and culture. Very similar to the pattern of such events in other countries.

The Palestinian-Israeli Jewish society has been portrayed to be divided along some very central lines, or cleavages (e.g., see Horowitz and Lissak 1989). In almost all of these cleavages we can find cases of political assassination events (or terrorism). For example, the secular-religious cleavage (e.g., the case involving Dov Pinkas, no. 85); Jews-Arabs; Jews-British and arguments between the "left" and the "right" regarding various issues (e.g., cooperation with the British, the "Shilumim" [reparations] agreement with Germany).

However, in one area, where there existed a very serious cleavage, that is the ethnic cleavage (mostly between Ashkenasi and Sephardi Jews), there are no known cases of political assassination events, and virtually no terror (despite some violent outbursts in the past mostly in the form of violent demonstrations). Obviously, this is an indirect measure for either the low perceived severity of the cleavage, or the absence of a clear cut political overlap between ethnic origin and power. This finding, in itself, can be taken as an encouraging sign for the amount of disintegrative forces in Israeli society in this regard.

This research has demonstrated, and confirmed, the theoretical stand that a true and valid interpretative sociological understanding of deviance must consider total social structures and/or processes by examining deviance as a relative phenomenon and as part of larger social processes of change and stability in the realm of symbolic-moral universes and their boundaries (see Piven 1981, Scull 1984, and Ben-Yehuda 1985, 1990). In this way, this study illustrated how deviance was indeed reframed, in Goffman's sense of the term, within general societal processes, in a dynamic historical and political perspective.

This research has also demonstrated, again, that what is, and what is not defined as deviance, depends on the particular culture in which it happened. Political assassination events were interpreted, and reinterpreted, by the different actors who participated in these dramatic events, (and later evaluators), as either negative or positive deviance. A crucial variable for the negotiations regarding the moral nature, and usefulness, of the events was the existence of cohesive ideological groups which could generate power and give legitimacy to the actors involved in the assassination events.[3] The rhetorical devices which were used illustrate this. Thus, there is a reluctance in all three pre-state groups to use the term political assassinations. They rather use such terms as "individual terror," or Hisul (meaning in Hebrew "elimination"). Many members of Lehi and Etzel are still very proud of those Hisulim. For example, in 1988 a few ex-Lehi members went to the daily press (the influential Yediot Aharonot), and openly (and proudly) admitted their part in the Bernadotte assassination (no.

83). What for members of some symbolic-moral universes (e.g., British, Swedish) looked like a simple murder, was not interpreted as such by others (e.g., Lehi).

The nature of political assassination events which was described in previous chapters fits very well the analytical characterization which was presented for politics and deviance (chapter 1). These events *are* problematic behavioral acts, which take place at the seams, where different symbolic-moral universe meet and touch, or from the periphery of a symbolic-moral universe towards its center, and vice versa. These events typically involve challenges, use or abuse, of power and morality. For example, political executions which are directed from the center to the periphery, or to other members of the very same center, or to another symbolic-moral universe. Likewise, there were political assassination events which were initiated by actors from a particular symbolic-moral universe, and directed towards other actors that were perceived to inhabit other symbolic-moral universes. The threat potential in such challenges was magnified in such cases as those of Eliahu Giladi (no. 38), Israel Pritzker (no. 39) and Yehuda Arie Levi (no. 75) where there may have been a threat directed at the legitimacy of the center's ideology and course of action.

The cases with Arlosoroff (1933, no. 7), Hilewitz (1944, no. 42), Baron Moyne (1944, no. 49), Levi (1948, no. 75), Tubianski (1948, no. 82), Count Folke Bernadotte (1948, no. 83), Kasztner (1957, no. 86) as well as the "Jewish Underground" (1980, no. 91) all point to the fact that political assassinations can be linked intimately with political trials where heated debates about moral boundaries and power take place.

With some very few exceptions (e.g., the cases involving Avneri [no. 89] and possibly Sadat [no. 90]) the political assassination events we encountered can indeed be conceptualized as rhetorical devices used to interpret situations where a discriminate, deliberate, intentional and serious attempt, some more successful than others, were made in order to kill a specific actor for political reasons that had typically something to do with the symbolic-moral universe out of which the assassin(s) acted, and which provided the legitimacy and justification for the act (in some cases even the integrity and future direction of the organization was invoked as the "reason" for the assassinations; for example, the cases involving Joseph Lishansky [no. 3], Zvi Frenkel [no. 9], Eliahu Giladi [no. 38], Yehuda Arie Levi [no. 75]).

The rest of this chapter will be divided into three main sections. The first deals with problems, and results, of sampling, analysis and methodology. The second section presents a few tables and an interpretative explanation about the nature and meaning of political assassination by Jews in Palestine and Israel. The main explanation rests with the concept of "justice." The nature of the specific assassins could not be determined, and even if it were—focusing on the assassins themselves as a route to explain the cases would have been theoretically useless. Based on the discussion in chapter 4 and on the different cases presented mainly in part 2, section three examines the relevant (to assassinations) characteristics, ideology, and structure, of the organizations which were involved in political assassination events.

SAMPLING, ANALYSIS, AND METHODOLOGY

Ninety-one cases of political assassination events were presented. However, and due to reasons suggested in the description of the cases themselves, four cases were not taken into the analysis of the aggregate data. These cases are the ones involving: Arlosoroff (case no. 7), Segal (case no. 74), Vilner (case no. 87) and the Jewish underground (case no. 91). Hence, only eighty-seven cases were taken into consideration for the final aggregate statistical analysis. Moreover, the cases included in the chapter on political executions were summarized in that chapter and were not taken into the statistical analysis. The reason is twofold: one, the problematic nature of the cases themselves and two, the very different type of morality and legitimation behind the two different types of assassinations. Perhaps not surprisingly, the general conclusions of the study presented in this part are valid for both political executions and assassinations.

When there was doubt as to who should be credited with the case, the choice was on the group which was most dominant. Thus, case nos. 53 and 60 were classified as Lehi. The case involving MacMichael (eight attempts) was dated as 1944, Lehi.

As was argued in chapter 3, the exact nature and representativeness of the sample of the eighty-seven cases we have are not entirely clear. Thus, I decided not to use inferential statistics and be satisfied only with descriptive statistics. In most cases, I rounded up the percentages to the closest figure. In this fashion, the emerging description is more convenient to digest and less confusing. This is also the reason that no 100% appears in the percentage total cells.

A key concept which was used in chapter 3 was Marx's (1984) "hidden and dirty data." How hidden are the data? We rated each case by the amount of information available. Each case could receive a grade from one to three. "Telegraphic" meant that the information available was brief and meager indeed. "Full" meant that the information was very full, including names of assassins, method, processes of decision making, reasons, and the like. The score "Partial" was given to anything which was anywhere between one and three. The results of the rating are presented in table 12–1:

TABLE 12–1
INFORMATION ABOUT THE CASE BY TYPE OF ASSASSIN(S)

Type of Assassin(s)	Information			
	Telegraphic	*Partial*	*Full*	*Total*
Individual Assassin		1	4	5
Hashomer		1	2	3
Etzel	3	9	3	15
Lehi	10	28	4	42
Hagana	9	6	1	16
Other Groups		5	1	6
TOTAL	22	50	15	87
% from total	25%	58%	17%	100%

Table 12–1 gives an empirical substantiation to Marx's terminology. In only about 17% of the cases we had full information.

Clearly, the Hagana gives telegraphic information about most of its cases (56%). Both Etzel and Lehi typically provide at least partial information about their cases (60% and 66.67%, respectively). Full information is available either on individual assassins (26.67%) or from Lehi (26.67%). It is thus evident that the least secretive are individual assassins, Lehi, Etzel and other groups. The most secretive group was the Hagana. Compared to the other cases, one is simply left pondering what it is that the Hagana had to hide, or what was their ideology that led to their hiding what others did not (more on this later). This is also the place to note that compared to *all* the three groups, the available information on cases of political executions is very meagre.

PATTERNS OF POLITICAL ASSASSINATION EVENTS BY JEWS—A RHETORICAL DEVICE FOR JUSTICE

General

TABLE 12–2
TYPE OF POLITICAL ASSASSINATION EVENT

	Frequency	Rounded Percentage
Preplanning	6	7
Planning	6	7
Unsuccessful	24	28
Successful— victim died	48	55
Successful— victim wounded	3	3
TOTAL	87	

Political assassination events constitute a serious matter (table 12–2). Most cases are located within the successful category. These data suggest that once serious preplanning begins, there is a fairly good chance for its successful completion. This conclusion, however, may be a result of a sampling bias because we simply may have more information about "unsuccessful" and successful cases than on "preplanning" and "planning."

The most obvious observation is that only in the minority of cases (6%) we have a *single* assassin. In the overwhelming majority of cases (94%) we have an *organized group* behind the assassination event (this conclusion is most certainly valid for cases of political execution as well) and therefore we are not dealing with a lone fanatic killer, but with a premeditated and planned act, committed by a group or by a representative of a group. Thus, the specific pattern of assassinations which emerges from this research is a very interesting one (and continues the pattern which developed in Europe—see chapter 5). I chose to call it *organized collective political assassination events*. There are two reasons for this name: first, most cases involve more than one assassin. While the actual assassin may be only one, in most cases this person is linked very intimately to a group which plans the assassination, gives the assassins a much needed moral support, the vocabularies of motives needed to justify and perform the task, and the means needed to execute the plan of assassination as well as shelter. In many cases the victim was warned, sometimes more than once by the group. The fact that most cases involve a group, (usually a secret one) is one of the reasons that it is so difficult to fully and thoroughly document these cases.

TABLE 12–3
WHO WAS RESPONSIBLE FOR THE
POLITICAL ASSASSINATION EVENT?

	Frequency	*Rounded Percentage*
An individual actor	5	6
Hashomer	3	3
Etzel	15	17
Lehi	42	48
Hagana	16	18
Another organized group	6	7
TOTAL	87	

In each of the cases the assassin felt part of a particular symbolic-moral universe, and by his/her act signified the boundaries not only of that universe but of a larger cultural matrix as well (e.g., see Ben-Yehuda, 1985). Therefore the second reason is that the rhetorical device called political assassination, as it has existed among Jews in Palestine and Israel, is associated with a similar pattern in Europe (as well as the Sicariis): an assassin who operates as part of, or representing, a larger more or less crystallized symbolic-moral universe. It is very rare indeed to find the "crazy" or "psychotic" killer in this study.

This finding can be easily connected to the discussion we had in the first chapter about politics and deviance, and particularly the possibility of giving a deviant, criminal act a political meaning. Schafer (1974) suggests the term "convictional criminal" to differentiate the political criminal from other types of criminals. A convictional criminal is one who is: "'convinced' about the truth and justification of his own beliefs.... It is a settled belief, essentially a deep-seated consideration in the political criminal's conscience that makes him feel that he has a rendezvous with destiny.... By contrast...the conventional offender almost always acts to fulfill his ego or personal interest, and his acts often lack an overarching coherence.... The convictional criminal...has an altruistic-communal motivation rather than an egoistic drive" (pp. 145–147). Hence, Schafer's convictional criminal could fit very well the type of assassin we have seen in this study. Moreover, and on a very different level of comparison, it is not too difficult to see how by taking the "insanity" plea the rather famous case of Daniel McNaughtan (see Moran 1981) was turned into a "psychiatric" issue. With the exceptions of case nos. 87 (involving Meir Vilner as a victim and not really included in the statistics) and 89 (involving Uri Avneri as a victim) the insanity or "mental stress" claims were not raised, even remotely.

The findings about the differential share of the major three pre-state underground Jewish groups must be contrasted against some other facts. Although accurate data about the size of the different groups in the different years is not available, there can be no doubt that the Hagana was, by far, the largest organization and the Lehi was the smallest. Thus, and in symbolic terms, the share of the latter is, obviously, significantly magnified. One must also be reminded at this point that our topic is political assassinations, as defined. If we take into consideration acts of indiscriminate terrorism, then all the numbers would have to be changed.[4]

The Pre-state Underground Jewish Groups and Political Assassination Events

Since seventy-three cases (83.9%) were committed by the 1920–1948 three pre-state underground Jewish groups, we shall next gradually focus our attention on those groups. The fact that most cases occurred between 1939–1948 and that *organizations* were involved in them raises some interesting questions such as *who* were the victims in *symbolic* terms and what was the nature of the process leading to a political assassination event? Who exactly committed the acts?

The last question is the easiest to answer. In only twenty-four cases (28% of the total number of cases) we could identify the specific assassin. This figure adds credibility to Marx's concept of hidden and dirty data.

TABLE 12–4

ETHNICITY/NATIONALITY OF VICTIM AND CATEGORY
OF POLITICAL ASSASSINATION EVENTS

	Category of Political Assassination Event						
Ethnicity	*Pre-planning*	*Planning*	*Unsuccessful*	*Successful (victim) Died*	*Successful Wounded*	*Total*	*% of Total*
Jewish	4	1	10	35	2	52	60%
British	2	2	12	6		22	25%
Arab		3		3	1	7	8%
Other			2	4		6	7%
TOTAL	6	6	24	48	3	87	100%

The fact that *most* victims were Jewish is surprising. This surprise is magnified when we realize that most successful cases (in the two subcategories) involve Jewish victims (73%). Dominant is also the British victim group in the unsuccessful category (50%). Since most assassinations were committed by the three pre-state Jewish underground groups who boasted of using such tactics as political assassination to help end the British occupation, how is one to explain the fact that there were only about 25% British victims vis-a-vis 60% Jewish victims? Before answering this important question we have to examine more data.

TABLE 12–5
ETHNICITY/NATIONALITY OF VICTIM,
PRE-STATE JEWISH UNDERGROUND GROUPS AND
CATEGORIES OF POLITICAL ASSASSINATION EVENTS

Category	Ethnicity	Hagana No.	%	Lehi No.	%	Etzel No.	%	Subtotal
	Jew	1	1.4	1	1.4	1	1.4	3
	British	1	1.4	1	1.4			2
Preplanning	Arab							
	Other							
	Subtotal	2		2		1		5
	Jew			1	1.4	1	1.4	2
	British							
Planned	Arab	1	1.4	1	1.4			2
	Other							
	Subtotal	1		2		1		4
	Jew			3	4.1	4	5.5	7
	British			12	16.4			12
Unsuccessful	Arab							
	Other							
	Subtotal			15		4		19
	Jew	9	12.3	15	20.6	8	11.0	32
	British	1	1.4	4	5.5	1	1.4	6
Successful	Arab	2	2.8	1	1.4			3
(dead and	Other	1	1.4	3	4.1			4
wounded)	Subtotal	13		23		9		45
TOTAL		16		42		15		73

How many Jews were victimized (actual or planned) by Lehi, Etzel, and the Hagana? Out of Lehi's forty-two political assassination events, twenty (48%) were directed against other Jews. Out of fifteen such cases by Etzel, fourteen (94%!) were directed against other Jews. Out of the Hagana's sixteen cases, ten (63%) were directed against other Jews. Hence, while Lehi was the group most involved in political assassinations, only less than half of its victims were Jews.

The share of Jews and non-Jews in the "preplanned" category is identical. Although it is different in the "planned" category, the numbers themselves are too small to allow a meaningful conclusion. The share of non-Jewish victims in the "unsuccessful" category is very pronounced, probably because the British were more protected. Clearly the largest concentration of cases is in the "successful" category—forty-five cases (62%). There, thirty-two of the victims were Jewish (44% from the number of cases in the table and 71% of the number of cases in the category). Of those thirty-two, fifteen (46.88%) were hit by Lehi; nine (28.13%) by the Hagana and eight (25%) by Etzel. Hence, while Etzel directed most of its political assassination plots against Jews, in terms of successful plots—Lehi led the trio.

The Reasons Given for Political Assassination Events— Squealers, Traitors, and Revenge

One more question must be addressed to the "reasons" given for the assassination events. To begin with, let me point out that only in one case was the reason unclear. In all other cases we have the reason, as given by the assassins. An almost obvious question is to what extent can we rely on the assassins' public justifications? Since the analysis uses rhetorical devices *as given*, and is based on social constructions of realities, this question—to a large extent—is meaningless. We take the assassins social construction of reality as given, and we examine the rhetorical devices which they used to construct that reality. If there is reason to suspect deliberate cheating (e.g., as in the case with the assassination of Schiff), it is taken into the account too.

An easy way to present the findings here is to go over the classifications of the reasons for political assassination events which were given in chapter 2. In three categories we had no cases at all: Elite Substitution, Tyrannicide, and Terroristic assassination. The lack of cases in the last category is self-evident because our definition of political assassination events excluded nonspecific targets. The lack of cases in the first two categories is probably linked to the structure of Jewish culture. No such cases could be found at all in all the history we surveyed. There was only one case of anomic assassination (the case involving Uri

Avneri, case no. 89), This one case in itself does not constitute a positive pattern and is totally insignificant as such. However, the fact that only one such case exists does support the collective pattern mentioned earlier.

The reasons given for the assassination events ranged from specific and detailed accusations (e.g., in the cases involving Max Schindler [no. 69], Mashiach [no. 63]) to cases where no specific charges were given and the reasons which were given were phrased in very broad term (e.g., Soffiof [no. 26], Zarfati [no. 71] or Gurevitz [no. 72]).

Some of the reasons which were given for the political assassination events constitute an interesting pattern of using particular vocabularies of motives. We tried to divide the reasons by the order of frequency in which they were presented. The category traitor/squealer was used most frequently (91.2%) in association with Jewish targets. The category "revenge" was used most frequently (63.2%) in association with British targets and 20.4% of the time in association with Arab targets.

TABLE 12–6
REASONS GIVEN FOR ASSASSINATION EVENTS
BY GIVEN PRIORITY

Reason (as given)	First Priority	Second Priority	Third Priority	More than One Reason No Prioritization
Traitor/squealer	34	4		4
Revenge	19	8	2	5
Propaganda by Deed	9	8	2	5
Inner organizational problems (e.g., Giladi)	5	1	1	2
To start/stop a process of social or political change	9	8		1

I tried to examine these categories in greater depth. There are 34 cases where the main reason for the assassination was that the victims were defined as traitors/squealers. Of those, 47.1% were with Lehi, 32.4% with Etzel, and 20.6% with the Hagana. However, 73.3% of Etzel's victims (N = 15) belonged to this category, as well as 46.7% of the Hagana's victims, and 38.1% of Lehi's victims. Hence, for Etzel, being defined as a traitor and/or squealer was a dangerous, moral boundary marker. The same meaning was true for the Hagana and Lehi, but much less so, especially for Lehi.

The major reason given for the assassination event was found to be, then, that the victim was a traitor/squealer or, as a revenge. The two, of course, do not exclude each other. The rhetorical devices "traitor," "squealer," "collaborator," and "spy" received special, and understandable, meaning particularly between 1939–1948.

The painful slow realization of the Yishuv of what was happening in Europe forced the issues of cooperation and collaboration to surface in the most powerful way. The limits of cooperation with occupation forces became a real issue. Hence, targeting specific action for assassinations because of squealing or of being defined as a traitor, collaborator, or spy made sense to many contemporaries (in Palestine and in Europe). Lehi (e.g., see *Ketavim* [A], pp. 196–197), Hagana (e.g., see S.T.H., vol. 3, part 1:141) and Etzel all denounced *fiercely* those who they saw as cooperating with the British against the Yishuv. While isolation and deportation, as forms of punishment, were sometimes used, the ultimate punishment—death—was used too. An assassination constituted not only a revenge, but gave a very bright warning signal to others about where exactly the moral boundaries were drawn. This issue simply boiled down to a *very* basic question of loyalty and commitment. Members of the Yishuv were faced with a painful dilemma phrased as "are you with us, or against us?" that is, the Jews, the British, and sometimes the Arabs (e.g., see case no. 76). Hence, Lehi's and Etzel's interest was in giving much echo and publicity for assassinations.

An important question in this context concerns the profession of the targets hit by Lehi, Etzel, and the Hagana. We divided these professions into three broad categories. There was "certified policeman" where we were quite sure that the potential victim was in fact such a policeman. Second was an "undercover agent," where there was enough satisfactory evidence to corroborate this claim. The third category was "suspected undercover agent." In this category we only have the group's accusation that the target was of such a nature, but *no* further corroboration.

TABLE 12–7
ASSASSIN GROUP BY VICTIM'S PROFESSION

| | Lehi | | | | Hagana | | | | Etzel | | | |
| | British | | Jewish | | British | | Jewish | | British | | Jewish | |
	No.	%	No.	%	No.	%	No.	%	No.	%	No.	%
Certified policeman	9	20.4	7	15.9	1	2.3			1	2.3	7	15.9
Undercover agent							1	2.3				
Suspected undercover agent			8	18.2			4	9.1			6	13.6
TOTAL	9	20.4	15	34.1	1	2.3	5	11.4	1	2.3	13	29.6
Total number of cases	24 (54.6%)				6 (13.6%)				14 (31.8%)			

Of all the above targets combined for the three groups (N = 44), 25 were certified policemen, 56% of whom were Jewish. There was one (2.3% of the total number) undercover agent (Jewish), and about 41% of the total (all Jewish) were *suspected* of being undercover agents. Lehi was the organization that hit these people most frequently. Clearly, the risk of being defined as a squealer or a traitor was correlated with professions that demanded a continuous friction of actors in the twilight zone between different, sometimes hostile, symbolic-moral universes. The cases with Davidesku (no. 50) and Pritzker (no. 39) illustrate how functioning in this twilight zone can become lethal when no good way exists to settle out the problem of "real" loyalties.

Revenge and vengeance were another *very* important and central issue. "Revenge is a universal pattern of behavior. It is also an ineradicable feature of our emotional lives" (Bar Elli and Heyd 1986:68). Revenge and vengeance provide an emotional outlet, and in situations where it assumes the form of an assassination (or a blood revenge) the potential assassin(s) must think that he/they have indeed suffered a very serious and grave injury and injustice. Here, vengeance becomes a quest for justice in a social ecology which is perceived to be unjust by the potential assassins (see Marongiu and Newman 1987). Using assassination as a form of revenge and vengeance, as can be recalled from chapter 5, characterized the pattern of assassinations outside Palestine-Israel, as well as in it. In both instances we have under-privileged and powerless groups (sometimes individuals) who feel that they do not stand a reasonable chance to receive a fair justice from the social system in which they live, and that the rules of distributive justice even operate against them. When their sense of justice is violated at its most delicate and vulnerable points (e.g., traitors, squealers, anti-semites, etc.), then in their own mind—assassination will be left as the only course of action. Cullen's (1983) question about the specific choice of the deviant behavior is, hence, answered again here.

One need not be mislead by the false impression that vengeance and revenge can be reduced primarily to *psychological* issues. As my study, and Rieder's discussion (1984) point out, they are, in fact *systemic* characteristics of many cultures. Underlying vengeance is a very strong moral character, guided by a simple principle of justice which stipulates that symmetry must be restored to what is perceived as an unbalanced situation. Therefore, it is not surprising to find that revenge and vengeance operate according to *socially* constructed and defined values and norms (and not as a result of some "irrational" psychological and individual motivation). This is a rational, nonemotional reaction, equal in logic to other forms of punishment and social control. As Rieder points out, the wish to retaliate for an injustice points to its logical nature. Thus, the "rationality of vengeance as a method of social control, not its unreasoning ravaging, emerges as one of its striking signatures" (1984:134).

Jacoby (1983) points out that "justice is a legitimate concept in the modern code of civilized behavior. Vengeance is not" (p. 1). Consequently, demanding revenge in our culture must be rephrased in rhetorical devices which will not be understood as simple vengeance. Rather, rhetorical devices which emphasize justice and proneness to future crimes (prevention), are used instead of "vengeance" and revenge. However, vengeance *has* been a major part of Western civilization and my study indicates that vengeance *can* become a chief component in an alternative system of popular justice.

Indeed the idea of justice and vengeance was also explored by Kirkham, Levy, and Crotty's landmark study (1970). There, among other things, they tried to examine the feelings of injustice on the individual level, as well as the potential rage experienced by different individuals and groups which is produced by living in a politically unjust society (241–258). "High assassination relief scores are related to political vengeance and that political vengeance is closely tied to the concept of political trust" (257–258). These topics are related directly to the discussion about political justice we had in chapter 2.

There were a few cases where an assassination event was initiated because of inner reasons of the organization (e.g., such cases as those involving Lishansky [no. 3], Zvi Frenkel [no. 9], Giladi [no. 38], Levi [no. 75]). The "inner" reasons for assassinating Lishansky and Frenkel were very different from those given for the assassination of Giladi and Levi (or even Pritzker—see case no. 39). In the first two cases the reason was a fear by the organization involved that Lishansky and Frenkel would not be able to resist an interrogation and would "squeal." Hence, the fear of potential future "squealing" propelled the organizations involved to choose the route of assassination. In the cases of Levi, but much more so in the case of Giladi, the assassinations were initiated because of a very bitter and severe argument about the very nature of the boundaries defining the symbolic-moral universe of Lehi.

The other few political assassination events were directed to achieve *some* change in policy (e.g., such cases as those involving Hitler [no. 13], Shaw [no. 46], MacMichael [no. 47], Moyne [no. 49]). The element of revenge and of hitting those who were defined as traitors/squealers is very salient. The pattern of revenge is certainly a continuation of the European cases, and the one to be found in some of the political executions described in chapter 9. Traitor/squealer as a vocabulary of motives used to justify assassinations is associated much closer with the legacy of the Sicariis, and the big revolt during the last year of the Jewish second temple.

Propaganda by Deed

Propaganda by deed has been portrayed in the literature as an important reason for political assassination event. As we shall see immediately, the importance of this category for this study is minimal.

"Propaganda by deed" was not used very frequently as *the* main reason for the initiation of a political assassination event. More often, it accompanied other reasons.

This specific issue was examined in some more depth (see table 12–8). We discovered that only in twenty-nine cases (33%) did the group publicize the assassination and took responsibility for it. In forty-nine cases (56%) no publicity, or taking responsibility, occurred (in nine cases [10.3%] no information was available regarding publicity). These findings indicate a rather strong tendency against publicizing the cases. This conclusion is consistent with the fact that most of the assassination attempts were directed against members of the "in-group" (other Jews). In this case, no large scale publicity is required. Table 12–8 illustrates this point.

TABLE 12–8
CONTEMPORARY PUBLICITY OF ASSASSINATION
BY ASSASSIN(S)

| Assassin(s) | Contemporary Publicity | | |
	No	Yes	Total
Individual assassin	4	1	5
Hashomer	3		3
Etzel	9	5	14
Lehi	15	19	34
Hagana	12	4	16
Another group	6		6
TOTAL	49	29	78

There are nine "unknown" cases.

The Hagana was obviously not interested in publicizing its cases (75%). Lehi, on the other hand, was more interested in publicizing its cases (56%). "Other groups," as well as most other individual assassins, were not interested in publicizing their acts. This is a rather surprising finding, compared to the widely accepted belief that a "hallmark" of political assassination events is the motivation for propaganda by deed. This belief, so it seems, has to be revised. It seems that only in some very particular political assassination events do the assassins *intend* to achieve a propaganda by deed effect. In most other cases, they do not seek publicity. This phenomenon may characterize other cultures as well.

A closer examination of the data reveals that in the nine cases where propaganda by deed was the first priority reason, six cases (66.7%) involved Lehi, and none involved the Hagana, Etzel or Hashomer (three cases involved other groups and one involved an individual).

Decisions to Assassinate

TABLE 12–9
DECISION TO ASSASSINATE AND ASSASSIN(S)

Assassin(s)	Decision to Assassinate		Total
	Command, Administrative	There was Some "Court"	
Individual assassins			
Hashomer	3		3
Etzel	7	1	8
Lehi	31	1	32
Hagana	5	2	7
Other groups	4		4
TOTAL	50	4	54
% of total	93%	7%	100%

In thirty-three cases (37.9% of the total number of cases) there either was no decision to assassinate, or that information was not available. In the overwhelming majority of cases the decision to assassinate had very little to do with any type of a formalized system of justice, or on anything which even resembled—remotely—a due process. In most cases the decision was either an administrative, or command, decision. Table 12–9 gives a quantitative backing to this, by the type of assassin(s).

Not much is known about decision making processes regarding political executions. However, from the few cases and the meager and partial information we have, it seems evident that decisions to make a political execution must have the approval of the highest levels in the Israeli political, security and military structure. How exactly this process works is not entirely clear (see chapter 9). In any event, again it seems that what we have here is a nonjudicial administrative process.

Towards an Integrative Sociological Interpretation: *Justice, Vilification, Deviantization, and Strangerization*

Alternative system of justice. How are we to integrate the data described in this section into a unified and coherent interpretation? To begin with, most cases of political assassination events occurred between 1939–1947. There were very few cases prior to 1939 and after 1948. Those 1939–1947 fateful years certainly marked a significant intensification of the Jewish efforts (mostly by the three pre-state underground groups) toward independence. Between 1896–1938, a period of forty-two years, we have eight cases. Between 1939–1948, a period of nine years, we have seventy-three cases. Between 1949 to 1988 a period of thirty-nine years, we have six cases (not including political executions).

In this sense, the necessary conditions for political assassination events which were presented in chapter 2, were found to be valid. Between 1930–1948 there were three parties with an ideology of direct action. These groups saw themselves as deeply involved in an actual *struggle* with the British and the Arabs for the creation of a new and independent Jewish state. From what we know about other works on underground pre-state movements (see also chapter 2) this particular aspect of political assassinations in Palestine and Israel is universalistic and not culture specific.

Taking into consideration the fact that the major reasons for the assassinations were that the victim was defined as a traitor/squealer, that revenge and vengeance were involved, and that most victims were Jewish leaves us with almost no choice but to arrive to the conclusion that, similar to the pattern of European cases of political assassinations by Jews, we have here too an interesting system of Justice.

The concept of justice which emerges from this study can be applied to two domains. One domain is focused on conflicts within the Yishuv, the other is focused on conflicts between members and groups of the Yishuv to external groups (e.g., Arabs, British).

Political assassination, as a particular rhetorical device, is invoked to explain and justify acts that seem like justice to the assassins in situations where they felt that they could not get a fair justice because the opportunities for such justice were felt to be blocked (see R. Cohen 1986). It is as if an alternative and popular system of justice was put into operation (see Abel 1982). Being secret and collective, however, makes it very difficult to fully expose in detail the ways through which this system worked.

The idea that political assassination events, in the context of this study, can be conceptualized as constituting a tool in an "alternative system of justice," both for insiders and for outsiders, is related to other works. The most salient works are those by Hobsbawm (1959) and others (e.g., Wilson 1988), and more recently by some British scholars (see S. Cohen 1986 for a short review) and Crummy (1986). These works, from a different point of view, focus on popular justice and on what Hobsbawm called "Primitive Rebels." In these perspectives, we take a hard and long look at societies with very problematic (and typically biased) formal mechanisms of justice. In such cultures, we can observe the rise of various mechanisms to enforce a different type of popular and alternative justice (Robin Hood being the example, but there are numerous other examples of banditry and other forms of "justice"). One of the central ideas which emerges from this tradition is that "crime under certain conditions serves equivalent functions to such recognized political forms as protest and resistance" (S. Cohen 1986:470). When such systems operate, we can witness justice done to members of the in-group, as well as to social actors outside the in-group.

Another group of scholars developed in the last few years a conceptualization that is most definitely related to the above interpretation. These scholars rely on Black's works (1983, 1984a) in the area of social control. Here is how one of them presents the approach:

Focusing upon the concept of self-help criminal justice, Black [1984b:1] argues that: "There is a sense in which conduct regarded as criminal is often quite the opposite. Far from being an intentional violation of a prohibition, much crime is moralistic and involves the pursuit of justice. It is a mode of conflict management, possibly a form of punishment, even capital punishment. Viewed in relation to law, it is self-help. To the degree that it defines or responds to the conduct of someone else—the victim—as deviant, crime is social control." (Weisburd 1989:5, 10)

In a very real sense, all the organizations that are mentioned in this study created a system of social control, in most cases a self-help type of justice followed, and this justice was focused on monitoring the moral boundaries of what these groups considered as the "collective." To some, and limited extend, this conceptualization will apply to cases of political executions as well.

Some comparisons.   I have noticed in previous chapters that while there are quite a few cases of political assassinations mentioned in this work, compared to other cultures, the society studied here does not present a culture which is characterized by strong supports for this particular type of violence. To give this claim an empirical base, let us try to examine briefly similar phenomena in other cultures, under similar conditions.

A study like this was not done before, hence finding information for a meaningful comparative comparison is virtually impossible. Our searches for such information yielded very little. However, the available information seems to indicate that similar systems of justice against collaborators were utilized by other underground groups. Hence, this type of system was utilized by the French resistance during World War II, and by the Kenyan Kikuyu Mau Mau. One conservative appraisal estimates that the Mau Mau killed about 11,500 Kikuyu and only about ninety-five Europeans, showing again that most of the lethal aggression was directed toward members of the in-group (Rosberg and Nottingham 1966:303). Political assassinations of those who were defined by such rhetorical devices as traitors, squealers, and "politically and ideologically dangerous opponents" characterized the activities of *Catchism* in the second half of the nineteenth-century Russia (including a secret student organization which called itself *Narodnaya Rasprova*, meaning "The People's Revenge") (Gaucher 1968:3–27); the struggle in Macedonia (and the involvement of the IMRO [Internal Macedonian Revolutionary Organization]) at the beginning of the twentieth century (Gaucher 1968:155–173; Ford 1985:259–260); the infamous Iron Guard in Bucharest, Rumania (Gaucher 1968:140–152; Ford 1985:268); some of the unrest in Germany during the 1920s (Gaucher 1968:128–130); the activities of the FLN (Front de libération Nationale) and OAS (Organization de L'Armee Secre'te) in Algiers in the 1950s and 1960s (Gaucher 1968:238–239, 260–264); and the assassinations committed by the Cypriot EOKA (Ethniki Orgánosis Kipriakou Agónos). Obviously, the underground groups in Northern Ireland utilized a similar system of justice as well (e.g., see Clutterbuck 1977:62–65; Corfe 1984 and Alexander and O'day 1984:21–22 who imply that the IRA even "occasionally obtained the services of professional assassins"). Similarly, Ford reports that: "by February 1972...a group of die-hards [from the Japanese Red Army] were surrounded in an abandoned hotel at Karuizawa.... When the Karuizawa fortress was stormed by police, the bodies of fourteen defenders were found already dead, killed as deviationists by the survivors in what one writer has described as 'an orgy of self purification'" (1985:310; quote is from Dobson and Payne 1977:187–191).

Clark (1986) points out that out of 696 attacks which were carried out by the Basque ETA (Euzkadi Ta Askatasuna) between 1968–1980, 29.45% were aimed at an individual target (1986: 132). Furthermore, Clark also notes that out of 287 dead victims as a result of ETA assaults, 5.6% were killed as "spies" or "informers" (that is about 2.3% out of all of ETA assaults for the above years; 1986:136, 138). Interestingly enough, the term Clark uses for these killings is "executions," and only about sixteen members (at least three of which were ETA members) were killed in this way. The typical charge against them was that they gave information to the police. As in my study, Clark notes that the *only* source that these sixteen people were traitors comes from ETA sources. In almost all the cases, the family of the victim denied the allegations and demanded open and public evidence (1986:138). The type of work done by Clark is quite rare, and despite our efforts we could not locate other and similar works on this particular issue.

Other, more impressionistic sources also tend to corroborate the above observations. This pattern exists in some South American countries; it also existed during the Arab revolt in Palestine between 1936–1939 when thousands of Arabs were killed by other Arabs (e.g., see *Davar*, November 21, 1938; Arnon-Ochana 1982:139–140); and emerged again when from December 1987 Arabs in the Israeli occupied West Bank and Gaza strip began their Intifada (uprising) and continued to assassinate other Arabs (see also *The New York Times*, November 12, 1989, p. 1 on a similar phenomenon within Abu Nidal terror group).[5] In all these cases we observe the unleashing of lethal forces mostly against actors from the in-group.

Clearly, these assassinations mark, in an unequivocal way, the symbolic-moral boundaries of the group, as well as cleanse and purify the group from what it evidently views as dirt (see Mary Douglas 1966 and Scott 1972). The Sicarii's and the Assassins' goals of purifying the in group reemerge again in all these cases. Accused of being a collaborator, in all these cases, is taken as the violation of trust—punishable by death. One can not avoid the irony that the way the original Assassins approached and killed was, again, by violating trust.

Justice, collaboration, and treason. What we have here is an interesting, and generalizable, sociological observation. We can observe an alternative, and popular, system of justice which operates on principles of *political* justice, and as a powerful system of social control as well. The emergence of this system is within the framework of a struggle for national independence and hence within a a process of nation building, against what the relevant social actors see as an occupying and alien force. We can most certainly expect to find a similar pattern of political assassinations under similar social conditions.

This is the main reason that the rhetorical devices which were used by the different pre-state Jewish underground groups to describe the acts of political assassinations are so meaningful and revealing. They talked about individual terror, Hisulim (eliminations), or "justice to collaborators." All these devices, and similar others, indeed corroborate the sociological observation that those who employed these rhetorical devices saw themselves as participating in processes of political and popular justice, and social control. These processes are obviously aimed at delineating the boundaries of symbolic-moral universes.

Nettler's perception of this issue was indeed illuminating: "Killing for justice translates homicide as execution rather than as murder. This is a translation that appeals to groups that regard themselves as legitimate possessors of moral authority. Thus both governments-in-power and revolutionary challengers of that power refer to their killing of enemies as homicides rationalized by their sense of justice, a sense that fluctuates between demands for revenge, retribution, deterrence, and submission" (1982:201).

The justice which was operating here was based on some information, sometimes on "confessions," and on command/administrative decisions. In such a system, the potential victim did not stand much of a chance to "prove his innocence." The cases involving Holianitzky (no. 78); Levi (no. 75), or Tubianski (no. 82), illustrate this point. Even where we have some evidence indicating to the existence of a "court," we typically do not have enough information to assess the nature of the evidence, the arguments for and against, the nature and evaluation of the "testimonies." However, while "trials" probably rarely took place, it was important for all the groups involved to use deliberately misleading rhetorical devices which utilized quasi legal jargon, and to give the faked impression that there was a "legal" procedure. Evidently, this was done with the explicit intent of gaining, and establishing, credibility, and legitimacy. Of course, what we view today as political was not defined as such, at the time, by the participants in the assassinations. One cultural analogy which comes to my mind is that between the type of justice mentioned above which actually prevailed, and the popular and public (perhaps mythical) image we have of the American Wild West, at its peak. The image of a fast justice, quick death, not too many questions asked, lack of a fair chance for due process seems to resemble the above type of justice. An obvious difference is that even in this mythical image no mention is made of underground groups struggling for national independence.

The three pre-state underground Jewish groups had to cope, like other movements, with a more or less ruthless occupying regime. A major part of that struggle was in the area of intelligence and information. The British were quite effective in being able to recruit "collaborators," and at different times they could seriously penalize the underground groups. The struggle against the collaborators, from the point of view of the underground groups, was one about survival.

The issue of the collaborators ("Shtinkers" in the prevailing intelligence slang) hides the one of treason. Treason implies betraying one's commitment and loyalty to a particular symbolic-moral universe, and violating the trust relationships which emerge from such a commitment. This is conceptualized as an almost universal "crime" by most cultures, and punishable very severely (e.g., see Ploscowe 1935; Hurst 1983). As Hurst points out, treason occurs when an obligation of allegiance to a particular social (and moral) order exists, on the individual level, and when an intention to violate that obligation exists, coupled with relevant action(s) (1983:1560). The *Encyclopaedia Hebraica* conceptualizes treason as the violation of trust of the sovereign, and views this as one of the most severe offenses in existence (vol. 7:603–607, Hebrew).

Treason has at least two sides. One is that of those who *recruit* the collaborators. Their motives are obvious. The other side is that of the collaborators themselves. Why are people willing to become Shtinkers? It is possible that, like spies, Shtinkers may present a variety of types like: ideological, mercenary, alienated, buccaneer, professional, compromised, deceived, and a few others (see Frank Hagan's 1987 typology of spies). There is reason to suspect that a similar typology may exist with Shtinkers. They are not very different than spies. Unfortunately, the data we have do not allow us to apply the above mentioned typology to the cases we have.

The existence of collaborators in so many cultures and periods may hint, perhaps, that there is a larger sociological puzzle here which requires some serious consideration. Possibly, a sociology of treason. While certainly beyond the scope of this volume, I will make a few observations about the sociological nature of treason.

Treason, first and foremost, violates trust, and it is considered to be the cultural opposite to loyalty. The question than becomes, what is so important, culturally, in "trust" and in "loyalty"? Two reasons can be offered.

The first is functional. Trust, as posited by exchange theory, enables exchange, without it no social exchange will be possible. Trust invokes the concepts of reliability, faithfulness and responsibility. Trust is one of the elements that Durkheim (1933) refers to in his discussion of the "pre-contractual" elements that are absolutely required for social cohesion and solidarity to exist. As such, and from the Durkheimian perspective, trust has an acquired quality of sacredness. In sanctifying trust society makes what it views as a most essential social relationship sacred. Undoubtedly trust is an essential ingredient of the "conscience collective," and it lies at the basis of the social construction of a symbolic-moral universe. Being sacred, the violation of trust is interpreted and reacted to emotionally.

The second reason is more ethnomethodological. What are the underlying assumptions of the social relationship called trust whose violation causes such a harsh reaction? Trust assumes such social relationships as loyalty, friendship, faith and belief. It also assumes that there is an implicit quality of such social relationship as primary relationship, and to some degree intimacy. Assuming these qualities constitutes both necessary and sufficient conditions for the social construction of realities. Without these, no such constructions are possible because it will not be feasible to maintain consistency, persistence, and prediction of social relationships. Faithfulness, as implied by trust and loyalty, is an essential and vital ingredient of social life. Without it, "society could simply not exist...for any length of time" (Simmel; in Wolff 1950, p. 379). Violation of trust shatters what actors will view as the "natural order of things" because it will destroy the perception of reality constructions. Moreover, violation of trust involves deception and lying which, according to Simmel, are among the most destructive forces in social interactions (Wolff 1950, pp. 312–316). Violation of trust disrupts the perception, or illusion, of a consensual reality constructions. But, the thing which is denied and shattered in treason is not only a social relationship, but another fundamental facet of the human existence: the social self.

Hence, it should not really surprise us to find out that trust can be classified as one of Durkheim's (1933) pre-contract conditions, as sacred. The violation of trust, namely treason, creates an emotional reaction in the form of hurt feelings. But these feelings are perceived as sacred and hence, it is common that treason is accompanied by feelings of being deceived and betrayed. The invocation of a charge in treason necessitates an *intention* to systematically betray conceal deceive and lie to the victim(s). Thus, traitors are typically punished severely as treason always elicits the motivation for revenge, or in its Western equivalent: justice.

The importance of the analytical argument focusing on justice may be magnified even further. Political deviance and political justice, as was pointed out in chapter 1, are associated variables. Certainly, members of the three pre-state Jewish underground groups experienced some very strong feelings of injustice and of being oppressed and repressed. The fact that assassinations were used either as revenge, or against those who were defined as traitors/squealers, only adds credibility to this hypothesis. Almost all the cases we have are concentrated around arguments about the nature, and definition, of the boundaries of symbolic-moral universes. Thus, the *interpretation* of the acts becomes important. For example, even today (1986–1988) many of our interviewees typically did not feel comfortable with the account political assassination and tended to use instead the Hebrew word "Hisulim" meaning "eliminations" or "liquidations." General MacMillan's (see case no. 66) request from his British soldiers to use the accounts "murderers," "criminals," and "robbers" to describe Jewish members of the pre-state underground groups (instead of "guerrillas" or even "terrorists") provides another example of attempting to enforce a criminal interpretation for a politically motivated behavior. Hence, while it was in the interest of members of the Lehi, Hagana and Etzel who were caught by the British to turn their trials into political trials—that was the *last* thing the British wanted.

Finally, one interesting question relates to the position of Judaism regarding collaborators and political assassination. Squealers and collaborators are called in the Jewish tradition Moser ("giver" in Hebrew), or Masor. Living for many years in the Galut (Diaspora), squealers could become very dangerous for the well being and survival of a persecuted minority. Such an expression as "and there shall be no hope for the squealers" became very relevant. It seems that the consensus was that if someone was known as a squealer, that person had to be killed *before* he/she actually squealed (there is an argument whether a warning was to be delivered or not). It must be emphasized that a *suspicion* of squealing was not enough. Proof had to be presented. Assassinating a squealer was justified on the ground that this act was meant as saving many others who were in danger because of the squealing. As can be inferred, deciding who exactly was a potentially dangerous squealer and why was not a simple matter. However, this was perceived as a preventive measure. Once a damaging squealing was in fact committed, a punishment was called for. Punishment, in any event, was a totally different issue because deciding on a proper punishment meant that a legitimate court had to be established, with an authority to pass a death sentence. The Jewish tradition is characterized by a very strong reluctance to pass death sentences, and there are very severe limitations on passing such a sentence. Furthermore, in only some very rare occasions Jewish courts *had* the authority to pass a death sentence. However, despite the severe limitations, there were a few cases of squealers who were executed (e.g., see Eisenstein 1951).[6]

While Jewish planners of political assassination events could use the above justifications to defend decisions to assassinate those that they felt were squealers—they typically did not. With the exception of De Hahn's (no. 6) assassination (where some reference was made to Jewish sources on what to do to squealers, see Nakdimon and Mayzlish 1985:194–195 and Meshi-Zahav and Meshi-Zahav 1985:242–243), we did not find any serious or meaningful references to the Jewish Halacha (Jewish legal codes on law and customs) in justifications of political assassinations. This could be due to four reasons. One, that those involved in the assassinations did not know the relevant Halacha. Second, that they knew the relevant Halacha but since they also knew that they were not acting according to the Halacha, they did not rely on it. Third, it is also possible that the early attempt to rely on the Halacha in the De Hahn case in 1924, and the criticisms which followed, indicated that reliance on the Halacha could not be used to justify the assassinations of suspected squealers. Finally, the three pre-state underground organizations, and the ones which were involved in assassinations and executions after 1948 (with the possible exception of the Jewish underground, case no. 91), viewed themselves primarily as secular-political, not religious, organizations. As such, it would not be reasonable or logical for them to justify acts of political assassinations on Halachic grounds.

Vilification, deviantization, and strangerization.   Before 1949, most cases of assassination were committed by the three main pre-state underground Jewish groups, with Lehi as the most prominent one. However, the majority of the victims of these groups were Jews. This conclusion was quite surprising. These groups, especially Lehi, boast of fighting the Arabs and of helping (and even causing) to drive the British occupation forces out of Palestine by their acts. How could so much lethal aggression and deadly force which was directed against members of the in-group accomplish that?

There are two superficial, and one more profound, answers for the above puzzle. One key to solve this puzzle lies with the fact that political assassinations are *discriminate*. The three pre-state underground Jewish groups killed *many* more Arabs and British by indiscriminatory terrorism acts than Jews. Hence, the narrow focus on the rather specific and discriminate political assassination events should not cloud the overall picture. Another, and most evident answer is that it was much easier—technically—to gather information about, and assassinate, unprotected members of the in-group.

A third symbolic reason requires a prior discussion about political assassination events generally. The real puzzle here is why was political assassination chosen as a route to begin with, as Cullen's (1983) work put it. The answer to this question is, necessarily, a functional one. It is that, from the point of view of those involved, they simply *had no other choice*. As we could see, the overwhelming majority of political assassination events revolved around very bitter arguments regarding the nature of the boundaries of symbolic-moral universes. The nature of the arguments was such that a physical liquidation and annihilation of the adversary seemed to the relevant actors as the only route possible. Moreover, for Lehi, the group which was most active and involved in political assassination events, that was a major modus operandi. In this context one may even reverse the question—why were there so *few* political assassination events? The answer is that the Etzel and Hagana simply restrained their members and Lehi was a rather small group. The decision to be involved in political assassination events was a deliberate, intentional and planned course of action. This decision can, and should, be interpreted and understood on the background of the period. Interpreting the choice of the more specific target—Jew— can now be attempted.

Indiscriminate terrorism is aimed at the "stranger" a la Simmel (1971:143–150): the one who is physically close but mentally and socially very far away. The British and the Arabs could be easily defined as strangers. No discrimination was required against those who were perceived as alien strangers because "they," the strangers, could and were defined as "enemies." Thus, with some reservations and exceptions, aggression and deadly force could be unleashed against them virtually indiscriminately.

However, one could not simply define all of the in-group as enemies, hence, discriminate political assassinations became a major way of dealing with what was regarded and perceived as severe threats (see chapter 2) to the symbolic-moral boundaries of those in the in-group. Once treason was suspected, the rhetorical devices traitor, squealer, cooperator were all used and served to mark the boundaries of what was permitted and acceptable and what not, in a degrading and stigmatizing process of vilification, focused on reputation making. This process made loyalties, commitments and the nature of trust very clear. Those from the in-group that were defined as deviant in this social context, were obviously portrayed as presenting a grave and a most serious threat for the integrity of the symbolic-moral universe of those in it.

The process which works here, if we are to adhere to the Simmelian terminology, may perhaps be called "strangerization," that is turning someone in the near and "in" group into a stranger. When this process is accompanied by parallel processes of stigmatization and deviantization, then the end product may be a "stranger," deviantized, stigmatized, and despised. Not being part of the in-group any more, perhaps a different (and dangerous) human being (sometimes to the point of being totally dehumanized), makes killing such an actor easier. This process gains importance in a culture which is in a struggle to assert itself in a revolutionary process, and where the different and individual members of that culture may not be sure where their loyalty lies.

The vocabularies of motives and the rhetorical devices which were frequently used in the strangerization process were such as squealer, spy, traitor, cooperator with the enemy. Such devices, regardless of their validity, could open the way to take the life of the actors against which the expressions were used. These rhetorical devices structured the deviantization process and helped to construct the social reality in which these deviants became defined as outsiders, pariahs—in short, aliens like the British and the Arabs only morally worse.

A comparable process works in other, somewhat similar, groups with the potential of leading to the development of dynamics resembling a so-called "totalitarian democracy" (see Cohen and Ben-Yehuda 1987). When a group representing a specific symbolic-moral universe decides to choose the route of terrorism, or of political assassinations, there is a very high probability—under specified conditions—that in the best tradition of developing a dynamic of totalitarian democracy, the group—sooner or later—would hit members who are in the in-group. It appears that the decision to use political assassinations can not be confined to "outsiders" only and it spills over into the in-group. That was true for the Sicariis as well as in the last century.

Using such a rhetorical device as traitor indicated a crossing of boundaries between symbolic-moral universes. Not just a marginal crossing, but a major violation of the boundaries. In times of a severe social and political conflict—both with the external world and between internal symbolic-moral universes—such a violation was magnified by a large factor. "Treason," in this context, entailed a death threat, and an assassination.

Once a process of strangerization, stigmatization and deviantization began in the direction of labeling a particular actor as a squealer/traitor (e.g., as a preparation for a revenge), a successful completion of the process almost had to be an assassi-

nation event. Before 1949, the Jewish underground groups had
no prisons, they could not isolate an accused/suspected actor for
very long periods. They had to act fast in order to get rid of what
they experienced as the problems. Assassination thus became a
valid solution. There were, however, a few (not very many) cases
of actors who were defined as traitors and squealers but who
were not assassinated. Unfortunately, the lack of enough details
in most such cases prevents us from an exploration for the differences between these cases and those that ended with death.

The collective pattern.   It is clear that political assassination
events, at least since the times of the Sicariis, illustrate much continuity. In most cases we have a pattern of *collective and organized
political assassination events.* Most of these events were used primarily as either a mechanism for revenge, or to hit those who were
defined as traitors and/or squealers. The incidence of these events
increased, quite dramatically, in times of stress and confusion in
Palestine. Once a formal state was established and institutionalized
mechanisms for justice—political and moral—began to function,
the incidence of the events tended to decline, dramatically too.
With the exception of political assassination events in Europe
(chapter 5), most events were directed against other Jews—which
also continues the pattern from the time of the Sicariis.

Hence, the pattern of political assassination events revealed
in this study is of collective political assassinations, carefully chosen and executed, as a pragmatic and alternative system of justice which functioned primarily as a tool in the struggle for independence. After 1948, the pattern was limited to discrete
incidences where an individual or a group felt cheated of the
political or social justice that they felt they deserved. This pattern
is very different from the wilder pattern of the Russian Revolutionary *Narodnaya Volya.* The Jewish pattern seems to be much
more restrained, calculated and selective.

Results of assassinations.   Ford's (1985) study implies that there
is no justification for political assassination in the pragmatic
sense—that is to say, "it does not work"; in his view, political
assassination is morally wrong and pragmatically useless. While
morally Ford's position is, perhaps, the easiest to identify with,
reality does not always concur (for more on the morality issue

see Ivianski 1982). Political assassination events may very well be morally wrong, but they *do* have an impact in reality, and the only problem is to decide which point of view to take in order to evaluate that impact—for example, how to assess the morality and "value" of a case where the assassin had revenge (or execution) in mind? Did the search for alternative justice not achieve a result, at least in the eyes of those who participated in this justice?—of course the answer to this question is "yes." Even in terms of achieving some desired impact, it can hardly be disputed that the assassinations of De Hahn, Arlosoroff, Eliahu Giladi, Count Bernadotte, and Pritzker achieved some very important (albeit controversial) results in terms of historical processes. Likewise, the executions of leaders of "Black September," the "Red Prince," Khalil el-Wazir and the attempts made to execute German scientists working in the Egyptian missile project all had important results and impacts. For example, the assassination of Count Bernadotte helped bring to a standstill the suggestion to divide Israel in a particular way. Likewise, hitting Shaka, Khalaf, and Tawil (case no. 91) probably helped to end the existence of the "National Steering Committee," an Arab group that tried to crystallize and steer the Palestinian struggle in the Israeli occupied West Bank and Gaza Strip. Lehi with Giladi would have been a very different organization than without him. Likewise, "liquidating" those who were suspected as traitors or informers, in a period when the British must have had quite a few informers, must have helped to intimidate other (or potential) informers. Making informers outcasts and assassinating them demarcated, in a very sharp way, between the boundaries of the different symbolic-moral universes. These liquidations marked the boundaries of moral, social, and political loyalty and commitment: to the old British rule or to the new emerging state of Israel. While the majority of such cases were not publicized very openly, the relevant officers in the British intelligence knew fairly well what was going on, and we must assume that many of the other informers knew about such cases as well. This, I must reemphasize, should not be taken to mean that there was (or, that there was not) any moral justification for such acts, just that they *had* results.

Furthermore, it is the case that getting involved in political assassination events was meant, certainly by Lehi, to receive popular and official recognition for the group, to gain recruits, to undermine the morale and prestige of the government and to push it into unpopular steps—the same functions mentioned by Snitch (1982) and reviewed in chapter 2. To some extent, these goals *were* achieved.

The pattern before and after 1948. The most salient feature of assassinations before and after 1948 is the dramatic decline in the frequency of cases after 1948, when the State of Israel was formally established. Only eight cases (9.2% of all the cases) took place after 1948. Of these, two (2.3%) were not counted (the cases involving Vilner [no. 87] and the Jewish Underground [no. 91]). Three of the cases occurred in the 1950s, and the rest are dispersed from 1967 to 1980. It is evident, therefore, that once the state of Israel was established in 1948, there was a significant drop in the frequency and vigor of political assassination events. This is also the period when we see more cases of a lone attackers and potential assassins (e.g., case nos. 87 [Vilner], 88 [Dayan], 89 [Avneri], and 90 [Sadat and Murtada]). In the rest of the cases, we had again a group involved.

How are we to explain the dramatic fact that after the State of Israel was formally established in 1948 the incidence of political assassination events declined very sharply and significantly? One simple explanation is that with the establishment of the State of Israel in 1948 everything "calmed down." True as this may be, it is too general. The "thing" which was established and contributed so significantly to the decline of political assassination events was, clearly, the establishment and institutionalization of two very important national systems: the system of justice, and the political system. Through these two systems the different groups, representing different symbolic-moral universes could, after a short period of adjustment, find a fair, open outlet—within formal and public new "rules of the game," for their views, wishes and values. Thus, the "need" for an alternative system of justice vanished to a very large degree, causing the sharp decline in the prevalence of the cases. This obviously did not just happen in one day. The 1950s witnessed this stormy and problematic passage. Furthermore, when in the late 1970s and early 1980s, a group of young and militant actors felt that they were not getting the type of justice they expected to get from the state of Israel, they organized a direct action group—the Jewish underground (see case no. 91; and Weisburd 1981).

In ordinary situations and States, we may have two types of alternative systems. One type consists of systems which claim that the State has *failed* to do something, and so a pretense to complement, or rectify, the failure is presented as the "reason" for the existence of the alternative system (e.g., the Jewish underground). Another possible alternative system may emerge as *antagonistic* to the State. These systems would emerge more rapidly in situations where the authority of the State itself is unclear. The Hagana, Etzel, and Lehi could not claim that the British authorities did not help, or that their authority was not clear. They created antagonistic systems to the British colonial rule.

While in general terms the pattern of political assassination events (and executions) throughout the period 1882–1988 is quite consistent, as well as with the European pattern and the Sicariis, there is one important difference between the pre-1948 period, and after 1948. To the extent that after 1948 there were cases of political assassination events committed by *groups*, in most cases these were groups whose description was closer to groups of *vigilantes*, that is, groups who resorted to the use of violence in order to preserve the order that they felt should have prevailed. The pre-1948 groups in Palestine were *revolutionary* groups whose use of violence was aimed to overthrow the British occupation forces. In this regard, the pattern in Europe was closer to the pattern in Israel after 1948. In both cases, however, a system of popular justice and control was in operation (see Karmen 1983).

The one new development which took place after 1948 was that of political executions. This development, however, had a fertile seed bed from which it grew. As far as we know, political executions were *not* aimed at members of the in-group, an observations which sets the pattern of political execution in a different category than political assassination. The fact that most political executions about which we know were primarily committed as acts of revenge and vengeance fits the pattern of political assassinations which we found.

POLITICAL ASSASSINATION EVENTS:
HASHOMER, LEHI, ETZEL, AND THE HAGANA

Since Hashomer Etzel Lehi and Hagana were the groups most frequently involved in political assassination events it becomes necessary to examine more closely their policies regarding this important issue. These groups were already presented in chapter four. However, at that point we could not delve into their policies about political assassinations for lack of information. Looking at the official histories of these groups for clues on this issue leads nowhere. However, much in the spirit of grounded theory now that we possess the crucial knowledge, we can try and extract from the different cases, and from fragmentary information, what the position of these groups toward political assassination was and why.

Hashomer

Hashomer was involved in three political assassination events (Lishansky—case no. 3; Storrs—case no. 4, and Tufik Bay—case no. 5). This group was characterized by a militant, direct action orientation and under the very strong influence of Russian revolutionary ideas. Mania Shochat, a key member, was herself involved in some political assassination events in Europe. Her brother, Gedalia, was involved in one event (case no. 1) and it seems that some leaders of the group, as well as other key members, were more than willing to consider political assassination whenever they thought it was justified. Overall, however, their activities only counted for 3.4% of the cases.

Hashomer's ideology did not endorse an active policy of political assassinations. However, it appears that Hashomer got into these acts out of what it felt was a necessity. Hashomer, though, probably did not spare expressing threats. It may have made a threat against Ben-Gurion's life (see chapter 2). According to Nakdimon and Mayzlish, Alexander Zeid (see case no. 36) told Ben-Gurion that he (Zeid) caught a messenger of Hashomer (Lukatcher, see also case no. 5) who wanted to kill him (Zeid) because of an alleged treason (Mania Shochat responded to this by stating that this was a "fantasy of Zeid"; 1985:228).

As far as we know Hashomer had no specific units, or other organizational structures, specializing in assassinations.

Lehi

In the 1919–1948 period Lehi was the most active organization in political assassination events. Out of eighty cases which took place in those fateful twenty-nine years, forty-two cases at least were carried out by Lehi—a hefty 53%. If one discounts the years 1919–August 1940 in which Lehi did not even exist, and the cases in those years (twenty-one cases, from case no. 4 to case no. 24), then Lehi's "share" becomes even more pronounced. Out of fifty-nine cases, forty-two can be attributed to Lehi—an astounding proportion of 71%.

Overall, 84% (table 12–5) of all preplanned, planned, unsuccessful, and successful political assassination events were committed by the three 1920–1948 pre-state underground organizations, with the involvement of Lehi the highest. The share of the different pre-state underground groups in the various categories of acts of political assassinations is different. Lehi was, by far, the most active: a share of 48% in all categories combined. In the specific category of successful political assassinations their effort is even more pronounced: 51% (from the specific category, see table 12–5). In this category, Lehi killed more Jews than non-Jews. In comparison for this particular category, the Hagana and Etzel clearly killed much less, and more Jews than non-Jews too. These figures obviously indicate that Lehi was much more committed—ideologically and pragmatically—to political assassinations than the other two groups. In fact, Lehi was involved in more cases than the Hagana and the Etzel combined.

Lehi was always a very small organization and, evidently, political assassination events were a major route that such a small organization could take to even hope to make a noticeable impact. The assassination of Baron Moyne (case no. 49) is a good illustration. The question regarding to what extent can this specific interpretation be expanded to a more generalizable conclusion, must await a much more detailed comparative study. It seems very reasonable to hypothesize that similar groups, under similar conditions and in other cultures, would behave similarly.

However, answering this hypothesis necessitates a very different study than this one.

Already in 1940, and even earlier than that, when Lehi did not exist as such, Abraham Stern (Yair) certainly authorized what became later known as "personal (or individual) terrorism," which Lehi always felt was a better rhetorical device than political assassinations (which is exactly what it is). This policy was clearly adopted by Lehi (e.g., see Ivianski 1987:36, J. Bowyer-Bell 1972). Eldad (1962:33) stated that assassination was a political statement for Lehi. After Stern was killed, his followers adopted this method. Strange as it may appear, it is very possible that in this particular aspect Giladi (see case no. 39) was much closer in spirit to Stern than Shamir, Eldad, or Yellin-Mor. However, the last three realized that Stern's policy led Lehi to a total destruction and disintegration, and that some restraints had to be exercised.

What did Lehi's three main leaders (Eldad, Shamir, and Yellin-Mor) think of political assassination? That Eldad approved political assassination is obvious (ibid.). Even in 1988 Eldad still approved it.[7] Bethell (1979:223) quotes Shamir who said that:

> to attack an army camp is guerrilla warfare and to bomb civilians is professional warfare. But I think it is the same from the moral point of view. Is it better to drop an atomic bomb on a city than to kill a handful of persons? I don't think so. But nobody says that President Truman was a terrorist. All the men we went for individually—Wilkin, Martin, MacMichael and others—were personally interested in succeeding in the fight against us. So it was more efficient and more moral to go for selected targets. In any case, it was the only way we could operate, because we were so small. For us it was not a question of the professional honor of a soldier, it was the question of an idea, an aim that had to be achieved. We were aiming at a political goal. There are many examples that what we did could be found in the Bible—Gideon and Samson, for instance. This had an influence on our thinking. And we also learnt the history of other peoples who fought for their freedom—the Russian and Irish revolutionaries, Garibaldi and Tito.

In another interview in 1983, Shamir told the interviewer (Shavit) that he approved of political assassinations, and added that:

under specific circumstances, the assassination of policy decision makers is legitimate...if it would have been possible to
assassinate Hitler in 1939 would you have done it? Is it legitimate or not?" (see *Ha'aretz*, September 7, 1983, p. 15).

Shamir's rhetoric reveals—in a crystal clear account—a point
which was made earlier, that a relatively powerless individual, or
group, can generate power, or use a pointed deadly force to try
and change what is felt to be the course of history. The assassinations of Moyne and Bernadotte illustrate this argument. The
assassinations of those that Lehi viewed as collaborators must
have had a deterrent effect and must have made the operations
(and intelligence work) of the British CID (Criminal Investigation Department) increasingly difficult.

Yellin-Mor's position was formally exposed in 1948, when he
was on trial in Israel, following the assassination of Count
Bernadotte (see case no. 83). There, Yellin-Mor stated before the
court that "it was Lehi's right to execute 'low level and degraded
traitors'.... Lehi maintained its own court. This court also dealt
with possible death sentences and was allowed to pass such sentences. In fact, death sentences were given.... In Lehi's death sentences there was no problem of age" (see e.g., *Ha'aretz*, December
12, 1948, p. 1). One must be reminded that no documentation (or
interviews) exist which support Yellin-Mor's claim about the existence of a court. Furthermore, the assassination events involving
Lewin (no. 57), as well as those of Giladi, Illin, Levi, and of others
support, at least prima facie, the interpretation that the decision
to assassinate in most of the cases was not based on a questionable quasi-procedure in court, but on command/administrative
decisions. As could be seen from table 12–9, in only two cases
(6% of the known cases which were committed by Lehi) we could
establish, with a reasonable certainty, that there actually may
have been something like a court in operation.

Political assassinations is not the kind of activity most people
will commit as a matter of course. Hence, Lehi had to develop a
socializing effort in the direction of persuading its members in the
morality and importance of this method. To begin with, Lehi
emphasized that recruits swore to dedicate their life to the struggle for freedom. On the particular topic of assassinations, Lehi's
indoctrination emphasized not only possible martyrology but

focused on relevant exotic and rare examples from the history of the Jews. Hence, Masada's lesson was reviewed and learned (even through Stern's nickname—Yair—after the name of Masada's commander); the cases of Lekert (Lehi, *Ketavim* [B]: 525–527; Cohen Y. 1973) and of Schwartzbard were learnt. Lehi's indoctrination also used such Biblical heroes as Ehud Ben-Gera who assassinated the king of Moab (see, Lehi, *Ketavim*, [A]:143), or Yehudit (who assassinated Holofornes [see ibid.]), Yael (who assassinated Sisera), and Moses (who assassinated an Egyptian). One of the key leaders of Lehi was code named Gera, which could be taken to mean "father of the assassin (Ehud)." The connection here to some cases mentioned in chapter 5 becomes very obvious. Moreover, Lehi used numerous examples of assassination and terrorism which were used by liberating movements in other nations as providing legitimacy for Lehi's choice of this particular form of warfare in a struggle for freedom (e.g., see Lehi, *Ketavim* [A]: 194–195). Tzameret (1974), whose work focused on the forms and contents of the socialization and indoctrination processes which Lehi used on its new recruits, documents how Lehi's commitment to political assassinations was translated into the training process of the new recruits. For example, by providing Biblical examples, or examples from other underground groups, the practice was justified. Particular emphasis was placed on the nineteenth-century Russian revolutionary group—*Narodnaya Volya*, which emphasized both means—terrorism *and* political assassinations (individual terror was the rhetorical device they chose; see Ivianski 1977; Shmuelevitz 1973:10; Ginosar 1973:2). Ivianski even points out that when Stern was killed, the platform of the *Narodnaya Volya* (in Russian) was on his desk (1987:38).

One of Lehi's moral codes allowed hitting *any* British person in Palestine. However, while Tzameret (1974:67) points out that Lehi from 1943 decided not to hit other Jews, the data we have do not support this statement.

From 1941 till 1948, we listed forty-two cases of political assassination events by Lehi. The following table presents the cases, divided by two periods: 1940–1942 (Stern's period) and afterwards. It is very easy to see from the table that overall, close to 50% of Lehi's targets were Jews and 65% of the successful cases were aimed against Jews.

TABLE 12–10
SUMMARY OF CASES BY YEARS BY LEHI

		Cases		
Years	Total No. of Cases by Lehi	No. of Cases against Jews	No. of Successful Cases—Jews & Non-Jews	No. of Successful Cases against Jews
1940–1942	8	4 (50%)	2 (25%)	2 (100%)
1943–1948	34	16 (47%)	21 (61.8%)	13 (61.9%)
TOTAL	42	20 (47.6%)	23 (54.8%)	15 (65%)

That Lehi contrasted its own symbolic-moral universe against that of the British is obvious. The British were portrayed as ruthless oppressors, and hitting them was thus permitted, indeed required. To a very large extent, Lehi ignored the Arabs and most of its struggle was directed against the British.

How do we explain, then, the lethal aggression directed by Lehi against other Jews? Examining the major reason given for assassinations of other Jews revealed that in 31% (N = 13) of Lehi's targets the main reason was revenge; in 38% (N = 16) of the cases the main reason given was treason, in three (7%) cases the reason had to do with Lehi itself (e.g., Levi, Giladi) and in six cases (14%) the event was primarily meant to achieve a propaganda by deed effect.

Tzameret (1974:69) points out that assassinating other Jews by Lehi was permitted only once the invocation of the above mentioned rhetorical devices against them was authorized. Lehi legitimized these actions on a few grounds. First, acts against traitors were already justified in the Bible. Such Biblical heroes as Gideon and the prophet Eliahu (who also assassinated traitors) were quoted. Kotzer (no date:18) quotes Stern who allegedly stated that: "Eliahu is not a legend, the Kishon is not a fairy tale, and the false prophets existed and still exist, their assassination is a divine command." One must be reminded at this point that Brit Habirionim, which preceded Lehi, adopted explicitly the legacy of the Sicariis, as well as Lehi. The Sicariis, as mentioned in chapter 5, gave a very strong legitimization for political assassinations. Lehi certainly used the example of the Sicariis in its socialization processes (e.g., see Y. Cohen 1973:6). Second, Lehi pointed out that almost all underground revolutionary groups, worldwide, were involved in political assassination events. Third, Lehi claimed to have warned all traitors (prior to their assassination) to stop their activities. Fourth, Lehi justified the assassinations on pragmatical grounds. If these traitors were allowed to continue to live, they could endanger Lehi (e.g., see the cases with Schnell [case no. 62] and Lewin [case no. 57], see Tzameret also 1974:71).

Lehi's publications (see *Ketavim* [A]:196–198) explicitly state that "the underground has two enemies: the external enemy, the oppressor; the internal enemy; the traitor-squealer.... The traitors, who made themselves available to the service of the alien regime by squealing on their friends must die. Their treason leads to the death of the freedom fighters. It may cause the destruction of all of the underground, or of important parts in it. Because of their actions, fighting the enemy is being given a blow, it creates defeats.... The life of many idealistic freedom fighters is endangered by the despised activities of the traitor. Thus, we have on the one hand the life of idealistic freedom fighters and on the other hand the life of one traitor squealer. Who should prevail?... Death to the traitor squealer. The underground judges the traitor by the evidence it has. The sentence is executed at the first opportunity available..."

Hence, and as analyzed earlier, Lehi's use of such rhetorical devices as traitor or squealer to describe another Jew, opened the way for an assassination events. It could also justify an assassination retroactively (e.g., the case with Schiff, [case no. 30]).

While most sources on Lehi typically tend to use the account court by stating that "victim X was put in front of Lehi's court, found guilty and sentenced to death," there are absolutely no indications that such a court existed; on the contrary, it is evident that the decision to assassinate, in the overwhelming majority of cases, was a command (or administrative) decision.

Thus, for example, Stern's use of the account that "officers Schiff and Goldman were sentenced to death by the supreme court of the organization" (see case no. 30) has, simply put, no basis in historical facts or reality.

Furthermore, Shamir (1973:3) stated that "regarding Shmuel

Levi [case no. 75—Ed.]—I was then in Africa. The court which sentenced him to death *was the only one we created*" (my emphasis—Ed.).

In contradistinction, Yellin-Mor (*Ha'aretz*, December 21, 1948, p. 1) stated that "...in the trials Lehi conducted, there was no procedure for an appeal. After the condemned was given the verdict he could process an application for clemency to a special institution or committee.... Lehi maintained its own court, and it was authorized to pass death sentences too. In fact, death sentences were executed.... In cases where the facts were visible, open and apparent, the trial took place not in the presence of the accused, and the verdict was also not given in their presence, according to the procedure common in every underground movement." What Yellin-Mor meant by "visible open and apparent" is not at all clear. As far as political assassinations are concerned, I very much doubt the validity of Yellin-Mor's account about the existence of a court in such cases. That was also probably not the first, or last, time he lied in his 1948–1949 trial (e.g., see Harel 1979).

The issue of a "due process" is very crucial. It is no coincidence that all three pre-state underground groups insist that they had courts. The existence of such a court, its procedures and decisions, was a very important issue for public consumption and perhaps more so in the eyes of the people who may have participated in them. The existence of a reasonably fair court, *is* the difference between justice and deviance. Looking at two more or less known courts—those of Tubianski (no. 82, Hagana) and Levi (no. 75, Lehi) do not leave one with a strong feeling of confidence about either the procedures of the court, or what the command group did with the decisions.

Answering a question of who deserved a death sentence, Yellin-Mor stated (ibid., p. 1) that:

This was [used] against degraded traitors.... These deeds are not like "Jews shooting Jews" first because they [the death sentences] were not executed against movements but against representatives and loners who committed an act of treason for money, provocateurs and the like. And secondly, they did not assassinate "insignificant people" but usually those in charge, who gave orders.

There is a contradiction here, since many of the so-called traitors and squealers were, in fact, insignificant people. It is interesting, though, to see how Yellin-Mor was delineating the boundaries of a symbolic-moral universe, the crossing of which may have meant death. Shamir adds to this that: "all the men we went for individually—Wilkin, Martin, MacMichael, and others—*were personally interested in the success of the struggle against us*" (Bethell, 1979:223. Emphasis mine—ED.). Hence, Shamir adds that another criterion for an assassination plot was not only an actor's formal role, but his *personal* involvement in the struggle, which went beyond the formal criteria.

According to Tzameret (1974:70), assassinating squealers and traitors was done by orders from Lehi's center "the 'center' usually created an *emergency court* of its own which examined the accusations...and (later) passed the verdict..." As we could see, this account probably reflects the rhetoric used by Lehi's center, and not the reality. One example which can easily shatter this "theory" is the assassination of Holianitzky (case no. 78). This case proves that local initiatives in assassination events did happen and, contrary to the rhetoric, Lehi's center was not aware of, or controlled, all the cases.

Did Lehi have (a) special assassination squad(s)? The answer to this question is, with all probability, negative. As far as we know, Lehi did not create a specific organizational structure for the purpose of planning and executing assassinations and assassinating became just another aspect of Lehi's operational activities. A strange fact for an organization which stated, explicitly, that it was interested in individual terrorism. What Lehi had were a few members who had a higher chance for being selected to take part in such acts because of their integrity, loyalty, valor and courage, and their reliability (e.g., Banai, Yehoshua Cohen, Eliav, Shomron, Dov, and others).

Etzel

Like Lehi and Hashomer, Etzel had a militant, direct action right wing ideological orientation. There is very little in writing which can be found on Etzel's attitude toward political assassination events. Etzel, however, is responsible for about 17% of the cases, distributed as follows:

TABLE 12–11
POLITICAL ASSASSINATION EVENTS BY ETZEL BY YEARS

Year	Frequency	Rounded Percentage
1937	1	7
1939	6	40
1941	1	7
1943	1	7
1944	2	13
1947	4	27
TOTAL	15	

The year of Etzel's highest activity was 1939, a turbulent year in Palestine and in Europe, and of severe upheavals in Etzel. Of the six events in 1939, five were directed against other Jews. All four events in 1947 were directed against other Jews. Overall, fourteen (93%) of the victims (actual or potential) of Etzel—an obvious majority—were Jewish. Judging by the case of Hilewitz (case no. 42)—one of the very few cases where we have a fairly detailed description of a court, it is possible that Etzel, at least after Menachem Begin became its commander, did use this procedure. This is, though, an hypothesis, since there are no valid indications for the existence of such a court (except, that is, in the case of Hilewitz).

Meridor, who was Etzel's commander between 1941–1943, certified that executions were sometimes a justified necessity, required to maintain the inner morale, and the continuity of the organization. Etzel's history of political assassination events certainly justifies this view (Koren 1986:11).

Lankin (1974:61), a key member of Etzel, describes how the group called "Am Lochem" (see case no. 47, involving MacMichael as a possible target, for a short description of the group) discussed possible suggestions to assassinate various British intelligence officers. The discussions were held by those who saw themselves as warriors, commanders or administrators and no framework which even remotely resembled a court was mentioned. While "Am Lochem" was indirectly associated with Etzel, the group's discussions certainly reflected a tradition of *how* contemporary members thought about political assassination events, and how decisions were made.

According to Niv (vol. 1:224–226) Etzel had what he calls "inner courts," whose jurisdiction was broad. This specific issue, however, gets only seven lines[!] in Niv's six volumes. No further information is provided at all as to how this/these court(s) (system?) functioned, what were its procedures, and the like. *Ha'aretz,* however, in a very short and cryptic message on June 25, 1948, told its readers that "Military Courts of Etzel debate whether some Etzel members should be found guilty as traitors."

While Etzel had a right wing, direct action ideology, it never stated that one of its major ways of action was individual terror. Etzel, however, did not shy away from committing acts of political assassination, and never said that it was *against* it. As far as we can tell, Etzel had no specialized organizational structures (operational or administrative) dealing specifically with political assassinations.

Hagana

The Hagana was a very different organization than Etzel and Lehi. It was under the authority of a larger political organization (most of the time it was the Jewish Agency). The Hagana constitutes a puzzle in terms of political assassination events. Officially, and according to the open Hagana's archives, the Hagana was simply not involved in political assassination events. However, we uncovered, briefly, at least sixteen cases in which the Hagana was involved. The Hagana was certainly the largest pre-state underground Jewish group. It was active and it had an ideology of direct action (much less so though, than Lehi and Etzel). Why then was this group involved, relative to its size, in only a few cases? Why the silence?

I shall next try to indicate why it is reasonable to assume that the Hagana was involved in more cases than what it admits to, and why the Hagana maintains such a silence on this particular topic (see also tables 12–1 and 12–5).

Already in 1939 the Hagana established the Pum (see case nos. 10, 11, 19, 21–24, and 35 for descriptions of Pum). Reading very carefully the few meager sources available about Pum makes it evident that it was planned to be used as an instrument in planning and executing political assassination events. Pum would have clearly functioned along this route. However, the leadership of the Hagana apparently realized what was lying ahead and dissolved Pum only seven to nine months after it had been created. Judging from the available sources, Pum was probably involved in more cases of political assassination events than those which are described openly and officially. Pum was very tightly controlled by the Hagana's high command, and specifically by Yitzhak Sade.

In one of our interviews, we talked to an assassin from the Hagana. During the interview, this assassin told us that the Hagana had three assassination squads ("Yehidot Hisul"), one in each town—Haifa, Tel Aviv, and Jerusalem. Each unit had five to eight members, had a car, weapons and a relatively unrestricted budget. According to the informant, who was a member in one of the units, Yitzhak Sade came to them with requests to assassinate specific actors. What usually followed was a long discussion whether the assassination was justified. If the group felt that it was justified, then an execution followed. Sometimes, the unit itself decided—without a direct suggestion from the Hagana's command—to assassinate specific actors, when the unit felt that there were some good reasons for doing so. What this process describes is a *negotiation*, and not orders, courts, and verdicts. Clearly, these units (certainly the informant's unit) committed many more assassinations than S.T.H. admits. The informant specified that in most cases, no publicity was given to the acts. This information, of course, is crucial. However, it needs further corroboration. Unfortunately, and despite many efforts, we could not find more direct sources to validate this account. We tried to talk to some experts on the history of pre-1948 Israeli society to evaluate the possible validity of the account, and all agreed that the likelihood that the account is valid is very high. One partial reinforcement can be found in Kanaan (1968:113) who states that in 1945 the Hagana's high command decided to create units for "special operations." Among these special operations he mentions terroristic acts against British intelligence officers, kidnaping of British hostages, and the like. Kanaan actually attributes the 1946 assassination of Wagner (see case no. 54) to one of those units.

One must be reminded here too about the intelligence unit Hashachar ("Mista'arvim") which was not only involved directly in at least two cases of political assassination events (no. 58 and no. 77), but was involved in a full scale plan (operation Zarzir, from January of 1948) to assassinate various Arab leaders.

The case involving Corporal Berger (see chapter 10, case no. 6 in the section which details cases that look like political assassinations, but are really not) indicates that the Hagana in Tel Aviv had the Pelugot Meiuchadot which were involved in attacking individual targets.

One must also note that it is possible that death sentences which passed by supposedly a secret court of the Hagana were later replaced by a decision to deport the accused. Joseph Israeli, (1972:59) recalls a case of an unknown young man, at an unknown date, who was found guilty by the Hagana's underground court of squealing to the British. The verdict was guilty and a death sentence followed. Yisraeli, who was supposed to approve the verdict hesitated and finally decided to deport the squealer. According to Israeli, that young man was in fact deported and "there were many other serious cases" (ibid.). Israeli's account indicates not only that there sometimes was a valid functional equivalent to assassination-deportation, but that there were many cases.

The last piece of information I would like to use here is the case involving Kurfirst (case no. 52). The case is not mentioned in S.T.H., or in any other record, and had it not been to some chance factors, we would probably have not been made aware of the case. How many more cases like it happened? Yet, the Kurfirst case provides a fairly detailed account of an interrogation and a court procedure.

Taking all the above cases together, the unavoidable conclusion must simply be that the Hagana was probably involved in many more cases than what S.T.H. (or other related sources) admit.

The Hagana kept quiet about most of its cases, and very little is known about the procedures and ways through which a decision to assassinate was made, or about the units which were involved in these events. The case with Kurfirst hints that the Hagana may have had (a) court(s), but from what we know about

Pum, from our informant and about Hashachar ("Mista'arvim"), we may also conclude that (a) the Hagana had, at different times, *specialized organizational units* whose activity focused either fully, or partially, on political assassinations; (b) the decision to assassinate may have frequently originated in command or administrative echelons. The ongoing and persistent organizational effort in creating and maintaining the above special units was not a small one. No organization would invest such an effort for nothing. These units must have been used. Furthermore, the organizational effort indicates that there probably was a persistent ideological, as well as operational, interest and justification for this route. Alas, it is also the case that the Hagana's high command wanted full control over such acts as political assassinations. Since the official policy of the Hagana was against political assassinations, they used this political stand to help them construct a clear moral and operational boundary between the Hagana Etzel and Lehi. The Hagana's official line was that it was against political assassinations, that it was a responsible organization, and would not take the routes of Etzel or Lehi. The Hagana's command was evidently quite hesitant about creating possible assassination units, or making their existence known (e.g., see the very short life of Pum). Consequently, the Hagana became extremely reluctant to even admit that its units were involved in assassinations, or expose the true magnitude of the Hagana's involvement in such acts. With such a strong ideological stand, the very existence of such units as Pum may have become embarrassing and problematic, not to mention that "assassination units" even existed. Repressing information about political assassination events by the Hagana thus becomes almost a logical must, at least from the Hagana's point of view. Furthermore, the tragic "Tubianski Syndrome" (case no. 82) and the possibility that other such mistakes were made only reinforces this.

Hence, the Hagana exhibits a real puzzle. It presented an official stand which was against political assassinations. However, it was involved in political assassination events, at least as much as Etzel was involved in them (and probably more). It was probably the only organization which established, and institutionalized, special organizational units which dealt with political assassination events. The existence of an organizational specialization and effort indicates that the Hagana had a system's view about, and commitment to, the subject. This finding, coupled with what we know from the cases of Kurfirst (no. 52) and Tubianski (no. 82), gives ground to the hypothesis that the Hagana was not only the only organization with structural assassination units, but probably had some form of a court for that purpose too. The actual activities of the Hagana were, thus, not in full harmony with its explicitly stated ideology. The Hagana's strange silence regarding political assassination events thus receives another partial explanation (i.e., the incongruity between ideology and actions).

INTERGRATIVE SUMMARY OF THE CHAPTER

The first observation made in this chapter pointed to the relative overall low number of political assassination events within the cultural matrix of Judaism. The findings indicate that most assassination events involved *organized groups* as initiators. These groups were characterized by particular symbolic-moral universes. Hence, one of the hallmarks of the pattern of political assassination events which emerges from this analysis is the fact that they are organized collective political assassination events. Since an obvious majority of the cases were committed by the three main pre-state Jewish underground groups—Hagana, Etzel, and Lehi, our attention was focused on these groups.

Much of the information available on assassination events from these groups is still not available. However, it seems that while these groups used extensively rhetorical devices which implied that political assassination events which were initiated by them were the result of a quasi-legal procedure (e.g., trial, sentence, etc.)—in most cases this was a vacuous rhetoric, with no real basis in reality. Most decisions regarding assassination events were either command or administrative decisions. It is worth noting that the contemporary use of quasi-legal rhetorical devices by the above groups was probably done in what the users felt was a very sincere motivation. They probably believed in that rhetoric and were convinced in its validity. They evidently thought that they were in the business of doing popular and political justice in a particular area, and this was the way they were doing it. It is only from a perspective of thirty years and more that we can use the rhetoric "vacuous" to describe those quasi-legal procedures.

The extent to which those involved in procedures leading to assassinations believed that these "procedures" were trials or functional equivalents of trials, raises the need to reconsider the concept of a "political trial" and of "political justice" mentioned earlier (see also Ben-Yehuda 1990:88–90). The cases with Lishansky (no. 3); Hilewitz (no. 42); Kurfirst (no. 52); Schnell (no. 62); Levi (no. 75) and Tubianski (no. 82) amplify this hypothesis. Becker (1971) characterized a political trial as the activation of the criminal procedure by members of the ruling elite (that is, the *center*) against a political dissident. My study implies that the *periphery* may activate a procedure (to which it will refer to as a "trial") which can be conceptualized as a political trial within a process of "doing political justice." Furthermore, although we lack good information about how a decision to carry out a political execution is made, something like a political trial may take place there as well.

Most political assassination events were directed against other Jews who were defined as traitors or squealers. Another typical reason for assassination events was revenge. We concluded that political assassination events, as particular rhetorical devices, were invoked to explain and justify acts that seemed like justice to the assassins, in situations where they felt that they could not get a fair justice because the opportunities for such justice were felt to be blocked. It is as if an alternative system of justice was put into operation. Once a formal system of justice—political and legal—was established when the state of Israel was created in 1948, the frequency of political assassination events dropped dramatically. The above interpretation also explains why we found virtually no cases of political assassination events in the categories of "Elite Substitution," "Tyrannicide," "Terroristic Assassination," and very few in "Anomic Assassination."

The fact that a majority of the targets were other Jews was explained by interpreting these events as markers of boundaries of symbolic-moral universes, in a period of a deep and a severe crisis and struggle over the very nature of the emerging and crystallizing

Jewish state. We used Simmel's concept of the stranger and Schur's concept of deviantization to point out that a political assassination event directed against another Jew involved a process of strangerization and "deviantization" of that Jew. A group provided the social context where such a process could take place as well as the legitimization for it. The above considerations also explain why, under the specific circumstances given, political assassination events became the chosen form of deviance.

We examined the structure and ideology of the Hagana, Etzel, and Lehi regarding political assassination events. We found that while Lehi had an explicit ideology favoring political assassination events, and Etzel did not shy away from being involved in such events, the Hagana rejected such an ideological stand. Strangely, however, it was the Hagana which was the only organization that established specially selected structural units, one of whose goals was political assassinations. Political assassinations were translated in the Hagana into a bureaucratic specialization. This disparity between ideology and practice is probably one of the major reasons that information about political assassination events has become so "dark" and "discreditable" for the Hagana, and much less so for Etzel and Lehi.

The information regarding political executions is scarce indeed. It does not allow us to reach the same analytical depth as do the data on political assassinations. However, even from the meager information we have, it is possible to conclude that political executions, at least in terms of motivation, do not seem to present a radically different picture than the one which emerges from political assassinations. Again revenge is a major reason.

CHAPTER 13

Integrative Summary

This book has two theoretical foci, addressed to two integrated puzzles. The first focuses on political assassination events and how they are socially constructed and interpreted. The second focuses on developing a particular sociology of deviance approach to understand political assassination events. To answer these two intellectual puzzles, an in-depth inquiry about the nature, scope and meaning of political assassination events in Palestine and Israel between 1882 1988 was launched.

BACKGROUND

Contrary to most works done on political assassination events, this book takes a *sociological* perspective, in particular the sociology of deviance. Within that sociology, we placed political assassination events within the area of politics and deviance. The analytical goal of this work is to describe, explain and understand the meaning of political assassination events within the specific social context where they occurred.

The view taken in this book is that deviance and societal reactions to it, are relative phenomena which should be analyzed in a dynamic context of history and politics. A clear and valid understanding of deviance cannot be achieved without placing the complex phenomenon of deviance, and reactions to it, with a much broader cultural and institutional context. Using this approach redirects the study of deviance into the mainstream of sociological analysis.

The above theoretical stand requires that we pay close attention to politics and deviance. There, we can encounter two types of combinations. One focused on political elements in so-called "regular" deviance. The other focused on political deviance. We defined "politics and deviance" (in chapter 1) as "problematic behavioral acts which take place at the realm of the seams, where the boundaries of different symbolic-moral universe touch and meet, or which are directed from the periphery of a symbolic-moral universe toward its center and vice versa, and which involve challenges (use or abuse) of power and morality."

ASSASSINATIONS

The social construction and interpretation of political assassination events most certainly place them in the area of politics and deviance. We characterized a homicidal event as a political assassination or execution as a social construction. It was defined as: "a rhetorical device which is used to socially construct and interpret (that is, to make a culturally meaningful account) the discriminate, deliberate, intentional and serious attempt(s), whether successful or not, to kill a specific social actor for political reasons having something to do with the political position (or role) of the victim, his/her symbolic-moral universe, and with the symbolic-moral universe out of which the assassin(s) act(s). This universe generates the legitimacy and justifications required for the act, which are usually presented in quasi-legal terms. However, decisions to assassinate are typically *not* the result of a fair legal procedure, based on a 'due process'." Hence, built into the very nature of political assassination is their interpretative character.

Political assassination events are a particular form of deviance which can be classified under the rubric of politics and deviance. As such, it is very conducive to an analysis which emphasizes total social structures, history and politics.

This is one of the few studies which attempted to investigate, in depth, *all* the known, and on the available public record, cases of political assassination events within a particular culture. The methodology which we used consisted of a combination of direct methods (e.g., interviews, as well as using primary sources) and of indirect methods (e.g., using secondary sources). Marx's characterization of this type of inquiry as looking for "hidden and dirty" data was fully corroborated.

This research aimed to solve the empirical, analytical and intellectual puzzle of political assassination events. Achieving this goal was made possible by an in-depth inquiry into the nature, scope, meaning and results of political assassination events within what may be considered a more or less similar, albeit infinitesimally complex, cultural matrix of Judaism, and Jewish life in Palestine and Israel particularly. To do this, we had, first, to look into the historical place of assassinations in Judaism. Chapter 5 indeed examined the issue of political assassinations in the Bible, the Sicariis, and in Europe. The cases described in the Bible lead us to the conclusion that political assassinations were simply used there as a means for social and political control—in different situations, with some very pragmatic ends.

RESULTS

The Sicariis constituted the first known group in the history of the Jews which was involved in what we termed in chapter 12 as *collective political assassination events,* that is, events which originate, and are legitimized, by a specific symbolic-moral universe of *a group.* The ideology, and practice, of the Sicariis had a strong influence on other Jewish groups. Certainly such groups as "Brit Habirionim," Etzel and Lehi in the 1930s in Palestine. Another established pattern, which was emulated later, was the fact that the lethal force which was used in political assassination events was mainly directed "inwards," that is toward other Jews.

The legacy of the European cases was in two areas. The first was that most of the cases again involved assassins that were members of ideological *groups.* The second was the fact that the motive of revenge was *very* salient in those cases. This pattern was to be emulated, in full force, in Palestine-Israel.

Looking at the cases in Palestine-Israel, we covered a period of over a century: 1882–1988. In this period we located ninety-one cases of political assassination events, some cases of political executions and some problematic cases which were presented in chapter 10. The pattern which emerges from *all* the cases is clear and consistent. Generally and comparatively speaking, the number of cases for almost a century seems very low. Unfortunately, no such study exists for other cultures, so this conclusion is based on impressions only. One must also be reminded that the size of the population in Palestine till 1948 was small. An obvious conclusion is that there is, perhaps, "something" in the Judaic cultural matrix which act(s) as (a) break(s) for possible and potential tendencies toward political assassination. What is/are this/these break(s)? What I can offer are a few possible educated guesses as to possible directions for answer(s). A full and persuasive answer is too elusive at the present state of our knowledge.

One background factor to remember is that violence, crime, and delinquency have not been traditional hallmarks of the Jewish cultural matrix, in or outside Israel (e.g., see Landau 1984; Barlow 1984:144–145; Conklin:1986:229–230). Second, it is quite clear that *individual* Jews are very reluctant to get involved in political assassination events. This tendency can be neutralized when these reluctant individuals either form, or join, groups with an active, direct action, ideology, particularly in situations when there is a very strong, and shared, collective feeling of lack of political justice and of blocked opportunities of having access to a system of fair justice. These groups are capable of generating ideologies which redefine new boundaries for new symbolic-moral universes and hence break the old moral boundaries and barriers. In this fashion, new modes of action are contemplated, debated, approved and legitimized. The "danger" of such a process is that, historically, breaking the old boundaries usually meant that—in the case of political assassination events—there was a spill-over effect and many of the victims were actors from the in-group, that is other Jews. This analysis is particularly valid when ideological and practical arguments among different Jewish groups revolve around such central issues as the future of the society, typically *in* Palestine-Israel and not outside it.

Aside from the detailed ninety-one cases presented, we delved into a few possible cases of political executions and detailed a few problematic cases. There, we surveyed cases that looked like political assassination events, but were actually not and we surveyed cases that looked like political assassination events, but lacked sufficient details and/or corroboration. Although the cases are not likely to represent all the cases, the motive of revenge in the available cases is very salient, as well as the attempt to use political assassination as a mean to prevent worse catastrophes, very similar to what Rapoport (1971) call the "Christian approach" (see chapter 2 for a review).

INTERPRETATION

The thrust of the sociological analtic interpretation is in presenting political assassinations as a particular form of a rhetorical device. The invocation of this rhetorical device was involved in what was perceived by relevant actors as either a situation of oppression and under a foreign rule, or in situations of bitter arguments about the boundaries of some of the myriad symbolic-moral universes which constitute the cultural matrix of Judaism. In *both* situations, the invocation, and use, of political assassination events should be conceptualized, in the overwhelming majority of cases, as an alternative system of justice. This system begins to operate once the formal, or established system of justice, from the point of view of the relevant Jewish actors, fails on what they perceive as very important issues and they feel that the balance of the prevailing distributive justice is consistently biased against them. Organizing into (or joining) ideological groups is a necessary (but not sufficient) condition for the initiation of political assassination events.

This approach is also consistent with contextual constructionism, as characterized. On the one hand we chartered the basic facts, and presented the relevant information. On the other hand, we could see how this information served as the basis for social constructions of political assassinations.

An important element in the pattern of political assassination events presented in this work is the fact that very rarely did we encounter the "lone" assassin. In the overwhelming majority of cases we encountered a pattern which we labeled in chapter 12 as *collective and organized* political assassination events. Behind most political assassination events we found a group, characterized by its own peculiar and distinguishable symbolic-moral universe.

The above patterns fit political assassination events in the cultural matrix of Judaism since at least the Sicariis (chapter 5) till 1988, including cases of political executions. Furthermore, the above patterns also explain why we found *no* cases of Tyrannicide, terroristic assassination, elite substitution and very few in Anomic assassination. In most cases the motives for the assassination events were revenge, and/or as a warning signal to actors which had been defined as "traitors" and/or "squealers." The use of such vocabularies of motives which consisted of rhetorical devices as traitor, squealer, (or "treason"), characterized the Sicariis and the 1892–1980 period. These accounts were used to justify political assassination events against the majority of victims—other Jews.

The reason that most victims were other Jews was explained by resorting to the concept of clashing symbolic-moral universes and the inability to use unspecified terror against inhabitants of these universes. Once the potential victim was perceived to present a grave threat to a particular symbolic-moral universe, a process of vilification and strangerization began, to be accompanied by processes of stigmatization and deviantization (Schur 1980). The end result was that a process of physical annihilation against the violator was initiated.

Once a formal and satisfactory system of political and social justice was institutionalized during 1948 and the early 1950s, the frequency of political assassination events dropped dramatically. Difficult and emotional questions of statehood, loyalty, commitment and political expression for a variety of ideologies were gradually allowable in public.

An obvious conclusion from this work is that as the mechanisms of social and political justice develop and become institutionalized to operate in a fair manner, the probability of their being perceived as such increases, hence, the probability of organized and collective political assassination declines.

The type of political assassination event which emerges from this study is very unusual in the literature on political assassinations. For example, the "typical" political assassination (e.g., assassinating a prominent political figure) is not characteristic of our data. Most political assassination events in our study were aimed against other Jews who were defined as traitors/collaborators/squealers/informers who, in most cases, were not very important political figures in central political processes of decision making. In very few cases we encountered assassination plots against major political leaders. In this particular respect, political executions may be closer to the typical case.

Therefore, political assassination events must be conceptualized within a popular system of justice, operated (and justified) typically by a relevant collective group (and not the individual). Vengeance and revenge (for example, as reactions to suspicions of treason) thus become identified with systemic moral and rational characteristics (and not individual irrational idiosyncrasies).

Consequently, two conclusions are unavoidable. The first is that there apparently is very much reluctance in the culture of Judaism to get involved in political assassination events. If political assassinations are carried out, it usually emerges from ideological groups, and it particularly occurs within a fierce struggle for national independence, in a conflict over the definition of moral boundaries of the collective. Within this context, political assassination events emerge as a tool in an alternative system of popular, political and social justice. The invocation of the label "political assassination" within this context by the ones involved in it is done very reluctantly. The rhetorical devices favored by the participants are typically more neutral like "eliminations," "individual terror."

This brings us to the second conclusion—which is a sociological generalization of a broader nature. We can most certainly expect that a similar pattern of political assassination events would exist in other cultures, under similar situations and conditions. Hence, this study implies that we should look at political assassination events through a different prism, and in a different way, than what we have done in the past. In essence, we must concede that political assassinations and executions are probably more prevalent than what we think. They are not unpredictable, exceptional and cataclysmic events carried out by (a) crazy person(s). Rather, they constitute a systemic characteristic which emerges under a specific set of conditions. We can make a very plausible sociological interpretation of political assassination events in which these events are seen as part of a system of a popular justice, consisting of political trials, political justice and as a very special and powerful system of social control. This formulation means that the concept of political trials must also be revised to include the type of "trials" carried out by the different underground groups.

Another issue concerns an important question—what "determines" history, personal actors or so-called "objective" processes? This question is particularly pertinent in the context of political assassinations, and is tied directly to another issue, that of the results of political assassinations.

There can hardly be a question that the cases of political assassinations and executions which we encountered in this study *had* results. To a very large extent, political assassinations and executions achieved such results as deterring collaborators, intimidating and eliminating opponents, achieving a propaganda effect, and more frequently achieving revenge. However, achieving societal level effects was much more difficult. The three pre-state underground Jewish groups most certainly wanted the British occupation forces out of Palestine. Lehi was at the forefront of that demand, and resorted to political assassinations. However, they usually did not hit major figures, and when they tried, the impact on policy was not clear. Lehi's two most important attempts—on Moyne (no. 49) and Bernadotte (no. 83) may have achieved results. In the first case, the results were a mixed bag for Lehi. It achieved a propaganda effect for Lehi, at the possible cost of the season and of delaying the decision on creating the State of Israel (see case no. 49). In the second case, the assassination marked the end of Lehi as an organization, but Lehi may have prevented the adoption of a partition plan which was not acceptable to many contemporary Israeli politicians. The attempts on MacMichael's life (no. 47) probably did not achieve any visible result. It is very doubtful, to say the least, whether any of the political assassination events "persuaded" Britain to withdraw from Palestine. However, it is possible that the continuous intimidation, and "liquidation" of collaborators was slowly rendering the British most important intelligence service useless. Without good intelligence, the British must have realized that controlling and subordinating the population was becoming exceedingly difficult, if not impossible. Coupled with the growing terror, and the willingness of many countries in the world to support the establishment of Israel, the British may have realized that the price of continuing the occupation was more than what they were willing to pay.

In the main, however, the major result of most of the assassination events was, no doubt, that of achieving an effect of revenge.

Hence, questions regarding the morality and usefulness of political assassination events must finally be addressed. Since taking somebody else's life against his/her wish cannot typically be morally justified, no political assassination can be justified either. However, political assassination events *do* have an impact in reality. Are they useful in any way? The obvious question is "useful to *whom*?" When looked upon in this way, it is not difficult to realize that political assassination events were committed in the past, and will probably be committed in the future, as long as there would be either individuals, or groups, that would feel that these acts are useful, or "positive"—from *their* particular point of view.

The sociological model which was used in this study viewed the social system as composed of a number of different and competing centers, each one enveloped by a particular symbolic-moral universe. These universes compete for a variety of resources and consequently are in an eternal process of negotiations. Political assassination events must be interpreted within this particular sociological conceptualization. This model emphasizes that conflict (non-Marxist) is an essential part of every cultural and social system. However, this model also emphasizes the social function of political assassinations as boundary markers in a particular system of social and political control and popular justice.

The data collected for, and analyzed in, this research support the theoretical approach taken in it; both the choice of the sociology of deviance, deviance and politics and the very definition of political assassinations. The basic sociological conceptualization of this research, namely its focus on center-periphery relationships was corroborated too. That this conceptualization is totally valid for interpreting political executions and the post-1948 period is obvious. It is also valid for the pre-1948 period. We must be reminded that the organized Yishuv had a center: the Zionist Federation and more specifically, the Jewish Agency (which was even recognized as such by the British). The Hagana was the operational arm of that political organization. Both Etzel and Lehi were called (in Hebrew) Irgunim Porshim, meaning "dissident organizations" *because* they challenged the authority of the center. Hence, the center-periphery conceptualization is valid for the pre-1948 period as well.

Consequently, political assassination events may be interpreted as either "good" or as "bad" events, depending on the point of view of the one making the interpretation. This brings us back to the concept of deviance which was presented in the first chapter—as a relative rhetorical device. Again and again, we could see how political assassination events were the result of ideas presented by different moral entrepreneurs in a moral crusade (e.g., see the cases involving De Hahn [no. 6]; Opler [no. 20]; Waksman [no. 25]; Lyttelton [no. 29]; Giladi [no. 38]; Hilewitz [no. 42]; MacMichael [no. 47]; Wagner [no. 54]; Barker [no. 60]; Schnell [no. 62]; Levi [no. 75]; Zeidenberg [no. 76]; Tubianski [no. 82]; Pinkas [no. 85]; Kasztner [no. 86]). While these cases were directed from the periphery, political executions which were directed from the center carry a similar signature of equivalent moral entrepreneurs in a similar moral crusade (e.g., the elimination of "Black September").

This study seems to justify Turk's observation that: "Assassination is most likely to be an effective tactic when the goal is a limited one (such as retaliation, discipline, or elimination of a rival or an obstacle) and when it has organizational support" (1983:87).

Taking the cases themselves together with the theory yields support to the generalization which views political assassinations as a systemic property of cultural and social systems subject to similar conditions under which the Yishuv existed. Furthermore, because of the approach taken in this study, we were able to shed light on a previously uncharted form of political assassination, and to arrive at some special generalizations about political assassinations.

NOTES

CHAPTER ONE. THEORETICAL ORIENTATION

1. Ellis and Gullo (1971) even suggest how to treat assassins.

2. The discussion is based on, and continues, chap. 1 in my 1985 and 1990 books.

3. The sociological concept of a "subculture" is close to the concept of a "symbolic-moral universe." Because the emphasis in this type of work is on a *symbolic interpretation*, use of "symbolic-moral universes" is much more appropriate and accurate than subculture.

4. See Orcutt 1983:59–62; Geertz 1973; Waltzer 1987. A cultural interpretation means for Geertz: "man is an animal suspended in webs of significance he himself has spun. I take culture to be those webs, and the analysis of it to be therefore not an experimental science in search of law but an interpretive one in search of meaning. It is explication I am after, constructing social expressions on their surface enigmatical.... Analysis, then, is sorting out the structures of signification...and determining their social ground and import" (1973:5, 9).

5. See Hills 1980:8–11; Douglas and Waksler 1982:8–25; Orcutt 1983:3–29; Thio 1988:3–24; and a similar argument by Woolgar and Pawluch 1985. Sagarin's 1985 programmatic paper advocates, uncompromisingly and sharply, the absolutist position. Typical of this approach, Sagarin's paper fails to take into a serious consideration the problem of power, and of the vitally important role of the relevant societal reactions. The really interesting problem is not whether a particular behavioral act is defined as deviant or not—but instead who wants to define it as deviant, where, when and why; and under what conditions such social actors may be successful in enforcing their views upon the rest of society.

6. For a related argument, see Dodge 1985; Sagarin 1985; Heckert 1989; Ben-Yehuda 1990a; and Goode 1990.

7. For more on this, see Durkheim's original essays (1933, 1938) on the functionality of deviance and later formulations by Cohen

1966:6–11; Box 1981; Farrel and Swigert 1982 chap. 2; Pfohl 1985, chap. 6; Harris 1977; Lauderdale 1976; Shapiro, Lauderdale and Lauderdale 1985 and Ben-Yehuda 1985:3–10. For some recent formulations on the Durkheimian views see Inverarity, Lauderdale and Feld 1983 and Inverarity 1987.

8. I have used this particular approach in other works. See for example, Ben-Yehuda 1980, 1985; 1987, 1990.

CHAPTER TWO. POLITICAL ASSASSINATIONS: THEORETICAL BACKGROUND

1. A significantly different version of this chapter, entitled "Political Assassinations as Rhetorical Devices" was published in *Terrorism and Political Violence*, 1990, 2 (3):324–350, (published by Frank Cass and Co. Ltd., London, Publishers).

2. For more on the Assassins see Franzius 1969; Ford 1985:96–104; Hammer 1835; Hodgson 1955; Hurwood 1970:5–13; Lerner 1930; Lewis 1967; Wilson 1975:15–301.

3. Camellion (1977:1) even discusses "the art of assassination." See also Clarke 1982; Crotty 1971; Ford 1985; Havens, Leiden and Schmitt 1970; Heaps 1969; Hurwood 1970; Hyams 1969; Kirkham, Levy and Crotty 1970; Lentz 1988; Paine 1975; Rapoport 1971; Schmid 1983:57–63; Snitch 1982; Wilkinson 1976; Wilson 1972.

4. Rapoport expressed concern in his 1982 paper that in the field of terrorism there developed a tendency to abuse language to the point that the original meaning of terms may be confused and murky. The use of the analytical concept "rhetorical device" should not mislead the reader into thinking that there is any intention here of confusing the issue. On the contrary. Using the term "event" to describe the act, and using specific rhetorical devices to describe the cultural and social construction of meaning attached to the "events" is meant, *explicitly*, to create a sharply defined terminology.

5. Another example is a threat (or a suggestion?) made in January 6, 1980 by a member (Gad Serotman) of the late Rabbi Kahana's Kach movement to poison Menachem Begin, then Israel's prime minister. This threat was made during a regular meeting of activists for Kach, on Osishkin Street in Jerusalem. Gad served then as a cook in a military base of the Israeli airforce and his idea was to poison Begin. Kahana negated and rejected the idea/suggestion/threat (Koren 1989:29).

CHAPTER THREE. METHODOLOGY AND RESEARCH EXPERIENCE

1. A significantly different version of this chapter entitled "Gathering Dark Secrets, Hidden and Dirty Information: Some Methodological Notes on Studying Political Assassinations" was published in *Qualitative Sociology*, 1990, 13 (4):345–372 (published by Human Science Press, Inc., New York).

2. I find that "Dripping" is a more accurate descriptive term for this process than "leaking."

CHAPTER FOUR. HISTORICAL AND POLITICAL BACKGROUND

1. For example, Yitzhak Ben-Zvi (later, the second president of Israel); Alexander Zeid; Israel Giladi; Yehezkel Hankin; Israel Shohat and a few others.

2. See S.T.H., vol. 1: 193–312, 396–421; Lev U. 1985; Shva 1969; Sefer Hashomer; Encyclopaedia Hebraica vol. 31:619–620.

3. Or, "Shohat's folks" because of the centrality of Israel Shohat— former chief of Hashomer—in this group. See S.T.H., vol. 2, part 1:219–241.

4. The Zionist Federation is the administrative framework of the world Zionist movement. It was established due to Dr. Theodore Herzl's (1860–1904) initiative in the first Zionist congress in Basel (Switzerland) in 1897. The Zionist Federation was recognized by the British mandate authorities as the *Jewish Agency*. According to article 4 of the 1922 mandate over Palestine, the main function of the Jewish Agency was to advice and help in creating and building a national homeland for the Jews, and in matters concerning Jewish settlement in Palestine.

5. Niv, vol. 1:156–194; S.T.H., vol. 2, part 1:574–585 and vol. 2, part 1:420–434.

6. See Yevin 1986:105–106; Niv, vol. 2:17–20; S.T.H., vol. 2, part 2:722–734.

7. Niv., vol. 2:75; Yevin 1986, 125–130; Naor 1990.

8. Niv, vol. 3:45–46; Yevin 1986:190, 310–311; Livni 1987: 25–26.

9. Apparently, it was a German air raid. See Niv, vol. 3:72–77; Yevin 1986:232–238; S.T.H., vol. 3, part 1:481–482; Naor 1990:265–279.

10. S.T.H., vol. 3, part 2:1541; Cohen N., ed., 1981:534–535. For a bibliographical review, and history of Etzel see Amrami 1975:29–70; Niv; Begin 1950; Livni 1987; Naor 1990.

11. S.T.H., vol. 3, part 1:494; Eliav 1983:171–178.

12. For the history of Lehi, consult Amrami 1975:73–90; Banai 1958; Eliav 1983; Gilboa 1986; Harel 1979; Harel 1985; 1987:193–205; Heller 1989; Katz 1987; Niv, dispersed information in all six volumes; Shavit 1987:153–179; S.T.H., vol. 3, part 1: 474–543; Shomron 1985; Weinshall 1978; Yevin 1986; Yellin-Mor 1974.

CHAPTER FIVE. POLITICAL ASSASSINATIONS BY JEWS IN THE BIBLE, THE SICARIIS, AND IN EUROPE

1. See also Encyclopaedia Hebraica, vol. 6:302–304 and vol. 10:277–278.

2. For example, see Kasher 1983; Avi Yonah and Beres 1983; Stern 1984.

3. For example, see also Aberbach 1985; Flusser 1985; Hangel 1983; Horsely 1979; Rapoport 1982, 1984; 1988; Smith 1983; Stern 1983, 1984, 1987; .

4. Book 4 of his "The History of the Wars Between the Jews and the Romans," chap. 7:b [Hebrew]; see also Flavius 1981; Hoenig 1970; Spero 1970; Zeitlin 1965 and 1967.

5. See Rapoport, 1984 and Stern, 1983.

6. See Basok 1944; Encyclopaedia Judaica 1971, vol. 11:1–3; Encyclopaedia Hebraica, vol. 21:196.

7. See also Niv, vol. 5, 1976:70–73; S.T.H., vol. 2, part 3:914–915.

8. See Dashewski 1903; S.T.H., vol. 2, part 1:160–161; Encyclopaedia Hebraica, vol. 13:222–223.

9. "Ataman" was a name given to the head of the Cossacks in Russia and the Ukraines.

10. See Encyclopaedia Hebraica 1979, vol. 31:676; Encyclopaedia Judaica 1971, vol. 14:1027 and vol. 13:340–341; Fuerstein 1986:83–92; Nedava 1979:70; S.T.H., vol. 2, part 1:32–33.

11. See, Frankfurter 1984; Encyclopaedia Hebraica, vol. 28:332–333; Encyclopaedia Judaica 1971, vol. 7:94; Ludwig 1936.

12. See Fuerstein 1986:101–108; *Ha`aretz* July 1, 1941 p. 2; *Ha`aretz* May 29, 1941, p. 1; *Ha`aretz* December 3, 1941 p. 2.

13. See Fuerstein 1986:101–108; Encyclopaedia Hebraica, reserve vol., pp. 790–791; Gross 1988; Harpaz 1988; Nevo 1988c.

14. Gross 1988; Harpaz 1988; Kliger 1988; Nevo 1988c.

15. Gutman 1988:119; Social Science Encyclopaedia, Hebraica, 1962, vol. 1:251–252; Zuckerman 1990:180, 207–209. See footnote no. 17 too.

16. The major part of that revolt began on April 19, 1943 and ended on May 16, 1943. The Jewish fighters' headquarters fell to the Germans already on May 8 (see, Encyclopaedia Hebraica, vol. 10:618–620).

17. Zuckerman's testimony contradicts—in the details of attributing repsonsibility—the details given by Niv. Focusing on cases of suspected collaborators with the Nazis (and the Gestapo), Zuckerman (1990) mentions the cases of Joseph Sherinski, Ya'acov Leikin and Israel Furst (pp. 179–180, 207–209, 574). However, he adds to this list the names of Anna Milewitz, Machislaw Shmerling, Dr. Alfred Nusig (pp. 231–232, 266, 268–270), Herman Katz (p. 268) and Furstenberg (p. 271). Two people against whom "death sentences" were not executed were Adam Jorabin (pp. 370–377) and Michael Vaichart (pp. 381–387). It is quite clear that different Jewish groups assassinated, or tried to assassinate, different collaborators in the Ghetto.

18. The Judenraete was the council of Jews set up as the self-governing body of the various ghettos constructed by the Nazis in occupied Eastern Europe (e.g., see Trunk 1972, 1977).

19. Social Science Encyclopaedia, Hebrew, 1969, vol. 2:486–488.

20. See Ben-Horin, 1987; Carmi 1960:99–107, 158–161; S.T.H., vol. 3, part 2:1070–1072; Haber and Schiff 1976:223; Bar-Zohar 1969; Naor M. 1988:139–150; Black and Morris 1991:188; Segev 1991:126–137. These activities got a dramatic exposure when in May 5, 1987 Israel Carmi himself appeared in the Israeli Television in the

program "Erev Hadash" (meaning, "New Evening") and told this story.

21. Ben Horin 1987:41; S.T.H., vol. 3, part 2:1072–1074; Black and Morris 1991:188; Segev 1991:131.

CHAPTER SIX: POLITICAL ASSASSINATIONS BY JEWS IN PALESTINE-ISRAEL BETWEEN 1882–1918

1. For example, see Encyclopaedia Judaica 1971, vol. 14:342–345; Encyclopaedia Hebraica, vol. 30:667–670.

2. These were collected and published in a 1887 book.

3. For a brief biographical sketch see Encyclopaedia Judaica 1971, vol. 14:952.

4. See Encyclopaedia Judaica 1971, vol. 14:952; S.T.H., vol. 1, Part 2:681 and p. 12 in Schwartzfux's introduction to Scheid 1983.

5. Dizengoff was one of the founders of the Ahuzat Bayit Company for establishing a modern Jewish quarter near Jaffa. This quarter, later called Tel Aviv, was founded in 1909. In 1911 Dizengoff was elected head of the local council. Later, when Tel Aviv became a city (1921), Dizengoff was elected its first mayor (Encyclopaedia Judaica, vol. 6, p. 138).

6. For more on Nily, see Encyclopaedia Judaica, vol. 12, pp. 1162–1165; Aharonson 1970; Blankfort 1965 (this is a "fiction" book based on the story of Nily. A Hebrew translation was published in 1965 too); Engle 1959.

7. See S.T.H., vol. 1, part 1:353–385; Ya'ari Poleskin 1937; Engle 1959; Aharonson 1970; Livneh 1961, 1969; Nedava 1977; Encyclopaedia Hebraica, vol. 21:883–884 and vol. 25:151–152; Amrami 1975:3–16.

8. Livneh 1961:290–291; Nedava 1977:310–311; see also Nedava 1986 and Nadav 1954:139–150; Engle 1959:211–219.

CHAPTER SEVEN: POLITICAL ASSASSINATIONS BY JEWS IN PALESTINE-ISRAEL BETWEEN 1919–1948

1. Herbert Louis Samuel (1870–1963) was appointed the first British high commissioner of Palestine from 1920 till 1925. The offer to

become the first high commissioner was probably made to Herbert Samuel in April of 1920 by Lloyd George (Katzburg, in Makover R. 1988:1–22). His letter of appointment dates June 19, 1920 (Encyclopaedia Judaica, vol. 14, p. 799). He actually arrived to Palestine in January of 1920 (see Makover R. 1988:54).

2. For another, probably even less reliable, version see Nakdimon and Mayzlish 1985:229.

3. Shva 1969:326–327; Tidhar 1960:99 and S.T.H., vol. 2, part 1:226–227; Ben-Zvi 1976:111; Harel 1987:213–219.

4. See also Shva 1969:254; Tidhar 1960:129–136; S.T.H., vol. 2, part 1:426–432; S.T.H., vol. 1, part 3:250–253; Niv Volume one:133, 271; Arzi 1982; Narkis 1986; Nakdimon 1986.

5. For a bibliographical survey on that group see Amrami 1975:19–25.

6. See Teveth 1982; Nedava 1986b; Ornstein 1973; Ahimair and Shatzki 1978; Brit Habirionim 1953; Rosenberg 1974; S.T.H., vol. 1 part 3:492–499.

7. For an account of the 1930s see Teveth 1982; Tidhar 1960:377–426; Niv, vol. 1:197–204; Kotzer 1977:124–125. For the 1982–1985 committee see Bechor, Kenneth, and Berkowitz 1985. Before leaving this case it is well worth noting that despite the 1985 committee's report, this case has a very strong "smell" of a political assassination. Both the situational "reason" for the killing, as well as the method, seem to point to it. The committee's report, one must add, is so pale that one wanders whether the next report would even deny the act, or that there even was a person named Arlosoroff. Farther than this is not possible to speculate at this point. It is doubtful that it will ever be possible to find out who exactly (and why) killed Arlosoroff. Despite the strong circumstances it must be added that one cannot fully discredit the hypothesis that Arlosoroff was killed by Arab nationalists or, perhaps, even criminals.

8. That treaty was signed during World War I by Britain, France, Italy, and Russia.

9. Niv, vol. 2:17–20; S.T.H., vol. 2, part 2:1054–1056.

10. Niv, vol. 2:20; S.T.H., vol. 2, part 2:1056 and part 3:1255; Bowyer Bell 1987:49; *Davar*, supplement, February 12, 1971, p. 33; The Ben-Amram file in the Jabotinsky archive "cannot be found."

11. Ibid, see also Bauer 1966:52–55; S.T.H., vol. 3 part 1:76–77. It is possible that not all units of Pum were dissolved and some small units remained operational.

12. Abraham Stern was probably aware of the possibility of a provocation, but he nevertheless wanted to go along with it, even if only to signal to the British that Lehi was willing to cooperate with a foreign power—even an enemy of Britain—in order to advance its goals (Yevin 1986:202).

13. Most commanders were transferred there in February 1940 and released in June 1940; Niv, vol. 3:38,43.

14. S.T.H., vol. 3, part 1:60; Niv, vol. 2:251.

15. Niv, vol. 2:251; Ha'aretz May 30, 1939 p. 1 and May 31, p. 1; Palestine Post, May 31, 1939:1.

16. S.T.H., vol. 3, part 1:65; Niv, vol. 2:251–252.

17. Niv, vol. 2:251; S.T.H., vol. 3 part 1:60; Arieh Kotzer may have described the case in his novel The Morning Comes in Blood, no date:72–83.

18. Ha'aretz, August 27, 1939:8; see also Yevin 1986:159; Eliav 1983:60; Yellin-Mor 1974:54–55; Niv, vol. 2:257–258. For a detailed report of Zerony's torture see Eliav 1983:124–132 and S.T.H., vol. 3, part 1:66 and part 3:1614; Illin 1985:89–90.

19. Niv, vol. 2:275; Weinshall 1978:146, 200; Yevin 1986:160.

20. Eshel 1978:267–268; S.T.H., vol. 3, part 1:76. Eshel's dating is probably more accurate, see also Mardor 1970:24.

21. Another reminder how these assassination episodes are still in the Israeli public's mind, more than fifty years after they occurred.

22. See Koren 1986; Niv, vol. 3:41; Davar, May 23, and May 30, 1986.

23. For example, see Kotzer 1977:247, 249; Weinshall 1978: 199–202; Yevin 1986:246–250.

24. See case no. 50. See also Jones 1979:22; Cohen M. J. 1978:114, 213 n. 46; Katzburg 1977; Casey 1962:94–97, 101, 129; Woodward 1970, vol. 2:27.

25. Yevin 1986:267; Eliav 1983:196; Shomron 1985:21; Yellin-Mor 1974:85; Banai 1958:81.

26. Morton 1957:137–140; Okev 1949:7–9; Niv, vol. 3:184–185; Weinshall 1978:218–225; Eliav 1983:196–203 and 353–355. See also Niv, vol. 3:185; S.T.H., vol. 3, part 1:503; *Ha'aretz*, January 21, 1942:1; *Ha'aretz*, January 22, 1942:1.

27. Weinshall 1978:271–272; Yellin-Mor 1974:86; Niv, vol. 3:192; Banai 1958:113.

28. There is a strong contradiction between the description of the method by which the mine was supposed to explode. Some sources suggest that the handle of the car's door was supposed to be the trigger for the explosion. The version I believe was mentioned by Eliav. I tend to trust his version and discard the others. Eliav was apparently an intimate insider for this assassination plot, and Lehi's contemporary expert on explosives.

29. Yevin 1986:280–293; Morton 1957; *Ha'aretz*, March 10, 1989, p. 5. Morton has claimed that they were killed when they attempted to escape.

30. Morton 1957:149; Niv, vol. 3:192; Banai 1958:112; Weinshall 1978:271.

31. See Yevin 1986; Yellin-Mor 1974:86; Banai 1958:113; Niv, vol. 3:183; S.T.H., vol. 3, part 1:505; Katz 1987:20.

32. See Chabas 1937; Smilansky 1953, vol. four:239–249; Argaman 1991:88–102.

33. In the evening of Monday, January 1, 1988 the Israeli Television broadcasted an interview with Itzhak Hankin (from Kefar Giladi) in the program "A Year in an Hour: 1938." There, Hankin stated that he was the one who actually shot Taubash. This version is consistent with Argaman (1991:99)

(34) Kotzer's book (1977:243) implies that Shmuel Kaplan was involved in the Wilenchik case, and that Wilenchik's assassination was not really called for.

35. Ziv 1973:17; S.T.H., vol. 3 part 3:1689; Segev 1981; interviews Anshell Shpillman and Hanna Armony.

36. Yevin 1986:216–217, 219, 316. On Giladi's part in the course see Cohen 1973:5 and Yellin-Mor 1974:91.

37. Eldad 1962:26; Kotzer 1977:246; Ziv 1973:17; Shmuelevitz 1973:12; Gilboa 1986:117.

38. Kotzer 1977:252–255; Gilboa 1986:117–119. Banai (1950:143) has no doubt that Giladi ("Shaul") was behind the escape attempt.

39. Who, years later, became the director of Lehi's museum.

40. It seems safe to assume that the two main "heroes" Nadel talks about are probably Giladi and Yehuda Arie Levi (see case no. 75). We contacted Nadel (who lives now in New York) in March of 1988, but he (rudely) refused to answer any of our questions.

41. See also my paper entitled "Conflict Resolution in an Underground Group: The Shamir-Giladi Clash," published in 1989 in *Terrorism 12* (no. 3):199–212 (published by Crane, Russak and Company, New York).

42. See also S.T.H., vol. 3, part 1:477–478 and vol. 3, part 1:471.

43. S.T.H., vol. 3, part 1:500; Eliav 1983:164; Shmuelevitz 1973:6.

44. At that time, and after Giladi's assassination and Yellin-Mor still in Mazra, Lehi was headed by Shamir.

45. Eliav 1983:164; Niv, vol. 2:196–197; S.T.H., vol. 3, part 1:507; Koren 1986:11.

46. Niv, vol. 4:42; *Ha'aretz*, May 11, 1944:4; Jabotinski's archives, file number 1/21, 4ב.

47. Yellin-Mor 1974:154–155; Lehi *Ketavim* (A):539–540 and 919–922; S.T.H., vol. 3, part 1:512, 523; *Ha'aretz*, March 20, 1944:20 and March 22, 1944:4.

48. Yellin-Mor 1974:155; Banai 1958:141; Katz 1987:32; *Ha'aretz*, April 11, 1944:1.

49. Nedava 1983; Niv, vol. 4:43.

50. Lehi even warned publicly Hilewitz in 1944 that his life was in danger (Lehi, *Ketavim* [A], pp. 532–532).

51. Niv, vol. 4:28–30; S.T.H., vol. 3, part 1:523–524.

52. Begin lived in hiding at 25 Alfasi Street. See Begin's account 1950:150–155.

53. Interesting to note that in his memories Menachem Begin mentions this affair. However, the *names* he uses in the original Hebrew version differ from the ones which he uses in the English version. In the Hebrew edition (1950) Hilewitz is identified in his real name (pp.

150–155). However, in the English version (*The Revolt*, Jerusalem: Steimatzky's Agency Limited, 1951), instead of using Hilewitz's name, Begin calls him "Tsorros" (pp. 101–102) and the affair is not given in the same details as in the original Hebrew text. Why would Begin do a thing like this? It may be that he did not want to expose Hilewitz to a potential readership in the United States where Hilewitz resided at the time. The name that he chose, though, Tsorros can be read to mean Tsorres, that is "troubles" in Yiddish.

54. See *Yediot Aharonot*, 1958, October 26, weekend Supplement (7 Days), p. 3; December 28 till December 31, daily reports on p. 3. *Yediot Aharonot*, 1959, January 1 to January 6, daily reports on p. 3. See also the responses to Dr. Rosenblum's accounts by Dr. Altman in *Yediot Aharonot*, January 7, 1959 p. 3; of Meridor in *Yediot Aharonot*, January 8, 1959 p. 3; and of others in *Yediot Aharonot*, January 9, 1959 p. 3, January 11, 1959 p. 3 and January 12, 1959 p. 3. In 1987 Rosenblum published his memoirs. There (pp. 78–79) he refers again to the Hilewitz affair, totally from his memory. Rosenblum "remembered" in 1987 that Hilewitz had told him that he did not betray. He said that he had just slipped because he had a weak character and owed a lot of money. Hilewitz told Rosenblum that he was not the only informer the British had, and that blaming him for everything was simply untrue and not justified. See also Nedava 1983:33; Yellin-Mor 1974:184–186; Begin 1950:154–155.

55. This, however, was not the only case where a provocateur-squealer in Etzel was not assassinated. *Ma'ariv* (July 12, 1973) tells (telegraphically) about another such case in 1939, involving a person named Epstein, who was not assassinated.

56. See Niv, part 2, p. 275 and Yevin 1986:160. For the most authentic version see Illin 1985:87–88.

57. Today Israel's Ben-Gurion International Airport.

58. Borochov is considered as one of the "fathers" of socialist Zionism.

59. Shomron 1985:81; Banai 1958:254; Niv, vol. 4:67; Yevin 1986:266; Weinshall 1978:214.

60. Although Wilkin left the room earlier. See Yevin 1986:287–291.

61. Banai 1958:254–258; Shomron 1985:80–92; Yellin-Mor 1974:197–199; *Ha'aretz*, October 1, 1944:1.

62. Shomron 1985:93–94 and 100–102; Yellin-Mor 1974:199–201; Banai 1958:259–260; Nevo 1986.

63. This act supposedly was planned as a joint venture for the three pre-state underground Jewish groups. However, its rationale and necessity became a focus of controversy. Eventually, this act of terror became identified with Etzel. It was directed against what was perceived as an important center of the British occupation forces in Palestine. See also n. 91 and n. 1 in chap. 10.

64. For example, see Margalit 1982; Bauer 1982:148–191; for more of this see Brand 1966; 1974 and case no. 86.

65. See S.T.H., vol. 3 part 1:562–564 and Niv, vol. 4:80–81. On the destruction of Hungarian Jews see Braham 1981; Hilberg 1985, vol. 2:796–860 and Wyman 1984:235–254 (chap. 13). After his release, Brand joined Lehi.

66. Nedava 1974:83–85; Frank 1963:101. Beit-Zuri was involved in 1944 in the assassination of Baron Moyne, see case no. 49.

67. See Niv, vol. 3:270–273; Livni 1987:47–51; Lankin 1974:61–64.

68. Eliav 1983:376–377; Frank 1963:137–138; Shomron 1985:71; Yellin-Mor 1974:190–191; Niv, vol. 3:261.

69. Nedava 1974:70; Shomron 1985:71–72.

70. Banai 1958:244–245; Yellin–Mor 1974:191–192; Shomron 1985:73–74.

71. Banai 1958:246–247; Yellin–Mor 1974:192–193; Shomron 1985:74.

72. Nedava 1974:74–75; Shomron 1985:77–80; Yellin–Mor 1974:193–195; S.T.H., vol. 3 part 1:514; Niv, vol. 4:53–55; *Ha'aretz* August 9, 1944:1.

73. See Kanaan 1975; Bowyer Bell 1987:98–105; Frank 1963; Yellin–Mor 1974:210–259; Katz 1966:191; Banai 1958:261–316; Lehi *Ketavim* [A]:929–934; S.T.H., vol. 3 part 1:512–517; Ayalon 1982; Hyams 1969:168–196; Heaps 1969:110–112.

74. This "strange" reaction has not yet been fully and sufficiently explained. See Shavit 1976:61–87; Jabotinski archive file number 4ב no. 10/19; *Ma'ariv*, August 8, 1972:10–11; Shomron 1985:114; Lev Ami 1972:100–126; Begin 1950:208; Milshtein 1973; Avidar 1970:198–201; Nakdimon 1978:26–31; Galili 1987:68–74; Yellin–Mor 1974:210–273; Katz S. 1966:160, 184.

75. The Gideonites was the name given to a defense organization which was established in Zichron Ya'acov toward the end of 1913 (around or during Sukkot). Alexander Aharonson was the chairman of this organization. The Gideonites only lasted for about fourteen months (see S.T.H., vol. 1, part 1, pp. 282–286). They ceased to exist because members were recruited to the Turkish Army as a result of the beginning of World War I.

76. Livneh 1961:330; Niv, vol. 2:40, 263; Yevin 1986:201, 212; S.T.H., vol. 3 part 1:519.

77. Karpel (1990) attributes the difference in the versions as to how many bullets were fired at Davidesku to Lehi's attempt to show the supposedly high professional standards and accuracy of its assassins. She also adds a few interesting details. According to her report, the four assassins were: Moshe Bar-Giora [Israel] (died two and a half months later in action against the refineries in Haifa); Avraham Yehudai [Elhanan] (died ten months later in Kefar Atta in the attack on the machine shops of the train); Moshe Armony [Nadav] (died about ten years ago in a car accident); Hanna Armony [Sarah], who later married Moshe, and is today (1990) the secretary of Anshell Shpillman. She was then nineteen years old. Karpel adds that Julie, Davidesku's second wife, left Palestine after the assassinations to London with their two children. Jack, who was six years old at the time of assassination and Sarah who was one year old. Both children's name were associated to Nily. Jack was named Ya'acov Ephraim, after the father of the father of the Aharonsons (who established Nily), and Sarah was named after Sarah Aharonson. Jack returned later to Israel, but Sarah remained in England.

78. Encyclopaedia Judaica, vol. 5:784–785; Encyclopaedia Hebraica, vol. 7:760–762; McDonald 1951:30–36; Niv, vol. 5:185; Kanaan 1958:28–29.

79. Encyclopaedia Hebraica, vol. 18:799–800; Carmel 1973; Encyclopaedia Judaica vol. 15:994–996; Kanaan 1964, 1968.

80. See Gilad 1955, vol. 1:587; S.T.H., vol. 3 part 2:1317–1318; Kanaan 1968:113–115; and an interview with one of the assassins on December 25, 1987.

81. See Pearlman 1947; Elath 1968;l Schechtman 1965; Encyclopaedia Judaica, vol. 8:1132–1133; Encyclopaedia Hebraica, vol. 7:829–827; Bar-Zohar and Haber 1984:37–64; Kanaan 1968:105–110; Dekel 1953:190–191.

82. Which indicates, again, that while the Hagana's command was aware of Hanokmim's actions, it may have felt uneasy about them.

83. He remained there until January 14, 1947, when he managed to escape. See Bowyer-Bell 1987:168–169; R. D. Wilson 1949:71; S.T.H., vol. 3 part 2:903, 908 and vol. 3:1747; Niv, vol. 5:31.

84. Shomron 1985:208; Banai 1958:482–485; Bowyer-Bell 1987:169.

85. Interview on July 5, 1987, "Beit Yair." Shpillman is head of the Lehi's museum, and a former Lehi member.

86. The settlers were actually the "religious group" of the Hagana/Palmach. See S.T.H., vol. 3, part 2:871–874.

87. The store existed at Jaffa Road, no. 36, at the corner of what is called today Donuas Street and Jaffa Road, downtown Jerusalem (the actual place of the store is occupied now [1988] by a speedy photo-finishing store and a pharmacy).

88. Professor Moshe Lissak told me (March 27, 1989) that Meir Pail told him that he was involved in the act. According to Pail's account to Lissak, Yigal Allon (commander of the Palmach) called him to Haifa and instructed him to prepare a plan to eliminate Bruce. Pail prepared the plan and was involved in its execution. It is not clear whether he (a) was only the planner; (b) was the commander of the assassins; (c) was the one who actually shot Bruce. Pail refused to grant us an interview, and failed to respond to any of my queries to him.

89. S.T.H., vol. 3, part 3:1743. See also *Ha'aretz*, October 20, 1946:1; *Ha'aretz* October 18, 1946:1; Gilad 1955, vol. 1:575.

90. *Ha'aretz*, November 20, 1946:6; Okev 1949:17–18; Israel Galili's testimony in the Friedman Yellin-Mor trial, see *Davar*, January 5, 1949:2.

91. See S.T.H., vol. 3, part 2:898–899; Niv, vol. 4:278–288. See also n. 63 above and note 1 in chap. 10.

92. S.T.H., vol. 3, part 2:401; Begin 1961, vol. 2:207–208; Niv, vol. 5:25.

93. S.T.H., vol. 3, Part two:934; Bowyer Bell 1987:303–305; Clarke 1981:230–231; Lankin 1974:203,211; Niv, vol. 5:219–221.

94. He was executed on April 26, 1947, see case no. 67.

95. Translated by the author from the document in Jabotinski's archives.

96. The Jabotinski archives have a special file on the Leon Mashiach affair, file number 4/21 4ב. At the time of the data collection (winter 1987) we were denied access to it and were told that the file was still classified.

97. Both committed suicide in their prison cell. They used a grenade that was smuggled into their cell and blew themselves up. For more details, see case no. 68.

98. These were Shomron, Drora, Yachin, Geula, and others.

99. Probably Ya'acov Panso—"Goel" and Chaim Akheiser "Avner"—see Banai 1958:585.

100. See n. 63 and 91 above.

101. Niv, vol. 5:49–50; Eliav 1983:333; Bowyer-Bell 1987:142 n. 3; Beit Jabotinsky's archives, document number 12/19 4ב.

102. Niv, vol. 5:50, 221; Eliav 1983:333–334; *Ma'ariv*, July 23, 1954, p. 4; Tavin 1973:172–174.

103. *Ha'aretz*, November 13, 1947, p. 1; *Ha'aretz*, November 25, 1947, p. 3; Banai 1959:585; Yellin-Mor 1974:412.

104. Tzameret (1974:68) indicates that Lehi actually pressed different Jewish industrialists into contributing money (as well as other "equivalents" like radio transmitters, printing machine, blankets, etc.) to Lehi. It is possible that Lehi used severe threats to force various people into cooperating and/or contributing money to Lehi (e.g., see *Ha'aretz*, January 7, 1979 and December 14, 1948).

105. This in fact shows to what extent members of the underground were really not aware of what was actually going on. Kotzer refers here to the capture of Ya'acov Kutik on August 20, 1938 by the British intelligence, probably due to "squealing" by Valentin Back. Back was shot to death by Etzel on June 22, 1939 (see case no. 16). The case with Holianitzky (no. 78) is another example for such a break in communications.

106. See *Ha'aretz*, November 21, 1947, p. 8 and the *Palestine Post*, November 21, 1947, p. 1.

107. S.T.H., vol. 3, part 2:1544–1555; Niv, part 6:121–123; Vinitzky 1950; Gavriel 1950; Bowyer-Bell 1987:264; Begin 1961, vol. 4:155–157; Begin 1950:419–429; Shavit 1976:140–141.

108. There are a few disturbing discrepancies concerning the details of this case. In "Beit Yair," the official museum of Lehi, the headline under Levi's picture states that he "was killed by mistake" on January 4, 1948. Okev (1949:26) and Nevo (1987) state that Levi was kidnapped only on January 15. Okev also states that Levi's body was found near the moshava Hadar in the Sharon. S.T.H. (vol. 3, part 2:1544) states that it was found buried in an orange grove near Ra'anana. Nevo states that the body was found near the road.

109. See also my "Violence aggression and conflict resolution in an underground group: the case of Lehi and Levi," published in 1989 in *Violence, Aggression and Terrorism*, 3(3):173–190.

110. Interesting to note that in 1989 Gideon Ganani directed a sensitive Israeli movie which was based on this affair. The movie was called "Esh Tzolevet" in Hebrew, meaning "crossfire."

111. October 1937. See also case no. 9 and chap. 4.

112. When the Germans stormed and conquered Poland in 1939 General Wladislaw Sikorski (1881–1943) became prime minister of the Polish government in exile. On July 30, 1941, Sikorski's government in exile signed an agreement with the USSR. This agreement created the basis for the formation of a Polish army, on Soviet territory, under a Polish command (who was subordinated to the Soviet military command). The Polish General Wladislaw Anders (1892–1970) was appointed as the commander of that Polish army, which later became known as "Anders Army." Part of that army was transferred, via Iran, to the Middle East and took part in some battles in this arena and in Italy.

113. At 9 King George Street, downtown Jerusalem. Today (1988) the place is occupied by a Brother-Empisal agency.

114. For example, see Yellin-Mor 1974:418–419; Bowyer-Bell 1987:242; Lehi, *Ketavim* [B], 524–526; Niv, vol. 6:36; Niv, vol. 5:148–150; S.T.H., vol. 3, part 2:929–930; Banai 1958:574–575; Yachin 1984:196–203.

115. On June 7, 1948, three separate intelligence services were formally created instead of the Hagana's Shai. One was a military intelligence service (headed by Isser Be'ery and Chaim Herzog). This service was put in charge of military and combat intelligence, counter espionage, censorship, listening-in and special operations. Second was an inner intelligence service (headed by Isser Halperin and Yoseph Israeli). Third was an external (political) intelligence service (headed by Reuven

Shiloach) (see Eshed 1988:120). As can be easily seen, the Tubianski case was unfolding during a period of structural uncertainty when the Israeli intelligence community was changing from a pre-state intelligence service, to a post state differentiation of services. It is evident that the Tubianski case, in spirit, reflects much more the legacy and tradition of the pre-state Shai than the post-state formal and legal system (Bar-Zohar 1970:37–38; Black and Morris 1991:1–97; Granot 1981:13–16; Nevo 1988b and Harel 1989:101–104; Raviv and Melman 1990).

116. Isser Be'ery acted as the prosecutor. The other Be'ery appointed judges were Binyamin Gibly, Abraham Kidron, and David Caron.

117. Commanded by Matitiahu Goldman.

118. The Tubianski case received extensive coverage in contemporary written media. For sources see, *Ha'aretz* archive, file on Tubianski. See also *Ha'aretz*, July 7, 1948, p. 1; July 20, 1948; August 14, 1949, p. 1; August 15, 1949, p. 1; October 25, 1949, p. 2; August 12, 1949, p. 1. During the months of July–October 1949 *Ha'aretz* provided good coverage of the affair. Israeli Television had a special program on the affair in May of 1981.

119. Actually, the *first* such appeal ever, criminal file number 1/48.

120. *Yediot Aharonot*, on April 6 and 7 of 1988 (p. 9 and pp. 8–11, respectively) published interviews with Etai Be'ery, Isser Be'ery's son. According to Etai, Ben-Gurion himself approved, in writing, the creation of the "court" and the death sentence. This, of course, has no bearing on the case itself. Besides, if this account is true, then it only reflects on Ben-Gurion's integrity in willing to admit publicly a possible mistake. Furthermore, and this is much more serious, Etai claimed that his father had told him that he had certain "information," which Isser Be'ery never revealed, which supposedly may have proved that Tubianski was, in fact, a traitor. That is, Etai implies that while Tubianski who was cleared of all the charges of treason and espionage, was in fact guilty—Isser Be'ery who was found guilty in the killing of Tubianski, WAS in fact not guilty. A serious, however totally unfounded, accusation. According to Etai, his father refused to reveal the information so as not to hurt Tubianski's innocent family. Supposedly, that was the reason that Isser Be'ery took the full responsibility upon himself. Finally, Etai hints that although his father asked to have a trial before a closed military court, his request was denied and he was put before an

open civilian court. That, according to Etai, caused his father not to expose all the information he had because his father was anxious not to hurt either Ben-Gurion or what he saw as the security of Israel.

I tend to doubt this account. First, why was Be'ery willing not to hurt Tubianski's family but hurt his own family and reputation? Second, Be'ery was involved in some of ugliest affairs in the history of Israel; For example, the execution of Ali Qassem (see chapter 9); fabricating telegrams which were intended to criminalize Haifa's mayor— Abba Hushi; ordering the unjustified arrest and torture of Yehuda ("Jule") Amster in May of 1948 (see Bar-Zohar 1970:32–38; Black and Morris 1991:58–61; Nevo 1988a and 1988b; Harel 1989:138–160; Raviv and Melman 1990:23–25). Isser Be'ery apparently had very few inhibitions in lying for various manipulations which he saw as justified. Thus, the integrity and trustworthiness of Isser Be'ery's accounts are suspicious and questionable, to say the least. Third, I very much doubt the very existence of a definite (albeit "secret" and/or "hidden") "information" which could "prove" Tubianski's guilt. We must remember that Be'ery was found guilty in court, after a long investigation and trial. To "fish" and hint that there was a secret information which could, perhaps, "clear" Be'ery is a claim which can not be taken too seriously. Fourth, Be'ery was put once before a closed military court (in the case of killing Ali Kasem [see chap. 9] in the part on the Israeli Army), and was found guilty.

As head of military intelligence, Isser Be'ery was probably very sure about what he was doing, and felt a deep commitment to Ben-Gurion, then Israel's prime minister. He must have been extremely zealous—in his own way—for what he saw as the security needs of the emerging state of Israel. The combination of the authority Be'ery enjoyed in 1948 as head of military intelligence, the chaotic social and political conditions which prevailed, as well as his ruthless personality, helped Be'ery into committing some very tragic and fatal mistakes.

The April 1988 public exposure was a gambit which probably constituted an attempt on Be'ery's son's part to try to cleanse the memory of his father. This 1988 attempt was not the first one. Already in 1964 Etai tried to "pull" a similar plan (see Bar-Zohar 1970:39–45). The "dripping" of partial information by Etai did not, of course, "solve" any riddle and only helped to create an explicit and intentional confusion. Etai consistently refused to present the "documents" his father supposedly "left" him, hence one was left with a simple choice: either believe Etai or not. I chose the latter alternative. During the course of this research I have become very suspicious of those interested parties who "drip" unsubstantiated and supposedly secret information aimed to change, in some major way, particular historiographies (for a similar stand see Tzachor's article in *Al Hamishmar* [Chotam supplement], April 15, 1988, pp. 20–21 [Hebrew]).

121. There are some very good and unanswered questions about the nature of Bernadotte's dealings with the Nazis. Some researchers raised the possibility (or accusation) that he even was anti-semitic (e.g., Trevor Roper or Nadel). However, this accusation has become very problematic, and may be based on false documentation. See Amitzur, 1989:25–47.

122. General Assembly resolution 186 [S–2], adopted by a vote of 31 to 7 with 16 abstentions.

123. For example, see Avituv 1986; *Ha'aretz*, July 5, 1948, p. 1; see also Tzameret 1988.

124. In Bernadotte's place the UN appointed Ralph Bunche (see *Ha'aretz*, September 19, 1948, pp. 1–2. See also news and evaluations in the following days in the same newspaper).

125. There is less consensus as to who was/were the rest, if any. It seems that an anonymous person whose code name was "Gingi" ("the red") was there too. The following names were mentioned in the past in connection with the assassination (one of the names may be "Gingi"): Shmuel Rosenblum (who was probably the person in whose home four of the assassins were hidden for three or four days after the assassination), David Effratti and Yitzhak Markowitz.

126. It is possible that another member of Lehi, Shmuel Rosenbloom, may have also joined the group of assassins. See Avituv 1988.

127. See also Kanaan and Margalit 1968; Persson 1979:208–209; Avituv 1986; 1988; Heaps 1969:112–115; Israeli 1986; Stanger 1988.

128. The act itself was passed by "Moetzet Ha'am" ("The People's Council") only on September 23, 1948.

129. See Harel 1985:14–48; 1987:193–205 and the daily coverage in *Ha'aretz* from December 6, 1948 till January 20, 1949 and February 11, 1949, p. 1 and February 13, 1949, p. 4.

130. See also another interview with Heller, by Yoram Harpaz, in *Kol Ha'ir*, October 7, 1988 (vol. 526, pp. 33–34, 62 [Hebrew]), and Heller's retraction/correction/apology a week later in *Kol Ha'ir*, October 14, 1988 (vol. 527, p. 8).

131. This particular case constitutes an illustrative part of my paper: "Criminalization and Deviantization As Properties of The Social Order," the *Sociological Review*, 1992, vol. 40 (1):73–108.

CHAPTER EIGHT: POLITICAL ASSASSINATIONS BY JEWS IN ISRAEL BETWEEN 1949–1980

1. See *Ha'aretz*, September 7, 1953, p. 1; September 9, 1953, p. 4; September 22, 1953, p. 4 and October 4, 1953, p. 4.

2. See newspaper coverage during the months of July–September 1952.

3. For example, see Yevin 1986:7–8; see also Yellin-Mor 1974:59–60.

4. For some background materials on the group see Gretz and Weisbroad (1986); Ratosh (1976) and Shavit (1984).

5. A.A., on August 8, 1986 in Jerusalem.

6. See Braham 1981; Hilberg 1985, vol. 2:796–868; Laqueur 1980.

7. For example, see Ayalon 1980; Rosenfeld 1955; Keren 1978:187–238; Hecht 1970; Prat 1955; Segev 1991:239–303.

8. See *Ma'ariv*, March 12, 1968, p. 7 and the verdict in criminal file number 799/67, Tel Aviv, p. 188–192.

9. See *Ha'aretz*, September 9, 1968, p. 7 and September 26, 1968, p. 10 as well as the appeal itself, Criminal Appeal no. 255/68, pp. 427–441.

10. Examining the coverage of the daily newspapers at the time of the incident and at the time of the trial illustrates this very vividly.

11. See *Ha'aretz*, December 19, 1975, p. 1, December 21, 1975, p. 8, December 23, 1975, p. 4, 11, and December 31, 1975, p. 3; *Haolam Haze*, December 24, 1975, p. 16–17, 20–21, 28; and December 31, 1975, p. 17; *Ha'aretz*, January 1, 1976, p. 3.

12. It is virtually impossible to give a detailed account of the complex phenomenon of Gush Emunim here. For recent and general descriptions of the development of Gush Emunim see Aran 1986; 1987; Weisburd 1989. For a discussion of Gush Emunim with a primer on the Jewish Underground see Sprinzak 1986; Gal-Or 1990; see also Cromer 1988.

13. See Karaim 1982; IDF Spokesman 1982; see also *Ha'aretz*, January 18, 1980, p. 1; May 16, pp. 24–25; June 3, p. 3; July 7, p. 14; Segal 1987:83–95.

14. See Black and Morris 1991:348–360.

15. Despite our request, the Israeli prison service refused to let us interview members of the "underground" who, at the time of gathering data for the research, were still in prison. By December 1990 all members of the "Jewish underground" were released from prison (e.g., see *Yediot Aharonot*, December 14, 1990 [front page] and it's December 22, 1990 weekly magazine, pp. 8, 9–10, 62).

CHAPTER NINE: POLITICAL EXECUTIONS

1. For example, see Bar-Zohar 1972; Black and Morris 1991; Deacon 1977; Eisenberg, Dan and Landau 1978; Hoy and Ostrovsky 1990; Laqueur 1985:220–224; Raviv and Melman 1990; Rosner 1987; Steven 1980.

2. For example, see Bar-Zohar and Haber 1984:23–80; Niv, vol. 6:47; S.T.H., vol. 3, part 2:1561–1562.

3. Livni 1987:99, 296–297; Bar-Zohar and Haber 1984:82–83; Niv, vol. 6:221–222; Talmi 1979.

4. *Ma'ariv*, January 1, 1989, supplement, pp. 10–13; *Yediot Aharonot*, January 1, 1989, p. 2. According to Dagan (1989:29), Zidon, who was the pilot of the Israeli interception plane, identified the wrong airplane and by mistake shot the escort airplane which only had twelve low ranking officers and four journalists.

5. Meir Har-Zion (1968) himself was involved in a blood-revenge affair. In December of 1958, his seventeen-year-old sister—Shoshana—and her eighteen-year-old boyfriend—Oded Vegmeister—were on a trip from Ein Gedi to Jerusalem. They disappeared and for a month no one knew where they had disappeared to. It turned out that along the trip they were attacked, cruelly abused and later murdered by Bedouins. About two months after the incident, in 1959, Meir Har-Zion, then in the Israeli paratrooper units, with three friends, crossed the border to Jordan, kidnaped six Bedouins from the tribe where Shoshana's and Oded's killers came from. They killed five as a "blood revenge" and sent the sixth back to tell the story (some other versions state that they kidnaped only five and killed four).

6. *Ha'aretz*, July 22, 1956, p. 1 and July 23, 1956, p. 1; Argaman 1991:16–30; Avneri, no date:208–213; Deacon 1977:245–246; Steven 1980:107–112; Granot 1981:51–53; Bar-Zohar and Haber 1984:142–149; Black and Morris 1991:123–125.

7. For a shot description of the "Sinai Campaign" see e.g., Haber and Schiff 1976:334–337, 361.

8. See Haber and Schiff 1976:289–290; Deacon 1977:246–247; Steven 1980:158–194; Bar-Zohar and Haber 1984:147–148; Harel 1982; Bar-Zohar 1965; Eisenberg, Dan, and Landau 1978:134–157; Lotz 1970; Avneri 1978; Carmi and Lotz 1978; Raviv and Melman 1990:122–124; Black and Morris 1991:192–202.

9. See Jonas 1984:191–207; Bar-Zohar and Haber 1984:170–180; Deacon 1977:268–283; Steven 1980:327–332; *The New York Times*, April 11, 1973, p. 14; Milshtein 1987:1613–1637. Raviv and Melman (1990:188–189) imply that the main reason for the operation was a vengeance for the massacre of the Israeli athletes by PLO members during the 1972 Munich Olympic games.

10. Hoy and Ostrovsky imply that Golda Meir "signed death warrants for about thirty-five known Black September terrorists" (1990:179). Raviv and Melman (1990:185–186) imply that Golda Meir with a secret cabinet committee ("committee x"—chaired by Golda Meir and Moshe Dayan) made the actual decision to avenge the Munich massacre. However, giving a full corroborated list of names, dates and methods is difficult. The names of the victims mentioned by most public sources are Abu Daud, Mahmoud Hamshari, Wael Zwaiter, Dr. Baril al-Kubaisi, Dr. Waddi Haddad, Hussein Abad al-Chir, Mohammed Boudia, Kamal Nasser, Mahmoud Yussuf Najjer. How accurate is this list is difficult to determine. It is possible that Dr. al-Kubaisi was a member of another terrorist organization and not "Black September." If so, then it is possible that the authorization given to execute leaders of Black September was used to execute members of other terrorist organizations who were considered dangerous.

11. See Bar-Zohar and Haber 1984; Dobson 1974; Tinnin and Christensen 1977; Deacon 1977:244–267; Steven 1980:313–333; Jonas 1984; Posner 1987:287–289; Hoy and Ostrovsky 1990; Black and Morris 1991:267–275.

12. Hoy and Ostrovsky (1990:206) imply that the tragic misidentification of Bushiki in Lillehammer as Salame was not an innocent mistake. According to this version, the Mossad was deliberately led to this misidentification by Salame's agents who penetrated the Mossad. Hoy and Ostrovsky imply that the purpose of this plot was to present the Mossad and Israel in a bad and problematic light. For contemporary newspaper coverage of this fiasco see *Ma'ariv*, January 15, 1974, p. 18; see also *Yediot Aharonot* of 1974, of January 7, p. 1; January 1, p. 3

and January 13, p. 2). See also Bar-Zohar and Haber 1984:192–200; Steven 1980:339–351; Tinnin and Christensen 1977; Raviv and Melman 1990:189–192; Black and Morris 1991:275–277.

13. Posner states that Salame "was chief of intelligence for the PLO and as such, in charge of contacts with the United States which agreed only to communicate with that organization at CIA level." Consequently, Posner raises the possibility that Salame was executed not because of what he calls "romantic revenge," but because "he was opening a 'back channel' to Washington." This possibility does not make much sense. If Israel was to use this as a reason for executions, we could expect *many* more executions. Posner himself is aware of this and states indeed that while he does not believe in the "romantic vengeance" theory, Salame's assassination was "designed to both undermine the PLO infrastructure and serve as a warning to other terrorist leaders that there would be a price for their attacks against Jews" (1987:287–288). This statement, in itself, admits some vengeance. Posner's "romantic" vengeance probably does not exist, but vengeance as such, pure and simple, does exist and probably *was* the motivating force behind Salame's execution. See also Bar-Zohar and Haber 1984:214–220; Finkelston 1979; Granot 1979; Dan 1979; Steven 1980:352–354; *The New York Times*, January 23, 1979, front page; Raviv and Melman 1990:191–192.

14. See *Yediot Aharonot* and *Ha'aretz* from April 17, 1988; *Yediot Aharonot* from April 19, 1988; *Time*, April 25, 1988, pp. 10–11.

15. See *New York Times*, April 19, 1988, p. 1; *Yediot Aharonot* and *Ha'aretz* from April 22, 1988; *The Sunday Times*, April 24, 1988, p. A4; *Time*, May 2, 1988, pp. 18–20.

16. Kidon can be translated to mean bayonet (in slang Hebrew it also means the handles of bicycles).

17. For more on "Committee X" see Raviv and Melman 1990:185–186.

18. On June 21, 1991 the Israeli State controlled television, in its Friday night prime time news show, broadcasted a program on top secret Israeli units. Soldiers in these units were reported to be impersonating Arabs (including women) and, under this guise, arresting key Arab activists in the Intifada (see *Yediot Aharonot*, June 23, 1991, front page and inner pages). There were also hints that soldiers in these units were responsible for killing a few selected Arab activists (activities

attributed to units called "Duvdevan" [meaning in Hebrew "cherry"] and "Shimshon"). The above public exposure, however, emphasized that these soldiers were involved in arrests and not executions. According to Arab sources these camouflaged units executed forty-seven Palestinians (twenty-six in 1989, eleven in 1990, and ten between January and May 1991. See *Yediot Aharonot,* June 26, 1991, p. 5. These figures are attributed to the Department of Human Rights from the Center for Arab Studies, headed by Faisal Husseini. For a dissenting view on these figures see Nachum Barnea: "How to sell fear," *Yediot Aharonot,* June 28, 1991, pp. 4–5 [Hebrew]). On November 20, 1991 (p. 9) *Ma'ariv* told its readers that a commander of 'Shimshon" was accused in a military court of giving orders that authorized the killing of an Arab in a refugee camp on October 4, 1989 (the first Israeli officer that had to face such a charge since the Intifada began). The man denied all the accusations against him. According to *Ma'ariv*'s headline, he stated explicitly that "Shimshon" was not an "elimination unit" and was not above the law.

CHAPTER TEN: POLITICAL ASSASSINATIONS, TERROR, AND TANGENIAL CASES

1. S.T.H., vol. 3, part 2:818–899; Niv, vol. 4:278–281. See notes 63 and 91 in chap. 7.

2. Haber and Schiff 1976:139–140; S.T.H., vol. 3, part 2:1546–1548; Niv, vol. 6:79–94; Begin 1961:274–277.

3. *Ha'aretz,* June 11, 1939, p. 1; Eliav 1983:106–108; Niv, vol. 2:244.

4. Niv, vol. 3:256; Eliav 1983:116–118; *Ha'aretz,* August 3, 1939, p. 1 and August 4, 1939, p. 1.

5. See *Ha'aretz,* October 6, 1952, p. 1; *Ha'aretz,* October 7, 1952, p. 4 and October 8, p. 4.

6. See *Ha'aretz,* December 15, 1952 p. 4; *Ma'ariv,* September 9, 1956, p. 8; Segev 1980; Shilanski 1977:9–32.

7. Duek surfaced again in the summer of 1988, when he established a new political party—Tarshish—and tried to be elected to the twelfth Knesset in the general elections which took place in Israel on November 1, 1988. He failed. Only 1,654 people voted for him, which constituted 0.07% of the votes for those elections (see *Yediot Aharonot,* October 28, p. 9 and November 6, p. 2).

8. See Haber and Schiff 1976:344–345; *Ha'aretz*, June 14, 1948, p. 1; *Davar*, March 22, 1983, p. 3 and 30–33; S.T.H., vol. 3, part 2:1482–1484s; Berkman 1965. A 1966 movie, *Cast a Giant Shadow,* was made on Stone's life.

9. During his trial, Avrushmi kept very quiet, did not admit anything. In March 1990, Avrushmi wrote to the president of Israel (Haim Herzog) asking for clemency. In his letter, he admitted the act, and explained it as a result of the public instigation ("hasata") he was exposed to from the right against the left. Avrushmi attributed his act of throwing a hand grenade into a "peace now" demonstration to his conviction, at that time, that the people in the left were endangering the state of Israel. He claimed that his agitated state of mind which led to his act, was induced by instigation of various leaders from the Israeli right. He expressed deep Harata (regret, remorse) and his realization that he was wrong. He also wrote to parliament member Yossi Sarid (from Ratz party), a prominent spokesman for what is considered the "left" in Israel expressing the same thoughts, and asking for Sarid's forgiveness and help. Sarid wrote him back that Avrushmi had no authority to ask forgiveness, and he—Sarid—had no authority to pardon him. Sarid stated that "I have no authority like this, and I do not have the strength to forgive and forget" (p. 5). See *Yediot Aharonot*, April 9, 1990, pp. 4–5.

10. We made many efforts to try and get more information—to no avail. The archives of the Israeli government do not have a police file on Rosa Beizer nor is the case known to the Israeli police headquarters. After many efforts we managed to find a family relative of her in Jerusalem. At first, she agreed to be interviewed but two days later decided that she was not interested in giving us an interview. I tend to accept Shpillman's account, which makes the case even stranger.

11. Water is a precious resource in the Middle East, and a potential source for explosive regional conflicts. In October of 1953, U.S. President Dwight David Eisenhower appointed Erik Johnston as a water mediator between Israel, Lebanon, Jordan, and Syria. His mediation was focused on suggestions on how to divide the water from the river Jordan among the four countries. He submitted a detailed plan in February 1955. The United States was supposed to provide financial aid for this joint, and agreed upon, division of water. Eventually, the Arab countries rejected the plan on principle grounds because they did not want to be part of a plan in which Israel was a partner (see, Haber and Schiff 1976:112–113).

CHAPTER ELEVEN: THE CRIMINOLOGICAL PATTERN OF POLITICAL ASSASSINATIONS IN A COMPARATIVE PERSPECTIVE

1. For the general description of the pattern called "Criminal Homicide" consult Barlow 1984:135–164; Bonn 1984:187–191; Conklin 1986; Eitzen and Timmer 1985:132–155; Luckenbill 1977; Reid 1982:214–219; Sanders 1983:230–253; Sykes 1978:130–135; Thio 1988:107–133; Von Hentig 1948; Wolfgang 1957; 1958; Wolfgang and Ferracuti 1967.

2. Only two studies were done on homicide in Israel. Both are very old. One was Landau et al., in 1974, the other by Zonshein's in 1976. Zonshein's work is the last research on murder and killing events in Israel. This research focused on 129 units of such events in the central area of Israel between 1966–1974. The pattern of homicide which emerges from the study is similar—in broad lines—to the pattern described here. There were, however, a few cultural variations. Thus, drinking was then a-typical in Israeli culture. While 11% of the offenders (and 4% of the victims) were females, males were found to be much more active in killing and murder. About 78% of the events involved Jews; 56% of the killers were Sefardi and 21% Ashkenasi. There was a clear tendency for killers and victims to be of the same ethnic group. Generally, killers had a higher level of education than the level of education of the equivalent group in the general population. Guns and knives were the typical murder weapons, but beating the victim to death was very common too (especially for older victims). No significant dispersion in time of day, or day was found. Most events occurred in an urban area, killer and victim typically knew each other, and the crime was committed as part of committing other crimes. It is clearly the case that the age of the above two studies, in a rapidly changing cultural matrix, makes meaningful comparisons very difficult. Furthermore, Zonshein points out—and I agree—that the Israeli complex culture in the late 1960s and early 1970s was so different than potentially similar other Western cultures, that making a cross cultural comparison may be doomed to fail even before making it.

CHAPTER TWELVE: POLITICAL ASSASSINATIONS AS RHETORICAL DEVICES: PATTERNS, REASONS, AND INTERPRETATIONS

1. See n. 5.

2. From a different angle, Wagner-Pacifici's most impressive work

(1986) also interpreted the kidnapping and killing of Italian Aldo Moro within the context of a total social structure, history and politics—all in a dramaturgical perspective.

3. For a somewhat similar process see Ben-Yehuda 1987.

4. For example, the Etzel and Lehi action in the village of Dir Yassin on April 9, 1948, when some two hundred fifty Arab villagers were killed; or the bomb planted in July 22, 1946 by the Etzel in the King David Hotel in Jerusalem, causing the death of eighty and wounding forty (see n. 63 and 91 in chap. 7).

5. The estimation is that since the "Intifada" began in 1987 and until the summer of 1990 around two hundred Arabs were assassinated by other Arabs (the number rose to 310 in the winter of 1991. See *The Globe and Mail* [Canada], February 28, 1991, p. A18) on charges "collaboration" or "cooperation" (some of the victims were interrogated and tortured before they were killed), around 573 others were severely beaten and/or targeted for unsuccessful assassinations, and there may have been a few cases of brutal group rape (Shalev 1990; Amnesty International report of November 1989; Schiff and Ya'ari 1990; Shaked, Broida, and Regev 1990).

6. I am deeply grateful for the help and guidance of Prof. Berachyahu Lifshitz, from the faculty of law, Hebrew University, whose assistance in this particular issue was indispensable.

7. See Eldad's article in *Yediot Aharonot*, April 22, 1988, p. 15 (as well as his appearance in April 1990 in the Israeli Television ("This is Your Life" program).

APPENDIX

INTRODUCTION

This appendix presents four diagrams which summarize, in a focused and condensed form, the cases which were discussed in previous chapters. Diagram AP–1 corresponds to chapter 5. Obviously, the political assassinations which were carried out by the Sicariis, the NOKMIM and by Jewish defense groups during World War II could not be fit into the diagram. Diagram AP–2 corresponds to chapter 6; diagram AP–3 corresponds to chapter 7, and diagram AP–4 to chapter 8.

The following codes were used in the diagrams: asterisk (*) means Jewish; The sign (=) was used in diagrams AP–2, AP–3, and AP–4 (on the left side of the case) whenever the case was not used in any further statistical analysis for reasons explained in each case separately in the previous chapters. None of the cases in diagram AP–1 was used in the statistical analysis. The numbers of the cases, in each diagram, correspond fully to the numbers of the cases as they appear in the different chapters. This was done explicitly so as not to confuse the consistency in numbering between this appendix and the chapters on which it is based.

DIAGRAM AP-1
PRE-ISRAEL EUROPE
(CHAPTER 5)

Case No.	Date	Method/ Weapon	Victim(s)	Assassin(s)	"Reason" (Suspicion) Given for Act
A	May 18, 1902	hand gun	von Val —unsuccessful	*Hirsch Lekert, a member in a small group of Bund members	flogging Jewish prisoners following a political demonstration
B	June 4, 1903	knife	Pavolaki Krushevan —unsuccessful	*Pinhas Dashewski (not clear whether a member of a Jewish defense group)	initiator of the Kishinov Pogrom
C	Between 1903– 1905	guns	3 victims: 1. Zubatov (planning) 2. Fleve (planning) 3. Akimov	*Mania Shochat (member in different defense groups)	either as a revenge, or to prevent a dangerous situation for the group.
D	May 25, 1926	hand gun	Simon Peteliura	*Shalom Schwarzbard	responsible for persecutions of Jews in Ukraine

DIAGRAM AP-1 (Continued)

Case No.	Date	Method/ Weapon	Victim(s)	Assassin(s)	"Reason" (Suspicion) Given for Act
E	May 27, 1926	gun shooting	The Ataman Askilko	*Yankoviak, Feldman and Blai	to prevent persecutions of Jews
F	February 4, 1936	hand gun	Wilhelm Gustloff	*David Frankfurter	revenge for the Nazi "treatment" of Jews; propaganda by deed; prevent Nazi influence
G	November 7, 1938	hand gun	Ernst von Rath	*Herschel Feibel Grynszpan	revenge for the Nazi "treatment" of Jews

DIAGRAM AP-2
FROM 1892 TILL 1918
(CHAPTER 6)

Case No.	Date	Method/ Weapon	Victim(s)	Assassin(s)	"Reason" (Suspicion) Given for Act
1	Between 1892–1899	hand gun	*Eliahu Scheid —unsuccessful	Gedalia Vilbuschevitz	corruption, abuse of funds.
2	Between 1916–1917	gun shooting	Aref El-Arsan	David Tidhar and Joshua Levi	by "order" from Dizengof, an enemy
3	October 9, 1917	gun shooting	*Joseph Lishansky	HASHOMER	Dangerous to HASHOMER & Yishuv

DIAGRAM AP–3
FROM 1919 TO 1948
(CHAPTER 7)

Case No.	Date	Method/ Weapon	Victim(s)	Assassin(s)	"Reason" (Suspicion) Given for Act
4	Spring 1920	—	Sir Ronald Storrs —planned	HASHOMER	held responsible for Arab riots in Jerusalem in 1920
5	January 17, 1923	gun shooting	Tufik Bay	Lukatcher—from the "kibbutz" of GDUD HAAVODA and HASHOMER	held responsible for murdering of Jews in Beit Haolot (1921)
6	June 30, 1924	gun shooting	*Dr. Yaacov Israel De Hahn	Tehomy[?] from the HAGANA, or a group within it	was perceived as dangerous to the emerging new state
7	=June 16, 1933	gun shooting	*Dr. Haim Arlosoroff	Not established	—
8	1933 (?)	gun shooting	King Abdalla (Jordan) —planned	Raia Berman (Regev) formerly of "Brit Habirionim"	was perceived as a dangerous political enemy

DIAGRAM AP-3 (Continued)

Case No.	Date	Method/ Weapon	Victim(s)	Assassin(s)	"Reason" (Suspicion) Given for Act
9	September 6 1937	Drowning[?]	*Zvi (Ben-Amram) Frenkel	ETZEL	fear of squealing once arrested.
10	1939	—	Robert Frier Jardine —preplanned	Berl Katzenelson demanded; Ben-Gurion vetoed. (PUM?)	dangerous political enemy
11	1939	—	The Arab Mufti Haj Amin Al-Husseini. —preplanned	Berl Katzenelson demanded; Ben-Gurion vetoed. (PUM?)	dangerous political enemy
12	1939	—	*Moshe Rotstein —unsuccessful	ETZEL	suspected as a British provocateur
13	March 15, 1939	hand grenade	Adolf Hitler —unsuccessful	Itzhak Shimkin	Dangerous for Jewish existence
14	May 3, 1939	gun shooting	*Joseph Brawerman	ETZEL	cooperation with British intelligence
15	May 29, 1939	gun shooting	*Arieh Polonski	ETZEL	cooperation with British intelligence

DIAGRAM AP-3 (Continued)

Case No.	Date	Method/ Weapon	Victim(s)	Assassin(s)	"Reason" (Suspicion) Given for Act
16	June 22, 1939	gun shooting	*Valentin Back	ETZEL	betrayed a BEITAR/ ETZEL member to British
17	August 18, 1939	gun shooting	*Gordon —unsuccessful	ETZEL	cooperation with British dangerous to ETZEL
18	August 26, 1939	electric mine	Ralf Cairns	ETZEL	torturing prisoners
19	October 1939	gun shooting	*Baruch Weinshall	HAGANA in Haifa (PUM)	helped British intelligence against Jewish immigration; killed HAGANA man
20	January– February (?) 1940	gun shooting	*Oscar Opler	HAGANA	squealed to British on illegal secret armouries in Mishmar Hashlosha (and Ben-Shemen)
21	May 3, 1940	gun shooting	*Moshe Savtani	HAGANA	cooperation with British, squealer

DIAGRAM AP–3 (Continued)

Case No.	Date	Method/ Weapon	Victim(s)	Assassin(s)	"Reason" (Suspicion) Given for Act
22	May 12, 1940	gun shooting	*Itzhak Sharanski	HAGANA	cooperation with British, squealer
23	June 25, 1940	gun shooting	*Baruch Manfeld	HAGANA	cooperation with British, squealer
24	July 3, 1940	gun shooting	*Walter Strauss	HAGANA	squealed to British on illegal secret armoury in Gan-Yavne
25	May 16, 1941	gun shooting	*Michael Waksman	ETZEL	cooperation with British
26	November 16, 1941	gun shooting	*Ya'acov Soffioff	LEHI	cooperation with British, squealing
27	1941	a four kilogram bomb	*Major Shlomo Schiff —unsuccessful	ETZEL	cooperation with British
28	January 18, 1942	probably shooting	*Binyamin Zerony —planning	LEHI	treason

DIAGRAM AP–3 (Continued)

Case No.	Date	Method/ Weapon	Victim(s)	Assassin(s)	"Reason" (Suspicion) Given for Act
29	January 18, 1942	—	Oliver Lyttelton —planning	LEHI	propaganda by deed
30	January 20, 1942	bomb	*Major Shlomo Schiff *Inspector Nachum Goldman *Inspector Dichter (wounded) Inspector Turton	LEHI	cooperation with British
31	April 22, 1942	bomb in car	Michael Joseph McConnel —unsuccessful	LEHI	revenge for Yair's killing; warning to British
32	April 22, 1942	bomb	Alan Saunders —unsuccessful	LEHI	revenge for Yair's killing
33	January 20, to May 1, 1942	mines	Jeffrey Morton —3 or 4 unsuccessful attempts	LEHI	dangerous for underground; killed Stern

DIAGRAM AP-3 (Continued)

Case No.	Date	Method/ Weapon	Victim(s)	Assassin(s)	"Reason" (Suspicion) Given for Act
34	May 1942	mines	*Itzhak Zelnik —preplanned (?)	LEHI	traitor; gave information to British
35	August 21, 1942	gun shooting	*Moshe Yaacov Marcus	HAGANA	cooperation with British, squealer
36	Autumn 1943	—	Kasem Taubash	HAGANA/ PALMACH	revenge for killing Alexander Zeid; propaganda by deed
37	February 25, 1943	gun shooting	*Avraham Wilenchik	LEHI	treason, wanted to leave LEHI
38	Summer 1943 (?)	gun shooting	*Eliahu Giladi	LEHI	dangerous to LEHI and to other leaders
39	September 3, 1943	gun shooting	*Israel Pritzker	LEHI	traitor, gave names to British
40	March 13, 1944	gun shooting	*Zeev Falsh	LEHI	undercover British intelligence agent

DIAGRAM AP-3 (*Continued*)

Case No.	Date	Method/ Weapon	Victim(s)	Assassin(s)	"Reason" (Suspicion) Given for Act
41	April 10, 1944	submachine gun	Major Y. P. W. Ford —unsuccessful	LEHI	revenge for killing LEHI's Yerachmiel Aharonson in Tel Aviv by British on March 19
42	March– May 1944	—	*Ya'acov Hilewitz —planned	ETZEL	treason, betrayal to British
43	May 10, 1944	gun shooting	*Chaim Gotowitz	LEHI	undercover British intelligence agent
44	Winter 1944	rifle	*Ephraim Illin —unsuccessful	LEHI	cooperation with British
45	2 attempts: June 1941 September 29, 1944	probably gun shots hand guns	T. I. Wilkin —unsuccessful —successful	LEHI	dangerous to LEHI; tortured prisoners; involved in Stern's killing
46	October– December 1944	probably gun shots	Sir John Shaw —planned	LEHI	propaganda by deed

DIAGRAM AP-3 (*Continued*)

Case No.	Date	Method/ Weapon	Victim(s)	Assassin(s)	"Reason" (Suspicion) Given for Act
47	8 attempts:		Sir Harold MacMichael	LEHI	held responsible for: sinking *Struma* and death of its 800 Jewish refugees; the *Patria* tragic affair;blocking entrance of tormented European Jewish refugees into Palestine-Israel; anti-Jewish, anti-Zionist
	–March 1941	gun, knife	–planning		
	–November 1943	mine	–planned kidnapping	ETZEL	
	–February 1944	submachine gun	–unsuccessful		
	–February 1944	submachine gun	–unsuccessful		
	–February 1944	grenade submachine guns,	–unsuccessful		
	—1944	grenades	–unsuccessful		
	—1944	hand gun	–unsuccessful		
	–August 8, 1944	grenades, submachine guns	–unsuccessful (wounded)		

DIAGRAM AP–3 (*Continued*)

Case No.	Date	Victim(s)	Method/ Weapon	Assassin(s)	"Reason" (Suspicion) Given for Act
48	October 4, 1944	*Wolf Fiedler	gun shooting	ETZEL	giving information to British
49	November 6, 1944	Baron Walter Edward Guinnes Moyne	gun shooting	LEHI	dangerous to the emerging Jewish State; propaganda by deed
50	August 20 1945	*Joseph Davidesku	gun shooting	LEHI	treason, gave his contact to British
51	6 attempts: 1945 to 1948	Ernest Bevin —preplanning —planning —unsuccessful	bombs, gun shots	LEHI	dangerous anti-zionist, anti-Jewish positions
52	January–March 1946	*Binyamin Kurfirst	handgun shooting	HAGANA/ PALMACH	British agent—tried to frame a kibbutz
53	February 15, 1946	Raymond Cafferata —unsuccessful	gun shooting, bomb	ETZEL and LEHI	dangerous persecuter of underground
54	March 22, 1946	Guthelf Wagner	gun shooting	HAGANA/ PALMACH	to help expel Germans from Israel

DIAGRAM AP-3 (Continued)

Case No.	Date	Method/ Weapon	Victim(s)	Assassin(s)	"Reason" (Suspicion) Given for Act
55	May 1946	bomb in his car	Mufti-Haj Amin Al Husseini —planning	LEHI	dangerous political enemy, revenge
56	September 9, 1946	hand gun shooting	T. G. Martin	LEHI	dangerous to underground
57	December 24, 1946	—	*Israel Lewin	LEHI	helped British against ALIA (Jewish immigration), blackmail
58	October 17, 1946	gun shooting	William H. Bruce	HAGANA/ PALMACH (Mista'arvim)	tortured prisoners from the underground (Hagana/Palmach)
59	November 19, 1946	gun shooting	*Moshe Ben-Betzalel	LEHI	cooperation with British intelligence
60	August 1946 to 1947	mine; booby-trapped stroller; 7 or 8 planned attempts; shooting; explosive envelope	Lieutenant General Sir Evelyn U. Barker	LEHI-ETZEL	projecting dangerous anti-semitic position

DIAGRAM AP-3 (Continued)

Case No.	Date	Method/ Weapon	Victim(s)	Assassin(s)	"Reason" (Suspicion) Given for Act
61	March 8, 1947	gun shooting	*Kadia Mizrahi	ETZEL	cooperation with British intelligence
62	March 8, 1947	gun shooting	*Michael Ernest Schnell	LEHI	traitor, squealer
63	March 21, 1947	gun shooting	*Leon Mashiach	ETZEL	betrayed ETZEL for money
64	March 27, 1947	—	*Sergeant Weighorn —unsuccessful	LEHI	cooperation with British intelligence
65	April 3, 1947	gun shooting	*Joseph Frumkin	LEHI	cooperation with British intelligence
66	3 attempts:		General Sir Gordon MacMillan	LEHI	anti-zionist; authorizing executions of ETZEL & LEHI members
	-April 1947	mine	—unsuccessful		
	-June 30, 1947	mine	—unsuccessful		
	-July 3 or 4, 1947	mine	—unsuccessful		
67	April 26, 1947	submachine gun	A. A. Conquest	LEHI	war crimes against underground

DIAGRAM AP-3 (Continued)

Case No.	Date	Method/ Weapon	Victim(s)	Assassin(s)	"Reason" (Suspicion) Given for Act
68	May 13, 1947	—	*Hans Reinhold ("Yanai") —unsuccessful	ETZEL	squealer to British intelligence
69	May 16, 1947	mine	*Max Schindler (badly wounded)	ETZEL	British officer, active against Jewish underground
70	3 attempts:		Sergeant Joseph Killy	LEHI	dangerous to the underground
	-July 23, 1947	mine	—unsuccessful		
	-August 10, 1947	gun shooting	—unsuccessful		
	-November 12, 1947	submachine gun	—unsuccessful (wounded)		
71	October 1947	gun shooting	*Yehoshua Zarfati	LEHI	cooperation with British intelligence
72	November 3, 1947	gun shooting	*Shalom Gurevitz	LEHI	Intelligence Sergeant active against underground

DIAGRAM AP–3 (Continued)

Case No.	Date	Method/ Weapon	Victim(s)	Assassin(s)	"Reason" (Suspicion) Given for Act
73	November 19, 1947	submachine gun	Shubaki's family; 4 died, 1 wounded	LEHI	cooperation with British; 5 LEHI members killed
74	=January 10–12, 1948	gun, knife	*Yedidia Segal	HAGANA (?)	not clear
75	January 15, 1948	hand-gun shooting	*Yehuda Arie Levi	LEHI	the victim wanted to "defect" to HAGANA
76	February 1, 1948	gun shooting	*Chaya Zeidenberg	LEHI	planned to put a bomb in Tel Aviv
77	February 19, 1948	automatic weapons	sheikh Nimer al-Khatib (wounded)	HAGANA/ PALMACH (Mista'arvim)	Poisonous anti-Jewish arab preacher and agitator
78	February– March 1948	probably shooting	Vitold Holianitzky	LEHI	espionage
79	February– March 1948	probably shooting	Stephen Arnold	LEHI	espionage
80	March 27, 1948	probably shooting	*Vera Duksova	LEHI	spied for the British

DIAGRAM AP-3 (*Continued*)

Case No.	Date	Method/ Weapon	Victim(s)	Assassin(s)	"Reason" (Suspicion) Given for Act
81	May 4, 1948	booby-trapped books by mail	Major Roy Farran —unsuccessful (brother opened envelope and was fatally wounded)	LEHI	revenge for torture and murder of a LEHI member: Alexander Rubowitz (16 years old) on May 6, 1947
82	June 30, 1948	firing squad	*Captain Meir Tubianski	Supposedly a field court of IDF. In fact a remnant of the HAGANA/SHAI	espionage
83	September 17, 1948	submachine gun	Count Folke Bernadotte	"Hazit Hamoledet" a LEHI operation	dangerous to the emerging state

DIAGRAM AP–4
FROM 1949 TO 1980
(CHAPTER 8)

Case No.	Method/ Date	Weapon	Victim(s)	Assassin(s)	"Reason" (Suspicion) Given for Act
84	March 27, 1952	bomb in a mail parcel	West German Chancellor Konrad Adenauer —unsuccessful	a group in France sympathetic to "Herut" and ETZEL	propaganda by deed
85	June 22, 1952	bomb	*Dov Pinkas —unsuccessful	Amos Keinan and Shealtiel Ben-Yair (?) (acquitted in court)	enforcing religious laws
86	March 3, 1957	gun shooting	*Rudolf Kasztner	Dan Shemer, Zeev Ekstein and Joseph Menkes	cooperation with with Nazis
87	=October 15, 1967	knife	*Parliament member Meir Vilner —unsuccessful (wounded)	Avraham Ben-Moshe (intent to kill was not proven in court)	representing the Russian oppression of Jews
88	November 1973	gun shooting	*Moshe Dayan —planned	Brigadier Shmuel Gonen (Gorodish)	"sacrificing" officers as responsible for the 1973 war

DIAGRAM AP–4 (Continued)

Case No.	Date	Method/ Weapon	Victim(s)	Assassin(s)	"Reason" (Suspicion) Given for Act
89	March 24, 1974	knife	*Uri Avneri —unsuccessful	Eliahu Galili	victim bothering him: planted microphones in his head; reading his thoughts
	December 18, 1975	knife			
90	Between 1979 and 1980	hand gun	Anwar Sadat and Saad Murtada —planning	Ze'ev-Miron Eltagar	revenge for his son's death in the 1973 Israel-Egypt war; propaganda by deed
91	=June 2, 1980	bombs	Basam Shaka, Karim Halaf, Tawil Ibrahim —unsuccessful (all three were wounded)	Jewish "underground" (accused denied intent to assassinate; court accepted claim)	members of the "Vaada Lehachvana Leumit"—a poisonous antizionist & anti-Jewish group

BIBLIOGRAPHY

Note: The names of the Hebrew Books are either translated into English by the author, or the English name of the book, if it appears in the book, are given in the list. Hebrew books are identified as such by (Hebrew) at the end of the reference.

Abel, Richard L., ed. 1982. *The Politics of Informal Justice*, 2 vol. New York: Academic Press.

Aberbach, Moses. 1985. "Josephus and His Critics—A Reassessment." *Midstream*, 31 (5):25–29.

Aharonson, Aharon. 1970. *The Diary of Aharon Aharonson 1916–1919*. Edited by Yoram Efrati, translated from French by Uri Keissarri. Tel Aviv: Karni (Hebrew).

Aharonson, Shlomo. 1988. "A New Light on the Season," *Al Hamishmar*, Chotam supplement, March 18, no. 12 (894):20–21 (Hebrew).

Ahimair, Joseph and Shmuel Shatzki. 1978. *We Are Sicariis*. Tel Aviv: Nitzanim (Hebrew).

Alexander, Yonah and Robert A. Kilmarx, ed. 1979. *Political Terrorism and Business*. New York: Praeger.

Alexander, Yonah and Alan O'day, eds. 1984. *Terrorism in Ireland*. London: Croom Helm.

Amitzur, Illan. 1989. *Bernadotte in Palestine, 1948*. London: Macmillan.

Amrami, Yoel. 1954. *Testimony of Ya'acov Meridor About his Activities in ETZEL between the Years 1934–1941*. Tel Aviv: Beit Jabotinsky (Hebrew).

Amrami, Ya'akov (Yoel). 1975. *Practical Bibliography*. Tel Aviv: Hadar (Hebrew).

Aran, Gideon. 1986. "From Religious Zionism to Zionist Religion," *Studies in Contemporary Jewry*, 2:116–143.

———. 1987. *From Religious Zionism to Zionist Religion. The Origins and Culture of Gush Emunim: A Messianic Movement in Modern Israel*. Ph.D. diss., Department of Sociology, Hebrew University (Hebrew).

Archer, Dane and Rosemary Gartner. 198: *Violence in Cross-National Perspective*. New Haven: Yale University Press.

Argaman, Joseph. 1991. *It was Top Secret*. Tel Aviv: Ministry of Defense (Hebrew).

Arnon-Ochana, Yuval. 1982. *Falachs in the Arab Revolt in Eretz Israel 1936–1939*, Tel Aviv: Tel Aviv University, Papirus (Hebrew).

Arzi, Oded. 1982. "'Hamiphal'—the history of a revolutionary cell in the intimate pioneer group and the case of De Hahn." *Katedra*, 22:173–200 (Hebrew).

Avidar, Joseph. 1970. *On the Road to Zahal—Memories*. Tel Aviv: Ma'arachot (Hebrew).

Avituv, Yaron. 1986. "Father took part in Bernadotte's assassination." *Kol Ha'ir* (Jerusalem), December 26, pp. 25–27, 29 (Hebrew).

———. 1988. "The Truth on Bernadotte's Assassination." *Kol Ha'ir* (Jerusalem), September 16, p. 19 (Hebrew).

Avi-Yonah, Michael and Zvi Beres, eds. 1983. *Society and Religion During the Period of the Second Temple*. Tel Aviv and Jerusalem: Alexander Peli Ltd. and Am Oved Ltd. (Hebrew).

Avner. 1959. *Memoirs of an Assassin*. Translated from the French by Burgo Partridge. London: Anthony Blond.

Avneri, Arieh. No date. *The Israeli Commando. A Short History of Israeli Commando—1950–1969*. Tel Aviv: Sifriat Madim (Hebrew).

Avneri, Arieh. 1978. *Lotz—The Spy on the Horse*. Tel Aviv: Y. Guttman (Hebrew).

Ayalon, Amos. 1980. *Timetable*. Jerusalem: Edanim Publishers, Yediot Aharonot Edition (Hebrew).

———. 1982. "Three Contemporary Heroes." *Ha'aretz*, February 19, p. 13 (Hebrew).

Banai, Ya'acov. 1958. *Anonymous Soldiers*. Tel Aviv: Hug Yedidim (Hebrew).

Bar-Elli, Gilead and David Heyd. 1986. "Can revenge be just or otherwise not justified?" *Theoria*, 21 (1–2):68–86.

Barlow, Hugh D. 1984. *Introduction To Criminology*. 3d ed. Boston: Little, Brown and Company.

Barnea, Nahum and Dany Rubinstein. 1982. "A-Profo the blood of your brother." *Davar*, March 3, p. 14 (Hebrew).

Bar-On, Mordechai. 1985. *Peace Now*. Tel Aviv: Hakibbutz Hameuchad (Hebrew).

Bar-Zohar, Michael. 1965. *Hunting the German Scientists*. Tel Aviv and Jerusalem: Schochen (Hebrew).

———. 1969. *The Avengers*. Tel Aviv: Lewin Epstein (Hebrew).

———. 1970. *Issar Harel and Israel's Security Services*. Jerusalem: Weidenfeld and Nicolson (Hebrew).

———. 1972. *Spies in the Promised Land*. London: Houghton Mifflin.

————— and Eitan Haber. 1984. *The Quest for the Red Prince*. Tel Aviv: Zmora, Bitan (Hebrew); (an English edition was published in 1983 by Weidenfeld and Nicolson, London).

Basok, Moshe. 1944. "Introduction." Pp. 3–8 in Leivich A.: *Hirsch Lekert: A Dramatical Poem*, translated by Basok M. Tel Aviv: Hakibbutz Hameuchad (Hebrew).

Bauer, Yehuda. 1966. *Diplomacy and Underground in Zionist Policy 1939–1945*. Merchavia: Sifriat Poalim (Hebrew).

Bauer, Yehuda. 1970. *Flight and Rescue: Bricha*. N.Y.: Random House.

—————. 1974. *The Escape*. Tel Aviv: Sifriat Poalim (Hebrew).

—————. 1982. *The Holocaust—Some Historical Aspects*. Jerusalem and Tel Aviv: Moreshet; Institute on Contemporary Judaism, Hebrew University; Sifriat Poalim (Hebrew).

Bechor, David, Kenneth Max, and Eliezer Berkowitz. 1985. *The Final Report of the Committee for the Investigation of the Assassination of Dr. Haim Arlozorov*. Jerusalem: Government Printing Press (Hebrew).

Becker, Howard S. 1963. *Outsiders*. New York: The Free Press.

—————. 1967. "Whose side are we on?" *Social Problems*, 14 (3):239–247.

—————. 1986. *Doing Things Together*, Evanston, Illinois: Northwestern University Press.

Becker, Theodore L., ed. 1971. *Political Trials*. Indianapolis and New York: The Bobbs-Merrill Co., Inc.

Begin, Menachem. 1950. *The Revolt*. Jerusalem: Achiasaf (Hebrew).

—————. 1961. *In the Underground* (Bamachteret). Tel Aviv: Hadar (Hebrew).

Bender, Arieh. 1988. "LEHI's member Mechoulam Makover: I took part in the assassination of Count Folke Bernadotte in 1948 in Jerusalem." *Ma'ariv*. January 29, pp. 1 and 5 (Hebrew).

Ben-Horin, Izhak. 1987. "Hanokmim." Pp. 6–8, 41 in *Ma'ariv*, weekend supplement, May 29, 1987, (Hebrew).

Ben, Philip. 1954. "Face to face with MacMichael and Shaw." *Ma'ariv*, April 16, p. 3 (Hebrew).

Bensman, Joseph. 1971. "Social and Institutional Factors Determining the Level of Violence and Political Assassination in the Operation of Society: A Theoretical Discussion." Pp. 345–388 in William J. Crotty, ed. *Assassination and the Political Order*. New York: Harper and Row.

Ben-Yehuda, Nachman. 1980. "The European Witch Craze of the 14th to 17th Centuries: A Sociologist's Perspective." *American Journal of Sociology* 86 (1), 1–31.

————. 1985. *Deviance and Moral Boundaries*. Chicago: The University of Chicago Press.

————. 1987. "The Politicization of Deviance: Resisting and Reversing Degradation and Stigmatization." *Deviant Behavior*, 8:259–282.

————. 1990. *The Politics and Morality of Deviance*. Albany: State University of New York Press (forthcoming).

————. 1990a. "Positive and Negative Deviance: More Fuel for a Controversy," *Deviant Behavior*, 11:221–243.

Ben-Zvi, Rachel Yanait. 1976. *Mania Shohat*. Jerusalem: Yad Yitzhak Ben-Zvi (Hebrew).

Berger, Peter L. and Thomas M. Luckmann. 1966. *The Social Construction of Reality*. Baltimore: Penguin Books.

Bergesen, Albert. 1984. "Social Control and Corporate Organization: A Durkheimian Perspective." Pp. 141–170 in Donald Black, ed. *Toward A General Theory of Social Control*. Vol. 2. New York: Academic Press, Inc.

Berkman, Ted. 1965. *Ha'aluf. Cast A Giant Shadow. The Story of Mickey Marcus*. Tel Aviv: Am Hasefer (Hebrew).

Bernadotte, Folke. 1945. *The Curtain Falls: Last Days of the Third Reich*. New York: A.A. Knopf.

————. 1951. *To Jerusalem*. London: Hodder and Stoughton (translated from the Swedish by Joan Bulman).

Best, Joel, ed. 1989. *Images of Issues: Typifying Contemporary Social Problems*, New York: Aldine de Gruyter.

————. 1990. *Threatened Children*. Chicago: University of Chicago Press.

Bethell, Nicholas. 1979. *The Palestine Triangle*. Jerusalem: Edanim (Hebrew).

Bilms, Jack. 1986. *Discourse and Behavior*. New York: Plenum Books.

Black, Donald. 1983. "Crime as social control," *American Sociological Review*, 43:34–45.

———— Ed. 1984a. *Toward a General Theory of Social Control*, Two volumes, New York: Academic Press.

————. 1984b. "Crime as Social Control." Pp. 1–27 in his *Toward a General Theory of Social Control*. Vol. 2. New York: Academic Press.

Black, Ian and Benny Morris. 1991. *Israel's Secret Wars*, London: Hamish Hamilton.

Blankfort, Michael. 1965. *Behold the Five*, New York: New American Library.

Boehm, Christopher. 1984. *Blood Revenge*, University of Pennsylvania Press (A 1987 edition).

Bonn, R. L. 1984. *Criminology*. New York: McGraw-Hill Book Company.

Bowyer-Bell, J. 1972. "Assassination in International Politics." *International Studies Quarterly*, 16(1):59–82.

———. 1987. *Fighting Zion*. Jerusalem: Achiasaf (Hebrew).

Box, Steven. 1981. *Deviance, Reality and Society*. 2d ed. New York: Holt, Rinehart and Winston.

———. 1983. *Power, Crime, and Mystification*. London: Tavistock Publications.

Braham, Randolph L. 1981. *The Politics of Genocide: The Holocaust in Hungary*. New York: Columbia University Press.

Brand, Yoel. 1957. *On a Mission for the Condemned to Death*. Tel Aviv: Ayanot (Hebrew).

Brand, Hansy and Yoel. 1966. *The Devil and the Soul*. Tel Aviv: Ledori (Hebrew).

Brand, Yoel. 1974. "Testimony in the Trial of Eichman." Pp. 869–909 in *The Legal Advisor to the Government Against Adolf Eichman*. Testimonies, (B). Jerusalem: Publication Service, Mercaz Hahasbara (Hebrew). (See also Henzi's testimony, pp. 910–935.)

Brit Habirionim, 1953, published by the Jabotinsky Institute, Tel Aviv. Author/s unknown, (Hebrew).

Burton, Frank and Pat Carlen. 1979. *Official Discourse: On Discourse Analysis, Government Publications, Ideology and the State*. London: Routledge and Kegan Paul.

Byas, Hugh. 1942. *Government by Assassination*. New York: Alfred A. Knopf.

Camellion, Richard. 1977. *Assassination Theory and Practice*. Boulder, Colorado: Paladin Press.

Carmel, Alex. 1973: *The Settlments of Germans in Eretz-Israel at the end of the Ottoman Period*. Jerusalem: The Israeli Eastern Society (Hebrew).

Carmi, Eliezer and Naomi Lotz. 1978. *Look Back Naomi: The Story of a Spy's Wife*. Tel Aviv: Bustan (Hebrew).

Carmi, Israel. 1960. *In the Road of Warriors*. Tel Aviv: Israel Defense Forces, Ma'arachot (Hebrew).

Casey, Lord. 1962. *Personal Experience 1939–1946*. New York: David McKay Company.

Chabas, Bracha. 1937. *Alexander Zeid. His Life Story*. Tel Aviv: The Center for Youth of the Histadrut (Hebrew).

Chalk, Frank, and Kurt Jonassohn. 1990. *The History and Sociology of Genocide*. New Haven: Yale University Press. Published in cooperation with the Montreal Institute for Genocide Studies.

Cheatwood, Derral. 1988. "Is there a season for homicide." *Criminology*, 26 (2):287–306.

Clark, Robert P. 1986. "Patterns of ETA Violence: 1968–1980." Pp. 123–141 in Merkl, Peter H., ed. *Political Violence and Terror. Motifs and Motivation.* Berkeley: University of California Press.

Clarke, James W. 1982. *American Assassins. The Darker Side of Politics.* Princeton, New Jersey: Princeton University Press.

Clarke, Thurston. 1981. *By Blood and Fire.* Hebrew Edition. Jerusalem: The Domino Press.

Cline, Ray S. and Alexander Yonah. 1986. *Terrorism as State Sponsored Covert Warfare.* Fairfax, Virginia: Hero Books.

Clutterbuck, Richard. 1973. *Protest and The Urban Guerrilla.* New York: Abelard-Schuman.

———. 1977. *Guerrillas and Terrorists.* London: Faber and Faber Limited.

Cohen, Albert. 1966. *Deviance and Control.* New Jersey: Prentice Hall.

Cohen, Arthur A. and Paul Mendes-Flohr, eds. 1987. *Contemporary Jewish Religious Thought.* New York: Charles Scribner's Sons.

Cohen Erik and Nachman Ben-Yehuda. 1987. "Counter Cultural Movements and Totalitarian Democracy." *Sociological Inquiry*, 57 (4):372–393.

Cohen Erik, Nachman Ben-Yehuda, and Janet Aviad. 1987. "Recentering the World: the quest for 'elective' centers in a secularized universe." *The Sociological Review*, 35 (2):320–346.

Cohen, Gavriel. 1975. "Harold MacMichael and the Question of the Future of Eretz Israel." *Hamizrach Hahadash* (the new East), 97–98 (1–2):52–68 (Hebrew).

Cohen, Michael J. 1978. *Palestine Retreats from the Mandate.* London: Paul Elek.

Cohen, Michael J. 1979. "The Moyne Assassination, November, 1944: A Political Analysis." *Middle Eastern Studies.* October, pp. 370–371.

Cohen, Mordechai (Marko), ed. 1981. *Chapters in the History of Eretz Israel.* Vol. 2. Tel Aviv: Ministry of Defense (Hebrew).

Cohen, Ronald, ed. 1986. *Justice: Views from the Social Sciences.* New York: Plenum Press.

Cohen, Stanley, 1986. "Bandits, Rebels or Criminals: African History and Western Criminology (Review Article)." *Africa*, 56 (4):468–483.

Cohen, Yehoshua, 1972. *Interview*, given to Zvi Zameret on July 8. The Hebrew University, The Institute for the Study of Contemporary Judaism, Center for Oral Documentation (Hebrew).

Cohen, Yehoshua. 1973. *Interview*, given to Zvi Zameret on March 14. The Hebrew University, The Institute for the Study of Contermporary Judaism, Center for Oral Documentaiton (Hebrew).

Cohen, Yeroham. 1969. *By Light and in Darkness*. Tel Aviv: Amikam (Hebrew).

Conklin, John E. 1986. *Crminiology*. 2d ed. New York: MacMillan Publishing Company.

Conrad, Peter and Joseph W. Schneider. 1980. *Deviance and Medicalization*. St. Louis: The C. V. Mosby Company.

Corbin, Juliet and Anselm Strauss. 1990. "Grounded Theory Research: Procedures, Canons, and Evaluative Criteria." *Qualitative Sociology*, 13(1):3–21.

Corfe, Tom. 1984. "Political Assassination in The Irish Tradition." Pp. 106–120 in Alexander Y. and A. O'Day, eds., 1984, *Terrorism in Ireland*. London: Croom Helm.

Coser, Lewis A. 1962. "Some Functions of Deviant Behavior and Normative Flexibility." *American Journal of Sociology*, 68 (2):172–181.

Crenshaw, Martha, ed. 1983. *Terrorism, Legitimacy, and Power*. Middletown, Connecticut: Wesleyan University Press.

Cromer, Gerald. 1985. "The Beer Affair: Israeli Social Reaction to a Soviet Agent." *Crossroads*, 15:55–75.

———. 1986. "Secularization is the Root of all Evil—The Response of Ultra-Orthodox Judaism to Social Deviance." Pp. 397–404 in *Proceedings of the 9th World Congress on Jewish Studies* (August 1985, 2d div., 3d vol. Jerusalem: World Association for Jewish Studies.

———. 1988. "'The Roots of Lawlessness': The coverage of the Jewish Underground in the Israeli Press." *Terrorism*, 11 (1):43–51.

Crotty, William J., ed. 1971. *Assassinations And the Political Order*. New York: Harper and Row Publications.

Crummey, Donald, ed. 1986. *Banditry, Rebellion and Social Protest in Africa*. London: James Currey.

Cullen, Francis T. 1983. *Rethinking Crime and Deviance Theory*. Totowa, New Jersey: Rowman and Allanheld.

Dagan, Amichai. 1988. "A Trap in Nachmani Street." *Ha'aretz*, weekly supplement, June 10, pp. 23–25, 31 (Hebrew).

———. 1989. "A hundred years on the firing line." *Ha'aretz*, supplement, May 5, pp. 27–31 (Hebrew).

Daly, Marti and Margo Wilson. 1988. *Homicide*, New York: Aldine De Gruyter.

Dan, Uri. 1979. "Munich's invoice was paid in Beirut." *Ma'ariv*, January 26, supplement, pp. 6–7. (Hebrew).

Dashewski, Pinhas. 1903. *Biagraphi*. London (Yiddish).

Davis, F. J. and R. Stivers, eds. 1975. *The Collective Definition of Deviance*. New York: The Free Press.

Deacon, Richard. 1977. *The Israeli Secret Service*. London: Hamish Hamilton.

Dekel, Ephraim. 1953. *The Ventures of SHAI*. Tel Aviv: Ma'arachot (Hebrew).

Dewar, Hugo. 1951. *Assassins at Large*. New York: Wingate.

Dietz, Mary Lorenz. 1983. *Killing for Profit: The Social Organization of Felony Homicide*. Chicago: Nelson-Hall.

Dinur, Dov. 1987. *Kasztner. New light on the man and his activities*. Haifa: Gestlit, Inc. (Hebrew).

Dobson, Christopher. 1974. *Black September: Its Short Violent History*. New York: Macmillan Publishing Company.

Dobson, C. and Ronald Payne. 1977. *The Carlos Complex: A Study in Terror*. London: Coronet Books/Hodder and Stoughton.

Dodge, David L. 1985. "The Over-Negativised Conceptualization of Deviance: A Programmatic Exploration." *Deviant Behavior*, 6:17–37.

Dothan, Shmuel. 1991. *REDS. The Communist Party in Palestine*. Kefar Saba: Shevana Hasofer (Hebrew).

Douglas, Jack D. 1967. *The Social Meaning of Suicide*. Princeton: Princeton University Press.

———. 1970. "Deviance and Order in a Pluralistic Society." Pp. 367–401 in Mckinney, J. C. and Tiryakian, E. A., eds. *Theoretical Sociology: Perspectives and Developments*. New York: Appleton-Century-Crofts.

———. 1970a. *Deviance and Respectability*. New York: Basic Books.

———. 1977. "Shame and Deceit in Creative Deviance." Pp. 59–86 in Sagarin, Edward, ed. *Deviance and Social Change*. California: Sage.

——— and Francis Waksler. 1982. *The Sociology of Deviance: An Introduction*. Boston: Little, Brown and Company.

Douglas, Mary. 1966. *Purity and Danger*. London and Henley, Routledge and Kegan Paul.

Dror, Zevika. 1986. *The Mista'arvim of the PALMACH*. Tel Aviv: Ministry of Defense, Hakibbutz Hameuchad (Hebrew).

Durkheim, E. 1933, 1964. *The Division of Labor in Society*. New York: The Free Press.

———. 1938: *The Rules of Sociological Method*. New York: The Free Press.

———. 1973. *On Morality and Society*. Chicago: University of Chicago Press.

Edelist, Ran. 1987. "Yehoshua the Saint." *Monitin*, April, 103:21–23, 74–77 (Hebrew).

Eisenberg Dennis, Dan Uri, and Eli Landau. 1978. *The Mossad*. New York: A Signet Book, New American Library.

Eitzen, Stanley D. and Doug A. Timmer. 1985. *Criminology: Crime and Criminal Justice.* New York: John Wiley and Sons.

Eisenstein, Yehuda David. 1951. *Ozar Israel: An Encyclopedia of all Matters Concerning Jews and Judaism.* New York: Pardes Publishing. Vol. 6:229–231 (Hebrew).

Elam, Yigal. 1990. *The Executors.* Jerusalem: Keter Publishing House, Ltd. (Hebrew).

Elath, Eliahu. 1968. *Haj Amin AL-Husseini.* Tel Aviv: Reshafim (Hebrew).

Eldad, Israel. 1962. "Who and What were Yair and Lehi." *Sulam*, 3–4:5–50 (Hebrew).

Eliav, Binyamin. 1990. *Memoirs.* Tel Aviv: Am Oved (Hebrew).

Eliav Ya'acov. 1983. *Wanted.* Jerusalem: Bamachteret (Hebrew).

Ellis, Albert and John M. Gullo. 1971. *Murder and Assassination.* New York: Lyle Stuart, Inc.

Eltagar, Zeev-Miron. 1988. "To assassinate an Ambassador." *Ma'ariv*, January 29, pp. 19 (Hebrew).

Engle, Anita. 1959. *The Nili Spies.* London: The Hogarth Press, Ltd. (A 1989 edition is available from Jerusalem: Phoenix Publications).

Erikson, K. T. 1966. *Wayward Puritans.* New York: Wiley.

Eshed, Haggai. 1988. *One Man "Mossad." Reuven Shiloach: Father of Israeli Intelligence.* Jerusalem: Edanim Publishers, Yediot Aharonot Edition (Hebrew).

Eshel, Zadok, ed. 1978. *The Fights of the HAGANA in Haifa.* Tel Aviv: Ministry of Defense publishing House (written by Sinai, Zvi) (Hebrew).

Farran, Roy. 1948. *Winged Dagger. Adventures on Special Service.* London: Collins.

Farrel, Ronald A. and Victoria L. Swigert. 1982. *Deviance and Social Control.* Glenview, Illinois, Scott, Foresman and Company.

Feierabend, Ivo K. et al. 1971. "Political Violence and Assassination: A Cross-National Assessment." Pp. 54–140 in Crotty, William J., ed. *Assassinations and the Political Order.* New York: Harper and Row, Publishers.

Feierabend, Ivo K. and Rosalind Feierbend. 1976. "Cross-National Comparative Study of Assassination." Pp. 151–213 in Doris Y. Wilkinson, ed. *Social Structure and Assassination Behavior.* Cambridge, Massachusetts: Schenkman Publishing Company.

Felson, Richard B. and Henry J. Steadman. 1983. "Situational Factors in Disputes leading to Criminal Violence." *Criminology*, 21:59–74.

Fiala, Robert and Gary LaFree. 1988. "Cross National Determinants of Child Homicide." *American Sociological Review*, 53 (3):421–431.

Finkelston, Y. 1979. "The Terrorists arrested Foreign Correspondents who came to cover Salame's funeral." *Ma'ariv*, January 1, p. 1 (Hebrew).

Flavius, Josephus. 1981. *The Complete Works of Josephus*. Translated by William Whiston. Grand Rapids, Michigan: Kregel Publications.

Flusser, David. 1985. *Josephus Flavius*. Tel Aviv: Ministry of Defense, Transmitted University (Hebrew).

Ford, Franklin L. 1985. *Political Murder From Tyrannicide to Terrorism*. Cambridge, Massachusetts: Harvard University Press.

Frank, Gerold. 1963. *The Deed*. Tel Aviv: Reshafim (Hebrew).

Frankfurter, David. 1984. *The First Fighter Against The Nazis*. An enlarged and revised edition of his book *Nakam* which was published originally in 1948. Tel Aviv: Reshafim. (Hebrew).

Franzius, Enno. 1969. *History of the order of Assassins*. New York: Funk and Wagnalls.

Freedman, Lawrence Zelic and Alexander Yonah, ed. 1983. *Perspectives on Terrorism*. Wilmington, Delaware, Scholarly Resources Inc.

Friedman, Menachem. 1977. *Society and Religion. The Non-Zionist Orthodoxy in Eretz-Israel 1918–1936*. Jerusalem: Yad Itzhak Ben-Zvi Publications (Hebrew).

Fuerstein, Emil. 1986. *Political Murder in Our Time*. Jerusalem: Keter Publishing House, Ltd. (Hebrew).

Galili, Israel. 1987. *In the center of doing and deciding*. Tel Aviv: Yad Tabenkin (Hebrew).

Galliher, John F. and John R. Cross. 1983. *Moral Legislation Without Morality*. New Brunswick: Rutgers University Press.

Gal-Or, Naomi. 1990. *The Jewish Underground: Our Terrorism*, Tel Aviv: Hakibbutz Hameuchad Publishing House, Ltd. (Hebrew).

Garfinkel, Harold. 1950. "Conditions of successful degradation ceremonies." *American Journal of Sociology*, 61:420–424.

Gavriel, Y. 1950. *I Accuse*. Tel Aviv: Unknown Publisher (Tel Aviv University Library). (Hebrew).

Gaucher, Roland. 1968. *The Terrorists From Tsarist Russia to the O.A.S.* London: Secker and Warburg.

Geertz, Clifford. 1973. *The Interpretation of Cultures*. New York: Basic Books.

Geter, Miriam. 1967. *The Ideology of Lehi*. Unpublished M.A. thesis. Tel Aviv University (Hebrew).

Geva, Moshe. 1990. "Maybe He Was Not Guilty At All." *Yedioth Aharonot*, Friday, June 29, 1990, "7 Days" supplement, pp. 29–31 (Hebrew).

Giddings, Franklin H. 1898: "Introduction." In Proal Louis (1898):

Political Crime. Reprinted in 1973. Montclair, New Jersey: Patterson Smith.

Gilad, Zerubavel. 1955: *The Palmach Book*. 3d ed. Tel Aviv: Hakibbutz Hameuchad (Hebrew).

———. 1971. *Palmach's Chapters*. A new Edition. Tel Aviv: Hakibbutz Hameuchad (Hebrew).

Gilbert, Martin. 1983. *Finest Hour. Winston S. Churchill 1939–1941*. London: Heinemann.

Gilbert, Nigel G. and Peter Abell, eds. 1983. *Accounts and Action. Survey Conference on Sociological Theory and Method*. Hampshire, England: Gower.

Gilbert, Nigel G. and Michael Mulkay. 1984. *Opening Pandora's Box. A Sociological Analysis of Scientists' Discourse*. New York: Cambridge University Press.

Gilboa (Polany) Ya'acov. 1986. *As You Walk the Fields of Terror*. Tel Aviv: Yair (Hebrew).

Gildenman, Moshe. 1956. "The End of the Ataman Askilko." Pp. 49–51 in Avatihi Arieh, ed. *Rovno—A Memorial Book*. Tel Aviv: Published by "Yalkut Wohlin"—the organization of people who came from Rovno, in Israel (Hebrew).

Ginat, Joseph. 1984. "The Role of Mediator: With Special Reference to Blood Disputes." Pp. 98–131 in Shoham S. G., ed. *Israel Studies in Criminology*. Vol. 7. New York: Sheridan House, Inc.

Ginosar, Pinhas. 1973. *Interview*, given to Zvi Zameret on January 12. The Hebrew University, The Institute for the Study of Contemporary Judaism, Center for Oral Documentaiton (Hebrew).

———. 1985. *Lehi Revealed*. Ramat Gan: Bar Ilan University (Hebrew).

Glaser, Barney G. and Anselm L. Strauss. 1967. *The Discovery of Grounded Theory: Strategies For Qualitative Research*. Chicago: Aldine Publishing Co.

Glines, Carroll V. 1990. *Attack on Yamamoto*. New York: Orion Books.

Goffman, Erving. 1963. *Stigma*. Middlesex, England: Penguin Books.

———. 1969. *Stigma*. Englewood Cliffs, New Jersey: Prentice Hall.

———. 1974. *Frame Analysis: An Essay on the Organization of Experience*. New York: Harper and Row.

Golan, Aviezer. 1975. "The riddle of the Disappearance of Alexander Rubowitz." *Yediot Aharonot*, April 17, p. 19 (Hebrew).

Goldscheider, Calvin and Alan S. Zuckerman. 1984. *The Transformation of the Jews*. Chicago: the University of Chicago Press.

Goldstein, Yaacov. 1991. *Mania Vilbuschevitz-Shochat*. Haifa: Haifa University Press (Hebrew).

Goode, Erich. 1984. *Deviant Behavior*. New Jersey: Prentice Hall, Inc. 2d ed.

———. 1989. "The American Drug Panic of the 1980s: Social Construction or Objective Threat?" *Violence, Aggression and Terrorism*, 3 (4):327–348 (reprinted in *The International Journal of the Addictions*, 1990, 25 (9):1083–1098).

———. 1990. "Positive Deviance: A Viable Concept?" *Deviant Behavior,* 12 (3):289–309.

Granot, Oded. 1979. "A woman detonated the bomb which killed Salame." *Ma'ariv*, January 25, p. 1. (Hebrew).

———. 1981. *Intelligence*. Vol. 6 of Zahal, Encyclopaedia for Army and Security. Tel Aviv: Revivim (Hebrew).

Grant, Dale. 1991. *Wilderness of Mirrors. The Life of Gerald Bull*. Scarborough, Ontario: Prentice-Hall Canada, Inc.

Gretz, Nurit and Rachel Weisbroad, eds. 1986. *The Canaanite Group: Literature and Ideology*. Tel Aviv: Everyman's University (Hebrew).

Gross, Feliks. 1970. "Political Violence and Terror in 19th and 20th Century Russia and Eastern Europe." Pp. 519–598 in James F. Kirkham, Sheldon G. Levy, William J. Crotty, eds. *Assassination and Political Violence*. New York: Praeger Publishers.

Gross, S. 1988. "Kristallnacht—Introduction to the Holocaust." *Ha'aretz*, November 4:3 (Hebrew).

Groussard, Serge. 1975. *The Blood of Israel*. New York: William Morrow.

Guelke, Adrian. 1986. "Loyalist and Republican Perceptions of the Northern Ireland Conflict: The UDA and the Provisional IRA." Pp. 91–122 in Merkl, Peter H., ed. *Political Violence and Terror. Motifs and Motivation*. Berkeley: University of California Press.

Gurion, Itzhak. 1973. *The Lawyers of LEHI*. Tel Aviv: Jabotinski Institute (Hebrew).

Gurr, Ted Robert. 1988. "Empirical research on Political Terrorism: The State of the Art and How it Might be Improved." Pp. 115–154 in Robert O. Slater, and Michael Stohl, eds. *Current Perspectives on International Terrorism*, London: Macmillan Press.

Gusfield, Joseph R. 1963. *Symbolic Crusade*. Chicago: The University of Illinois Press.

———. 1981. *The Culture of Public Problems: Drinking—Driving and the Symbolic Order*. Chicago: The University of Chicago Press.

Gutman, Israel. 1988. *Fighters Among the Ruins*. Jerusalem: Keter (Hebrew).

Haber, Eitan and Ze'ev Schiff, eds. 1976. *Israel, Army and Defense: A Dictionary*. Tel Aviv: Zmora, Bitan, Modan (Hebrew).

Hacker, Frederick J. 1976. *Crusaders Criminals Crazies. Terror and Terrorism in Our Time.* New York: W. W. Norton and Company, Inc.

Hadar, David. 1971. "The attitude of the Superpowers to Yoel Brand's Mission." *Molad,* 4 (19–20), new series:112–125 (Hebrew).

Hagan, Frank E. 1987. *Espionage as Political Crime: A Typology of Spies,* Paper presented at the American Society of Criminology Annual Meeting, Montreal, P.Q., Canada, November.

Hagan, J. 1977. *The Disreputable Pleasures.* Toronto: McGraw Hill, Ryrson, Ltd.

Hakim, Shimeon. 1982. "Was it really an act of total madness?" *Zemanim,* 9:82–86. (Hebrew).

Halevi, D. 1987. *Murder in Jerusalem.* Jerusalem: Tefutza (Hebrew).

Hammer, Joseph Vaughn. 1835 *The History of the Assassins.* London: Smith and Elder, Cornhill.

Hangel, Martin. 1983. "Zealots and Sicariis." Pp. 339–364 in Kasher Arieh, ed. *The Big Revolt, Reasons and Circumstances for its Occurrence.* Jerusalem: Mercaz Zalman Shazar (Hebrew).

Harel, Israel. 1979. "Dr. Israel Eldad (Sheib) 'Begin in a Sad Episode'." *Monitin,* September, 13:56–63, 87, 144 (Hebrew).

Harel, Isser. 1982. *The Crisis of the German Scientists 1963–1962.* Tel Aviv: Sifriat Ma'ariv (Hebrew).

————. 1985. *The Truth About the Kasztner Murder.* Jerusalem: Edanim Publishers, Yediot Aharonot Edition (Hebrew).

————. 1987. *Soviet Espionage. Communism in Israel.* Jerusalem: Edanim Publishers, Yediot Aharonot Edition (Hebrew).

————. 1989. *Security and Democracy.* Tel Aviv: Edanim Publishers (Hebrew).

Harff, Barbara and Ted Robert Gurr. 1989. "Victims of the State: Genocide, Politicides and Group Repression Since 1945." *International Review of Victimology,* 1:23–41.

Harpaz, Yoram. 1988. "A Hero without a Certificate." *Kol Ha'ir* (Jerusalem), November 4, no. 530:23, 25 (Hebrew).

Harris, Anthony R. 1977. "Sex and Theories of Deviance: Toward a Functional Theory of Deviant Type-Scripts." *American Sociological Review,* 42:3–16.

Har-Zion, Meir. 1968. *Chapters of a Diary.* Tel Aviv: A. Lewin-Epstein (Hebrew).

Haskell, M. R. and L. Yablonsky. 1983. *Criminology: Crime and Criminality.* Boston: Houghton Mifflin Company.

Havens, Murray C., Carl Leiden, and Karl M. Schmitt. 1970. *The Politics of Assassination.* Englewood Cliffs, New Jersey: Prentice Hall, Inc.

Heaps, Willard A. 1969. *Assassination. A Special Kind of Murder.* New York: Meredith Press.

Hecht, Ben. 1970. *Perfidy.* Tel Aviv: Dfus Israel (Hebrew).

Heckert, Druann Maria. 1989. "The Relativity of Positive Deviance: The Case of the French Impressionists." *Deviant Behavior,* 10:131–144.

Heller, Joseph. 1979. "Failure of a Mission: Bernadotte and Palestine, 1948." *Journal of Contemporary History,* 14:515–534.

Heller, Joseph. 1989. *LEHI: Ideology and Politics, 1940–1949.* Jerusalem: Mercaz Zalman Shazar and Keter (Hebrew).

Hepworth, Mike and Bryan S. Turner. 1974. "Confessing to Murder: Critical Notes on the Sociology of Motivation." *British Journal of Law and Society,* 1 (1):31–49.

———. 1984. *Confession.* London: Routledge and Kegan Paul.

Hewins, R. 1950. *Count Folke Bernadotte: His Life and Work.* London: Hutchinson and Company.

Hilberg, Paul. 1985. *The Destruction of the European Jews.* New York: Holmes and Meier.

Hills, Stuart L. 1980. *Demystifying Social Deviance.* New York: McGraw Hill Book Company.

Hobsbaum, E. J. 1959. *Primitive Rebels.* Manchester: Manchester University Press.

Hodgson G. S. 1955: *The Order of Assassins.* The Hague: Mouton and Co. Reprinted in New York by AMS Press.

Hoenig, Sidney B. 1970. "The Sicarii in Masada—Glory or Infamy." *Tradition,* 11 (1):5–30.

Holmes, Ronald M. and James DeBurger. 1988. *Serial Murder.* London: Sage Publications.

Homans, George C. 1974. *Social Behavor: Its Elementary Forms.* Rev. ed. New York: Harcourt, Brace Jovanovich.

Horowitz, Dan and Moshe Lissak. 1989. *Overburdened Policy: Society and Politics in Israel.* New York: State University of New York Press.

Horseley, Richard. 1979. "Josephus and the Bandits." *Journal for the Study of Judaism,* 10 (1):37–63.

Hoy, Claire and Ostrovsky Victor. 1990. *By Way of Deception,* Toronto: Stoddart Publishing Co. Limited.

Hoyt, Edwin P. 1990. *Yamamoto.* New York: McGraw Hill.

Hughes, E. C. 1971. *The Sociological Eye: Selected Papers.* Chicago: Aldine.

Hurst, James Willard. 1983. "Treason." Pp. 1559–1562 in Sanford H. Kadish, ed. *Encyclopedia of Crime and Justice.* New York: The Free Press.

Hurwood, Bernhardt J. 1970. *Society and the Assassin*. New York: Parents' Magazine Press.

Hyams, Edward. 1974. *Terrorists and Terrorism*. New York: St. Martin's Press.

————. 1969. *Killing No Murder*. London: Thomas Nelson and Sons, Ltd.

Israel Defense Forces spokesman. 1982. *The National Steering Committee (Hava'ada Lehachvana Leumit)* and *A Political Portrait of Karim Halaf and Basam Shaka*. Tel Aviv: Mimeographed background. distributed by the IDF (Hebrew).

Illin, Ephraim. 1985. *Signed (Al Hachatum)*. Tel Aviv: Ma'ariv Library (Hebrew).

Inverarity, James P. 1987. *Durkheim's Theory of Sanctions and Solidarity: A defense*. Unpublished paper. Bellingham, Washington: Department of Sociology, Western Washington University.

Inverarity, J., Pat Lauderdale, and B. Feld. 1983. "Sanctions and Solidarity: The Contribution of Emile Durkheim." Pp. 126–160 in *Law and Society*. Boston: Little, Brown and Co.

Israeli, Chaim. 1986. "Yehoshua Cohen, A Fighter and a Pioneer." *Yediot Aharonot*, August 19, p. 22 (Hebrew).

Israeli, Joseph. 1972. *On a Mission of Security*. Tel Aviv: Am Oved (Hebrew).

Ivianski, Ze'ev. 1977. "Individual Terror: Concept and Typology." *Journal of Contemporary History*, 12:43–63.

————. 1981. "Individual terror." Pp. 409–414 in David Kna'ni, ed. *Encyclopedia of Social Sciences*. Vol. 6. Tel Aviv: Al Hamishmar (Hebrew).

————. 1982. "The Moral Issue: some Aspects of Individual Terror." Pp. 229–266 in David C. Rapoport and Yonah Alexander, eds. *The Morality of Terrorism*. New York: Pergamon.

————. 1987. "LEHI and the Limits To Terror." Pp. 24–59 in Carmel Moshe et al., edited by Orna Makover-Katlav: *Struggle and Terror*. Ramat Efal, Yad Tabenkin, The Center for the Study of the History of the Defense Forces—"Hahagana" (Hebrew).

Jacoby, Susan. 1983. *Wild Justice: The Evolution of Revenge*. New York: Harper and Row.

Johnson, Doyle Paul. 1981. "Integration and Social Order in Society: The Functional Approach." Pp. 385–445 in: *Sociological Theory*. New York: John Wiley and Sons.

Jonas, George. 1984. *Vengeance*. New York: Bantam Books.

Jones, Philip, comp. 1979. *Britain and Palestine 1914–1948. Archival Sources for the History of the British Mandate*. London: Published for The British Academy by The Oxford University Press.

Kafra, Michal. 1986. "Mother Says the Devil got into Them." *Ma'ariv*, December 19, supplement, p. 6–10 (Hebrew).

Kanaan, Habib. 1958. *As the British were Leaving*. Tel Aviv: Gadish Books (Hebrew).

———. 1964. "The Nazis from Eretz Israel have not given Hope." *Hauma*, 10 (2.):368–374 (Hebrew).

———. 1968. *The Nazi Fifth Column in Palestine*. Tel Aviv: Hakibbutz Hameuchad Publishing House, Ltd. (Hebrew).

———. 1975. "Sons return to their homeland." *Ha'aretz*, supplement, June 27, pp. 16–18 (Hebrew).

——— and Dan Margalit. 1968. "LEHI members Assassinated Bernadotte." *Ha'aretz*, September 17, p. 14 (Hebrew).

Karaim, Zadok. 1982. "The Political Leadership in Judea, Samaria and the Gaza Strip vis-a-vis the Camp David Agreement." *Ma'arachot*, 283:22–26 (Hebrew).

Karmen, Andrew A. 1983. "Vigilantism." Pp. 1616–1618 in Sanford H. Kadish, ed. *Encyclopedia of Crime and Justice*. New York: The Free Press.

Karpel, Dalia. 1990. "1945. A Bullet in the Head." *Ha'ir*, March 2, pp. 25–29 (Hebrew).

Kasher, Arieh, ed. 1983. *The Big Revolt*. Jerusalem: Mercaz Zalman Shazar (Hebrew).

Katz, Immanuel. 1987. *Lohamei Herout Israel (LEHI)*. Tel Aviv: Beit Yair (Hebrew).

Katz, Shmuel. 1966. *Inside The Miracle (Day of Fire)*. Tel Aviv: Karni (Hebrew).

Katzburg, Netanel. 1977. *A Policy in a Maze. British Policy in Eretz-Israel 1940–1945*. Jerusalem: Yad Itzhak Ben-Zvi (Hebrew).

Keinan, Amos. 1988. "On Amos Keinan." *Yediot Aharonot*, weekend supplement "7 Days," no. 1258, March 11, pp. 38–39 (Hebrew).

———. 1990. "Vili, the horse that is finished." *Yediot Aharonot*, weekend supplement "7 Days," no. 1390, September 19, pp. 20–23 (Hebrew).

Keren, Moshe. 1978. *Transitory and Permanent Problems*. Edited by Eli Shealtiel. Jerusalem: A.S., P.O. Box 4070 (Hebrew).

Kirk, William R. 1984. "Economic Sources of Homicide: Reestablishing the Effects of Poverty and Inequality." *American Sociological Review*, 49:283–289.

Kirkham, James F., Sheldon G. Levy, and William J. Crotty, ed. 1970. *Assassination and Political Violence*. New York: Praeger Publishers.

Klein, Menachem. 1986. *Chapters in the Relationships Between Israel and the Arabs Between the Years 1957–1967*. Jerusalem: The

Hebrew University, the Harry S. Truman Institute for the Advancement of Peace (Hebrew).

Kliger, Noah. 1988. "This was Only the Beginning." *Yediot Aharonot,* "7 Days" weekend supplement, November 4, no. 1292:27 (Hebrew).

Koren, Yehuda. 1986. "Why was Michael Waksman Murdered." *Davar,* May 30, pp. 10–11. (See also *Davar* from May 23 (Hebrew).

———. 1989. "When we deal with a Jewish soul." *Ha'aretz,* May 12, weekend supplement, pp. 25–29. (Hebrew).

Kotzer, Arieh. 1977. *Red Carpet (Marvad Adom).* Tel Aviv: Makeda. (Hebrew).

———. No date. *The Morning Comes in Blood (Bedam Maftzia Hashachar).* Tel Aviv: Israel. A novel. (Hebrew).

Kuper, Leo. 1982. *Genocide: Its Political Use in the Twentieth Century.* New Haven: Yale University Press.

———. 1986. *The Prevention of Genocide.* New Haven:Yale University Press.

Kupperman, Robert H. and Darrel M. Trent, ed. 1979. *Terrorism. Threat, Reality, Response.* Stanford, California: Stanford University, Hoover Institution Press.

Lam, Amira. 1987. "A 40 Year Tragedy." *Tzomet Hasharon* (supplement to *Hadashot*), November 17, 240:1, 15, 34 (Hebrew).

Landau, Simha F., Drapkin I., Arad S. 1974. "Homicides, Victims and Offenders: An Israeli Study." *The Journal Of Criminal Law and Criminology.* Vol. 65 (3).

Landau, Simha F. 1984. "Trends in Violence and Aggression: A Cross-Cultural Analysis." *International Journal of Comparative Sociology,* 25 (3–4):133–158.

Lankin, Eliahu. 1974. *The Story of Altalena's Commander.* Tel Aviv: Hadar (Hebrew; Original edition 1950.

Lapidot, Arie and Gad Leor. 1988. "The Consolation Letter of President Hertzog Did Not Appease Sweden." *Yediot Aharonot,* September 19, p. 1. (Hebrew).

Laqueur, Walter. 1980. *The Terrible Secret. Suppression of the Truth about Hitler's 'Final Solution'.* Boston: Little, Brown and Company.

———. 1985. *A World of Secrets. The Use and Limits of Intelligence.* New York: Basic Books.

———, ed. 1978. *The Terrorism Reader. A Historical Anthology.* New York: New American Library.

Lauderdale, Pat. 1976. "Deviance and Moral Boundaries." *American Sociological Review,* 41:660–664.

Lentz, Harris M. 1988. *Assassinations and Executions.* Jefferson, North Carolina: McFarland and Company, Inc.

Lerner, Max. 1930: "Assassination." In Edwin Seligman, ed. *Encyclopedia of the Social Sciences*. Vol. 2. New York: The MacMillan Company.

Lester, David. 1986. *The Murderer and His Murder*, New York: AMS Press, Inc.

Lev Ami, A. 1972. *The Underground Organizations in Eretz-Israel 1941–1943*. Unpublished Ph.D. diss. Jerusalem: Hebrew University (Hebrew).

Lev, Uziel. 1985. *"Bar Giora" and "Hashomer." The Roots of Jewish Military Concept and Organization (1907–1914)*. Tel Aviv: Ministry of Defense, Ma'arachot (Hebrew).

Levi, Avrahami. 1959. "'The Hagana will kill you'—they threatened 'Dov' the driver—but he did not talk." *Yediot Aharonot*, April 30, supplement "7 Days," (407), p. 7, 16. (Hebrew).

Levi, Ken. 1981. "Becoming a Hit Man: Neutralization in a Very Deviant Carreer." *Urban Life*, 10 (1):47–63.

Levin, Jack and James Alan Fox. 1985. *Mass Murder: Amerca's Growing Menace*. New York: Plenum Press.

Levinson, Amit. 1987. "The Last Refuge." *Yediot Aharonot*, supplement ("New Times"), November 11, pp. 15–16 (Hebrew).

Lewis, Bernard. 1967. *The Assassins. A Radical Sect in Islam*. London: Weidenfeld and Nicolson (a 1985 edition by London: Al Saqi Books).

Leyton, Elliot. 1980. *Compulsive Killers: The Rise of the Modern Multiple Murderer*. New York: New York University Press.

Lidz, Charles W. and Andrew L. Walker. 1980. *Heroism Deviance and Morality*. Beverly Hills: Sage Publications.

Lifshitz, Roni. 1987. "Yehoshua Offir's Slik.' *Jerusalem* (local newspaper), December 4, pp. 23–24 (Hebrew).

Litani, Yehuda. 1980. "Bloody Saturday in Hebron." *Ha'aretz*, May 4, p. 3 (Hebrew).

Livneh, Eliezer .1961. *NILI—The History of a Political Daring*. Jerusalem: Schocken Books (Hebrew).

———. 1969. *Aharon Aaronson, His Life and Times*. Jerusalem: Mosad Bialik (Hebrew).

Livni, Eitan. 1987. *E.Z.L.—Operation and Underground*. Jerusalem: Edanim/Yediot Aharonot (Hebrew).

Lodge, Juliet, ed. 1981. *Terrorism: A Challenge to the State*. Oxford: Martin Robertson.

Lofland, John. 1969. *Deviance and Identity*. New Jersey: Prentice Hall.

Lotz, Wolfgang. 1970. *A Mission in Cairo*. Tel Aviv: Sifriat Ma'ariv (Hebrew).

Louis, Roger W. and Robert W. Stookey, ed. 1986. *The End of the Palestine Mandate*. Austin: University of Texas Press.

Lowther, William. 1991. *Arms and the Man. Dr. Gerald Bull, Iraq and the Supergun*. Toronto: Doubleday Canada Limited.

Luckenbill, David F. 1977. "Criminal Homicide as a Situated Transaction." *Social Problems*, 25:176–186.

Ludwig, Emil. 1936. *The Davos Murder*. Translated by Eden and Cedar Paul. New York: Viking Press.

Maimon Yehuda et al. 1984. *The Fighting Pioneer ("Hechalutz Halochem"). Organ of the Chalutz Underground Movement in occupied Cracow. August–October 1943*. Israel: Ghetto Fighters House, and Hakibbutz Hameuchad (Hebrew).

Makover, Mechoulam .1988. "Mechoulam Makover ("Yoav"), from the LEHI unit which assassinated Bernadotte, tells—for the first time—his story." Pp. 155–156 in *Idan*, no. 10, Jerusalem: Yad Yitzhak Ben-Zvi (Hebrew).

Makover, Rachela. 1988. *Government and Administration of Palestine 1917–1925*. Jerusalem: Yad Ben-Zvi (Hebrew).

Mardor, Meir. 1970. *On a Secret Mission*. Tel Aviv: Ma'arachot (Hebrew).

———. 1988. "The Pum." Pp. 87–95 in *Army on the way to a state*. Tel Aviv: Ministry of Defense, The Israel Galili Center for the History of the Defense Force "Hagana," editors unknown (Hebrew).

Margalit, Elkana. 1980. *Kibbutz, Society and Politics. The Gdud Ha'avoda named after J. Trumpeldor*. Tel Aviv: Am Oved (Hebrew).

Margalit, Dan. 1982. "Murder at 6 Emmanuel Boulevard." *Ha'aretz*, supplement, April 30, pp. 12–13 (Hebrew).

Marongiu, Pietro and Graeme Newman. 1987. *Vengeance: The Fight Against Injustice*. Totowa, N.J. : Rowman and Littlefield.

Marx, Gary T. 1984. "Notes on the Discovery, Collection, and Assessment of Hidden and Dirty Data." Pp. 78–113 in Joseph W. Schneider and John I. Kitsuse, eds. *Studies in the Sociology of Social Problems*. Norwood, New Jersey: Ablex.

Meridor, Ya'acov. 1950. *The Long Road to Freedom*. Jerusalem: Achiasaf (Hebrew).

Merton, R. K. 1968. *Social Theory and Social Structure*. New York: Free Press.

Meshi-Zahav Zvi and Meshi-Zahav Yehuda. 1985. *De Hahn. The First Zionist Murder in Eretz Israel*. Jerusalem: The Institute of the Jewish Haredim (Hebrew).

Mickolus, Edward F. 1980. *Transnational Terrorism. A Chronology of Events, 1968–1979*. London: Aldwych Press.

Mills, C. W. 1940: "Situated Actions and Vocabularies of Motives." *American Sociological Review*, 5:904–913.

———. 1943: "The Professional Ideology of Social Pathologists." *American Journal of Sociology*, 49:165–180.

Milshtein, Uri. 1973. "The Season." *Ha'aretz*, supplement, February 23, pp. 25–28. (Hebrew).

———. 1987. *The History of the Israeli Paratroopers*. Vol. 4. Tel Aviv: Shalgi (Hebrew).

Moran, Richard. 1981. *Knowing Right from Wrong. The Insanity Defense of Daniel McNaughtan*. New York: The Free Press.

Morton, G. J. 1957. *Just The Job*. London: Hodders and Stoughton.

McDonald, James. 1951. *My Mission in Israel*. Jerusalem: Achiasaf (Hebrew).

McTague, John J. 1983. *British Policy in Palestine 1917–1922*. London: University Press of America.

Nadav, Zvi. 1954. *From Days of Guarding and Defense*. Tel Aviv: Ma'arachot (Hebrew).

Nadel, Baruch. 1968. *The Assassination of Bernadotte*. Tel Aviv: Y. Guttman (Hebrew).

———. 1976. *The Story of the Fighter Yonatan*. Tel Aviv: Ministry of Defense/Tarmil Books (Hebrew).

Nakdimon, Shlomo. 1978. *Altalena*. Jerusalem: Edanim (Hebrew).

———. 1986. "The Deposit," *Yediot Aharonot*, November 21, weekend supplement, 34–35, (Hebrew).

———. 1986a. *Tammuz in Flames*, Jerusalem: Edanim Publishers (Yediot Aharonot Edition. Hebrew).

———. 1987. "Executed by Palmach." *Yediot Aharonot*, July 3, weekend supplement (Hebrew).

——— and Mayzlish, Shaul. 1985. *De Haan: The First Political Assassination in Palestine*. Tel Aviv: Modan (Hebrew).

Naor, Arye. 1990. *David Raziel. The life and times of the commander-in-chief of the 'Irgun' underground in Palestine*. Tel Aviv: Ministry of Defense (Hebrew).

Naor, Mordecai. 1988. *Laskov*. Jerusalem and Tel Aviv: Ministry of Defense and Keter Publishing House (Hebrew).

Narkis, Uzi. 1986. "More on De Hahn's Assassination." Letters to editor in *Yediot Aharonot*, November 30, p. 19 (Hebrew).

Nedava, Joseph. 1974. *The Book of The Executed*. Tel Aviv:Hadar (Hebrew).

———, ed. 1977. *Joseph Lishansky, Papers and Letters*. Tel Aviv: Hadar (Hebrew).

———. 1979. "Some Aspects of Individual Terrorism: A Case Study of the Schwartzbard Affair." *Terrorism*, 3 (1–2):69–80.

———. 1983. "The Squealer." *Ha'aretz*, January 28, supplement, pp. 28–29, 33 (Hebrew).

———, ed. 1986. *Joseph, Member of NILI—An Epilogue*. Jerusalem: Agudat Hashmonai (Hebrew).

———, ed. 1986b. *Zvi Rosenblatt's Struggle for the Truth*. Tel Aviv: Jabotinsky Institute in Israel (Hebrew).

Nettler, Gwynn. 1982. *Killing One Another*. Criminal Carreers. Vol. 2. Cincinnati, Ohio: Anderson Publishing Company.

Nevo, Amos. 1986. "The Man from Lehi who Loved Ben-Gurion." *Yediot Aharonot*, August 15, p. 6. (Hebrew).

———. 1987. "The Fighter Shmuel." *Yediot Aharonot*, "7 Days," weekend supplement, November 27, pp. 20–23, 45 (Hebrew).

———. 1988a. "B. G. Approved in Writing the Execution of Meir Tubianski." *Yediot Aharonot*, April 6, p. 9 (Hebrew).

———. 1988b. "Big Isser." *Yediot Aharonot*, "7 Days," weekend supplement, April 7, no. 1262, pp. 8–11 (Hebrew).

———. 1988c. "The Shot," *Yediot Aharonot*, "7 Days," weekend supplement, November 4, no. 1292:25–26 (Hebrew).

Ngor, Haing with Roger Warner. 1987. *Haing Ngor: A Cambodian Odyssey*. New York: Macmillan Publishing Company.

Niv, David. *The Battles of the National Military Organization (Ma'archot Hairgun Hatzvai Haleumi)*. 6 vol. set. Published between 1965–1980. Tel Aviv: Mossad Klosner (Hebrew).

Ofer, Dalia. 1988. *Illegal Immigration During the Holocaust*. Jerusalem: Yad Ben-Tzvi (Hebrew).

Okev, Y. 1949. *The Black Deed (Hama'as Hashachor)*. Tel Aviv: Oz (Hebrew).

Olzak, Susan. 1988. *Were the Causes of Racial Conflicts and Lynchings in Late 19th and Early 20th Century America the Same?* Paper presented at the session on Collective Behaviour and Social Movements: Unruly Events, at the American Sociological Association Meetings in Atlanta, United States, August 1988.

Orcutt, James D. 1983. *Analyzing Deviance*. Homewood, Illinois: The Dorsey Press.

Ornstein, Ya'acov. 1973. *In Chains. The Memories of a Warrior*. Tel Aviv: Hug Yedidim (Hebrew).

Padover, Saul K. 1943. "Patterns of Assassination in Occupied Territory." *Public Opinion Quarterly*, 7:680–693.

Pail, Meir. 1979. *The Emergence of ZAHAL (I.D.F.)*. Tel Aviv: Zmora, Bitan, Modan (Hebrew).

Paine, Lauran. 1975. *The Assassin's World*. New York: Taplinger Publishing Company.

Palgi, Arieh. 1979. *Peace now and no more*. Tel Aviv: Sifriat Poalim (Hebrew).

Parsons, Talcott. 1971. *The System of Modern Societies*. Englewood Cliffs, New Jersey: Prentice Hall.

Pearce, Frank. 1976. *Crimes of the Powerful*, London: Pluto.

Pearlman, Moshe. 1947. *Mufti of Jerusalem: The Story of Haj Amin Al-Husseini*. London: V. Gollancz.

Perlmutter, Amos, Michael Handel, and Uri Bar-Joseph. 1982. *Two Minutes Over Baghdad*. London: Vallentine, Mitchell and Co., Ltd.

Persson, Sune O. 1979. *Mediation and Assassination: Count Bernadotte's Mission to Palestine 1948*. London: Ithaca Press.

Petersburg, Offer and Reuven Kastro. 1988. "I Planned to Assassinate the Egyptian Ambassador in Tel Aviv." *Ma'ariv*, January 8, pp. 12–14. (Hebrew).

Pfohl, Stephen J. 1985. *Images of Deviance and Social Control. A Sociological History*. New York: McGraw-Hill Book Company.

Pfuhl, Edwin H., Jr. 1986. *The Deviance Process*. 2d ed. Belmond, California: Wadworth Publishing Company.

Piers, Maria W. 1978. *Infanticide*. New York: W. W. Norton and Company.

Piven, Frances Fox. 1981. "Deviant Behavior and the Re-making of the World." *Social Problems*, 28:489–508.

Ploscowe, Morris. 1935: "Treason." Pp. 93–96 in Edwin Seligman, and R. A. and Alvin Johnson, ed. *Encyclopaedia of The Social Sciences*. New York: Macmillan.

Polany. See Gilboa 1986.

Political Killings By Governments. 1983 London: An Amnesty International Report.

Posner, Steve. 1987. *Israel Undercover*, Syracuse: Syracuse University Press.

Potter, Jonathan and Margaret Wetherell. 1987. *Discourse and Social Psychology*. London: Sage Books.

Prat, Immanuel. 1955. *The Big Trial: The Kasztner Affair*. Tel Aviv: Or Publications (Hebrew).

Rabinov, Baruch. 1969. "Hagana." Pp. 31–47 in David Kena'ani, ed. *Encyclopaedia of Social Sciences*. Vol. 11. Tel Aviv: Sifriat Poalim (Hebrew).

Rafter, Nicole Hahn. 1990. "The Social Construction of Crime and Crime Control." *Journal of Research in Crime and Delinquency*, 27 (4):376–389.

Rapoport, David C. 1971. *Assassination and Terrorism*. Canadian Publishing Corporation.

——. 1982. "Introduction." Pp. 1–7 in David C. Rapoport and Yonah Alexander, eds. *The Rationalization of Terrorism*. Frederic, MD: Altheia Books, University Publications of America.

——. 1984. "Fear and Trembling: Terrorism in Three Religious Traditions." *The American Political Science Review*, 78 (30):658–677.

——. 1988. "Messianic Sanctions for Terror." *Comparative Politics*, 20 (2):195–213.

Rapoport, Uriel, ed. 1982. *Josephus Flavius*. Jerusalem: Yad Itzhak Ben-Zvi (Hebrew).

Ratosh, Jonathan. 1976. *From Victory to Disaster*. Tel Aviv:Hadar (Hebrew).

Raviv, Dan and Yossi Melman. 1990. *Every Spy a Prince. The Complete History of Israel's Intelligence Community*. Boston: Houghton Mifflin.

Read, Anthony and David Fisher. 1989. *Kristallnacht*. New York: Peter Bedrick Books.

Rechav, Shlomo. 1963. "Gdud Ha'avoda." *Encyclopedia of Social Sciences*. Merchavia: Sifriat Poalim (Hebrew).

Reicher, Gideon. 1968. "The female spy was shot." *Yediot Aharonot*, October 13, p. 14 (Hebrew).

Reid, Sue Titus. 1982. *Crime and Criminology*. New York: Holt, Rinehart and Winston.

Resnik, Shlomo. 1986. *An Underground Movement in a Sectorial Society. A Social Profile of the Fighters of Lehi*. M.A. thesis. Department of Sociology and Anthropology, Ramat Gan, Bar Ilan University (Hebrew).

Rieder, Jonathan. 1984. "The Social Organization of Vengeance." Pp. 131–162 in Donald Black, ed. *Toward A General Theory of Social Control*. New York: Academic Press, Inc.

Ringel-Hoffman, Ariella. 1988. "Shots in the Air." *Yediot Aharonot*, January 22, supplement "7 Days," 1251:8–10 (Hebrew).

Rock, Paul. 1973a. *Deviant Behavior*. London: Hutchinson University Library.

——. 1973b. "Phenomenalism and and Essentialism in the Sociology of Deviancy." *Sociology*, 7:17–29.

——. 1974. "The Sociology of Deviance and Conceptions of Moral Order." *British Journal of Criminology*, 14 (2):139–149.

——. 1985. "Deviance." Pp. 199–202 in Kuper Adam and Jessica Kuper, eds. *The Social Science Encyclopedia*. London: Routledge and Kegan Paul.

Rosberg, Carl and John Nottingham. 1966. *The Myth of "Mau Mau": Nationalism in Kenya*. New York: Praeger.

Rosenberg, Moshe. 1968. *Interview*, given to Nathan Cohen on May 30. The Hebrew University, The Institute for the Study of Contemporary Judaism, Center for Oral Documentation (Hebrew).

Rosenberg, Shoshana. 1974. *Brit Habirionim*. Tel Aviv: Hamidrasha Haleumit (Hebrew).

Rosenbloom, Herzl. 1987. *Drops From the Sea*. Jerusalem: Edanim Publishers (Hebrew).

Rosenfeld, Shalom. 1955. *Criminal File Number 124. The Greenwald-Kasztner Trial*. Tel Aviv: Karni (Hebrew).

Rubinstein, Shimon. 1985. "The De Hahn Affair—A Political Assassination or an Execution by the Institutions of "the Coming State." *Kivunim*, May, vol. 27:5–29 (Hebrew).

Sagarin, Edward. 1985. "Positive Deviance: An Oxymoron." *Deviant Behavior*, 6 (2):169–181.

Salomon, Chezi. 1987. "The Influence of the Intelligence Organizations of the 'Yishuv' on Ben-Gurion's Assessment of the Situation: 1946–1947." *Ma'arachot*, 309 (July–August):28–36 (Hebrew).

Salpeter, Eliahu and Yuval Elitzur. 1973. *Who Runs Israel*. Tel Aviv: A Lewin-Epstein (Hebrew).

Samet, Moshe. 1979. *Religion and State in Israel*. Department of Sociology, Hebrew University of Jerusalem (Hebrew).

Sanders, William R. 1983. *Criminology*. Reading, Massachusetts: Addison-Wesley Publishing Company.

Sarna, Yigal. 1987. "Chancellor on the sight." *Yediot Aharonot*, weekend supplement, July 31, pp. 34–39 (Hebrew).

Schafer, Stephen. 1974. *The Political Criminal*. New York: The Free Press.

Scharf, Peter and Binder Arnold. 1983. *The Badge and the Bullet: Police Use of Deadly Force*. New York: Praeger.

Schechtman, Joseph B. 1965. *The Mufti and the Fuehrer*. New York: A.S. Barnes and Compay Inc. (Reprinted by Thomas Yoseloff).

Scheid, Eliahu. 1983. *Memories about the Jewish settlements and the trips in Israel and Syria 1883–1899*. Translated by Aharon Amir, introduction by Shimon Shcwartzfux. Jerusalem: Yad Yitzhak Ben-Zvi (Hebrew).

Schiff, Ze'ev and Ehud Ya'ari. 1990. *Intifada*, Tel Aviv: Schocken Publishing House, Ltd. (Hebrew).

Schmid, Alex P. 1983. *Political Terrorism*. Amsterdam: North-Holland Publishing Company.

Schur, Edwin M. 1971. *Labeling Deviant Behavior*. New York: Harper and Row.

————. 1979. *Interpreting Deviance*. New York: Harper and Row.

————. 1980. *The Politics of Deviance*. Englewood Cliffs, New Jersey: Prentice Hall, Inc.

Schwartz, Barry, Yael Zerubavel, and Bernice M. Barnett. 1986. "The Recovery of Masada: A Study in Collective Memory." *The Sociological Quarterly*, 27 (2):147–164.

Schwartz, Stephen. 1988. "Intellectuals and Assassins—Annals of Stalin's Killerati." *The New York Times Book Review*, January 24, pp. 3, 30–31.

Scott, Marvin B. and Stanford M. Lyman 1968. "Accounts, Deviance and Social Order." Pp. 89–119 in J. D. Douglas, ed. *Deviance and Respectability*. New York: Basic Books.

Scott, Robert A. 1972. "A Proposed Framework for Analyzing Deviance as a property of Social Order." Pp. 9–36 in R. A. Scott and J. D. Douglas, eds. *Theoretical Perspectives on Deviance*. New York: Basic Books.

Scull, Andrew. 1984. "Competing Perspectives on Deviance." *Deviant Behavior*, 5:275–289.

Segal, Haggai. 1987. *Dear Brothers*. Jerusalem: Keter (Hebrew).

Segal, Ze'ev. 1988. "The Verdicts of the Israeli Supreme Court in the First Year." *Idan*, 10:99–104. Jerusalem: Yad Yitzhak Ben-Zvi (Hebrew).

Segev, Tom. 1980. "Israel and Germany: Relations of the Third Kind." *Ha'aretz* (supplement) March 14, pp. 8–9, 27. (Hebrew).

————. 1981. "The Mystery of the Skeleton in the Closet." *Ha'aretz*, November 13, supplement, pp. 8–9, 31. (Hebrew).

————. 1988. "Bernadotte Hits Again," *Ha'aretz*, September 16, p. 7. (Hebrew).

————. 1991. *The Seventh Million. The Israelis and the Holocaust*. Jerusalem: Keter Publishing House and Domino Press, Ltd. (Hebrew).

Shaked, Roni. 1988. "This is how we liquidated Bernadotte." *Yediot Aharonot*, September 11, 1988, A Special Rosh Hashana supplement, issue no. 17736, pp. 2–5 (Hebrew).

————, Haim Broida, and David Regev. 1990. "Yesterday the 200th victim from the beginning of the Intifada, was murdered by Reulei Panim." *Yediot Aharonot*, March 22 (Hebrew).

Shalev, Aryeh. 1990. *The Intifada Causes and Effects*. Tel Aviv: Papirus and the Institute for Strategic Studies, University of Tel Aviv (Hebrew).

Shamir, Itzhak. 1973. *Interview,* given to Zvi Tzameret on January 12. The Hebrew University, The Institute for the Study of Contemporary Judaism, Center for Oral Documentaiton (Hebrew).

Shapiro, Rhonda J., Pat Lauderdale, and Michael Lauderdale. 1985. *The Changing Forms of Deviance: Salem Witchcraft.* Paper presented at the 80th Annual Meeting of the American Sociological Association, Washington D.C.

Shargel, Baila R. 1979. "The Evolution of the Masada Myth." *Judaism,* 28 (1–3):357–371.

Shavit, Ya'acov. 1976. *The Hunting Season: The Sezon.* Tel Aviv:Hadar (Hebrew).

————. 1984. *From Hebrew To Canaanite. Aspects in the History, Ideology and Utopia of the 'Hebrew Renaissance'—From Radical Zionism to Anti-Zionism.* Jerusalem: The Domino Press (Hebrew).

————. 1987. *The Mythologia of the Zionist Right Wing.* Tel Aviv: EMDA Library—Academia Series. Published by Beit-Berl and the Moshe Sharett Institute (Hebrew).

Shilanski, Dov. 1977. *In a Hebrew Prison. From the Diary of a Political Prisoner.* Tel Aviv: Armoni (Hebrew).

Shils, E. 1975. *Center and Periphery: Essays in Macrosociology.* Selected paper of Edward Shils. Vol. 2. Chicago: University of Chicago Press.

Shmuelevitz, Matitiahu. 1973. *Interview,* given to Zvi Tzameret on March 5. The Hebrew University, The Institute for the study of Contemporary Judaism, Center for Oral Documentation (Hebrew).

Shneurson, Pinhas. 1957. "Eradicating the mob's nests in Jaffa." Pp. 291–292 in *Sefer Hashomer,* edited by Y. Ben-Zvi et al. Tel Aviv: Dvir (Hebrew).

Shochat, Israel. 1957. "A Mission and a Road (Shlihut and Derech)." Pp. 1–80 in *Sefer Hashomer,* edited by Y. Ben-Zvi et al. Tel Aviv: Dvir (Hebrew).

Shochat, Mania. 1957. "My way in the Hashomer." Pp. 385–395 in Itzhak Ben-Zvi et al., eds. *The Book of the Hashomer: Members' Memories.* Tel Aviv: Dvir (Hebrew).

Shomron, David ("Eli"). 1985. *We Were Recruited for Life.* Tel Aviv: Ministry of Defense (Hebrew).

Shpiellman, Anshell, ed. 1986. *Historic Encounter: A Symposium on the United Resistance Movement 1945–1946.* Tel Aviv: Yair Publications (Hebrew).

Shragai, Nadav. 1984. "6 members of the underground were accused of murder, 19 with attempted murder and membership in a terroristic organization." *Ha'aretz,* May 24, p. 3. (Hebrew).

Shva, Shlomo. 1969. *The Tribe of the Darings: The Status of Mania and Israel Shohat and their friends in the Hashomer.* Merhavia: Sifriat Poalim (Hebrew).

Simmel, Georg. 1971. *On Individuality and Social Form.* Edited with an introduction by Donald Levine. Chicago: The University of Chicago Press.

Smelser, Neil J. 1962. *Theory of Collective Behavior,* New York: The Free Press.

Smilanski, Moshe. 1953: *The Family of the Land.* Vol. 4. Tel Aviv: Am Oved (Hebrew).

Smith, Morton. 1983. "The Zealots and Sicariis, Their Origins and Connections." Pp. 319–337 in Arieh Kasher, ed. *The Big Revolt, Reasons and Circumstances for its Occurence.* Jerusalem: Mercaz Zalman Shazar (Hebrew).

Snitch, Thomas H. 1982. "Terrorism and Political Assassinations: A Transnational Assessment, 1968–1980." *The Annals of the American Academy of Political and Social Science.* September, 463:54–68.

Spero, Shubert. 1970. "In Defense of the Defenders of Masada." *Tradition,* 11 (1):31–43.

Sprinzak, Ehud. 1986. *Fundamentalism, Terrorism and Democracy: The Case of Gush Emunim Underground.* Washington, D.C.: The Wilson Center, Smithsonian Institution Building, occasional paper no. 4.

Stanger, Cary David. 1988. "A Haunting Legacy: The Assassination of Count Bernadotte." *The Middle East Journal,* 42 (2):260–272.

Stern, Menachem. 1983. "Sicariis and Zealots." Pp. 167–196 in Avi Yonah Michael and Zvi Beres, eds. *Society and Religion During the Period of the Second Temple.* Tel Aviv and Jerusalem: Alexander Peli, Ltd and Am Oved, Ltd (Hebrew).

———, ed. 1984. *The History of the Land of Israel. The Roman-Byzantian Period.* Vol. 4. Jerusalem: Yad Itzhak Ben-Zvi and Keter (Hebrew).

———. 1987. "Yoseph Ben-Matitiahu, Historian of 'Wars of the Jews'." Pp. 41–51 in Salmon Joseph, Menachem Stern and Moshe Zimmermann, eds. *Studies in Historiography.* Jerusalem: The Zalman Shazar Center for Jewish History (Hebrew).

Steven, Stewart. 1980. *The Spymasters of Israel.* New York:Ballantine Books.

S.T.H.—*Sefer Toldot HaHagana. (The History of the Hagana).* 8 vol. set. Published between 1954 and 1973. First five vol. published by Tel Aviv: Ma'arachot and last three vol. published by Tel Aviv: Am Oved (Hebrew).

Stohl, Michael, ed. 1983. *The Politics of Terrorism.* New York: Marcel Dekker.

Stohl, Michael and George Lopez, eds. 1984. *The State As Terrorist.*

The Dynamics of Governmental Violence and Repression. London: Aldwych Press.

Storrs, Sir Ronald. 1937. *The Memoirs of Sir Ronald Storrs*. New York: G. P. Putnam.

Strauss, Anselm L. 1987. *Qualitative Analysis For Social Scientists*, Cambridge: Cambridge University Press.

Sykes G. M. 1978. *Criminology*. New York: Harcourt Brace Jovanovich, Inc.

Talmi, Menachem. 1979. "When the target was Hassan Salame the father." *Ma'ariv*, January 26, p. 29. (Hebrew).

Tavin, Eli. 1973. *The Second Front. The ETZEL in Europe 1946–1948*. Tel Aviv: Ron (Hebrew).

Terry, Robert M. and Darrell J. Steffensmeier. 1988. "Conceptual and Theoretical Issues in the Study of Deviance." *Deviant Behavior*, 9:55–76.

Teveth, Shabtai. 1968. *Exposed in the Turret*. Tel Aviv: Schochen (Hebrew).

———. 1982. *The Murder of Arlosorov*. Jerusalem: Shocken Books (Hebrew).

Thio, Alex. 1983. *Deviant Behavior*. Boston, Houghton Mifflin, 2d ed.

———. 1988. *Deviant Behavior*, 3d ed. New York: Harper and Row.

Tidhar, David. 1938: *With and Without Uniform: 25 Years of Public Work 1912–1937*. Tel Aviv: Hotza'at Yedidim (Hebrew).

———. 1960. *In the Service of the Homeland: 1912–1960*. Tel Aviv: Hotza'at Yedidim (Hebrew).

Tinnin, David B. and Dag Christensen. 1977. *The Hit Team*. Boston: Little, Brown and Company.

Trunk, Isaiah. 1972, 1977. *Judenrat*, New York: Stein and Day. A Scarborough Book.

Turk, Austin. 1975. *Political Criminality and Political Policing*. New York: MSS Modular Publishers.

———. 1982. *Political Criminality*. Beverly Hills: Sage.

———. 1983. "Assassination." Pp. 82–88 in Sanford H. Kadish, ed. *Encyclopedia of Crime and Justice*. New York: The Free Press.

Tzameret, Zvi. 1974. *The Educational Activity in LEHI*. Unpublished M.A. thesis, Faculty of Humanities, School of Education, Jerusalem: The Hebrew Univerity (Hebrew).

———. 1988. "The mediation affair by Count Folke Bernadotte." *Idan*, no. 10:143–154. Jerusalem: Published by Yad Yitzhak Ben-Zvi (Hebrew).

van den Bergh, Pierre. 1988. *The Ixil Triangle: Vietnam in Guatemala*. Unpublished paper. Seattle: The University of Washington.

Vinitzky, Joseph, ed. 1950. *My Blood is not Quiet: The Yedidia Segal Affair in Front of the Tel Aviv District Court.* Tel Aviv: Shelach (Hebrew).

Von Hentig, Hans. 1948: *The Criminal and His Victim.* New Haven: Yale University Press.

Wagner-Pacifici, Robin Erica. 1986. *The Moro Morality Play: Terrorism as Social Drama.* Chicago: University of Chicago Press.

Walliman, Isidor and Michael M. Dobkowski, eds. 1987. *Genocide and the Modern Age.* Westport. CT: Greenwood Press.

Wallwork, E. 1972. *Durkheim: Morality and Milieu*, Cambridge: Harvard University Press.

Walzer, Michael. 1987. *Interpretation and Social Criticism.* Cambridge, Masseahusetts: Harvard University Press.

Wardlaw, Grant. 1982. *Political Terrorism.* New York: Cambridge University Press.

Wasserstein, Bernard. 1982. "New Light on the Assassination of Lord Moyne." *Zemanim* (a quarterly journal on history), 7:4–17 (Hebrew).

Watson, Francis M. 1976. *Political Terrorism: The Threat and the Response.* Washington and New York: Robert B. Luce Company, Inc.

Weinshall, Ya'acov. 1978. *The Blood on the Threshold.* Tel Aviv: Yair Publishing House (Hebrew).

Weisburd, David. 1981. "Vigilantism as rational social control: The Case of Gush Emunim Settlers." Pp. 69–87 in M. J. Aronoff, ed. *Cross-currents in Israeli Culture and Politics.* New Brunswick:Transaction Books.

———. 1989. *Jewish Settler Violence. Deviance as Social Reaction.* University Park and London: The Pennsylvania State University Press.

Weisman, Richard. 1984. *Witchcraft, Magic and Religion in 17th Century Massachusetts.* Amherst: The University of Massachusetts Press.

Wellford, Charles. 1975. "Labelling Theory and Criminology: An Assessment," *Social Problems,* 22 (3):332–345.

Wilbanks, William. 1984. *Murder in Miami: An Analysis of Homicide Patterns and Trends in Dade County (Miami) Florida, 1917–1983.* Lanham, Maryland: University Press of America.

Wilkinson, Doris Y., ed. 1976. *Social Structure and Assassination Behavior.* Cambridge, Massachusetts: Schenkman Publishing Company.

Wilkinson, Kenneth P. 1984. "A Research Note on Homicide and Rurality." *Social Forces,* 63:445–452.

Williams, Kirk R. and Robert L. Flewelling. 1988. "The Social Production of Criminal Homicide: A Comparative Study of Disaggregated Rates In American Cities." *American Sociological Review*, 53 (3):421–431.

Wilson, Colin. 1975. *Order of Assassins*. England: Panther Books.

Wilson, R. D. 1949. *Cordon and Search*. Aldershot:Gale and Polden Limited.

Wilson, Stephen. 1988. *Feuding, Conflict and Banditry in Nineteenth-Century Corsica*. New York: Cambridge University Press.

Wolff, Kurt H. 1950. *The Sociology of Georg Simmel*. Translated, edited, and with an introduction by Kurt H. Wolff. Glencoe, Illinois: Free Press.

Wolfgang, Marvin E. 1957. "Victim-Precipitated Criminal Homicide." *Journal of Criminal Law, Criminology, and Police Science*, 48:1–11.

———. 1958. *Patterns of Criminal Homicide*. Philadelphia: University of Pennsylvania Press.

——— and Franco Ferracuti. 1967. *The Subculture of Violence: Towards an Integrated Theory in Criminology*. London: Tavistock.

Wolfgang, Marvin E. and Margaret A. Zahn. 1983. "Homicide: Behavioral Aspects." Pp. 849–855 in Sanford H. Kadish, ed. *Encyclopedia of Crime and Justice*, New York: The Free Press.

Woodward, Llewellyn. 1970. *British Foreign Policy in the Second World War*. London: Her Majesty's Stationary Office.

Woolgar, Steve and Dorothy Pawluch. 1985. "Ontological Gerrymanding: The Anatomy of Social Problems Explanations." *Social Problems*, 32:214–227.

Wyman, David. 1984. *Abandonment of The Jews*. New York: Pantheon Books.

Ya'akubovitz, Mordechai (captain). 1953: *From Palmach to Zahal*. Tel Aviv: Amichai (Hebrew).

———. 1967. *From Palmach to Suetz*. Tel Aviv: N. Tversky (Hebrew).

Ya'ari-Poleskin, J. 1937. *NILI*. Tel Aviv: Masada (Hebrew).

Yachin, Ezra. 1984. *The Story of Elnakam*. Tel Aviv: Yair Publications (Hebrew).

Yellin-Mor, Natan. 1974. *Lohamei Herouth Israel (LEHI)*. Tel Aviv: Shikmona. (Hebrew).

Yerushalmi, Shalom and Avituv Yaron. 1986. "Who Shot Yedidia Segal." *Kol Hair*, (Jerusalem) November 11, pp. 25–27, 29, 77 (Hebrew).

Yevin, Amichal Ada. 1986. *In Purple. The Life of Yair—Abraham Stern*. Tel Aviv: Hadar (Hebrew).

Zeitlin, Solomon. 1965. "Masada and the Sicarii." *Jewish Quarterly Review*, 55 (4):299–317.

————. 1967. "The Sicarii and Masada." *Jewish Quarterly Review*, 57 (4):251–270.

Zerubavel, Gilad. 1955: *The Book of the Palmach*. 3d ed. Hakkibutz Hameuchad (Hebrew).

Ziv, Shimon. 1973. *Interview,* given to Zvi Tzameret on July 2. The Hebrew University, The Institute for the Study of Contemporary Judaism, Center for Oral Documentation. (Hebrew).

Zonshein, Eliezer. 1976. *A Profile of Murder and Killing in Israel.* Unpublished M.A. thesis, Faculty of Law, University of Tel Aviv (Hebrew).

Zuckerman (Antek), Itzchak. 1990. *Those Seven Years 1939–1946*. Tel Aviv: HaKibbutz Hameuchad Publishing House, Ltd. and Bet Lochamei Hagetaot (Hebrew).

Zunz, Olivier, ed. 1985. *Reliving the Past. The Worlds of Social History*. Chapel Hill: The University of North Carolina Press.

INDEX

24 96 9I   dup

1 -00